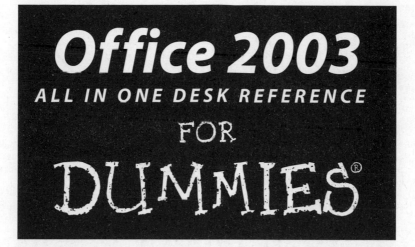

Office 2003
ALL IN ONE DESK REFERENCE
FOR
DUMMIES®

by Peter Weverka

WILEY

Wiley Publishing, Inc.

Office 2003 All in One Desk Reference For Dummies®

Published by
Wiley Publishing, Inc.
111 River Street
Hoboken, N.J. 07030
www.wiley.com

Copyright © 2003 by Wiley Publishing, Inc., Indianapolis, Indiana

Published by Wiley Publishing, Inc., Indianapolis, Indiana

Published simultaneously in Canada

For general information on our other products and services or to obtain technical support, please contact our Customer Care Department within the U.S. at 800-762-2974, outside the U.S. at 317-572-3993, or fax 317-572-4002.

Wiley also publishes its books in a variety of electronic formats. Some content that appears in print may not be available in electronic books.

Library of Congress Control Number: 2003101797

ISBN: 0-7645-3883-7

Manufactured in the United States of America

10 9 8 7 6 5 4

1B/RZ/QZ/QT/IN

 is a trademark of Wiley Publishing, Inc.

About the Author

Peter Weverka is the bestselling author of several *For Dummies* books, including *Word for Dummies Quick Reference* and *Microsoft Money For Dummies,* as well as 25 other computer books about various topics. Peter's humorous articles and stories — none related to computers, thankfully — have appeared in *Harper's, SPY,* and other magazines for grown-ups.

Dedication

For Sofia and Henry.

Author's Acknowledgments

This book owes a lot to many hard-working people at Wiley Publishing in Indiana. I would especially like to thank Steve Hayes for his encouragement and for giving me the opportunity to write this and other books for Wiley.

As usual, Susan Christophersen wielded the editorial scalpel with great skill and shrewdness. Susan is always a pleasure to work with, and it was delightful to have her aboard for all 792 pages of this long book.

Technical editor Allen Wyatt made sure that all the instructions in this book are indeed accurate and offered many excellent suggestions for using Office programs, and I thank him for his work. I would also like to thank Jason Gerend for helping me with parts of Book V, Rich Tennant for the witty cartoons you will find on the pages of this book, and for writing the index.

These people at the Wiley offices in Indianapolis gave their all to this book, and I want to acknowledge all of them:

Kristie Rees, Seth Conley, Jacque Schneider, Lynsey Osborn,
John Greenough, Evelyn Still.

Finally, I want to thank my family — Sofia, Henry, and Addie — for putting up with my vampire-like working hours and eerie demeanor at daybreak.

Publisher's Acknowledgments

We're proud of this book; please send us your comments through our online registration form located at www.dummies.com/register/.

Some of the people who helped bring this book to market include the following:

Acquisitions, Editorial, and Media Development

Project Editor and Copy Editor:
Susan Christophersen

Acquisitions Editor: Steve Hayes

Technical Editor: Allen Wyatt

Editorial Manager: Carol Sheehan

Media Development Supervisor:
Richard Graves

Editorial Assistant: Amanda Foxworth

Cartoons: Rich Tennant
(www.the5thwave.com)

Production

Project Coordinator: Kristie Rees

Layout and Graphics: Amanda Carter, Seth Conley, Joyce Haughey, LeAndra Hosier, Michael Kruzil, Lynsey Osborn, Jacque Schneider, Julie Trippetti

Proofreaders: John Greenough, Angel Perez, Carl William Pierce, Evelyn Still

Indexer: Stever Rath

Publishing and Editorial for Technology Dummies

    Richard Swadley, Vice President and Executive Group Publisher

    Andy Cummings, Vice President and Publisher

    Mary C. Corder, Editorial Director

Publishing for Consumer Dummies

    Diane Graves Steele, Vice President and Publisher

    Joyce Pepple, Acquisitions Director

Composition Services

    Gerry Fahey, Vice President of Production Services

    Debbie Stailey, Director of Composition Services

Contents at a Glance

Table of Contents

Book II: Outlook 135

Chapter 1: Getting Acquainted with Outlook 137

Chapter 2: Maintaining the Contacts Folder 151

Chapter 4: Making Your Presentation Livelier 253

Chapter 5: Giving the Presentation 267

Book IV: Excel 277

Chapter 1: Up and Running with Excel 279

Chapter 2: Refining Your Worksheet 295

Introduction

This book is for users of Office who want to get to the heart of the program without wasting time. Don't look in this book to find out how the different programs in the Office suite work. Look in this book to find out how *you* can get *your* work done better and faster with these programs.

I show you everything you need to make the most of the different Office programs, and Windows XP as well. On the way, you have a laugh or two. No matter how much or how little skill you bring to the table, the guidance of this book will make you a better, more proficient, more confident user of the Office programs.

What's in This Book, Anyway?

This book is jam-packed with how-to's, advice, shortcuts, and tips for getting the most out of the Office programs. Here's a bare outline of the nine parts of this book:

✦ **Part I: Word:** Explains the numerous features in Office's word processor, including how to create documents from letters to reports.

✦ **Part II: Outlook:** Shows you how to send and receive e-mail messages and files, as well as track tasks, maintain an address book, and keep a calendar with Outlook.

✦ **Part III: PowerPoint:** Demonstrates how to make a meaningful presentation that makes the audience say, "Wow!"

✦ **Part IV: Excel:** Shows the many different ways to crunch the numbers with the bean counter in the Office suite.

✦ **Part V: FrontPage:** Explains how to create a Web site, including one with sophisticated layouts and graphics.

✦ **Part VI: Access:** Describes how to create a useful database for storing information, as well as query the database and create reports from it.

✦ **Part VII: Publisher:** Shows how to create brochures and other publications with the "print shop in a can."

✦ **Part VIII: One Step Beyond Office:** Explores miscellaneous programs in the Office suite. You'll discover how to use and write macros with VGA (Visual Basic for Applications), customize the different Office programs, handle and create line art and graphics, manage graphics in an Office file, and brainstorm with OneNote.

✦ **Part IX: Windows XP:** Looks into the many ways to customize the Windows operating system, store files, and use Windows XP as an entertainment center.

What Makes This Book Special

You are holding in your hands a computer book designed to make learning the Office programs as easy and comfortable as possible. Besides the fact that this book is easy to read, it's different from other books about Office. Read on to see why.

Easy-to-look-up information

This book is a reference, and that means that readers have to be able to find instructions quickly. To that end, I have taken great pains to make sure that the material in this book is well organized and easy to find. The descriptive headings help you find information quickly. The bulleted and numbered lists make following instructions simpler. The tables make options easier to understand.

I want you to be able to look down the page and see in a heading or list the name of the topic that concerns you. I want you to be able to find instructions quickly. Compare the table of contents in this book to the book next to it on the bookstore shelf. The table of contents in this book is put together better and presents topics so that you can find them in a hurry.

A task-oriented approach

Most computer books describe what the software is, but this book explains how to complete tasks with the software. I assume that you came to this book because you want to know how to *do* something — print form letters, create a worksheet, query a database, build a Web site. You came to the right place. This book describes how to get tasks done.

Meaningful screen shots

The screen shots in this book show only the part of the screen that illustrates what is being explained in the text. When instructions refer to one part of the screen, only that part of the screen is shown. I took great care to make sure that the screen shots in this book serve to help you understand the Office programs and how they work. Compare this book to the next one on the bookstore shelf. Do you see how clean the screen shots in this book are?

Foolish Assumptions

Please forgive me, but I made one or two foolish assumptions about you, the reader of this book. I assumed that:

✦ You own a copy of Office 2003, the latest edition of Office, and you have installed it on your computer.

✦ You use a Windows operating system, preferably Windows XP. Part IX of this book explains how to use Windows XP, but all people who have the Windows operating system installed on their computers are invited to read this book. It serves for people who have Windows 95, Windows 98, and Windows NT, as well as Windows XP or higher.

✦ You are kind to foreign tourists and small animals.

Conventions Used in This Book

I want you to understand all the instructions in this book, and in that spirit, I've adopted a few conventions.

To show you how to step through command sequences, I use the ⇨ symbol. For example, you can choose File⇨Save to save a file. The ⇨ is just a shorthand method of saying "Choose Save on the File menu."

Notice how the *F* in File and the *S* in Save are underlined in the preceding paragraph. Those same characters are underlined in command names. Underlined letters are called *hot keys*. You can press them along with the Alt key to give commands and make selections in dialog boxes. Where a letter is underlined in a command name or in a dialog box, it is also underlined in the step-by-step instructions in this book.

Besides pressing hot keys to give commands, you can press combinations of keys. For example, pressing Ctrl+S is another way to save a file. In other words, you can hold down the Ctrl key and press the S key. Where you see Ctrl+, Alt+, or Shift+ and a key name or key names, press the keys simultaneously.

Yet another way to give a command is to click a toolbar button. When I tell you to click a toolbar button, you see a small illustration of the button in the margin of this book. The button shown here is the Save button, the one you can click to save a file.

Where you see boldface letters or numbers in this book, it means to type the letters or numbers. For example, "Enter **25** in the Percentage text box" means to do exactly that: Enter the number 25.

Icons Used in This Book

To help you get the most out of this book, I've placed icons here and there. Here's what the icons mean:

Next to the Tip icon, you can find shortcuts and tricks of the trade to make your visit to Officeland more enjoyable.

Where you see the Warning icon, tread softly and carefully. It means that you are about to do something that you may regret later.

When I explain a juicy little fact that bears remembering, I mark it with a Remember icon. When you see this icon, prick up your ears. You will discover something that you need to remember throughout your adventures with Word, Excel, PowerPoint, or the other Office program I am demystifying.

When I am forced to describe high-tech stuff, a Technical Stuff icon appears in the margin. You don't have to read what's beside the Technical Stuff icons if you don't want to, although these technical descriptions often help you understand how a software feature works.

Good Luck, Reader!

If you have a comment about this book, a question, or a shortcut you would like to share with me, address an e-mail message to me at this address: weverka@sbcglobal.net. Be advised that I usually can't answer e-mail right away because I'm too darned busy. I do appreciate comments and questions, however, because they help me pass my dreary days in captivity.

Book I

Word

Contents at a Glance

Chapter 1: Entering, Editing, and Formatting Text

In This Chapter

- ✔ Creating new documents
- ✔ Opening documents
- ✔ Saving versions of documents
- ✔ Changing text fonts and the size of text
- ✔ Spell-checking a document

Chapter 1 is where you get your feet wet. Don't be shy. Walk right to the shore and sink your toes in the water. Don't worry; I won't push you from behind. This chapter explains how to create and open documents, save different versions of documents, and change the look of the text. For poor typists and spellers, it also tells how to spell-check a document.

Getting Acquainted with Word

Seeing the Word screen for the first time is sort of like trying to find your way through Tokyo's busy Ikebukuro subway station. It's intimidating. But when you start using Word, you quickly learn what everything is. To help you get going, Table 1-1 gives you some shorthand descriptions of the different parts of the Word screen. Figure 1-1 shows precisely where these screen parts are.

Table 1-1	Parts of the Word Screen
Part of Screen	*What It Is*
Title bar	At the top of the screen, the title bar tells you the name of the document you're working on.
Control menu	Click here to pull down a menu with options for minimizing, maximizing, moving, and closing the window.
Minimize, Restore, Close buttons	These three magic buttons make it very easy to shrink, enlarge, and close the window you are working in.
Menu bar	The list of menu options, from File to Help, that you choose from to give commands.

(continued)

Table 1-1 *(continued)*

Part of Screen	*What It Is*
Task Pane	The pane that appears on the right side of the screen and provides options for opening Word documents and doing other tasks.
Toolbars	A collection of buttons you click to execute commands. To display or remove toolbars, right-click a toolbar and choose a toolbar name on the shortcut menu.
Scroll bars	The scroll bars help you get from place to place in a document.
View buttons	Click one of these to change your view of a document.
Status bar	The status bar gives you basic information about where you are and what you're doing in a document. It tells you what page and what section you're in, the total number of pages in the document, and where the insertion point is on the page.

To see the Standard toolbar and Formatting toolbar in two separate rows, click the Toolbar Options button and choose <u>S</u>how Buttons on Two Rows. You will find the miniscule Toolbar Options button on the far right side of the Standard or Formatting toolbar.

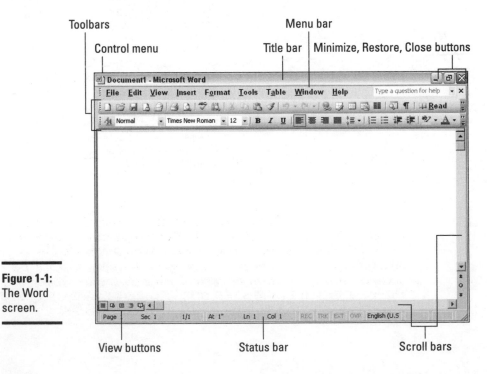

Figure 1-1: The Word screen.

Creating a New Document

Document is just a fancy word for a letter, report, announcement, or procla-
mation that you create with Word. When you first start Word, you see a document with the generic name "Document1." Apart from the new document
that appears when you start Word, the program offers a bunch of ways to
create a brand-new document:

✦ **Starting from a blank document:** Click the New Blank Document
button, press Ctrl+N, or click the Blank Document hyperlink in the New
Document task pane. Go this route and you get a blank document made
from the Normal template. For most occasions, the blank document is a
fine place to start.

✦ **Starting with a sophisticated template:** Click the On My Computer
hyperlink in the New Document task pane to open the Templates dialog
box and choose a template there, as shown in Figure 1-2. You'll find the
On My Computer hyperlink under the "Other Templates" in the New
Document task pane. If you don't see the task pane, press Ctrl+F1 or
choose <u>V</u>iew⇨Tas<u>k</u> Pane.

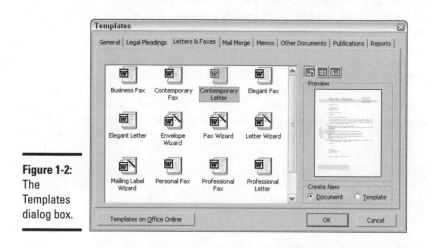

Figure 1-2:
The
Templates
dialog box.

Select a tab in the dialog box, select a template or wizard, and click the
OK button. Each template comes with its own sophisticated styles so
that you don't have to create fancy layouts yourself (Chapter 4 explains
styles). A *wizard* is a series of dialog boxes in which you make choices
about the kind of document you want. If you are in the market for a fancy
document, you can save a lot of time by doing it with a template or wizard
because you don't have to do most of the formatting yourself.

✦ **Starting with a template from the Microsoft Web site:** Click the Templates Home Page hyperlink on the New Document task pane to go to Microsoft.com and choose a template there.

Speedy Ways to Open Documents

Rooting around in the Open dialog box to find a document is a bother, so Word offers these handy techniques for opening documents:

✦ **File menu:** If you want to open a document you worked on recently, it may be on the File menu. Check it out. Open the File menu and see whether the document you want to open is one of those listed at the bottom of the menu. If it is, click its name or press its number (1 through 4).

✦ **Document list in New Document task pane:** The same documents that are listed on the File menu can also be found at the top of the New Document task pane. Click a file there to open it.

✦ **My Recent Documents button in the Open dialog box:** Click the My Recent Documents button in the Open dialog box to see a list of the last three dozen documents and folders that you opened. Double-click a document to open it; double-click a folder to see its contents.

✦ **My Documents button in the Open dialog box:** Click the My Documents button to see the contents of the My Documents folder. Double-click a document to open it. The My Documents folder is a good place to keep documents you are currently working on. When you're done with a current document, you can move it to a different folder for safekeeping.

✦ **Windows Documents menu:** Click the Start button and choose Documents to see a list of the last 15 files you opened (in Word and in other programs). Choose a Word document on the list to open it in Word.

✦ **Open the Recent Documents Menu:** Click the Start button, choose My Recent Documents, and select from the last several files you opened. This way, you open a file and a program at the same time.

To list more than four documents at the bottom of the File menu and the top of the New Document task pane, choose Tools⇨Options, select the General tab in the Options dialog box, and enter a number higher than 4 in the Recently Used File List box.

The New Document task pane appears when you start Word, but if you prefer not to see it when you start the program, choose Tools➪Options, select the View tab in the Options dialog box, and uncheck the Startup Task Pane check box.

All about Saving Documents

Everybody, or nearly everybody, knows how to save a document. All you have to do is press Ctrl+S, click the Save button, or choose File➪Save. The first time you save a document, you are asked to give it a descriptive name and choose the folder where it belongs. Word also offers the File➪Save As command for saving a file under a different name. You can also save versions of a document or save documents under a different format. Better read on.

Saving versions of documents

In a lengthy document such as a manual or a report that requires many drafts, saving different drafts can be helpful. That way, if you want to retrieve something that got dropped from an earlier draft, you can do so. One way to save drafts of a document is to save them under different names, but why do that when you can rely on the Versions command on the File menu?

Follow these steps to save different versions of a document as it evolves into a masterpiece:

1. **Choose File➪Versions.**

   The Versions In dialog box appears, as shown in Figure 1-3. It lists past versions of the document that you saved.

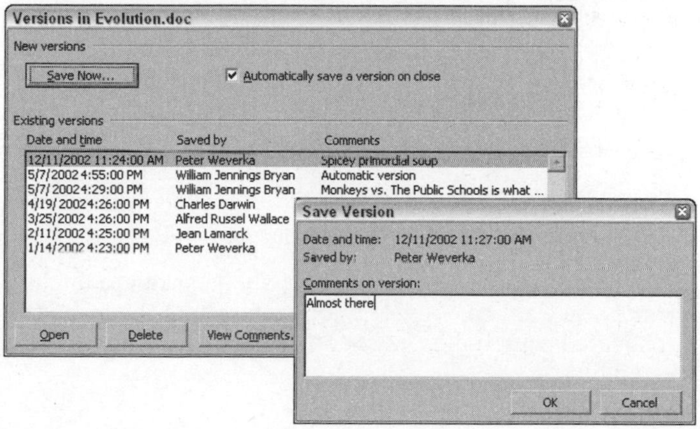

Figure 1-3:
Saving
different
versions of
a document.

Versions in Evolution.doc

New versions

Save Now...   ☑ Automatically save a version on close

Existing versions

Date and time	Saved by	Comments
12/11/2002 11:24:00 AM	Peter Weverka	Spicey primordial soup
5/7/2002 4:55:00 PM	William Jennings Bryan	Automatic version
5/7/2002 4:29:00 PM	William Jennings Bryan	Monkeys vs. The Public Schools is what ...
4/19/2002 4:26:00 PM	Charles Darwin	
3/25/2002 4:26:00 PM	Alfred Russel Wallace	
2/11/2002 4:25:00 PM	Jean Lamarck	
1/14/2002 4:23:00 PM	Peter Weverka	

Open   Delete   View Comments.

Save Version

Date and time: 12/11/2002 11:27:00 AM
Saved by: Peter Weverka

Comments on version:

Almost there|

OK   Cancel

2. **Click the Save Now button.**

3. **In the Save Version dialog box, write a descriptive comment about this version of the document and click OK.**

To review an earlier version of a document, choose File➪Versions. In the Versions In dialog box, read comments to find the version you want to open, select the version, and click the Open button. The earlier version appears in its own window next to the up-to-date version. You can tell which version you are dealing with by glancing at the title bar, which lists the date that the earlier version was saved. If a version of a document deserves to be a document in its own right, open it, choose File➪Save As, and save it under its own name. That way, you can get at it more easily.

Saving under a different file format

Suppose that a friend or co-worker isn't as sophisticated as you and doesn't have the latest version of Word. All is not lost: You can save Word documents under different formats and thereby permit others to open them. To save under a different format, choose File➪Save As, open the Save As Type drop-down list in the Save As dialog box, and choose a format. You will find many formats on the Save As Type drop-down list, including earlier versions of Word (97– 2002 and 6.0/95, as well as Rich Text Format), WordPerfect, and Macintosh formats. I should warn you, however, that converting a file to a different format is always a dicey proposition, because little things such as special characters often get mangled in the translation.

Word also offers the Batch Conversion Wizard for converting numerous files to a different format simultaneously. To use this wizard, start by creating a new folder and copying files you want to convert to the folder. While you're at it, create a new folder for storing the converted files. The Batch Conversion Wizard will ask you which files to convert and where to place the converted files. By creating the two folders to begin with, you can make the process go more smoothly. To run the Batch Conversion Wizard:

1. **Choose File➪New and select the On My Computer hyperlink in the New Document task pane.**

   Press Ctrl+F1 or choose View➪Task Pane to display the task pane.

2. **In the Templates dialog box, select the Other Documents tab.**

3. **Double-click the Batch Conversion icon.**

   The Conversion Wizard starts. You will be asked to declare which format you want to convert to or from, where the to-be-converted files are located, which files need converting, and where to place the converted files.

TIP

If everybody you work with is running an older version of Word and you want to save all your Word files under an older format, you can arrange to save files this way automatically. Choose Tools➪Options, select the Save tab in the Options dialog box, and choose a format from the Save Word Files As drop-down list.

Changing the Font and Size of Text

Font is the catch-all name for type style and type size. When you change fonts, you choose another style of type or change the size of the letters. Word offers a whole bunch of different fonts. You can see their names by clicking the down arrow next to the Font drop-down list and scrolling down the list. To change the font:

1. **Select the text or place the cursor where you want the font to change.**

2. **Click the down arrow on the Font drop-down list and select a font name.**

   As shown in Figure 1-4, you see the names of fonts, each one dressed up and looking exactly like itself. Word puts all the fonts you've used so far in the document at the top of the Font drop-down list to make it easier for you to find the fonts you use most often.

   To quickly scroll down the list, press a letter on your keyboard. Press S, for example, to scroll to fonts whose names begin with an S. Fonts with *TT* beside their names are TrueType fonts. Use these fonts if you can because they look the same on-screen as they do when printed on paper.

   Book IX, Chapter 1 explains how to load and unload fonts from your computer. Unload fonts when the Font menu gets too crowded.

Figure 1-4:
Choosing a
font and font
size.

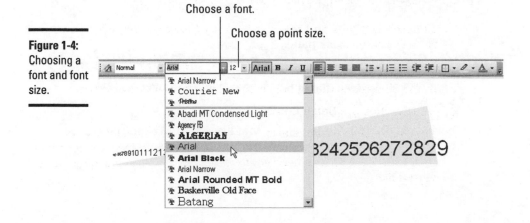

Choose a font.

Choose a point size.

Constructing your default document

When you open a brand-new document by clicking the New Blank Document button or pressing Ctrl+N, does the document meet your specifications? When you start typing, does the text appear in your favorite font? Are the margins just-so?

You can get a head start in creating documents by telling Word what you want new documents to look like. To do that, open the Font dialog box (choose Format⇨Font), the Page Setup dialog box (choose File⇨Page Setup), and the Language dialog box (choose Tools⇨Language⇨Set Language), in turn, make your choices, and click the Default button in these dialog boxes. Changes you make this way are made to the Normal document template (Chapter 4 explains what templates are).

Type is measured in *points*. A point is 1/72 of an inch. The larger the point size, the larger the letters. To change the size of letters:

1. **Select the letters or place the cursor where you want the larger or smaller letters to start appearing.**

2. **Click the down arrow on the Font Size drop-down list and choose a Font size.**

   Enter a point size in the Font Size box if the font sizes on the menu don't do the trick.

You can also change font sizes by selecting the text and pressing Ctrl+Shift+< or Ctrl+Shift+>. Doing so increases or decreases the font size by the next interval on the Font Size menu. Press Ctrl+] or Ctrl+[to increase or decrease the font size by 1 point.

To change fonts and font sizes at the same time, choose Format⇨Font and make your choices in the Font dialog box.

Changing lowercase to UPPERCASE and Vice Versa

What do you do if you look at your screen and discover — to your dismay — that you entered characters iN tHe wRONg casE! It happens. And sometimes Word does mysterious things to letters at the start of sentences and to capital letters in the middle of words. What can you do about that? You can fix uppercase and lowercase problems in two ways.

The fastest way is to select the text you entered incorrectly and press Shift+F3. Keep pressing Shift+F3 until the text looks right. Shift+F3 first changes the characters to all lowercase, then to Initial Capitals, then to ALL UPPERCASE, and then back to all lowercase again.

Microsoft Weird is very presumptuous about how it thinks capital letters should be used. You've probably noticed that already. You can't type a lowercase letter after a period without Word uppercasing it. You can't enter lowercase computer code at the start of a line without Word capitalizing the first letter. If Word capitalizes a letter against your will, move the pointer over the letter. You see the AutoCorrect Options button. At that point, you can click the button to open a drop-down menu and choose an option to undo the capitalization. For that matter, you can click the Control AutoCorrect Options command to open the AutoCorrect dialog box and choose for yourself what is "corrected" automatically (Chapter 2 explains the AutoCorrect options).

Spell-Checking a Document

Don't trust the smell checker — it can't catch all misspelled words. If you mean to type *middle* but type *fiddle* instead, for example, the spell-checker won't catch the error because *fiddle* is a legitimate word. The moral is: If you're working on an important document, proofread it carefully. Don't rely on the spell checker to catch all your smelling errors.

The spell-checker is great, however, for taking care of the majority of spelling errors. Figure 1-5 demonstrates the two ways to run the spell-checker. Red wiggly lines appear under words that Microsoft Word thinks are misspelled. Right-click a misspelled word and choose the correct word on the shortcut menu. Otherwise, go the whole hog and spell- or grammar-check an entire document or text selection by starting in one of these ways:

✦ Click the Spelling and Grammar button.

✦ Choose Tools➪Spelling and Grammar.

✦ Press F7.

The Spelling and Grammar dialog box appears. Options in this dialog box are self-explanatory, I think, except for these beauties:

✦ **Ignore Once:** Ignores the misspelling, but stops on it again if it appears later in the document.

✦ **Ignore All:** Ignores the misspelling wherever it appears in the document. Not only that, it ignores the misspelling in all your other open documents.

✦ **Add to Dictionary:** Adds the word in the Not in Dictionary box to the words in the dictionary that Microsoft Word deems correct. Click this button the first time that the spell checker stops on your last name to add your last name to the spelling dictionary.

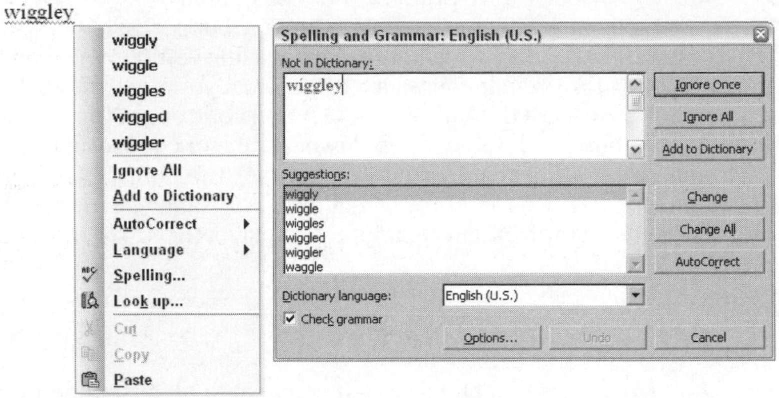

Figure 1-5:
Two ways to
fix spelling
errors.

✦ **Change All:** Changes not only this misspelling to the word in the Suggestions box, but also all identical misspellings in the document.

✦ **AutoCorrect:** Adds the suggested spelling correction to the list of words that are corrected automatically as you type them (Chapter 2 explains the AutoCorrect mechanism).

✦ **Undo:** Goes back to the last misspelling you corrected and gives you a chance to repent and try again.

✦ **Check Grammar:** Uncheck this box to run the spell checker and ignore what Word thinks are grammatical errors.

You can click outside the Spelling dialog box and fool around in your document, in which case the Ignore button changes names and becomes Resume. Click the Resume button to start the spell-check again.

Suppose that you have a bunch of computer code or French language text that you would like the spell checker to either ignore or check against its French dictionary instead of its English dictionary. To tell the spell checker how to handle text like that, select the text and choose Tools➪Language➪ Set Language. In the Language dialog box, choose a new language for your words to be spell-checked against, or else click the Do Not Check Spelling or Grammar check box.

From Word's standpoint, a dictionary is merely a list of words in a file, not a list of words and their definitions. To find spelling errors, Word compares each word on the page to the words in its main dictionary (Mssp3en.lex, if you write in U.S. English) and a second dictionary called Custom.dic. The Custom.dic dictionary lists words, proper names, and technical jargon that you deemed legitimate when you clicked the Add to Dictionary button in the course of a spell check. To edit a custom dictionary, choose Tools⇨Options, select the Spelling & Grammar tab in the Options dialog box, click the Custom Dictionaries button, select the dictionary that needs editing in the Custom Dictionaries dialog box, and click the Modify button. A dialog box appears with all the words in the dictionary in a list. Edit away.

What's with the red and green wiggly lines?

As you must have noticed by now, red wiggly lines appear under words that are misspelled, and green wiggly lines appear under words and sentences that Word thinks are grammatically incorrect. Correct spelling and grammar errors by right-clicking them and choosing an option from the shortcut menu. If the red or green lines annoy you, however, you can remove them from the screen by choosing Tools⇨Options and selecting the Spelling & Grammar tab in the Options dialog box:

✦ **Stop the wiggly lines from appearing:** Unselect the Check Spelling as You Type and Check Grammar as You Type check boxes.

✦ **Stop the lines from appearing in one document only:** Select the Hide Spelling Errors in This Document or Hide Grammatical Errors in this Document check boxes.

Chapter 2: Speed Techniques for Using Word

In This Chapter

✔ Changing views of a document

✔ Splitting the screen

✔ Selecting text

✔ Fixing mistakes quickly

✔ Going here and there in documents

✔ Entering text quickly

✔ Finding and replacing text and formats

Computers are supposed to make your work easier and faster. And if you can cut through all the jargon and technobabble, they can really do that. This chapter explains shortcuts and commands that can help you become a speedy user of Word. Everything in this chapter was put here so that you can get off work earlier and take the slow, scenic route home.

Getting a Better Look at Your Documents

A computer screen can be kind of confining. There you are, staring at the darn thing for hours at a stretch. Do you wish the view were better? The Word screen can't be made to look like the Riviera, but you can examine documents in different ways, zoom in and zoom out, and work in two places at one time in the same document. Better read on.

Viewing documents in different ways

In word processing, you want to focus sometimes on the writing, sometimes on the layout, and sometimes on the organization of your work. To help you stay in focus, Word offers different ways of viewing a document. Figure 2-1 shows what these views are. To change views, click a View button in the lower-left corner of the screen or choose a command from the View menu. Word offers no fewer than six ways to examine documents:

Figure 2-1:
Clockwise
from upper
left: Normal
view, Web
Layout view,
Outline
view,
Reading
Layout view,
Print
Preview,
and Print
Layout view.

✦ **Normal view:** Choose View➪Normal or click the Normal View button (in the lower-left corner of the screen) when you want to focus on the words. Normal view is best for writing first drafts and proofreading. You can see section breaks clearly in Normal view. You can't, however, see floating graphics in documents.

✦ **Web Layout view:** Choose View➪Web Layout or click the Web Layout View button to see what your document would look like as a Web page. Background colors appear. Text is wrapped to the window. Want to see precisely what your document would look like in a Web browser? Choose File➪Web Page Preview. The document opens in your default Web browser (probably Internet Explorer).

✦ **Print Layout view:** Choose View➪Print Layout or click the Print Layout View button to see the big picture. You can see graphics, headers, footers, and even page borders in Print Layout view. This is what your document will look like when it's printed.

✦ **Outline view:** Choose View➪Outline or click the Outline View button to see how your work is organized. In Outline view, you see only the headings in a document and can easily move chunks of a document from place to place. Chapter 7 explains outline view.

✦ **Reading Layout view:** Click the Read button on the Standard toolbar, choose View➪Reading Layout, or click the Reading button when you want to focus on the words. The Reading Mode toolbars appear on-screen. Click the Document Map or Thumbnails button to get from heading to heading or page to page. By clicking the Increase Text Size or Decrease Text Size button, you can make the type larger or smaller. Press Esc or click the Close button to exit Reading Layout view.

✦ **Full Screen view:** Choose View➪Full Screen if you want to get rid of everything except the text you're working on. When you choose Full Screen, everything gets stripped away — buttons, menus, scroll bars, and all. Only a single button called Close Full Screen remains. Click it or press Esc when you want the buttons, menus, and so on to come back. You can give commands from the menus on the menu bar in Full Screen view by moving the pointer to the top of the screen to make the menu bar appear. You can also press shortcut key combinations and right-click to see shortcut menus.

✦ **Print Preview view:** Choose File➪Print Preview or click the Print Preview button to see what entire pages look like. Use this view to see the big picture and find out whether documents are laid out correctly. By clicking the Multiple Pages button, you can see one, two, or several pages simultaneously.

Zooming in, zooming out

Eyes were not meant to stare at computer screens all day, which makes the Zoom command all the more valuable. Use this command freely and often to enlarge or shrink the text on your screen and preserve your eyes for important things, such as gazing at the horizon.

Give this command in one of these ways:

✦ Click the down arrow in the Zoom menu and choose a magnification percentage from the drop-down list, as shown in Figure 2-2. You will find the Zoom menu on the Standard toolbar.

✦ Click inside the Zoom menu, type a percentage of your own, and press the Enter key.

✦ Choose View➪Zoom and, in the Zoom dialog box, choose a setting.

Sometimes it pays to shrink the text way down to see how pages are laid out. For instance, after you lay out a table, shrink it down to see how it looks from a bird's-eye view.

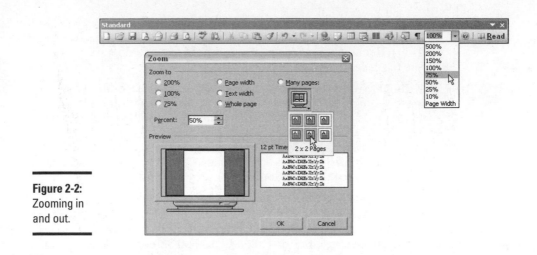

Figure 2-2:
Zooming in
and out.

Book IX, Chapter 3 explains Windows XP techniques for making the screen easier to see and read.

Working in two places in the same document

You can open a window on two different places simultaneously in a document. One reason you might do this: You are writing a long report and want the introduction to support the conclusion, and you also want the conclusion to fulfill all promises made by the introduction. That's difficult to do sometimes, but you can make it easier by opening the document to both places and writing the conclusion and introduction at the same time.

Word offers two methods for opening the same document to two different places: Opening a second window on the document or splitting the screen.

Opening a second window

To open a second window on a document, choose <u>W</u>indow⇨<u>N</u>ew Window. Immediately, a second window opens and you see the start of your document.

✦ Select the <u>W</u>indow menu and you'll see that it now lists two versions of your document, number 1 and number 2 (the numbers appear after the filename). Choose number 1 to go back to where you were before.

✦ You can move around in either window as you please. Changes you make in either window also appear in the other window. Choose the <u>F</u>ile⇨<u>S</u>ave command in either window and you save all the changes you made in both windows. The important thing to remember here is that you are working on a single document, not two documents.

✦ When you want to close the second or third window, just click its Close Window button. This button is located in the upper-right corner of the screen, below the Close button.

Splitting the screen

Splitting a window means to divide it into north and south halves, as shown in Figure 2-3. In a split screen, two sets of scroll bars appear so that you can travel in one half of the screen without disturbing the other half. Word offers two ways to split the screen:

✦ Move the mouse cursor to the *split box* at the top of the scroll bar on the right. Move it just above the arrow. When the cursor turns into double-arrows, click and drag the gray line down the screen. When you release the mouse button, you have a split screen.

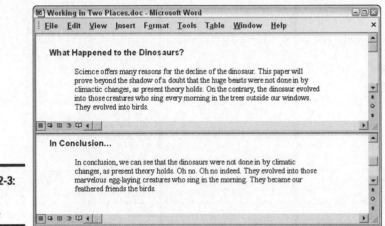

Figure 2-3:
A split
screen.

✦ Choose <u>W</u>indow⇨<u>S</u>plit. A gray line appears on-screen. Roll the mouse down until the gray line is where you want the split to be, and click. You get two screens split down the middle.

When you tire of this schizophrenic arrangement, choose <u>W</u>indow⇨Remove Split, drag the gray line to the top or bottom of the screen, or double-click on the line that splits the screen in two.

In a split screen, you can choose a view for the different halves. For example, choose Outline view for one half and Normal view for the other to see the headings in a document while you write the introduction.

Selecting Text in Speedy Ways

To move text or copy it from one place to another, you have to select it first. You can also erase a great gob of text merely by selecting it and pressing the Delete key. So it pays to know how to select text. Table 2-1 describes shortcuts for selecting text.

Table 2-1	Shortcuts for Selecting Text
To Select This	*Do This*
A word	Double-click the word.
A line	Click in the left margin next to the line.
Some lines	Drag the mouse over the lines or drag the mouse pointer down the left margin.
A paragraph	Double-click in the left margin next to the paragraph.
A mess of text	Click at the start of the text, hold down the Shift key, and click at the end of the text.
A gob of text	Put the cursor where you want to start selecting, press F8 or double-click EXT (it stands for Extend) on the status bar, and press an arrow key, drag the mouse, or click at the end of the selection.
Yet more text	If you select text and realize you want to select yet more text, double-click EXT on the status bar and start dragging the mouse or pressing arrow keys.
Text with the same formats	Right-click text that is formatted a certain way and choose Select Text with Similar Formatting.
A document	Hold down the Ctrl key and click in the left margin, or triple-click in the left margin, or choose Edit⇨Select All, or press Ctrl+A.

If you have a bunch of highlighted text on-screen and you want it to go away but it won't (because you pressed F8 or double-clicked EXT to select it), double-click EXT again.

After you press F8 or double-click EXT, all the keyboard shortcuts for moving the cursor also work for selecting text. For example, press F8 and then press Ctrl+Home to select everything from the cursor to the top of the document. Double-click EXT and press End to select to the end of a line.

Tricks for Editing Text

Following are some tried-and-true techniques for editing faster and better. On these pages, you find out how to take some of the drudgery out of repetitive work, fix errors, fit text on the screen, and view format symbols so that you can tell why text lies where it does on the page.

Undoing a mistake

Fortunately for you, all is not lost if you make a big blunder in Word, because the program has a marvelous little tool called the Undo command. This command "remembers" the editorial and formatting changes you made since you opened your document. As long as you catch your error before you do five or six new things, you can "undo" your mistake. Try one of these undo techniques:

✦ Choose Edit⇨Undo (or press Ctrl+Z). The name of this command changes on the menu, depending on what you did last. For example, if you just typed a sentence, it says `Undo Typing`.

✦ Click the Undo button to undo your most recent change. If you made your error and went on to do something else before you caught it, click the down arrow next to the Undo button. You see a menu of your previous six actions. Click the one you want to undo or, if it isn't on the list, use the scroll bar until you find the error and then click it, as shown in Figure 2-4. However, if you do this, you also undo all the actions on the Undo menu above the one you're undoing. For example, if you undo the 98th action on the list, you also undo the 97 before it.

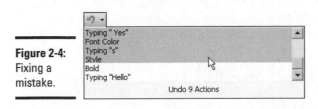

Figure 2-4:
Fixing a
mistake.

Contrary to the Undo command is the Redo command. It "redoes" the commands you "undid." If you've "undone" a bunch of commands and regret having done so, pull down the Redo menu by clicking its down arrow and then choose the commands you thoughtlessly "undid" the first time around.

Repeating an action — and quicker this time

The Edit menu contains a command called Repeat that you can choose to repeat your last action, and it can be a mighty, mighty time-saver. For example, if you just changed a heading style and you want to change another heading in the same way, move the cursor to the next heading and choose Edit⇨Repeat (or press F4 or Ctrl+Y). Rather than go to the trouble of clicking the Style menu and choosing a heading style from the drop-down list, all you have to do is choose a simple command or press a key or two.

If you had to type "I will not talk in class" a hundred times, all you would have to do is write it once and choose Edit⇨Repeat (or press F4 or Ctrl+Y) 99 times.

Viewing the hidden format symbols

Sometimes it pays to see the hidden format symbols when you are editing and laying out a document. The symbols show where lines break, where tab spaces are, where one paragraph starts and another ends, and whether two spaces instead of one appear between words. To see the hidden format symbols, click the Show/Hide¶ button. Click the button again to hide the symbols. Here's what the hidden symbols look like on-screen.

Symbol	How to Enter
Line break (()	Press Shift+Enter
Optional hyphen (_)	Press Ctrl+hyphen
Paragraph (¶)	Press Enter
Space (·)	Press the spacebar
Tab ((tm))	Press tab

Moving Around Quickly in Documents

Besides sliding the scroll bar, Word offers a handful of very speedy techniques for jumping around in documents: pressing shortcut keys, browsing in the Select Browse Object menu, using the Go To command, and navigating with the Document Map or thumbnails. Read on to discover how to get there faster, faster, faster.

Keys for getting around quickly

One of the fastest ways to go from place to place is to press the keys and key combinations listed in Table 2-2.

Table2-2	Keys for Moving Around Documents
Key to Press	*Where It Takes You*
PgUp	Up the length of one screen
PgDn	Down the length of one screen
Ctrl+PgUp	To the previous page in the document
Ctrl+PgDn	To the next page in the document
Ctrl+Home	To the top of the document
Ctrl+End	To the bottom of the document

If pressing Ctrl+PgUp or Ctrl+PgDn doesn't get you to the top or bottom of a page, it's because you clicked the Select Browse Object button at the bottom of the vertical scroll bar, which makes Word go to the next bookmark, comment, heading, or whatever. Click the Select Browse Object button and choose Browse by Page to make these key combinations work again.

TIP

Here's a useful keystroke for getting from place to place: Shift+F5. Press it once to go to the previous location where you edited text, and twice or three times to go to the one or two places previous to that. Press Shift+F5 after you open a document and you will go to the last edit you made prior to saving and closing it.

Viewing thumbnail pages

In lengthy documents such as the one shown in Figure 2-5, the best way to get from place to place is to use Thumbnails view. In Thumbnails view, a thumbnail of each page in the document appears in the window pane on the left side of the screen. Each thumbnail is numbered so that you always know which page you are viewing. To quickly move from page to page, use the scroll bar on the left side of the screen. To switch to Thumbnails view, choose View⇨Thumbnails.

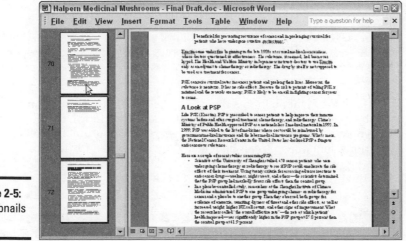

Figure 2-5:
Thumbnails
view.

"Browsing" around a document

A really fast way to move around quickly is to click the Select Browse Object button in the lower-right corner of the screen. When you click this button, Word presents 12 "Browse by" icons.

Select the icon that represents the element you want to go to, and Word takes you there immediately. For example, click the Browse by Heading icon to get to the next heading in your document (provided that you assigned heading styles to headings). After you have selected a "Browse by" icon, the navigator buttons — the double-arrows directly above and below the Select Browse Object button — turn blue. Click a blue navigator button to get to the next example or the previous example of the element you chose. For example, if you selected the Browse by Heading icon, all you have to do is click the blue navigator buttons to get from heading to heading, backward or forward in a document.

Going there fast with the Go To command

Another fast way to go from place to place in a document is to use the Edit⇨Go To command. Choose this command or press either Ctrl+G or F5 to see the Go To tab of the Find and Replace dialog box, shown in Figure 2-6.

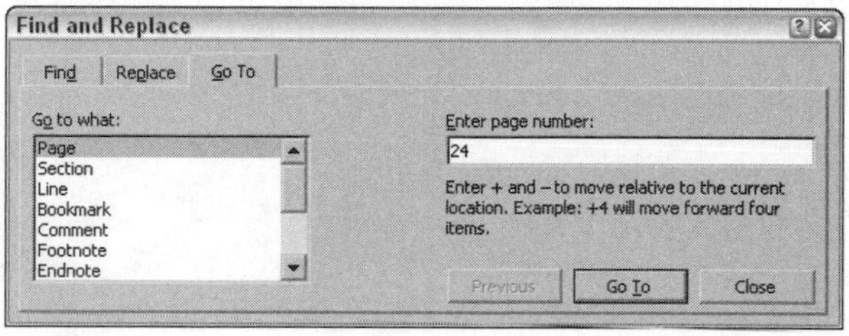

Figure 2-6: Using the Go To command.

Find and Replace	? ✕

Find | Replace | Go To

Go to what:

Page
Section
Line
Bookmark
Comment
Footnote
Endnote

Enter page number:

24

Enter + and – to move relative to the current location. Example: +4 will move forward four items.

Previous | Go To | Close

The Go to What menu in this dialog box lists everything that can conceivably be numbered in a Word document, and other things, too. Everything that you can get to with the Select Browse Object button, as well as lines, equations, and objects, can be reached by way of the Go To tab. Click a menu item and enter a number, choose an item from the drop-down list, or click the Previous or Next button to go elsewhere.

Hopping from place to place in the Document Map

Yet another way to hop from place to place is by turning on the document map. To do so, click the Document Map button or choose View⇨Document Map. The headings in your document appear along the left side of the screen, as shown in Figure 2-7.

Select an item in the Document Map, and Word takes you there in the twinkling of an eye. The Document Map is like a table of contents whose headings you can click to get from place to place. Right-click the document map and choose a heading level option on the shortcut menu to tell Word which headings to display in the map. You can also select Expand or Collapse on the shortcut menu to see or hide lower-level headings.

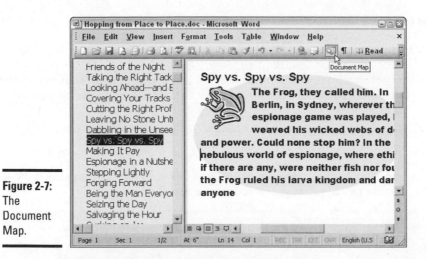

Figure 2-7:
The
Document
Map.

Bookmarks for hopping around

Rather than press PgUp or PgDn or click the scroll bar to thrash around in a long document, you can use bookmarks. All you do is put a bookmark in an important spot in your document that you'll return to many times. When you want to return to that spot, choose Insert⇨Bookmark, double-click the bookmark in the Bookmark dialog box, and click the Close button. True to the craft, the mystery writer whose bookmarks are shown in Figure 2-8 wrote the end of the story first and used bookmarks to jump back and forth between the beginning and end to make all the clues fit together.

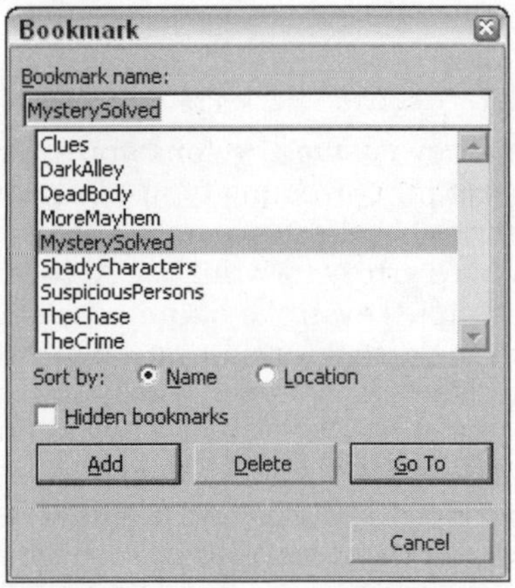

Figure 2-8:
The
Bookmark
dialog box.

Follow these instructions to handle bookmarks:

✦ **Adding a bookmark:** To place a bookmark in a document, click where you want the bookmark to go, choose Insert⇨Bookmark (or press Ctrl+Shift+F5), type a descriptive name in the Bookmark Name box, and click the Add button. Bookmarks can't start with numbers or include blank spaces.

✦ **Deleting a bookmark:** To delete a bookmark, select it in the Bookmark dialog box and click the Delete button.

Word uses bookmarks for many purposes. For example, bookmarks indicate in a document where cross-references are located.

Inserting a Whole File in a Document

One of the beautiful things about word processing is that you can recycle documents. Say that you wrote an essay on the Scissor-Tailed Flycatcher that would fit very nicely in a broader report on North American birds. You can insert the Scissor-Tailed Flycatcher document into your report document:

1. **Place the cursor where you want to insert the document.**

2. **Choose Insert⇨File.**

3. **In the Insert File dialog box, find and select the file you want to insert.**

4. **Click the Insert button.**

Making Fewer Typing Errors

Most people are clumsy typists. They mistype certain words time and time again. Word's spell checker is great for correcting typos, but you can correct typos literally as you make them with the features described in the following pages. With AutoCorrect, Word fixes errors for you. Use AutoText to enter whole words or phrases with a simple keystroke or menu selection. The Autoformat As You Type options make text formatting a little bit easier.

AutoCorrect: Correcting typos on the fly

As part of its AutoCorrect mechanism, the divine and invisible hand of Word corrects certain typos after you enter them and press the spacebar. Try misspelling *weird* by typing *wierd* to see what I mean. You can have Word correct the typos that you make often, and with a little cunning, you can even use the AutoCorrect feature to enter long company names and hard-to-spell names on-the-fly. AutoCorrect entries apply to all the Office programs, not just Word.

As shown in Figure 2-9, the AutoCorrect dialog box offers a comprehensive list of words that are "autocorrected," as well as options for telling Word what to autocorrect. To open this dialog box, choose Tools⇨AutoCorrect Options.

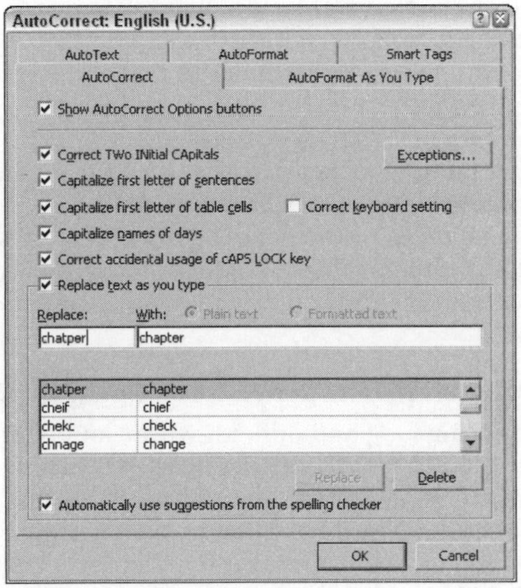

Figure 2-9:
Add words
you often
misspell
to the
AutoCorrect
list.

When you have a spare moment, open the AutoCorrect dialog box and do the following:

✦ Remove the check marks from the AutoCorrect features that you don't want. For example, if you enter a lot of computer code in your manuscripts, you don't necessarily want the first letter of sentences to be capitalized automatically, so you should uncheck the Capitalize First Letter of Sentences check box to deselect it.

✦ If you want, remove the check mark from the Replace Text as You Type box to keep Word's invisible hand from correcting idiosyncrasies in capitalization and spelling as you enter them.

✦ Scroll through the list and take a look at the words that are "autocorrected." If you don't want a word on the list to be corrected, select it and click Delete.

✦ If a word that you often misspell isn't on the list, you can add it to the list and have Word correct it automatically. Enter the misspelling in the Replace box, enter the right spelling in the With box, and click the Add button.

✦ If you don't like one of the replacement words, select the word on the list, enter a new replacement word in the With box, and click the Replace button.

If Word makes an autocorrection that you don't care for, move the pointer over the spot where the correction was made. You see the AutoCorrect Options button. By clicking it, you can get a drop-down menu with options for reversing the correction, telling Word never to make the correction again, and opening the AutoCorrect dialog box.

Most people consistently misspell certain words. Yours truly, for example, always trips over the word *chapter,* which I usually spell *chatper.* You can add the words you misspell often to the list of "autocorrected" words by right-clicking a misspelling, choosing AutoCorrect on the shortcut menu, and choosing the option that describes how the word is correctly spelled.

AutoText: Entering graphics and text quickly

The "AutoCorrect for entering long and difficult words and names" sidebar describes a way to enter graphics and text quickly with the AutoCorrect command. Here's another way to do it: Put the text and graphics that you often use on the Insert⇨AutoText list (Word has already placed a few common entries there). That way, you can enter the long-winded text or a complicated graphic simply by clicking a few menu commands or typing a couple of letters. Addresses, letterheads, and company logos are ideal candidates for the AutoText list because they take so long to enter.

AutoCorrect for entering long and difficult words and names

With a little cunning, you can use AutoCorrect to enter long words, long e-mail addresses, and even graphics. Suppose that you are writing the definitive work on Gaetano Donizetti, the Italian opera composer. To keep from having to type his long name again and again, choose Tools⇨AutoCorrect Options, enter **/gd** (or something similar) in the Replace box, enter Donizetti's full name in the With box, and click the Add button. Now all you have to do is type **/gd** and a blank space, and AutoCorrect writes out the entire name. The catch is that you have to enter a sequence of letters in the Replace box that you won't ever, ever, ever need to really use.

Word has already created a handful of AutoText entries for — month, days of the week, and others. To see what I mean, try typing "September." After you type the first four letters, a bubble appears: "September (Press ENTER to Insert)." As the man says, you can press the Enter key (or Tab or F3) to insert months and days of the week without typing them from start to finish.

AutoText entries are stored in templates. That means they are available only in the template in which you are working, although AutoText entries can be copied from template to template with the Organizer. If you try to make an AutoText entry and it doesn't work, you're in the wrong template. Chapter 4 explains what templates are and how to copy AutoText and styles between templates.

To create an AutoText entry, type the text or import the graphic, select it, and choose Insert⇨AutoText⇨New (or press Alt+F3). The Create AutoText dialog box appears. Type a name for the text or graphic in the text box and click OK.

Word offers several ways to insert an AutoText entry:

✦ Start typing the entry's name. Midway through, a bubble appears with the entire entry. Press Enter at that point to insert the whole thing.

✦ Type the entry's name and then press F3.

✦ Display the AutoText toolbar, click the All Entries button, select a sub-menu name, and choose an AutoText entry.

✦ Choose Insert⇨AutoText, select a submenu name, and choose an AutoText Entry.

To delete an AutoText entry, choose Insert⇨AutoText⇨AutoText to open the AutoCorrect dialog box, select the entry that you want to delete, and click the Delete button.

Some people find the AutoText bubbles annoying. They pop up in the oddest places. To keep the bubbles from appearing, choose Insert⇨ AutoText⇨AutoText and uncheck the Show AutoComplete Suggestions check box.

AutoFormat As You Type

You must have noticed by now that Word occasionally formats text and paragraphs for you. To see what I mean, open a new document, type **The Title** (be sure to capitalize both words), and press Enter twice. Word assigns the Heading 1 style to the words you typed because it assumes that you entered a heading. Now try this: Type **1.**, press the spacebar, type **one**, and press the Enter key. On the next line, Word enters a 2 on the idea that you want to create a numbered list. Try typing **1st**, **2nd**, or **3rd** — Word formats these ordinal numbers like so: 1st, 2nd, 3rd.

Mysterious changes like these are made as part of Word's AutoFormat as You Type options. For the most part, these changes are good, but at some point in your career as a Microsoft Word double-agent, go over these options and choose the ones that are right for you. To check out these options, choose Tools⇨AutoCorrect Options, select the AutoFormat As You Type tab in the AutoCorrect dialog box, and choose which options you want. Figure 2-10 shows the AutoFormat as You Type tab.

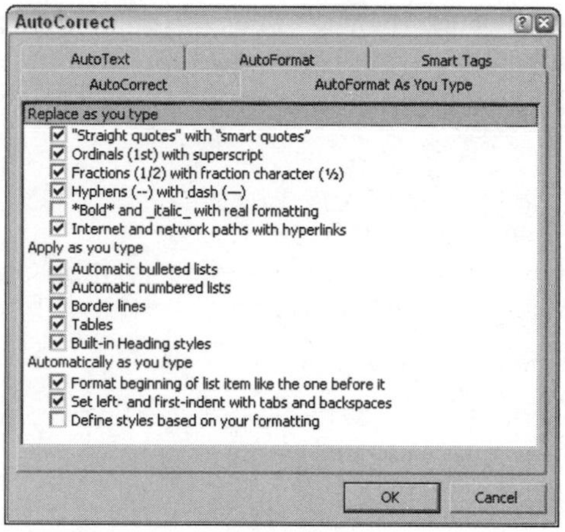

Figure 2-10: The AutoFormat As You Type options.

Finding and Replacing

The Find and Replace commands are some of the most powerful commands in Office. Use them wisely and you can find passages in documents, correct mistakes *en masse,* change words and phrases throughout a document, and even reformat a document. These pages explain how to find errant words and phrases and replace them if you so choose with different words and phrases.

Finding a word, paragraph, or format

You can search for a word in a document, and even search for fonts, special characters, and formats. Here's how:

1. **Choose Edit⇨Find, press Ctrl+F, or click the Select Browse Object button in the lower-right corner of the screen and choose Find.**

The Find and Replace dialog box appears, as shown in Figure 2-11. In the figure, the More button is clicked so that you can see all the Find options.

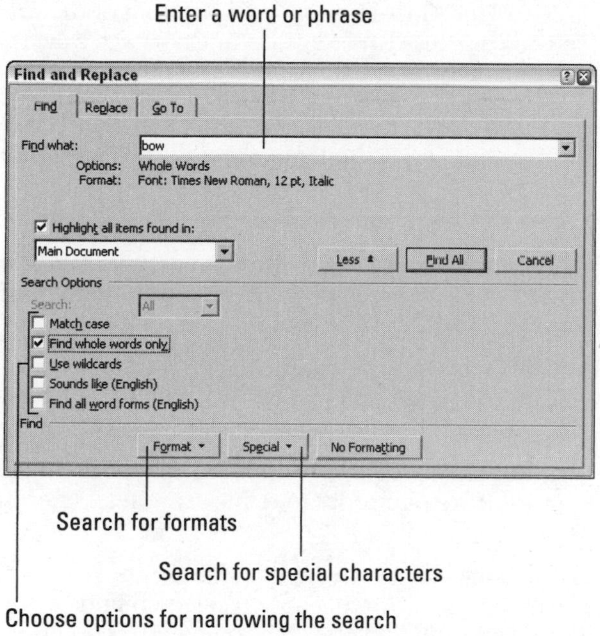

Enter a word or phrase

Figure 2-11:
Conducting a find operation.

Search for formats

Search for special characters

Choose options for narrowing the search

2. **Enter the word, phrase, or format that you're looking for in the Find What text box (I explain how to search for formats shortly).**

   The words and phrases you looked for recently are on the Find What drop-down menu. Open the Find What drop-down menu and make a selection from that list if you want.

3. **To search for all instances of the thing you are looking for, check the Highlight All Items Found In check box and make a choice from the drop-down menu.**

   If you go this route, Word highlights all instances of the thing you are looking for.

4. **Click the Find Next button if you are looking for a simple word or phrase, or the Find All button to highlight all instances of a word or phrase in your document.**

   Click the More button, if necessary, to open the bottom half of the dialog box and conduct a sophisticated search.

If Word finds what you're looking for, it highlights the thing — or Word highlights all instances of the thing if that is the way you chose to search. To find the next instance of the thing you are looking for, click Find Next again. You can also close the Find and Replace dialog box and click either the Previous Find/Go To or Next Find/Go To button at the bottom of the scroll bar to the right of the screen (or press Ctrl+Page Up or Ctrl+Page Down) to go to the previous or next instance of the thing you're looking for.

By clicking the More button in the Find and Replace dialog box, you can get very selective about what to search for and how to search for it:

✦ **Search:** Open the menu and choose a direction for searches.

✦ **Match Case:** Searches for words with upper- and lowercase letters that exactly match those in the Find What box. With this box selected, a search for *bow* finds that word, but not *Bow* or *BOW*.

✦ **Find Whole Words Only:** Normally, a search for *bow* yields *elbow, bowler, bow-wow,* and all other words with the letters *b-o-w* (in that order). Click this option and you get only *bow.*

✦ **Use Wildcards:** Click here if you intend to use wildcards in searches (see "Using wildcard operators to refine searches," later in this chapter).

✦ **Sounds Like:** Looks for words that sound like the one in the Find what box. A search for *bow* with this option selected finds *beau,* for example. However, it doesn't find *bough.* This command isn't very reliable.

✦ **Find All Word Forms:** Takes into account verb conjugations and plurals. With this option clicked, you get *bows, bowing,* and *bowed,* as well as *bow.*

To search for words, paragraphs, tab settings, and styles, among other things, that are formatted a certain way, click the Format button and choose an option from the menu. You see the familiar dialog box you used in the first place to format the text. In Figure 2-11, I chose Font from the Format menu and filled in the Font dialog box in order to search for the word *bow* in Times Roman, 12-point, italicized font.

That No Formatting button is there so that you can clear all the formatting from the Find What box.

Searching for special characters

Table 2-3 describes the special characters you can look for in Word documents. To look for the special characters listed in the table, enter the character directly in the Find What text box or click the Special button in the

Find and Replace dialog box and choose a special character from the menu. Be sure to enter lowercase letters. For example, you must enter **^n**, not **^N**, to look for a column break. And take note: A caret (^) precedes special characters.

Before searching for special characters, click the Show/Hide¶ button. That way, you will see the special characters — also known as the hidden format symbols — on-screen when Word finds them. See "Tricks for Editing Text," earlier in this chapter, if you need to know how the hidden format symbols work.

Table 2-3	Special Characters for Searches
To Find/Replace	*Enter*
Manual Formats That Users Insert	
Column break	^n
Manual line break (()	^l
Manual page break	^m
Paragraph break (¶)	^p
Section break[1]	^b
Tab space (()	^t
Carets, Hyphens, Dashes, and Spaces	
Caret (^)	^^
Em dash (—)	^+
En dash (–)	^=
Nonbreaking hyphen	^~
Optional hyphen	^-
White space (one or more blank spaces)	^w
Characters and Symbols	
Foreign character	You can type foreign characters in the Find What and Replace With text boxes
ANSI and ASCII characters and symbols	^*nnnn*, where *nnnn* is the four-digit code
Clipboard contents[2]	^c
Contents of the Find What box[2]	^&
Elements of Reports and Scholarly Papers	
Endnote mark[1]	^e
Footnote mark[1]	^f
Graphic[1]	^g

[1]*For use in search operations; can be entered only in the Find What text box*

[2]*For use in replace operations; can be entered only in the Replace With text box*

Before searching for special characters, click the Show/Hide¶ button. That way, you'll see the special characters — also known as the hidden format symbols — on-screen when Word finds them.

Creative people find many uses in the Find and Replace dialog box for special characters. The easiest way to find section breaks, column breaks, and manual line breaks in a document is to enter ^b, ^n, or ^l, respectively, in the Find What text box and start searching. By combining special characters with text, you can make search operations more productive. In Figure 2-12, for example, special characters and text are used in a find-and-replace operation to find all double hyphens in a document and replaces them with em dashes. This kind of find-and-replace operation is especially useful for cleaning up documents that were imported into Word.

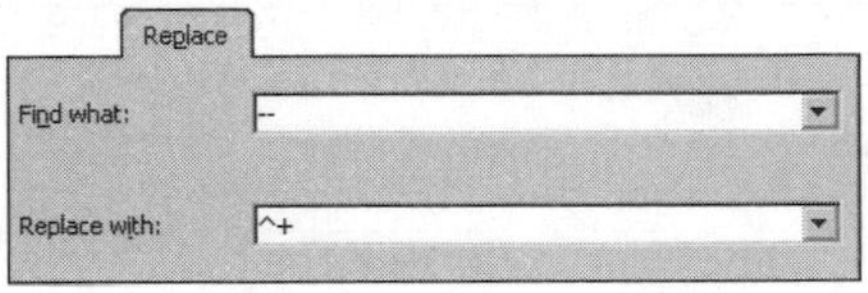

Figure 2-12:
Special
characters
search and
replacing.

Replace
Find what: | --
Replace with: ^+

Using wildcard operators to refine searches

A *wildcard operator* is a character that represents characters in a search expression. Wildcards aren't for everybody. Using them requires a certain amount of expertise, but after you know how to use them, wildcards can be very valuable in searches and macros. Table 2-4 explains the wildcard operators you can use in searches.

Table 2-4	Wildcards for Searches	
Operator	**What It Finds**	**Example**
?	Any single character	**b?t** finds *bat, bet, bit,* and *but.*
*	Zero or more characters	**t*o** finds *to, two,* and *tattoo.*
[*xyz*]	A specific character, *x, y,* or *z*	**t[aeiou]pper** finds *tapper, tipper,* and *topper.*
[*x-z*]	A range of characters, *x* through *z*	**[1-4]000** finds 1000, 2000, 3000, and 4000, but not 5000.
[!*xy*]	Not the specific character or characters, *xy*	**p[!io]t** finds *pat* and *pet,* but not *pit* or *pot.*
<	Characters at the beginning of words	**<info** finds *information, infomaniac,* and *infomercial.*
>	Characters at the end of words	**ese>** finds *these, journalese,* and *legalese.*

Operator	What It Finds	Example
@@	One or more instances of the previous character	**sho@@t** finds *shot* and *shoot.*
{*n*}	Exactly *n* instances of the previous character	**sho{2}t** finds *shoot* but not *shot.*
{*n,*}	At least *n* instances of the previous character	**^p{3,}** finds three or more paragraph breaks in a row, but not a single paragraph break or two paragraph breaks in a row.
{*n,m*}	From *n* to *m* instances of the previous character	**10{2,4}** finds 100, 1000, and 10000, but not 10 or 100000.

You can't conduct a whole-word-only search with a wildcard. For example, a search for **f*s** not only finds "fads" and "fits" but also all text strings that begin with *f* and end with *s*, such as "for the birds." Wildcard searches can yield many, many results and are sometimes useless.

To search for an asterisk (*), question mark (?), or other character that serves as a wildcard search operator, place a backslash before it in the Find What text box.

Finding and replacing text and formats

The Edit⇨Replace command is a very powerful tool indeed. If you're writing a Russian novel and you decide on page 816 to change the main character's last name from Oblonsky to Oblomov, you can change it on all 816 pages with the Edit⇨Replace command in about half a minute.

But here's the drawback: You never quite know what this command will do. Newspaper editors tell a story about a newspaper that made it a policy to use the word *African-American* instead of *black*. A laudable policy, except that a sleepy editor made the change with the Edit⇨Replace command and didn't review it. Next day, a lead story on the business page read, "After years of running in the red, US Steel has paid all its debts, and now the corporation is running well in the African-American, according to company officials."

Always save your document before you use the Edit⇨Replace command. Then, if you replace text that you shouldn't have replaced, you can close your document without saving it, open your document again, and get your original document back.

To replace words, phrases, or formats throughout a document:

1. **Choose Edit⇨Replace, or press Ctrl+H.**

2. **As shown in Figure 2-13, fill in the Find What box just as you would if you were searching for text or formats.**

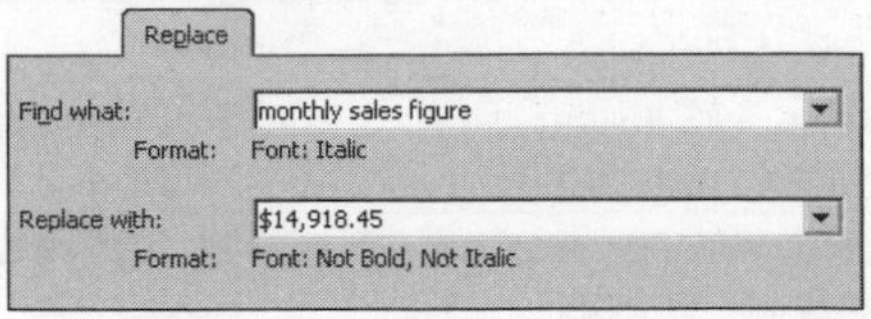

Figure 2-13:
A search-
and-replace
operation.

Replace		
Find what:	monthly sales figure	▾
Format:	Font: Italic	
Replace with:	$14,918.45	▾
Format:	Font: Not Bold, Not Italic	

However, be sure to click the Find Whole Words Only check box if you want to replace one word with another. Depending on which options appear in the dialog box, you might have to click the More button to see all of them. (Earlier in this chapter, "Finding a word, paragraph, or format," explains how to conduct a search.)

3. **In the Replace With box, enter the text that will replace what is in the Find What box. If you're replacing a format, enter the format.**

4. **Either replace everything simultaneously or do it one at a time.**

   Click one of these buttons:

   • Click Replace All to make all replacements in an instant.

   • Click Find Next and then either click Replace to make the replacement or Find Next to bypass it.

The sleepy newspaper editor I told you about clicked the Replace All button. Do that only if you're very confident and know exactly what you're doing. In fact, one way to keep from making embarrassing replacements is to start by using the Edit⇨Find command. When you land on the first instance of the thing you're searching for, click the Replace tab and tell Word what should replace the thing you found. This way, you can rest assured that you entered the right search criteria and that Word is finding exactly what you want it to find.

Entering Information Quickly with Forms

A *form* is a means of soliciting and recording information. Besides creating paper forms, you can create computerized forms that make entering data easy. Instead of entering every piece of information, you can choose it from drop-down lists and check boxes. Designing computerized forms is a tricky business and is too complicated for this little book, but this section will at least get you started.

Creating a paper form

To create paper forms, use commands on the Table menu. By shading cells, by merging cells, by drawing borders around different parts of the table, and by using different fonts, you can create a form like the one shown in Figure 2-14. (Chapter 5 in this mini-book explains how to work with tables.)

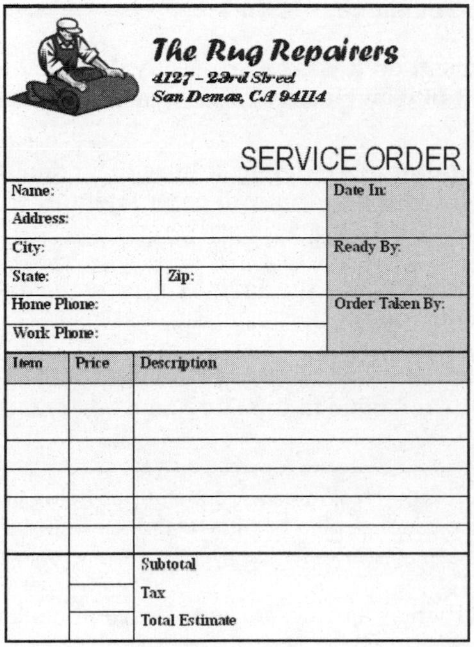

The Rug Repairers
4127 – 23rd Street
San Demas, CA 94114

SERVICE ORDER

Name:		Date In:
Address:		
City:		Ready By:
State:	Zip:	
Home Phone:		Order Taken By:
Work Phone:		

Item	Price	Description
		Subtotal
		Tax
		Total Estimate

Figure 2-14: Create paper forms with Table menu commands.

Creating a computerized form

A computerized form is an electronic version of a paper form. Computerized forms make entering data easier because the person who enters the data can type only in predefined areas — the person can't erase the names of the fields where data is entered. If you were to turn the paper form in Figure 2-14 into a computerized form, you or someone else could then enter the data from the paper forms into a computer file very quickly and cleanly.

The first step to creating a computerized form is to design the form. Enter the names of the fields — the places where information goes — and leave empty spaces for the information itself. Rather than design the computerized form from scratch, you can use a paper form that you created with Microsoft Word.

After you have designed the form, you turn it into a template and tell Word where the fields are. With that done, you choose File⇨New, choose the template that you created for your new file, and open the file. Then you enter the raw data itself. You can enter data in the predefined fields only. When you are done, you have a file with all the data in it.

Here is how to create a computerized form:

1. **Open a new document or, if you have already designed a paper form and want to turn it into an electronic form, open the paper form's file on your computer.**

2. **Label the fields appropriately and make sure that enough room is on the form to enter the raw data you will enter later.**

3. **Choose File➪Save As to save the document as a template.**

4. **Click the down arrow to open the Save As Type menu and choose Document Template (*.dot).**

   The Template folder's name appears in the Save In box.

5. **Type a name for the template in the File Name box and click the Save button.**

Now that the form is a template, you have to put input fields in it so that raw data can be entered into them. A *field* is simply a place to put information. Input fields fall into three categories:

✦ **Text:** A text entry, such as a name, address, or telephone number.

✦ **Check box:** A "multiple choice," such as two or three check boxes, only one of which can be selected.

✦ **Drop-down:** A drop-down menu of choices.

To enter input field types, open the Forms toolbar. Do that by right-clicking a toolbar and choosing Forms from the shortcut menu. To enter the input fields, go to the first place in the template where data is to be entered and click the Text Form Field, Check Box Form Field, or Drop-Down Form Field button on the Forms toolbar, depending on the type of field you need. When you do so, Word puts shading on the form where the field is. (If you don't see the shading, click the Form Field Shading button on the Forms toolbar).

 ✦ **Text Form Field:** For entering text on the form. You can double-click the field (or click the Form Fields Options button) to open the Text Form Field Options dialog box. From there, you can enter default text or establish a limit to the number of characters that can be entered in the field.

 ✦ **Check Box Form Field:** For entering a check box that the data-entry person can click to show agreement or disagreement. Double-click the field (or click the Form Fields Options button) to enter a default value (checked or unchecked).

✦ **Drop-Down Form Field:** For entering multiple choices on the form. Double-click the field (or click the Form Fields Options button) to open the Drop-Down Form Field Options dialog box and enter the multiple choices, as shown in Figure 2-15. To enter a choice, type it in the Drop-Down Item text box and click the Add button. Click a Move button to arrange choices on the menu.

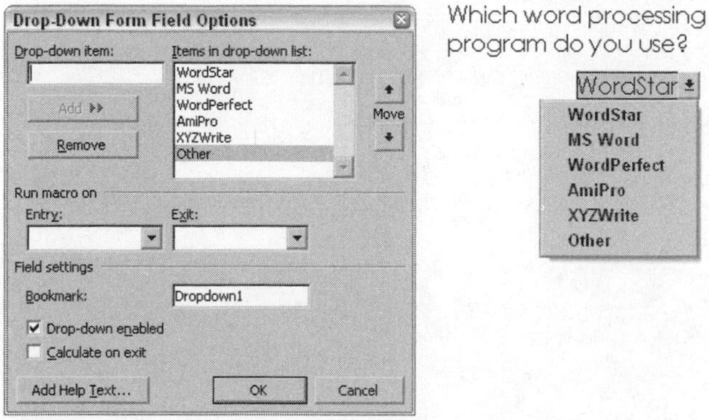

Drop-Down Form Field Options

Drop-down item:

Items in drop-down list:
WordStar
MS Word
WordPerfect
AmiPro
XYZWrite
Other

Add ▸▸

Remove

Move
▲
▼

Run macro on
Entry:

Exit:

Field settings
Bookmark: Dropdown1

☑ Drop-down enabled
☐ Calculate on exit

Add Help Text...   OK   Cancel

Which word processing program do you use?

WordStar ▾
WordStar
MS Word
WordPerfect
AmiPro
XYZWrite
Other

Figure 2-15:
Creating a drop-down field for a form.

Keep going down the template and entering form fields. Don't worry about the fields' length. Unless you click the Form Fields Options button and change the settings, text of any length can be entered in input fields. However, you may want to change the length setting in a ZIP Code field to keep anyone from inputting more than nine numbers, for example.

 When you're done entering the input fields, click the Protect Form button. Now whoever enters the data on the form cannot disturb the field names. He or she can type only in the input fields. Finally, save the template and close it.

Now that you have the template, you or someone else can enter data cleanly in easy-to-read forms:

1. **Choose File⇨New to open a new document to enter the data in.**

2. **In the New Document task pane, select On My Computer Templates (you'll find it under the Other Templates).**

   The Templates dialog box opens.

3. **On the General tab, double-click the template you created for entering data in your form.**

4. **Enter information in the input fields.**

   Press the up or down arrow, or press Tab and Shift+Tab to move from field to field. You can also click input fields to move the cursor there. Notice that you can't change the field labels.

5. **When you're done, print the document or save it.**

Chapter 3: Laying Out Text and Pages

In This Chapter

- ✔ Entering a section break
- ✔ Starting a new page
- ✔ Changing the margins
- ✔ Indenting text
- ✔ Handling bulleted and numbered lists
- ✔ Hyphenating the text

This chapter explains how to format text and pages. A well-laid-out document says a lot about how much time and thought was put into a document. This chapter presents tips, tricks, and techniques for making pages look just right.

In this chapter, you learn what section breaks are and why they are so important to formatting. You discover how to establish the size of margins, determine how much space appears between lines of text, indent text, handle lists, and hyphenate text, as well as number the pages and handle headers and footers.

Paragraphs and Formatting

Back in English class, your teacher taught you that a paragraph is a part of a longer composition that presents one idea or, in the case of dialogue, presents the words of one speaker. Your teacher was right, too, but for word-processing purposes, a paragraph is a lot less than that. In word processing, a paragraph is simply what you put on-screen before you press the Enter key.

For instance, a heading is a paragraph. If you press Enter on a blank line to go to the next line, the blank line is considered a paragraph. If you type **Dear John** at the top of a letter and press Enter, "Dear John" is a paragraph.

It's important to know this because paragraphs have a lot to do with formatting. If you choose the Format➪Paragraph command and monkey around with the paragraph formatting, all your changes affect everything in the paragraph that the cursor is in. To make format changes to a whole paragraph, all you have to do is place the cursor there. You don't have to select the paragraph. And if you want to make format changes to several paragraphs in a row, all you have to do is select those paragraphs first.

Inserting a Section Break for Formatting Purposes

Every document has at least one *section.* That's why "Sec 1" appears on the left side of the status bar at the bottom of the screen. When you want to change page numbering schemes, headers and footers, margin sizes, and the page orientation, you have to create a *section break* to start a new section. Word creates one for you when you create newspaper-style columns or change the size of margins.

Follow these steps to create a new section:

1. **Click where you want to insert a section break.**

2. **Choose Insert➪Break.**

You see the Break dialog box, shown in Figure 3-1.

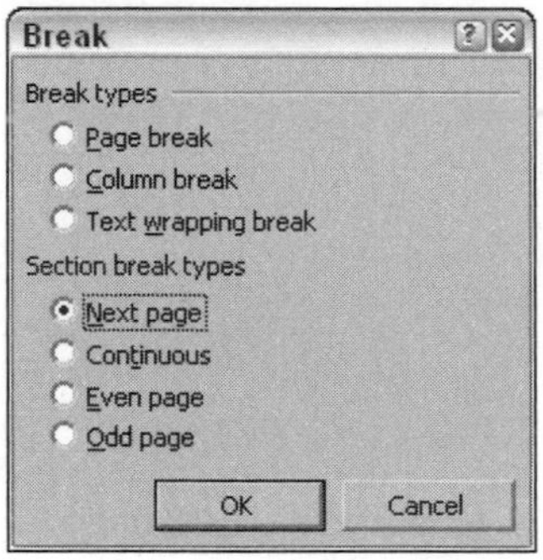

Figure 3-1:
Creating a section break.

Break

Break types
- ◯ Page break
- ◯ Column break
- ◯ Text wrapping break

Section break types
- ◉ Next page
- ◯ Continuous
- ◯ Even page
- ◯ Odd page

OK   Cancel

3. **Under Section Break Types, tell Word which kind of section break you want and then click OK.**

All four section break options create a new section, but they do so in different ways:

✦ **Next Page:** Inserts a page break as well as a section break so that the new section can start at the top of a new page (the next one). Select this option to start a new chapter, for example.

✦ **Continuous:** Inserts a section break in the middle of a page. Select this option if, for example, you want to introduce newspaper-style columns in the middle of a page.

✦ **Even Page:** Starts the new section on the next even page. This option is good for two-sided documents in which the headers on the left- and right-side pages are different.

✦ **Odd Page:** Starts the new section on the next odd page. You might choose this option if you have a book in which chapters start on odd pages. (By convention, that's where they start.)

To delete a section break, make sure that you are in Normal view, click the dotted line, and press the Delete key.

Editing a document with many sections can be confusing, and if you accidentally delete a section break, you can turn a perfectly good document into guacamole. In the same way that paragraph marks store formats for a paragraph, section breaks store formats for an entire section. If you accidentally delete a section break, you apply new formats, because the section is folded into the section that formerly followed it and adopts that next section's formats. Because it's easy to accidentally delete a section break and create havoc, I recommend working in Normal view when your document has many section breaks. In Normal view, you can tell where a section ends because Section Break and a double dotted line appear on-screen. The only way to tell where a section ends in Print Layout view is to glance at the "Sec" listing on the status bar or click the Show/Hide¶ button.

Breaking a Line

To break a line of text in the middle before it reaches the right margin without starting a new paragraph, press Shift+Enter or choose <u>I</u>nsert⇨<u>B</u>reak and select the Text <u>W</u>rapping Break option button in the Break dialog box. Figure 3-2 shows how you can press Shift+Enter to make lines break better. The paragraphs are identical, but I broke lines in the right-side paragraph to make the text easier to read. Line breaks are marked with the (symbol. To erase line breaks, click the Show/Hide¶ button to see these symbols; then backspace over them.

Figure 3-2:
Break lines
to make
reading
easier.

| "A computer in every home and a chicken in every pot is our goal," stated Rupert T. Verguenza, President and CEO of the New Technics Corporation International at the annual shareholder meeting this week. | "A computer in every home and a chicken in every pot is our goal," stated Rupert T. Verguenza, President and CEO of the New Technics Corporation International at the annual shareholder meeting this week. |

Starting a New Page

Word gives you another page so that you can keep going when you fill up one page. But what if you're impatient and want to start a new page right away? Whatever you do, *don't* press Enter again and again until you fill up the page. Instead, create a page break by doing either of the following:

✦ Press Ctrl+Enter.

✦ Choose Insert➪Break and select the Page Break option in the Break dialog box.

In Normal view, you know when you've inserted a page break because you see the words Page Break and a dotted line appear on-screen. In Print Layout view, you can't tell where you inserted a page break. To delete a page break, switch to Normal view, click the words Page Break, and press the Delete key. Change views by clicking the View buttons in the lower-left corner of the screen.

Setting Up and Changing the Margins

Margins are the empty spaces along the left, right, top, and bottom edges of a page, as shown in Figure 3-3. Headers and footers fall, respectively, in the top and bottom margins. And you can put graphics, text boxes, and page numbers in the margins as well. Margins serve to frame the text and make it easier to read.

When you start a new document, give a moment's thought to the margins. Changing the size of margins after you have entered the text, clip art, graphics, and whatnot can be disastrous. Text is indented from the left and right margins. Pages break on the bottom margin. If you change margin settings, indents and page breaks change for good or bad throughout your document. By setting the margins carefully from the beginning, you can rest assured that text will land on the page where you want it to land.

Seeing what the formats are

Especially if you are a convert from WordPerfect, seeing how text was formatted merely by looking is difficult. WordPerfect users are accustomed to looking at the Reveal Codes, which show precisely where formats begin and end. There are no Reveal Codes in Word, but you can find out how text was formatted with this command: Format➪Reveal Formatting (press Shift+F1). The Reveal Formatting task pane opens and tells you plain as day how your text is formatted — how it is aligned, indented, and spaced, for example.

Reveal Formatting

Selected text

Sample Text

☐ Compare to another selection

Formatting of selected text

⊟ **Font**
Font:
(Default) Times New Roman
12 pt
Language:
English (U.S.)

⊟ **Paragraph**
Alignment:
Left
Indentation:
Left: 0"
Right: 0"

⊞ **Section**

Options

☐ Distinguish style source
☐ Show all formatting marks

While the Reveal Formatting task pane is open, you can take advantage of these amenities:

✦ **Compare one part of a document to another:** Check the Compare to Another Section check box and then click another part of your document. The Reveal Formatting task pane describes how the two parts differ. Knowing how parts of a document differ can be invaluable when you're creating and modifying styles.

✦ **Find out which style was assigned:** Check the Distinguish Style Source check box. The task pane lists the style you assigned to the part of your document the cursor is in.

✦ **See the formatting marks:** Check the Show All Formatting Marks check box. Checking this box has the same results as clicking the Show/Hide¶ button on the Standard toolbar — you can tell where paragraphs end, where line breaks are, and where tab spaces were entered.

Don't confuse margins with indents. Text is indented from the margin, not from the edge of the page. If you want to change how far text falls from the page edge, indent it. To change margin settings in the middle of a document, you have to create a new section.

To set up or change the margins, start by choosing File➪Page Setup. You see the Page Setup dialog box. The Margins tab offers commands for handling margins:

Outside margin   Inside margins   Outside margin

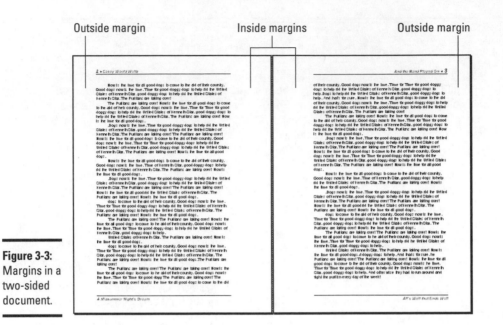

Figure 3-3:
Margins in a
two-sided
document.

✦ **Margins:** Enter measurements in the <u>T</u>op, <u>B</u>ottom, <u>L</u>eft, and <u>R</u>ight boxes to tell Word how much blank space to put along the sides of the page.

✦ **Gutter:** The *gutter* is the part of the paper that the binding eats into when you bind a document. Enter a measurement in the <u>G</u>utter box to increase the left or inside margin and make room for the binding. Notice on the pages of this book, for example, that the margin closest to the binding is wider than the outside margin. Choose Top on the G<u>u</u>tter Position menu if you intend to bind your document from the top, not the left, or inside, of the page. Some legal documents are bound this way.

✦ **Two-sided documents (inside and outside margins):** In a bound document in which text is printed on both sides of the pages, the terms "left margin" and "right margin" are meaningless. What matters instead is in the *inside margin*, the margin in the middle of the page spread next to the bindings, and the *outside margin*, the margin on the outside of the page spread that isn't affected by the bindings (refer to Figure 3-3). Choose Mirror Margins on the Multiple Pages drop-down menu and adjust the margins accordingly if you will print on both sides of the paper.

✦ **App<u>l</u>y To:** Choose Whole Document to apply your settings to the entire document, This Section to apply them to a section, or This Point Forward to change margins for the rest of a document. When you choose This Point Forward, Word creates a new section.

To get a good look at where boundaries are, choose <u>T</u>ools⇨<u>O</u>ptions, select the View tab in the Options dialog box, and select the Te<u>x</u>t Boundaries check box.

Indenting Paragraphs and First Lines

An *indent* is the distance between a margin and the text, not the edge of the page and the text. Word offers a handful of different ways to change the indentation of paragraphs.

The fastest way is to use the Increase Indent and Decrease Indent buttons on the Formatting toolbar to move the paragraph away from or toward the left margin:

1. **Click in the paragraph whose indentation you want to change; if you want to change more than one paragraph, select those paragraphs.**

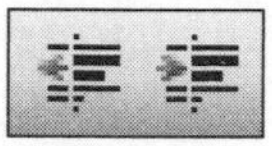

2. **Click the Increase Indent or Decrease Indent button (or press Ctrl+M or Ctrl+Shift+M) as many times as necessary to indent the text.**

You can also change indentations by using the ruler to "eyeball it." This technique requires some dexterity with the mouse, but it allows you to see precisely where paragraphs and the first lines of paragraphs are indented.

1. **Choose <u>V</u>iew⇨<u>R</u>uler, if necessary, to put the ruler on-screen.**

2. **Select the paragraph or paragraphs whose indentation you want to change.**

3. **Slide an indent marker with the mouse.**

   Figure 3-4 shows where these markers are:

Figure 3-4:
Indenting
with the
ruler.

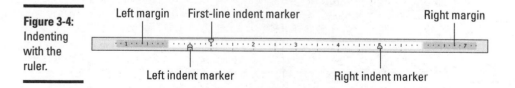

Left margin   First-line indent marker   Right margin

Left indent marker   Right indent marker

- **First-line indent marker:** Drag the down-pointing arrow on the ruler to indent only the first line of the paragraph.

- **Left indent marker:** This one, on the bottom-left side of the ruler, comes in two parts. Drag the arrow that points up (called the hanging indent marker), but not the box underneath it, to move the left margin independently of the first-line indentation. To move the left indentation *and* the first-line indentation relative to the left margin, slide the box. Doing so moves everything on the left side of the ruler.

- **Right indent marker:** Drag this one to move the right side of the paragraph away from or toward the right margin.

If you're not one for "eyeballing it," you can use the Format⇨Paragraph command to indent paragraphs. Choose Format⇨Paragraph or double-click the Left or Right indent marker on the ruler to open the Paragraph dialog box, and then make selections in the Indentation area.

Numbering the Pages

Word numbers the pages of a document automatically, which is great, but if your document has a title page and table of contents and you want to start numbering pages on the fifth page, or if your document has more than one section, page numbers can turn into a sticky business. The first thing to ask yourself is whether you've included headers or footers in your document. If you have, go to "Putting Headers and Footers on Pages," the next section in this chapter. It explains how to put page numbers in a header or footer.

Use the Insert⇨Page Numbers command to put plain old page numbers on the pages of a document. You see the Page Numbers dialog box, shown in Figure 3-5. This dialog box actually inserts a {Page} field inside a frame in the header or footer. In the Position and Alignment boxes, choose where you want the page number to appear. Click to remove the check mark from the Show Number on First Page box if you're working on a letter or other type of document that usually doesn't have a number on page 1.

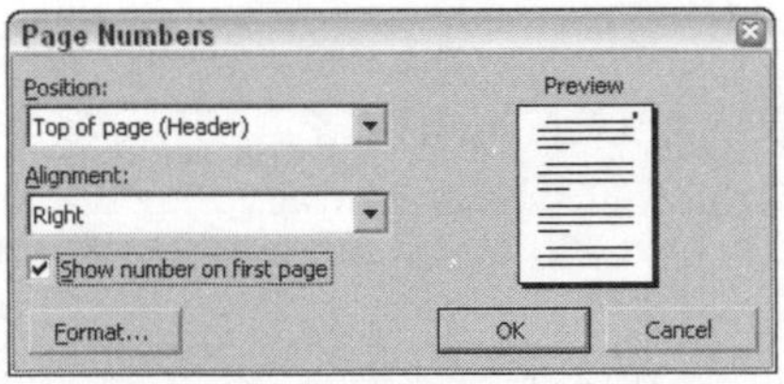

Figure 3-5:
Simple page
numbers.

Putting Headers and Footers on Pages

A *header* is a little description that appears along the top of a page so that the reader knows what's what, as shown in Figure 3-6. Usually, headers include the page number and a title. A *footer* is the same thing as a header except that it appears along the bottom of the page, as befits its name. To change headers or footers in the middle of a document, you have to create a new section.

To put a header or a footer in a document, follow these steps:

1. **Choose View⬎Header and Footer.**

If you're in Print Layout view and you've already entered a header or footer, you can edit it by double-clicking the header or footer text.

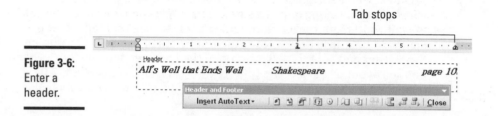

Figure 3-6:
Enter a
header.

2. **Type your header in the box, or if you want a footer, click the Switch between Header and Footer button and type your footer.**

While you're typing away in the Header or Footer box, you can call on most of the commands on the Standard and Formatting toolbars. You can change the text's font and font size, click an alignment button, and paste text from the Clipboard. Tabs are set up in headers and footers to make it possible to center, left-align, and right-align text. To center a header or footer, for example, press the Tab key once to go to the Center tab mark and start typing.

3. **Click the Close button.**

To remove a header of footer, choose View⬎Header and Footer or double-click the header or footer in Print Layout view, and then delete the text.

Here are some header and footer features that may be useful to you:

✦ **Inserting a page number:** Click the Insert Page Number button on the Header and Footer toolbar (or press Alt+Shift+P). While you're at it, you can type the words *page* and *of* and click the Insert Number of Pages button to list the total number of pages, like so: page 4 of 16.

✦ **Inserting the date and time:** By clicking the Insert Date and Insert Time button, you can enter the date and time at which the document is printed.

✦ **Changing headers and footers from section to section:** Click the Same As Previous button to change headers and footers (you must first divide the document into sections). "Unpressing" (clicking to release it) this button tells Word that you don't want this header or footer to be the same as the header or footer in the previous section of the document. When this button is pressed down, the header or footer is the same, and the Header or Footer box reads Same as Previous, but when you "unpress the button," the words Same as Previous don't appear. You can click the Show Previous or Show Next button to examine the header or footer in the previous or next section and see what the header of footer there is.

✦ **Different headers and footers for odd and even pages:** As I explain previously in "Setting Up and Changing the Margins," documents in which text is printing on both sides of the page can have different headers and footers for the left and right side of the page spread (refer to Figure 3-3). Choose File➪Page Setup or click the Page Setup button on the Header and Footer toolbar to open the Page Setup dialog box. Then, on the Layout tab, select the Different Odd and Even check box. The header or footer box now reads "Odd" or "Even" to tell you which side of the page spread you are dealing with.

✦ **Removing headers or footers from the first page**: To remove a header or footer from the first page of a document or section, choose File➪Page Setup or click the Page Setup button on the Header and Footer toolbar. In the Page Setup dialog box, select the Layout tab, check the Different First Page check box, and click OK.

Adjusting the Space Between Lines

To change the spacing between lines, select the lines whose spacing you want to change or simply put the cursor in a paragraph if you're changing the line spacing in a single paragraph (if you're just starting a document, you're ready to go). Then click the down-arrow beside the Line Spacing button and choose an option on the drop-down menu.

To take advantage of more line-spacing options, choose Format➪Paragraph (or select More, the last option on the Line Spacing button menu). Then, in the Paragraph dialog box, select a Line Spacing option:

✦ **At Least:** Choose this one if you want Word to adjust for tall symbols or other unusual text. Word adjusts the lines but makes sure there is, at minimum, the number of points you enter in the At box between each line.

✦ **Exactly:** Choose this one and enter a number in the At box if you want a specific amount of space between lines.

✦ **Multiple:** Choose this one and put a number in the At box to get triple-, quadruple-, quintuple-, or any other number of spaced lines.

To quickly single-space text, click it or select it if you want to change more than one paragraph, and press Ctrl+1. To quickly double-space text, select the text and press Ctrl+2. Press Ctrl+5 to put one and a half lines between lines of text.

Creating Numbered and Bulleted Lists

What is a word-processed document without a list or two? It's like an emperor with no clothes. Numbered lists are invaluable in manuals and books like this one that present a lot of step-by-step procedures. Use bulleted lists when you want to present alternatives to the reader. A *bullet* is a black, filled-in circle or other character.

Simple numbered and bulleted lists

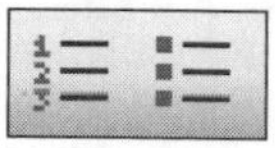

The fastest, cleanest, and most honest way to create a numbered or bulleted list is to enter the text without any concern for numbers or bullets. Just press Enter at the end of each step or bulleted entry. When you're done, select the list and click the Numbering or Bullets button on the Formatting toolbar.

Meanwhile, here are some tricks for handling lists:

✦ **Ending a list:** Press the Enter key twice after typing the last entry in the list. You can also choose Format➪Bullets and Numbering or right-click the list and choose Bullets and Numbering to open the Bullets and Numbering dialog box, shown in Figure 3-7. From there, click the None option on the Numbered or Bulleted tab and click OK.

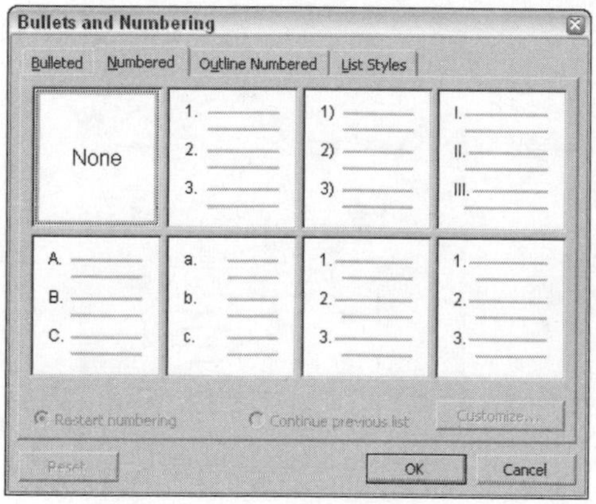

Figure 3-7:
The Bullets
and
Numbering
dialog box.

✦ **Picking up where you left off:** Suppose that you want a numbered list to resume where a list you entered earlier ended. In other words, suppose that you left off writing a four-step list, put in a graphic or some paragraphs, and now you want to resume the list at Step 5. Click the Numbering button to start numbering again. The AutoCorrect Options button appears on-screen. Click it and choose Continue Numbering. You can also open the Bullets and Numbering dialog box and select the Continue Previous List option button.

✦ **Starting a new list:** Suppose that you want to start a brand-new list right away. Right-click the number Word entered and choose Restart Numbering on the shortcut menu. You can also open the Bullets and Numbering dialog box (refer to Figure 3-7) and choose Restart numbering.

Constructing lists of your own

If you are an individualist and you want numbered and bulleted lists to work your way, start from the Bullets and Numbering dialog box shown in Figure 3-7 (choose Format⇨Bullets and Numbering to get there). On the Bulleted and Numbered tabs, you can choose among different kinds of bullets and different numbering schemes.

If those choices aren't good enough for you, click the Customize button to open the Customize Bulleted List or Customize Numbered List dialog box, shown in Figure 3-8. These dialog boxes offer opportunities for indenting numbers or bullets and the text that follows them in new ways. You can also choose fonts for the numbers and symbols for the bullets. The card shark in Figure 3-8 created bulleted entries for hearts, clubs, spades, and diamonds. Be sure to watch the Preview area of these dialog boxes. It shows exactly what you are doing to your bulleted or numbered lists.

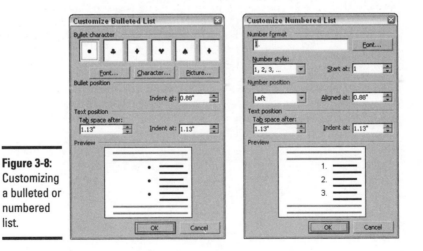

Figure 3-8: Customizing a bulleted or numbered list.

Working with Tabs

Tabs are a throwback to the days of the typewriter, when it was necessary to make tab stops in order to align the next item. Except for making leaders and aligning text in headers and footers, everything you can do with tabs can also be done by creating a table — and it can be done far faster. All you have to do is align the text inside the table and then remove the table borders. Chapter 5 explains tables.

Automatic lists and what to do about them

Word creates automatic lists for you whether you like it or not. To see what I mean, type the number 1, type a period, press the spacebar, type the first entry in the list, and press Enter to get to the next line and type the second entry. As soon as you press Enter, Word inserts the number 2 and formats the list for you. In the same manner, Word creates bulleted lists when you type an asterisk (*), press the spacebar, type the first entry in the list, and press Enter.

Some people find this kind of behind-the-scenes skullduggery annoying. If you are one such person, either click the AutoCorrect Options button — it appears automatically — and choose Stop Automatically Creating Lists, or else choose Tools⇨AutoCorrect Options, select the AutoFormat As You Type tab in the AutoCorrect dialog box, and uncheck the Automatic Numbered Lists and Automatic Bulleted Lists check boxes.

A *tab stop* is a point on the ruler around which or against which text is formatted. When you press the Tab key, you advance the text cursor by one tab stop. Tab stops are set at half-inch intervals on the ruler, but you can change that if you want. You can also change the type of tab. By default, tabs are left-aligned, which means that when you enter letters after you press the Tab key, the letters move toward the right in the same way that they move toward the right when text is left-aligned. However, Word also offers right, center, decimal, and bar tabs. Figure 3-9 shows the differences between the tab settings. Notice the symbols on the ruler — they tell you what type of tab you are dealing with.

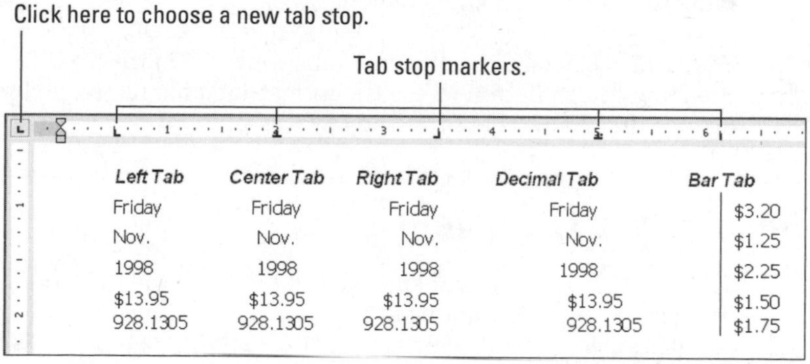

Click here to choose a new tab stop.

Tab stop markers.

Figure 3-9:
The five kinds of tab stops.

Left Tab	Center Tab	Right Tab	Decimal Tab	Bar Tab
Friday	Friday	Friday	Friday	$3.20
Nov.	Nov.	Nov.	Nov.	$1.25
1998	1998	1998	1998	$2.25
$13.95	$13.95	$13.95	$13.95	$1.50
928.1305	928.1305	928.1305	928.1305	$1.75

To change tabs or change where tabs appear on the ruler, start by selecting the paragraphs for which you need different tabs. Then click in the box on the left side of the ruler as many times as necessary to choose the kind of tab you want, and click on the ruler where you want the tab to go. You can click as many times as you want and enter more than one kind of tab.

All about tab leaders

In my opinion, the only reason to fool with tabs and tab stops is to create tab leaders like the ones shown in the following figure. A *leader* is a series of punctuation marks — periods in the illustration — that connects text across a page. Leaders are very elegant. For the figure, I used left-aligned tab stops for the characters' names and right-aligned tab stops for the players' names. I included leaders so that you can tell precisely who played whom.

Follow these steps to create tab leaders:

1. **Enter the text and, in each line, enter a tab space between the text on the left side and the text on the right side.**

2. **Select the text and choose Format⇨Tabs to open the Tabs dialog box.**

3. **Enter a position for the first new tab in the Tab Stop Position box.**

4. **Under Leader in the dialog box, select the punctuation symbol you want.**

5. **Click OK, display the ruler, and drag tab markers to adjust the space between the text on the left and right.**

The Players

Romeo	McGeorge Wright
Juliet	Gabriela Hernandez
Mercutio	Chris Suzuki
Lady Capulet	Mimi Hornstein

To move a tab, simply drag it to a new location on the ruler. Text that has been aligned with the tab moves as well. To remove a tab, drag it off the ruler. When you remove a tab, the text to which it was aligned is aligned to the next remaining tab stop on the ruler or to the next default tab stop if you didn't create any tab stops of your own.

Sometimes it's hard to tell where tabs were put in the text. To find out, click the Show/Hide¶ button to see the formatting characters, including the arrows that show where the Tab key was pressed.

Hyphenating a Document

The first thing you should know about hyphenating the words in a document is that you may not need to do it. Text that hasn't been hyphenated is much easier to read, which is why the majority of text in this book, for example, isn't hyphenated. It has a *ragged right margin,* to borrow typesetter lingo. Hyphenate only when text is trapped in columns or in other narrow places, or when you want a very formal-looking document.

Do not insert a hyphen simply by pressing the hyphen key, because the hyphen will stay there even if the word appears in the middle of a line and doesn't need to be broken in half. Instead, when a big gap appears in the right margin and a word is crying out to be hyphenated, put the cursor where the hyphen needs to go and press Ctrl+hyphen. This way, you tell Word to make the hyphen appear only if the word breaks at the end of a line. (To remove a manual hyphen, press the Show/Hide¶ button so that you can see it; then backspace over it.)

Hyphenating a document automatically

To hyphenate a document automatically:

1. **Choose Tools⇨Language⇨Hyphenation.**

You see the Hyphenation dialog box, shown in Figure 3-10.

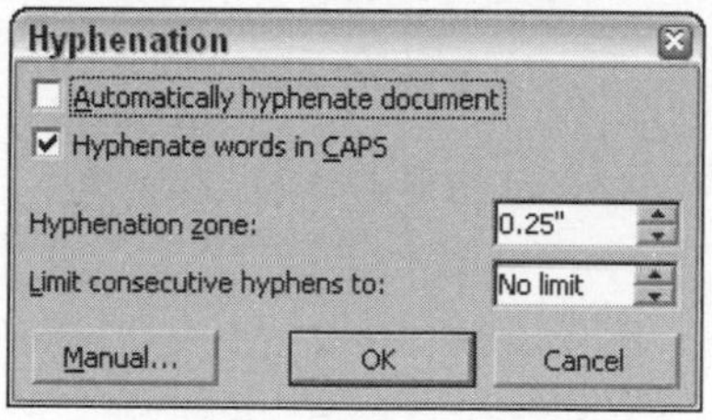

Figure 3-10:
Hyphen-
ating the
text.

2. **Click Automatically Hyphenate Document to let Word do the job.**

While you're at it, click Hyphenate Words in CAPS to remove the check mark if you don't care to hyphenate words in uppercase.

If the text isn't justified — that is, if it's "ragged right" — you can play with the Hyphenation Zone setting (but I don't think you should hyphenate ragged-right text anyway). Words that fall in the Zone are hyphenated, so a large zone means a less ragged margin but more ugly hyphens, and a small zone means fewer ugly hyphens but a more ragged right margin.

3. **Having more than two consecutive hyphens on the right margin looks bad, so enter 2 in the Limit Consecutive Hyphens To box.**

4. **Click OK.**

Hyphenating a document manually

The other way to hyphenate is to see where Word wants to put hyphens, and you can then "Yea" or "Nay" them one at a time:

1. **Select the part of the document you want to hyphenate, or place the cursor where you want hyphens to start appearing.**

2. **Choose Tools⇨Language⇨Hyphenation to display the Hyphenation dialog box (refer to Figure 3-10).**

3. **Click the Manual button.**

   Word displays a box with some hyphenation choices in it. The cursor blinks on the spot where Word suggests putting a hyphen.

4. **Click Yes or No to accept or reject Word's suggestion.**

   Keep accepting or rejecting Word's suggestions. A box appears to tell you when Word has finished hyphenating. To quit hyphenating before Word finishes, click the Cancel button in the Manual Hyphenation dialog box.

Unhyphenating and other hyphenation tasks

More hyphenation esoterica:

✦ To "unhyphenate" a document you hyphenated automatically, choose Tools⇨Language⇨Hyphenation, remove the check from the Automatically Hyphenate Document box, and click OK.

✦ To prevent a paragraph from being hyphenated, choose Format⇨Paragraph, select the Line and Page Breaks tab, and put a check mark in the Don't Hyphenate box. (If you can't hyphenate a paragraph, it's probably because this box was checked unintentionally.)

✦ To hyphenate a single paragraph in the middle of a document — maybe because it's a long quote or some other thing that needs to stand out — select the paragraph and hyphenate it manually by clicking the Manual button in the Hyphenation dialog box.

Em and en dashes

Here is something about hyphens that editors and typesetters know but the general public does not know: There is a difference between hyphens and dashes. Most people insert a hyphen where they ought to use an em dash or an en dash:

✦ An *em dash* looks like a hyphen but is wider — it's as wide as the letter m. The last sentence has an em dash in it. Did you notice?

✦ An *en dash* is the width of the letter *n*. Use en dashes to show inclusive numbers or time periods, like so: pp. 45–50; Aug.–Sept. 1998; Exodus 16:11–16:18. An en dash is a little bit longer than a hyphen.

To place em or en dashes in your documents and impress your local typesetter or editor, not to mention your readers, press Alt+Ctrl+– (the minus sign key on the Numeric keypad) to enter an em dash, or Ctrl+– (on the numeric keypad) to enter an en dash. You can also choose Insert⇨Symbol, and, on the Special Characters tab in the Symbol dialog box, choose Em Dash or En Dash.

Chapter 4: Word Styles

*W*elcome to what may be the most important chapter of this book — the most important in Book I, anyway. Styles can save a ridiculous amount of time that you would otherwise spend formatting and wrestling with text. And many Word features rely on styles. You can't create a table of contents or use the Document Map unless each heading in your document has been assigned a heading style. Nor can you take advantage of Outline view and the commands on the Outline toolbar. You can't cross-reference headings or number the headings in a document.

If you want to be stylish, at least where Word is concerned, you have to know about styles.

All about Styles

A *style* is a collection of commands and formats that have been bundled under one name. With styles, you don't have to visit a bunch of dialog boxes to change the formatting of text or paragraphs. Instead, you simply choose a style from the Styles and Formatting task pane or the Style drop-down list. You can be certain that all parts of the document that were assigned the same style look the same. In short, you can fool everybody into thinking your documents were created by a pro.

Which styles are available depends on which template you used to create your document. Each template comes with its own set of styles, and you can create your own styles, too. A simple document created with the Normal template — a document that you created by clicking the New Blank Document button or pressing Ctrl+N — has but a few basic styles, but a document that was created with an advanced template comes with many styles. (Later in this chapter, "Creating and Managing Templates" explains templates.)

To see which styles are available in the document you are working on, choose Format⇨Styles and Formatting or click the Styles and Formatting button to open the Styles and Formatting task pane. Want to know which style has been assigned to text or a paragraph? Click the text or paragraph and glance at the Style menu or the Styles and Formatting task pane.

On the Style menu and the task pane, each style name is formatted to give you an idea of what it does when you apply it in your document. Word offers four types of styles:

✦ **Paragraph styles:** Determine the formatting of entire paragraphs. A paragraph style can include these settings: font, paragraph, tab, border, language, and bullets and numbering. Paragraph styles are marked with the paragraph symbol (¶). By far the majority of styles are paragraph styles.

✦ **Character styles:** Apply to text, not to paragraphs. You select text before you apply a character style. Create a character style for text that is hard to lay out and for foreign-language text. A character style can include these settings: font, border, and language. When you apply a character style to text, the character-style settings override the paragraph-style settings. If the paragraph style calls for a 14-point Arial text but the character style calls for 12-point Times Roman font, the character style wins. Character styles are marked with an underlined *a*.

✦ **Table styles:** Apply to tables (Chapter 5 describes creating and formatting tables). Table styles are marked with a grid icon.

✦ **List styles:** Apply to lists (see Chapter 3). List styles are marked with a list icon.

The beauty of styles is this: After you modify a style, all paragraphs or text to which the style has been assigned are instantly changed. You don't have to go back and format text and paragraphs throughout your document.

Applying a Style to Text and Paragraphs

Follow these steps to apply a style:

1. **Click the paragraph you want to apply the style to, or, to apply a style to several paragraphs, select all or part of them; if you're applying a character style, select the letters whose formatting you want to change.**

2. **Apply the style:**

As shown in Figure 4-1, Word offers two ways to apply a style:

- Open the Style drop-down list on the Formatting toolbar and select a style. To make all styles in the template appear on the Style menu, hold down the Shift key as you click to open the menu.

- Click the Styles and Formatting button to open the Style and Formatting task pane; then select a style there.

Choose a style from the Style menu...   ... or the Styles and Formatting task pane

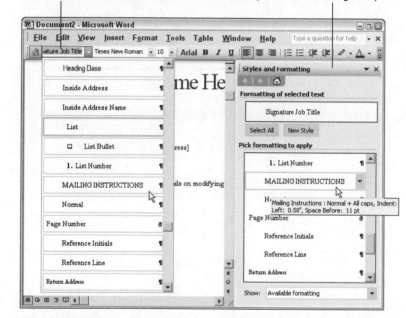

Figure 4-1:
Applying
a style.

Sometimes distinguishing one style from another is hard when you're working on a complex document, especially if the Style menu is crowded with a number of styles. To help make style choices in complex documents, you can see style names on the left side of the document window. To see style names there, switch to Normal view and choose Tools➪Options, select the View tab in the Options dialog, and, under Outline and Normal Options at the bottom of the dialog box, enter .5 or .7 inches in the Style Area Width box.

Creating a New Style

You can create new styles in two ways: using the New Style dialog box and directly from the screen. To do a thorough job, use the New Style dialog box. Styles you create there can be made part of the template you are currently working in and can be copied to other templates (later in this chapter, "Creating and Managing Templates" explains templates).

Shortcuts for applying styles

Here's a handful of keyboard shortcuts that can be very handy when applying paragraph styles:

✦ Normal: Ctrl+Shift+N

✦ Bulleted List: Ctrl+Shift+L

✦ Heading 1: Ctrl+Alt+1

✦ Heading 2: Ctrl+Alt+2

✦ Heading 3: Ctrl+Alt+3

✦ Next higher heading: Alt+Shift+→

✦ Next lower heading: Alt+Shift+←

You can assign keyboard shortcuts to styles and even create toolbar buttons for styles. Book VIII, Chapter 1 explains these customization techniques.

Creating styles directly from the screen

First, the directly-from-the-screen method, which you can use to create paragraph styles for a document you are working on:

1. **Click a paragraph whose formatting you would like to turn into a style and apply to other paragraphs in your document.**

   Remember, a heading is also a paragraph as far as Word is concerned, so if you're creating a style for a heading, click the heading.

2. **Click in the Style drop-down list and type a name for the style.**

3. **Press the Enter key.**

A style you create this way becomes a part of the document you are working on — it isn't made part of the template from which you created your document.

Creating styles using the New Style dialog box

If you want to make a style available in documents you will create in the future, make it part of a template and use the New Style dialog box method. Follow these steps:

1. Click the Styles and Formatting button.

   The Styles and Formatting task pane opens.

2. **Click the New Style button in the task pane to open the New Style dialog box.**

   Figure 4-2 shows the New Style dialog box.

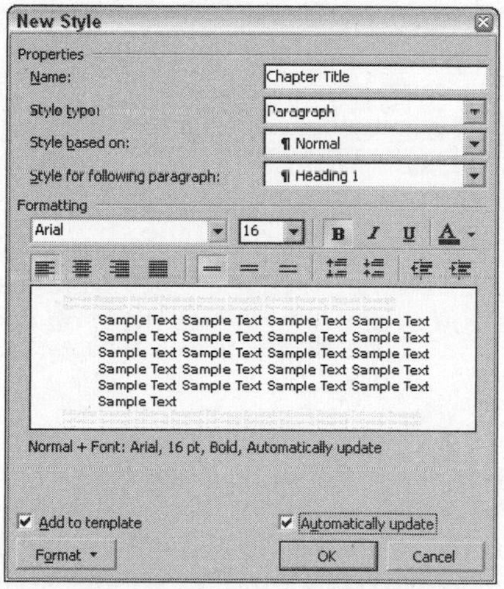

New Style

Properties

Name: Chapter Title

Style type: Paragraph

Style based on: ¶ Normal

Style for following paragraph: ¶ Heading 1

Formatting

Arial   16   **B** *I* <u>U</u> <u>A</u> ·

Sample Text Sample Text Sample Text Sample Text
Sample Text Sample Text Sample Text Sample Text
Sample Text Sample Text Sample Text Sample Text
Sample Text Sample Text Sample Text Sample Text
Sample Text Sample Text Sample Text Sample Text
Sample Text

Normal + Font: Arial, 16 pt, Bold, Automatically update

☑ Add to template   ☑ Automatically update

Format ▾   OK   Cancel

Figure 4-2:
Creating a
new style.

3. **Fill in the New Style dialog box.**

   As you do so, keep your eyes on the Preview box. It shows you what
   your new style will look like when you apply it to a document.

   Here's a rundown of the options in the New Style dialog box:

   ✦ **Name:** Enter a descriptive name for the style. The name you enter will
   appear on the Style menu and in the Styles and Formatting task pane.

   ✦ **Style Type:** On the drop-down list, choose a style type ("All about
   Styles," earlier in this chapter, describes the four style types).

   ✦ **Style Based On:** If your new style is similar to a style that is already part
   of the template with which you created your document, choose the
   style to get a head start on creating the new one. Be warned, however,
   that if you or someone else changes the Based On style, your new style
   will inherit those changes and be altered as well.

   ✦ **Style for Following Paragraph:** Choose a style from the drop-down list
   if the style you're creating is always followed by an existing style. For
   example, a new style called "Chapter Title" might always be followed by
   a style called "Chapter Intro Paragraph." If that were the case, you
   would choose "Chapter Intro Paragraph" from this drop-down list.

   ✦ **Formatting:** Choose options from the menus or click buttons to fashion
   or refine your style (you can also click the Format button to do this).

   ✦ **Add to Template:** Adds the style to the document's template so that
   other documents based on the template you are using can also make
   use of the new style.

✦ **Automatically Update:** Normally, when you make a formatting change to a paragraph, the style assigned to the paragraph does not change at all, but the style does change if you check this box. By checking this box, you tell Word to alter the style itself each time you alter a paragraph to which you've assigned the style. With this box checked, all paragraphs in the document that were assigned the style are altered each time you change a single paragraph that was assigned the style.

✦ **Format:** This is the important one. Click the button and make a formatting choice. Word takes you to dialog boxes so that you can create or refine the style.

Modifying a Style

What if you decide at the end of an 80-page document that all 35 introductory paragraphs to which you've assigned the "Intro Para" style look funny? If you clicked the Automatically Update check box in the New Style dialog box when you created the style, all you have to do is alter a paragraph to which you assigned the Intro Para style to alter all 35 introductory paragraphs. However, if you decided against updating styles automatically, you can still change the introductory paragraphs throughout your document.

Follow these steps to modify a style that isn't updated automatically:

1. **Click any paragraph, table, or list to which you've assigned the style; if you want to modify a character style, select the characters to which you assigned the style.**

2. **Click the Styles and Formatting button.**

The Styles and Formatting task pane appears. The style you want to modify should be selected in the task pane. If it isn't, select it.

3. **Select the name of the style that needs modifying, open its drop-down list, and choose Modify.**

You see the Modify Style dialog box. Does the box look familiar? That's because it's virtually identical to the New Style dialog box that you used to create the style in the first place (refer to Figure 4-2). The only difference is that you can't choose a style type in the Modify Style dialog box.

4. **Change the settings in the Modify Styles dialog box and click OK.**

The previous section in this chapter explains the settings.

While the Modify Style dialog box is open, you can check the Automatically Update check box if you want future modifications that you make to the style to be applied automatically. This way, when you change a paragraph or text to which the style has been applied, all other paragraphs and text in your document are changed accordingly. Check the Add to Template button if you want the style change to be made not only in the document you are working on but also in any other documents that you create in the future with this template.

Creating and Managing Templates

Every document you create is founded upon a *template*. When you click the New Blank Document button or press Ctrl+N, you create a document founded on the Normal template. And if you click the On My Computer hyperlink in the New Document task plane, you get the chance to open the Templates dialog box and create a complex document from a template of your choice — Contemporary Report, for example, or Brochure, or Elegant Memo.

Each template comes with its own styles and also its own AutoText entries, toolbars, and macros. Suppose that you create a complex document and you want to be able to use its styles, AutoText entries, and so on in other documents. To be able to do that, you can create a template from your document. For that matter, you can create a template from scratch by assembling styles from other templates and documents.

Creating a new template

Here are the ways to create a new template:

✦ **Creating a template from a document:** With your document open, choose File➪Save As. In the Save As dialog box, choose Document Template (*.dot) in the Save As Type drop-down list. Then enter a name for your template and click the Save button. Next time you open the Templates dialog box (by selecting On My Computer hyperlink in the New Document task pane), you will see the name of the template you created on the General tab of the Templates dialog box.

✦ **Assembling styles from other templates:** Create a new template by following the preceding instructions and then copy styles (and AutoText entries, toolbars, and macros as well, if you want) to the new template ("Copying styles from different documents and templates," later in this chapter, explains the details). To choose a template from which to copy styles, click the Close File button on the left side of the Organizer dialog box, click the Open File button, select the template in the Open dialog box, and click the Open button.

Where templates are stored depends on which version of Windows your computer runs under:

✦ **Windows XP:** C:\Documents and Settings*Username*\Application Data\ Microsoft\Templates folder.

✦ **Windows NT, 95, 98, 2000, and ME:** C:\Windows\Profiles\Application Data*Username*\Application Data\Microsoft\Templates folder, or the C:\Windows\Profiles\Application Data\Application Data\Microsoft\ Templates folder.

Suppose that you need to delete styles or rename styles in a template. Follow these steps:

1. **Choose Tools⇨Templates and Add-Ins.**

   You see the Templates and Add-Ins dialog box.

2. **Click the Organizer button to open the Organizer dialog box.**

3. **Click the Close File button on the right side of the dialog box.**

4. **Click the Open File button and, in the Open dialog box, select the template that needs modifying; then, click the Open button.**

   The names of items in the template — styles, AutoText entries, toolbars, and macros — appear in the right side of the dialog box. Click a tab, if necessary, to find the item that needs renaming or deleting.

5. **Select the item you want to rename and delete.**

   Follow these steps to rename or delete the item:

   • **Rename an item:** Click the Rename button, enter a new name in the Rename dialog box, and click OK.

   • **Delete an item:** Click the Delete button and then click Yes in the dialog box.

Copying styles from different documents and templates

Suppose that you like a style in one document and you want to copy it to another so that you can use it there. How you make the copy depends on whether you want to copy the style into a document or into a template. By copying it into a template, you make the style part of the template, and the style will be available in all documents that were created with that template. However, if you need the style solely for a particular document, you may as well copy it into the document. Doing that is easy enough.

Copying a style from one document to another

Copy a style from one document to another when you need the style on a one-time basis. Follow these steps:

1. **Select a paragraph that was assigned the style you want to copy.**

Be sure to select the entire paragraph. If you want to copy a character style, select text to which you have assigned the character style.

2. **Choose Edit⇨Copy or press Ctrl+C to copy the paragraph to the Clipboard.**

3. **Switch to the document you want to copy the style to and choose Edit⇨Paste or press Ctrl+V.**

4. **Delete the text.**

The style remains on the Style menu and the Styles and Formatting task pane even though the text is deleted. You can call upon the style whenever you desire.

Copying styles (and AutoText entries and macros) between templates

Use the Organizer to copy styles into other templates. By making the style a part of a template, you can call upon the style later on, in other documents. You can call upon it in each document you create or created with the template. Follow these steps to copy a style into a template:

1. **Open the document or template you want to copy styles from.**

2. **Choose Tools⇨Templates and Add-Ins and then click the Organizer button in the Templates and Add-Ins dialog box.**

You see the Organizer dialog box shown in Figure 4-3. Styles in the document that you opened appear in the In box on the left side of the dialog box.

3. **Click the Close File button on the right side of the dialog box.**

The button changes names and becomes the Open File button.

4. **Click the Open File button and, in the Open dialog box, find and select the template to which you want to copy styles; then, click the Open button.**

Where the templates are stored depends on which version of Windows you are working in:

- **Windows XP:** C:\Documents and Settings*Username*\Application Data\Microsoft\Templates folder.

- **Windows NT, 95, 98, 2000, and ME:** C:\Windows\Profiles\Application Data*Username*\Application Data\ Microsoft\Templates folder, or the C:\Windows\Profiles\Application Data\Application Data\Microsoft\Templates folder.

Attaching a different template to a document

It happens in the best of families. You create or are given a document only to discover that the wrong template is attached to it. For times like those, Word gives you the opportunity to switch templates. Follow these steps:

1. **Open the document that needs a new template and choose Tools⇨Templates and Add-Ins. You see the Templates and Add-Ins dialog box.**

2. **Click the Attach button. You see the Attach Template dialog box.**

3. **Find and select the template you want, and click the Open button. You return to the Templates and Add-ins dialog box, where the name of the template you chose appears in the Document Template box.**

4. **Click the Automatically Update Document Styles check box. Doing so tells Word to**

apply the styles from the new template to your document.

5. **Click OK.**

Select styles you want to copy.

Figure 4-3: Copying styles from one template to another.

Click to close one template and open another.

The names of styles in the template you chose appear on the right side of the Organizer dialog box. Notice the AutoText, Toolbars, and Macro Project Names tabs. They are for copying AutoText entries, toolbars, and macros between templates.

5. **In the Organizer dialog box, Ctrl+click the names of styles on the left side of the dialog box that you want to copy to the template listed on the right side of the dialog box.**

   As you click the names, they become highlighted.

6. **Click the Copy button.**

   The names of styles that you copied appear on the right side of the Organizer dialog box.

7. **Click the Close button and click Yes when Word asks whether you want to save the new styles in the template.**

Chapter 5: Constructing the Perfect Table

In This Chapter

✔ **Creating a table and working with table formats**

✔ **Repeating heading rows on subsequent pages**

✔ **Sorting, or reordering, your table**

✔ **Working with AutoFormats and other fancy elements**

✔ **Using math formulas in tables**

The best way to present a bunch of data at one time is to do it in a table. Provided that the row labels and column headings are descriptive, looking up information in a table is the easiest way to look up information. However, as everyone who has worked on tables knows, tables are a chore. Getting all the columns to fit, making columns and rows the right width and height, and editing the text in a table is not easy. So problematic are tables that Word has devoted an entire menu to constructing them: The Table menu. This chapter explains how to create tables, enter text in tables, change the number and size of columns and rows, sort tables, format tables, and, to start you off on the right foot, I begin with table jargon.

Talking Table Jargon

As is true of so much else in Computerland, tables have their own jargon. Figure 5-1 describes table jargon. Sorry, but you need to catch up on these terms to construct the perfect table:

✦ **Cell:** The box that is formed where a row and column intersect. Each cell holds one data item.

✦ **Heading row:** The name of the labels along the top row that explain what is in the columns below.

✦ **Row labels:** The labels in the first column that describe what is in each row.

✦ **Borders:** The lines in the table.

✦ **Gridlines:** The gray lines that show where the columns and rows are. Gridlines are not printed — they appear to help you format your table. (Choose Table➪Show Gridlines or Table➪Hide Gridlines to display or hide them). Word prints only the borders, not the gridlines, when you print a table.

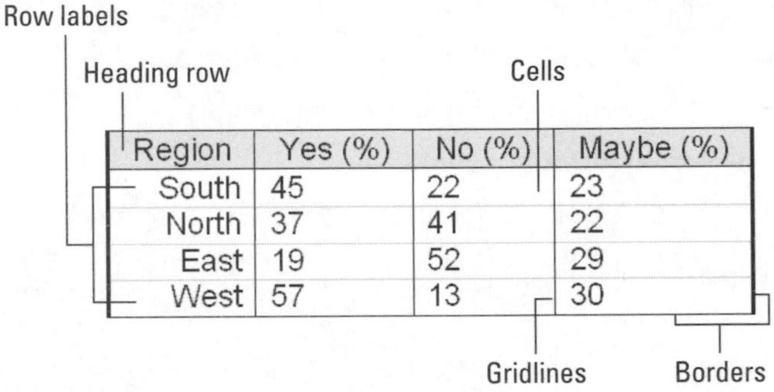

Row labels

Heading row   Cells

Figure 5-1:
Parts of a
table.

Region	Yes (%)	No (%)	Maybe (%)
South	45	22	23
North	37	41	22
East	19	52	29
West	57	13	30

Gridlines   Borders

Creating a Table

Word offers no fewer than four ways to create the cells and rows for a table. On your marks, get set, go:

✦ **Insert table button:** Click the Insert Table button, drag out the menu to the number of rows and columns you want, and let go of the mouse button.

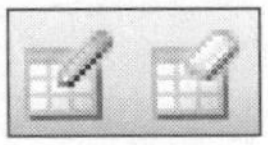

✦ **Drawing a table:** Choose Table➪Draw Table or click the Draw Table button on the Tables and Borders toolbar. The cursor changes into a pencil. Use the pencil to draw the table borders. If you make a mistake, click the Eraser button on the Tables and Border toolbar. The pointer changes into an eraser. Drag it over the parts of the table you regret drawing. When you're finished drawing the table, press Esc or click the Draw Table button to put the pencil away.

✦ **Insert Table dialog box:** The only advantage of the Insert Table dialog box, as shown in Figure 5-2, is that it gives you the opportunity to decide how wide to make the table. Choose Table➪Insert➪Table. Enter the number of columns and rows you want and click OK.

✦ **Converting text to a table:** Press Tab or enter a comma in the text where you want columns to be divided. For example, if you are turning an address list into a table, put each name and address on one line and press Tab or enter a comma after the first name, the last name, the street address, the city, the state, and the ZIP Code. For this feature to work, each name and address — each line — must have the same number of tab spaces or commas in it. Choose Table➪Convert➪Text to Table. Under Separate Text At in the Convert Text to Table dialog box, choose Tabs or Commas to tell Word how the columns are separated. Then click OK.

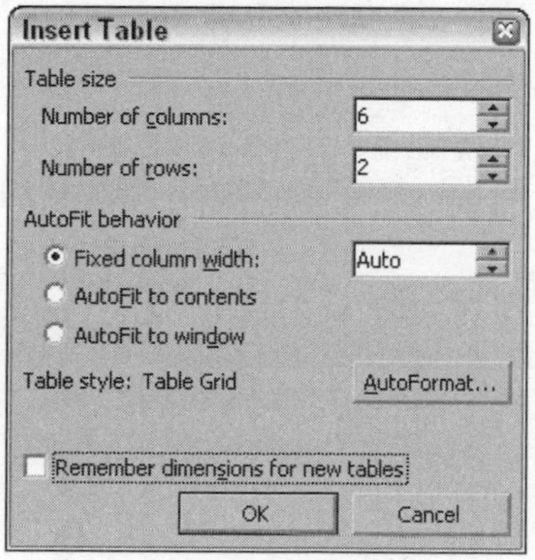

Figure 5-2:
Creating a
table.

Entering the Text and Numbers

After you've created the table, you can start entering text and numbers. All you have to do is click in a cell and start typing. To help you work more quickly, here are some shortcuts for moving the cursor in a table:

Press	Moves the Cursor to
Tab	Next column in row
Shift+Tab	Previous column in row
Alt+Home	Start of row
Alt+End	End of row
↓	Row below
↑	Row above
Alt+PgUp	Top of column
Alt+PgDn	Bottom of column

Fitting a table on the page

Sometimes fitting a table on a page is difficult. One way to get around this problem is to print the page or pages that the table is on in Landscape mode (Chapter 6 explains how to do this). In Landscape mode, pages are turned on their ears so that they are wider than they are tall. To print in Landscape mode, however, you must create a new section for the pages in question (Chapter 3 explains sections). Chances are, if your table can't fit on one page, presenting the information in a table is not the best option. Try presenting it in bulleted or numbered lists. Or present the information in short paragraphs under small fourth- or fifth-level headings.

If you need to add a row at the bottom of the table to enter more text, place the cursor in the last column of the last row and press the Tab key.

Here's a neat trick for entering data: Enter the heading row and two empty rows, open the Database toolbar, and click the Data Form button. You see a Data Form dialog box like the one in Figure 5-3. For each column in the heading row, you can enter the data in a text box. Click the Add New button after you enter the data.

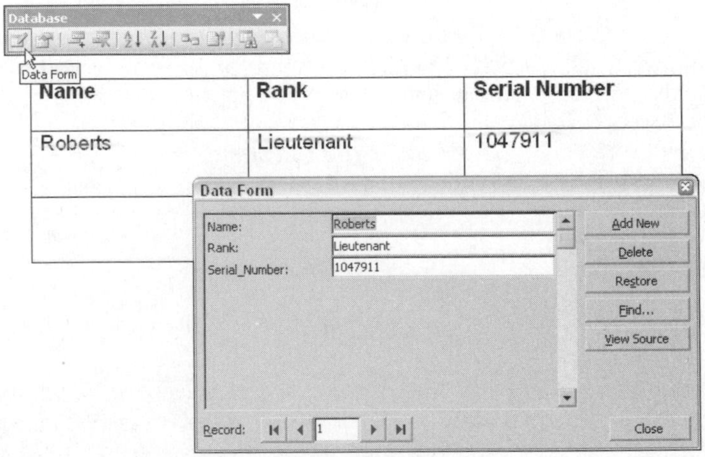

Figure 5-3: Entering table data using the Data Form dialog box.

Name	Rank	Serial Number
Roberts	Lieutenant	1047911

Data Form

Name:	Roberts	Add New
Rank:	Lieutenant	Delete
Serial_Number:	1047911	Restore
		Find...
		View Source

Record: |◀ ◀ 1 ▶ ▶| Close

Aligning Text in Columns and Cells

The easiest way to align text in the columns or cells is to rely on the Align Left, Center, Align Right, and Justify buttons on the Standard toolbar. Select a cell, a column, or columns and click one of those buttons to align the text in a column the same way.

 However, if you want to get really fancy, you can use the Align button on the Tables and Borders toolbar. Select the cells that need aligning, click the down arrow to open the Align button drop-down menu, and select one of the nine buttons to align text in a new way.

Merging and Splitting Cells and Tables

In the table in Figure 5-4, the cells in rows 2, 4, and 6 have been merged to create three cells for the baseball players' names. Where these rows should have nine cells, they have only one. To merge the cells in a table, select the cells you want to merge and choose Table⇨Merge Cells or click the Merge Cells button on the Tables and Borders toolbar.

Figure 5-4:
Merge cells
to create
larger cells.

1994	1995	1996	1997	1998	1999	2000	2001	2002
Mark McGuire's Home Runs								
53	51	52	58	70	65	32	20	–
Sammy Sosa's Home Runs								
11	38	37	48	64	63	50	64	49
Barry Bonds' Home Runs								
37	33	42	40	37	34	49	73	46

 In the same vein, you can split a cell into two or more cells by selecting the cell and choosing Table⇨Split Cells or clicking the Split Cells button on the Tables and Borders toolbar. In the Split Cells dialog box, declare how many columns and rows you want to split the cell into and click OK.

Still in the same vein, you can split a table by placing the cursor in what you want to be the first row of the new table and choosing Table⇨Split Table.

Modifying the Table Layout

Very likely, you created too many or too few rows or columns for your table. Some columns are probably too wide, and others may be too narrow. If that is the case, you have to change the layout of the table by deleting, inserting, and changing the size of columns and rows ("Sprucing Up Your Table," later in this chapter, explains how to put borders around tables and embellish them in other ways). In other words, you have to modify the table layout.

Selecting different parts of a table

Before you can fool with cells, rows, or columns, you have to select them:

✦ **Cells:** To select a cell, click in it. You can select several cells simultaneously by dragging the cursor over them.

✦ **Rows:** Place the cursor in the left margin and click to select one row, or click and drag to select several rows. You can also select rows by placing the cursor in the row you want to select and then choosing the Table⇨Select⇨Row command. To select several rows, select cells in the rows and then choose Table⇨Select⇨Row.

✦ **Columns:** To select a column, move the cursor to the top of the column. When the cursor changes into a fat down-pointing arrow, click once. You can click and drag to select several columns. The other way to select a column is to click anywhere in the column and choose Table⇨Select⇨Column. To select several columns with this command, select cells in the columns before giving the Select command.

✦ **A table:** To select a table, click in the table and choose Table⇨Select⇨Table; hold down the Alt key and double-click; or press Alt+5 (the 5 on the numeric keypad, not the one on the main part of the keyboard).

Inserting and deleting columns and rows

Here's the lowdown on inserting and deleting columns and rows:

✦ **Inserting columns:** To insert a blank column, select the column to the right of where you want the new column to go, right-click, and choose Insert Columns. You can also choose Table⇨Insert⇨Columns to the Left (or Columns to the Right). Word inserts the number of columns you select, so, to insert more than one, select more than one before choosing the Insert Columns command.

✦ **Deleting columns:** To delete columns, select them. Then choose Table⇨Delete⇨Columns, or right-click and choose Delete Columns. (Pressing the Delete key deletes the data in the column.)

✦ **Inserting rows:** To insert a blank row, select the row below which you want the new one to appear. If you want to insert more than one row, select more than one. Then right-click and choose Insert Rows, or choose Table⇨Insert⇨Rows Above (or Rows Below). You can also insert a row at the end of a table by moving the cursor into the last cell in the last row and pressing the Tab key.

✦ **Deleting rows:** To delete rows, select them and choose
Ta̲ble⇨De̲lete⇨R̲ows, or right-click and choose Delete Rows. (Pressing
the Delete key deletes the data in the row.)

A fast way to insert columns or rows is to insert one and then press F4 (or
choose E̲dit⇨R̲epeat) as many times as necessary to insert all the columns
or rows you need.

Moving columns and rows

Because there is no elegant way to move a column or row, you should move
only one at a time. If you try to move several simultaneously, you open a can
of worms that is best left unopened. To move a column or row:

1. **Select the column or row you want to move.**

2. **Right-click in the selection and choose Cu̲t on the shortcut menu.**

The column or row is moved to the Clipboard.

3. **Move the column or row:**

• **Column:** Click in the topmost cell in the column to the right of where
you want to move the column. In other words, to make what is now
column 4 column 2, cut column 4 and click in the topmost cell of
column 2. Then right-click and choose P̲aste Columns from the
shortcut menu.

• **Row:** Move the cursor into the first column of the row below which
you want to move your row. In other words, if you're placing the row
between what are now rows 6 and 7, put the cursor in row 7. Then
right-click and choose P̲aste Rows on the shortcut menu.

Resizing columns and rows

The fastest way to adjust the width of columns and the height of rows is to
"eyeball it." To make a column wider or narrower, move the cursor onto a
gridline or border between rows or columns. When the cursor changes into
a double-headed arrow, start dragging. Tug and pull, tug and pull until the
column is the correct width or the row is the correct height. You can also
slide the column bars on the ruler or the rows bars on the vertical ruler (if
you're in Print Layout View) to change the width of columns and height of
rows.

Because resizing columns and rows can be problematic, Word offers these
commands on the Ta̲ble⇨A̲utoFit submenu for adjusting the width and
height of rows and columns:

✦ **AutoFit to Contents:** Makes each column wide enough to accommodate its widest entry.

✦ **AutoFit to Window:** Stretches the table so that it fits across the page between the left and right margin.

✦ **Fixed Column Width**: Fixes the column widths at their current settings.

 ✦ **Distribute Rows Evenly:** Makes all rows the same height as the tallest row. You can also click the Distribute Rows Evenly button on the Tables and Borders toolbar. Select rows before giving this command to make the command affect only the rows you selected.

 ✦ **Distribute Columns Evenly:** Makes all columns the same width. You can also click the Distribute Columns Evenly button. Select columns before giving this command if you want to change the size of a few columns, not all the columns in the table.

Yet another technique for adjusting row heights and columns widths is to choose Table➪Table Properties and visit the Row tab and Column tab in the Table Properties dialog box. There, you can enter specific measurements for row heights and columns widths. Click the Previous or Next button to go from row to row or column to column. This technique isn't nearly as useful as the others, however, because the Table Properties dialog box doesn't have a Preview box and you can't see what your choices do to the table.

Repeating Heading Rows on Subsequent Pages

 Making sure that the heading row, sometimes called the header row, appears on a new page if the table breaks across pages is absolutely essential. The header row is the first row in the table, the one that usually describes what is in the columns below. Without a header row, readers can't tell what the information in a table is or means.

To make the header row (or rows) repeat on the top of each new page, place the cursor in the header row (or select the header rows if you have more than one) and choose Table➪Heading Rows Repeat. By the way, header rows appear only in Print Layout view, so don't worry if you're in Normal view and you can't see them.

 In a top-heavy table such as the one in Figure 5-5 in which the heading row cells contain text and the cells below contain numbers, you can make the entire table narrower by changing the orientation of the text in the heading row. To turn text on its ear, select the cells whose text needs a turn and click the Change Text Direction button on the Tables and Borders toolbar. Keep clicking until the text turns the direction you want.

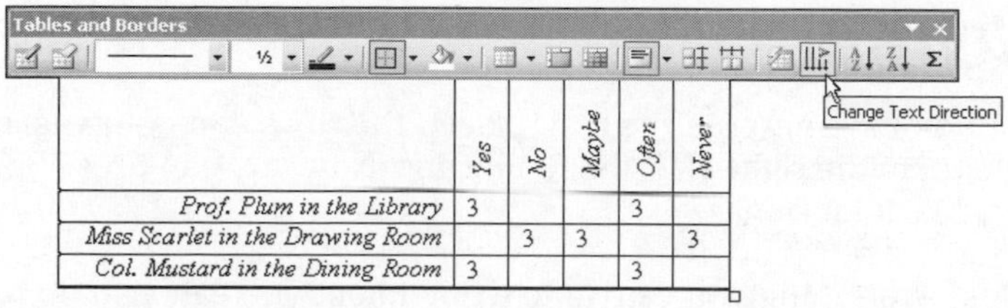

Figure 5-5:
Changing
text
direction.

	Yes	No	Maybe	Often	Never
Prof. Plum in the Library	3			3	
Miss Scarlet in the Drawing Room		3	3		3
Col. Mustard in the Dining Room	3			3	

Change Text Direction

Sorting, or Reordering, a Table

The fastest way to rearrange the rows in a table is to use the Table⇨Sort command or click one of the Sort buttons on the Tables and Borders toolbar. *Sorting* means to rearrange all the rows in a table on the basis of data in one or more columns. For example, a table that shows candidates and the number of votes they received could be sorted in alphabetical order by the candidates' names or in numerical order by the number of votes they received. Both tables present the same information, but the information is sorted in different ways.

The difference between ascending and descending sorts is as follows:

✦ Ascending arranges text from A to Z, numbers from smallest to largest, and dates from earliest to latest.

✦ Descending arranges text from Z to A, numbers from largest to smallest, and dates from latest to earliest.

When you rearrange a table by sorting it, Word rearranges the formatting as well as the data. Do your sorting before you format the table.

For simple sorts, select the column that is to be the basis of the sort and click the Sort Descending button on the Tables and Borders toolbar for a descending sort, or the Sort Ascending button for an ascending sort. You can also select a column and choose Table⇨Sort, select the Ascending or Descending option button in the Sort dialog box, and click OK.

When you sort a table, Word ignores the header row — the first row in the table — and doesn't move it. However, if you want to include the header row in the sort, sort your table with the Table⇨Sort command and select the No Header Row option button in the Sort dialog box.

Sprucing Up Your Table

After you have entered the text, placed the rows and columns in place, and made them the right size, the fun begins. Now you can dress up your table and make it look snazzy.

Almost everything you can do to a document you can also do to a table by selecting parts of it and choosing menu commands or clicking buttons. You can change text fonts, align data in the cells in different ways, and even import a graphic into a cell. You can also play with the borders that divide the rows and columns and "shade" columns, rows, and cells by filling them with gray shades or a black background. Read on to find out how to do these tricks and how to center a table or align it with the right page margin.

Formatting a table with Word's AutoFormats

By far the fastest way to get a good-looking table is to let Word do the work for you: Click your table and choose Table➪Table AutoFormat. You see the Table AutoFormat dialog box, shown in Figure 5-6. Rummage through the Table Styles until you find a table to your liking. The Preview box shows what the different tables look like. (On the Category drop-down list, you can choose an option to put a cap on the number of styles offered in the Table Style menu.) Under Apply Special Formats To, check and uncheck the boxes to modify the table format. As you do so, watch the Preview box to see what your choices do.

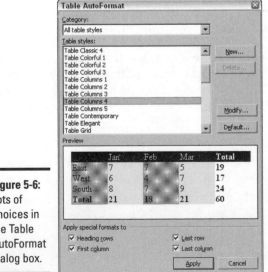

Figure 5-6:
Lots of
choices in
the Table
AutoFormat
dialog box.

Borders, shading, and color

Rather than rely on Word's Table⇔Table AutoFormat command, you can draw borders yourself and shade or give color to different parts of a table as well. Figure 5-7 shows these tools. Decorating a table by means of the Tables and Borders toolbar is easier than you might think. Click the Tables and Borders button on the Standard toolbar to display the Tables and Borders toolbar. Then select the part of the table you want to decorate and go to it:

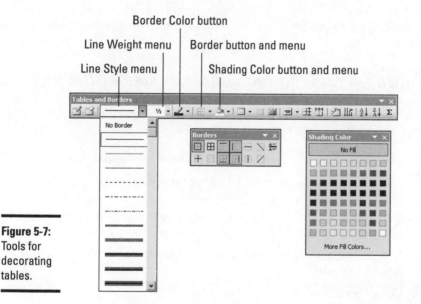

Border Color button
Line Weight menu | Border button and menu
Line Style menu | Shading Color button and menu

Figure 5-7:
Tools for
decorating
tables.

+ **Choosing lines for borders:** Click the down arrow beside the Line Style button and choose a line, dashed line, double line, or wiggly line for the border. (Choose No Border if you don't want a border or you are removing one that is already there.) Then click the down arrow beside the Line Weight button to choose a line width for the border.

+ **Choosing line colors:** Click the down arrow beside the Border Color button and choose one of the colors on the drop-down menu. Use the Automatic choice to remove colors and gray shades.

+ **Drawing the border lines:** Click the down arrow beside the Border button and choose one of the border styles on the drop-down menu. (Choose No Border to remove borders.) For example, choose Top Border to put a border along the top part of the table you selected in Step 1; choose Inside Border to put the border on the interior lines of the part of the table you selected. You will find the Border button on the Formatting toolbar as well as the Tables and Borders toolbar.

✦ **Shading or giving a color background to table cells:** Click the down arrow beside the Shading Color button and choose a color or gray shade on the drop-down menu.

After you make a choice from a menu on the Tables and Borders toolbar, the choice you made appears on the button that is used to open the menu. Choose Blue on the Shading Color menu, for example, and the Shading Color button turns blue. If the choice you want to make from a menu happens to be the last choice you made, you can click the button instead of opening a drop-down menu. To make a blue background show in a table, for example, you can simply click the Shading Color button as long as the Shading Color button is blue.

Putting a table in the middle or side of the page

As long as a table doesn't fill the page, you can lean it against the left or right margin or put it squarely between the margins. You can even make text wrap around the table. Follow these steps to do so:

1. **Click the table and choose T͟able➪Table P͟roperties.**

2. **On the T͟able tab, choose an Alignment option — L͟eft, C͟enter, or Rig͟ht.**

   If you choose L͟eft, you can enter a measurement in the I͟ndent from Left box to indent the table from the left margin.

3. **If you want text to wrap around the side of your table, click the A͟round option.**

4. **Click OK.**

Using Math Formulas in Tables

Σ

No, you don't have to add the figures in columns and rows yourself; Word gladly does that for you. Word can perform other mathematical calculations as well. To total the figures in a column or row, place the cursor in the cell that is to hold the total and click the AutoSum button on the Tables and Borders toolbar. The AutoSum button, however, is good only for adding figures. Follow these steps to perform other mathematical calculations and tell Word how to format sums and products:

1. **Put the cursor in the cell that will hold the sum or product of the cells above, below, to the right, or to the left.**

2. **Choose T͟able➪F͟ormula.**

The Formula dialog box appears, as shown in Figure 5-8. In its wisdom, Word makes a very educated guess about what you want the formula to do and places a formula in the Formula box.

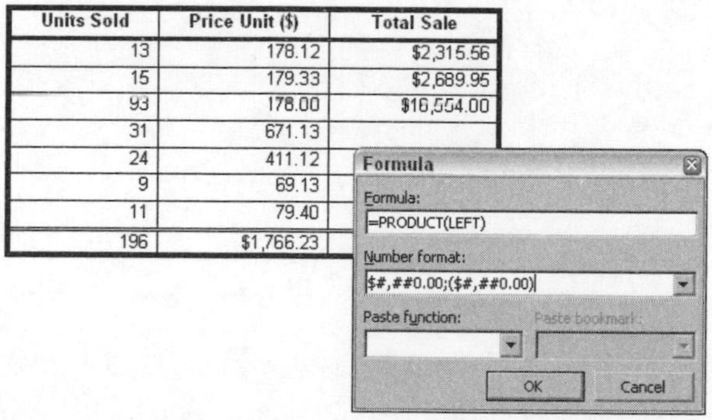

Units Sold	Price Unit ($)	Total Sale
13	178.12	$2,315.56
15	179.33	$2,689.95
93	178.00	$16,554.00
31	671.13	
24	411.12	
9	69.13	
11	79.40	
196	$1,766.23	

Formula

Formula:
=PRODUCT(LEFT)

Number format:
$#,##0.00;($#,##0.00)

Paste function:　　　Paste bookmark:

OK　　Cancel

Figure 5-8:
A math
formula in a
table.

3. **If this isn't the formula you want, delete everything except the equal sign in the Formula box, open the Paste Function drop-down list, and choose another function for the formula.**

   For example, choose PRODUCT to multiply figures. You may have to type **left, right, above,** or **below** in the parentheses beside the formula to tell Word where the figures that you want it to compute are.

4. **In the Number Format drop-down list, choose a format for your number.**

5. **Click OK.**

Word does not calculate blank cells in formulas. Enter a **0** in blank cells if you want them to be included in calculations. You can copy functions from one cell to another to save yourself the trouble of opening the Formula dialog box.

Chapter 6: Desktop Publishing with Word

In This Chapter

✓ Running text in newspaper-style columns

✓ Putting text boxes in documents

✓ Putting borders on pages

✓ Decorating pages with drop caps and watermarks

✓ Printing landscape documents

*O*nce upon a time, word processors were nothing more than glorified typewriters. They were good for typing and basic formatting, and not much else. But over the years, Microsoft Word has become a desktop publishing program in its own right. This chapter explains a few desktop publishing features that can make your documents stand out in the crowd — columns, text boxes, page borders, watermarks, and drop caps, to name a few.

Putting Newspaper-Style Columns in a Document

Columns look great in newsletters and similar documents. And you can pack a lot of words in columns. I should warn you, however, that the Columns command is only good for creating columns that will appear on the same page. Running text to the next page with the Columns command can be problematic. If you are serious about running text in columns, I suggest either constructing the columns from text boxes or using Publisher, another Office program. Book VII explains Publisher.

Before you put text in newspaper-style columns, write it. Take care of the spelling, grammar, and everything else first because making text changes to words after they've been arranged in columns is hard. Columns appear only in Page Layout view.

Sometimes it is easier to create columns by creating a table or by text boxes, especially when the columns refer to one another. In a two-column résumé, for example, the left-hand column often lists job titles ("Facsimile Engineer") whose descriptions are found directly across the page in the right-hand column ("I Xeroxed stuff all day long"). Creating a two-column résumé with Word's Format⇨Columns command would be futile because making the columns line up is nearly impossible. Each time you add something to the left-hand column, everything "snakes" — it gets bumped down in the left-hand column and the right-hand column as well.

There are two ways to create columns: with the Columns button on the toolbar and with the Format⇨Columns command. Format⇨Columns gives you considerably more leeway because the Columns button lets you create only columns of equal width. To use the Columns button:

1. **Select the text to be put in columns or simply place the cursor in the document to "columnize" all the text.**

2. **Click the Columns button on the toolbar.**

   A menu drops down so that you can choose how many columns you want.

3. **Click and drag to choose how many columns you want.**

Word creates a new section if you selected text before you columnized it, and you see your columns in Print Layout View. Very likely, they don't look so good. It's hard to get it right the first time. You can drag the column border bars on the ruler to widen or narrow the columns, but it's much easier to choose Format⇨Columns and play with options in the Columns dialog box. If you want to start all over, or if you want to start from the beginning with the Columns dialog box, here's how:

1. **Select the text to be put in columns, or put the cursor in the section to be put in columns, or place the cursor at a position in the document where columns are to start appearing.**

2. **Choose Format⇨Columns.**

   You see the Columns dialog box shown in Figure 6-1.

3. **Choose options in the Columns dialog box and, as you do so, keep your eye on the Preview box in the lower-right corner.**

Here are the options in the Columns dialog box:

✦ **Preset columns:** Select a Presets box to choose a preset number of columns. Notice that, in some of the boxes, the columns aren't of equal width. Choose One if you want to remove columns from a document.

✦ **Number of Number of Columns:** If a preset column doesn't do the trick, enter the number of columns you want in the Number of Columns box.

Figure 6-1:
Running text
in columns.

+ **Line between columns:** A line between columns is mighty elegant and is difficult to do on your own. Choose the Line Between check box to run lines between columns.

+ **Columns width:** If you uncheck the Equal Column Width check box, you can make columns of unequal width. Change the width of each column by using the Width boxes.

+ **Space between columns:** Enter a measurement in the Spacing boxes to determine how much space appears between columns.

+ **Start New Column:** This box is for putting empty space in a column, perhaps to insert a text box or picture. Place the cursor where you want the empty space to begin, open the Columns dialog box, select this check box, and choose This Point Forward from the Apply To drop-down menu. Text below the cursor moves to the next column.

To "break" a column in the middle and move text to the next column, click where you want the column to break and press Ctrl+Shift+Enter or choose Insert⇨Break and select the Column Break radio button.

Working with Text Boxes

Put text in a text box when you want a notice or announcement to stand out on the page. Text boxes can be shaded, filled with color, and given borders, as the examples in Figure 6-2 demonstrate. You can also lay them over graphics to make for interesting effects. I removed the borders and the fill color from the text box on the right side of Figure 6-2, but rest assured, the text in this figure lies squarely in a text box.

Announcing a
FROG JUMPING
CONTEST
~~Calaveras County~~
July 5-6

Announcing a
FROG JUMPING
CONTEST
~~Calaveras County~~
July 5-6

Figure 6-2:
Examples of
text boxes.

You can move a text box around at will on the page until it lands in the right place. You can even use text boxes as columns and make text jump from one text box to the next in a document — a nice feature, for example, when you want a newsletter article on page 1 to be continued on page 2. Instead of cutting and pasting text from page 1 to page 2, Word moves the text for you as the column on page 1 fills up. (Book VIII, Chapter 3 explains how to give borders, shading, and color to objects such as text boxes.)

Inserting a text box

To put a text box in a document, follow these steps:

1. **Choose Insert➪Text Box or click the Text Box button on the Drawing toolbar.**

   The pointer turns into a cross and the drawing canvas appears on-screen.

2. **Click and drag to draw the text box.**

   Lines show you how big it will be when you release the mouse button.

3. **Release the mouse button.**

   After you've inserted the text box, you can type text in it and call on all the formatting techniques in Word to boldface it, align it, or do what you will with it.

You can use an autoshape from the Drawing toolbar as a text box. Create the shape, right-click it, and choose Add Te_x_t on the shortcut menu.

Shades and borders for text boxes

Shade a text box to make it stand out on the page. A shaded text box, or a text box with white letters and a black background, is great for announcements and important notices. Word offers two ways to shade a text box:

✦ Select it and choose Format➪Borders and Shading. Then select the Shading tab in the Borders and Shading dialog box and select a color or gray shade. The No Fill option removes shading and color.

✦ Select it, click the arrow beside the Fill Shade button on the Drawing toolbar, and choose a shade or color from the pop-up menu.

To select a border and line size for a text box, click the arrow beside the Line Color and Line Style buttons and make a choice from the pop-up menu.

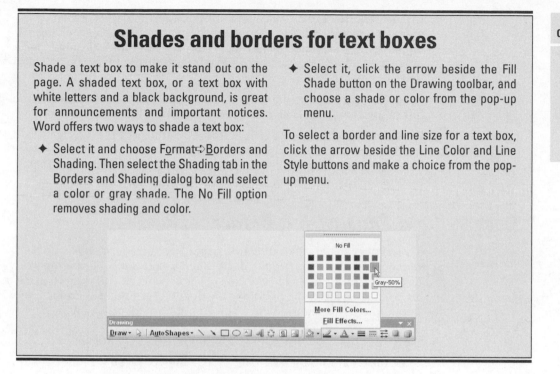

Manipulating text boxes

The fun begins after you create the text box and enter the text:

✦ **Handling the drawing canvas:** The drawing canvas appears when you create a text box. Drag a corner or side of the drawing canvas to change its size. To drag it elsewhere on the page, right-click it, choose Format Drawing Canvas, select the Layout tab in the Format Drawing Canvas dialog box, and select any wrapping style except In line with Text. Then drag the drawing canvas to a new location.

✦ **Moving a text box:** Place the mouse pointer over the border of the text box, and click and drag when you see the four-headed arrow.

 ✦ **Changing the direction of text:** On the Text Box toolbar is a little toy called the Change Text Direction button. Click a text box and click this button to make the text in the text box change orientation.

As I mention earlier, you can link text boxes so that the text in the first box is pushed into the next one when it fills up. To link text boxes, start by creating all the text boxes that you will need. You cannot link one text box to another if the second text box already has text in it. Use these buttons on the Text Box toolbar to link the text boxes in a document:

✦ **Create Text Box Link:** Click a text box and then click this button to create a forward link. When you click the button, the pointer changes into a very odd-looking pointer that is supposed to look like a pitcher. Move the odd-looking pointer to the next text box in the chain and click there to create a link.

✦ **Break Forward Link:** To break a link, click the text box that is to be the last in the chain, and then click the Break Forward Link button.

✦ **Previous Text Box and Next Text Box:** Click these buttons to go backward or forward through the text boxes in the chain. Click the Previous Text Box button to go backward through the chain and the Next Text Box button to merrily skip forward.

Decorating a Page with a Border

Word offers a means of decorating title pages, certificates, menus, and similar documents with a page border. Besides lines, you can decorate the sides of a page with stars, pieces of cake, and other artwork. If you want to place a border around a page in the middle of the document, you must create a section break where the page is. Here's how to put borders around a page:

1. **Place the cursor on the page where the border is to appear.**

Place the cursor on the first page of a document if you want to put a border around only the first page. If your document is divided into sections and you want to put borders around certain pages in a section, place the cursor in the section — either in the first page, if you want the borders to go around it, or in a subsequent page.

2. **Choose Format⇨Borders and Shading.**

3. **Select the Page Border tab in the Borders and Shading dialog box, as shown in Figure 6-3.**

4. **Under Setting, choose which kind of border you want.**

The Custom setting is for putting borders on one, two, or three sides of the page, not four. Use the None setting to remove borders.

5. **Under Apply To, tell Word which page or pages in the document get borders.**

6. **Select options to construct the border you want and then click OK.**

The Page Border tab offers a bunch of tools for fashioning a border:

✦ **Line for borders:** Under Style, scroll down the list and choose a line for the borders. You will find interesting choices at the bottom of the menu. Be sure to look in the Preview window to see what your choices in this dialog box add up to.

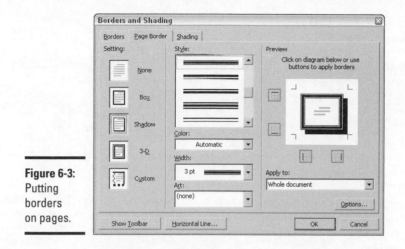

Figure 6-3:
Putting
borders
on pages.

✦ **Color for borders:** Open the Color drop-down list and choose a color for the border lines if you want a color border and you have a color printer.

✦ **Width of borders:** If you chose artwork for the borders, use the Width drop-down list to tell Word how wide the lines or artwork should be.

✦ **Artwork for borders:** Open the Art drop-down list and choose a symbol, illustration, star, piece of cake, or other artwork, if that is what you want for the borders. You will find some amusing choices on this long list, including ice cream cones, bats, and umbrellas.

✦ **Borders on different sides of the page:** Use the four buttons in the Preview window to tell Word on which sides of the page you want borders. Click these buttons to remove or add borders, as you wish.

✦ **Distance from edge of page:** Click the Options button and fill in the Border and Shading Options dialog box if you want to get specific about how close the borders can come to the edge of the page or pages.

Dropping In a Drop Cap

A *drop cap* is a large capital letter that "drops" into the text, as shown in Figure 6-4. Drop caps appear at the start of chapters in many books, this book included, and you can find other uses for them, too. In Figure 6-4, one drop cap marks the "A" side of a list of songs on a homemade tape. To create a drop-cap:

1. **Click anywhere in the paragraph whose first letter you want to "drop."**

If you want to "drop" more than one letter, select the letters.

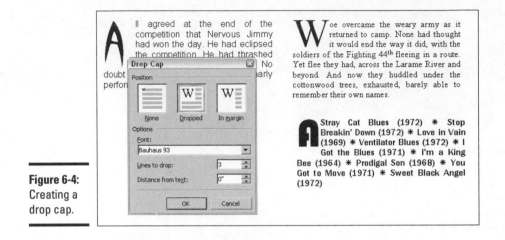

Figure 6-4:
Creating a
drop cap.

2. **Choose Format⇨Drop Cap.**

   You see the Drop Cap dialog box shown in Figure 6-4.

3. **Choose which kind of drop cap you want by clicking a box. The None setting is for removing drop caps.**

4. **Choose a font from the Font drop-down list.**

   Choose one that's different from the text in the paragraph. You can come back to this dialog box and get a different font later, if you want.

5. **In the Lines to Drop box, enter the number of text lines that the letter should "drop on."**

6. **Keep the 0 setting in the Distance from Text box unless you're dropping an *I*, *1*, or other skinny letter or number.**

7. **Click OK.**

You see your drop cap in Print Layout View. The drop cap appears in a text frame. To change the size of the drop cap, choose Format⇨Drop Cap again and play with the settings in the Drop Cap dialog box.

Watermarking for the Elegant Effect

A *watermark* is a pale image or set of words that appears behind text on each page in a document. True watermarks are made in the paper mold and can be seen only when the sheet of paper is held up to a light. You can't make true watermarks with Word, but you can make the closest thing to them that can be attained in the debased digital world in which we live. Figure 6-5 shows two pages of a letter in which the paper has been "watermarked." Watermarks are one of the easiest formatting tricks to accomplish in Word.

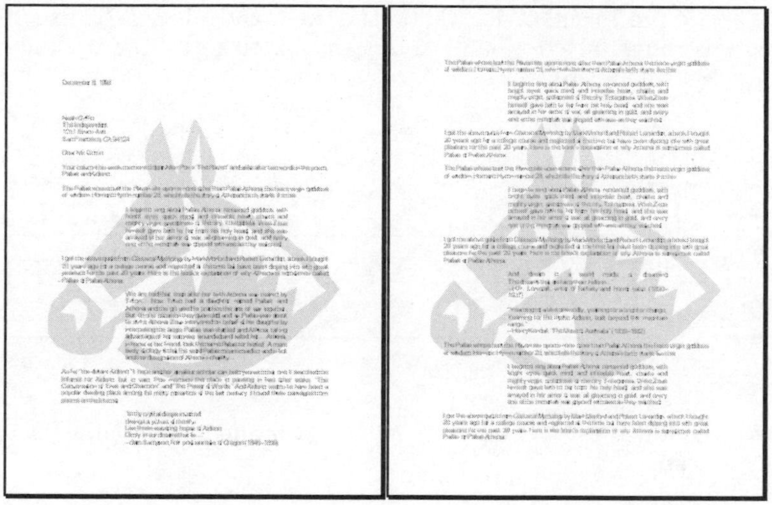

Figure 6-5:
Watermarks
showing
faintly on
the page.

To create a watermark for every page of a document, start by choosing Format➪Background➪Printed Watermark. You see the Printed Watermark dialog box. From here, you can create a picture watermark or a text watermark:

✦ **Picture watermark:** Select the Picture Watermark option button and then click the Select Picture button. In the Insert Picture dialog box, select a clip art file to use for the watermark and click the Insert button. Back in the Printed Watermark dialog box, choose a size for the clip-art image from the Scale drop-down menu. I don't recommend unchecking the Washout check box — do so and your image may be too dark and obscure the text.

✦ **Text watermark:** Click the Text Watermark option button and type a word or two in the Text box (or choose an AutoText entry from the drop-down menu). Choose a font, size, color, and layout for the words. If you uncheck the Semitransparent check box, you do so at your peril because the watermark words may be too dark on the page.

Click OK in the Printed Watermark dialog box to see your watermark. To tinker with it or remove it, choose Format➪Background➪Printed Watermark and change the settings in the Printed Watermark dialog box. To remove the watermark, click the No Watermark option button.

Fixing Spacing Problems in Headings

Sometimes when you enlarge text for a heading, one or two letters in the words end up being too close together or too far apart. For example, in the first heading shown in Figure 6-6, the *T* and *W* in *TWINS* are too far apart, as are the *Y*s and *O*s in *YO-YOS* and the *O* and *S* in *LOST*. I fixed this problem by kerning the letter pairs. *Kerning* means to adjust the amount of space between two letters.

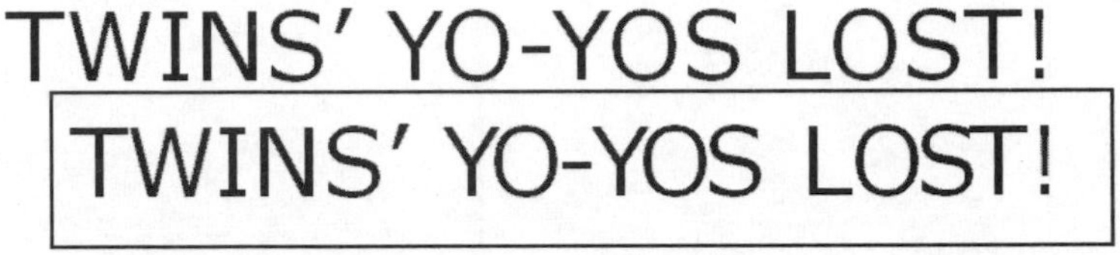

Figure 6-6:
Kerning
letters.

TWINS' YO-YOS LOST!
TWINS' YO-YOS LOST!

Follow these steps to kern a letter pair and make a large heading easier to read:

1. **Select the two letters that are too far apart or too close together.**

2. **Choose Format⇨Font or press Ctrl+D.**

3. **Select the Character Spacing tab in the Font dialog box.**

4. **In the Spacing drop-down list, choose Expanded to spread the letters out or Condensed to pack them in.**

5. **Word changes the number in the By box for you, but you can do yet more packing or spreading by clicking the down or up arrow yourself.**

   Watch the Preview box to see how close or far apart you have made the letters.

6. **Click the Kerning for Fonts check box and enter a point size in the Points and Above box if you want Word to kern fonts above a certain point size automatically.**

7. **Click OK.**

Landscape Documents

A *landscape* document is one in which the page is wider than it is long, like a painting of a landscape, as shown in Figure 6-7. Most documents, like the pages of this book, are printed in *portrait* style, with the short sides of the page on the top and bottom. However, creating a landscape document is sometimes a good idea because a landscape document stands out from the usual crowd of portrait documents and sometimes printing in landscape mode is necessary to fit text, tables, and graphics on a single page. Create a new section for your landscape page if you want to place it in a document of portrait pages (Chapter 3 explains sections).

Figure 6-7:
A portrait document (left) and landscape document (right).

To turn the page on its ear and create a landscape document, follow these steps:

1. **Choose File⇨Page Setup to open the Page Setup dialog box.**

2. **Select the Margins tab.**

3. **In the Orientation area, click the Landscape button.**

4. **In the Apply To box, choose Whole Document to print landscape pages throughout the document, This Section to print only the section the cursor is in, or This Point Forward to make the rest of the pages in the document landscape pages.**

5. **Click OK.**

Printing on Different-Size Paper

You don't have to print exclusively on standard 8.5 x 11 paper; you can print on legal-size paper and other sizes of paper as well. A 'zine or newsletter with an unusual shape really stands out in a crowd and gets people's attention. To change the size of the paper on which you intend to print a document, choose File⇨Page Setup, select the Paper tab in the Page Setup dialog box, and choose a setting on the Paper Size drop-down list. If none of the settings suits you, enter your own settings in the Width and Height text boxes.

If you keep legal-size paper in one tray of your printer and standard-size paper in another, for example, select the Paper tab in the Page Setup dialog box and choose Upper Tray or Lower Tray on the First Page and Other Pages menus.

Chapter 7: Getting Word's Help with Office Chores

In This Chapter

✔ Commenting on others' work

✔ Tracking revisions to documents

✔ Printing on envelopes and labels

✔ Mail merging for form letters and bulk mailing

*T*his chapter is dedicated to the proposition that everyone should get their work done sooner. It explains how Word can be a help in the office, especially when it comes to working on team projects. This chapter also explains mail merging, Microsoft's term for generating form letters, labels, and envelopes for mass mailings.

Highlighting Parts of a Document

In my work, I often use the Highlight command to mark paragraphs and text that need reviewing later. And on rainy days, I use it to splash color on my documents and keep myself amused. Whatever your reasons for highlighting text in a document, follow these steps to do it:

1. **If necessary, click the down arrow beside the Highlight button and choose a color.**

   If the stripe on the bottom of the button is the color you want, just click the button.

2. **Drag the cursor over the text you want to highlight.**

3. **Click the Highlight button again when you're done.**

You can also highlight text by selecting it and then clicking the Highlight button to choose a new color from the Highlight drop-down menu.

Highlight marks are printed along with the text. To temporarily remove the highlights in a document, choose Tools⇨Options, select the View tab in the Options dialog box, and unselect the Highlight check box. To permanently remove highlights, select the document or the text from which you want to remove the highlights, click the down arrow to open the Highlight drop-down menu, and select None.

Commenting on a Document

In the old days, comments were scribbled illegibly in the margins of books and documents, but in Word, comments are easy to read. Highlights, displaying in a different color for each commenter, appear on-screen where comments have been made in a document, and brackets appear around words and passages as well. As shown in Figure 7-1, you can read a comment in Normal view and Outline view by moving the cursor over bracketed text; in Page Layout view and Web Layout view, comments appear in bubbles. (Choose Tools⇨Options, select the View tab in the Options dialog box, and check the ScreenTips check box if comments don't appear when you move the pointer over them in Normal or Outline view.)

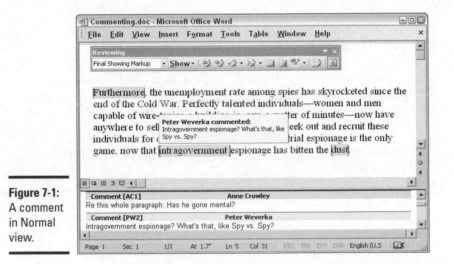

Figure 7-1:
A comment
in Normal
view.

If you are putting together a proposal, you can pass it around the office and invite everyone to comment. If someone makes an especially good comment, you can include it in the main text merely by copying and pasting it. To write a comment:

1. **Select the word or sentence that you want to criticize or praise.**

2. **Choose Insert⇨Comment or click the Insert Comment button on the Reviewing toolbar.**

The Reviewing pane opens at the bottom of the screen with comments that have already been made and the names of the people who made them. You see the Reviewing toolbar as well.

3. **In the Reviewing pane, type your comment in the space provided under the word "Comment" and your name.**

If your name doesn't appear in the Reviewing pane, choose Tools⇨Options, select the User Information tab, and type your name in the Name box.

Here is a handful of tasks that deserve comment (if you'll pardon my little pun):

✦ **Seeing and hiding the Reviewing pane:** Click the Reviewing Pane button on the Reviewing toolbar to hide or display the Reviewing pane. You can also click the Show button on the toolbar and Reviewing Pane on the drop-down menu.

✦ **Seeing and hiding comment brackets:** Click the Show button on the Reviewing toolbar and choose Comments to hide or display the brackets that appear in the text where a comment was made.

✦ **Deleting a comment:** Click a highlighted comment in brackets or a comment in the Reviewing pane and then click the Reject Change/Delete Comment button on the Reviewing toolbar. You can also right-click a comment in your document and choose Delete Comment on the short-cut menu.

✦ **Deleting all the comments in the document:** Click the down arrow beside the Reject Change/Delete Comment button and choose Delete All Comments in Document on the drop-down menu.

✦ **Deleting comments made by one or two people:** First, isolate comments made by people whose comments you want to delete. To do that, click the Show button on the Reviewing toolbar, choose Reviewers, and, on the submenu, deselect the name of a commenter whose comments you want to keep. Do this as many times as necessary until brackets appear only around the comments you want to delete. Then click the down arrow beside the Reject Change/Delete Comment button and choose Delete All Comments Shown on the drop-down menu.

✦ **Editing a comment:** Rewrite it in the Reviewing pane. You can right-click a phrase in brackets and choose Edit Comment to open the Reviewing pane to a comment you want to edit.

Showing Revisions to Documents

When many hands go into revising a document, figuring out who made revisions to what is impossible. And more important, it's impossible to tell what the first draft looked like. Sometimes it's hard to tell whether the revision work was for the good or the ill.

To help you keep track of changes to documents, Word offers the Tools⇨Track Changes command. When this command is in effect, all changes to the document are recorded in a different color, with one color for each reviewer. New text is underlined, a vertical line appears in the margin to show where changes were made, and text that has been deleted either appears in balloons (in Print Layout and Web Layout view) or is crossed out (in Normal and Outline view). By moving the pointer over a change, you can read the name of the person who made it as well as the words that were inserted or deleted. Then you can accept or reject each change. You can also see the original document or a copy with revisions simply by making a choice from a drop-down list.

To give you an idea of what tracking marks look like, Figure 7-2 shows the first two lines of Vladimir Nabokov's autobiography *Speak, Memory* in Normal view, with marks showing where additions were made and text was scratched out.

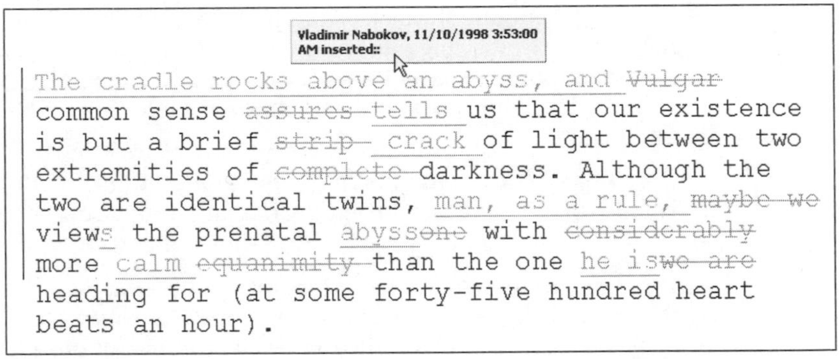

Figure 7-2: A document with revision marks.

> Vladimir Nabokov, 11/10/1998 3:53:00 AM inserted::
>
> The cradle rocks above an abyss, and ~~Vulgar~~ common sense ~~assures~~ tells us that our existence is but a brief ~~strip~~ crack of light between two extremities of ~~complete~~ darkness. Although the two are identical twins, man, as a rule, ~~maybe we~~ views the prenatal ~~abyss~~one with ~~considerably~~ more calm ~~equanimity~~ than the one he is~~we are~~ heading for (at some forty-five hundred heart beats an hour).

Marking the changes

To start tracking where editorial changes are made to a document, do one of the following:

- ✦ Double-click TRK on the status bar.
- ✦ Choose Tools⇨Track Changes (or press Ctrl+Shift+E).

✦ Click the Track Changes button on the Reviewing toolbar.

The Reviewing toolbar appears on-screen. If you are the first author to have a crack at this document, your changes appear in red. If you are the second author, they appear in a different color. Word can tell when a new reviewer has gotten hold of a document and assigns a new color accordingly.

To track formatting changes as well as editorial changes, click the Show button on the Reviewing toolbar and choose Formatting on the drop-down menu. If you prefer not to see balloons within balloons in Print Layout and Web Layout view, click the Show button and choose Baloons⇨Never Use Balloons.

Marking changes when you forgot to turn on revision marks

Suppose that you write the first draft of a document and someone revises it but that someone doesn't track revisions. How can you tell where changes were made? For that matter, suppose that you get hold of a document, you change it around without turning on revision marks, and now you want to see what your editorial changes did to the original copy. I have good news: You can see where changes were made, as long as you have a clean copy of the first draft.

To see where changes were made to the first draft of a document, use the Tools⇨Compare and Merge Documents command. After you are done comparing and merging, revision marks appear where changes were made. Follow these steps to compare and merge documents:

1. **Open the copy of the document that you or someone else made changes to.**

In other words, open the second or a subsequent draft.

2. **Choose Tools⇨Compare and Merge Documents.**

You see the Compare and Merge Document dialog box.

3. **Find and select the first-draft file.**

4. **Click the down arrow beside the Merge button and choose an option on the drop-down menu.**

Here are the options:

- **Merge:** Makes the changes and revision marks appear in the first draft of the document.

- **Merge into Current Document:** Makes the changes and revision marks appear in the subsequent draft, that is, in the document you opened in Step 1.

- **Merge into New Document:** Makes the changes and revision marks appear in a new document.

Compare documents when you want to see where the original and revised document differ, not what was inserted or deleted. If both reviewers deleted the same paragraph, for example, you won't see the paragraph crossed out; instead, it doesn't appear at all in the compared copy. To compare documents, follow the procedure you use to merge them, but click the Legal Blackline check box in the Compare and Merge Documents dialog box, and then click the Compare button.

Reading and reviewing a document with revision marks

Reading and reviewing a document with revision marks isn't easy. The revision marks can get in the way. Fortunately, Word offers a handful of techniques for dealing with documents that have been scarred by revision marks:

- **Temporarily remove the revision marks:** Click the Show button on the Reviewing toolbar and deselect the Insertions and Deletions option on the drop-down menu. Select the command again when you want to see revision marks.

- **See what the document would look like if you accepted all revisions:** Open the Display for Review menu on the Reviewing toolbar and choose Final (or choose View⇨Markup).

- **See what the document would look like if you rejected all revisions:** Open the Display for Review menu and choose Original.

- **See more clearly where text has been deleted:** Open the Display for Review menu and choose Original Showing Markup. Now a line appears through text that has been deleted. Text that has been deleted does not appear in balloons as it does when you choose Final Showing Markup on the Display for Review menu.

- **Focus on revisions made by one or two reviewers:** Click the Show button, choose Reviewers, and deselect a reviewer's name on the submenu. Do this as many times as necessary to remove names and be able to see only revisions made by one or two people. Choose All Reviewers on the submenu when you want to see all the revision marks.

Accepting and rejecting changes

Word gives you the chance to accept or reject changes one at a time, but in my considerable experience with revisions (I am a sometime editor), I find that the best way to handle changes is to go through the document, reject the changes you don't care for, and, when you have finished reviewing, accept all the remaining changes. That way, reviewing changes is only half as tedious.

Whatever your preference for accepting or rejecting changes, start by selecting a change. To do so, either click it or click the Previous or Next button on the Reviewing toolbar to locate it in your document. With the change selected, do one of the following:

+ **Accept the change:** Click the Accept Change button or right-click and choose Accept on the shortcut menu.

+ **Reject the change:** Click the Reject Change button or right-click and choose Reject on the shortcut menu.

To accept all the changes in a document, click the down arrow beside the Accept Change button and choose Accept All Changes in Document.

Printing an Address on an Envelope

Printing addresses gives correspondence a formal, official look. It makes you look like a big shot. (Later in this chapter, "Churning Out Letters, Labels, and Envelopes for Mass Mailings" explains how to print more than one envelope at a time). Here's how to print an address and a return address on an envelope:

1. **To save a bit of time, open the document that holds the letter you want to send; then select the name and address of the person you want to send the letter to.**

   By doing so, you save yourself from having to type the address again. However, you don't have to open a document to start with.

2. **Choose Tools⇨Letters and Mailings⇨Envelopes and Labels.**

   The Envelopes tab of the Envelopes and Labels dialog box appears, as shown in Figure 7-3.

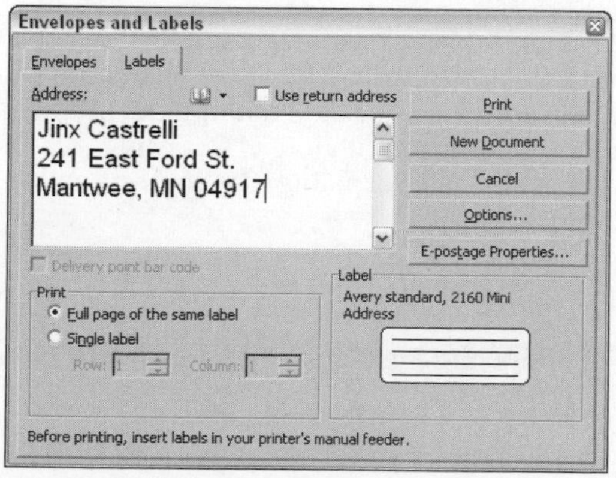

Figure 7-3:
Printing
on an
envelope.

Envelopes and Labels

Envelopes | Labels

Address: ☐ Use return address

Jinx Castrelli
241 East Ford St.
Mantwee, MN 04917

Print
New Document
Cancel
Options...
E-postage Properties...

☐ Delivery point bar code

Print
● Full page of the same label
○ Single label
Row: 1   Column: 1

Label
Avery standard, 2160 Mini
Address

Before printing, insert labels in your printer's manual feeder.

3. **Enter a name and address in Delivery Address box (the address is already there if you selected it in Step 1).**

   Your name and address should appear in the Return Address box. (If they aren't there, enter them for now, but be sure to read the Tip at the end of this section to find out how to put them there automatically.)

4. **Check the Omit check box if you don't want your return address to appear on the envelope.**

5. **Click the Print button.**

Two commands on the Envelopes tab tell Word how your printer handles envelopes and what size your envelopes are.

 Click the envelope icon below the word *Feed* to open the Envelope Options dialog box and choose the right technique for feeding envelopes to your printer. Consult the manual that came with your printer, select one of the Feed Method boxes, click the Face Up or Face Down option button, and open the Feed From drop-down list to tell Word which printer tray the envelope is in or how you intend to stick the envelope in your printer. Click OK when you're done.

After you've fed the envelope to your printer, click the envelope icon below the word *Preview* — that's right, click the icon — to tell Word what size your envelopes are and whether you want to print bar codes on the envelope.

 To make your name and return address appear automatically in the Envelopes and Labels dialog box, choose Tools⇨Options, select the User Information tab, and enter your name and address in the Mailing Address box.

Printing a Single Address Label (or a Page of the Same Label)

If you need to print a single label or a sheet of labels that are all the same, you can do it. Before you start printing, however, take note what size and what brand your labels are. You are asked about label brands and sizes when you print labels. (Later in this chapter, "Churning Out Letters, Labels, and Envelopes for Mass Mailings" explains how to print multiple labels as part of a mass mailing).

Follow these steps to print a single label or a sheet full of identical labels:

1. **Choose Tools⇨Letters and Mailings⇨Envelopes and Labels.**

   You see the Envelopes and Labels dialog box.

2. **Select the Labels tab, as shown in Figure 7-4.**

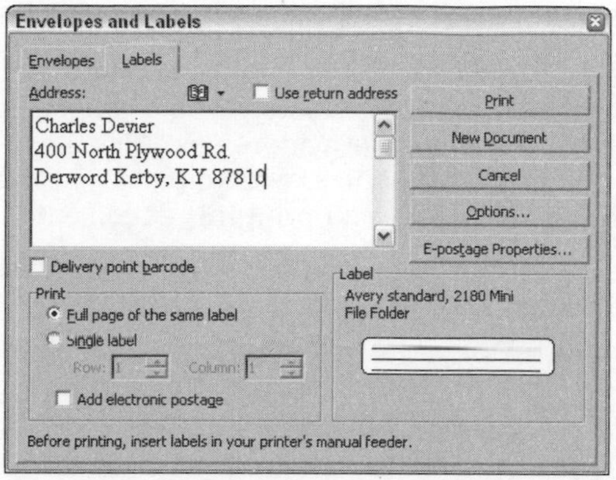

Figure 7-4:
Printing
labels.

3. **Enter the label — the name and address — in the Address box.**

   If you're printing your return address on labels, check the Use Return Address check box. Your return address appears automatically if you entered it in the Options dialog box by choosing Tools⇨Options and entering it on the User Information tab. If your return address doesn't appear, however, enter it now.

4. **Either click the Options button or click the label icon in the Label box to see the Label Options dialog box appear.**

5. **In the Printer Information area, select either Dot Matrix or Laser and Ink Jet to say which kind of printer you have; on the Tray drop-down list, choose the option that describes how you will feed labels to your printer.**

6. **Open the Label Products drop-down list and choose the brand or type of labels that you have.**

   If your brand is not on the list, you can choose Other/Custom (found at the bottom of the list), click the Details button, and describe your labels in the extremely confusing Address Information dialog box. A better way, however, is to measure your labels and see whether you can find a label of the same size by experimenting with Product Number and Label Information combinations.

7. **In the Product Number menu, select the product number listed on the box that your labels came in.**

   Look in the Label Information box on the right to make sure that the Height, Width, and Page Size measurements match those of the labels you have.

8. **Click OK to return to the Envelopes and Labels dialog box.**

9. **Choose a Print option and click the <u>P</u>rint button.**

   Tell Word whether you're printing a single label or a sheet full of labels:

   • **F<u>u</u>ll Page of the Same Label:** Select this option button if you want to print a pageful of the same label. Likely, you'd choose this option to print a pageful of your own return addresses. Click the New <u>D</u>ocument button after you make this choice. Word creates a new document with a pageful of labels. Save and print this document.

   • **Sin<u>g</u>le Label:** Select this option button to print one label. Then enter the row and column where the label is and click the <u>P</u>rint button.

Churning Out Letters, Labels, and Envelopes for Mass Mailings

Thanks to the miracle of computing, you can churn out form letters, labels, and envelopes for a mass mailing in the privacy of your home or office, just as the big companies do. Churning out form letters, labels, and envelopes is easy, as long as you take the time to prepare the source file. The *source file* is the file that the names and addresses come from. A Word table, an Excel worksheet, a Microsoft Access database table or query, or an Outlook Contacts list or Address Book can serve as the source file. (Book II explains Outlook; Book IV explains Excel; Book VI explains Access.)

To generate form letters, labels, or envelopes, you merge the source file with a form letter, label, or envelope document. Word calls this process *merging*. During the merge, names and addresses from the source file are plugged into the appropriate places in the form letter, label, or envelope document. When the merge is complete, you can either save the form letters, labels, or envelopes in a new file or start printing right away.

The following text explains how to prepare the source file and merge addresses from the source file with a document to create form letters, labels, or envelopes. Then I explain how to print the form letters, labels, or envelopes.

Preparing the source file

If you intend to get addresses for your form letters, labels, or envelopes from an Outlook Contact List or Address Book on your computer, you're ready to go. However, if you haven't entered the addresses yet or you are keeping them in a Word table, Access database table, or Access query, make sure that the data is in good working order:

✦ **Word table:** Save the table in its own file and enter a descriptive heading at the top of each column. In the merge, when you tell Word where to plug in address and other data, you will do so by choosing a heading name from the top of a column. In Figure 7-5, for example, the column headings are Last Name, First Name, Street, and so on. (Chapter 5 explains how to construct a Word table.)

Figure 7-5:
A source
table for a
mail merge.

Last Name	First Name	Street	City	State	Zip	Birthday	Sign
Haines	Clyde	1289 Durham Lane	Durban	MA	64901	January 1	Aquarius
Yee	Gladys	1293 Park Ave.	Waddle	OR	98620	May 3	Libra
Harmony	Esther	2601 Estner Rd.	Pecos	TX	34910	April 10	Taurus
Sings	Melinda	2789 23rd St.	Roburgh	NE	68912	June 14	Gemini
Stickenmud	Rupert	119 Scutter Lane	Nyad	CA	94114	August 2	Leo
Hines	Martha	1263 Tick Park	Osterville	MA	03874	March 16	Sagittarius

✦ **Excel table:** Arrange the worksheet in table format with a descriptive heading atop each column. Word will plug in address and other data by choosing heading names.

✦ **Access database table or query:** Make sure that you know the field names in the database table or query where you keep the addresses. During the merge, you will be asked for field names. By the way, if you are comfortable in Access, query a database table for the records you will need. As you will find out shortly, Word offers a technique for choosing only the records you want for your form letters, labels, or envelopes. However, by querying first, you can start off with the records you need and spare yourself from having to choose records in Word.

A Word table or Access table or query can include more than address information. Don't worry about deleting information that isn't required for form letters, labels, and envelopes. As you will find out soon, you get to decide which information to include from the table or query.

Merging the source file with the document

The next step in generating form letters, labels, or envelopes for a mass mailing is to merge the source file with the document. Follow these general steps to do so:

1. **Open a new document if you want to print labels or envelopes en masse; if you want to print form letters, either open a new document or open a letter you have already written and delete the addressee's name, the address, and other parts of the letter that will differ from recipient to recipient.**

2. **Choose Tools⇨Letters and Mailings⇨Mail Merge.**

The Mail Merge task pane appears, as shown in Figure 7-6. As you complete each step in the Mail Merge Wizard, you will click the Next hyperlink at the bottom of the task pane.

Choose an option.

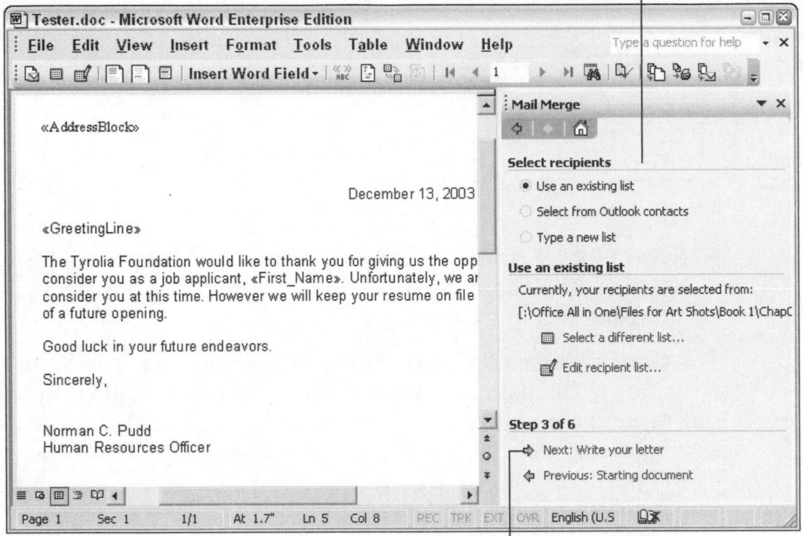

Figure 7-6:
The Mail
Merge task
pane.

Go to the next step.

3. **Under "Select Document Type" in the task pane, select the Letters, Envelopes or Labels option button; and, under "Step 1 of 6," click the Next: Starting Document hyperlink.**

4. **Under "Select Starting Document" in the task pane, choose the type of document with which you are dealing; and, under "Step 2 of 6," click the Next: Select Recipients hyperlink.**

   Here are your choices in Step 2:

   • **Form letters:** With the Use the Current Document option button already selected, you're ready to go. The text of your form letter already appears on-screen if you followed the directions for opening it or writing it in Step 1. (To use a form letter you have used before, select the Start from Existing Document option button, click the Open button, find and select the letter in the Open dialog box, and click the Open button. Your form letter appears on-screen.)

- **Labels:** With the Change Document Layout option button already selected, click the Label Options hyperlink under "Change Document Layout." You see the Label Options dialog box, where you tell Word what size labels you will print on (see "Printing a Single Address Label [or a Page of the Same Label])," earlier in this chapter, if you need advice for filling out this dialog box.) A sheet of sample labels appears on-screen.

- **Envelopes:** With the Change Document Layout option button already selected, click the Envelope Options hyperlink under "Change Document Layout." You see the Envelope Options dialog box, where, on the Envelope Options and Printing Options tabs, you tell Word what size envelope you will print on (see "Printing an Address on an Envelope," earlier in this chapter, for instructions about filling out these tabs). A sample envelope appears on-screen.

5. **Tell Word what your source file or the source of your address and data information is.**

   Earlier in this section, "Preparing the source file" explains what a source file is. Your options are as follows:

   - **Addresses from a Word table, Excel table, Access database table, or Access query:** Under "Select Recipients," make sure that the Use an Existing List option button is selected and then click the Browse hyperlink under "Use an Existing List." You see the Select Data Source dialog box. Locate the Word file or Excel table with the table or the Access database with the table or query, select it, and click the Open button. The Mail Merge Recipients dialog box appears, as shown in Figure 7-7.

   If you select an Access database, you see the Select Table dialog box. Select the table or query you want and click the OK button.

Choose the names of recipients.

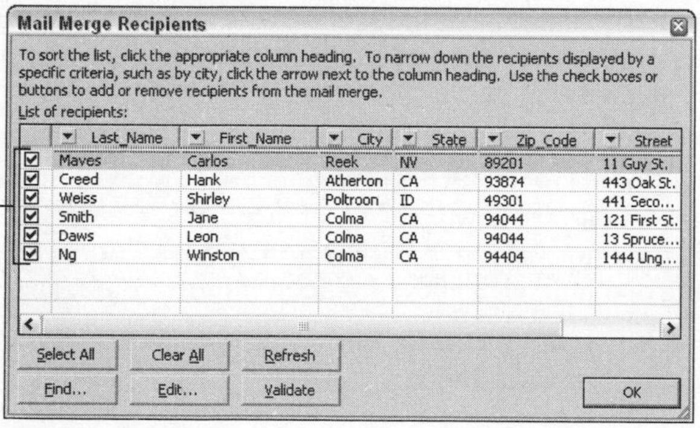

Figure 7-7: Choosing which records to print.

- **Addresses from Microsoft Outlook:** Under "Select Recipients," select the Select from Outlook Contacts option button. Then, under "Select from Outlook Contacts," click the Choose Contacts Folder hyperlink. The Choose Profile dialog box appears. Click OK in this dialog box. You see the Select Contacts List folder dialog box. Double-click the Contacts folder there. Now you're getting somewhere. You see the Mail Merge Recipients dialog box, with its list of contacts.

6. **In the Mail Merge Recipients dialog box, select the names of people to whom you will send mail; then click OK.**

   To select recipients' names, check or uncheck the boxes on the left side of the dialog box, or else click the Clear All button to remove all the checks and then check recipients' names one at a time.

7. **Click the Next hyperlink in the bottom of the task pane to go to Step 4 of the mail merge.**

8. **Enter the address block on your form letters, labels, or envelopes.**

   The *address block* is the address, including the recipient's name, company, title, street address, city, state, and ZIP Code. If you are creating form letters, click in the sample letter where the address block will go. If you are printing on envelopes, click in the middle of the envelope where the delivery address will go. Then follow these steps to enter the address block:

   - Either click Insert Address Block button on the Mail Merge toolbar or click the Address Block hyperlink in the Mail Merge task plane. The Insert Address Block dialog box appears.

   - Choose a format for entering the recipient's name in the address block (watch the Preview window as you do so).

   - Click the Match Fields button. You see the Match Fields dialog box, shown in Figure 7-8.

   - Using the drop-down lists on the right side of the dialog box, match the fields in your source file with the address block fields on the left side of the dialog box. In Figure 7-8, for example, the Street field is the equivalent of the Address 1 field on the left side of the dialog box, so Street is being chosen from the drop-down menu.

   - Click OK in the Match Fields dialog box and the Insert Block Address dialog box. The <<AddressBlock>> field appears in the document where the address will go. Later, when you merge your document with the data source, real data will appear where the field is now. Think of a field as a kind of placeholder for data.

9. **Click the View Merged Data button on the Mail Merge toolbar to see real data rather than fields.**

Now you can see clearly whether you entered the address block correctly. If you didn't enter it correctly, click the Match Fields button on the Mail Merge toolbar to open the Match Fields dialog box and make new choices.

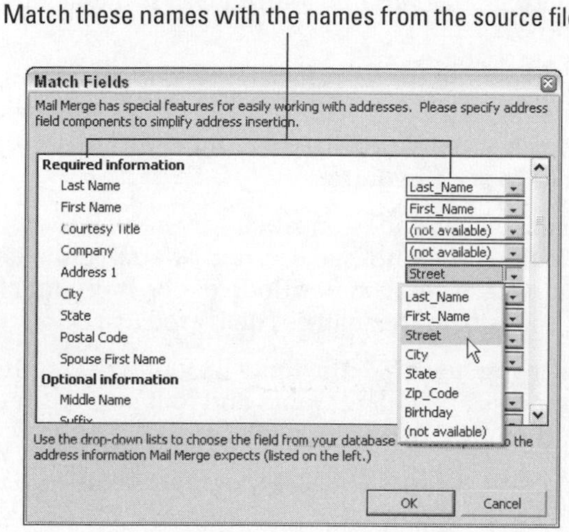

Match these names with the names from the source file.

Figure 7-8:
The Match
Fields dialog
box.

10. **Put the finishing touches on your form letters, labels, or envelopes:**

- **Form letters:** Click where the salutation ("Dear John") will go and then click the Insert Greeting Line button on the Mail Merge toolbar or the Greeting Line hyperlink. You see the Greeting Line dialog box, shown in Figure 7-9. Make choices in this dialog box to determine how the letters' salutations will read.

Figure 7-9:
Entering the
greeting.

The body of your form letter may well include other variable information such as names and birthdays. To enter that stuff, click where variable information goes and then click the Insert Merge Fields button or the More Items hyperlink. The Insert Merge Field dialog box appears and lists fields from the source file. Select a field, click the Insert button, and click the Close button.

If you are editing your form letter and you need to see precisely where the variable information you entered is located, click the Highlight Merge Fields button. The variable information is highlighted in your document.

- **Labels:** Click the Update All Labels button on the bottom of the task pane to enter all recipients' labels in the sample document. (You may have to click the down arrow on the bottom of the task pane several times to see the button.)

  To include postal bar codes on labels, click the Postal Bar Code hyperlink in the task pane, make sure that a ZIP Code field is selected in the Insert Postal Bar Code dialog box, and click OK. Postal bar codes help the mail get delivered faster.

- **Envelopes:** If you don't like the fonts or font sizes on the envelope, select an address and change fonts and font sizes with the drop-down menus on the Formatting toolbar.

  To enter a return address, click in the upper-right corner and enter it by hand.

  To include postal bar codes on envelopes, click below the delivery address, click the Postal Bar Code hyperlink in the task pane, and fill in the Insert Postal Bar Code dialog box.

11. **Click the Next Record and Previous Record buttons on the Mail Merge toolbar to skip from recipient to recipient and make sure that you have entered information correctly.**

    The items you see on-screen are the same form letters, envelopes, or labels you will see when you have finished printing. (Click the View Merged Data button if you see field names rather than people's names and addresses.)

If an item is incorrect, open the source file and correct it there. When you save the source file, the correction is made in the sample document.

At last — you're ready to print the form letters, labels, or envelopes. Better keep reading.

Printing form letters, labels, and envelopes

After you have gone to the trouble to prepare the data file and merge it with the document, you're ready to print your form letters, labels, or envelopes. Start by loading paper, sheets of labels, or envelopes in your printer:

✦ **Form letters:** Form letters are easiest to print. Just put the paper in the printer.

✦ **Labels:** Load the label sheets in your printer.

✦ **Envelopes:** Not all printers are capable of printing envelopes one after the other. Sorry, but you probably have to consult the dreary manual that came with your computer to find out the correct way to load envelopes.

Now, to print the form letters, labels, or envelopes, save the material in a new document or send it straight to the printer:

✦ **Saving in a new document:** Click the Merge to New Document button on the Mail Merge toolbar (or press Alt+Shift+N) to create a new document for your form letters, labels, or envelopes. You see the Merge to New Document dialog box. Click OK. After Word creates the document, save it and print it. You can go into the document and make changes here and there before printing. In form letters, for example, you can write a sentence or two in different letters to personalize them.

✦ **Printing right away:** Click the Merge to Printer button (or press Alt+Shift+M) to print the form letters, labels, or envelopes without saving them in a document. Click OK in the Merge to Printer dialog box and then negotiate the Print dialog box.

Chapter 8: Tools for Reports and Scholarly Papers

In This Chapter

- ⋼ Looking for synonyms with the Thesaurus
- ⋼ Working in Outline view
- ⋼ Managing footnotes and endnotes
- ⋼ Indexing your work
- ⋼ Putting cross-references in documents

This chapter is hereby dedicated to everyone who has had to delve into the unknown and write a report about it. Writing reports, manuals, and scholarly papers is not easy. You have to explore uncharted territory. You have to contemplate the ineffable. And you have to write bibliographies and footnotes and maybe an index, too. Word cannot take you directly to uncharted territory, but it can take some of the sting out of it.

This chapter explains how to handle footnotes and endnotes, generate a table of contents, index a document, and include cross-references in documents. You also find out how the Thesaurus can help you find *le mot juste*.

Finding the Right Word with the Thesaurus

If you can't seem to find the right word, or if the word is on the tip of your tongue but you can't quite remember it, you can always give the Thesaurus a shot. To find synonyms for a word in your document, start by right-clicking the word and choosing Synonyms on the shortcut menu, as shown in Figure 8-1. With luck, the synonym you are looking for appears on the submenu, and all you have to do is click to enter the synonym in your document. Usually, however, finding a good synonym is a journey, not a Sunday stroll.

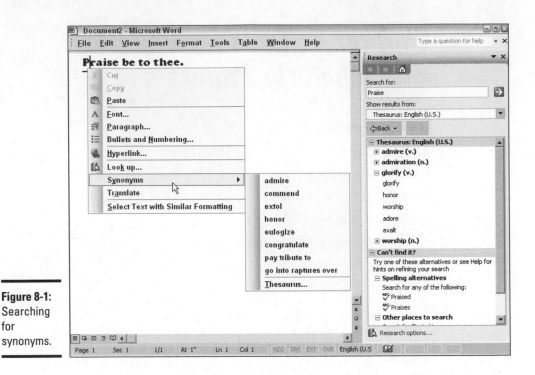

Figure 8-1:
Searching
for
synonyms.

To search for a good synonym, click the word in question and then press Shift+F7, choose Tools⇨Language⇨Thesaurus, or right-click and choose Synonyms⇨Thesaurus. The Research task pane opens, as shown in Figure 8-1. Now you're getting somewhere:

✦ **Choosing a synonym:** Move the pointer over the word, open its drop-down menu, and choose Insert.

✦ **Finding a synonym for a synonym:** If a synonym intrigues you, click it. The task pane displays a new list of synonyms.

✦ **Searching for antonyms:** If you can't think of the right word, try typing its antonym and then looking for an antonym in the Research task pane. The task pane sometimes lists antonyms for words.

✦ **Revisit a word list:** Click the Back button as many times as necessary. If you go back too far, you can always click its companion Forward button.

Outlines for Organizing Your Work

Outline view is a great way to see at a glance how your document is organized and whether you need to organize it differently. To take advantage of this feature, you must have assigned heading levels to the headings in your document (Chapter 4 explains styles.) In Outline view, you can see all the headings in your document. If a section is in the wrong place, you can move it simply by dragging an icon or by pressing one of the buttons on the Outlining toolbar. To change the rank of a heading, simply choose an option on the Outlining toolbar.

Choose View⇨Outline or click the Outline View button in the lower-left corner of the screen to switch to Outline view. Rather than see text, you see the headings in your document, as well as the first line underneath each heading. Now you get a sense of what is in your document and whether it is organized well. By choosing an option from the Show Level menu, you can decide which headings to see on-screen, as Figure 8-2 demonstrates.

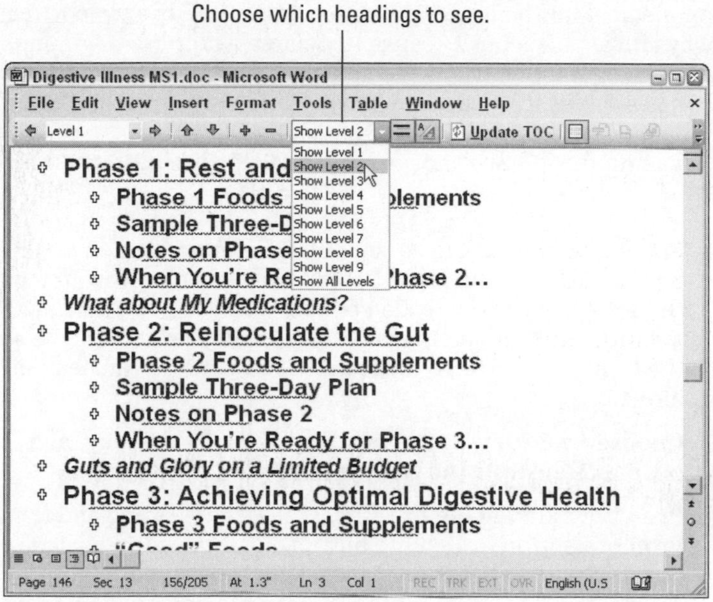

Choose which headings to see.

Figure 8-2:
A document in Outline view.

Before you start rearranging your document in Outline view, get a good look at it by taking advantage of buttons and menus on the Outlining toolbar:

✦ **View some or all headings:** Choose an option from the Show Level drop-down list. To see only first-level headings, for example, choose Show Level 1. To see first-, second-, and third-level headings, choose Show Level 3. Choose Show All Levels to see all the headings.

✦ **View heading formats:** Click the Show Formatting button. When this button is selected, you can see how headings were formatted and get a better idea of their ranking in your document.

✦ **View or hide the headings in one section:** To see the headings and text in only one section of a document, select that section by clicking the plus sign beside it; then, click the Expand button. To hide the headings and text in a section, select the minus sign beside its name and then click the Collapse button.

✦ **View or hide paragraph text:** Click the Show First Line Only button (or press Alt+Shift+L). When this button is selected, you see only the first line in each paragraph. First lines are followed by an ellipsis (. . .) so that you know that more text follows.

Notice the plus and minus icons next to the headings and the text. A plus icon means that the item has subtext under it. For example, headings almost always have plus icons because text comes after them. A minus icon means that nothing is found below the item in question. For example, body text usually has a minus icon because body text is lowest on the Outline totem pole.

You can do the following tasks with the lists and buttons on the Outlining toolbar:

✦ **Move a section in the document:** To move a section up or down in the document, click the Move Up or Move Down button. You can also drag the plus sign or square icon to a new location. If you want to move the subordinate text and headings along with the section, be sure to click the Collapse button to tuck all the subtext into the heading before you move it.

✦ **Choose a new level for a heading:** Click the heading and choose a new heading level from the Outline Level drop-down list.

✦ **Promote and demote headings:** Click the heading and then click the Promote button or Demote button. For example, you can promote a Level 3 heading to Level 2 by clicking the Promote button. Click the Promote to Heading 1 button to promote any heading to a first-level heading.

Generating a Table of Contents

A book-size document isn't worth very much without a table of contents (TOC). How else can readers find what they're looking for? Generating a table of contents with Word is easy, as long as you give the headings in the document different styles — Heading 1, Heading 2, and so on (Chapter 4 explains styles). The beautiful thing about Word TOCs is the way they can be updated nearly instantly. If you add a new heading or erase a heading, you can update the TOC with a snap of your fingers. Moreover, you can quickly go from a TOC entry to its corresponding heading in a document by Ctrl+clicking the entry.

Before you create your TOC, create a new section in which to put it and number the pages in the new section with Roman numerals (Chapter 2 explains sections). TOCs, including the TOC in this book, are usually numbered in this way. The first entry in the TOC should cite page number 1. If you don't take my advice and create a new section, the TOC will occupy the first few numbered pages of your document, and the numbering scheme will be thrown off.

Creating a TOC

To create a table of contents:

1. **Place the cursor where you want the TOC to go.**

2. **Choose Insert⇨Reference⇨Index and Tables.**

3. **Select the Table of Contents tab in the Index and Tables dialog box, as shown in Figure 8-3.**

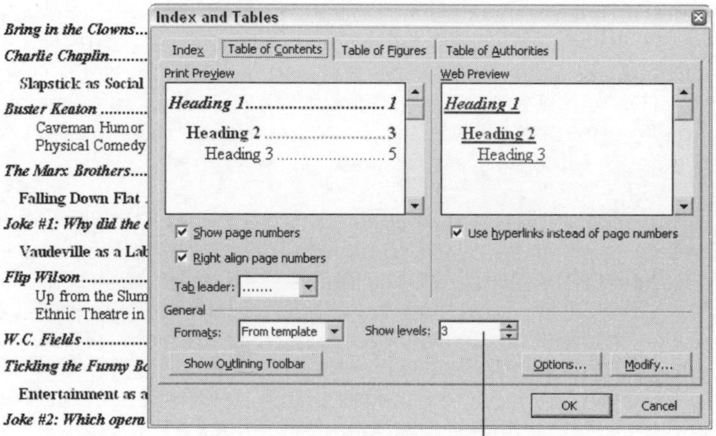

Figure 8-3:
Creating a
TOC.

Choose which headings to list.

4. **Choose options in the dialog box and click OK when you're done.**

As you make your choices, watch the Print Preview and Web Preview boxes to see what effect your choices have.

The Table of Contents tab gives you several ways to control what goes in your TOC and what it looks like:

✦ **Showing page numbers:** Uncheck the <u>S</u>how Page Numbers box if you want your TOC to be a simple list that doesn't refer to headings by page.

✦ **Aligning the page numbers:** Select the <u>R</u>ight Align Page Numbers check box if you want page numbers to line up along the right side of the TOC so that the ones and tens line up under each other.

✦ **Choosing a tab Leader:** A *leader* is the punctuation mark that appears between the heading and the page number the heading is on. If you don't want periods as the leader, choose another leader or choose "(None)."

✦ **Choosing a format:** Choose a format from the Forma<u>t</u>s list if you don't care to use the one from the template. Just be sure to watch the Print Pre<u>v</u>iew and <u>W</u>eb Preview boxes to see what your choice amounts to.

✦ **Choosing a TOC depth:** The Show <u>L</u>evels box determines how many heading levels are included in the TOC. Unless your document is a legal contract or other formal paper, enter a **2** or **3** here. A TOC is supposed to help readers find information quickly. Including lots of headings that take a long time to read through defeats the purpose of having a TOC.

If you add a new heading to your document or if you remove one, you can easily get an up-to-date TOC. To do so, click the Update TOC button on the Outlining toolbar, click in the TOC and press F9, or right-click anywhere in the TOC and choose <u>U</u>pdate Field on the shortcut menu. A dialog box asks how to update the TOC. Choose to update the page numbers only or update the entire table, TOC entries, and page numbers.

Suppose that you want to copy a TOC to another document. It can be done. Before copying it, however, you need to unlock it. *Unlocking* means to disconnect TOC entries from the headings to which they refer. To unlock a TOC, click in the margin to the left of the first entry to select the TOC. Next, press Ctrl+Shift+F9. Now you can successfully copy or move the TOC to another document. Because Word gives the text of TOCs the Hyperlink character style, you have to change the color of the text in the TOC (it's blue) and remove the underlines. After you unlock a TOC, however, you can't update it automatically.

Tinkering with the look and structure of a TOC

Sometimes the conventional TOC that Word generates doesn't do the trick. Just because a heading has been given the Heading 1 style doesn't mean that it should receive first priority in the TOC. Suppose that you created another style called ChapterTitle that should stand taller in the hierarchy than Heading 1. In that case, you need to rearrange the TOC such that Heading 1 headings rank second, not first, in the hierarchy.

Marking TOC entries with the TC Field

Table of contents entries can refer to a particular place in a document, not just to headings that have been assigned heading styles. For example, to include a caption or word in a TOC, select it and press Alt+Shift+O. Then, in the Mark Table of Contents Entry dialog box, make sure that the words you want to appear in the TOC appear in the Entry text box (edit the words if need be), and make sure that C (for Contents) appears in the Table Identifier box. In the Level box, enter a number to tell Word how to treat the entry when you generate the table of contents. For example, entering 1 tells Word to treat the entry like a first-level heading and give it top priority. A 3 places the entry with the third-level headings. Finally, click Mark button.

When you generate the table of contents, be sure to include TOC fields. To do that, click the Options button on the Table of Contents tab of the Index and Tables dialog box and, in the Table of Contents Options dialog box, select the Table Entry fields check box.

Use the Table of Contents Options and Style dialog boxes to tinker with a TOC. These dialog boxes are shown in Figure 8-4. To open them, click, respectively, the Options button or Modify button on the Table of Contents tab of the Index and Tables dialog box (refer to Figure 8-3).

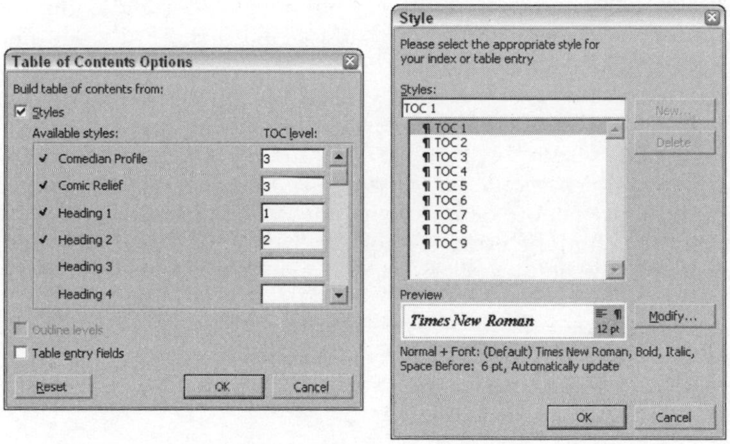

Figure 8-4:
Customizing
a TOC.

+ **Assigning TOC levels to paragraph styles:** The Table of Contents Options dialog box lists each paragraph style in the document you're working in. For headings you want to appear in the TOC, enter a number in the TOC Level text box to determine the headings' rank. If headings assigned the Heading 1 style are to rank second in the TOC, for example, enter a 2 in Heading 1's TOC Level text box. You can exclude headings from a TOC by deleting a number in a TOC Level box.

✦ **Including TOC field entries:** To include text you marked with a TC field in the TOC, select the Table Entry Field check box in the Table of Contents Options dialog box (earlier in this chapter, the sidebar "Marking TOC entries with the TC Field" explains how TC fields work).

✦ **Changing the look of TOC entries:** The Style dialog box you see when you click the Modify button on the Table of Contents tab gives you the chance to choose new fonts, character styles, and font sizes for TOC entries. Click the Modify button. Then, in the Modify Styles dialog box, choose options to format the TOC style. For example, click the Bold button to boldface TOC entries. (Chapter 4 explains modifying styles.)

Putting Footnotes and Endnotes in Documents

A *footnote* is a reference, bit of explanation, or comment that appears at the bottom of the page and is referred to by a number or symbol in the text. An *endnote* is the same thing, except that it appears at the end of the chapter or document. If you've written a scholarly paper of any kind, you know what a drag footnotes and endnotes are.

Word takes some of the drudgery out of footnotes and endnotes. For example, if you delete or add a note and you instruct Word to automatically number your footnotes and endnotes, all notes after the one you added or deleted are renumbered. And you don't have to worry about long footnotes because Word adjusts the page layout to make room for them. You can change the numbering scheme of footnotes and endnotes at will. When you are reviewing a document, all you have to do is move the pointer over a footnote or endnote citation. The note icon appears, as does a pop-up box with the text of the note, as shown in Figure 8-5. Meanwhile, footnotes appear at the bottom of the page and endnotes at the end of the section.

Inserting a footnote or endnote

To insert a footnote or endnote in a document:

1. **Place the cursor in the text where you want the note's symbol or number to appear.**

2. **Choose Insert⇨Reference⇨Footnote.**

   The Footnote and Endnote dialog box appears (refer to Figure 8-5). I explain the many options in this dialog box shortly.

3. **Choose the Footnotes or Endnotes option button.**

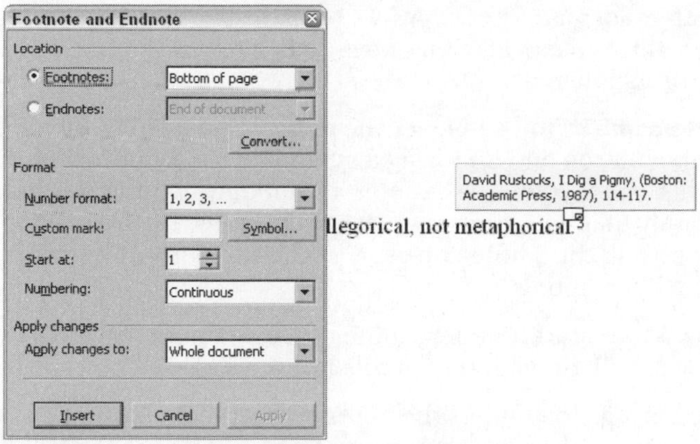

Figure 8-5:
Formatting
and viewing
footnotes.

David Rustocks, I Dig a Pigmy, (Boston: Academic Press, 1987), 114-117.

llegorical, not metaphorical.

4. **Click the Insert button.**

   If you are in Normal view, a notes box opens at the bottom of the screen with the cursor beside the number of the note you're about to enter. In Print Layout view, Word scrolls to the bottom of the page or end of the document or section so that you can enter the note.

5. **Type your footnote or endnote.**

6. **Click Close if you're done in Normal view; in Print Layout view, scroll upward to return to the main text.**

Choosing the numbering scheme and position of notes

Changing the numbering scheme and positioning of endnotes and footnotes is quite easy. Start by choosing Insert➪Reference➪Footnote. The Footnote and Endnote dialog box appears (refer to Figure 8-5). Do the following in the dialog box.

Tell Word where to place your notes:

✦ **Footnotes:** Choose Bottom of Page to put footnotes at the bottom of the page no matter where the text ends; choose Below Text to put footnotes directly below the last text line on the page.

✦ **Endnotes:** Choose End of Section if your document is divided into sections (such as chapters) and you want endnotes to appear at the back of sections; choose End of Document to put all endnotes at the very back of the document.

In the Format area, tell Word how to number the notes if you haven't done so already:

✦ **Number Format:** Choose A B C, i ii iii, or another numbering scheme, if you want. You can also enter symbols by choosing the last option on this drop-down list.

✦ **Custom Mark:** You can mark the note with a symbol by clicking the Symbol button and choosing a symbol in the Symbol dialog box. If you go this route, you have to enter a symbol each time you insert a note. Not only that, but you may have to enter two or three symbols for the second and third notes on each page or document because Word can't renumber symbols.

✦ **Start At:** To start numbering the notes at a place other than 1, A, or i, enter **2**, **B**, **ii**, or whatever in this box.

✦ **Numbering:** To number the notes continuously from the start of your document to the end, choose Continuous. Choose Restart Each Section to begin anew at each section of your document. For footnotes, you can begin anew on each page by choosing Restart Each Page.

By the way, the Convert button in the Footnote and Endnote dialog box is for fickle scholars who suddenly decide that their endnotes should be footnotes, or vice versa. Click it and choose an option in the Convert Notes dialog box to turn footnotes into endnotes, turn endnotes into footnotes, or — in documents with both endnotes and footnotes — make the endnotes footnotes and the footnotes endnotes.

Deleting, moving, and editing notes

If a devious editor tells you that a footnote or endnote is in the wrong place, that you don't need a note, or that you need to change the text in a note, all is not lost:

✦ **Editing:** To edit a note, double-click its number or symbol in the text. You see the note on-screen. Edit the note at this point.

✦ **Moving:** To move a note, select its number or symbol in the text and drag it to a new location; or you can cut and paste it to a new location.

✦ **Deleting:** To delete a note, select its number or symbol and press the Delete key.

Footnotes and endnotes are renumbered when you move or delete any.

Indexing a Document

A good index is a thing of beauty. User manuals, reference works of any length, and reports that readers will refer to all require indexes. Except for the table of contents, the only way to find information in a long document is to look in the index. An index at the end of a company report reflects well on the person who wrote the report. It gives the appearance that the author put in a fair amount of time to complete the work, even if he or she didn't really do that.

An index entry can be formatted in many ways. You can cross-reference index entries, list a page range in an index entry, and break out an index entry into subentries and sub-subentries. To help you with your index, Figure 8-6 explains indexing terminology.

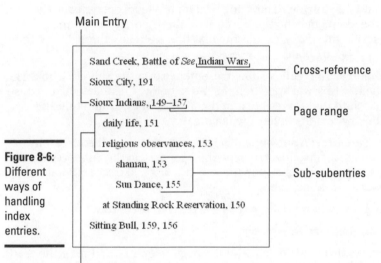

Figure 8-6:
Different
ways of
handling
index
entries.

Writing a good index entry is as hard as writing good, descriptive headings. As you enter index entries in your document, ask yourself how you would look up information in the index if you were reading it, and enter your index entries accordingly.

Marking index items in the document

Marking index items yourself is easier than it seems. After you open the Mark Index Entry dialog box, it stays open so that you can scroll through your document and make entries.

1. **If you see a word in your document that you can use as a main, top-level entry, select it; otherwise, place the cursor in the paragraph or heading whose topic you want to include in the index.**

You can save a little time by selecting a word, as I describe shortly.

2. Press Alt+Shift+X.

The Mark Index Entry dialog box appears. If you selected a word, it appears in the Main Entry box.

3. Choose how you want to handle this index entry (refer to Figure 8-6 to see the various ways to make index entries).

When you enter the text, don't put a comma or period after it. Word does that when it generates the index. The text that you enter will appear in your index.

- **Main Entry:** If you're entering a main, top-level entry, leave the text in the Main Entry box (if it's already there), or type new text to describe this entry, or edit the text that's already there. Leave the Subentry box blank.

- **Subentry:** To create a subentry, enter text in the Subentry box. The subentry text will appear in the index below the main entry text, so make sure that there is text in the Main Entry box and that the subentry text fits under the main entry.

- **Sub-subentry:** A sub-subentry is the third level in the hierarchy. To create a sub-subentry, type the subentry in the Subentry box, enter a colon (:), and type the sub-subentry, like so: **religious observances:shaman**.

4. Decide how to handle the page reference in the entry.

Again, your choices are many:

- **Cross-reference:** To go without a page reference and refer the reader to another index entry, click Cross-reference and type the other entry in the text box after the word *See*. What you type here appears in your index, so be sure that the topic you refer the reader to is really in the index.

- **Current Page:** Click this option to enter a single page number after the entry.

- **Page Range:** Click this option if you're indexing a subject that covers several pages in your document. A page range index entry looks something like this: "Sioux Indians, 149–157." To make a page range entry, you must create a bookmark for the range. Click outside the dialog box to get back to your document, and select all the text in the page range. Then choose Insert⇨Bookmark, type a name in the Bookmark Name box (you may as well type the name of the index entry), and click Add. Back in the Mark Index Entry dialog box, select the Page Range option button, open the Bookmark drop-down list, and select your bookmark. Click Mark, not Mark All, when you get to Step 6.

5. **You can boldface or italicize a page number or page range by clicking a Page Number Format check box.**

   In some indexes, the page or page range where the topic is explained in the most depth is italicized or boldfaced so that readers can get to the juiciest parts first.

6. **If you selected a word in Step 1, you can click the Mark All button to have Word go through the document and mark all words identical to the one in the Main Entry box; click Mark to put this single entry in the index.**

   Click outside the Mark Index Entry dialog box and find the next topic or word that you want to mark for the index. Then press Alt+Shift+X and make another entry.

¶ A bunch of ugly field codes appear in your document. You can render them invisible by clicking the Show/Hide¶ button. Now you can go ahead and generate the index.

Generating the index

After you mark the index entries, it's time to generate the index:

1. **Place the cursor where you want the index to go, most likely at the end of the document.**

   You might type the word **Index** and format the word in a decorative way.

2. **Choose Insert➪Reference➪Index and Tables and select the Index tab, if necessary.**

   Figure 8-7 shows the Index tab of the Index and Tables dialog box.

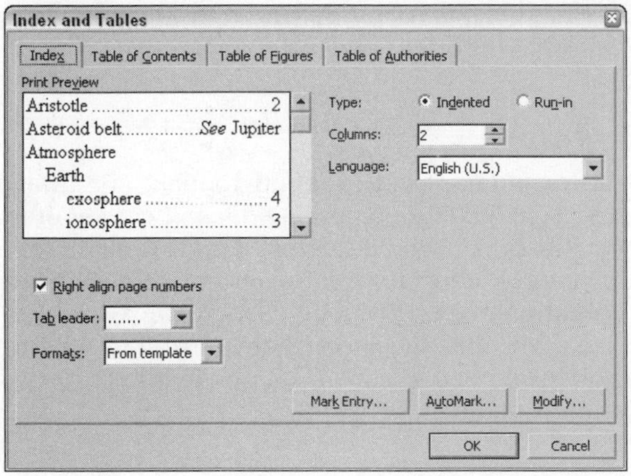

Figure 8-7:
Generating
an index.

3. **Choose options in the Index tab of the Index and Tables dialog box and click OK.**

   As you make your choices, watch the Print Preview box to see what happens.

Here are the options on the Index tab of the Index and Tables dialog box:

✦ **Type:** Choose Run-in if you want subentries and sub-subentries to run together. Otherwise, stick with the Indented option to indent them.

✦ **Columns:** Stick with 2, unless you don't have subentries or sub-subentries and you can squeeze three columns on the page.

✦ **Language:** Choose a language for the table, if necessary and if you have installed a foreign language dictionary. By doing so, you can run the spell-checker over your index and make sure that the entries are spelled correctly.

✦ **Right Align Page Numbers:** Normally, page numbers appear right after entries and are separated from entries by a comma, but you can right-align the entries so that they line up under one another with this option.

✦ **Tab Leader:** Some index formats (such as Formal) place a *leader* between the entry and the page number. A leader is a series of dots or dashes. If you're working with a format that has a leader, you can choose a leader from the drop-down list.

✦ **Formats:** Word offers a number of attractive index layouts. You can choose one from the list.

✦ **Modify:** Click this button if you're adventurous and want to create an index style of your own (Chapter 4 explains styles).

To update an index after you create or delete entries, right-click the index and then choose Update Field on the shortcut menu, or click the index and press F9.

Editing an index

After you generate an index, read it carefully to make sure that all entries are useful to readers. Inevitably, something doesn't come out right, but you can edit index entries as you would the text in a document. Index field markers are enclosed in curly brackets with the letters *XE* and the text of the index entry in quotation marks, like so: { XE: "Wovoka: Ghost Dance" }. To edit an index marker, click the Show/Hide¶ button to see the field markers and find the one you need to edit. Then delete letters or type letters as you would do with normal text.

Here's a quick way to find index field markers: After clicking the Show/Hide¶ button, with the index fields showing, choose Edit➪Go To (press Ctrl+G), select Field in the Go to What box, type **XE** in the Enter Field Name box, and click the Next button until you find the marker you want to edit. You can also use the Edit➪Find command to look for index entries. Word finds those as well as text — it does that as long as you clicked the Show/Hide¶ button and displayed index fields in your document.

Putting Cross-References in a Document

Cross-references are very handy indeed. They tell readers where to go to find more information on a topic. The problem with cross-references, however, is that the thing being cross-referenced really has to be there. If you tell readers to go to a heading called "The Cat's Pajamas" on page 93, and neither the heading nor the page exists, readers curse and tell you where to go, instead of the other way around.

Fortunately for you, Word lets you know when you make errant cross-references. You can refer readers to headings, page numbers, footnotes, endnotes, and plain-old paragraphs. And as long you create captions for your cross-references with the Insert➪Reference➪Caption command, you can also make cross-references to equations, figures, graphs, listings, programs, and tables. If you delete the thing that a cross-reference refers to and render the cross-reference invalid, Word tells you about it the next time you update your cross-references. Best of all, if the page number, numbered item, or text that a cross-reference refers to changes, so does the cross-reference.

To create a cross-reference:

1. **Write the first part of the cross-reference text.**

For example, you could write **To learn more about these cowboys of the pampas, see page** and then enter a blank space. The blank space separates the word *page* from the page number you're about to enter with the Insert➪Reference➪Cross-reference command. If you are referring to a heading, write something like **For more information, see** **".** Don't enter a blank space this time because the heading text will appear right after the double quotation mark.

2. **Choose Insert➪Reference➪Cross-reference.**

The Cross-reference dialog box shown in Figure 8-8 appears.

3. **Choose what type of item you're referring to in the Reference Type drop-down list.**

If you're referring to a plain old paragraph, choose Bookmark. Then click outside the dialog box, scroll to the paragraph you're referring to and place a bookmark there with the Insert⇨Bookmark command. (Chapter 2 explains bookmarks.)

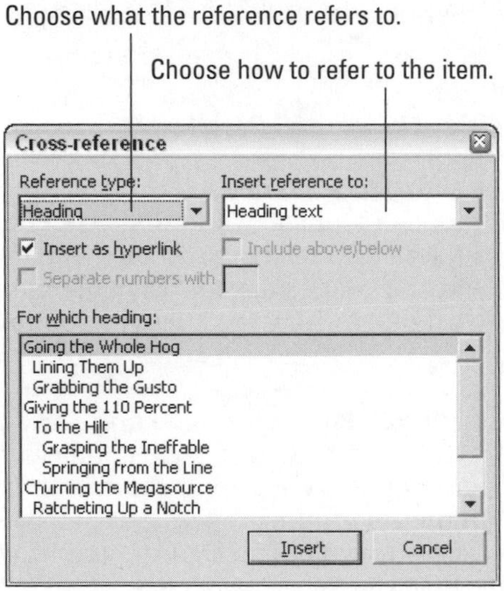

Choose what the reference refers to.

Choose how to refer to the item.

Figure 8-8: Entering a cross-reference.

4. **Make a choice in the Insert Reference To box to refer text, a page number, or a numbered item.**

   The options in this box are different, depending on what you chose in Step 3.

   - **Text:** Choose this option (Heading Text, Entire Caption, and so on) to include text in the cross-reference. For example, choose Heading Text if your cross-reference is to a heading.

   - **Number:** Choose this option to insert a page number or other kind of number, such as a table number, in the cross-reference.

   - **Include Above/Below:** Check this box to include the word "above" or "below" to tell readers where, in relation to the cross-reference, the thing being referred to is in your document.

5. **If you wish, leave the check mark in the Insert as Hyperlink check box to create a hyperlink as well as a cross-reference.**

   This way, someone reading the document online can Ctrl+Click the cross-reference and go directly to what it refers to. (The person can click the Back button on the Web toolbar or press Alt+← to return to the cross-reference as well.)

6. **In the For Which box, tell Word where the thing you're referring to is located.**

To do so, select a heading, bookmark, footnote, endnote, equation, figure, graph, or whatnot in the menu. In long documents, you will surely have to click the scrollbar to find the one you want.

7. **Click the Insert button and then click the Close button.**

8. **Back in your document, enter the rest of the cross-reference text, if necessary.**

When you finish creating your document, update all the cross-references. To do that, press Ctrl+A to select the entire document. Then press F9 or right-click in the document and choose Update Field from the shortcut menu.

If the thing referred to in a cross-reference is no longer in your document, you see `Error! Reference source not found` where the cross-reference should be. To find cross-reference errors in long documents, look for the word *Error!* with the Edit⇨Find command. Investigate what went wrong, and delete the cross-reference or make a new one.

Numbering the Headings in a Document

In scholarly papers and formal documents, the headings are sometimes numbered so that cross-references and commentary can refer to them by number as well as by name. The Format⇨ Bullets and Numbering command makes numbering the headings in a document very easy. The beauty of this command is that Word renumbers the headings automatically if you remove a heading or add a new one.

To use the Format⇨Bullets and Numbering command, you must have assigned heading styles to your document (Chapter 4 explains styles.) First-level heads are given top billing in the numbering scheme. Subheadings get lower billing.

To number the headings in a document:

1. **Switch to Outline view by clicking the Outline View button in the lower-left corner of the screen or choosing View⇨Outline.**

2. **Choose an option on the Show Level drop-down menu (you'll find it on the Outlining toolbar) so that you see only headings in Outline view.**

Earlier in this chapter, "Outlines for Organizing Your Work" describes how to choose which levels are displayed.

3. **Select the headings you want to number.**

   Select all the headings or a handful of headings:

   - To select all the headings, choose Edit⇨Select All (or press Ctrl+A).
   - To select groups of headings, hold down the Shift key and click the plus or minus sign beside heading names.

4. **Choose Format⇨Bullets and Numbering.**

5. **Select the Outline Numbered tab in the Bullets and Numbering dialog box.**

6. **Select a numbering scheme in the Outline Numbered tab.**

   Notice that some choices place words as well as numbers or letters before headings.

   Click the Customize button if you want to devise your own numbering scheme or put a word before all headings. You can even choose new fonts for headings. If you experiment, be sure to watch the Preview box to see what kind of damage you're doing. Click OK when you're done experimenting.

7. **Click OK to close the Bullets and Numbering dialog box.**

If you regret having numbered the headings in your document, choose Edit⇨Undo Bullets and Numbering (or press Ctrl+Z), or go back to the Outline Numbered tab and choose None.

Book II

Outlook

The 5th Wave   By Rich Tennant

"It's a ten step word processing program. It comes with a spell—checker, grammar—checker, cliche—checker, whine—checker, passive/aggressive—checker, politically correct—checker, hissy—fit—checker, pretentious pontificating—checker, boring anecdote—checker and a Freudian reference—checker."

Contents at a Glance

Chapter 1: Getting Acquainted with Outlook

In This Chapter

- ✔ Getting around in Outlook
- ✔ Viewing folders in different ways
- ✔ Categorizing items so that you can locate them easily
- ✔ Searching in folders
- ✔ Deleting items
- ✔ Backing up your Outlook file
- ✔ Importing e-mail and contact information from other software programs

This chapter pulls back the curtain and gives you a first glimpse of Outlook, the e-mailer and personal organizer in the Office suite of programs. Read on to find out once and for all what Outlook does, how to get from folder to folder, and the different ways to view the stuff in folders. You can find advice about keeping folders well organized in this chapter, deleting stuff, backing up an Outlook file, and cleaning out items in folders that you no longer need.

What Is Outlook, Anyway?

Outlook is not in character with the rest of the Office programs. It's a little different — you can tell as soon as you glance at the screen. The familiar Standard and Formatting toolbars are nowhere to be found. Toolbars change altogether when you click a Navigation pane button and go to a different Outlook window.

Outlook can be confusing because the program serves many different purposes. To wit, Outlook is all this:

- ✦ **An e-mail program:** You can use it to send and receive e-mail messages and files, as well as organize e-mail messages in different folders so that you can keep track of them. (See Chapter 3.)

✦ **An appointment scheduler:** Outlook is also a calendar for scheduling appointments and meetings. You can tell at a glance when and where you are expected, as well as be alerted to upcoming appointments and meetings. (See Chapter 4.)

✦ **An address book:** The program can store the addresses, phone numbers, and e-mail addresses of friends, foes, clients, and family members. Looking up this information in the Contact List is easy. (See Chapter 2.)

✦ **A task reminder:** Outlook is a means of planning projects. You can tell when deadlines fall and plan your workload accordingly. (See Chapter 5.)

✦ **A notes receptacle:** The program is a place to jot down notes and reminders. (See Chapter 5.)

Outlook is a lot of different things all rolled into one. For that reason, the program can be daunting at first. But hang in there. Soon you will be running roughshod over Outlook and making it suffer on your behalf.

Navigating the Outlook Windows

Figure 1-1 shows the Outlook Today window with the Folder List on display. The Outlook Today window lists calendar appointments, tasks that need doing, and the number of messages in three folders that pertain to e-mail (Inbox, Drafts, and Outbox). Not that it matters especially, but all Outlook jobs are divided among folders, and these folders are all kept in a master folder called Personal Folders.

Here are the ways to get from window to window in Outlook and undertake a new task:

✦ **Navigation pane:** Click a button — Mail, Calendar, Contacts, Tasks, or Notes — on the Navigation pane to change windows and use Outlook a different way.

✦ **Go menu:** Choose an option on the Go menu — Mail, Calendar, Contacts, Tasks, Notes — to go from window to window. You can also change windows by pressing the Ctrl key and a number 1 through 5.

✦ **Folder List:** Click the Folder List button to see all the folders in the Personal Folder, and then select a folder (refer to Figure 1-1). For example, to read incoming e-mail messages, select the Inbox folder. The Folder List button is located at the bottom of the Navigation pane. You can also see the Folder List by pressing Ctrl+6 or choosing Go⇨Folder List.

✦ **Outlook Today button:** No matter where you go in Outlook, you can always click the Outlook Today button to return to the Outlook Today window. You can find this button on the Advanced toolbar.

Folder List

Book II
Chapter 1

Getting Acquainted
with Outlook

Figure 1-1:
The Outlook
Today
window.

Click here to move to another window.

Navigation pane

✦ **Back, Forward, and Up One Level buttons:** Click these buttons to return to a window, revisit a window you retreated from, or climb the hierarchy of personal folders. The three buttons are found on the Advanced toolbar.

By the way, you can open a folder in a new window. To do so, right-click a Navigation pane button and choose Open in New Window. To close a window you opened this way, click its Close button (the *X* in the upper-right corner).

When you start Outlook, the program opens to the window you were looking at when you exited the program. If you were staring at the Inbox when you closed Outlook, for example, you see the Inbox next time you open the program. However, if you prefer to see the Outlook Today window each time you start Outlook, click the Customize Outlook Today button (it's on the right side of the Outlook Today window). Then, in the Outlook Today Options window, select the When Starting, Go Directly to Outlook Today check box and click the Save Changes button.

Getting a Better View of a Folder

Because you spend so much time gazing at folders, you may as well get a good view. To find the items you're looking for and help prioritize your work, Outlook offers different views of each folder. Each option on the menu gives you a different insight into the task at hand. Do one of the following to change views:

✦ Open the Current View drop-down menu on the Advanced toolbar and make a choice, as shown in Figure 1-2.

✦ Choose <u>V</u>iew⇨<u>A</u>rrange By⇨Current <u>V</u>iew and an option on the submenu.

✦ Select a Current View option button in the Navigation pane, as shown in Figure 1-2. Current View option buttons are available in the Contacts, Tasks, and Notes folders.

Click here to change views.

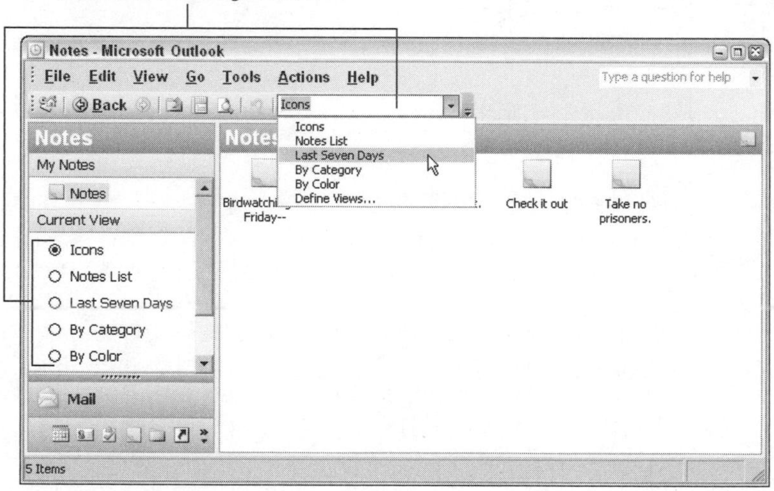

Figure 1-2:
Changing views of a folder's contents.

Categorizing Items in a Folder

One of your biggest tasks in Outlook, if you choose to accept it, is to organize items in folders so that you can find and deal with them. Finding items can be a chore in a folder with a lot of items. As the previous section mentions, changing views of a folder by making a choice on the Current View menu is one way to reorganize items and find the one you're looking for. Another way is to categorize items. After you assign a category to an item, you can arrange items in folders by category and, in so doing, find items. Categorizing is a great way to stay on top of all the tasks you have to do.

Choosing what's on the Navigation pane

 Click the Configure Buttons button on the Navigation pane to decide which buttons belong on the Navigation pane and which buttons to display. Not everyone needs all the buttons. Some people, for example, forsake the Tasks and Notes parts of Outlook, so they don't need the Tasks and Notes buttons.

After you click the Configure Buttons button, you can rearrange the Navigation pane like so:

✦ **Remove or add a button:** Select Add or Remove buttons on the shortcut menu and select the name of a button to add or remove.

✦ **Show fewer or more buttons:** Select Show More Buttons or Show Fewer Buttons on the shortcut menu.

✦ **Rearrange the buttons:** Select Navigation Pane Options and, in the Navigation Pane Options dialog box, select button names and click the Move Up or Move Down button.

By the way, you can hide the Navigation pane altogether if the thing gets in your way. To hide (or display) the Navigation pane, choose View➪Navigation Pane or press Alt+F1.

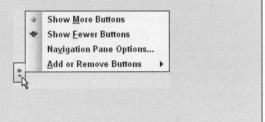

Assigning items to categories

Outlook offers 21 ready-made categories, and you can invent your own as well. Follow these steps to assign a category to a folder item:

1. Select the item.

2. Right-click and choose Categories or choose Edit➪Categories.

You see the Categories dialog box, shown in Figure 1-3.

3. Select a category in the Available Categories box.

You can select more than one category.

 If none of the categories suits you, create a new category by entering its name in the Item(s) Belong to These Categories text box and then clicking the Add to List button. To delete a category, click the Master Category List button in the Categories dialog box and, in the Master Category List dialog box, select the name of the category you want to delete and click the Delete button.

4. Click OK.

To recategorize an item, open the Categories dialog box and remove the check marks next to category names. The Item(s) Belong to These Categories box tells you which categories were assigned to an item.

Create a category

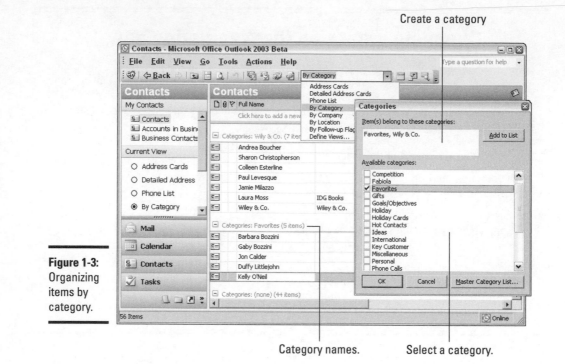

Figure 1-3:
Organizing
items by
category.

Category names.   Select a category.

Arranging items by category

To arrange items by category in a folder, open the Current View drop-down
menu and choose By Category. As shown in Figure 1-3, items in the folder are
grouped by category name. You can hide or display items in categories by
clicking the plus (+) or minus (–) sign next to a category name.

Finding Items in Folders

If you can't locate an item in a folder by scrolling, changing views, or switching to By Category view, you have to resort to the Find command. Outlook
offers two Find commands, a simple Find command that's available on the
Standard toolbar and an Advanced Find command that requires more effort
but can yield more exacting results. Keep reading.

The Contacts folder offers a very convenient means of finding stray contact
information. In the Find a Contact text box (you can find it on the Standard
toolbar), enter a name or an e-mail address and press Enter. If the name or
e-mail address can be found, you see the person's Contact information.

Searching in the Find pane

Is it just me, or do others think "pain" instead of "pane" when they hear that the Outlook windows are composed of different panes — the Navigation pane, Reading pane, and so on? As if you aren't already in enough pain, simple searches are conducted in the Find pane. Follow these steps to conduct a simple search in the Find pane:

1. **Click the Find button in any window.**

   You see a Find pane like the one in Figure 1-4.

**Book II
Chapter 1**

**Getting Acquainted
with Outlook**

Figure 1-4:
Conducting
a simple
search.

2. **If necessary, tell Outlook which folders to search by opening the Search In drop-down menu and making a choice.**

   Choose one of the options on the menu or select Choose Folders and choose a folder name in the Select Folder(s) dialog box. You can search more than one folder by opening this dialog box and selecting folders.

   In mail folder searches, Outlook searches the text in messages as well as the subject of messages, but if that kind of search produces too many messages to look through, open the Options menu on the Find pane and unselect Search All Text in Each Message (refer to Figure 1-4). This way, Outlook searches messages' subjects only, and fewer messages appear in the search results.

3. **Enter what you're searching for in the Look For text box.**

4. **Click the Find Now button.**

   If your search doesn't bear fruit, click the Clear button and start all over, or open the Options drop-down menu and choose Advanced Find to embark on an advanced search. The next section explains advanced searching. Click the Find button or the Close button on the Find pane to remove the Find pane from the screen.

Conducting an advanced search

Run an advanced search when a simple search doesn't do the job, you want to search using more than one criterion, or you want to search in several different folders. To start an advanced search, either press Ctrl+Shift+F or click the Find button, open the Options menu on the Find pane (refer to Figure 1-4), and select Advanced Find. You see the Advanced Find dialog box. If your search is a successful one, found items will appear at the bottom of the dialog box, as shown in Figure 1-5. You can double-click to open found items in the search results.

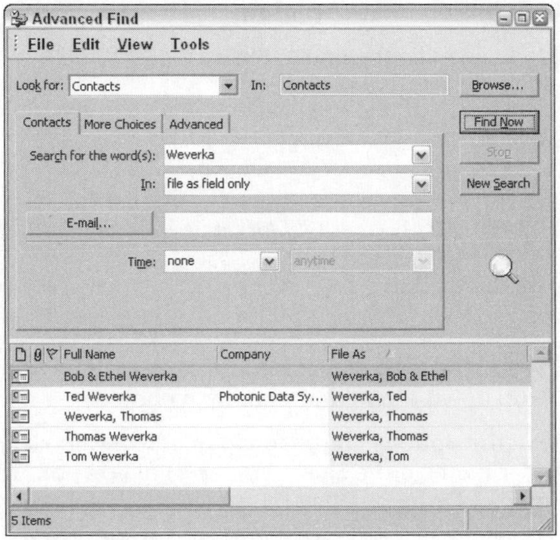

Figure 1-5: Conducting an advanced search.

In the Look For drop-down menu, choose where you want to search. If the folder isn't on the menu, click the Browse button and choose it in the Select Folder(s) dialog box. Then choose options on the three tabs — Contacts, More Choices, and Advanced — in the dialog box. Which options are available depends on which folder you are searching.

The Advanced Find dialog box offers handy commands for dealing with items after you find them. Select the items and choose Edit➪Move to Folder to move the items into a new folder. Choose Edit➪Delete to delete the items. Ctrl+click, Shift+click, or choose Edit➪Select All to select items in the Advanced Find dialog box.

Deleting E-Mail Messages, Contacts, Tasks, and Other Items

Outlook folders are notorious for filling very quickly. E-mail messages, contacts, and tasks soon clog the folders if you spend any time in Outlook. From time to time, go through the e-mail folders, Contacts window, Task window, and Calendar to delete items you no longer need. To delete items, select them and do one of the following:

+ Click the Delete button (or press the Delete key).

+ Choose Edit⇨Delete (or press Ctrl+D).

+ Right-click and choose Delete.

Deleted items — e-mail messages, calendar appointments, contacts, or tasks — land in the Deleted Items folder in case you want to recover them. To delete items once and for all, open the Deleted Items folder and start deleting like a madman.

To spare you the trouble of deleting items twice, once in the original folder and again in the Deleted Items folder, Outlook offers these amenities:

+ **Empty the Deleted Items folder when you close Outlook:** If you're no fan of the Deleted Items folder and you want to remove deleted items without reviewing them, choose Tools⇨Options, select the Other tab in the Options dialog box, and select Empty the Deleted Items Folder Upon Exiting.

+ **Empty the Deleted Items folder yourself:** Choose Tools⇨Empty "Deleted Items" Folder to remove all the messages in the Deleted Items folder. You can also right-click the Deleted Items folder in the Folder List and choose Empty "Deleted Items" Folder.

You can search for items and delete them in the Advanced Find dialog box. See "Conducting an advanced search," earlier in this chapter.

Saving a search so that you can run it later

If you find yourself searching for the same stuff repeatedly, save the search criteria in a file. That way, you don't have to enter the search criteria each time you run the search. All you have to do is open the Advanced Find dialog box, choose File⇨Open Search in the dialog box, and choose a search file in the Open Saved Search dialog box. Searches are saved in special files with the extension .OSS (Office Saved Searches).

To save a search, start by creating a folder for storing OSS files. After you have conducted a search you want to save, choose File⇨Save Search in the Advanced Save dialog box. You see the Save Search dialog box. Locate the folder where you save searches, enter a descriptive name for the search, and click OK.

Finding and Backing Up Your Outlook File

All the data you keep in Outlook — e-mail messages, names and addresses, calendar appointments and meetings — is kept in a file called Outlook.pst. Locating this file on your computer sometimes requires the services of Sherlock Holmes. The file isn't kept in a standard location. It can be any number of places, depending on the operating system on your computer and whether you upgraded from an earlier version of Office.

The all-important Outlook.pst file is hiding deep in your computer, but you need to find it. You need to know where this file is located so that you can back it up to a floppy disk, Zip drive, or other location where you keep backup material. The Outlook Contacts List holds clients' names and the names of relatives and loved ones. It holds the e-mail messages you think are worth keeping. It would be a shame to lose this stuff if your computer failed.

Here's a quick way to find the Outlook.pst file on your computer and back it up:

1. **Choose File⇨Data File Management.**

   You see the Outlook Data Files dialog box, shown in Figure 1-6.

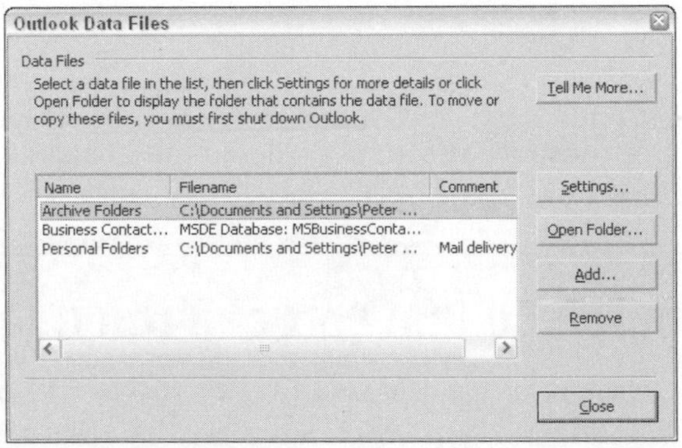

Figure 1-6:
The Outlook
Data Files
dialog box.

2. **Select Personal Folders and click the Open Folder button.**

   Windows Explorer opens and you see the folder where the Outlook.pst file is kept.

3. **Click the Folders button in Windows Explorer to see the folder hierarchy on your computer.**

By scrolling in the Folders pane on the left side of the window, you can determine where on your computer the elusive Outlook.pst file really is.

4. **Close Outlook.**

   Sorry, but you can't back up an Outlook.pst file if Outlook is running.

5. **To back up the file, right-click it in Windows Explorer, choose Send To on the shortcut menu, and choose the option on the submenu that represents where you back up files.**

   You can also copy the Outlook.pst file to a floppy disk or Zip drive in Windows Explorer by Ctrl+dragging or copying and pasting. Book IX, Chapter 2 describes Windows Explorer in detail.

**Book II
Chapter 1**

Importing E-Mail and Addresses from Another Program

Suppose that you've been using Outlook Express, Eudora, or Lotus Organizer to handle your e-mail and contact addresses, but now you've become a convert to Outlook. What do you do with the e-mail messages and names and addresses in the other program? You can't let them just sit there. You can import them into Office and pick up where you left off.

To import e-mail and contact addresses from another program, start by choosing File➪Import and Export. You see the Import and Export Wizard. What you do next depends on where you now do your e-mailing and address tracking:

✦ **Outlook Express:** Select Import Internet Mail and Addresses and click Next. In the Outlook Import Tool dialog box, select Outlook Express, click check boxes to decide what to export (Mail, Addresses, and/or Rules), and click Next again. In the next dialog box, choose options to decide what to do about duplicate entries; then click the Finish button.

✦ **Eudora:** Select Import Internet Mail and Addresses and click Next. In the Outlook Import Tool dialog box, select Eudora, choose options to decide what to do about duplicate entries, and click Next again. In the Browser for Folder dialog box, select the file where the Eudora data is kept and click OK.

✦ **Lotus Organizer:** Select Import from Another Program or File, click Next, select a Lotus Organizer version (4.*x* or 5.*x*), and click Next again. Clicking Next as you go along, you're asked how to handle duplicate items, to locate the Lotus Organizer data file, and to select an Outlook folder to put the data in.

Cleaning Out Your Folders

Getting rid of unneeded items in folders is essential for good mental health. All that clutter can be distressing. Earlier in this chapter, "Deleting E-Mail Messages, Tasks, Contacts, and Other Items" explains how to muck out folders by emptying them. These pages explain two more techniques for removing detritus from folders — archiving and the Mailbox Cleanup command.

Archiving the old stuff

In some cases, Outlook puts e-mail messages, tasks, and appointments older than six months in to the Archive folder, a special folder for items that Outlook thinks are stale and not worth keeping anymore. Outlook calls sending these items to the Archive folder "autoarchiving." Items that have been archived are not lost forever. You can visit them by opening the Archive folder and its subfolders on the Folders List. The Archive folder and its subfolders is created automatically the first time you archive items.

Archiving is a way of stripping your mail folders, tasks lists, and Calendar of items that don't matter anymore. How and when items are archived is up to you. To archive items, you establish a default set of archiving rules that apply to all folders, and if a folder needs individual attention and shouldn't be subject to the default archiving rules, you can establish special rules for that folder. Each folder can have its own set of archiving rules or be subject to the default rules.

To tell Outlook how to archive old stuff, start by displaying an AutoArchive dialog box, as shown in Figure 1-7:

✦ **Establishing default archiving rules:** Choose Tools⇨Options, and, in the Options dialog box, select the Other tab. Then click the AutoArchive button.

✦ **Establishing rules for a specific folder:** Either right-click the folder and choose Properties or display the folder and choose File⇨Folder⇨ Properties for *Folder Name*. Then, in the Properties dialog box, select the AutoArchive tab. (Because no date is connected to items in the Contacts folder, you can't autoarchive names and addresses.)

Negotiate these options to establish default archiving rules (refer to Figure 1-7):

✦ **Run AutoArchive Every:** Enter a number to tell Outlook how often to archive items.

✦ **Prompt Before Archive Runs:** If this check box is selected, you see a message box before archiving begins, and you can decline to archive if you want by selecting No in the message box.

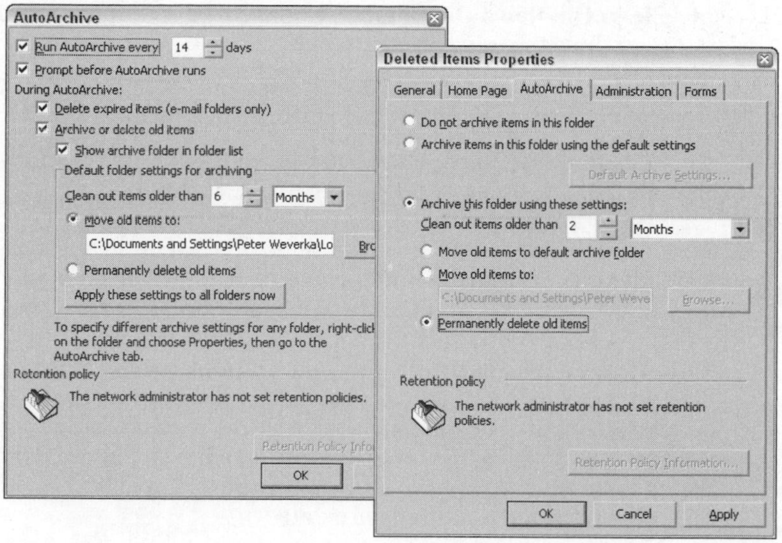

Figure 1-7:
Making the
default
archiving
rules (left)
and rules for
a folder
(right).

✦ **Delete Expired Items (E-Mail Folders Only):** Select this check box to delete all e-mail messages when the time period has expired.

✦ **Archive or Delete Old Items:** Unselect this option if you *don't* want to archive items.

✦ **Show Archive Folder in Folder List:** Select this option if you want to keep the Archive folder in the Folder List. Archived items are kept in this folder.

✦ **Clean Out Items Older Than:** Choose a cut-off time period after which to archive items.

✦ **Move Old Items To:** Click the Browse button and select a folder if you want to store the Archive file in a certain location.

✦ **Permanently Delete Old Items:** Select this option if you want to delete, not archive, old items.

Choose among these options to establish archiving rules for a specific folder (refer to Figure 1-7):

✦ **Do Not Archive Items in This Folder:** Select this option if items in the folder aren't worth archiving.

✦ **Archive Items in This Folder Using the Default Settings**: Select this option to defer to the default archiving rules for the folder.

✦ **Archive This Folder Using These Settings:** Choose this option to establish archiving rules for the folder.

✦ **Clean Out Items Older Than:** Choose a cut-off time period after which to archive the items in the folder.

✦ **Move Old Items To:** Click the Browse button and select a folder if you want to store the archived items in a specific location.

✦ **Permanently Delete Old Items:** Select this option if you want to delete, not archive, items in this folder.

Besides archiving, another way to remove bric-a-brac automatically is to take advantage of the Rules Wizard to delete certain kinds of messages as they arrive. See "Yes, You Can Prevent Junk Mail (Sort Of)" in Chapter 3.

Periodically compact the file in which Outlook data is stored to shrink the file and get more room on your hard disk. To compact the Outlook data file, choose File➪Data File Management, select Personal Folders in the Outlook Data Files dialog box, and click the Settings button. In the Personal Folders dialog box, select the Compact Now button. Compacting an Outlook file can take time if the file is stuffed with data.

Running the Mailbox Cleanup command

The Mailbox Cleanup command is an all-purpose command for finding e-mail messages, archiving items, deleting items, and deleting alternate versions of items. To use the command, choose Tools➪Mailbox Cleanup. You see the Mailbox Cleanup dialog box. The dialog box offers a speedy entrée into these different Outlook tasks:

✦ **Seeing how much disk space folders occupy:** Click the View Mailbox Size button and take note of folder sizes in the Folder Size dialog box.

✦ **Finding items:** Select an option button to find items older than a certain number of days or larger than a certain number of kilobytes, enter a days or kilobytes number, and click the Find button. You land in the Advanced Find dialog box. Earlier in this chapter, "Conducting an advanced search" explains this dialog box. Use it to select items and delete them.

✦ **Archiving items:** Click the AutoArchive button to archive items in your folders. See "Archiving the old stuff," the previous section in this chapter, for details.

✦ **Emptying the deleted items folder:** Click the Empty button to empty out the Deleted Items folder. See "Deleting E-Mail Messages, Contacts, Tasks, and Other Items" earlier in this chapter.

Chapter 2: Maintaining the Contacts Folder

In This Chapter

✔ Recording information about a new contact

✔ Using the Activities tab on the Contact form

✔ Locating a contact in the Contacts folder

✔ Printing contact information in the Contacts folder

In pathology, which is the study of diseases and how they are transmitted, a contact is a person who passes on a communicable disease, but in Outlook, a contact is someone about whom you keep information. Information about contacts is kept in the Contacts folder. This folder is a super-powered address book. It has places for storing people's names, addresses, phone numbers, e-mail addresses, Web pages, pager numbers, birthdays, anniversaries, nicknames, and other stuff besides. When you address an e-mail, you can get it straight from the Contacts folder to be sure that the address is entered correctly. As Book I, Chapter 7 explains, you can also get addresses from the Contacts folder when you generate form letters, labels, and envelopes for mass mailings.

This short but happy chapter explains how to maintain a tried-and-true Contacts folder, enter information about people in the folder, edit information, find a missing contact, and print the information in the Contacts folder.

Maintaining a Happy and Healthy Contacts Folder

A Contacts folder is only as good and as thorough as the information about contacts that you put into it. These pages explain how to enter information about a contact and update the information if it happens to change.

Don't despair if you have been using another software program to track addresses. Chapter 1, "Importing E-Mail and Addresses from Another Program," explains how to bring those addresses into Outlook without having to re-enter them.

Entering a new contact in the Contacts folder

To place someone on the Contacts list, open the Contacts folder and start by doing one of the following:

+ Click the <u>N</u>ew button.

+ Press Ctrl+N (in the Contacts Folder window) or Ctrl+Shift+C.

+ Choose <u>F</u>ile⇨<u>N</u>ew⇨<u>C</u>ontact.

You see the Contact form, shown in Figure 2-1. On this form are places for entering just about everything there is to know about a person except his or her love life and secret vices. Enter all the information you care to record, keeping in mind these rules of the road as you go along:

+ **Full names, addresses, and so on:** Although you may be tempted to simply enter addresses, phone numbers, names, and so on in the text boxes, don't do it! Click the Full <u>N</u>ame button on the General tab, for example, to enter a name (refer to Figure 2-1). Click the Business or Home button to enter an address in the Check Address dialog box (refer to Figure 2-1). By clicking the buttons and entering data in dialog boxes, you permit Outlook to separate out the component parts of names, addresses, and phone numbers. As such, Outlook can use names and addresses as a source for mass mailings and mass e-mailings.

When entering information about a company, not a person, leave the Full <u>N</u>ame field blank and enter the company's name in the Co<u>m</u>pany field.

+ **Information that matters to you:** If the form doesn't appear to have a place for entering a certain kind of information, try clicking a triangle button and choosing a new information category from the pop-up menu. Click the triangle button next to the Business button and choose Home, for example, if you want to enter a home address rather than a business address (refer to Figure 2-1).

+ **File As:** Open the Fi<u>l</u>e As drop-down menu and choose an option for filing the contact in the Contacts folder. Contacts are filed alphabetically by last name, first name, company name, or combinations of the three. Choose the option that best describes how you expect to find the contact in the Contacts folder.

+ **Mailing addresses:** If you keep more than one address for a contact, display the address to which you want to send mail and select the This Is the Mailing Add<u>r</u>ess check box. This way, in a mass mailing, letters are sent to the correct address.

+ **E-mail addresses:** You can enter three e-mail addresses for each contact (click the triangle button and choose E-mail 2 or E-mail 3 to enter a second or third address). In the Displa<u>y</u> As text box, Outlook shows you what the To: line of e-mail messages will look like when you send e-mail to a contact. By default, the To: line shows the contact's name followed by his or her e-mail address in parentheses. However, you can enter whatever you wish in the Display As text box, and if entering something different will help you distinguish between e-mail addresses, enter something different. For example, enter Lydia – Personal so that you can tell when you send e-mail to Lydia's personal address as opposed to her business address.

✦ **Photos:** To put a digital photo on a Contact form, click the Add Contact Photo button and, in the Add Contact Picture dialog box, select a picture and click OK.

Be sure to write a few words on the General tab to describe how and where you met the contact. When the time comes to weed out contacts in the Contacts folder list, reading the descriptions will help you decide who gets weeded and who doesn't.

When you're done entering information, click the Save and Close button. If you're in a hurry to enter contact information, click the Save and New button. Doing so opens an empty form so that you can record information about another contact.

Click buttons to enter information.

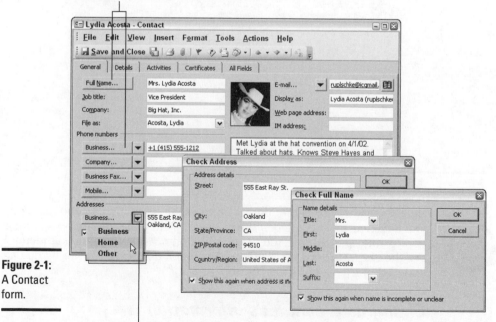

Figure 2-1:
A Contact
form.

Click to choose new information categories.

Tracking your dealings with a contact

The Activities tab in the Contacts form is a nifty place to keep track of your comings and goings with a client, friend, or co-worker. E-mail messages you sent to a contact, tasks and journal entries that pertain to a contact, and calendar appointments with a contact can be placed on the Activities tab. To examine your dealings with a contact, all you have to do is open the Activities tab. By double-clicking an item on the tab, you can open an e-mail message, Calendar form, Task form, or Journal form and see what's what.

Follow these instructions to track your dealings with a contact on the Activities tab of the Contacts form:

> ✦ **Calendar items, tasks, and journal entries:** On the Appointment, Task, or Journal Entry form you

Contacts...

use to set up a calendar appointment, task, or journal entry, click the Contacts button (it's in the lower-left corner) and select a contact in the Select Contacts dialog box. You can select more than one contact by Ctrl+clicking.

> ✦ **E-mail messages:** As long as the e-mail address on a message is on file somewhere in the Contacts folder, a record of the e-mail message being received or sent is recorded on the Activities tab.

The Activities tab is an excellent place for deleting e-mail messages, because you can see in one place the messages you sent to or received from a client. To delete the messages, select them and click the Delete key.

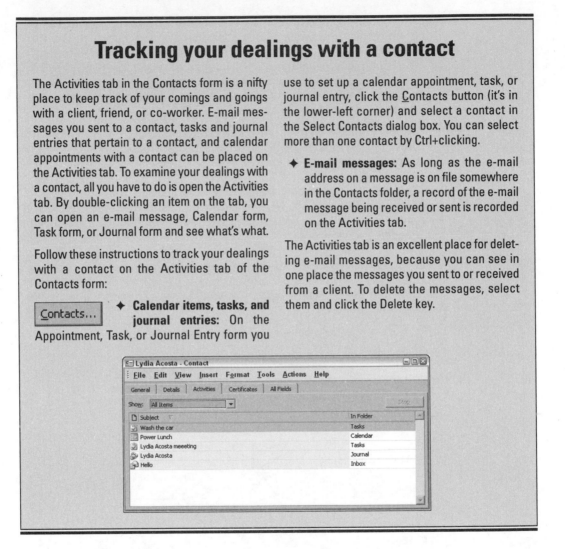

Here's a fast way to enter contact information for someone who has sent you an e-mail message: Open the message, right-click the sender's name on the To: line, and choose Add to Outlook Contacts on the shortcut menu. You see the Contact form. Enter more information about the sender if you can and click the Save and Close button.

Changing a contact's information

Changing a contact's information is a chore if you do it by going from field to field on the General and Details tabs of the Contact form. Fortunately for you, there is a faster way to update the information you have about a contact — go to the All Fields tab in the Contact form. As Figure 2-2 shows, this tab lists fields in alphabetical order. Choose an option on the Select From drop-down menu, scroll in the form, and update fields as necessary.

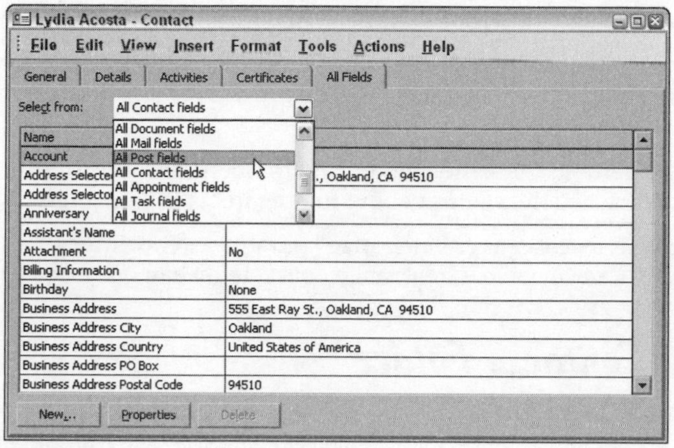

Figure 2-2: Editing data on the All Fields tab.

Book II Chapter 2

Maintaining the Contacts Folder

Finding a Contact

The Contacts folder, which is shown in Figure 2-3, can grow very large, so Outlook offers a number of ways to search it. After you have found the contact you're looking for, double-click it to open the Contact form. Here are some techniques for finding a contact in the Contacts folder:

Figure 2-3: Address Cards view of Contacts folder.

✦ **The scrollbar:** Click the arrows or drag the scroll box to move through the list.

✦ **Letter buttons:** Click a letter button on the right side of the window to move in the list to a specific letter.

✦ **Change views:** Changing views often helps in the search. Choose a new view from the Current View drop-down menu on the Advanced toolbar.

✦ **Find a Contact text box:** Enter a name or e-mail address in this text box and press Enter. The Find a Contact text box is located on the Standard toolbar.

✦ **Find button:** Click the Find button to open the Find pane and look for a contact. See the section about finding items in folders in Chapter 1.

✦ **Search by category:** Categorize contacts as you enter them and switch to By Category view to arrange contacts by category. See Chapter 1.

Printing the Contacts Folder

The paperless office has not arrived yet in spite of numerous predictions to the contrary, and sometimes it's necessary to print the Contents folder on old-fashioned paper. For times like those, I hereby explain the different ways to print the Contents folder and how to fiddle with the look of the print pages.

To print information about a single contact, double-click his or her name to open the Contact form. Then click the Print button in the Contact form.

Different ways to print Contact information

Outlook offers several attractive ways to print contact information in the Contacts folder. Which printing options you get depends on which view of the Contacts window is showing when you give the command to print (open the Current View menu and choose an option to change views).

Starting in Address Cards view or Detailed Address Cards view, you can print Contact information like so:

✦ **Card Style:** Prints all information on display in the Contacts window, with each contact name appearing in a gray shade.

✦ **Small Booklet Style:** Similar to Card Style, except the page is shrunk to an eighth of its size and pages are designed to be printed on both sides so that they can be bound and distributed.

✦ **Medium Booklet Style:** Similar to Small Booklet Style, except pages are shrunk to a fourth of their original size.

✦ **Memo Style:** Information for each contact is printed on one page, and you get one page for each contact in the Contacts folder.

✦ **Phone Directory Style:** Similar to Card Style, except only phone numbers and fax numbers are printed.

Starting in all views apart from Address Cards and Detailed Address Cards, you can print contact information in Table style. In Table style, the information is printed in a simple table with column headings.

The basics of printing contact information

Follow these steps to print information about contacts in the Contacts folder:

Book II
Chapter 2

1. **Select the contacts whose information you want to print, if you don't want to print information about everybody.**

You can select contacts by Ctrl+clicking names. Another way to select contacts is to run the Find command, as explained in Chapter 1.

2. **Click the Print button or press Ctrl+P.**

You see the Print dialog box, shown in Figure 2-4.

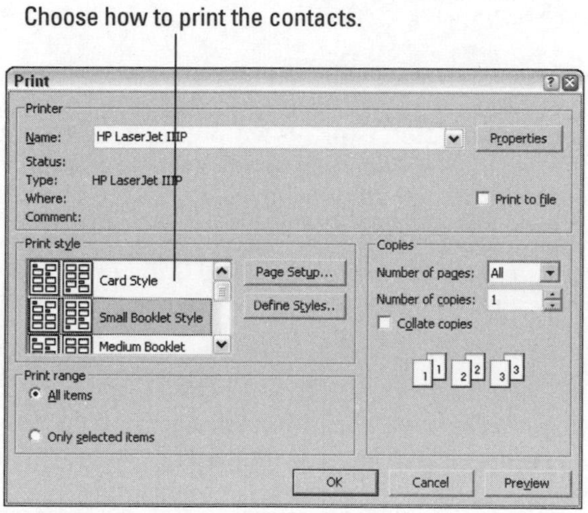

Choose how to print the contacts.

Figure 2-4:
Printing contact information.

3. **Under Print Style, select an option.**

To get a better idea what the print styles are, select one, click the Page Setup button, and, in the Page Setup dialog box, click the Print Preview button. The Print Preview window shows what the pages will look like when you print them. Click the Print button in this window to start printing right away.

If you start in a view apart from Address Cards or Detailed Address Cards, Table Style is the only Print Style option.

4. **Choose Page Setup options if you want to change the number of columns that are printed, change fonts, change headers and footers, or otherwise fiddle with the printed pages.**

   The next section in this chapter explains these options.

5. **If you selected contacts to print in Step 1, choose the Only Selected Items option button.**

6. **Click OK to start printing.**

Changing the look of printed pages

By default, contact information is printed in 12-, 10-, or 8-point Tahoma font. Your name, a page number, and the date and time you print the contact information appears on a footer at the bottom of the pages. To change these and other settings, click the Page Setup button in the Print dialog box (refer to Figure 2-4). You see the Page Setup dialog box. You can click the Print Preview button in this dialog box to open the Print Preview window and see what your Contacts will look like when you print them (click the Page Setup button to return to the Page Setup dialog box).

Change these settings on the Format tab of the Page Setup dialog box:

+ **Where contact information is printed:** Contact information is printed alphabetically with a letter heading to mark where the As, Bs, Cs, and so on begin. To place contacts that begin with each letter on separate pages, select the Start on a New Page option button.

+ **Number of columns:** Enter a number in the Number of Columns text box to tell Outlook how many columns you want.

+ **Contact index:** Select the Contact Index on Side check box to print thumbnail letter headings on the sides of pages.

+ **Letter headings:** To remove the letter headings that mark where contacts starting with a certain letter begin, uncheck the Headings for Each letter check box.

+ **Fonts and fonts sizes:** Click a Font button and choose a different font or font size for headings and body text.

+ **Gray shades:** Gray shades appear behind contact names, but you can remove them by unchecking the Print Using Gray Shading check box.

On the Header/Footer tab, the three boxes are for deciding what appears on the left side, middle, and right side of headers and footers. Type whatever you please into these text boxes. You can also click buttons in the dialog box to enter fields — a page number, total page number, printing date, printing time, or your name — in headers or footers.

Mapping out an address

 On the Contact form is an obscure but very useful little button that can be a great help when you need to go somewhere but aren't sure how to get there. This button is called Display Map of Address. As long as your computer is connected to the Internet and an address is on file for a contact, you can click the Display Map of Address button (or choose Actions⇨Display Map of Address) to go online to the Microsoft Expedia Web site and see a map with the address at its center. Double-click a contact name to open the contact in a form. Good luck getting there!

Book II
Chapter 2

Maintaining the
Contacts Folder

Chapter 3: Handling Your E-Mail

In This Chapter

✔ Addressing, sending, replying to, and forwarding e-mail messages

✔ Creating distribution lists to send messages to groups

✔ Sending files and pictures with e-mail

✔ Understanding HTML and plain-text formats

✔ Receiving e-mail and files over the Internet

✔ Organizing and managing your e-mail

✔ Creating and using different folders to store e-mail

"**N**either snow nor rain nor heat nor gloom of night stays these couriers from the swift completion of their appointed rounds," reads the inscription on the Eighth Avenue New York Post Office Building. E-mailers face a different set of difficulties. Instead of snow, rain, or gloomy nights, they face junk mail blizzards, pesky colleagues, and the occasional co-worker who believes that all e-mail messages should be copied to everyone in the office.

This chapter explains the basics of sending and receiving e-mail, but it also goes a step further to help you organize and manage your e-mail messages. This chapter unscrews the inscrutable. It shows you how to send files and pictures with e-mail messages, make a distribution list so that you can e-mail many people simultaneously, and postpone sending a message. You can also find out how to be advised when someone has read your e-mail, re-organize e-mail in the Inbox window, and be alerted to incoming messages from certain people or from people writing about certain subjects. Finally, this chapter shows how to create folders for storing e-mail and explains what you can do to prevent junk e-mail from arriving on your digital doorstep.

Addressing and Sending E-Mail Messages

Sorry, you can't send chocolates or locks of hair by e-mail, but you can send pictures and computer files. These pages explain how to do it. You also discover how to send copies and blind copies of e-mail messages, reply to forwarded e-mail, create a distribution list, send e-mail from different accounts, and postpone sending a message. Better keep reading.

The Basics: Sending an E-Mail Message

After you get the hang of it, sending an e-mail message is as easy as falling off a turnip truck. The first half of this chapter addresses everything you need to know about sending e-mail messages. Here are the basics:

1. **In the Mail folder, click the <u>N</u>ew button or choose Ctrl+N.**

   A Message window like the one in Figure 3-1 appears.

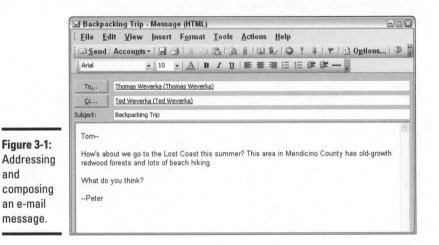

Figure 3-1: Addressing and composing an e-mail message.

2. **Enter the recipient's e-mail address in the To text box.**

   The next section in this chapter, "Addressing an e-mail message," explains the numerous ways to address an e-mail message. You can address the same message to more than one person by entering more than one address in the To text box. For that matter, you can send copies of the message and blind copies of the message to others (see "Sending copies and blind copies of messages," later in this chapter).

3. **In the Subject text box, enter a descriptive title for the message.**

   When your message arrives on the other end, the recipient will see the subject first. Enter a descriptive subject that helps the recipient decide whether to read the message right away. After you enter the subject, it appears in the title bar of the Message window.

   Outlook offers different ways to get a recipient's attention. For example, you can give your message a priority rating. See the sidebar "Prioritizing the messages you send," later in this chapter.

4. **Type the message.**

Whatever you do, don't forget to enter the message itself! You can spell-check your message by pressing F7 or choosing Tools⇨Spelling.

As long as you compose messages in HTML format and the person receiving your e-mail messages has software capable of reading HTML, you can decorate messages to your heart's content (later in this chapter, "All about Message Formats" explains the HTML issue). Experiment with fonts and font sizes. Boldface and underline text. Throw in a bulleted or numbered list. You will find many formatting commands on the Format menu and Formatting toolbar.

To choose the default font and font size with which messages are written, choose Tools⇨Options, select the Mail Format tab in the Options dialog box, and click the Fonts button. You see the Fonts dialog box. Click a Choose Font button and, in the dialog box that appears, select a font, font style, and font size.

5. **Click the Send button.**

As "Postponing sending a message" explains later in this chapter, you can put off sending a message. And if you have more than one e-mail account, you can choose which one to send the message with, as "Choosing which account to send messages with" explains. Messages remain in the Outbox folder if you postpone sending them or if Outlook can't send them right away because your computer isn't connected to the Internet.

If you decide in the middle of writing a message to write the rest of it later, choose File⇨Save or press Ctrl+S; then close the Message window. The message will land in the Drafts folder. When you're ready to finish writing the message, open the Drafts folder and double-click your unfinished message to resume writing it.

Copies of e-mail messages you have sent are kept in the Sent Items folder. If you prefer not to keep copies of sent e-mail messages on hand, choose Tools⇨Options and, on the Preferences tab of the Options dialog box, click the E-Mail Options button. You see the E-Mail Options dialog box. Uncheck the Save Copies of Messages in Sent Items Folder check box.

Addressing an e-mail message

How do you address an e-mail message in the To text box of the Message window (refer to Figure 3-1)? Let me count the ways:

✦ **Get the address (or addresses) from the Contacts folder:** Click the To (or Cc or Bcc) button to send a message to someone whose name is on file in your Contacts folder. You see the Select Names dialog box, shown in Figure 3-2. Click or Ctrl+click to select the names of people to whom you want to send the message. Then click the To-> button (or Cc-> or Bcc-> button) to enter addresses in the To text box (or Cc or Bcc text boxes) of the Message window. Click OK to return to the Message window. This is the best way to address an e-mail message to several different people.

Select names.

Select Names

Type Name or Select from List: Show Names from the:
                                                                   Contacts

Name	Display Name	E-mail Address	E-mail Type
Sy Weverka	Weverka (Weverka)	weverka@net.net	SMTP
Ted Weverka	Ted Weverka (Ted Weverka)	weverka@net.net	SMTP
Ted	Weverka (Weverka)	weverka@net.net	FAX
Teresa Weverka	Weverka (Weverka)	weverka@net.net	SMTP
Thomas Weverka	Weverka (Weverka)	weverka@net.net	SMTP
Tom Weverka	Weverka (Weverka)	weverka@net.net	SMTP
Weverka, Cindy	Weverka (Weverka)	weverka@net.net	SMTP
Weverka Press	Weverka (Weverka)	weverka@net.net	SMTP
Weverka, Thomas	Weverka (Weverka)	weverka@net.net	SMTP
Wiley & Co.	Weverka (Weverka)	weverka@net.net	SMTP

Message Recipients

To ->	Thomas Weverka (Thomas Weverka)
Cc ->	Ted Weverka (Ted Weverka)
Bcc ->	

Advanced ▼   OK   Cancel

Figure 3-2: Getting addresses from the Contacts folder.

Click a button.

✦ **Type a person's name from the Contacts folder:** Simply type a person's name if the name is on file in the Contacts folder. (See the Tip at the end of this list to find out what to do if you aren't sure whether the name is really on file or you aren't sure whether you entered the name correctly.) To send the message to more than one person, enter a comma (,) or semicolon (;) between each name.

✦ **Type the address in the To text box:** If you have entered the address recently or the address is on file in your Contacts folder or Address Book, a pop-up message with the complete address appears. Press Enter to enter the address without your having to type all the letters. To send the message to more than one person, enter a comma (,) or semicolon (;) between each address.

✦ **Reply to a message sent to you:** Select the message in the Inbox folder and click the Reply button. The Message window opens with the address of the person to whom you're replying already entered in the

To text box. This is the most reliable way (no typos on your part) to enter an e-mail address. You can also click the Reply to All button to reply to enter the e-mail addresses of all the people to whom the original message was sent.

These days, many people have more than one e-mail address, and when you enter an e-mail address in the To text box of the Message window, it's hard to be sure whether the address you entered is the right one. To make sure that you send an e-mail address to the right person, click the Check Names button or choose Tools⇨Check Names. You see the Check Names dialog box, shown in Figure 3-3. Select the correct name and address in the dialog box and click OK. You can also click the Check Names button if you aren't sure whether a name was entered correctly in the To text box or you aren't sure whether a name is really on file in the Contacts folder.

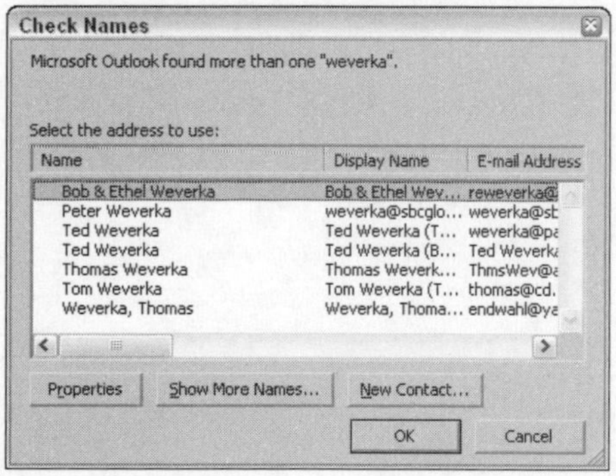

Book II
Chapter 3

Handling Your
E-Mail

Figure 3-3:
Checking
the
accuracy of
an e-mail
address.

Making Outlook your default e-mail program

If you switched to Outlook from Outlook Express or another e-mail program and you like Outlook, you need to tell your computer that Outlook is henceforward the e-mail program you want to use by default. The default e-mail program is the one that opens when you click an e-mail link on a Web page or give the order to send an Office file from inside an Office program. Follow these steps to make Outlook the default e-mail program on your computer:

1. **Click the Start button and choose Control Panel.**

2. **Double-click Internet Options. You see the Internet Properties dialog box.**

3. **On the Programs tab, choose Microsoft Outlook on the E-Mail drop-down menu and click OK.**

Sending e-mail from inside another Office program

As long as Outlook is your default e-mail program (I explain how to make it the default program earlier in this chapter), you can send e-mail messages or file attachments from other Office programs without opening Outlook. If the Word document, Excel worksheet, PowerPoint presentation, Publisher brochure, or Access database table or query needs sending right away, follow these steps to send it either as a file attachment or in the body of an e-mail message:

1. **With the file you want to send on-screen, choose File⇨Send To.**

2. **On the Send To submenu, choose Mail Recipient to send the item in the body of an** e-mail message, or **Mail Recipient (As Attachment) to send the item as a file. The To, Cc, Subject, and other text boxes appear so that you can address the e-mail message and write a note to accompany the file you're about to send.**

3. **Click the Send button.**

 In some Office programs you can click the E-Mail button rather than choose File⇨Send To⇨Mail Recipient when you want to send a file in the body of an e-mail message. You can find the E-Mail button on the Standard toolbar.

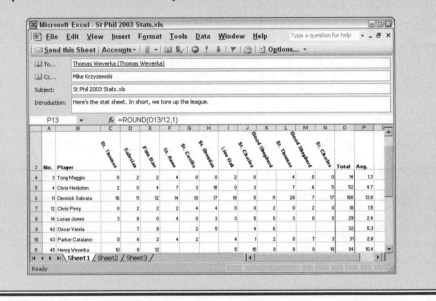

Sending copies and blind copies of messages

Sending copies of messages and blind copies of messages is simple enough, but think twice before you do it. In my experience, a dysfunctional office is one where people continuously send copies of messages to one another, often to supervisors, to itemize their quarrels or document their work. However, sending copies of messages can clog mailboxes and waste everyone's time.

When you send a copy of a message, the person who receives the message knows that copies have been sent because the names of people to whom copies were sent appear at the top of the e-mail message. But when you send blind copies, the person who receives the message does not know that others received it.

Follow these instructions to send copies and blind copies of messages:

✦ **Send a copy of a message:** Enter e-mail addresses in the Cc text box of the Message window or, in the Select Names dialog box (refer to Figure 3-2), select names and click the Cc->button.

✦ **Send a blind copy of a message:** In the Message window, click the To or Cc button to open the Select Names dialog box (refer to Figure 3-2). Then select the names and click the Bcc-> button or else enter addresses in the Bcc-> text box.

People who often send blind copies can make the Bcc text box appear in all Message windows. To do so, choose View⇨Bcc Field in any Message window.

You may well ask yourself why these buttons are called Cc and Bcc. Why the extra *C*? Actually, the Cc stands for "carbon copy" and the Bcc stands for "blind carbon copy." These terms originated in the Mesozoic era when letters were composed on the typewriter and, to make a copy of a letter, you inserted carbon paper between two paper sheets and typed away. The carbon paper turned your fingers black. You left black fingerprints on your fedora hat or angora sweater. Those were the days!

Replying to and forwarding e-mail messages

Replying to and forwarding messages is as easy as pie. For one thing, you don't need to know the recipient's e-mail address to reply to a message. In the Inbox, select the message you want to reply to or forward and do the following:

✦ **Reply to author:** Click the Reply button. The Message window opens with the sender's name already entered in the To box and the original message in the text box below. Write a reply and click the Send button.

✦ **Reply to all parties who received the message:** Click the Reply to All button. The Message window opens with the names of all parties who received the message in the To and Cc boxes and the original message in the text box. Type your reply and click the Send button.

✦ **Forward a message:** Click the Forward button. The Message window opens with the text of the original message. Either enter an e-mail address in the To text box or click the To button to open the Select Names dialog

Book II
Chapter 3

Handling Your
E-Mail

box and select the names of the parties to whom the message will be forwarded. Add a word or two to the original message if you like; then click the Send button.

Forwarding a message to a third party without the permission of the original author is a breach of etiquette and very bad manners. How would you like your opinions or ideas scattered hither and yon to strangers you don't know? I could tell you a story about an e-mail message of mine that an unwitting editor forwarded to a cantankerous publisher, but I'm saving that story for the soap opera edition of this book.

To find the e-mail address of someone who sent you an e-mail message, double-click the message to display it in the Message window, and then right-click the sender's name in the To box and choose Outlook Properties. The e-mail address appears in the E-Mail Properties dialog box. To add a sender's name to the Contacts folder, right-click the name and choose Add to Outlook Contacts.

By default, the text of the original message appears in the Message window when you click the Reply or Reply to All button to respond to a message. However, Outlook offers the option of not displaying the original text by default. The program also offers different ways of displaying this text. To scope out these options and perhaps select one, choose Tools⇨Options and, on the Preferences tab of the Options dialog box, click the E-Mail Options button. You see the E-Mail Options dialog box. Chose an option on the When Replying to a Message drop-down menu to tell Outlook how or whether to display original messages in replies.

Distribution lists for sending messages to groups

Suppose you're the secretary of the PTA at a school and you regularly send the same e-mail messages to ten or twelve other board members. Entering e-mail addresses for the ten or twelve people each time you want to send an e-mail message is a drag. Some would also consider it a violation of privacy to list each person by name in a message. To see why, consider Figure 3-4. Anyone who receives the message shown at the top of the figure can learn the e-mail address of anyone on the To list by right-clicking a name and choosing Outlook Properties. Some people don't want their e-mail addresses spread around this way.

To keep from having to enter so many e-mail addresses, and to keep e-mail addresses private as well, you can create a *distribution list*, a list with different e-mail addresses. To address your e-mail message, you simply enter the name of the distribution list. You don't have to enter ten or twelve different e-mail addresses. People who receive the message see the name of the distribution list on the To line, not the names of ten or twelve people, as shown in Figure 3-4.

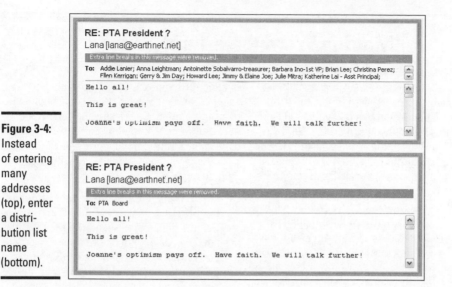

Figure 3-4:
Instead
of entering
many
addresses
(top), enter
a distri-
bution list
name
(bottom).

Creating a distribution list

Follow these steps to bundle e-mail addresses into a distribution list:

1. **Choose File⇨New⇨Distribution List or press Ctrl+Shift+L.**

   You see the Distribution List window, as shown in Figure 3-5.

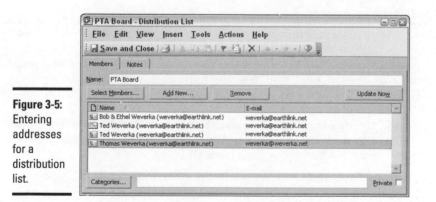

Figure 3-5:
Entering
addresses
for a
distribution
list.

2. **Enter a descriptive name in the Name text box.**

3. **Click the Select Members button to get names and addresses from the Contacts folder.**

   You see the Select Members dialog box.

Making Word the e-mail editor

Fans of Microsoft Word will be glad to know that you can compose and edit e-mail messages using Microsoft Word. If you make Word your e-mail editor, you can do everything to an e-mail message that you can do to a Word document — lay out a table, make a bulleted list, or choose a background theme, for example. All the Word commands are available to you. That's the good news. The bad news is that not everyone uses e-mail software that is capable of displaying the tables, bulleted lists, themes, and other fancy doodads you can put in your e-mail messages. To view this stuff, recipients' e-mail software must be able to display e-mail messages in HTML (hypertext markup language) or rich-text format; moreover, recipients must have opted to display their e-mail messages in HTML or rich-text format.

Here are the two ways to make Word an e-mail editor:

 ✦ **Compose messages in Word:** In Microsoft Word, click the E-Mail button (you'll find it on the Standard toolbar) or choose File➪Send To➪Mail Recipient. Text boxes for addressing the message, entering the subject, and composing the message appear. Compose your message and click the Send a Copy button. (If you change your mind about composing a message, just click the E-Mail button to make all the Outlook stuff go away.)

✦ **Make Word the default e-mail editor in Outlook:** Choose Tools➪Options, and, in the Options dialog box, select the Mail Format tab. Then select the Use Microsoft Word to Edit E-Mail Messages check box and click OK. Now when you click the New button to compose an e-mail message, the Message window offers every command that Word offers. If you don't believe me, open the Table menu or display the Drawing toolbar. You won't find either of them in a conventional Outlook window.

---

4. **Hold down the Ctrl key and select the name of each person you want to be on the list, click the Members button, and click OK.**

   The names you chose appear in the Distribution List window.

5. **To add the names of people who aren't in your Contacts folder, click the Add New button and, in the Add New Member dialog box, enter a name and e-mail address; then click OK.**

6. **Click the Save and Close button in the Distribution List dialog box.**

   You did it — you created a distribution list.

Addressing e-mail to a distribution list

To address an e-mail message to a distribution list, click the New button to open the Message window, click the To button to open the Select Names dialog box, and select the distribution list name. Distribution list names appear in boldface and are marked with a Distribution List icon.

Editing a distribution list

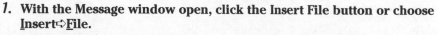

The names of distribution lists appear in the Contacts folder, where they are marked with an icon showing two heads in profile. You can treat the lists like regular contacts. In the Contacts folder, double-click a distribution list name to open the Distribution List window (refer to Figure 3-5). From there, you can add names to the list, remove names from the list, or select new members for the list.

Sending a file along with a message

Sending a file along with an e-mail message is called "attaching" a file in Outlook lingo. Yes, it can be done. You can send a file or several files along with an e-mail message by following these steps:

Book II
Chapter 3

1. **With the Message window open, click the Insert File button or choose Insert⇨File.**

    You see the Insert File dialog box.

2. **Locate and select the file that you want to send along with your e-mail message.**

    Ctrl+click filenames to select more than one file.

3. **Click the Insert button.**

    The name of the file (or files) appears in the Attach text box in the Message window. Address the message and type a note to send along with the file. You can right-click a filename in the Attach text box and choose Open on the shortcut menu to open a file you're about to send.

Here's a fast way to attach a file to a message: Find the file in Windows Explorer or My Computer and drag it into the message window. The file's name appears in the Attach box as though you placed it there with the Insert⇨File command.

Including a picture in an e-mail message

As shown in Figure 3-6, you can include a picture in the body of an e-mail message, but in order to see it, the recipient's e-mail software must display messages using HTML (hypertext markup language). As "All about Message Formats" explains later in this chapter, not everyone has software that displays e-mail by using HTML. People who don't have HTML e-mail software will get the picture anyhow, but it won't appear in the body of the e-mail message; it will arrive as an attached file (see "Handling Files that Were Sent to You," later in this chapter, to find out about receiving files by e-mail). To view the attached file, the recipient has to open it with a graphics software program such as Paint or Windows Picture and Fax Viewer.

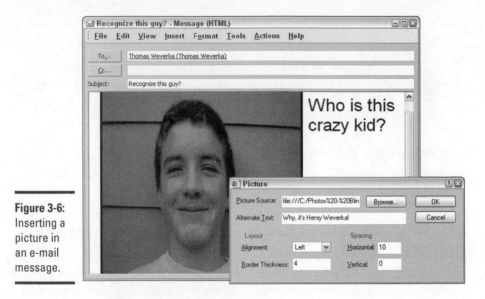

Figure 3-6:
Inserting a
picture in
an e-mail
message.

Follow these steps to adorn an e-mail message with a picture:

1. **In the Message window, click in the body of the e-mail message where you want the picture to go, and choose Insert⇨Picture.**

   You see the Picture dialog box, shown in Figure 3-6.

2. **Click the Browse button and, in the Picture dialog box, find and select the digital picture you want to send; then click the Open button.**

3. **In the Picture dialog box, click OK.**

   The picture lands in the Message window. Don't worry about the other settings in the Picture dialog box for now. You can fool with them later.

To change the size of a picture, click to select it and then drag a corner handle. Otherwise, right-click the picture and choose Properties to re-open the Picture dialog box (refer to Figure 3-6) and experiment with these settings:

✦ **Alternate Text:** The description you enter here appears while the picture is loading or, if the recipient has turned off images, appears in place of the image.

✦ **Alignment:** Experiment with these settings to determine where the picture is in relation to the text of the e-mail message.

✦ **Border Thickness:** Determines, in pixels, how thick the border around the picture is. One pixel equals 1/72 of an inch.

✦ **Horizontal and** **Vertical:** Determines, in pixels, how much empty space appears between the text and the side, top, or bottom of the picture.

Want to remove a picture from an e-mail message? Select it and press the Delete key.

Choosing which account to send messages with

If you have set up more than one e-mail account, you can choose which one to send an e-mail message with. Follow these instructions to choose an account for sending e-mail messages:

✦ **Choosing the default account for sending messages:** When you click the Send button in the Message window, the e-mail message is sent by way of the default e-mail account. To tell Outlook which account that is, choose Tools⇨E-Mail Accounts. You see the E-Mail Accounts dialog box. Select the View or Change Existing E-Mail Accounts option button and click Next. The next dialog box lists e-mail accounts that have been set up for your computer. Select an account and click the Set As Default button.

Accounts ▾

✦ **Sending an individual message:** To bypass the default e-mail account and send a message with a different account, click the Accounts button in the Message window and choose an account name on the drop-down menu. Then click the Send button.

Postponing sending a message

As you probably know, e-mail messages are sent immediately when you click the Send button in the Message window if your computer is connected to the Internet. If it isn't connected, the message lands in the Outbox folder, where it remains until you connect to the Internet.

But suppose you want to postpone sending a message? Outlook offers two techniques for putting off sending a message:

✦ **Moving messages temporarily to the Drafts folder:** Compose your message, click the Save button in the Message window (or press Ctrl+S), and close the Message window. Your e-mail message goes to the Drafts folder. When you're ready to send it, open the Drafts folder, double-click your message to open it, and click the Send button in the Message window.

✦ **Postponing the send date:** Click the Options button in the Message window. You see the Message Options dialog box, the bottom of which is shown in Figure 3-7. Select the Do Not Deliver Before check box, choose a date in the drop-down calendar, and, if you so desire, select a time from the drop-down menu. Then click the Close button. In the Message window, click the Send button. Your message goes to the Outbox folder, where it remains until the time arrives to send it.

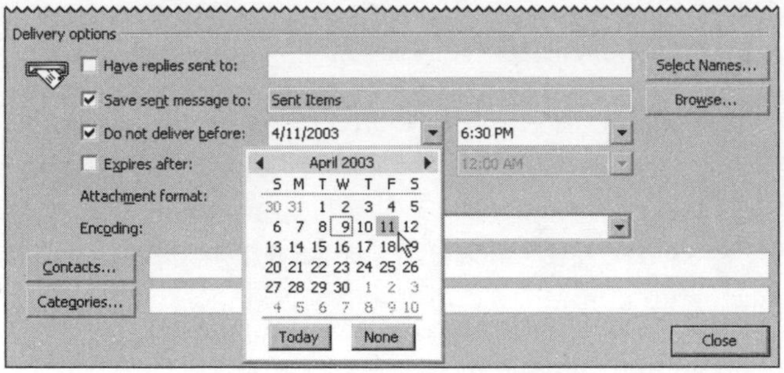

Figure 3-7:
Putting off
sending an
e-mail
message.

Being Advised When Someone Has Read Your E-Mail

Outlook offers a command whereby you can be informed when someone has received or read an e-mail message you sent. You can even send a mini-ballot to someone else, solicit their vote, and have the vote sent to you by e-mail. To perform this magic trick, start in the Message window and click the Options button. You see the Message Options dialog box. Under Voting and Tracking Options, select one of these check boxes:

✦ **Use Voting Buttons:** Voting buttons are included in the e-mail message you send, as shown in Figure 3-8. Choose a set of buttons from the drop-down menu. The recipient clicks a button to respond, and the response is sent to you in the form of an e-mail message with the word Approve, Reject, Yes, No, or Maybe in the subject line.

Voting buttons   Read receipt message box

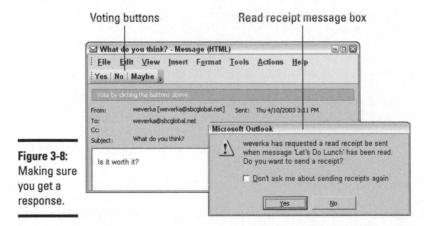

Figure 3-8:
Making sure
you get a
response.

✦ **Request a Read Receipt for This Message:** The message box shown in Figure 3-8 appears. If the recipient clicks the Yes button, a Message window appears immediately so that he or she can send an e-mail informing you that the message was read. The message, when It arrives on your end, lists the date and time that the response message was sent.

✦ **Request a Delivery Receipt for This Message:** You are informed by e-mail when the message is delivered. To be informed, however, you and the recipient must use the same Exchange Server and the recipient must choose to inform you that the message was delivered. Don't count on this one really working.

Book II
Chapter 3

Handling Your
E-Mail

Prioritizing the messages you send

Every day, billions of e-mail messages arrive on peoples' computers, each one begging for the recipient's attention, each one crying out, "Read me first." With this kind of cut-throat competition, how can you give your e-mail messages a competitive advantage? How can you make yours stand out in the crowd?

The best way is to write a descriptive title in the Subject box of the Message window. The subject is the first thing people see in their Inboxes. They decide whether to read a message now, later, or never on the basis of what they see on the Subject line.

Another way to (maybe) get other's attention is to assign a high priority rating to your message. If the recipient reads his or her e-mail with

Outlook or Outlook Express, a red exclamation point appears beside the message in the Inbox folder. Conversely, you can assign a low priority to messages as well, in which case a downward-pointing arrow appears next to the message heading in the Inbox folder. However, prioritizing this way is only worthwhile if the recipient runs Outlook or Outlook Express, because other e-mail programs don't know what to make of the exclamation point or the arrow.

To assign a priority to a message, click the Importance: High or Importance: Low button in the Message window. In the Inbox folder, click the Sort By: Importance button to arrange messages by their priority ratings.

!	D	@	From	Subject	Received	Size	⚑
			Sort by: Importance	gh (2 items, 2 unread)			
!	✉		Lana	To the Barricades!	3:35 PM	1 KB	⚑
!	✉		Mark	Get the lead out!	3:34 PM	1 KB	⚑
⊟ Importance: Normal (2 items, 2 unread)							
	✉		Marc Ball	"Medicinal Mushrooms" Index	5/31/2002	34 KB	⚑
	✉		Becky	Mark's family	5/15/2002	33 KB	✓
⊟ Importance: Low (2 items, 2 unread)							
⬇	✉		Mark	Out to Lunch	3:36 PM	1 KB	⚑
⬇	✉		Becky	Time To Kill	3:35 PM	1 KB	⚑

Inbox

All about Message Formats

Outlook offers three formats for sending e-mail messages: HTML (hypertext markup language), plain text, and rich text. What are the pros and cons of the different formats?

These days, almost all e-mail is transmitted in HTML format, the same format with which Web pages are made. If HTML is the default format you use for creating messages in Outlook — and it is unless you tinkered with the default settings — the e-mail messages you send are, in effect, little Web pages. HTML gives you the most opportunities for formatting text and graphics. In HTML format, you can place pictures in the body of an e-mail message, use a background theme, and do any number of sophisticated formatting tricks.

However, the HTML format has it share of detractors. First, the messages are larger because they include sophisticated formatting instructions, and being larger, they take longer to transmit over the Internet. Some e-mail accounts allocate a fixed amount of disk space for incoming e-mail messages and reject messages when the disk-space allocation is filled. Because they are larger than other e-mail messages, HTML messages fill the disk space quicker. Finally, some e-mail software can't handle HTML messages. In this software, the messages are converted to plain-text format.

In plain text format, only letters and numbers are transmitted. The format does not permit you to format text or align paragraphs in any way, but you can rest assured that the person who receives the message will be able to read it exactly as you wrote it.

The third e-mail message format, rich text, is proprietary to Microsoft e-mailing software. Only people who use Outlook and Outlook Express can see rich text formats. I don't recommend choosing the rich text format. If formatting text in e-mail messages is important to you, choose the HTML format because more people will be able to read your messages.

When someone sends you an e-mail message, you can tell which format it was transmitted in by looking at the title bar, where the letters HTML, "Plain Text," or "Rich Text" appear in parentheses after the subject of the message. Outlook is smart enough to transmit messages in HTML, plain text, or rich text format when you reply to a message that was sent to you in that format.

Follow these instructions if you need to change the format in which e-mail messages are transmitted:

✦ **Changing the default format:** Choose Tools➪Options and, in the Options dialog box, select the Mail Format tab. From the Compose in This Message Format drop-down list, choose an option.

✦ **Changing the format for a single e-mail message:** In the Message window, open the F<u>o</u>rmat menu and choose <u>H</u>TML, Plain <u>T</u>ext or <u>R</u>ich Text.

✦ **Always using the plain-text or rich-text format with a contact:** To avoid transmitting in HTML with a contact, start in the Contacts folder, double-click the contact's name, and, in the Contact form, double-click the contact's e-mail address. You see the E-Mail Properties dialog box. In the Internet Format drop-down menu, choose Send Plain Text Only or Send Using Outlook Rich Text Format.

Stationery for Decorating E-Mail Messages

Apart from the standard formatting commands, the other way to decorate e-mail messages is to do it with stationery. In Outlook lingo, stationery is a background design meant to give an e-mail message the appearance of having been written on real-life stationery, as shown in Figure 3-9. Some kinds of stationery — Holiday Letter, Party Invitation — are designed for sending certain kind of notices or invitations. As you choose stationery for your e-mail messages, remember that some people find the stuff extremely annoying.

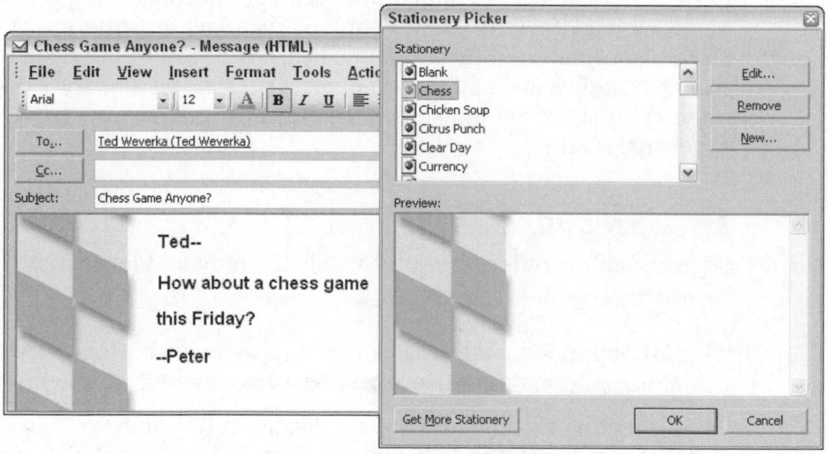

Figure 3-9:
Using
stationery to
adorn e-mail
messages.

Follow these steps to choose a stationery for the e-mail messages you send:

1. **Choose <u>T</u>ools⇨<u>O</u>ptions to open the Options dialog box.**

2. **Select the Mail Format tab.**

3. **Click the Stationery Picker button.**

You see the Stationery Picker dialog box, shown in Figure 3-9.

4. **Select a stationery and click OK.**

5. **Click OK again in the Options dialog box.**

To quit using stationery in your e-mail, return to the Mail Format tab of the Options dialog box, open the Use This Stationery by Default drop-down list, and choose <None>.

Earlier in this chapter, "Making Word the e-mail editor" explains how you can compose and edit e-mail messages in Microsoft Word and in so doing take advantage of that program's many formatting commands. If Word is the e-mail editor at your house, you can choose stationery for your e-mail messages in the following way: Choose Tools⇨Options in Word and, on the General tab of the Options dialog box, click the E-Mail Options button. The E-Mail Options dialog box opens. On the Personal Stationery tab, click the Theme button and choose a theme in the Theme or Stationery dialog box.

Receiving E-Mail Messages

Let's hope that all the e-mail messages you receive carry good news. These pages explain how to collect your e-mail and all the different ways that Outlook notifies you when e-mail has arrived. You will find several tried-and-true techniques for reading e-mail messages in the Inbox window. Outlook offers a bunch of different ways to rearrange the window as well as the messages inside it.

Getting your e-mail

Here are all the different ways to collect e-mail messages that were sent to you:

> Send/Receive

✦ **Collecting the e-mail:** Click the Send/Receive button, press F9, or choose Tools⇨Send/Receive⇨Send/Receive All.

✦ **Collecting e-mail from a single account (if you have more than one):** Choose Tools⇨Send/Receive and, on the submenu, choose the name of an e-mail account or group (see the sidebar "Groups for handling e-mail from different accounts," later in this chapter to find out what groups are).

✦ **Collect e-mail automatically every few minutes:** Press Ctrl+Alt+S or choose Tools⇨Send/Receive⇨Send/Receive Settings⇨Define Send/Receive Groups. You see the Send/Receive Groups dialog box, the bottom of which is shown in Figure 3-10. Select a group (groups are explained in the sidebar "Groups for handling e-mail from different accounts), select a Schedule an Automatic Send/Receive Every check box and enter a minute setting. To temporarily suspend automatic e-mail collections, choose Tools⇨Send/Receive⇨Send/Receive Settings⇨ Disable Scheduled Send/Receive.

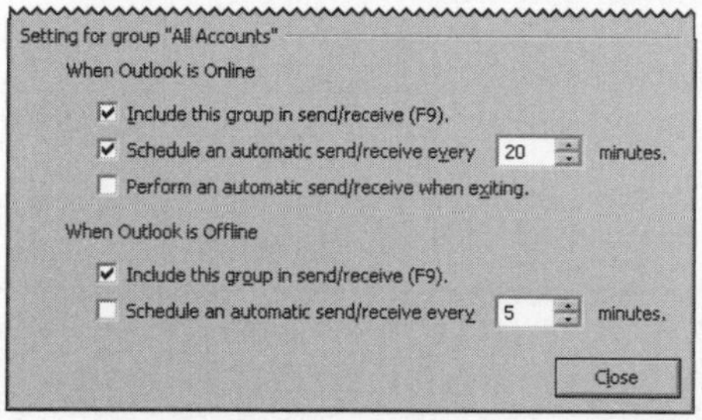

Figure 3-10: Entering Group settings.

If you're not on a network or don't have a DSL or cable connection, you shortly see a Connection dialog box. Enter your password, if necessary, and click the Connect button. The Outlook Send/Receive dialog box appears to show you the progress of messages being sent and received.

Being notified that e-mail has arrived

Take the e-mail arrival quiz. Winners get the displeasure of knowing that they understand far more than is healthy about Outlook. You can tell when e-mail has arrived in the Inbox folder because:

A) You hear this sound: *ding*.

B) The mouse cursor briefly changes to a little envelope.

C) A little envelope appears in the system tray to the left of the Windows clock (and you can double-click the envelope to open the Inbox folder).

D) A pop-up "desktop alert" with the sender's name, the message's subject, and the text of the message appears briefly on your desktop.

E) All of the above.

The answer is E, "All of the above," but if four arrival notices strikes you as excessive, you can eliminate one or two. Choose Tools⇨Options and, on the Preferences tab of the Options dialog box, click the E-Mail Options button. Then, in the E-Mail Options dialog box, click the Advanced E-Mail Options button. At long last, in the Advanced E-Mail Options dialog box, select or unselect the four When New Items Arrive in My Inbox options. To make desktop alerts stay on-screen longer, click the <u>D</u>esktop Alert Settings button and drag the Duration slider in the Desktop Alert Settings dialog box. While you're at it, click the <u>P</u>review button to see what the alerts look like.

Reading your e-mail in the Inbox window

Messages arrive in the Inbox window, as shown in Figure 3-11. Unread messages are shown in boldface type and have envelope icons next to their names; messages that you've read (or at least opened to view) are shown in Roman type and appear beside open envelope icons. To read a message, select it and look in the Reading pane or, to focus more closely on a message, double-click it to open it in a Message window, as shown in Figure 3-11.

Devising a signature for your e-mail messages

An *e-mail signature* is an address, word, phrase, or pithy saying that appears at the bottom of all the e-mail messages you send. Sometimes signatures list company information or instructions for reaching the sender. You can create more than one signature and choose different signatures for different e-mail messages.

Follow these steps to create an e-mail signature:

1. **Choose Tools⇨Options, select the Mail Format tab in the Options dialog box, and click the Signatures button. You see the Create Signature dialog box.**

2. **Click the New button. The Create New Signature dialog box appears.**

3. **Enter a descriptive name for the signature in the first text box and click the Next button.**

4. **In the Edit Signature dialog box, type the signature.**

5. **Click the Font button and, in the Font dialog box, choose a font and font size for the signature. You can also click the Paragraph button and choose an alignment option.**

6. **Click OK three times to return to the Create Signature dialog box, return to the Mail Format tab of the Options dialog box, and close the Options dialog box.**

If you change your mind about putting a signature in your e-mail messages, return to the Mail Format tab of the Options dialog box and choose <None> on the Signature for N<u>e</u>w Messages drop-down menu.

To choose which signature to use if you created more then one, choose <u>I</u>nsert⇨Signature and a signature name in the Message window. To choose a new default signature, return to the Mail Format tab of the Options dialog box and select a signature in the Signature for N<u>e</u>w Messages drop-down list.

If Word is your e-mail editor (see "Making Word the e-mail editor," earlier in this chapter), create a signature starting in Word. Choose <u>T</u>ools⇨ Options, select the General tab in the Options dialog box, and click the E-Mail Options button. You see the E-Mail Options dialog box and its many self-explanatory commands. Create your signature there.

In the Folder List, a number beside the Inbox tells you how many unread messages are in the Inbox folder.

Navigation pane.   Reading pane.

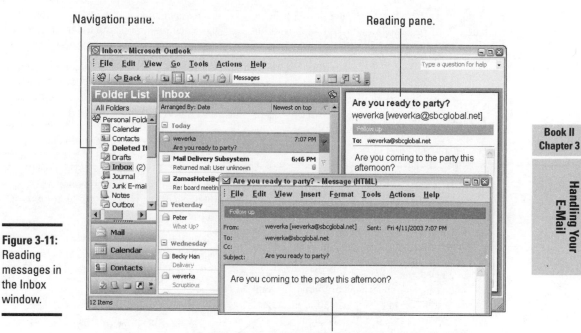

Figure 3-11: Reading messages in the Inbox window.

Book II
Chapter 3

Handling Your
E-Mail

Double-click a message to read it in a Message window.

Later in this chapter, "Techniques for Managing E-Mail Messages" explains how to organize messages in the Inbox folder. Meanwhile, here are some simple techniques you can use to unclutter the Inbox folder and make it easier to manage:

✦ **Hiding and displaying the Reading Pane:** Click the Reading Pane button to make the Reading pane appear or disappear. With the Reading pane gone, column headings — From, Subject, Received, Size, and Flagged — appear in the Inbox window, as shown in Figure 3-12. You can click a column heading name to sort messages in different ways. For example, click the From column name to arrange messages by sender name.

You can eat your cake and have it too by displaying column names *and* the Reading pane, as shown in Figure 3-12. To do so, choose View⇨ Reading Pane⇨Bottom on the submenu.

Groups for handling e-mail from different accounts

Groups are meant to help people who have more than one e-mail account handle their e-mail. To begin with, all e-mail accounts belong to a group called All Accounts. Unless you change the default settings, all accounts belong to the All Accounts group, and e-mail is sent by and received from all your e-mail accounts when you click the Send/Receive button. If you want to change these default settings, press Ctrl+Alt+S or choose Tools⇨Send/Receive⇨Send/Receive Settings⇨Define Send/Receive Groups. You see the Send/Receive Groups dialog box. Follow these instructions in the dialog box to change how you handle e-mail from different accounts:

✦ **Excluding an account from the All Accounts group:** Exclude an account if you don't want to collect its e-mail when you press the Send/Receive button. Maybe you want to collect mail from this account sporadically. To exclude an account, select the All Accounts group in the Send/Receive Groups dialog box and click the Edit button. You land in the Send/Receive Settings – All Accounts dialog box. In the Accounts list,

select the account you want to exclude and unselect the Include the Selected Account in this Group check box.

✦ **Creating a new group:** Create a new group if you want to establish settings for a single e-mail account or group of accounts. Click the New button in the Send/Receive Groups dialog box, enter a name in the Send/Receive Group Name dialog box, and click OK. You see the Send/Receive Settings dialog box. For each account you want to include in your new group, select an account name and then select the Include the Select Account in This Group check box.

✦ **Choosing settings for a group:** In the Send/Receive Groups dialog box, select the group whose settings you want to establish. At the bottom of the dialog box (refer to Figure 3-10), select whether to send and receive e-mail when you click the Send/Receive button or press F9, whether to send and receive automatically every few minutes, and whether to send and receive when you exit Outlook.

✦ **Hiding and displaying the Navigation pane:** Choose View⇨Navigation Pane or press Alt+F1. By hiding the Navigation pane, you get even more room to display messages.

 ✦ **"Autopreviewing" messages:** Click the AutoPreview button or choose View⇨AutoPreview to read the text of all on-screen messages in small type. The message text appears below the subject heading of each message.

✦ **Changing views:** Choose an option on the Current View menu to reduce the number of messages in the window. For example, you can see only unread messages, or messages that arrived in the past week.

Suppose you open an e-mail message but you regret doing so because you want it to look closed. You want the unopened envelope icon to appear beside the message's name so you know to handle it later on. To make a message in the Inbox window appear as if it has never been opened, right-click it and choose Mark As Unread.

Figure 3-12:
Another
way to look
at the Inbox.

Handling Files That Were Sent to You

You can tell when someone has sent you files along with an e-mail message because the word "Attachments" appears in the Reading pane along with the file names, as shown in Figure 3-13. The word "Attachments" and a file name appears as well in the Message window. And if columns are on display in the Inbox window (see the previous section of this chapter), a paperclip icon appears in the Sort By Attachment column to let you know that the e-mail message includes a file or files, as Figure 3-13 also shows.

Files that are sent to you over the Internet land deep inside your computer in a subfolder of the Temporary Internet Files folder. This is the same obscure folder where Web pages you encounter when surfing the Internet are kept. The best way to handle an incoming file is to open it or save it right away to a folder where you are likely to find it when you need it.

To save a file that was sent to you in a new folder:

✦ Right-click the filename and choose Save As, as shown in Figure 3-13.

✦ Choose File➪Save Attachments➪*Filename*.

Attached file.

Figure 3-13:
Receiving
a file.

Right-click to handle incoming files.

To open a file that was sent to you, do one of the following:

✦ Double-click the filename in the Reading pane or Message window.

✦ Right-click the filename and choose <u>O</u>pen, as shown in Figure 3-13.

✦ Right-click the paperclip icon in the Inbox window and choose View Attac<u>h</u>ments⊅*Filename.*

Techniques for Organizing E-Mail Messages

If you are one of those unfortunate souls who receives 20, 30, 40 or more e-mail messages daily, you owe it to yourself and your sanity to figure out a way to organize e-mail messages such that you keep the ones you want, you can find e-mail messages easily, and you can quickly eradicate the e-mail messages that don't matter to you. These pages explain the numerous ways to manage and organize e-mail messages. Pick and choose the techniques that work for you, or else try to convince the Postal Service that you are entitled to your own ZIP Code and you should be paid to handle all the e-mail you receive.

In a nutshell, here are all the techniques for organizing e-mail messages:

✦ **Change views in the Inbox window:** Open the Current View drop-down menu on the Advanced toolbar and choose Last Seven Days, Unread Messages in This Folder, or another view to shrink the number of e-mail messages in the Inbox window.

✦ **Rearrange, or sort, messages in the Inbox window:** If necessary, click the Reading Pane button to remove the Reading pane and see column heading names in the Inbox window. Then click a column heading name to rearrange, or sort, messages by sender name, subject, receipt date, size, or flagged status. See "Reading your e-mail in the Inbox window," earlier in this chapter, for details.

✦ **Delete the messages that you don't need:** Before they clutter the Inbox, delete messages you're sure you don't need as soon as you get them. To delete a message, select it and click the Delete button, press the Delete key, or choose Edit➪Delete.

✦ **Move messages to different folders:** Create a folder for each project you're involved with and, when an e-mail message about a project arrives, move it to a folder. See "All about E-Mail Folders," later in this chapter.

✦ **Move messages automatically to different folders as they arrive:** See "Earmarking messages as they arrive," later in this chapter.

✦ **Destroy junk mail as it arrives:** You can delete junk mail automatically. See "Yes, You Can Prevent Junk Mail (Sort Of)," later in this chapter.

✦ **Flag messages:** Flag a message with a color-coded flag to let you know to follow up on it. See "Flagging e-mail messages," the next section in this chapter.

✦ **Categorize messages:** Assign e-mail messages to categories; then, arrange e-mail messages by category in the Inbox window by choosing View➪Arrange By➪Categories. See Chapter 1 of this mini-book for info on categorizing items in a folder.

✦ **Have Outlook remind you to reply to a message:** Instruct Outlook to make the Reminder message box appear at a date and time in the future so that you know to reply to a message. See "Being reminded to take care of e-mail messages," later in this chapter.

✦ **Make liberal use of the Find command:** You can always find a stray message with the Find command. (See Chapter 1 to know more about finding items in folders.) To quickly find all the messages from one person, right-click an e-mail message from the person and choose Find All➪Messages from Sender. Choose Find All➪Related Messages to find messages that are part of the same conversation (the original message and all replies).

✦ **Archive messages you no longer need:** Archiving is a good way to strip the Inbox folder of items that you don't need. See Chapter 1 of this mini-book for more about archiving.

✦ **Use the Mailbox Cleanup command:** This handy command archives messages, deletes them, and deletes alternate versions of messages. See Chapter 1 for more about this command.

**Book II
Chapter 3**

**Handling Your
E-Mail**

Preventing computer viruses from spreading by e-mail

Outlook does not permit you to receive these kinds of files because they may contain computer viruses: batch program files (.bat), executable program files (.exe), JavaScript source files (.js), Microsoft Access Application files (.mdb), and Visual Basic Scripts (.vbs). If someone attempts to send you one of these files, you get this message instead: "Outlook blocked access to the following potentially unsafe attachments." What's more, because computer viruses can be hidden in macros, any file that can conceivably contain a macro is screened. When you try to open one of these files, a dialog box warns you to open files only from trustworthy sources. If you suspect that a file has a virus, don't open it. Save it to your hard disk and scan it for viruses with your anti-virus software. You do have anti-virus software, don't you?

Here's a little trick for getting around the problem of not being able to receive certain kinds of files: Have your friend or colleague send you the file as a Zip file (Book IX, Chapter 2 explains how to do this). Outlook does not screen Zip files or prevent them from being received.

If you think your computer has been struck by a virus, visit the Microsoft Virus Assistance Center at office.microsoft.com/assistance/9798/antivirus.aspx. You will find information there about viruses and virus prevention. Another good Web site for learning about viruses is Computer Virus Myths at www.vmyths.com, where you can read about virus hoaxes and virus hoaxsters. Next time someone sends you a panicky e-mail explaining that you were sent a virus, visit the Computer Virus Myths site to see whether the virus is really worth panicking over. So far in my experience (he said, knocking on wood), every virus I am supposed to have received turned out to be a hoax.

Flagging e-mail messages

One way to call attention to e-mail messages is to flag them. As shown in Figure 3-14, you can make color-coded flags appear in the Inbox window. You can use red flags, for example, to mark urgent messages and green flags to mark the not-so-important ones. Which color you flag a message with is up to you. Outlook offers six colors. As Figure 3-14 shows, you can click the Sort By Flag Status button in the Inbox window to arrange messages in color-coded flag order.

Follow these instructions to flag an e-mail message:

 ✦ **Starting in the Message window:** Click the Follow Up button. You see the Flag for Follow Up dialog box, as shown in Figure 3-14. If the color you prefer isn't showing, choose a color from the Flag Color drop-down menu. From the Flag To drop-down menu, choose follow-up notice, or else type one of your own in the text box. The notice will appear across the top of the e-mail message in the Message window.

✦ **Starting in the Inbox folder:** Select the message and choose <u>A</u>ctions➪ Follow <u>U</u>p and a flag color, or right-click and choose Follow <u>U</u>p and a flag color.

Click to flag a message.

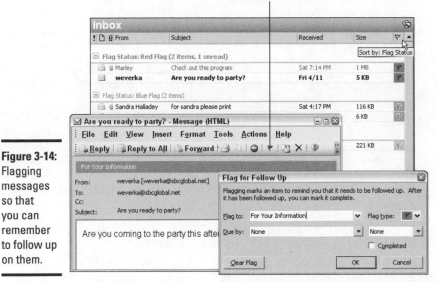

Figure 3-14: Flagging messages so that you can remember to follow up on them.

To "unflag" a message, right-click it and choose Follow <u>U</u>p➪Clear Flag. You can also right-click and choose Follow <u>U</u>p➪Flag Comp<u>l</u>ete to put a check-mark where the flag used to be and remind yourself that you're done with the message. Later in this chapter, "Earmarking messages as they arrive" explains how you can flag messages automatically as messages arrive.

Being reminded to take care of e-mail messages

If you know your way around the Calendar and Tasks windows, you know that the Reminders message box appears when an appointment or meeting is about to take place or a task deadline is about to fall. What you probably don't know, however, is that you can put the Reminders dialog box to work in regard to e-mail messages.

Follow these steps to remind yourself to reply to an e-mail message or simply to prod yourself into considering an e-mail message in the future:

1. **Select the message and choose Actions➪Follow Up➪Add Reminder.**

You see the Flag for Follow Up dialog box (refer to Figure 3-14). You can also right-click a message and choose Follow Up➪Add Reminder to see the dialog box.

2. **On the Flag To drop-down menu, choose an option that describes why the e-mail message needs your attention later on, or, if none of the options suits you, enter a description in the Flag To text box.**

The description you choose or enter will appear above the message in the Reading Pane and appear as well in the Reminders message box.

3. **Choose the date and time that you want the Reminders message box to appear.**

As Chapter 5 explains in detail, the Reminders message box will appear 15 minutes before the date and time you enter. If you enter a date but not a time, Outlook assigns the default time, 5:00 P.M.

4. **Click OK.**

Items flagged this way appear in red text with a red flag. When the reminder falls due, you see the Reminder message box, where you can click the Open Item button to open the e-mail message. See Chapter 5 of this mini-book if you need to find out how the Reminder message box works.

Earmarking messages as they arrive

To help you organize messages better, Outlook gives you the opportunity to mark messages in various ways and even move messages as they arrive automatically to folders apart from the Inbox folder. Being able to move messages immediately to a folder is a great way to keep e-mail concerning different projects separate. If you belong to a newsgroup that sends many messages a day, being able to move those messages instantly into their own folder is a real blessing, because newsgroup messages have a habit of cluttering the Inbox folder.

To earmark messages for special treatment, Outlook has you create so-called *rules*. To create a rule, start by trying out the Create Rule command, and if that doesn't work, test-drive the more powerful Rules Wizard.

Simple rules with the Create Rule command

Use the Create Rule command to be alerted when e-mail arrives from a certain person or the Subject line of a message includes a certain word. You can make the incoming message appear in the New Items Alerts window (as shown on the top of Figure 3-15), play a sound when the message arrives, or move the message automatically to a certain folder.

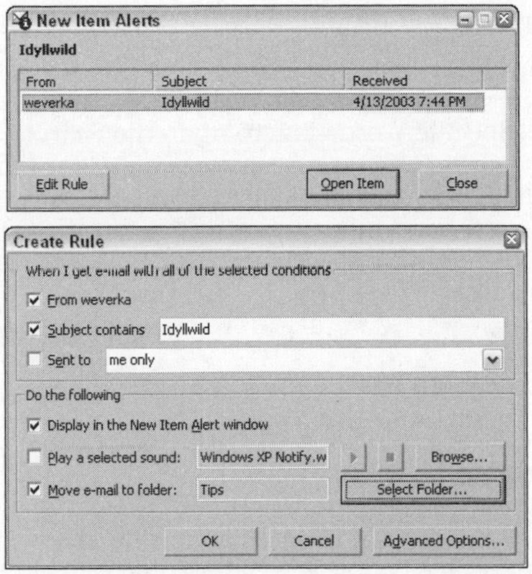

Figure 3-15:
The New
Item Alerts
window
(top) and
Create Rule
dialog box
(bottom).

Follow these steps to create a simple rule:

1. **If you want to be alerted when e-mail arrives from a certain person, find an e-mail message from the person, right-click it, and choose Create Rule; otherwise, right-click any message and choose Create Rule.**

   You see the Create Rule dialog box, shown on the bottom of Figure 3-15.

2. **Fill in the dialog box and click OK.**

   These commands are self-explanatory.

Another way to create a simple rule is to choose Tools➪Organize. The Ways to Organize Inbox panel appears. Starting here, you can move messages from a certain person to a folder or color-code messages as they arrive from a certain person.

Creating complex rules with the Rules Wizard

Use the Rules Wizard to create complex rules that earmark messages with words in the message body or earmark messages sent to distribution lists. You can also create a rule to flag messages automatically or delete a conversation (the original message and all replies).

To run the Rules Wizard, click the Rules and Alerts button or choose Tools➪Rules and Alerts. You see the Rules and Alerts dialog box. Click the New Rule button and keep clicking Next in the Rules Wizard dialog boxes as you complete the two steps to create a rule:

✦ **Step 1:** Choose the rule you want to create or how you want to be alerted in the New Item Alerts message box (refer to Figure 13-15).

✦ **Step 2:** Click a hyperlink to open a dialog box and describe the rule. For example, click the Specific Words link to open the Search Text dialog box and enter the words that earmark a message. Click the Specified link to open the Rules and Alerts dialog box and choose a folder to move the messages to. You must click each link in the Step 2 box to describe the rule.

To edit a rule, double-click it in the Rules and Alerts dialog box and complete Steps 1 and 2 all over again.

All about E-Mail Folders

Where Outlook e-mail is concerned, everything has its place and everything has its folder. E-mail messages land in the Inbox folder when they arrive. Messages you write go to the Outbox folder until you send them. Copies of e-mail messages you send are kept in the Sent folder. And you can create folders of your own for storing e-mail.

If you're one of those unlucky people who receive numerous e-mail messages each day, you owe it to yourself to create folders in which to organize e-mail messages. Create one folder for each project you're working on. That way, you know where to find e-mail messages when you want to reply to or delete them. These pages explain how to move e-mail messages between folders and create folders of your own for storing e-mail.

Moving e-mail messages to different folders

Click to select the message you want to move and use one of these techniques to move an e-mail message to a different folder:

✦ **With the Move To Folder button:** Click the Move To Folder button and, on the drop-down menu that appears, select a folder. The Move To Folder button is located on the Standard toolbar to the right of the Print button.

✦ **With the <u>M</u>ove To Folder command:** Choose <u>E</u>dit⇨<u>M</u>ove to Folder, press Ctrl+Shift+V, or right-click and choose <u>M</u>ove to Folder. You see the Move Items dialog box. Select a folder and click OK.

✦ **By dragging:** Click the Folder List button, if necessary to see all the folders; then drag the e-mail message into a different folder.

Earlier in this chapter, "Earmarking messages as they arrive" explains how to move e-mail messages automatically to folders as they are sent to you.

Creating a new folder for storing e-mail

Follow these steps to create a new folder:

1. **Choose File➪New➪Folder.**

You see the Create New Folder dialog box, shown in Figure 3-16. You can also open this dialog box by pressing Ctrl+Shift+E or right-clicking a folder in the Folder List and choosing New Folder.

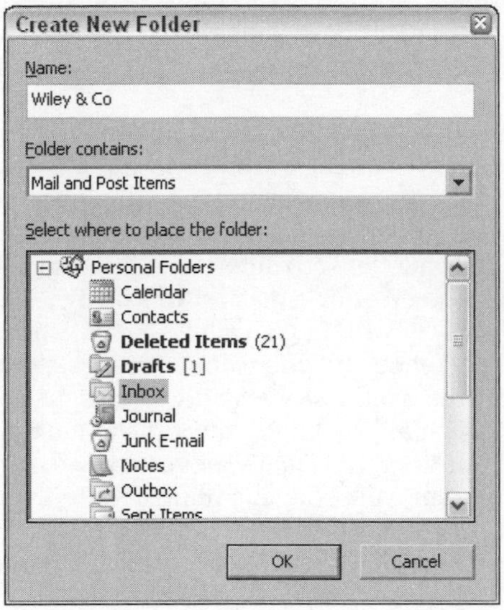

Book II
Chapter 3

Handling Your
E-Mail

Figure 3-16:
Creating a
new folder.

2. **Select the folder that the new folder will go inside.**

For example, to create a first-level folder, select Personal Folders.

3. **Enter a name for the folder.**

4. **Click OK.**

To delete a folder you created, select it and click the Delete button. To rename a folder, right-click it, choose Rename, and enter a new name.

Yes, You Can Prevent Junk Mail (Sort of)

Outlook maintains a folder called Junk E-Mail especially for storing junk mail, or *spam* as the digital variety is sometimes called. E-mail messages with certain words or phrases in the Subject line — *for free!*, *money-back guarantee*, *order now* — are sent automatically to the Junk E-Mail folder. (To see the list of words that qualify messages as junk mail, search for a file called FILTERS.TXT on your computer and double-click to open it in Windows Notepad.) Outlook can only, however, send plain-text messages to the Junk E-Mail folder. HTML messages can slip through. (Earlier in this chapter, "All about Message Formats" explains the differences between HTML and plain-text messages.)

If you get an e-mail message from a junk mailer, you can add the mailer's name to the list of Junk Senders and in so doing send future correspondence from the sender to the Junk E-Mail folder. To do so, right-click the Junk sender's name and choose Junk E-Mail⇨Add Sender to Blocked Senders List. To see the list of Junk senders, choose Actions⇨Junk E-Mail⇨Junk E-Mail Options and select the Blocked Senders tab in the Junk E-Mail Options dialog box.

As zealous as Outlook is about preventing junk mail, the program can't really do the job. Junk mailers change addresses frequently. They often send e-mail in HTML format. The only way to truly prevent junk mail is to be careful to whom you give your e-mail address. Junk senders get the majority of their addresses from commercial Web sites. When you register at a commercial Web site, choose to keep your e-mail address private if you're given that option. If you can get away with it, give a false e-mail address. If junk mail is the bane of your existence and you want to stamp it out cold, get a Hotmail address or other free e-mail address and submit it to commercial Web sites. That way, all junk mail will go to your official junk mail address, not the one you use most of the time. Finally, never reply to junk mail, even to say that you want to be removed from a mailing list. Replying only encourages these pests.

Chapter 4: Managing Your Time and Schedule

In This Chapter

- Understanding how to classify activities
- Going to different dates in the Calendar
- Scheduling appointments and events
- Rescheduling an activity
- Getting a better view of your schedule
- Customizing the Outlook window

The purpose of the Outlook Calendar is to keep you from arriving a day late and a dollar short. Use the Calendar to schedule meetings and appointments. Use it to make the most of your time. This chapter explains how to go from day to day, week to week, and month to month in the Calendar window. It shows you how to schedule and reschedule appointments and meetings, look at your schedule in different ways, and customize Outlook.

Introducing the Calendar

Use the Calendar to juggle appointments and meetings, remind yourself where you're supposed to be, and get there on time. Surveying your schedule in the Calendar window is easy. Merely by clicking a button, you can tell where you're supposed to be today, any given day, this week, this work week, this month, or any month. Figure 4-1 shows, for example, someone's schedule during the work week of April 21 through 25 (a work week comprises Monday through Friday, not Monday through Sunday). All you have to do to find out how busy you are on a particular day, week, or month is gaze at the Calendar window. If someone invites you to a meeting or wants to schedule an appointment, you can open the Calendar and see right away whether your schedule permits you to attend the meeting or make the appointment.

Outlook gives you opportunities to color-code meetings and appointments so that you can tell at a glance what they are all about. Moving a meeting or appointment is simply a matter of dragging it elsewhere in the Calendar window. By double-clicking a meeting or appointment in the Calendar window, you can open a form to find out where the meeting takes place or read notes you jotted down about the meeting. You can even make a bell ring and the Reminder message box appear when a meeting or appointment is forthcoming.

To make the TaskPad, an abbreviated Tasks window, appear beside the Calendar window, choose View➪TaskPad. Chapter 5 explains how to schedule tasks in the Tasks window.

The Different Kinds of Activities

For scheduling purposes, Outlook makes a distinction between appointments, events, and meetings. Meetings, however, are not everybody's concern. If your computer is connected to a network and the network uses the Microsoft Exchange Server, you can use Outlook to invite colleagues on the network to come to meetings. But if your computer is not on a network, don't bother with meetings. Schedule appointments and events instead. You can schedule the following activities:

✦ **Appointment:** An activity that occupies a certain time period on a certain day. For example, a meeting that takes place between 11 and 12 o'clock is an appointment.

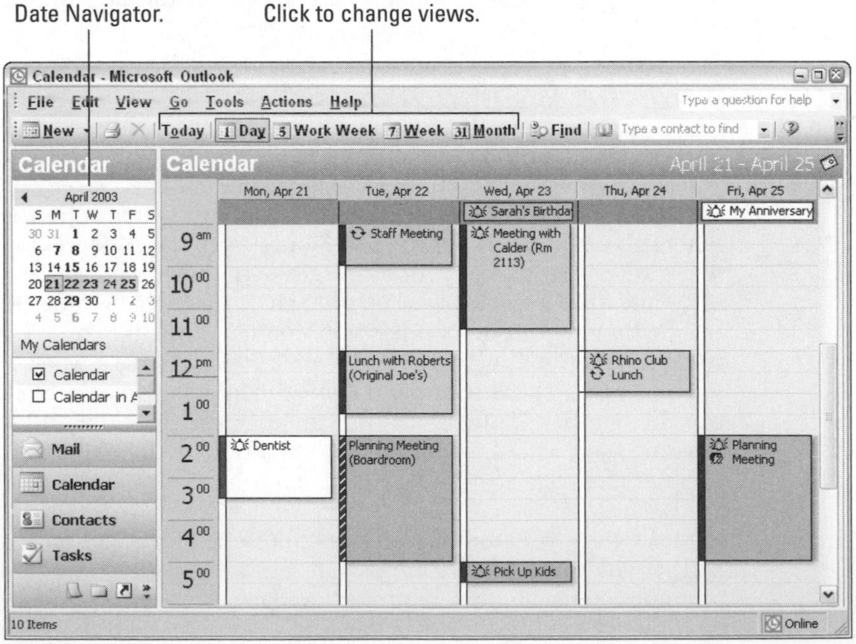

Date Navigator.   Click to change views.

Figure 4-1:
The Calendar in Work Week view.

✦ **Recurring appointment:** An appointment that takes place daily, weekly, or monthly on the same day and same time each day, week, or month. A weekly staff meeting is a recurring appointment. The beauty of recurring appointments is that Outlook enters them weeks and months in advance in the Calendar window. You don't have to enter these appointments one at a time.

✦ **Event:** An activity that lasts all day. A trade show, for example, is an event. A birthday is an event. A day spent on vacation is also an event (is it ever!). On the Calendar, events and recurring events appear first.

✦ **Recurring event:** An all-day activity that takes place each week, month, or year. Unromantic users of Outlook are hereby advised to schedule these recurring events in the Calendar: Valentine's Day, their significant other's birthday, and first-date and wedding anniversaries. Thanks to Outlook, no one will ever accuse you again of being cold-hearted or indifferent.

✦ **Meeting:** Same as an appointment, except that you can invite others to attend. Scheduling meetings is not covered in this book. See your network administrator for details.

**Book II
Chapter 4**

**Managing Your
Time and Schedule**

Getting around in the Calendar Window

Days on which meetings or appointments are scheduled appear in boldface in the *Date Navigator,* the calendar in the upper-left corner of the window (refer to Figure 4-1). Here are all the different ways to go from date to date in the Calendar window:

Today

✦ **To today:** Click the Today button on the Standard toolbar.

✦ **To a specific day:** Click a day in the Date Navigator. You can also press Ctrl+G and select a day in the Go To Date dialog box. In some views, you can press Alt+PageUp to go to the first day of the month, or Alt+PageDown to go to the last day.

✦ **To a different month:** Click an arrow beside the month name in the Date Navigator to go backward or forward by a month. Here's a quick way to go from month to month in the Calendar: Click the month name in the Date Navigator and hold down the mouse button. You see a list of month names. Drag the pointer to the name of the month you want to go to.

Use the scroll bar on the right side of the window to travel from hour to hour in Day view and Work Week view. In Week view and Month view, manipulating the scroll bar takes you from week to week.

Scheduling an Activity

Now that you know how the Calendar works, the next step is to fill the pages of the Calendar with all kinds of busywork. These pages explain how to schedule activities, schedule recurring activities, and magically transform an e-mail message into a Calendar item. You can find many intriguing shortcuts in these pages.

Scheduling an activity: The basics

Follow these basic steps to schedule an appointment, recurring appointment, event, or recurring event:

1. **Select the day in which you want to schedule the activity.**

   If the activity occupies a certain time period, you can select the time period in Day or Work Week view and save yourself the trouble of entering a time period in the Appointment dialog box. To select a time period, drag downward in the Calendar window. To create a half-hour appointment, simply double-click a half hour slot in Day or Work Week view. The Appointment dialog box opens with the Start and End time already entered.

2. **Click the New Appointment button, press Ctrl+N, or choose Actions⇨New Appointment.**

   As shown in Figure 4-2, you see a form for naming the activity, stating its starting and ending time, and choosing whether you want to be alerted to its occurrence. When you double-click an appointment or event in the Calendar window, this is the form you see.

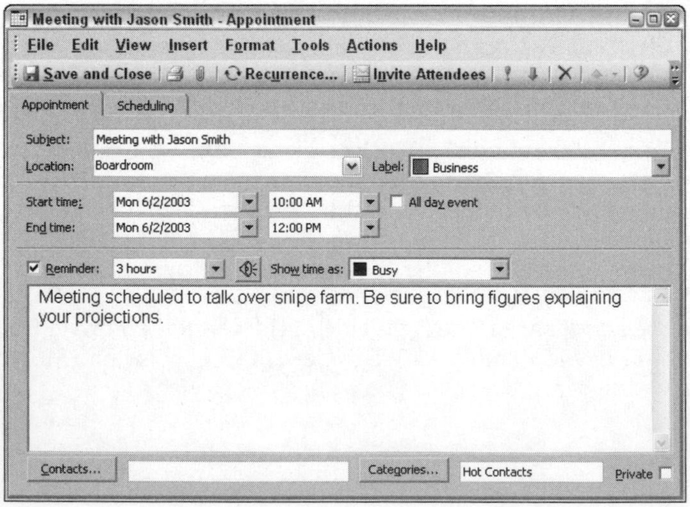

Figure 4-2:
The form for scheduling activities.

3. **Enter information in the form.**

   Table 4-1 explains what all the fields in the Appointment form are. To enter a recurring event or appointment, click the Recurrence button. To enter an event instead of an appointment, select the All Day Event check box.

4. **Click the Save and Close button when you're finished describing the appointment or event.**

   The appointment or event is entered in the Calendar window.

Table 4-1	Appointment Fields
Field	*What to Enter*
Subject	A description of the activity. What you enter will appear in the Calendar window.
Location	Where the activity will take place. You can open the drop-down window and choose from the last 10 locations you entered.
Label	A color from the drop-down list so that you can see at a glance what type of activity it is. Later in this chapter, "Customizing Outlook" explains how to customize the color codes.
Start Time	When the activity begins. Choose a date and time. In Day or Work Week view, you can enter start and end times before opening the Appointment dialog box by dragging to select time periods in the Calendar window.
End Time	When the activity ends.
All Day Event	When the activity is an event, not an appointment. Select this check box if you are describing an event.
Reminder	If you want to be reminded when the activity is imminent. Select the check box and choose an option from the drop-down menu to make the Reminder message box appear before the activity is to begin. In the Calendar window, activities about which you will be reminded are marked by the ringing bell icon. Chapter 5 of this mini-book explains how reminders work.
Show Time As	A setting that describes your availability to others on the network. This option is pertinent only if your computer is connected to a network that uses Microsoft Exchange Server and the administrator has activated the Delegate option.
Contacts	The contact name of a person associated with the activity. Click the Contacts button and, in the Select Contacts window, choose a name from your Contacts folder. In this way you can track your dealings with a contact. The appointment or event will appear on the Activities tab in the person's Contact form. See Chapter 2 of this mini-book for details.

(continued)

Table 4-1 *(continued)*

Field	What to Enter
Categories	A category name for tracking this activity. As Chapter 1 of this mini-book explains, you can choose By Category in the Current View drop-down menu in any window to arrange items by category.
Private	When you want others on the network to be able to view this activity on your schedule. This option pertains only if you're connected to a network that uses Microsoft Exchange Server.

Scheduling a recurring appointment or event

To enter a recurring appointment or event, click the Recurrence button in the Appointment form (refer to Figure 4-2). You see the Appointment Recurrence form shown in Figure 4-3. Describe how persistent the activity is and click OK:

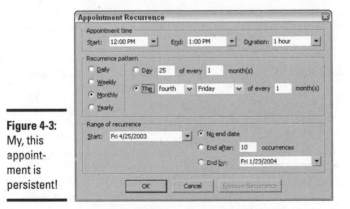

Figure 4-3:
My, this appoint-ment is persistent!

✦ **Appointment Time:** Enter the starting and ending time, if you didn't do so already in the Appointment form.

✦ **Recurrence Pattern:** Use the options and drop-down menus to describe how often the activity recurs.

✦ **Range of Recurrence:** Describe when the recurring events will cease recurring. Choose the No End Date option button if the activity occurs *ad infinitum, ad nauseum* (that's Latin for "unto infinity most nauseously").

 In the Calendar window, recurring activities are marked by the arrow chas-ing its tail icon. To change a recurring activity into a one-time activity, click the Recurrence button and, in the Recurrence dialog box, click the Remove Recurrence button.

Using an e-mail message to schedule an appointment

Here's a neat little trick that can save you time when e-mail correspondence has to do with scheduling an appointment. To get a head start on scheduling, drag the e-mail message from the Inbox window over the Calendar button on the Navigation pane. On the theory that you want to schedule an appointment around the information in the e-mail message, the Appointment form appears on-screen. For the subject of the appointment, Outlook enters the subject of the e-mail message. The text of the e-mail message appears on the form as well. Fiddle with the particulars of the appointment and click the Save and Close button.

Scheduling an event

Select the All Day Event check box in the Appointment window (refer to Figure 4-2) to schedule an event, not an appointment. As I explain earlier, an event is an activity that lasts all day. Here are some shortcuts for creating events:

✦ In Week view or Month view, double-click the day on which the event is to occur. The Event dialog box opens immediately.

✦ Choose Actions⇨New All Day Event to open the Event dialog box straightaway.

Canceling, Rescheduling, and Altering Activities

Canceling, rescheduling, and altering appointments and events is pretty easy. You can always double-click an activity to open the Appointment or Event form and change the particulars there. And you can take advantage of these shortcuts:

✦ **Canceling:** Select an activity and click the Delete button. When you cancel a recurring activity, a dialog box asks whether you want to delete all occurrences of the activity or just the activity on the day you selected. Choose an option and click OK.

✦ **Rescheduling:** Drag the activity to a new location on the schedule. Move the pointer over the left side of the activity and, when you see the four-headed arrow, start dragging.

✦ **Changing start and end times:** In Day or Work Week view, move the pointer over the top or bottom of the activity and start dragging when you see the double arrow.

✦ **Changing the description:** Click in the activity's box and start typing or editing.

Getting a Better Look at Your Schedule

Here are the various and sundry ways to organize and view the activities you so patiently entered in the Calendar window:

✦ **Change Calendar views:** Click one of the four View buttons — Today, Day, Work Week, Week, or Month — to read the fine print or get the bird's-eye view of activities you've scheduled in the Calendar window.

✦ **Change views of the Calendar window:** Open the Current View drop-down menu and choose Events, Recurring Appointments, or another view to isolate certain kinds of activities.

✦ **Color-code activities:** Color-coding is a great way to separate the important activities from the not-so-important ones. To change the color of an activity, right-click it, choose Label, and select a color on the submenu. The next section, "Customizing Outlook," explains how to set up your own color scheme.

✦ **Categorize messages:** Assign activities to categories and then arrange activities by category in the Calendar window. To do so, choose By Category in the Current View menu. Chapter 1 of this mini-book explains categorizing.

Customizing Outlook

In case you're in the mood to redecorate, here are a few ways to customize Outlook:

✦ **Choosing your own color codes:** As you probably know, you can assign a color code to an activity in the Appointment form by right-clicking an activity, choosing Label, and selecting a color. To decide for yourself what the colors mean, choose Edit⇨Label⇨Edit Labels. You see the Edit Calendar Labels dialog box, shown in Figure 4-4. Enter your own descriptions next to the color boxes and click OK.

✦ **Changing fonts and font sizes:** To change the look of the letters in the Calendar window, right-click an empty spot in the window and choose Other Settings. You see the Format dialog box. Starting here, you can click Font buttons to change fonts and font sizes in different parts of the Calendar window.

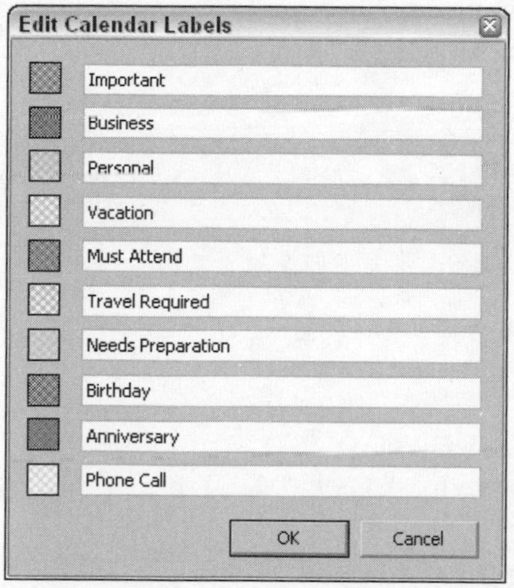

Figure 4-4: Setting up your own color scheme.

✦ **Changing the background color:** To choose a background color for the Calendar window, choose Tools➪Options and, on the Preferences tab of the Options dialog box, click the Calendar Options button. You see the Calendar Options dialog box. Choose a new color from the Background Color drop-down menu.

Be sure to visit Book VIII, Chapter 1 as well. It explains how to customize the toolbars, keyboard shortcuts, and menus in all the Office programs, Outlook included.

Chapter 5: Tasks, Reminders, and Notes

In This Chapter

✔ Creating, handling, and managing tasks

✔ Being reminded when deadlines and activities are forthcoming

✔ Jotting down digital notes

This short chapter describes some Outlook goodies that were neglected in the other chapters in Part II. It explains how the Tasks window can help you meet your deadlines and how to be alerted when an activity is looming, a task deadline is arriving, an e-mail needs your attention, or someone in your Contacts folder needs love and attention. Finally, this chapter explains Outlook's digital stick 'em notes.

Tasks: Seeing What Needs to Get Done

As shown in Figure 5-1, use the Tasks window to see what needs to be done, when it's due, and whether it's overdue. On this list, due dates clearly show how smartly the whip is being cracked and how close you are to meeting or missing deadlines. A gray line appears across tasks that are done. Tasks that are overdue appear in red. Read on to find out how to enter a task, attach a file to a task, and manage tasks in the Tasks window.

The best way to examine tasks is to display the Reading pane and move it to the bottom of the Tasks window. This way, you can select a task and read notes you've made about it, as shown in Figure 5-1. To display the Reading pane along the bottom of the Tasks window, choose View⇨Reading Pane⇨ Bottom. (You can make a mini-Tasks window appear alongside the Calendar by choosing View⇨TaskPad in the Calendar window.)

Entering a task in the Tasks window

Outlook offers two ways to enter a task in the Tasks window:

✦ **The fast way:** Click at the top of the window where it says "Click here to add a new Task," type a few words to describe the task, and enter the due date in the Due Date box. To enter the date, type it yourself or open the drop-down calendar and select a date there.

New ▾

✦ **The slower but thorough way:** Click the New button, press Ctrl+N, or choose Actions⇨New Task. You see the Task form, shown in Figure 5-2. On this form are places for describing the task, entering start and due dates, describing the task's status, prioritizing the task, and jotting down notes about it. Click the Save and Close button when you're finished describing the task.

Select a task.

Tasks

☐ ✓	Subject	Due Date
	Click here to add a new Task	
☑ ☐	Write the outline	Thu 5/1/2003
☑ ☐	Finish Chapter 4.	Wed 4/23/2003
☑ ☐	Wash the car	None
☑ ☑	~~Lydia Acosta meeting~~	~~None~~
☑ ☑	~~Take out the cat~~	~~Tue 1/1/2003~~
☑ ☑	~~Write Chapter 1~~	~~Sat 3/29/2003~~

Due in 9 days.

Subject: Write the outline
Due date: Due on 5/1/2003
Status: In Progress   Priority: High   % Complete: 25%
Owner: weverka

Go to the library and read the books to do the research. Consult Halpern as well.

Figure 5-1: The Tasks window shows what has been done and what needs doing.

Examine it in the Reading pane.

By clicking the Recurrence button in the Task form (refer to Figure 5-2), you can enter a sisyphian task that gets repeated over and over again. In the Task Recurrence dialog box, describe how often the task recurs. Recurring tasks are marked in the Tasks window with an unusual icon. What is that? Looks to me like a clipboard with a piece of toilet paper stuck to it.

Use the Details tab of the Task form to track the hours you worked on a project, the companies you worked for, and how many miles you logged going to and fro in your work.

Handling and managing tasks

When the time comes to manage the tasks in the Tasks window, I hope you are a stern taskmaster. Here's advice for handling and managing tasks:

✦ **Marking a task as complete:** Click the check box beside the task name in the Task window. Outlook draws a line through completed tasks.

✦ **Deleting a task:** Select the task and click the Delete button or press Ctrl+D.

✦ **Editing a task:** Double-click a task in the Task window to open the Task form and change the particulars there.

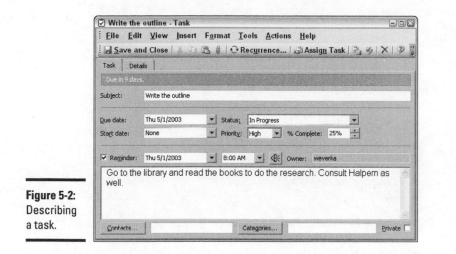

Figure 5-2:
Describing a task.

Outlook offers a number of techniques for locating tasks in a crowded Task window:

✦ **Change views in the Tasks window:** Open the Current View drop-down menu and choose the view that is most likely to turn up the task you are looking for.

✦ **Categorize tasks:** Assign tasks to categories and choose By Category in the Current View drop-down menu to arrange tasks by category. Chapter 1 of this mini-book explains categorizing.

✦ **Use the Find command:** If worse comes to worst, you can always resort to the Find command to find a stray task. Chapter 1 of this mini-book explains this command.

Reminders for Being Alerted to Activities and Tasks

Outlook offers the Reminders message box to alert you when an appointment or event from the Calendar is about to take place (see Chapter 4 of this mini-book), when a Task deadline is looming (see the previous section in this chapter), when an e-mail message needs a reply (see Chapter 3 of this mini-book), or when someone whose name is in your Contacts folder needs attention (see Chapter 2 of this mini-book). Figure 5-3 shows the Reminders message box. When Outlook is running and you least expect it, a Reminders message box such as the one in Figure 5-3 may appear to keep you on your toes.

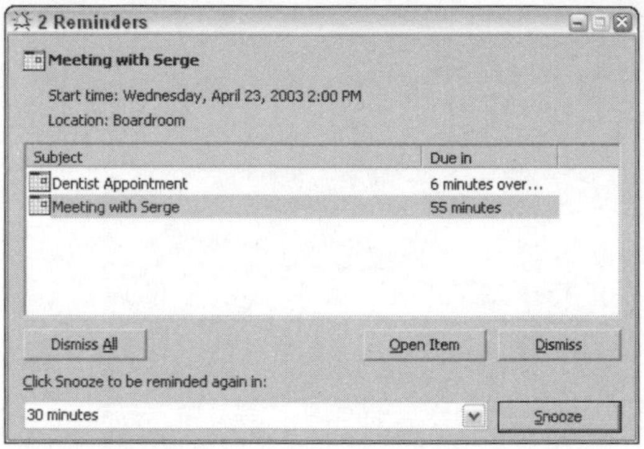

Figure 5-3:
The
Reminders
message
box.

Do the following in the Reminders message box to handle a reminder:

✦ **Dismiss it:** Click the Dismiss button to shelve the reminder notice. If more than one notice appears in the Reminders message box and you want to erase them all, click the Dismiss All button.

✦ **Be reminded later:** Click the Snooze button. The Click Snooze to Be Reminded Again In text box tells you when the next reminder message will arrive. To change this setting, open the drop-down menu and choose a different time period.

✦ **Open the item:** Click the Open Item button to examine the appointment, task, e-mail message, or contact to which the reminder pertains.

✦ **Procrastinate:** Click the Close button (the *X*) in the Reminders message box to make it disappear. To open the message box later on, choose View➪Reminders Window.

Attaching a file to a task

Attaching a file to a task is a neat way to get down to work quickly. Instead of fumbling in your computer for a Word document, Excel worksheet, or other type of file to work on, you can open it merely by double-clicking its name in the Task form or Reading pane of the Task window. To attach a file to a task, choose Insert➪File or click the Insert File button in the Task form (refer to Figure 5-2). Then, in the Insert File dialog box, select the file and click the Insert button.

Reminders work only for items that are stored in these folders: Tasks, Calendar, Inbox, and Contacts. Store an item in another folder or a subfolder of one of the folders I just named and you won't see the Reminders message box when the reminder is due. To make sure you get reminded, store items in these folders: Tasks, Calendar, Inbox, or Contacts.

Scheduling a reminder message

Follow these instructions to schedule a reminder message:

Book II
Chapter 5

✦ **A Calendar appointment or event:** In the Appointment or Event form, select the Reminder check box and, on the drop-down menu, choose how many minutes, hours, or weeks in advance to make the reminder appear, as shown in Figure 5-4.

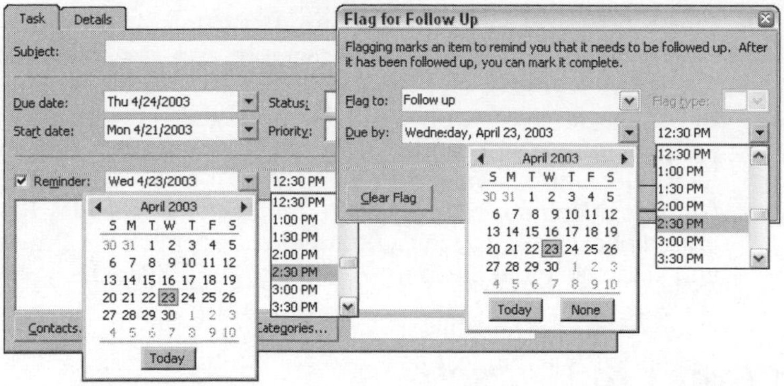

Tasks, Reminders, and Notes

Figure 5-4: Scheduling a reminder for appointments and tasks (left) and e-mail and contacts (right).

✦ **A Task deadline:** In the Task form, select the Reminder check box and choose a time period on the drop-down menu.

✦ **E-mail message:** If you're in the Message window, click the Flag button. In the Inbox window, right-click the message and choose Follow Up➪ Add Reminder. You see the Flag for Follow Up dialog box, as shown in Figure 5-4. Choose a date and time in the Due By drop-down menus. If you enter a date but not a time, the Reminders message box appears at 5:00 p.m.

✦ **Contacts name:** In a Contact form, click the Flag button; in the Contacts window, right-click a contact name and choose Follow Up. The Flag for Follow Up dialog box appears. Treat this dialog box the same way you treat the one for e-mail messages (see the previous item in this list).

Making reminders work your way

You can do two or three things to make reminders work your way:

✦ **Changing the reminder time for appointments and events:** By default, the Reminders message box appears 15 minutes before appointments and events are to start. To change this setting, choose Tools⇨Options and, on the Preferences tab of the Options dialog box, enter a new setting in the Default Reminder drop-down menu.

✦ **Changing the default time for task reminders:** When a task's deadline has arrived, the Reminders dialog box lets you know at 8:00 a.m. (or when you start Outlook, if you start the program after 8:00 a.m.). To change this default setting, choose Tools⇨Options and, on the Preferences tab of the Options dialog box, choose a new time from the Reminder Time drop-down menu.

✦ **Play a different sound (or no sound):** By default, you hear a little chime when the Reminders message box appears on-screen. To hear a different sound or no sound at all, choose Tools⇨Options and select the Other tab in the Options dialog box. Next, click the Advanced Options button and, in the Advanced Options dialog box, click the Reminder Options button. You arrive — at last — at the Reminder Options dialog box. To play no sound, unselect the Play Reminder Sound check box. To play a different sound, click the Browse button and select a sound file in the Reminder Sound File dialog box.

Making Notes to Yourself

As shown in Figure 5-5, notes resemble the yellow stick 'em notes that you often see affixed to manuscripts and refrigerator doors. Click the Notes button on the Navigation pane to go to the Notes window. Write a note to mark down a deadline, for example, or remind yourself to take out the cat. Here are instructions for doing all and sundry with notes:

✦ **Creating a note:** Click the New Note button and type the note in the Note window. Then press Esc or click outside the window.

✦ **Opening a note:** Double-click a note to read it in its Note window.

✦ **Forwarding a note:** To forward a note to someone in an e-mail message, right-click the note and choose Forward. A message window opens so that you can address the message. The note arrives in the form of a file attachment, and the recipient must have Outlook in order to read it.

✦ **Deleting a note:** Select the note and click the Delete button or press the Delete key.

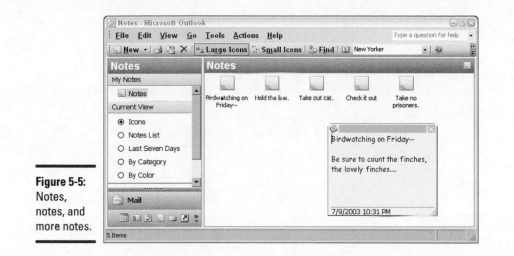

**Book II
Chapter 5**

Figure 5-5:
Notes,
notes, and
more notes.

**Tasks, Reminders,
and Notes**

Book III

PowerPoint

The 5th Wave   By Rich Tennant

"MY GIRLFRIEND RAN A SPREADSHEET OF MY LIFE, AND GENERATED THIS CHART. MY BEST HOPE IS THAT SHE'LL CHANGE HER MAJOR FROM 'COMPUTER SCIENCES' TO 'REHABILITATIVE SERVICES.'"

Contents at a Glance

Chapter 1: Getting Started in PowerPoint

In This Chapter

✔ **Starting a new presentation**

✔ **Making your presentation persuasive**

✔ **Changing views in the PowerPoint screen**

✔ **Creating a new slide**

✔ **Moving and deleting slides**

✔ **Designating a hidden slide**

PowerPoint presentations are now ubiquitous in the corporate world. It's impossible to sit through a conference, seminar, or trade show without seeing at least one PowerPoint presentation. PowerPoint has found its way into nearly every office and boardroom. I've heard of a man — a very unromantic man — who proposed to his wife by way of a PowerPoint presentation.

As nice as PowerPoint can be, it has its detractors. If the software isn't used properly, it can come between the speaker and the audience. In an article in the May 28, 2001, *New Yorker* titled "Absolute PowerPoint: Can a Software Package Edit Our Thoughts?," Ian Parker argued that PowerPoint may actually be more of a hindrance than a help in communicating. PowerPoint, Parker wrote, is "a social instrument, turning middle managers into bullet-point dandies." The software, he added, "has a private, interior influence. It edits ideas.... It helps you make a case, but also makes its own case about how to organize information, how to look at the world."

To make sure that you use PowerPoint wisely, this chapter offers more than instructions in using the software — it explains how to make your presentations meaningful. Along the way, you discover how to find your way around PowerPoint, create a presentation, change views, insert the slides, and designate some slides as "hidden."

Getting Acquainted with PowerPoint

Figure 1-1 shows the PowerPoint window. That thing in the middle is a *slide,* PowerPoint's word for an image that forms part of a presentation. Surrounding the slide are many tools for decorating and adorning slides.

When the time comes to show a presentation, you dispense with the tools and make the slide fill the screen, as shown in Figure 1-2. Don't worry about making slides as dazzling as the one in Figures 1-1 and 1-2. PowerPoint offers prefabricated slide designs that take most of the trouble out of decorating the slides.

To make PowerPoint do your bidding, you need to know a little jargon:

✦ **Presentation:** All the slides, from start to finish.

✦ **Slides:** The images you create with PowerPoint. During a presentation, slides appear on-screen one after the other. Don't be put off by the word *slide* and dreary memories of sitting through your uncle's slide-show vacation memories. You don't need a slide projector to show these slides. You can now plug a laptop or other computer into special monitors that display PowerPoint slides.

✦ **Speaker notes:** Printed pages that you, the speaker, write and print so that you know what to say during a presentation. Only the speaker sees the speaker notes.

✦ **Handout:** Printed pages that you may give to the audience after a presentation. A handout shows the slides in the presentation. Handouts are also known by the somewhat derogatory term "leave-behinds."

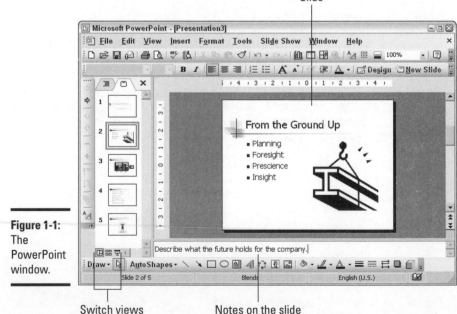

Figure 1-1:
The
PowerPoint
window.

Slide

Switch views

Notes on the slide

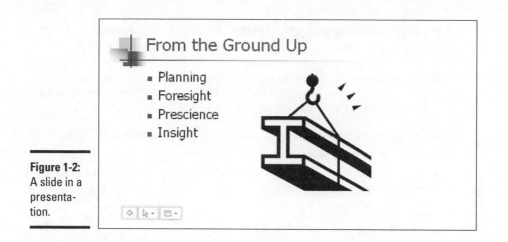

From the Ground Up

- Planning
- Foresight
- Prescience
- Insight

Figure 1-2:
A slide in a
presenta-
tion.

Creating a New Presentation

To create a new presentation, start by choosing File⇨New (or pressing
Ctrl+N). That's all there is to it. The New Presentation task pane appears on
the right side of the window. The next step is to choose a look for the slides
in the presentation, and PowerPoint offers no fewer than four ways to do
that: start with a blank presentation, start from a design template or color
scheme, make use of the AutoContent Wizard, or commandeer an existing
presentation.

No matter which look you choose for your presentation, you can change
your mind and choose a different look later on. To do so, click the Design
button or choose Format⇨Slide Design and select a new look in the Slide
Design task pane. You can choose a new look no matter how far along you
are in constructing a presentation.

Starting with a blank presentation

 Click the Blank Presentation link in the Slide Design task pane to create a
bare-bones presentation. You're on your own. With this technique, you have
to fashion a design yourself with the tools on the Drawing toolbar. I don't
recommend this technique unless you know PowerPoint well and have an
artistic flair. Why make your own design when you can rely on a design template, one created by a genuine artist?

**Book III
Chapter 1**

**Getting Started
in PowerPoint**

Starting from a slide design or color scheme

Click the Design button on the Formatting toolbar or the From Design
Template link in the task pane to make use of a slide design or color scheme.
As shown in Figure 1-3, the Slide Design task pane opens. Scroll through the
templates or color schemes, select one, glance at the slide on-screen, and
decide which design or color scheme tickles your fancy:

✦ **Slide design:** Click the Design button or the From Design Template link,
   if necessary, to see the designs and choose one.

✦ **Color scheme:** Click the Color Schemes link to choose a color scheme. If
   the Slide Design task pane isn't showing, click the Design button on the
   Formatting toolbar.

Click to select a color scheme.

Select a design.

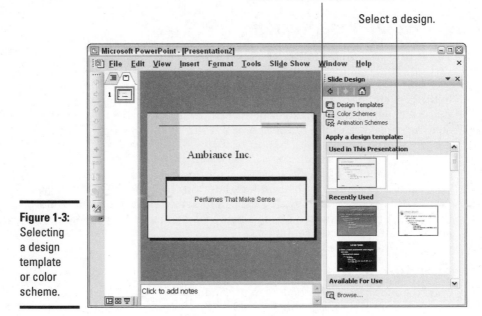

Figure 1-3:
Selecting
a design
template
or color
scheme.

Putting your own presentations in the AutoContent Wizard

For the benefit of co-workers, you can save a PowerPoint presentation in the AutoContent Wizard and thereby make it available to others who want to follow in your footsteps:

1. **Create and save the presentation under a descriptive name.**

2. **Choose File⇨New and click the From AutoContent Wizard link in the New Presentation task pane.**

   The AutoContent Wizard dialog box appears.

3. **Click the Next button to see presentation types.**

4. **Choose a category for your presentation (All, General, Corporate, Projects, or Sales/Marketing) and click the Add button.**

5. **In the Select Presentation Template dialog box, locate your presentation, select it, and click OK.**

6. **Click Cancel in the AutoContent Wizard dialog box.**

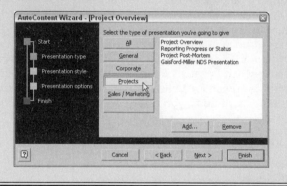

Starting from the AutoContent Wizard

Click the From AutoContent Wizard link in the New Presentation task pane to create a presentation with the help of the AutoContent Wizard. With this technique, PowerPoint asks questions about the kind of presentation you want. When you're done answering, the program chooses a presentation design for you, complete with generic headings and text, and you enter your own headings and text where the generic stuff is.

WARNING!

Unless you're in a big hurry, I strongly recommend against creating a presentation with the AutoContent Wizard. Presentations created this way are invariably cold and impersonal. As I explain in "Advice for Building Persuasive Presentations," later in this chapter, a presentation has to be an expression of who you are and what you stand for if it is to be successful.

Generic presentations made with the AutoContent Wizard are by definition dull and characterless. They are the primary reason that PowerPoint has a bad reputation in some boardrooms and conference halls.

Starting from an existing presentation

 If a PowerPoint presentation on your computer or computer network can be used as the starting point for your new presentation, click the From Existing Presentation link in the New Presentation task pane. You see the New from Existing Presentation dialog box. Select the presentation and click the Create New button. The presentation you selected appears in the window. Start tweaking it to your liking.

Advice for Building Persuasive Presentations

Once upon a time I was at a conference where someone was delivering a PowerPoint presentation and the computer with PowerPoint on it failed. Members of the audience clapped and cheered. It was the sixth or seventh PowerPoint presentation of the morning and the audience was thoroughly tired of PowerPoint. As I mentioned at the start of this chapter, PowerPoint in the wrong hands can make for a very dull presentation. To prevent dullness, here is advice for building a persuasive presentation, one that brings the audience around to your side.

Tips for creating presentations

 Here's a handful of tips to start you on your way as you create a PowerPoint presentation:

✦ **Start by writing the text in Word:** Start in Microsoft Word, not PowerPoint, and work from an outline. As I explain in the next section of this chapter, you can see your presentation take shape by working from a Word outline. Moreover, PowerPoint has a special command for importing text files from Word, so you won't lose any time by writing the early drafts of your presentation in Word. In Word, you can clearly see how a presentation develops. You can make sure that your presentation builds to its rightful conclusion.

✦ **When choosing a design, consider the audience:** A presentation to the American Casketmakers Association calls for a mute, quiet design; a presentation to the Cheerleaders of Tomorrow calls for something bright and splashy. Choose a slide design that sets the tone for your presentation and wins the sympathy of the audience.

✦ **Take control from the start:** Spend the first minute introducing yourself to the audience without running PowerPoint (or, if you do run PowerPoint, put a simple slide with your company name or logo on-screen). Make eye contact with the audience. This way, you establish your credibility. You give the audience a chance to get to know you.

✦ **Start from the conclusion:** Try writing the end of the presentation first. A presentation is supposed to build to a rousing conclusion. By writing the end first, you have a target to shoot for. You can make the entire presentation service its conclusion, the point at which your audience says, "Ah-ha! She's right."

✦ **Make clear what you're about:** In the early going, state very clearly what your presentation is about and what you intend to prove with your presentation. In other words, state the conclusion at the beginning as well as the end. This way, your audience will know exactly what you are driving at and be able to judge your presentation according to how well you build your case.

✦ **Personalize the presentation:** Make the presentation a personal one. Tell the audience what *your* personal reason for being there is or why *you* work for the company you work for. Knowing that you have a personal stake in the presentation, the audience is more likely to trust you. The audience will understand that you are not a spokesperson, but a speaker — someone who has come before them to make a case for something that you believe in.

✦ **Tell a story:** Include an anecdote in the presentation. Everybody loves a pertinent and well-delivered story. This piece of advice is akin to the previous one about personalizing your presentation. Typically, a story illustrates a problem for *people* and how *people* solve the problem. Even if your presentation concerns technology or an abstract subject, make it about people. "The people in Shaker Heights needed faster Internet access," not "the data switches in Shaker Heights just weren't performing fast enough."

✦ **Make like a newspaper:** Put a newspaper-style headline at the top of each slide, and think of each slide as a newspaper article. Each slide should address a specific aspect of your subject, and it should do so in a compelling way. How long does it take to read a newspaper article? It depends on how long the article is, of course, but a PowerPoint slide should stay on-screen for roughly the time it takes to explore a single topic the way a newspaper article does.

✦ **Follow the one-slide-per-minute rule:** At the very minimum, a slide should stay on-screen for at least one minute. If you have been given 15 minutes to speak, you are allotted no more than 15 slides for your presentation, according to the rule.

✦ **Beware the bullet point:** Terse bullet points have their place in a presentation, but if you put them there strictly to remind yourself what to say next, you are doing your audience a disfavor. Bullet points can cause drowsiness. They can be a distraction. The audience skims the bullets when it should be attending to your voice and the argument you are making. (As I explain in Chapter 2 of this mini-book, PowerPoint lets you write speaker notes that the audience doesn't see. If having notes to yourself is what you're after, use the speaker notes, not bullet points in slides.)

✦ **Use graphics and charts to make your point:** A good pie chart or bar chart that bolsters your argument is ideal and irrefutable. As shown in Figure 1-4, the clip art that comes with Office includes many cartoon-like graphics that I think are wonderful for PowerPoint presentations. If you can, use these humorous clip art images to make your case.

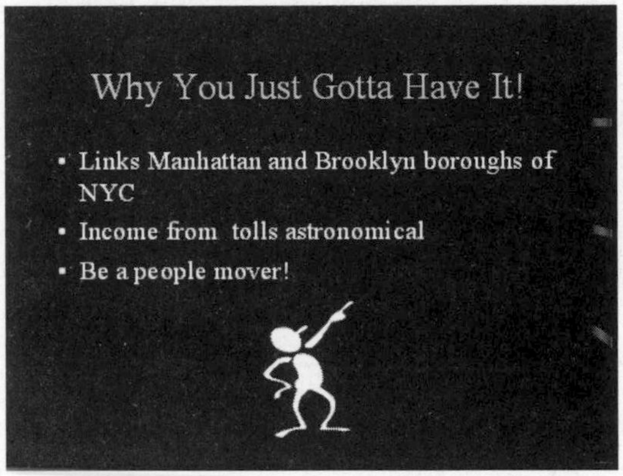

Figure 1-4:
A graphic
in a slide.

✦ **Blank out the screen for dramatic effect:** Show a blank screen when you come to the crux of your presentation and you want the audience's undivided attention. (You can blank out the screen by pressing B, which gives you a black screen, or pressing W, which gives you a white screen. Press B or W again and a slide reappears). When seeing the blank screen, the audience will focus all attention on you. What you say will have more impact. Sometimes PowerPoint comes between the speaker and the audience. By removing PowerPoint momentarily, you give yourself the chance to talk straight into the heart of your audience.

Want to see just how PowerPoint can suck the life and drama out of a dramatic presentation? Try visiting the Gettysburg PowerPoint Presentation, a rendering of Lincoln's Gettysburg Address in PowerPoint. Yikes! You'll find it here: www.norvig.com/Gettysburg/index.htm.

Start by writing the text

Here's the best piece of advice you will ever get about creating a PowerPoint presentation: Write the text of the presentation before going anywhere near PowerPoint. Focus on the words to begin with. This way, you focus on what you want to communicate, not slide layouts or graphic designs or fonts. If you work in Microsoft Word, you can take advantage of the outline feature to import your outline straight into a PowerPoint presentation.

I suspect that people actually enjoy doodling with PowerPoint slides because it distracts them from focusing on what really matters in a presentation — that is, what's meant to be communicated. Building an argument is hard work. People who can afford it pay lawyers and ghostwriters to do the job for them. Building an argument requires thinking long and hard about your topic, putting yourself in the place of an audience member who doesn't know the topic as well as you, and convincing the audience member that you're right. You can do this hard work better in Word, where the carnival atmosphere of PowerPoint isn't there to distract you.

In Word, simply write down the text you want to put on each slide. Later, you can copy the text into a PowerPoint presentation. If you're comfortable with Word's outline feature (Book I, Chapter 8 explains it), write the PowerPoint text in outline form. Moving headings around is easy in Outline view, and, as Chapter 2 explains, you can import a Word outline straight into a PowerPoint presentation. After the outline arrives in PowerPoint, you get one slide for each Level 1 heading. Level 1 headings form the titles of the slides, Level 2 headings form first-level bullets, and Level 3 headings form second-level bullets.

Book III Chapter 1

Getting Started in PowerPoint

Getting a Better View of Your Work

When you work on a presentation, some views are better than others. Figure 1-5 demonstrates different ways of viewing a presentation. To change views, click a View button in the lower-left corner of the window or open the View menu and choose Normal, Slide Sorter, Slide Show, or Notes Page. Click a tab at the top of the task pane in Normal view to see thumbnail slides or outline text. Why choose one view over the other? Here's why:

✦ **Normal/Outline view for fiddling with the text:** To enter text or read the text in a presentation, switch to Normal view and select the Outline tab (you can find it at the top of the task pane). The words on the slides appear in the task plane. You can select a slide and click a button on the Outlining toolbar to move the slide forward or backward in the presentation.

Normal/Slides   Slide sorter   Normal/Outline   Notes Page

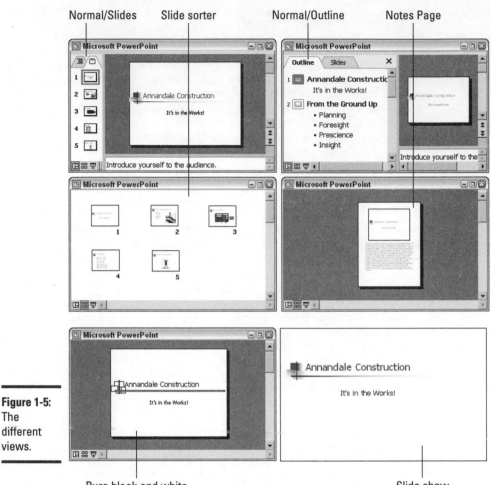

Figure 1-5:
The
different
views.

Pure black and white   Slide show

 ✦ **Normal/Slides view for moving from slide to slide:** Switch to Normal view and click the Slides tab when you want to move around in a presentation or work on a particular slide. Thumbnail slides appear in the task pane. Scroll to and select a slide to make it appear on-screen.

 ✦ **Slide Sorter view for moving and deleting slides:** In Slide Sorter view, you see thumbnails of all the slides in the presentation. From here, moving slides around is easy, and seeing many slides simultaneously gives you a sense of whether the different slides are consistent with one another.

 ✦ **Slide Show view for giving the show:** In Slide Show view, you see a single slide. This is what the slide will look like to the audience when you give the presentation. To quit Slide Show view, press the Esc key.

✦ **Notes Page view for reading your speaker notes:** In Notes Page view, you see notes you have written to aid in the presentation, if you've written any. This view is available only on the <u>V</u>iew menu.

 ✦ **Grayscale, Black and White:** Sometimes color on slides, not to mention animations and graphics, is a distraction. To strip down slides to their bare essence, click the Color/Grayscale button on the Standard toolbar and choose <u>G</u>rayscale or P<u>u</u>re Black and White on the drop-down menu. Pure Black and White is especially useful for focusing on text. These commands do not actually change the color on slides — they change the slides' appearance only on your computer monitor.

You can close the task pane in Normal view if it gets in your way. To close it, click the Close button. To see the task pane again, choose <u>V</u>iew➪<u>N</u>ormal (Restore Panes).

In Normal view, you can make the Outline tab show all the text on slides or just the titles. On the Outlining toolbar, click the Expand All button (or press Alt+Shift+9) to see all the text; click the Collapse All button (or press Alt+Shift+1) to see the titles.

Inserting Slides and Choosing Layouts

After you've written the text for the presentation, it's time to create the slides. To that end, PowerPoint offers *slide layouts,* preformatted slides into which you can plug headings, bulleted lists, graphics, tables, charts, and whatnot. You can also insert a slide by duplicating one you've already made or steal slides from another presentation. Better keep reading.

Inserting a new slide and layout

As shown in Figure 1-6, you choose a slide layout whenever you insert a new slide. Slide layouts appear in the Slide Layout task pane. The first layout is a *title slide* meant for the first slide in presentations; the other slides are known simply as *slides* in PowerPoint-speak (the sidebar "Slides and title slides" explains the difference between title slides and slides).

In Figure 1-6, I chose the Title and Text layout. The important thing to remember about these layouts is that you can change them whenever you want, although changing layouts can be problematic, for example, if you entered a graphic or bulleted list on the slide and you choose a layout that doesn't have placeholders for graphics or bulleted lists. To apply a layout to a slide, click the layout in the Slide Layout task pane.

Title slide. Click new slide.

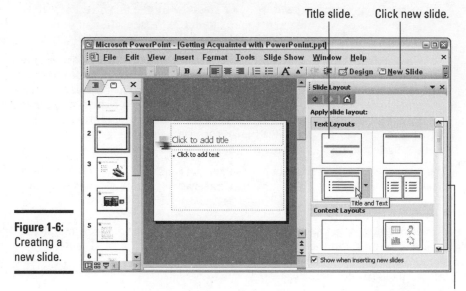

Figure 1-6:
Creating a
new slide.

Choose a slide layout.

Follow these steps to insert a new slide and give it a slide layout:

1. Select the slide that you want the new slide to go after.

In Normal view, select the slide on the Slides pane (select the Slides tab, if necessary). In Slide Sorter view, select the slide in the main window.

2. Click the New Slide button, press Ctrl+M, or choose Insert⇨New Slide.

A slide appears, as does the Slide Layout task pane (refer to Figure 1-6). The task pane offers 26 slide layouts. Try to find a layout that works for the slide you're creating. If you can't find one, choose the Blank layout and prepare to do a lot of formatting work on your own. Later, in Chapter 2 of this mini-book, I show you how to plug bulleted lists, graphics, and so on in a slide layout.

3. Scroll through the layouts and select the one you want.

Go ahead and experiment. When you select a layout in the task pane, the slide adopts the layout.

Here are a couple of shortcuts for inserting slides in presentations:

✦ Select a slide that's already there, choose Insert⇨Duplicate Slide, and then change the text on the duplicate slide and move it elsewhere.

✦ In Normal view, select a slide and press Enter. Doing so inserts a Title and Text slide (a slide with a placeholder for a heading and a bulleted list) after the slide you selected.

Slides and title slides

The Title Slide layout in the Slide Layout task pane (refer to Figure 1-6) is designed for the introductory slide in a presentation. Usually, the first slide is assigned the Title Slide layout. In a presentation that is divided into parts, the Title Slide layout is sometimes assigned to the first slide in each part. This way, the audience knows when one part ends and the next begins.

Whether you choose the Title Slide layout or one of the other slide layouts matters when it comes to formatting slides with a Slide Master. No, "Slide Master" is not the name of demonic super villain. As I explain in Chapter 3 of this mini-book, a Slide Master presents a way of formatting many slides simultaneously. Slide Masters give you the opportunity to save on formatting work and make sure that slides present a uniform appearance. PowerPoint offers two Slide Masters:

✔ **The Title Master for slides assigned Title Slide layout:** By changing the Title Master slide — by changing its background color or fonts, for example — you change all slides in the presentation that were assigned the Title Slide layout.

✔ **The Slide Master for slides assigned all the other layouts:** By changing the Slide Master, you change all slides *except* those assigned the Title Slide Layout.

The following figure shows the Title Master and Slide Master slide. Choose View⇨Master⇨Slide Master and select the Title Master or Slide Master in the task pane to work over a Master Slide.

If you mistakenly choose the wrong layout for a slide, you can choose another. Select the slide, choose Format⇨Slide Layout, and choose a different layout in the Slide Layout task pane (refer to Figure 1-6).

Stealing slides from other presentations

Stealing is wrong, of course, except when stealing slides from other PowerPoint presentations. If slides you developed for another presentation will do the trick, don't hesitate to steal them:

1. **Select the slide that you want the new slide or slides to follow.**

2. **Choose Insert⇨Slides from Files to open the Slide Finder dialog box, shown in Figure 1-7.**

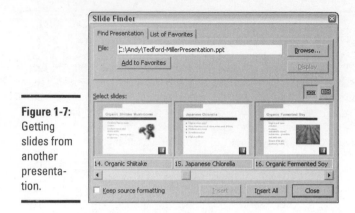

Figure 1-7:
Getting
slides from
another
presenta-
tion.

3. **Click the Browse button to open the Browse dialog box and select the PowerPoint presentation with the slides you want to steal.**

   Slides from the presentation appear in the Slide Finder dialog box.

4. **Select the files you need.**

   Click the Insert All button to grab all of them. Otherwise, Ctrl+click to select slides. You can click the unnamed buttons in the dialog box to see the slides in thumbnail or outline form.

5. **Click the Insert button to insert your slides in the presentation you're working on.**

All about summary slides

PowerPoint offers a command for creating a summary slide, although I'm not sure whether the command is worth very much. A *summary slide* is a slide that lists the titles of other slides in bullet points. Fans of summary slides put them at the start or end of presentations, but I think they're redundant. A presentation should end with a rock-solid conclusion, not a recap of what the audience just heard and saw, I believe, but of course you may disagree.

I'll let you be the judge of whether summary slides are worthwhile. Creating them (and deleting them) takes but a moment. Follow these steps to create a summary slide:

1. **Switch to Slide Sorter view, or, in Normal view, display the Slides tab.**

2. **Ctrl+click the slides whose titles you want for the bullet points on the summary slide.**

   If PowerPoint can't fit all the bullets on one slide, it creates two summary slides.

3. **Click the Summary Slide button on the Slide Sorter or Outlining toolbar (or press Alt+Shift+5).**

   The summary slide appears before the first slide you selected.

4. **Move the summary slide where you want it to be in the presentation.**

Slides that you copy this way adopt the slide design or color background of the presentation you're working on. Be sure to examine the slides to make sure that nothing on the new slides was lost, obscured, mutilated, or spindled by the new design. Dark backgrounds, for example, can sometimes obscure text. To copy slides with their designs intact, select the Keep Source Formatting check box in the Slide Finder dialog box.

Moving and Deleting Slides

As a presentation takes shape, you sometimes have to move a slide forward or backward in the presentation. And sometimes you have to delete a slide. To perform these relatively simple tasks, switch to Slide Sorter or Normal view and do the following:

✦ **Deleting a slide:** Click the slide and then press the Delete key or right-click it and choose Delete Slide.

✦ **Moving a slide:** Click the slide you want to move and drag it to a new position. A vertical line (in Slide Sorter view) or horizontal line (in Normal view) shows where the slide will land when you release the mouse button. With the Outline pane displayed, you can also move a slide by selecting it and clicking the Move Up or Move Down button on the Outlining toolbar.

In my experience, Slide Sorter view is best for moving slides around because you can grab the slides and move them more easily. You can move several slides simultaneously as long as they are next to each other. To select the slides, Ctrl+click them.

Hidden Slides for All Contingencies

Hide a slide when you want to keep it on hand "just in case." Hidden slides don't appear in slide shows, although you can see them in Normal view and Slide Sorter view, where their slide numbers are crossed through, and you can call on them for slide shows if you need them. Hide slides when you anticipate having to turn your presentation in a different direction — to answer a question from the audience, prove your point more thoroughly, or revisit a topic in more depth. Merely by right-clicking and choosing a couple of commands, you can display a hidden slide in the course of a slide show.

Put hidden slides at the end of the show so you know where to find them. Select a slide in the Slide pane or in Slide Sorter view and follow these instructions to hide it from the audience:

✦ Click the Hide Slide button. You will find this button on the Slide Sorter toolbar.

✦ Choose Slide Show➪Hide Slide.

✦ Right-click the slide and choose Hide Slide.

To "unhide" a slide, switch to Slide Sorter view, select the slide, and click the Hide Slide button on the Slide Sorter toolbar, or right-click and choose Hide Slide all over again.

Hidden slides don't appear during the course of a presentation, but suppose that the need arises to show one. Before showing a hidden slide, take careful note of which slide you're viewing now. You'll have to return to this slide after viewing the hidden slide. Then right-click the screen, choose Go to Slide, and select the hidden slide from the list of slides. You can tell which slides are hidden because their numbers are enclosed in parenthesis, as shown in Figure 1-8.

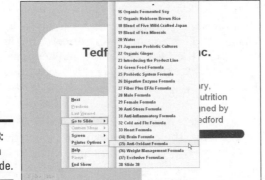

Figure 1-8:
Going to a
hidden slide.

If you look at only one hidden slide, you can right-click and choose Last Viewed on the shortcut menu to return to the slide you saw previous to the hidden slide. For that matter, you can put a Last Viewed Action button on the hidden slide and click it. See Chapter 4 for more about action buttons.

Chapter 2: Entering the Text

In This Chapter

- ✔ Getting the text from a Word outline
- ✔ Fitting text in frames
- ✔ Changing the look of text
- ✔ Writing the speaker notes
- ✔ Presenting lists and tables on slides

*I*t goes without saying, but you can't have much of a PowerPoint presentation without text. This chapter describes everything a mere mortal needs to know about putting the text on slides. It explains text frames, getting the text from a Word document, tending to the appearance of slide text, and putting lists and tables on slides. You also find out what speaker notes are, how they can assist you in giving a presentation, and how to enter and print the notes.

Entering Text on Slides

After you have decided what your presentation is all about, the next step is to enter the text on the slides. You can do that one slide at a time, or, if you're comfortable with Microsoft Word, import the presentation text from a Word document. Better keep reading.

The basics

As shown in Figure 2-1, the easiest way to enter text on slides is to click in a text frame and start typing where the placeholder frame is. The other way is to switch to Normal view, select the Outline tab to see the Outline pane, and enter text there. Text you type next to a slide icon in the Outline pane is made the title of the slide.

 To see formatting text in the Outline pane, click the Show Formatting button. When this button is selected, text that is boldfaced, italicized, and underlined in the presentation looks that way in the Outline pane as well.

On the outline pane   In a text frame

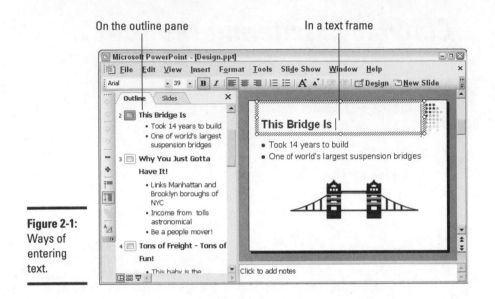

Figure 2-1:
Ways of
entering
text.

Getting the text from a Word outline

In Chapter 1 of this mini-book, I explain why starting in Word, not PowerPoint, is the best way to formulate a presentation. In Word, you can concentrate on developing a presentation without PowerPoint's many distractions. The makers of PowerPoint, it appears, agree with me. PowerPoint has a command for importing a Word outline into a presentation.

Book I, Chapter 8 explains how to work on an outline in Word. When you import the outline, you get one slide for each Level 1 heading (headings given the Heading 1 style) in the Word document. Paragraph text is not imported. Level 1 headings form the title of the slides. On the slides, Level 2 headings form first-level bullets, Level 3 headings form second-level bullets, and so on. Well, you get the picture, and if you don't, Figure 2-2 shows what a Word outline looks like after it lands in a PowerPoint presentation.

Follow these steps to use headings in a Word document as text for a PowerPoint presentation:

1. **Select the slide that the outline slides will follow if you want to insert the outline slides in the middle of a presentation.**

2. **Choose Insert➪Slides from Outline.**

   The Insert Outline dialog box opens.

3. **Locate and select the Word file you want to import; then click the Insert button.**

Each Level 1 heading becomes a slide.

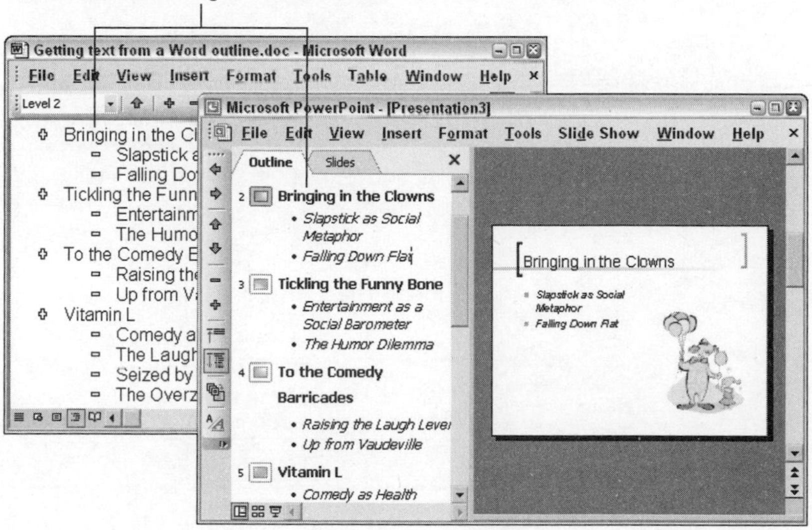

Figure 2-2:
A Word
outline (left)
imported
into a
presentation
(right).

Making Text Fit in Frames

When headings, paragraphs, and lists don't fit in a text frame, PowerPoint starts by shrinking the amount of space between lines. Then the program shrinks the text itself. You can tell when PowerPoint has shrunk the text because the AutoFit Options icon appears by the frame when the frame is selected. Click this icon and you get a menu of choices for handling the text, as shown in Figure 2-3.

Figure 2-3:
AutoFit
options.

Fixing a top-heavy headline

In typesetting terminology, a top-heavy headline is a headline in which the first line is much longer than the second. Whenever a headline runs to two lines, it runs the risk of being top-heavy. Unsightly top-heavy headlines look especially bad on PowerPoint slides, where text is blown up to 40-points or more. To fix a top-heavy headline, click where you prefer the lines to break and press Shift+Enter.

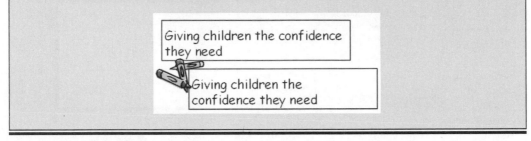

When text doesn't fit in a frame, the first question to ask yourself is, "Do I want to fool with the integrity of the slide design?" Making the text fit usually means shrinking the text, enlarging the text frame, or compromising the slide design in some way, but audiences notice design inconsistencies. Slides are shown on large screens where design flaws are easy to see. If heading text is shrunk on one slide and the heading frame is enlarged on the next one, the audience may notice the inconsistency and conclude that the presentation is the work of. . .an amateur!

Making text fit in a frame usually means making a compromise. Here are different ways to handle the problem of text not fitting in a frame. Be prepared to click the Undo button as you test these techniques:

✦ **Edit the text:** Usually when text doesn't fit in a frame, the text needs editing. It needs to be made shorter. A slide is not a place for a treatise. The words on the slide are supposed to tell the audience what you're talking about, not provide a full explanation. Editing the text is the only way to make it fit in the frame without compromising the design.

✦ **Enlarge the frame:** Click the AutoFit Options button and choose S̲top Fitting Text to Placeholder. Then select the frame and drag the bottom or top selection handle — the round white circle — to enlarge it.

 ✦ **Increase or decrease the font size:** The easiest way to change font sizes is to select the text and click the Increase Font Size or Decrease Font Size button as many times as necessary to make the text fit within the frame.

✦ **Change the frame's internal margins:** Similarly to the design of a page, text frames have internal margins to keep text from getting too close to the frame border. By shrinking these margins, you can make more room for text. Right-click the text frame and choose Format Placeholder. Then, on the Text Box tab of the Format Placeholder dialog box, enter smaller measurements for the margins.

✦ **Create a new slide for the text:** If you're dealing with a list or paragraph text, the AutoFit Options menu offers two ways to create a new slide. Choose Continue on a New Slide to run the text onto another slide; choose Split Text Between Two Slides to divide the text evenly between two slides. I don't recommend either option, though. If you need to make a new slide, do it on your own, and rethink how to present the material. Inserting a new slide to accommodate a long list throws a presentation off-track.

Making Your Own Text Frames

Intrepid travelers will be glad to know that you don't have to rely solely on the text frames in slide layouts. You can create text frames of your own. And PowerPoint permits you to turn an autoshape into a text frame as well. As Figure 2-4 shows, autoshape text frames are attractive and elegant.

Book III
Chapter 2

Entering the Text

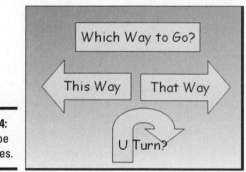

Figure 2-4:
Autoshape
text frames.

✦ **Text frame:** To insert a text frame of your own, choose Insert➪Text Box or click the Text Box button on the Drawing toolbar. The cursor changes into a cross-hair. Click and drag to draw the frame.

✦ **Autoshape:** To insert an autoshape, click the AutoShapes button on the Drawing toolbar and, on the pop-up menu, choose the kind of shape you want and then the shape itself from the submenu. Drag on the slide to draw the shape.

Click in a text box or autoshape and start typing to enter the text. Book VIII explains all the details of changing the size, the color, or the border of a text frame or autoshape. The Increase Font Size and Decrease Font Size buttons come in very handy when you are trying to make text fit in a text box or autoshape.

Changing the Look of Text

Most of the text-formatting commands that you know and love in Microsoft Word are also available in PowerPoint. These options are available in the Font dialog box, which you can open by choosing Format⇨Font. You can also take advantage of these text-formatting shortcuts:

✦ **Changing fonts:** Select the text and choose an option from the Font drop-down menu on the Formatting toolbar.

 ✦ **Changing font size:** Select the text and choose an option on the Font Size drop-down menu. For your convenience, you can also click the Increase Font Size or Decrease Font Size buttons until the text is just-so.

✦ **Choosing character styles:** Click the Bold, Italic, Underline, or Shadow button to change the look of the letters.

 ✦ **Changing the color of text:** Select the text, open the Font Color button's menu, and select a color.

✦ **Changing case:** Case refers to whether letters are upper- or lowercase. Press Shift+F as many times as necessary until the letters are the right case: Sentence case, lowercase, UPPERCASE, or Title Case. You can also choose Format⇨Change Case and make a choice in the Change Case dialog box.

To quickly change fonts throughout a presentation, PowerPoint offers the Format⇨Replace Fonts command. Going to the Slide Master is another way to change fonts throughout a presentation (see Chapter 3 of this mini-book).

All about Speaker Notes

Notes, also known as *speaker notes,* are printed pages that you carry to a presentation to remind yourself what to say while each slide is on-screen. Notes are strictly for the speaker. They are not for the unwashed masses. Don't hesitate to write notes to yourself as you put together your presentation. The notes may come in handy when you are delivering your presentation and you run out of things to say. Some people hand out speaker notes after the presentation instead of handouts.

Follow these instructions to enter notes:

Notes...

✦ **In Normal view:** Type the notes in the Notes pane, as shown in Figure 2-5.

✦ **In Slide Sorter view:** Select the slide that needs a note, click the <u>N</u>otes button on the Slide Sorter toolbar, and type a note in the Speaker Notes dialog box, as shown in Figure 2-5.

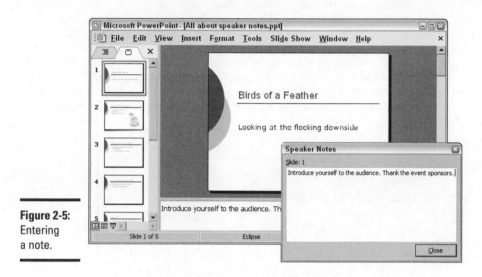

Figure 2-5:
Entering
a note.

To refer to the notes you have written, follow these instructions:

✦ **Viewing notes on-screen:** Select the slide whose notes need your attention and choose <u>V</u>iew➪Note<u>s</u> Page. The notes appear on a page along with the slide to which they refer. This is what the page will look like when you print it. Choose 75% or 100% from the Zoom menu to be able to read the notes.

✦ **Printing the notes pages:** Choose <u>F</u>ile➪<u>P</u>rint and, in the Print dialog box, select Notes Pages from the Print <u>W</u>hat drop-down list. You get one notes page for each slide in your presentation.

Similarly to the Slide Master, PowerPoint offers the Notes Master for laying out notes pages. Choose <u>V</u>iew➪<u>M</u>aster➪Notes Master to see the Notes Master. From the master, you can enter headers and footers for notes pages and decide for yourself which fonts and font sizes to use.

Fans of Microsoft Word will be glad to know that you can save notes and slide thumbnails in a Word file. Choose <u>F</u>ile➪Sen<u>d</u> To➪Microsoft Office <u>W</u>ord. In the Send to Microsoft Office Word dialog box, select one of the Notes options and click OK. Microsoft Word opens a file with the notes and slides. Save the file and print it.

**Book III
Chapter 2**

Entering the Text

Making a Numbered or Bulleted List

Everybody knows how to make a numbered or bulleted list: Click the Numbering or Bullets button and start typing. Each time you press Enter, a new bullet or number appears. To make a list out of text you've already entered, select the text and click the Numbering or Bullets button.

So much for conventional numbers and bullets. You will be glad to know that PowerPoint permits you to toy with bullets and numbers to create lists like the ones in Figure 2-6. To create an out-of-the-ordinary list, select the list if you've already entered it and choose Format⇨Bullets and Numbering. In the Bullets and Numbering dialog box, go to the Bulleted or Numbered tab to beautify your list:

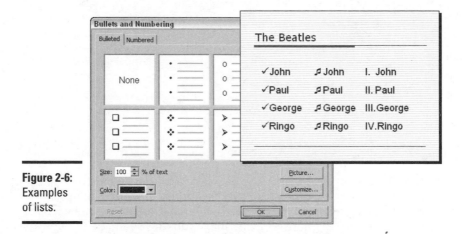

Figure 2-6:
Examples
of lists.

✦ **Bulleted list:** Choose a bullet on the Bulleted tab (this is where I got the check marks in Figure 2-6). If the choices don't suit you, click the Picture button to open the Picture Bullet dialog box and select small clip-art bullets; or click the Customize button to open the Symbol dialog box and select a symbol for the bullets (this is where I got the musical notes in Figure 2-6).

✦ **Numbered list:** On the Numbered tab, choose letters, Roman numerals, or another numbering scheme (notice the Roman numerals in Figure 2-6). Enter a number in the Start At box to resume numbering a list that starts on one slide and continues on another.

✦ **Changing the size of bullets and numbers:** Enter a percentage in the Size % of Text box to change the size of bullets or numbers relative to the text in the list. Entering 200, for example, makes bullets twice as big as the text.

+ **Changing the color of bullets and numbers:** Open the Color drop-down menu and select a color.

Putting Tables on Slides

Tables are excellent for strengthening an argument. Everyone in the audience who sees the table data on-screen can see that the data confirms your ideas. However, the easiest and best way to create a table is to forsake PowerPoint and do it in Word or Excel. Those programs offer many more commands for formatting and decorating tables than PowerPoint does.

The techniques for creating a table will be very, very familiar if you have spent any time in Word (Book I, Chapter 5 explains how to create tables in Word). Here are the ways to create a table:

+ **Starting from a placeholder:** PowerPoint offers 12 slide layouts with Insert Table placeholders for inserting a table. Click the Insert table placeholder icon on one of these layouts; the Insert Table dialog box appears. In the dialog box, enter the number of columns and rows you want and click OK.

+ **Inserting a table:** Choose Insert⇨Table to create a table on a slide that doesn't offer a convenient Insert Table placeholder. You see the Insert Table dialog box, where you enter the number of columns and rows you want.

**Book III
Chapter 2**

+ **Insert table button:** Click the Insert Table button, drag out the menu to the number of rows and columns you want, and let go of the mouse button.

Entering the Text

+ **Drawing a table:** Click the Draw Table button on the Tables and Borders toolbar and, when the cursor changes into a pencil, draw the table borders. If you make a mistake, click the Eraser button and drag over the parts of the table that you don't want.

+ **Copying a table from Word or Excel:** In Word or Excel, select the table data, choose Edit⇨Copy, and, on the PowerPoint slide, click and choose Edit⇨Paste.

Word's Table⇨Table AutoFormat command can come in very handy when you want a table for a PowerPoint slide. Autoformats save you the trouble of formatting tables and are very sophisticated. However, if you use them — and I recommend it highly — make sure that you choose the same autoformat design for all the tables in your presentation. Doing so gives the slides a uniform appearance, which in turn lends an overall professional look to your presentation.

Chapter 3: Advanced Formatting Techniques

The purpose of this chapter is to help your slide presentations stand out in a crowd. The chapter explains how to stretch the slide designs and color schemes that come with PowerPoint just a little bit further. You discover how to alter the color schemes and slide designs, get a professional look for your presentations with Slide Masters, handle footers, and make your presentations a little more dramatic with transitions and animations.

Changing or Tweaking a Slide Design or Color Scheme

Chapter 1 of this mini-book explains how you can click the Design button on the Formatting toolbar and choose a new slide design or color scheme from the Slide Design task pane. You can do that no matter how far along you are in constructing your presentation. The new slide design will take over from the old one, even if it means obscuring text or rendering graphics invisible. New slide designs usually change the background of slides. That can have untoward consequences.

Besides changing slide designs or color schemes, you can alter the designs or color schemes themselves by following these instructions:

✦ **Choosing a new background color:** Choose Format➪Background or right-click a slide in the presentation and choose Background. You see the Background dialog box, shown in Figure 3-1. Open the Background Fill drop-down menu and choose a new color or fill effect. Choose Automatic if you want to restore the slide design to its original background color.

✦ **Changing the color scheme:** Click the Design button to display the Slide Design task pane; then select the Color Schemes link. The Slide Design task pane shows color schemes. If none suits you, click the Edit Color Schemes link. You see the Custom tab of the Edit Color Scheme dialog box. From here, you can select a part of the color scheme, click the Change Color button to open the Background Color dialog box, and select a new color.

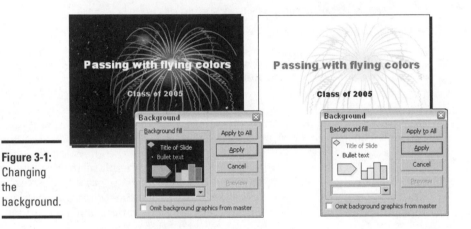

Figure 3-1:
Changing
the
background.

✦ **Changing the fonts:** The only way to change fonts in a slide design is to go to a master slide. Font changes made to the Slide Master slide are made to all slides except title slides; font changes made to the Title Master slide show up on all title slides. Choose View⇨Master⇨Slide Master to fiddle with master slides. Later in this chapter, "Slide Masters for Consistent Formatting" explains how to handle master slides.

Overriding the Slide Design or Color Scheme

Changing fonts, background colors, and whatnot on a single slide is simply a matter of switching to Normal view, going to the slide, and making the changes. To choose a different slide design or color scheme for a handful of slides in a presentation, not the whole shebang, follow these steps:

1. **Switch to Slide Sorter view.**

2. **Ctrl+click to select the slides that need a different slide design or new color scheme.**

3. **Click the Design button.**

The Slide Design task pane appears.

4. **Select a new slide design, or click the Color Schemes link and choose a new color scheme.**

The previous section of this chapter explains a bunch of ways to change the appearance of slides.

Slide Masters for Consistent Formatting

Consistency is everything in a PowerPoint presentation. The secret to a good layout is to make sure that the fonts and font sizes on slides are consistent from one slide to the next, that the text boxes for headings are relatively the same size, and that bulleted lists are formatted the same. If the corner of each slide is to show a company logo, the logo needs to appear in the same position on each slide.

To make slides consistent with one another, PowerPoint offers the Slide Masters. A Slide Master is similar to a Word template. Formatting changes made to a Slide Master are made as well to the slides that use the Slide Master as the basis for their design. Drop a logo or other image in the corner of a Slide Master, for example, and the logo appears as well on all slides that are governed by the Slide Master. To put slide numbers, footers, the date — anything that might appear on every slide in a presentation — on slides, insert them on a Slide Master.

When you click the New Slide button and choose a layout for a slide, you make either the Slide Master or the Title Master the basis for your new slide. The majority of slides are governed by the Slide Master, because the majority of slides are not title slides. Here's the lowdown on the Slide Master and Title Master:

✦ **Slide Master:** The master for all slides *except* those assigned the Title Slide layout, the layout designed for the introductory slide. Figure 3-2 shows a Slide Master. It has placeholders for entering a slide number, the date, and a footer. The placeholder text shows which font and font size is used for slide titles, first-level bulleted lists, second-level bulleted lists, and so on. By changing one of these fonts, you change fonts on all slides that the Slide Master governs. Drop a company logo onto this slide and it will appear on all slides except the title slide.

Book III Chapter 3

Advanced Formatting Techniques

Select the Slide Master or Title Master.

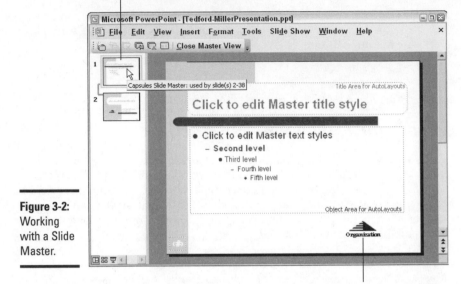

Figure 3-2:
Working
with a Slide
Master.

This graphic appears on all slides.

✦ **Title Master:** The master for slides assigned the Title Slide layout, the first layout in the Apply Slide Layout task pane. Most presentations have only one title slide, but some people use more than one to mark when a new stage of the presentation is forthcoming. If more than one slide in your presentation has been assigned the Title Slide layout, you can go to the Title Master, make formatting changes to it, and rest assured that your changes will appear on all title slides.

The following pages explain how to change formats on a Slide Master, apply Slide Master formats to slides, and create more than one Slide Master for a presentation.

Changing formats on the Slide Master

Follow these steps to open the Slide Master or Title Master and make formatting changes there:

1. **Choose View⇨Master⇨Slide Master.**

Slide Master thumbnails appear on the task pane (refer to Figure 3-2).

2. **Move the mouse pointer over a thumbnail to see which is the Slide Master and which is the Title Master.**

A pop-up box tells you the name of the slide design you are working on, whether the slide is the Slide Master or the Title Master, and how many slides in the presentation are title slides or normal slides.

3. **Select the Slide Master or the Title Master in the task pane.**

    Which slide you choose depends, of course, on whether you want to alter the appearance of a title slide or the other slides in your presentation.

4. **Change formats on the slide, insert a logo graphic, change the size of text frames, or do whatever it is you want done to slides throughout your presentation.**

    When you're finished doing your masterful work, click the Close Master View button or switch to Normal or Slide Sorter view.

Here are some other things worth knowing when it comes to Slide Masters:

✦ **Dealing with placeholder frames:** To remove a placeholder frame, select it and press the Delete button. Many people, for example, remove the Date Area, Footer Area, or Number Area to make room for a graphic or logo. If you remove a frame but regret doing so, click the Master Layout button or choose Format➪Master Layout and, in the Master Layout dialog box, select the name of the frame you regret deleting: Title, Text, Date, Slide Number, or Footer.

✦ **Working with footers:** To handle the footer along the bottom of slides — the Date Area, Footer Area, and Number Area — choose View➪Header and Footer. In the misnamed Header and Footer dialog box (misnamed because there are no headers on slides), enter the date, a footer, or slide numbers along the bottom of slides. Later in this chapter, "Handling Footers" takes up this subject in detail.

✦ **Getting the original design back:** When you change formats on a Slide Master, you are really tinkering with the slide design itself. Suppose that you regret tinkering with the design and you want the original design back? The only way to start all over with an original slide design is to choose a new design in the Slide Design task plane and immediately choose your original design a second time. Doing so has the effect of washing away all the changes you made on the Slide Master and Title Master of a presentation.

Removing a Slide Master item from one slide

The beauty of Slide Masters is that they permit you to put the same item — a company logo, a slide number, the date — on all the slides in a presentation and rest assured that the items will appear in the same place on each slide. Sometimes, however, Slide Master items get in the way. They occupy valuable space that you need for a chart. They clash with the clip-art illustration on the slide.

Applying Slide Master formats to formatted slides

If you change formats on an individual slide, PowerPoint assumes that you want the slide to stand out from the crowd, and it breaks the connection between the individual slide and its Slide Master. Thereafter if you make a change to the Slide Master, the change does not translate to the individual slide whose formats you changed, because that slide, PowerPoint reasons, is supposed to stand apart from the rest. Suppose, however, that you want a slide whose formats you changed to adopt the formats of a Slide Master. Follow these steps to reapply the formats on a Slide Master to a rebel slide:

1. **Select the slide. To select more than one slide, switch to Slide Sorter view and Ctrl+click the slides.**

2. **Choose Format⇨Slide Layout to display the Slide Layout task pane.**

3. **Find the slide layout that you applied originally to the slide or slides, open the layout's drop-down menu, and choose Reapply Layout.**

   Now the formats on the Slide Master, whatever they happen to be, whether you altered them or not, are applied to the slide or slides you selected.

PowerPoint offers two ways to remove Slide Master elements from a single slide:

✦ **Removing the footer and all Master Slide graphics:** Select the slide, choose Format⇨Background, and, in the Background dialog box, select the Omit Background Graphics from Master check box. Then click the Apply button.

✦ **Covering up the item:** With this technique, you block out the item. Click the Rectangle button on the Drawing toolbar and draw a rectangle over the item. Next, open the Fill Color menu on the Drawing toolbar and choose the same color that appears on the slide background. Finally, open the Line Color drop-down menu on the Drawing toolbar and choose No Line.

Working with more than one Slide Master

Sometimes a presentation can do with more than one Slide Master. Suppose, for example, that a sales presentation imparts "upside" and "downside" information. To help the audience distinguish between optimistic upside slides and their pessimistic downside counterparts, you can create an additional two Slide Masters, a rose-colored one called "Upside" and a murky green one called "Downside." This way, the audience will know immediately which side's views you are presenting when you display a new slide.

To prevent more than one Slide Master from being created, or for that matter to create more than one Slide Master if you are unable to create them, choose Tools➪Options, and, on the Edit tab of the Options dialog box, check or uncheck the Multiple Masters check box.

Creating a new Slide Master

To begin with, all slides in a presentation are associated with a single Title Master or Slide Master, but you can follow these steps to create secondary Slide Masters:

1. **Choose View➪Master➪Slide Master.**

2. **In the task pane, select the Slide Master thumbnail if you want to create a new Slide Master; select the Title Master thumbnail to create a new Title Master.**

3. **Choose Insert➪New Slide Master or click the Insert New Slide Master button.**

To insert a New Title Master, click the Insert New Title Master button. A new Slide Master or Title Master thumbnail appears in the task pane and the master itself appears in the window.

4. **Format the new Slide Master.**

You can call upon any formatting command you desire. To choose a slide design or color scheme for your new Slide Master, choose Format➪Slide Design and select the design or color scheme in the Slide Design task pane.

Another way to create a new Slide Master is to duplicate one that is already there and then change the duplicate's formats. In the task plane, select the Slide Master that needs duplicating and choose Insert➪Duplicate Slide Master. You can then rename the duplicate, as I describe shortly.

Assigning slides to a Slide Master

No slide can serve two masters. When a presentation includes more than one Slide Master or Title Master, you have to tell PowerPoint which master to assign to your slides. Follow these steps to assign a slide or slides to a Slide Master:

1. **Select the slide or slides.**

2. **Click the Design button to open the Slide Design task pane.**

3. **Under "Used in This Presentation," open the drop-down menu for the Slide Master you want to assign the slide or slides; then choose Apply to Selected Slides on the drop-down menu**

Doing this, that, and the other to Slide Masters

Here is some other stuff you may or may not need to know about working with more than one Slide Master:

+ **Renaming Slide Masters:** A newly made Slide Master is given the name "Custom Design," but you can give it a more descriptive name. To do so, select the slide, click the Rename Master button, and enter a new name in the Rename Master dialog box.

+ **Deleting a Slide Master:** Select the Slide Master and click the Delete Master button. Slides that were assigned the Slide Master you deleted are assigned to the first or only Slide Master in the Slide Master task pane.

Handling Footers

A footer is a line of text that appears at the foot, or bottom, of a slide. Figure 3-3 shows a footer and the dialog box for entering footers. Typically, a footer includes the date, a company name, and a slide number. The Slide Master includes frames for entering those very same items. Except for slide numbers, however, I don't recommend putting anything in the footer. Footers crowd slides and distract the audience from gazing at the slide itself.

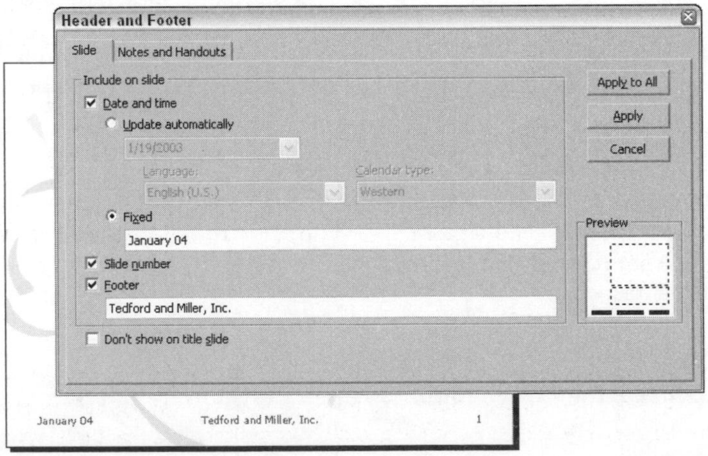

Figure 3-3: Entering a footer.

PowerPoint has a special command, View⇨Header and Footer, for entering the date, a word or two of text, and the slide number in footers. To put other items in footers, do so on your own by going to a Slide Master, drawing a text box, and placing the text box near the bottom of the slide (see "Slide Masters for Consistent Formatting," earlier in this chapter).

To enter a footer with PowerPoint's help, choose View⇨Header and Footer. You see the Header and Footer dialog box (refer to Figure 3-3) and its self-explanatory options. Keep your eye on the Preview window. It shows what your footer will look like.

Here are some things that are worth knowing as you play footsy with PowerPoint slides:

✦ **Adjusting the position of footer items:** To change where footer items are on the page, you have to go to a Slide Master. Choose View⇨Master⇨ Slide Master and select the Slide Master or Title Master thumbnail. Then drag the text frames in the footer to new locations.

✦ **Removing a footer from the first slide:** Choose View⇨Header and Footer, and, in the Header and Footer dialog box (refer to Figure 3-3), select the Don't Show on Title Slide check box. To remove a text box from footers that you placed there yourself, choose View⇨Master⇨ Slide Master, select the Title Master thumbnail, select the item you want to remove, and press the Delete key.

✦ **Removing the footers from slides:** Select the slides from which you want to remove footers, choose Format⇨Background, and, in the Background dialog box, check the Omit Background Graphics from Master check box. Then click the Apply to All button. However, this command also removes graphics on the Master Slide. It removes everything except the title placeholder and text placeholder.

Transitions and Animations

In PowerPoint-speak, a *transition* is a little bit of excitement that occurs as one slide leaves the screen and the next slide climbs aboard. An *animation* is movement on the slide. For example, you can animate bulleted lists on slides such that the bullet points appear on-screen one at a time when you click the mouse, rather than all at one time.

Before you know anything about transitions and animations, you should know that they can be distracting. The purpose of a presentation is to communicate with the audience, not display the latest, busiest, most dazzling presentation technology. For kiosk presentations, however, eye-catching transitions and animations can be useful, because they draw an audience (a kiosk-style presentation is one that plays on its own, as I explain in Chapter 5 of this mini-book). For audiences that enjoy high-tech wizardry, transitions and animations can be a lot of fun and add to a presentation.

Showing transitions between slides

Transitions include the dissolve, the wipe up, and the cover down. Don't worry, you get a chance to test-drive these transitions before you attach them to slides. Follow these steps to show transitions between slides:

1. **Switch to Slide Sorter view.**

2. **Click the Transition button or choose Slide Show⇨Slide Transition.**

| Transition |

The Slide Transition task pane appears, as shown in Figure 3-4.

Flying star icon   Choose a transition

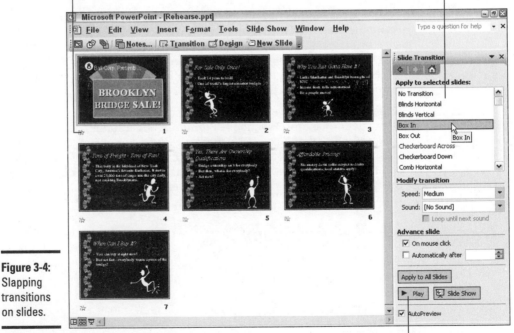

Figure 3-4:
Slapping
transitions
on slides.

Click to test transitions

3. **Select the slides that need transitions; or, to run transitions throughout your presentation, click the Apply to All Slides button or press Ctrl+A.**

4. **Select a transition in the Apply to Selected Slides menu.**

As soon as you choose a transition, the slide or slides you selected "transition" — they demonstrate the transition you chose. Click the Play button to see the transition again. Experiment with different transitions until you find Mr. Right.

Choose the same transition for all the slides, unless your goal is to make a wacky presentation. Transitions already call attention to themselves. Assigning a different transition to each slide has the effect of turning the audience's attention away from you and toward transitions.

5. **On the Speed menu, choose a speed for the transition — Slow, Medium, or Fast.**

Again, the slides demonstrate how fast or slow these options are.

6. **To play a sound during a transition, select the sound from the Sound menu.**

These canned sounds can be distracting, however, so choose wisely, or, better yet, don't choose a sound unless you are working on a kiosk presentation.

A flying star icon appears with slides that have been assigned transitions (the star appears as well with slides that have been animated). To remove a transition from slides, select them in Slide Sorter view, click the Transition button, and choose No Transition on the Apply to Selected Slides menu in the Slide Transition task pane.

Animating parts of a slide

When it comes to animations, you can choose between animation schemes, the pre-built special effects made by the elves of the Microsoft Corporation, or customized animations that you build on your own. Only fans of animation and people with a lot of time on their hands go the second route.

Choosing an animation scheme

Follow these steps to preview and choose an animation scheme for slides:

1. **In Normal view, select the slide or slides that need an animation scheme.**

2. **Choose Slide Show⇨Animation Schemes.**

   The Slide Design task pane opens, except that now it lists animation schemes, as shown in Figure 3-5. If you scroll down the list of schemes, you will see that they fall into these categories: Subtle, Moderate, and Exciting.

3. **Select an animation scheme.**

   As soon as you select a scheme, the on-screen slide is "animated." Click the Play button to see the scheme again. Keep trying animations until you find the one that suits you.

   The flying star icon appears beside animated slides in Slide Sorter view and on the Slide pane in Normal view (the star also appears next to slides that have been assigned a transition). To "unanimate" a slide, select it, choose Slide Show⇨Animation Schemes, and choose No Animation in the Slide Design task pane.

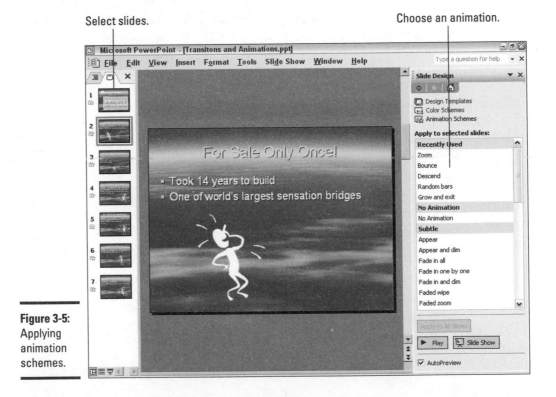

Figure 3-5: Applying animation schemes.

Fashioning your own animation scheme

To fashion an animation scheme of your own, you tell PowerPoint what part of the slide you want to animate, how you want to animate that part, in which order the different parts of the slides are animated, and how long each animation lasts.

To start, select a slide in Normal view and choose Slide Show⇨Custom Animation. Then click the slide to select which part to animate, click the Add Effect button, and choose options in the Custom Animation task pane. Which options you get depends on what kind of animation you're dealing with.

Chapter 4: Making Your Presentation Livelier

*T*his chapter is dedicated to the proposition that no presentation should be a dull one. It explains how to decorate slides with clip-art images and pictures and use charts to bolster your argument. You find out what action buttons are and how you can use them to get quickly from slide to slide. Finally, this chapter tells how to make a PowerPoint presentation resemble a radio or television station. It explains how to grace slides with music or play video on slides.

Putting a Picture or Clip-Art Image on a Slide

It goes without saying, but a picture or clip-art image makes an excellent addition to a slide. Company logos, digital photographs of company events, and illustrative clip-art images make a presentation livelier. They are a welcome contrast to the headlines and bulleted lists that comprise the majority of slides in presentations. Figure 4-1 shows an example of a clip-art image on a slide.

Book VIII explains more than a mortal needs to know about putting a picture or clip-art image in a PowerPoint presentation or other Office file. Meanwhile, here are the basics of inserting a picture or clip-art image:

✦ **Inserting a picture:** Click the Insert Picture placeholder icon if one is available on the slide you're working on. Otherwise, click the Insert Picture button on the Drawing toolbar or choose Insert➪Picture➪ From File. In the Insert Picture dialog box, locate and select the picture you want and click the Insert button.

✦ **Inserting a clip-art image:** Click the Insert Clip Art icon if one is located on the slide you're working on. Otherwise, click the Insert Clip Art button on the Drawing toolbar or choose Insert➪Picture➪Clip Art. The Clip Art task pane opens. Find a clip-art image you like and double-click it.

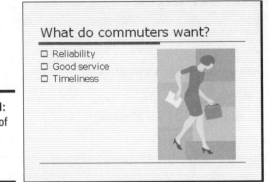

What do commuters want?

☐ Reliability
☐ Good service
☐ Timeliness

Figure 4-1:
Example of
a clip-art
image on
a slide.

Can't make up your mind which picture or clip-art image you want? You can park images in the gray area outside the slide and in so doing be able to compare and contrast them. Simply delete the images you don't want when you're finished comparing and contrasting.

Here are some helpful hints when it comes to handling pictures and clip-art images on a PowerPoint slide:

✦ **Positioning the object:** As you probably know, you can drag a clip-art image or picture to change its location on a slide. Objects "snap to the grid" as you move them. That is, they fall into place along the grid, but you can move objects without the grid interfering by pressing the Alt key as you move them. (The sidebar "The grid and drawing guides" explains the grid.)

✦ **Changing an object's size:** Drag a selection handle — a circle at the corner or side of an object — to change its size or shape. Drag a corner handle and the object maintains its proportions; drag a side handle to stretch or scrunch the object.

✦ **Handling objects that overlap:** Select one of the overlapping objects, right-click it, choose Order, and choose an option on the submenu. Select different objects in the stack and play with the Order commands — Bring to Front, Send to Back, Bring Forward, Send Backward — until you get it right.

✦ **Putting the same graphic on every page:** To put a company logo or other image on the corner of each slide in a presentation, place the image on a master slide. See "Master Slides for Consistent Formatting," in Chapter 3 of this mini-book.

✦ **Changing clip-art colors:** Often the colors in clip-art images don't sit well with the colors in the slide design you're using, but you can fix that. As long as the clip-art image you're working with is a Windows Metafile (.wmf) image, you can alter its colors. (To quickly find out whether you're dealing with a .wmf image, right-click it and choose Save As Picture. In the Save As Picture dialog box, glance at the Save As Type menu to see which kind of file it is and then click the Cancel button.)

To change colors, right-click the image and choose Show Picture Toolbar. On the Picture toolbar, click the Recolor Picture button. You see the Recolor Picture dialog box, where you can trade an original color in the clip-art image for a color of your choosing, as shown in Figure 4-2.

The grid and drawing guides

The grid is an invisible set of horizontal and vertical lines to which objects — clip-art images, pictures, shapes, and autoshapes — cling when you move them on a slide. The grid is meant to help objects line up squarely with one another. As you drag an object, it sticks to the nearest grid line. Besides the grid, PowerPoint offers the drawing guides for aligning objects. These guides divide a slide into vertical and horizontal planes.

When you want to align or place objects with precision, display the grid and the drawing guides with one of these commands:

✔ Click the Show/Hide Grid button.

✔ Press Shift+F9.

✔ Choose View⇨Grid and Guides and, in the Grid and Guides dialog box, select the Display Grid on Screen and Display Drawing Guides on Screen check boxes. Choose an option from the Spacing menu to draw a tighter or looser grid.

Even if the Snap Objects to Grid check box in the Grid and Guides dialog box is selected, you can move objects without them snapping to a gridline by holding down the Alt key as you drag.

Select the Snap Objects to Other Objects check box if you want shapes to abut each other or fall along a common axis.

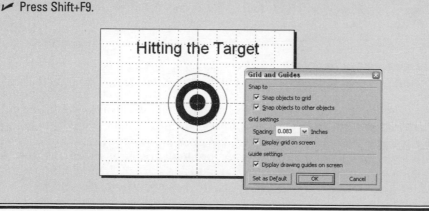

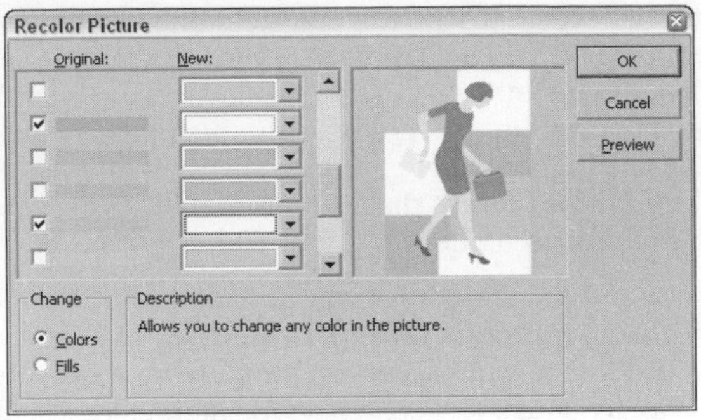

Figure 4-2:
Choosing
new colors
for clip art.

Putting Charts in Slides

Nothing is more persuasive than a chart. The bars, the pie slices, or the columns show the audience instantaneously that production is up or down, that cats are better than dogs or dogs better than cats, or that catsup tastes better than ketchup. Aficionados of Excel will be glad to know that putting an Excel chart on a PowerPoint slide is easy. And if you're not adept at Excel, you can use an auxiliary program called Microsoft Graph — it comes with Office — to create charts.

Don't pack too much information into a chart. It's hard for an audience to make sense of a crowded chart with too many bars, pie charts, or columns. And, as nice as three-dimensional charts are on paper, they can turn a simple chart into a maze when they're shown on the big screen.

Creating a chart in PowerPoint

A chart is constructed from data of some kind — Elvis sightings in Memphis, precipitation in Barstow, annual sales posted by different salespeople. The first step in creating a chart is to enter the data so that Microsoft Graph knows how wide or tall or thick to make the pie slices or bars or columns. With that done, you can tend to the chart's appearance.

Entering the raw data

Following are methods for starting the Microsoft Graph program and entering the data for the chart.

To construct a chart, click the Insert Chart placeholder icon if one is on the slide you're working with; otherwise, click the Insert Chart button or choose Insert⇨Chart. The Microsoft Graph program opens, as shown in Figure 4-3. Notice the new buttons on the Standard and Formatting toolbars. You, my friend, are in a new program. The Datasheet is for entering the data on which the chart is based. Click the View Datasheet button if you don't see the Datasheet.

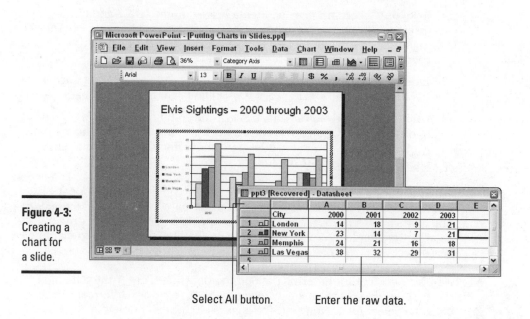

Figure 4-3:
Creating a
chart for
a slide.

Select All button.   Enter the raw data.

Enter the data you want to plot in the chart in the Datasheet. For now, don't worry about whether data appears in the right place on the chart. Later, I show you how to rearrange the various parts of a chart. Observe these technicalities as you enter the data; then, click outside the Datasheet and graph when you're done:

✦ **Entering the numbers:** Click in a cell — the place where a column and row intersect — and enter data or descriptive labels.

✦ **Formatting numbers:** Select numbers in the datasheet and click a Style button on the Formatting toolbar (Currency Style, Percent Style, or Comma Style) to change number formats. To increase or decrease the number of decimal places in a number, click the Increase Decimal or Decrease Decimal button.

✦ **Changing the width of columns:** If a row isn't wide enough to show data, you see scientific notation instead of numbers. To make a column wider, move to the top row of the datasheet, place the cursor on the divider line between letters, and click and drag toward the right when you see the two-headed arrow.

✦ **Deleting data, columns, and rows:** Drag across data and then press the Delete key to delete data. To delete an entire row or column, right-click its number or letter in the datasheet and choose Delete.

✦ **Inserting a column or row:** Right-click a column letter and choose Insert to insert a new column to the left of the column you right-clicked. Right-click a row number and choose Insert to insert a new row. The row appears above the row whose number you clicked.

✦ **Enlarging the datasheet:** Move the pointer to the lower-right corner of the datasheet and start dragging when you see the double-headed arrow.

✦ **Excluding data from the chart:** Select the column(s) or row(s) you want to exclude by dragging over their letters or numbers; then, choose Data⇨ Exclude Row/Col. To re-include a row or column that you excluded, choose Data⇨Include Row/Col.

When you want to edit a chart, double-click it. The Datasheet appears so that you can fool with the numbers and other data. A chart is an embedded object. As such, you can move it to a new position on-screen or drag one of its selection handles to change its size (Book VIII explains how to manipulate objects).

Here's a shortcut for entering data on the Datasheet: Enter the data in a Word table or Excel worksheet, select the data, return to Microsoft Graph, click the Select All button (refer to Figure 4-3), press the Delete key, and choose Edit⇨Paste. Your data appears in the Datasheet.

Tending to the chart's appearance

Getting it right the first time isn't easy when you're dealing with charts. Fortunately, Microsoft Graph offers about a hundred different ways to tinker with a chart's appearance and change the way that charts are laid out.

To tinker with a chart, double-click it to open Microsoft Graph and then either click buttons on the Standard toolbar or choose Chart⇨Chart Options to open the Chart Options dialog box shown in Figure 4-4. As you experiment with the different settings in the dialog box, watch the chart — the dialog box shows your chart and how it is affected by the settings you choose. Follow these instructions to make your chart just so:

✦ **Choosing a new chart type:** Open the drop-down menu on the Chart Type button and choose a new type of chart. Microsoft Graph offers pie charts, bar charts, area charts, column charts, and spider charts, among other types.

✦ **Changing the column data series orientation:** Click the By Column or By Row button on the Standard toolbar to reorient the graph and change which data appears in the legend and how values and categories are plotted.

✦ **Displaying or hiding the gridlines:** Gridlines mark value amounts. Click the Category Axis Gridlines and Value Axis Gridlines buttons on the Standard toolbar to see or display gridlines.

✦ **Handling legends, titles, and labels:** Click the Legend button on the Standard toolbar to display or hide the *legend,* the box on the graph that describes what is being plotted on the graph. To enter category and value names on your chart, choose <u>C</u>hart⇨Chart Opt<u>i</u>ons, select the Titles tab in the Chart Options dialog box, and enter the names.

✦ **Changing the chart's appearance:** A chart is composed of different areas — the category axis and chart area, among others. To change the look of an area, either click to select it or choose its name on the Chart Objects drop-down menu. Then double-click. The Format dialog box appears so that you can choose new borders, colors, fonts, or whatever for your chart.

Click the View Datasheet button to remove the datasheet from the screen and be able to see the chart better. Click the button again if you need to see the datasheet and edit the data from which the chart is plotted.

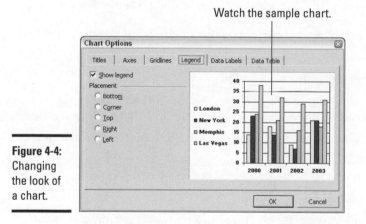

Figure 4-4:
Changing
the look of
a chart.

Getting a chart from an Excel worksheet

If you are fortunate enough to be adept at Excel, you will be glad to know that bringing an Excel chart into a PowerPoint presentation is a piece of cake. Of all the Office programs, Excel is best at creating charts. Book IV, Chapter 5 explains how to create an Excel chart.

To get a chart from Excel, select it in Excel, choose Edit⇨Copy (or press Ctrl+C), select a slide in PowerPoint, choose Edit⇨Paste (or press Ctrl+V). Charts arrive as what Office calls an *embedded object*, a pictorial representation of data (don't you hate computer terminology?). An embedded object is only a picture; it has no relationship to the data from which it was created. Being a picture, you can move an embedded object around by dragging, or change its shape by dragging a selection handle.

Action Buttons for Going from Slide to Slide

An *action button* is a handy button, usually found in a corner of a slide, that you may click to go elsewhere in a presentation. Action buttons are especially useful in kiosk-style presentations (Chapter 5 explains what those are). PowerPoint offers action buttons for going to the next slide, the previous slide, the first or last slide in a presentation, the last slide you viewed, or a specific slide. Figure 4-5 shows some action buttons and the dialog box where action buttons are born. Rather than click action buttons, you can tell PowerPoint to activate them when the mouse pointer moves over them.

Select the slide that needs action and follow these steps to adorn it with an action button:

1. Display the Action Buttons toolbar.

AutoShapes▾ To do so, either choose Slide Show⇨Action Buttons or click the AutoShapes button on the Drawing toolbar and choose Action Buttons.

2. Study the buttons carefully and click the one that best illustrates the action you want to take.

The pointer changes to a cross-hair cursor.

3. Draw the button on the slide.

To do so, drag the cross-hair cursor in a diagonal fashion. The Action Settings dialog box (refer to Figure 4-5) appears when you finish dragging.

4. Select the Mouse Over tab if you want to activate the button by moving the mouse pointer over it, not clicking it.

5. Select the Hyperlink To option button.

6. **On the Hyperlink To drop-down menu, choose the action you want for the button.**

7. **Click OK.**

Now to make the button look right and adjust its size and position:

✦ **Choosing a different button:** Sorry, the only way to choose a different button for an action is to start all over and redraw the button.

✦ **Changing a button's action:** Right-click the button and choose Edit Hyperlink. In the Action Settings dialog box, choose a new action.

✦ **Changing an action button's appearance:** Double-click the button or right-click it and choose Format AutoShape. You see the Format AutoShape dialog box. On the Colors and Lines tab, choose a color for the button and line for its border.

✦ **Changing the button's size:** Click the button to display its selection handles. Drag a corner handle — a white circle — to enlarge or shrink the button.

✦ **Changing the button's position:** Click the button to select it. Then drag the button elsewhere.

Book III
Chapter 4

Making Your
Presentation Livelier

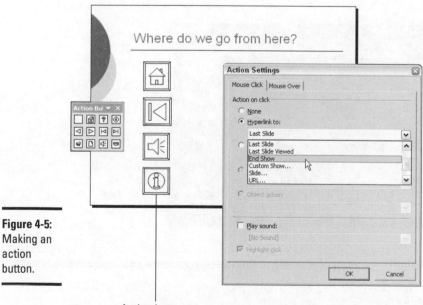

Figure 4-5:
Making an
action
button.

Action buttons

Sounding Off on Slides

Most everyone has had the experience of going to a site on the Internet and being greeted by a tinny, irritating noise that passes for music. Choose sounds carefully for slides and Web pages. Nothing turns people off more and has them reaching for the volume controls faster than squeaky, irksome sounds. That said, a well-chosen melody is an excellent choice for a kiosk presentation (Chapter 5 explains what those are).

PowerPoint offers two ways to make sound a part of a presentation:

✦ **As part of slide transitions:** The sound is heard as a new slide arrives on-screen. In the Slide Transition task pane, choose a sound from the Sound drop-down menu (see Chapter 3).

✦ **On the slide itself:** The means of playing the sound file appear on the slide. By clicking the Sound icon, you can play the sound. Figure 4-6 shows what the sound icon looks like on a slide. You can also make the sound play as soon as the slide arrives on-screen. Sound files placed on slides this way are linked to the PowerPoint file, not a part of it. As such, you can't move the sound file after you tell PowerPoint where to put it on a slide. If you move the file, PowerPoint won't know where it is and won't be able to play it.

Figure 4-6:
Making sound part of a slide.

Follow these steps to attach a sound file to a slide and be able to play it:

1. **In Normal view, select the slide that needs a sound file.**

2. **Choose Insert⇨Movies and Sounds⇨Sound from File.**

The Insert Sound dialog box appears. You can also locate sound files by choosing Insert⇨Movies and Sounds⇨Sound from Clip Organizer and selecting the file in the Clip Art task pane (Book VIII explains the Clip Art Organizer).

3. **Locate the sound file, select it, and click OK.**

4. **Click the Automatically button or the When Clicked button to tell PowerPoint whether to play the sound when the slide appears or wait for the presenter to give the signal.**

   The Sound icon appears on your slide.

5. **Drag the Sound icon to a convenient location. While you're at it, change its size by dragging a selection handle.**

   To test-drive the sound, right-click the Sound icon and choose Play Sound.

So much for inserting a sound file on a slide. Here are the other things you may or may not need to know about playing sound files:

✦ **Continuously playing a sound:** Right-click the movie and choose Edit Sound Object. Then select the Loop Until Stopped in the Sound Options dialog box.

✦ **Hiding the Sound icon:** Right-click the Sound icon and choose Edit Sound Object. In the Sound Options dialog box, select Hide Sound Icon During Slideshow. For this option to work, the sound file must play automatically. Otherwise, you won't see a Sound icon or be able to click it and make the file play.

✦ **Changing the Automatically or When Clicked status:** To play the sound automatically rather than have to click it, choose Slide Show⇨Custom Animation. Then select the Sound icon if it isn't already selected, right-click the sound file's name in the Custom Animation task pane, and choose Start On Click, Start With Previous, or Start After Previous.

Playing a Movie on a Slide

As long as they are meaningful and pertain to your presentation, movies and animated GIFs are a great way to make the audience say, "Wow!" Movies, however, can also look amateurish on slides if they aren't set up properly. Take into consideration these caveats before putting a movie on a slide:

✦ Make sure that the sound capabilities of your computer are up to playing sound if the video clip you intend to play has sound.

✦ Movies are linked to the PowerPoint presentation file, not embedded in it. When you insert a movie on a slide, you merely give PowerPoint instructions for feeding the movie into the slide. The movie itself is not part of the PowerPoint presentation. For that reason, put a copy of the movie in the same folder as the presentation file and don't move it elsewhere. If you do, PowerPoint won't be able to locate the movie file and the movie won't play.

✦ Movies are played on Windows Media Player (Book IX, Chapter 4 describes the Media Player). The Media Player appears in slides as the movie plays.

✦ Movies can look terribly grainy when they appear on a big computer screen. Unless you're a grain merchant, preview your movie to make sure it is suitable for showing on a PowerPoint slide.

Inserting the movie

Follow these instructions to place a movie on a slide:

1. **Place the movie on the slide.**

How you place a movie on a slide depends on what kind of slide and what kind of movie you're dealing with:

- **If the slide layout has a Media Clip placeholder:** Double-click the placeholder. The Media Clip dialog box appears (Book VIII explains how to organize clip and images in the Microsoft Clip Organizer). Select a clip and click OK.

- **If the movie is in the Microsoft Clip Organizer:** Choose Insert➪ Movies and Sounds➪Movie from Clip Organizer. The Clip Art task pane opens. Locate the movie and double-click it (Book VIII explains the Microsoft Clip Organizer).

- **If the movie is on your computer or network:** Choose Insert➪Movies and Sounds➪Movie from File. Then locate and double-click the movie file in the Insert Movie dialog box.

- **If the movie is an animated GIF:** If the GIF isn't stored in the Clip Organizer, choose Insert➪Picture➪From File and locate the GIF in the Insert Picture dialog box. Otherwise, choose Insert➪Movies and Sounds➪Movie from Clip Organizer and locate the animated GIF in the task pane. You can choose Preview/Properties on the GIF's drop-down menu to see what the animation looks like.

2. **Click the Automatically button or the When Clicked button when PowerPoint asks how you want the movie to start on the slide.**

Do you want the movie to play as soon as the slide arrives on-screen or when the presenter clicks the movie image?

The movie lands on the slide, as shown in Figure 4-7.

Figure 4-7:
A movie
on a slide.

3. **Right-click the movie and choose <u>P</u>lay Movie to see how (or whether) it plays.**

   In the case of an animated GIF, the only way to see what the animation looks like is to click the Slide Show button and view it at full-screen size.

Fine-tuning the movie presentation

The next step is to make the movie just-so:

✦ **Changing the movie's size and position:** Click the movie and drag to change its position. To change its size, drag a corner selection handle.

✦ **Continuously playing a movie:** Right-click the movie and choose Edit Movie <u>O</u>bject. Then select the Loop Until Stopped in the Movie Options dialog box. The movie will play continuously until you go to the next slide.

✦ **Hiding or displaying the movie on-screen:** You can arrange things so that the movie doesn't appear until it starts. Right-click the movie and choose Edit Movie <u>O</u>bject. Then select the Hide While Not Playing option in the Movie Options dialog box.

✦ **Changing the Automatically or When Clicked status:** If you change your mind about whether the movie should play automatically or play after it's clicked, choose Slide Show⇨Custo<u>m</u> Animation. Then select the movie, if necessary, right-click the movie's name in the task pane, and choose Start On Click or Start After Previous.

Chapter 5: Giving the Presentation

In This Chapter

- ✔ Making the last-minute preparations: Spell checks and style checks
- ✔ Printing handouts
- ✔ Showing the presentation slides
- ✔ Setting up a kiosk-style presentation
- ✔ Customizing a show
- ✔ Putting a presentation on the Internet

At last, the big day has arrived. It's time to give the presentation. "Break a leg," as actors say before they go on stage. These pages explain how to make the last-minute preparations, print handouts, and show the slides. You also discover how to give self-playing, kiosk-style presentations; customize a presentation for different audiences; and put a presentation on a Web page.

Getting Ready to Give Your Presentation

Don't be nervous. Everything is going to be all right. You'll come off like a champion, I'm sure. And to boost your confidence, these pages explain three last-minute preparations: spell-checking your slides, searching for style inconsistencies, and printing the speaker notes.

Running the spell-checker

Misspellings are glaringly apparent on PowerPoint slides. With headings in the 30-point and above range, an audience can spot misspellings and typos on a slide more readily than it can the printed page. Red squiggly lines appear below typos on slides (if you don't see the lines or don't care to see them, choose Tools⇨Options, select the Spelling and Style tab in the Options dialog box, and unselect the Check Spelling As You Type check box). You can fix spelling errors one at a time by right-clicking a redlined word and choosing the correct word on the drop-down menu.

To check for spelling errors from start to finish, choose the same command you choose throughout the Office programs: Tools➪Spelling (or press F7). The Spelling dialog box appears. It offers the standard buttons for correcting spelling errors — Ignore, Change, and so on. Go to it. Run the spell checker over your presentation. While you're at it, read the presentation one last time with an eye toward finding spelling errors. The spell checker can't find all your smelling errors. For example, if you mistype the word *spelling* and enter *smelling* instead, the spell-checker doesn't catch the error because *smelling* is a legitimate word.

Checking for style inconsistencies

PowerPoint also offers a "style checker" that goes over presentations in search of style inconsistencies. The inconsistencies are marked by a light bulb icon. What are these inconsistencies? To find out, choose Tools➪ Options, select the Spelling and Style tab in the Options dialog box, and click the Style Options button. You see the Style Options dialog box, as shown in Figure 5-1. Its two tabs permit you to decide for yourself what constitutes a style inconsistency. Back on the Spelling and Style tab, click the Check Style check box to flag inconsistencies with the light bulb icon.

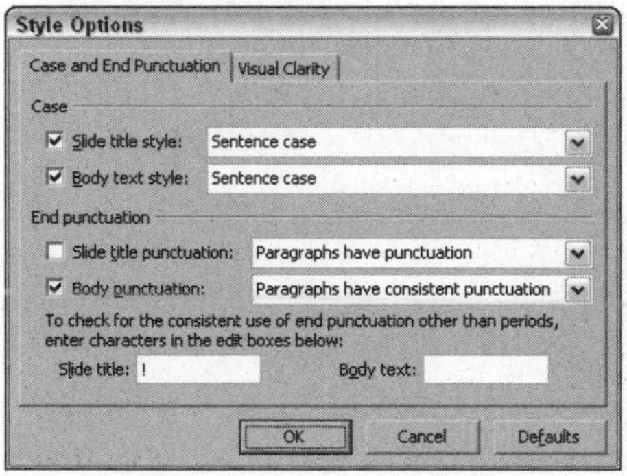

Figure 5-1:
The Style
Options
dialog box.

Printing the speaker notes

Chapter 2 explains what speaker notes are, how speaker notes assist in a presentation, and how to print speaker notes. Before you go into your presentation, be sure to print and bring along speaker notes if you sometimes get stage fright or you intend to speak from notes.

Rehearsing Your Presentation

Be sure to rehearse the presentation two or three times. Take note of how long it takes for you to give the presentation. Be sure to take into account time for questions from the audience. You might need to lengthen or shorten the presentation. And before it starts, make sure the machine on which you will give it is hooked up and in working order.

To help you rehearse, PowerPoint offers the Rehearse Timings command. This command keeps count of how long your presentation is and how long each slide is on-screen. When the dress-rehearsal is over, you can see in Slide Sorter view how long each slide was on-screen, as shown in Figure 5-2. You can tell whether a slide was on too long and perhaps needs to be divided into two slides. You can tell whether your presentation fits the time you'll be allotted.

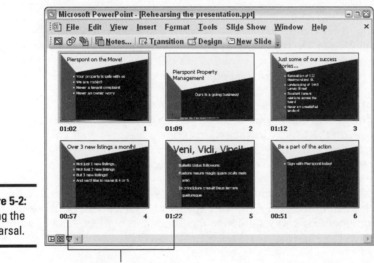

Figure 5-2:
Timing the
rehearsal.

Slide times

Book III
Chapter 5

Giving the
Presentation

Follow these steps to rehearse a presentation:

1. **Choose Slide Show⇨Rehearse Timings.**

The first slide appears on-screen, as does the Rehearsal toolbar. You can click the Pause button if during the presentation the dog needs walking or the postman rings twice.

2. **Go through your presentation as you expect to on the big day.**

   When the presentation is over, a dialog box tells you the total time of the presentation and asks whether you want to record how long each slide was on-screen.

3. **Click Yes to record the timings; click No to ignore them.**

   If you click Yes, the timings will appear in Slide Sorter view (refer to Figure 5-2).

Printing Handout Copies of a Presentation

One way to make a slide presentation more memorable is to print copies of it and hand out the copies after the presentation is over. That way, audience members can refer to your presentation or even marvel at it later on. Slides can be printed one, two, three, four, six, or nine to a page.

 Before printing handout copies of the slides in your presentation, tell PowerPoint how many slides to print on a page. Choose View➪Master➪ Handout Master. On the Handout Master View toolbar, click the button that corresponds to the number of slides per page you want. While you're looking at the Handout Master, you can enter a header or footer on the handouts.

To print a handout, choose File➪Print. In the Print dialog box, choose Handouts on the Print What drop-down menu. I also suggest choosing Grayscale on the Color/Grayscale drop-down menu even if you have a color printer. Slides, especially those with color backgrounds, are easier to see and examine in grayscale on the printed page.

 As long as the speaker notes you wrote for your slides are suitable for public consumption, you can print speaker notes instead of handouts for your audience. This way, audience members can read explanatory notes as well as see the slides themselves (see Chapter 2).

Showing Your Presentation

Compared to the preliminary work, giving a presentation is a piece of cake. To get off to a good start, press the Home key or select the first slide in the presentation. That way, you start at the beginning. Then do the following to show the slides:

 ✦ **Starting the show:** Choose View➪Slide Show, press F5, or click the Slide Show button.

♦ **Going forward:** To go forward from slide to slide, press the → key, click the mouse button, press N (for Next), press the Page Down key, press the Spacebar, right-click and choose Next, or click the Navigation button in the lower-left corner of the screen and choose Next.

♦ **Going backward:** To go backward through the slides, press the ← key, press P (for Previous), press the Page Up key, right-click and choose Previous on the shortcut menu, click the Navigation button in the lower-left corner of the screen and choose Previous, or click the Back button in the lower-left corner of the screen.

♦ **Going to a specific slide:** Either right-click or click the Navigation button, choose Go to Slide, and select the slide from the list. Press the Home key to go to the first slide.

♦ **Ending the show:** Press Esc, right-click and choose End Show from the shortcut menu, or click the button in the lower-left corner of the screen and choose End Show.

Book III
Chapter 5

**Giving the
Presentation**

Using the Pen for emphasis

To make presentations a little livelier, whip out the Pen and draw on a slide. Draw to underscore bullet points on a slide. Or draw check marks when you hit the key points. To use the Pen, right-click a slide and choose Pointer Options⇨Felt Tip Pen or chose one of the other pens. Now you can draw with the Pen.

Press Esc when you're finished using the pen (but be careful not to press Esc twice, because the second press tells PowerPoint to end the presentation). Pen marks are not permanent. At the end of a presentation in which someone has drawn on the screen, PowerPoint asks whether you want to discard or keep your scribblings. You can also choose Pointer Options⇨Eraser, and, with the eraser pointer, click lines you have drawn to erase them.

You can choose different colors for the Pen by right-clicking, choosing Pointer Options⇨Ink Color, and selecting a color on the submenu.

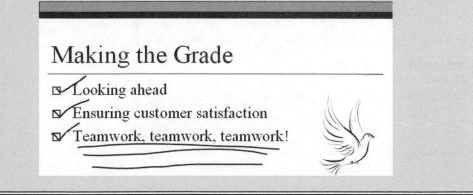

Presentations end with a blank screen and the words "End of slide show, click to exit." To end presentations without the blank slide, choose Tools⇨ Options, select the View tab in the Options dialog box, and unselect the End with Black Slide check box.

Giving a Self-Playing, Kiosk-Style Presentation

A kiosk-style presentation is one that plays on its own. You set the works in motion and it plays over and over on your computer until you or someone else comes along to press the Esc key. To give a kiosk-style presentation, you tell PowerPoint how long to leave each slide on-screen. Then you arrange for the presentation to be shown "kiosk-style."

Deciding how long to keep slides on-screen

Follow these steps to tell PowerPoint how long to keep each slide on-screen:

1. **Switch to Normal view and select the Slides tab.**

2. **Select the first slide in the presentation.**

3. **Choose Slide Show⇨Slide Transition.**

   The Slide Transition task pane appears, as shown in Figure 5-3.

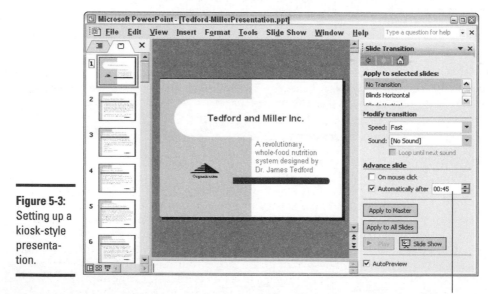

Figure 5-3: Setting up a kiosk-style presentation.

Enter the time period.

4. **Unselect the On Mouse Click check box.**

5. **Select the Automatically After check box.**

   Select both these check boxes If you want to give the people who view the presentation the option of moving ahead on their own. Whichever comes first, slides advance when the viewer clicks the screen or when each slide's time period comes to an end.

6. **Click the Apply to All Slides button.**

7. **Enter how long you want the slide or all the slides to remain on-screen.**

   How you do this depends on whether you want the slides to stay on-screen the same amount of time:

   • **All slides the same time:** Enter a time period in the Automatically After text box and click the Apply to All Slides button again.

   • **Each slide a different time:** One by one, select each slide on the Slide tab and enter a time period in the Automatically After text box.

   A fast way to enter time periods for individual slides is to rehearse the presentation and save the timings. If you save the timings, the time periods appear in the Automatically After text box. See "Rehearsing Your Presentation," earlier in this chapter.

Making the presentation "kiosk-style"

Follow these steps to make yours a "kiosk-style" presentation:

1. **Choose Slide Show⇨Set Up Show.**

   You see the Set Up Show dialog box.

2. **Under Show Type, select the Browsed at Kiosk (Full Screen) option.**

3. **Click OK.**

Customizing Shows for Particular Audiences

Here's a neat little trick: You can designate a subset of slides in a presentation as a *custom show* and show this shorter, customized version of the presentation to audiences instead of the entire show. Rather than set up four different presentations for four regional offices, a salesperson can keep all the slides he or she needs in one PowerPoint file. Then, from the collection of slides, the salesperson can put together four custom shows. This way, the salesperson has to deal with only one PowerPoint file, not four. Thanks to custom shows, the salesperson has the means to put together a presentation tailored for whatever audience he or she is addressing.

To set up a custom show, you choose which slides in a PowerPoint file belong in the show. Then you tell PowerPoint to run the custom show, not the full-blown one.

Assembling slides for a custom show

Follow these steps to assemble slides in a PowerPoint presentation for a custom show:

1. Choose Slide Show⇨Custom Shows.

The Custom Shows dialog box appears, as shown in Figure 5-4. It lists custom shows you've already put together, if you've put any together.

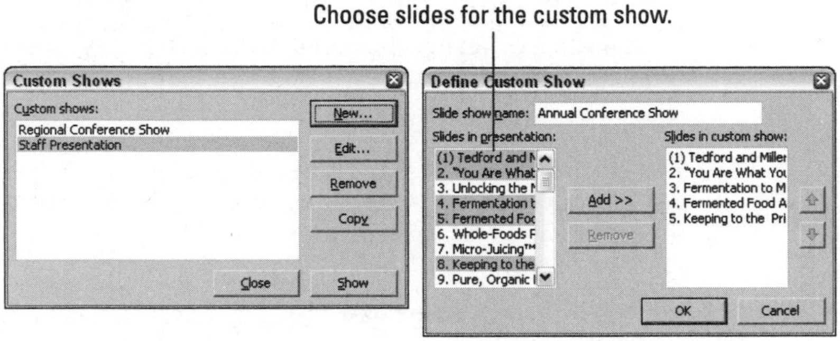

Choose slides for the custom show.

Figure 5-4: Tailoring a show for a particular audience.

2. Click the New button.

The Define Custom Show dialog box appears, as shown in Figure 5-4. The Slides in Presentation box lists all the slides in the presentation.

3. Enter a descriptive name for your custom show in the Slide Show Name text box.

4. Ctrl+click to select the slides you want for the custom show; then click the Add button.

The slides appear in the Slides in Custom Show box. To change the order of slides in the custom show, select slides and click an arrow button.

5. Click OK to return to the Custom Shows dialog box; then click Close.

The name you gave your custom show appears in the Custom Shows dialog box. To rehearse a custom show, select its name and click the Show button.

Presenting a custom show

PowerPoint offers two techniques for presenting a custom show:

+ **Starting from the Custom Shows dialog box:** Choose Slide Show➪ Custom Shows. In the Custom Shows dialog box (refer to Figure 5-4), select a show and then click the Show button.

+ **Making a custom show the one that is always shown:** With this technique, the custom show is presented whenever you give the command to start a slide show. Choose Slide Show➪Set Up Show. You see the Set Up Show dialog box. Under Show Slides, select the Custom Show check box and choose a custom show from the drop-down menu.

If you make a custom show the one that always appears, please, please, please remember that you have to return to the Set Up Show dialog box and check the All check box if you want to present the show in its entirety again. More than a few PowerPoint users have gnashed their teeth and pulled out their hair because they forgot how to go back to showing the entire show, not a custom one.

PowerPoint Presentations as Web Sites

By saving a PowerPoint presentation as a Web site and posting it on the Internet, you give people who don't have PowerPoint the opportunity to view your presentation. You give co-workers a chance to critique it as well. I once put together a presentation with people in Montana and Arizona. We posted the presentation on a team member's Web site. During several conference calls, we were able to critique and refine the presentation without having to e-mail it back and forth.

That said, however, PowerPoint presentations are not really meant to be made into Web pages. Something always gets lost in the translation. AutoShapes, WordArt, and charts don't make the translation at all.

To see what your presentation will look like in a Web browser, choose File➪Web Page Preview. Your browser opens and displays the Web page, as shown in Figure 5-5.

To save a PowerPoint file as a set of Web pages, create a new folder for storing the pages and choose File➪Save As Web Page. In the Save As dialog box, save the file in the folder you created. Book V explains how to upload Web pages to a Web site on the Internet.

Figure 5-5:
A presentation in Internet Explorer.

Book IV

Excel

The 5th Wave   By Rich Tennant

"Your database is beyond repair, but before I tell you our backup recommendation, let me ask you a question. How many index cards do you think will fit on the walls of your computer room?"

Contents at a Glance

Chapter 1: Up and Running with Excel

In This Chapter

↙ **Understanding what a worksheet is**

↙ **Entering text, as well as numeric, date, and time data**

↙ **Using the AutoFill command to enter lists and serial data**

↙ **Formatting text on a worksheet**

↙ **Setting up data-validation rules**

This chapter introduces Excel, the official number cruncher of Office. The purpose of Excel is to track, analyze, and tabulate numbers. Use the program to project profits and losses, formulate a budget, or analyze Elvis sightings in North America. Doing the setup work takes time, but after you enter the numbers and tell Excel how to tabulate them, you're on Easy Street. Excel does the math for you. All you have to do is kick off your shoes, sit back, and see how the numbers stack up.

This chapter explains what a workbook and a worksheet is, and how rows and columns on a worksheet determine where cell addresses are. You also discover tips and tricks for entering data quickly in a worksheet, how to format data, and how to construct data-validation rules to make sure that data is entered accurately.

Getting Acquainted with Excel

If you have spent any time in an Office program, much of the Excel screen will look familiar to you. The buttons on the Formatting toolbar — Bold, the Align button, and the Indent buttons, for example — work the same in Excel as they do in Word. The Font menu and Font Size menu work the same as well. Any command in Excel that has to do with formatting text and numbers works the same in Excel and Word. The commands for opening new files, closing files, and creating files are also the same.

An Excel file is called a *workbook.* Each workbook comprises one or more worksheets. A *worksheet,* also known as a *spreadsheet,* is a table where you enter data and data labels. Figure 1-1 shows a worksheet with data about rainfall in different counties. A worksheet works like an accountant's ledger — only it's much easier to use. Notice how the worksheet is divided by gridlines into columns (A, B, C, and so on) and rows (1, 2, 3, and so on). The rectangles where columns and rows intersect are called *cells,* and each cell can hold one data item, a formula for calculating data, or nothing at all. At the bottom of the worksheet are tabs for visiting the other worksheets in the workbook.

Each cell has a different cell address. In Figure 1-1, cell B7 holds 13, the amount of rain that fell in Sonoma County in the winter. Meanwhile, as the Formula bar at the top of the screen shows, cell F7 holds the formula =B7+C7+D7+E7, the sum of the numbers in cells — you guessed it — B7, C7, D7, and E7.

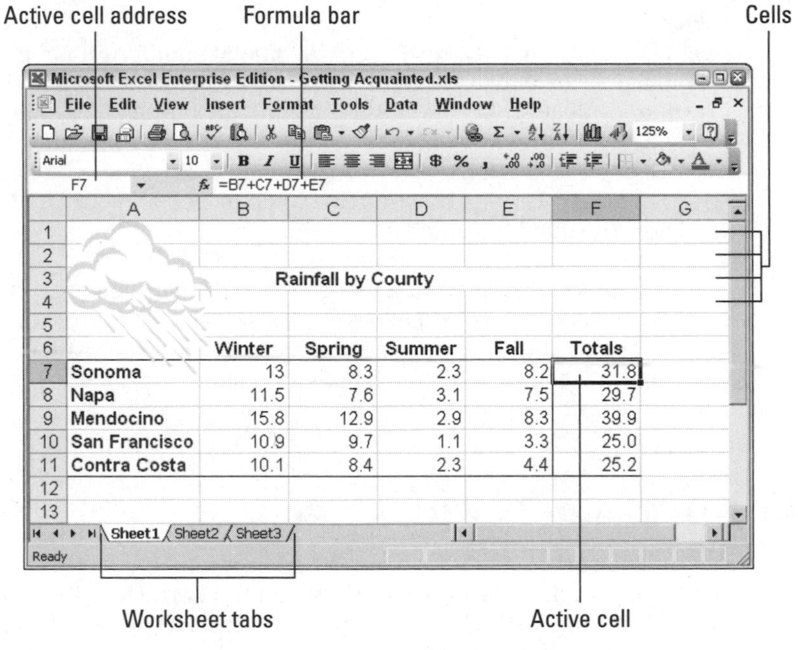

Active cell address   Formula bar   Cells

Figure 1-1:
The Excel
screen.

Worksheet tabs   Active cell

The beauty of Excel is that the program does all the calculations and recalculations for you after you enter the data. If I were to change the number in cell B7, Excel would instantly recalculate the total amount of rainfall in Sonoma County in cell F7. People like myself who struggled in math class will be glad to know that you don't have to worry about the math, because Excel does it for you. All you have to do is make sure that the data and the formulas are entered correctly.

After you have entered and labeled the data, entered the formulas, and turned your worksheet into a little masterpiece, you can generate charts like the one in Figure 1-2. Do you notice any similarities between the worksheet in Figure 1-1 and the chart in Figure 1-2? The chart is fashioned from data in the worksheet, and it took me exactly six seconds to create that chart. Chapter 5 explains charts.

Figure 1-2:
A chart generated from the data in Figure 1-1.

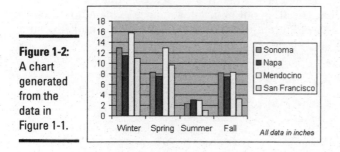

Rows, columns, and cell addresses

Not that anyone except an Enron accountant needs all of them, but an Excel worksheet has 256 columns and 65,536 rows. The rows are numbered, and columns are labeled A to Z, then AA to AZ, then BA to BZ, and so on. The important thing to remember is that each cell has an address whose name comes from a column letter and a row number. The first cell in row 1 is A1, the second is A2, and so on. You need to enter cell addresses in formulas to tell Excel which numbers to compute.

To learn a cell's address, either make note of which column and row it lies in, or click the cell and glance at the *Formula bar* (refer to Figure 1-1). The left side of the Formula bar lists the address of the *active cell*, the cell you clicked in the worksheet. In Figure 1-1, cell F7 is the active cell.

Workbooks and worksheets

 When you open a new Excel file, you open a workbook, a file with three worksheets in it. The worksheets are called Sheet1, Sheet2, and Sheet3 (you can change their names and add more worksheets). To get from worksheet to worksheet, click tabs along the bottom of the Excel screen. Why three worksheets? Because you might need more than one worksheet for a single project. Think of a workbook as a stack of worksheets. Besides calculating the numbers in cells across the rows or down the columns of a worksheet, you can make calculations throughout a workbook by using numbers from different worksheets in a calculation.

Entering Data in a Worksheet

Entering data in a worksheet is an irksome activity. Fortunately, Excel offers a few shortcuts to take the sting out of it. These pages explain how to enter data in a worksheet, the different types of data, and how to enter text labels, numbers, dates, and times.

The basics of entering data

What you can enter in a worksheet cell falls in four categories:

+ Text

+ A value (numeric, date, or time)

+ A logical value (True or False)

+ A formula that returns a value, logical value, or text

Still, no matter what type of data you are entering, the basic steps are the same:

1. **Click the cell where you want to enter the data or text label.**

As shown in Figure 1-3, a square appears around the cell to tell you that the cell you clicked is now the active cell. Glance at the left side of the Formula bar if you're not sure which cell you're about to enter data in. The Formula bar lists the cell address.

2. **Type the data in the cell.**

If you find typing in the Formula bar easier, click and start typing there. As soon as you type the first character, you see the Cancel button (an *X*), the Enter button (a check mark), and the Edit Formula button (an equal sign) on the Formula bar.

3. **Press the Enter key to enter the number or label.**

    Besides pressing the Enter key, you can also press an arrow key (←, ↑, →, ↓) or click the Enter button (the check mark) on the Formula bar.

    If you change your mind about entering data, click the Cancel button or press Esc to delete what you entered and start over.

Enter the data here...   ...or here.

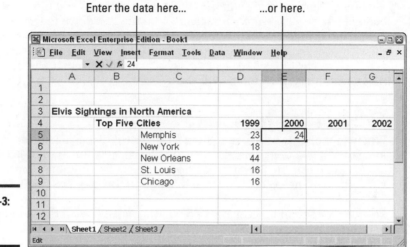

Figure 1-3:
Entering
data.

Chapter 3 explains how to enter logical values and formulas. The next several pages describe how to enter text labels, numeric values, date values, and time values.

The Edit⇨Paste Special command can come in very handy with worksheet data. As numbers are updated in the source file, they can be updated automatically in an Excel worksheet as well. Consider linking worksheets if your adventures in Excel enable you to keep source data in one place.

Entering text labels

Sometimes a text entry is too long to fit in a cell. How Excel accommodates text entries that are too wide depends on whether there is data in the cell to the right of the one you entered the text in:

✦ If the cell to the right is empty, Excel lets the text spill into the next cell.

**Book IV
Chapter 1**

**Up and Running
with Excel**

✦ If the cell contains data, the entry gets cut off. Nevertheless, the text you entered is in the cell. Nothing gets lost when it can't be displayed on-screen. You just can't see the text or numbers except by glancing at the Formula bar, where the contents of the cell can be seen in their entirety.

To solve the problem of text that doesn't fit in a cell, widen the column, shorten the text entry, re-orient the text (see the section in Chapter 4 of this mini-book about aligning numbers and text in columns and rows), or wrap the contents of the cell. *Wrapping* means to run the text down to the next line, much the way the text in this paragraph runs to the next line when it reaches the right margin. Excel makes rows taller to accommodate wrapped text in a cell. To wrap text in cells, select the cells, choose Format⇨Cells, select the Alignment tab in the Format Cells dialog box, and choose Wrap Text.

Entering numeric values

When a number is too large to fit in a cell, Excel displays pounds signs (###) instead of a number or displays the number in scientific notation. You can always glance at the Formula bar, however, to see a number. And you can always widen the column to make the number display in its entirety.

To enter a fraction in a cell, leave a blank space between the whole number and the fraction. For example, to enter 5⅜, type the **5**, press the spacebar, and type **3/8**.

Here's a little trick for entering numbers with decimals quickly. To spare yourself the trouble of pressing the period key (.), you can tell Excel to enter the period automatically. Instead of entering 12.45, for example, you can simply enter 1245. Excel enters the period for you: 12.45. To perform this trick, choose Tools⇨Options, select the Edit tab in the Options dialog box, choose Fixed Decimal, and, in the Places text box, enter the number of decimal places you want for numbers. Turn off this option when you want to go back to entering numbers the normal way.

Entering date and time values

Dates and times can be used in calculations, but entering a date or time value in a cell can be problematic because these values must be entered in such a way that Excel can recognize them as dates or times, not text.

Entering date values

Enter a date value in one of the following ways:

m/d/yy	7/31/04
m-d-yy	7-31-04
d-mmm-yy	31-Jul-04

After you enter a date this way, Excel converts it to the format it prefers for dates: 7/31/2004. If you don't enter the year, Excel assumes that the date you entered is in the current year. (You can enter fractions as well as dates in cells with the forward slash. However, to make sure that Excel recognizes the entry as a fraction, place a 0 in front of the fraction, if necessary. Excel interprets **3/8** as March 8, but if you enter **0 3/8**, Excel understands you're entering a fraction.)

When it comes to entering two-digit years in dates, the digits 30 through 99 belong to the 20th century (1930 – 1999), but the digits 00 through 29 belong to the 21st century (2000 — 2029). For example, 7/31/04 refers to July 31, 2004, not July 31, 1904. To enter a date in 1929 or earlier, enter four digits instead of two to describe the year: **7-31-1929**. To enter a date in 2030 or later, enter four digits instead of two: **7-31-2030**.

Dates entered in these formats are treated as text entries, not date values, and can't be used in calculations:

✦ July 31, 2004

✦ 31 July 2004

To enter a date directly in a formula, enclose the date in quotation marks (and make sure that the cell where the formula is entered has been given the Number format, not the Date format). For example, the formula =today()-"1/1/2003" calculates the number of days that have elapsed since January 1, 2003. Formulas are the subject of Chapter 3 of this mini-book.

Entering time values

Enter a time value in one of the following ways:

h:mm AM/PM	3:31 AM
h:mm:ss AM/PM	3:31:45 PM

Hours, minutes, and seconds must be separated by colons (:). Unless you enter AM or PM with the time, Excel assumes that you're operating on military time. For example, 3:30 is considered 3:30 a.m., not 3:30 in the afternoon. Don't enter periods after the letters am or pm (that is, not a.m., p.m.).

Combining date and time values

You can combine dates and time values by entering the date, a blank space, and the time:

✦ 7/31/04 3:31 am

✦ 7-31-04 3:31:45 pm

Here are shortcuts for entering the current time or current date in a cell: Press Ctrl+; (semicolon) to enter the current date; press Ctrl+Shift+; (semicolon) to enter the current time.

Not that you need to know it especially, but Excel converts dates and times to serial values for the purpose of being able to use dates and times in calculations. For example, July 31, 2004 is the number 38199. July 31, 2004 at noon is 38199.5. These serial values represent the number of whole days since January 1, 1904. The portion of the serial value to the right of the decimal point is the time, as a portion of a full day.

Entering Lists and Serial Data with the AutoFill Command

Data that falls in the "serial" category — month names, days of the week, and consecutive numbers and dates, for example — can be entered quickly with the AutoFill command. Believe it or not, Excel recognizes certain kinds of serial data and will enter it for you as part of the AutoFill feature. Instead of laboriously entering this data one piece at a time, you can enter it all at one time by dragging the mouse. Follow these steps to "autofill" cells:

1. **Click the cell that is to be first in the series.**

For example, if you intend to list the days of the week in consecutive cells, click where the first day is to go.

2. **Enter the first number, date, or list item in the series.**

3. **Move to the adjacent cell and enter the second number, date, or list item in the series.**

If you want to enter the same number or piece of text in adjacent cells, it isn't necessary to take this step, but Excel needs the first and second items in the case of serial dates and numbers so that it can tell how much to increase or decrease the given amount or time period in each cell. For example, entering **5** and **10** tells Excel to increase the number by 5 each time, so that the next serial entry is 15.

4. **Select the cells or cells you just entered data in.**

To select a single cell, click it; to select two, drag over the cells. The section in Chapter 2 of this mini-book about selecting cells in a worksheet describes all the ways to select cells.

5. **Click the AutoFill handle and start dragging in the direction in which you want the data series to appear on your worksheet.**

The *AutoFill handle* is the little black square in the lower-right corner of the cell. Finding it can be difficult. Carefully move the mouse pointer over the lower-right corner of the cell and, when you see the mouse pointer change into a black cross, click and start dragging. As you drag, the serial data appears in a pop-up box, as shown in Figure 1-4.

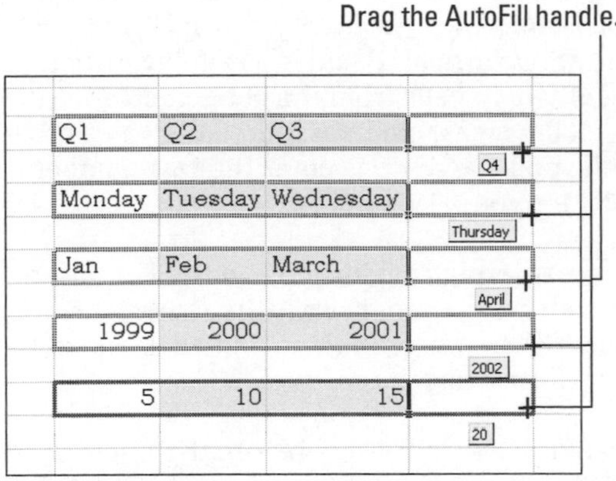

Drag the AutoFill handle.

Figure 1-4:
Entering
serial data
and text.

Creating an AutoFill list of your own

As you know, Excel is capable of completing lists on its own with the AutoFill feature. You can enter the days of the week or month names simply by entering one day or month and dragging the AutoFill handle to enter the others. Here's some good news: The AutoFill command can also reproduce the names of your co-workers, the roster of a softball team, street names, or any other list you care to enter quickly in a worksheet.

Follow these steps to enter items for a list so that you can enter them in the future by dragging the AutoFill handle:

1. **Choose Tools⇨Options to open the Options dialog box.**

2. **Select the Custom Lists tab.**

3. **Click the Add button.**

4. **In the List Entries box, enter items for the list, and enter a comma after each item.**

   You can see how it's done by glancing at the Custom Lists box.

5. **Click OK.**

The AutoFill Options button appears after you enter the serial data. Click it and choose an option if you want to copy cells or fill the cells without carrying along their formats.

 To enter the same number or text in several empty cells, drag over the cells to select them or select each cell by holding down the Ctrl key as you click. Then type a number or some text and press Ctrl+Enter.

Formatting Numbers, Dates, and Time Values

When you enter a number that Excel recognizes as belonging to one of its formats, Excel assigns the number format automatically. Enter **45%**, for example, and Excel assigns the Percent Style format. Enter **$4.25**, and Excel assigns the Currency Style format. Besides assigning formats by hand, however, you can assign them to cells from the get-go and spare yourself the trouble of entering dollar signs, commas, percent signs, and other extraneous punctuation. All you have to do is enter the raw numbers. Excel does the window dressing for you.

Excel offers five number-formatting buttons on the Formatting toolbar — Currency Style, Percent Style, Comma Style, Increase Decimal, and Decrease Decimal. Select cells with numbers in them and click one of these buttons to change the numbers' formatting:

✦ **Currency Style:** Places a dollar sign before the number and gives it two decimal places.

✦ **Percent Style:** Places a percent sign after the number and converts the number to a percentage.

✦ **Comma Style:** Places commas in the number.

✦ **Increase Decimal:** Increases the number of decimal places by one.

✦ **Decrease Decimal:** Decreases the number of decimal places by one.

To format dates and time values as well as numbers, choose Format➪Cells and make selections on the Number tab of the Format Cells dialog box. Figure 1-5 shows this dialog box. Select a category and choose options to describe how you want numbers or text to appear.

 To strip formats, including number formats, from the data in cells, choose Edit➪Clear➪Formats.

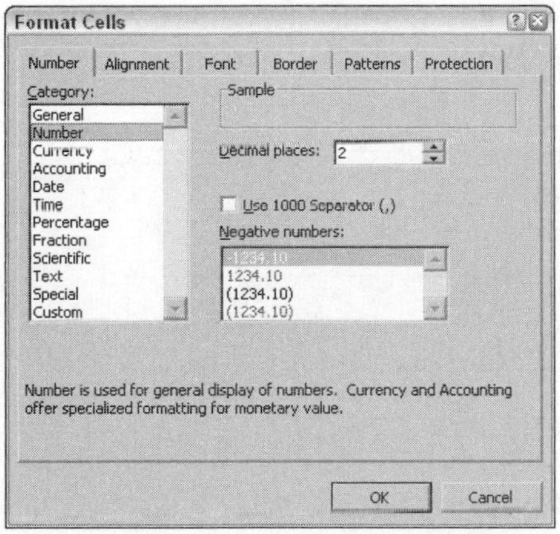

Figure 1-5:
The Format
Cells dialog
box.

Entering ZIP Codes can be problematic because Excel strips the initial 0
from a number if it begins with a 0. To get around that problem, visit the
Number tab of the Format Cells dialog box (refer to Figure 1-5), select
Special in the Category list, and choose a ZIP Code option.

Formatting Text and Numbers

You know the drill, I'm sure. To change the font or font size of text or numbers, select them and make choices from the Font and Font Size menus on
the Formatting toolbar. To boldface, italicize, or underline text or numbers,
click the Bold, Italic, or Underline button on the Formatting toolbar. Or, to
do a more thorough job of formatting, choose Format➪Cells, select the Font
tab in the Format Cells dialog box, and make your choices there.

Sometimes displaying cells slantwise can be a big advantage when your
worksheet is a big one. In Figure 1-6, for example, column labels are very
long. To pack them in a little, you can display them slantwise and reduce the
width of the worksheet considerably. Follow these steps to turn column
headings on their ear:

1. **Select the cells you want to slant.**

2. **Choose Format➪Cells or press Ctrl+1.**

   You see the Format Cells dialog box.

3. **Select the Alignment tab.**

**Book IV
Chapter 1**

**Up and Running
with Excel**

4. **Drag the marker in the Orientation box or enter an angle in the** **D**egrees **box; then click OK.**

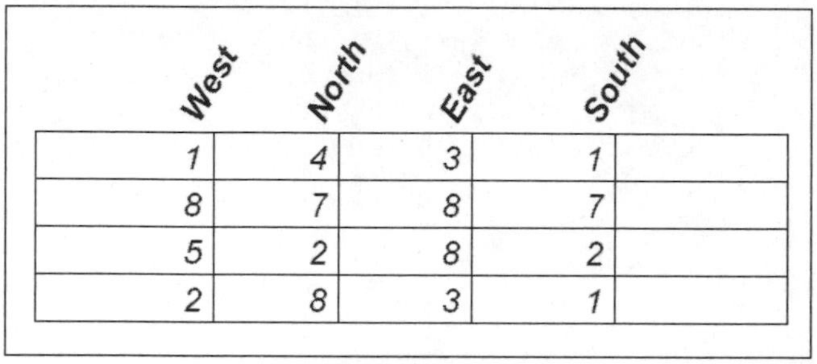

West	North	East	South	
1	4	3	1	
8	7	8	7	
5	2	8	2	
2	8	3	1	

Figure 1-6: Turning text on its ear.

Conditional formats for calling attention to data

A *conditional format* is one that applies when data meets certain conditions. To call attention to numbers greater than 10,000, for example, you can tell Excel to boldface those numbers automatically. To highlight negative numbers, you can tell Excel to display them in bright red. Select the cells that are candidates for conditional formatting and follow these steps to tell Excel when and how to format the cells:

1. **Choose Format⇨Conditional Formatting. You see the Conditional Formatting dialog box.**

2. **Use the condition text boxes and operator drop-down menu to describe a condition.**

   You can refer to a cell in your worksheet by selecting it. Doing so places the cell's address in a condition text box. To enter more than one condition, click the **A**dd button.

3. **Click the Format button and, in the Format Cells dialog box, choose a font, font size, font color, border, pattern, or background color for the cells that will set them apart from the other cells in the worksheet.**

4. **Click OK twice to return to the worksheet.**

To change or remove conditional formats, select the cells and choose Format⇨Conditional Formatting. In the Conditional Formatting dialog box, click the **D**elete button and, in the Delete Conditional Format dialog box, select a condition and click OK.

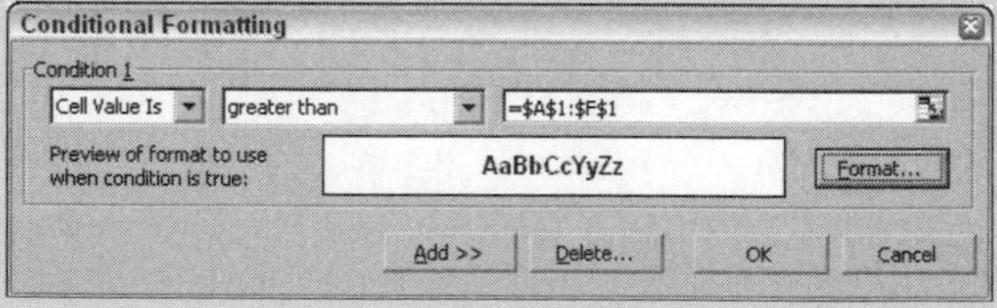

Conditional Formatting

Condition 1
Cell Value Is | greater than | =$A$1:$F$1

Preview of format to use when condition is true: | AaBbCcYyZz | Format...

Add >> | Delete... | OK | Cancel

Establishing Data-Validation Rules

By nature, people are prone to enter data incorrectly because the task of entering data is so dull, and this is why data-validation rules are invaluable. A *data-validation rule* is a rule concerning what kind of data can be entered in a cell. When you select a cell that has been given a rule, an input message tells you what to enter, as shown in Figure 1-7. And if you enter the data incorrectly, an error message tells you as much, as shown in Figure 1-7. If the Office Assistant is turned on, the input message comes from the Office Assistant, not a pop-up message.

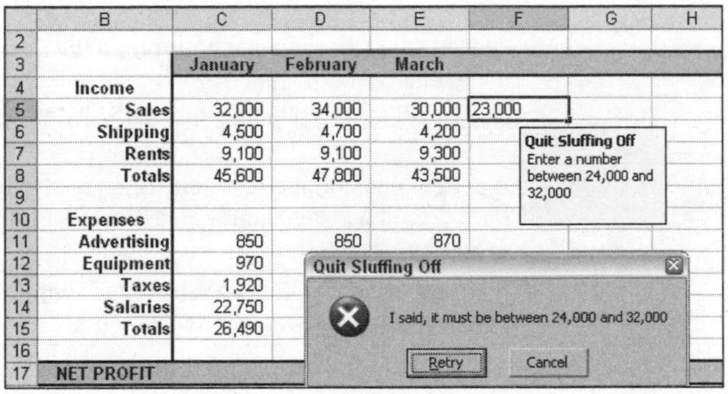

Figure 1-7:
A data-
validation
rule in
action.

Data-validation rules are an excellent defense against sloppy data-entry and that itchy feeling you get when you're in the middle of an irksome task. In a cell that records date entries, you can require dates to fall in a certain time frame. In a cell that records text entries, you can choose an item from a list instead of typing it yourself. In a cell that records numeric entries, you can require the number to fall in a certain range. Table 1-1 describes the different categories of data-validation rules.

Table 1-1	Data-Validation Rule Categories
Rule	*What Can Be Entered*
Any Value	Anything whatsoever. This is the default setting.
Whole Number	Whole numbers (no decimal points allowed). Choose an operator from the Data drop-down menu and values to describe the range of numbers that can be entered.
Decimal	Same as the Whole Number rule, except numbers with decimal points are permitted.

(continued)

Table 1-1 *(continued)*

Rule	What Can Be Entered
List	Items from a list. Enter the list items in cells on a worksheet, either the one you are working in or another. Then reopen the Data Validation dialog box, click the Return to Worksheet button (you will find it on the right side of the Source text box) and select the cells that hold the list. The list items appear in a drop-down list on the worksheet.
Date	Date values. Choose an operator from the Data drop-down menu and values to describe the date range. Earlier in this chapter, "Entering date and time values" describes the correct way to enter date values.
Time	Time values. Choose an operator from the Data drop-down menu and values to describe the date and time range. Earlier in this chapter, "Entering date and time values" describes the correct way to enter a combination of date and time values.
Text Length	A certain number of characters. Choose an operator from the Data drop-down menu and values to describe how many characters can be entered.
Custom	A logical value (TRUE or FALSE). Enter a formula that describes what constitutes a true or false data entry.

Follow these steps to establish a data-validation rule:

1. **Select the cell or cells that need a rule.**

2. **Choose Data⇨Validation.**

As shown in Figure 1-8, the Data Validation dialog box appears.

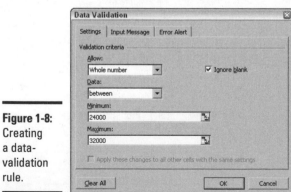

Figure 1-8:
Creating
a data-
validation
rule.

3. **On the Allow drop-down menu, choose the category of rule you want.**

   Table 1-1, earlier in this chapter, describes these categories.

4. **Enter the criteria for the rule.**

   What the criteria is depends on what rule category you are working in. Table 1-1 describes how to enter the criteria for rules in each category. You can refer to cells in the worksheet by selecting them.

5. **Select the Input Message tab and enter a title and input message.**

   You can see a title ("Quit Sluffing Off") and input message ("Enter a number between 24,000 and 32,000") in Figure 1-7. The title appears in boldface. Briefly describe what kind of data belongs in the cell or cells you selected.

6. **Select the Error Alert tab, choose a style for the symbol on the Message Alert dialog box, enter a title for the dialog box, and enter a warning message.**

   In the error message in Figure 1-7, the Stop symbol was chosen. The title you enter appears across the top of the dialog box and the message appears beside the symbol.

7. **Click OK.**

To remove data-validation rules from cells, select the cells, choose Data⇨ Validation, and, on the Settings tab of the Data Validation dialog box, click the Clear All button.

Chapter 2: Refining Your Worksheet

In This Chapter

- ✔ Changing and editing worksheet data
- ✔ Going here and there in a worksheet
- ✔ Freezing and splitting columns to make data entry easier
- ✔ Documenting a worksheet with comments
- ✔ Selecting cells
- ✔ Copying and moving data
- ✔ Moving among, deleting, and renaming worksheets

*T*his chapter delves into the workaday world of worksheets (say that three times quickly). It explains how to edit worksheet data and move quickly here and there in a worksheet. You also discover a couple of techniques for entering data quickly, how to select cells, and how to copy and move data in cells. Finally, this chapter describes how to find and replace data and how to move, delete, and rename worksheets.

Editing Worksheet Data

Not everyone enters the data correctly the first time. To edit data you have entered in a cell, do one of the following:

- ✦ **Double-click the cell.** Doing so places the cursor squarely in the cell, where you can start deleting or entering numbers and text.

- ✦ **Click the cell and press F2.** This technique also lands the cursor in the cell.

- ✦ **Click the cell you want to edit.** With this technique, you edit the data on the Formula bar.

If nothing happens when you double-click, or if pressing F2 lands the cursor in the Formula bar, not a cell, somebody has been fooling with Edit settings. Choose Tools➪Options, select the Edit tab in the Options dialog box, and select the Edit Data Directly in Cell check box.

Moving around in a Worksheet

Going from place to place gets progressively more difficult as a worksheet gets larger. Luckily for you, Excel offers keyboard shortcuts for jumping around. Table 2-1 describes these keyboard shortcuts. (If the keyboard shortcuts in Table 2-1 don't work on your machine, someone has told Excel to adopt the keyboard shortcuts of Lotus 1-2-3, another spreadsheet program. To remedy the problem, choose Tools➪Options, select the Transition tab in the Options dialog box, and uncheck the Transition Navigation Keys option.)

Table 2-1	Keyboard Shortcuts for Getting around Worksheets
Press. . .	*To Move the Cursor. . .*
Home	To column A
Ctrl+ Home	To cell A1, the first cell in the worksheet
Ctrl+End	To the last cell in the last row with data in it
←, →, ↑, ↓	To the next cell
Ctrl+←, →, ↑, ↓	In one direction toward the nearest cell with data in it or to the first or last cell in the column or row
PgUp *or* PgDn	Up or down one screenful of rows
Alt+PgUp *or* Alt+PgDn	Left or right one screen's worth of columns
Ctrl+PgUp *or* Ctrl+PgDn	Backward or forward through the workbook, from worksheet to worksheet

In addition to pressing keys, you can use these techniques to get from place to place in a worksheet:

✦ **Scroll bars:** Use the vertical and horizontal scroll bars to move to different areas. Drag the scroll box to cover long distances. To cover long distances very quickly, hold down the Shift key as you drag the scroll box on the vertical scroll bar.

✦ **IntelliMouse:** If your computer is equipped with an IntelliMouse, turn the wheel to quickly scroll up and down.

✦ **Name box:** Enter a cell address in the Name box and press Enter to go to the cell. The name box is found to the left of the formula bar. If you named cell ranges in your worksheet (see the section in Chapter 3 of this mini-book about naming cell ranges so that you can use them in formulas), you can go to a cell range by choosing its name in the Name box.

✦ **The Go To command:** Choose Edit⇨Go To (or press Ctrl+G or F5) and, in the Go To dialog box, enter a cell address in the Reference box and click OK. Cell addresses you've already visited with the Go To command are already listed in the dialog box, as are cell ranges you named. Click the Special button to open the Go To Special dialog box and visit a formula, comment, or other esoteric item.

✦ **The Find command:** Click the Find button, choose Edit⇨Find, or press Ctrl+F to open the Find dialog box. Enter the data you seek in the Find What box and click the Find Next button.

To scroll to the active cell, press Ctrl+Backspace.

Getting a Better Look at the Worksheet

Especially when you are entering data, it pays to be able to get a good look at the worksheet. You need to know which column and row you are entering data in. These pages explain techniques for changing your view of a worksheet so you always know where you are. Read on to discover how to freeze columns and rows, hide columns and rows, and zoom in and out.

Freezing and splitting columns and rows

Sometimes your adventures in a worksheet take you to a faraway cell address, such as X31 or C39. Out there in the wilderness, it's hard to tell where to enter data because you can't see the data labels in the first column or first row that describe what the data in the worksheet is.

To see one part of a worksheet no matter how far you stray from it, you can split the worksheet or freeze columns and rows on-screen. In Figure 2-1, I split the worksheet so that column A, "Property," always appears on-screen, no matter how far I scroll to the right. Similarly, row 1 also appears on-screen no matter how far I scroll down the worksheet. Notice how the row numbers and column letters are interrupted in Figure 2-1. Because I split the screen, I always know what data to enter in a cell.

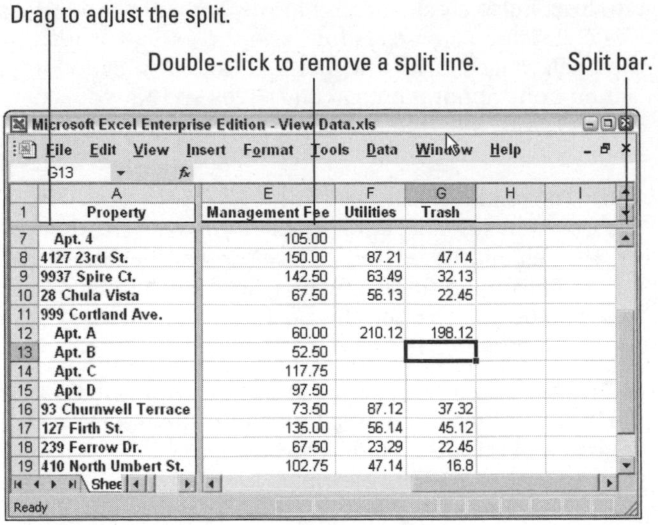

Drag to adjust the split.

Double-click to remove a split line.

Split bar.

	A	E	F	G	H	I
1	Property	Management Fee	Utilities	Trash		
7	Apt. 4	105.00				
8	4127 23rd St.	150.00	87.21	47.14		
9	9937 Spire Ct.	142.50	63.49	32.13		
10	28 Chula Vista	67.50	56.13	22.45		
11	999 Cortland Ave.					
12	Apt. A	60.00	210.12	198.12		
13	Apt. B	52.50				
14	Apt. C	117.75				
15	Apt. D	97.50				
16	93 Churnwell Terrace	73.50	87.12	37.32		
17	127 Firth St.	135.00	56.14	45.12		
18	239 Ferrow Dr.	67.50	23.29	22.45		
19	410 North Umbert St.	102.75	47.14	16.8		

Microsoft Excel Enterprise Edition - View Data.xls

File Edit View Insert Format Tools Data Window Help

G13

Figure 2-1:
Splitting a
worksheet.

Freezing columns or rows on a worksheet works much like splitting except that lines instead of gray bars appear on-screen to show which columns and rows are frozen.

Follow these steps to split or freeze columns and rows on-screen:

1. **Click the cell directly below the row you want to freeze or split, and click in the column to the right of the column that you want to freeze or split.**

In Figure 2-1, for example, I clicked cell B2, row 2 being below row 1, the row with the column labels (Property, Management Fee, and so on), and column B being to the right of column A, the column with the row labels (the property addresses).

2. **Choose <u>Window</u>⇨<u>Freeze</u> Panes or <u>Window</u>⇨<u>Split</u>.**

Gray bars or lines are drawn on-screen to show which row and column have been frozen or split. Move where you will in the worksheet. The column and row you froze stay on-screen.

The other way to split a worksheet is to grab hold of a *split bar*, the little division markers directly above the vertical scroll bar and directly to the right of the horizontal scroll bar (refer to Figure 2-1). You can tell where split bars are because the pointer turns into a double arrow when it's over a split bar. Click and drag a split bar to split the screen vertically or horizontally.

Choose <u>W</u>indow➪Un<u>f</u>reeze Panes or <u>W</u>indow➪Remove <u>S</u>plit when you no longer want a frozen or split worksheet. You can also double-click a split line to remove it from the screen.

Splitting the worksheet is superior to freezing columns or rows because, for one, you can drag the gray lines to new locations when you split the worksheet, and, moreover, you can remove the horizontal or vertical split by double-clicking it. Double-click the horizontal split line to remove it and divide the worksheet between sides, or double-click the vertical split to remove it and divide the worksheet between top and bottom.

Hiding columns and rows

Another way to take the clutter out of a worksheet is to temporarily hide columns and rows:

✦ **Hiding columns and rows:** Click anywhere in the row or column you want to hide and choose F<u>o</u>rmat➪<u>R</u>ow➪<u>H</u>ide or F<u>o</u>rmat➪<u>C</u>olumn➪<u>H</u>ide. You can hide more than one row or column by selecting them and then giving a Hide command.

✦ **Unhiding columns and rows:** Select columns to the right and left of the hidden column, or select rows above and below the hidden row, and choose F<u>o</u>rmat➪<u>R</u>ow➪<u>U</u>nhide or F<u>o</u>rmat➪<u>C</u>olumn➪<u>U</u>nhide. To unhide all columns and rows in the worksheets, click the Select All button (or press Ctrl+A) and give an Unhide command.

To unhide Row 1 or Column A, choose <u>E</u>dit➪<u>G</u>o To (or press F5) and, in the Go To dialog box, enter **A1** in the <u>R</u>eference text box and click OK. Then give an Unhide command.

Zooming in and out

The Zoom commands come in very handy when you're entering data. From the Zoom box on the Standard toolbar, select or enter a percentage and press the Enter key. You can also zoom in or out by choosing <u>V</u>iew➪<u>Z</u>oom and making a selection in the Zoom dialog box. Select the data in your worksheet, choose <u>V</u>iew➪<u>Z</u>oom, and select the <u>F</u>it Selection option in the Zoom dialog box to see all the data in a worksheet simultaneously.

If you have an IntelliMouse, the supercharged mouse manufactured by the Microsoft Corporation, you can zoom in and out by holding down the Ctrl key and turning the mouse wheel backward or forward. If you want to use the IntelliMouse strictly for zooming, not for scrolling, choose <u>T</u>ools➪<u>O</u>ptions, select the General tab in the Options dialog box, and choose <u>Z</u>oom on Roll with IntelliMouse.

Your own customized views

After you go to the trouble of freezing the screen or zooming in to a position you're comfortable with, you may as well save your view of the screen as a customized view. That way, you can call upon the customized view whenever you need it. View settings, the window size, the position of the grid on-screen, and cells that are selected can all be saved in a customized view.

To create a customized view, choose View⇨ Custom Views, click the Add button in the Custom Views dialog box, and enter a name for the view in the Add View dialog box. To switch

views, choose View⇨Custom Views, select a view, and click the Show button.

The catch to making customized views is to start by creating a view from the standard screen settings and calling it Normal or Standard or Ordinary. Without the Normal view, getting back to ordinary screen settings after you switch to a customized view is well-nigh impossible. The only way to do it is to change all the screen settings and undo the work you did to create the customized view in the first place.

Custom Views

Views:
Big View
Little View

Show
Close
Add...
Delete

Add View

Name: Middle View

Include in view
☑ Print settings
☑ Hidden rows, columns and filter settings

OK   Cancel

Comments for Documenting Your Worksheet

It may happen that you return to your worksheet days or months from now and discover to your dismay that you don't know why certain numbers or formulas are there. For that matter, someone else may inherit your worksheet and be mystified as to what the heck is going on. To take the mystery out of a worksheet, document it by entering comments here and there. As shown in Figure 2-2, a *comment* is a note that describes part of a worksheet. Each comment is connected to a cell. You can tell where a comment is because a small red triangle appears in the corner of cells that have been commented on. Move the pointer over one of these triangles and you see the pop-up box, a comment, and the name of the person who entered the comment.

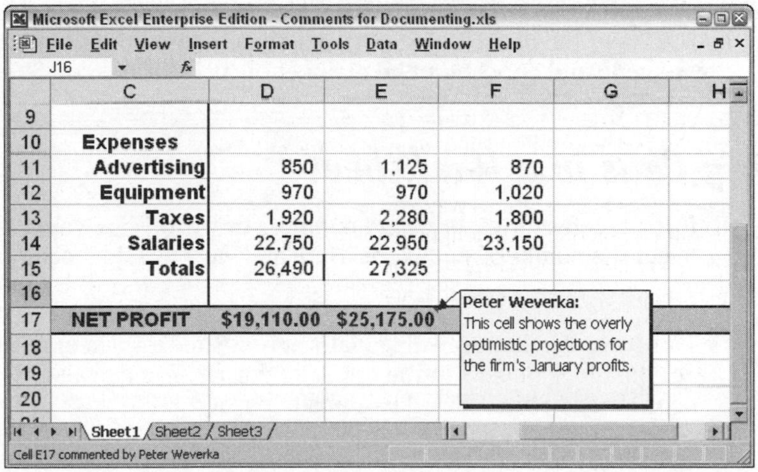

	C	D	E	F	G	H
9						
10	**Expenses**					
11	**Advertising**	850	1,125	870		
12	**Equipment**	970	970	1,020		
13	**Taxes**	1,920	2,280	1,800		
14	**Salaries**	22,750	22,950	23,150		
15	**Totals**	26,490	27,325			
16						
17	**NET PROFIT**	**$19,110.00**	**$25,175.00**			
18						
19						
20						

Peter Weverka:
This cell shows the overly optimistic projections for the firm's January profits.

Cell E17 commented by Peter Weverka

Figure 2-2: Press Shift+F2 to enter a comment.

Here's everything a mortal needs to know about comments:

✦ **Entering a comment:** Click the cell that deserves the comment, choose Insert⇨Comment (or press Shift+F2), and enter your comment in the pop-up box. Click in a different cell when you're done entering your comment.

✦ **Reading a comment:** Move the pointer over the small red triangle and read the comment in the pop-up box. To search for comments in a workbook, shrink your worksheet to 50 percent, choose Edit⇨Go To (or press Ctrl+G), and, in the Go To dialog box, click the Special button. Then, in the Go To Special dialog box, select Comments and click OK. All comments in your worksheet are highlighted.

✦ **Editing a comment:** Select the cell with the comment, choose Insert⇨ Edit Comment, and edit the comment in the pop-up box.

✦ **Deleting comments:** Right-click the cell with the comment and choose Delete Comment. To delete several comments, select them and choose Edit⇨Clear⇨Comments. To delete all the comments in a workbook, use the Edit⇨Go To command to highlight all of them; then right-click any highlighted cell with a comment and choose Delete Comment.

If your name doesn't appear in the pop-up box when you enter a comment and you want it to appear there, choose Tools⇨Options, select the General tab in the Options dialog box, and enter your name in the User Name text box.

You can print the comments in a worksheet. Choose File⇨Page Setup and, on the Sheet tab of the Page Setup dialog box, open the Comments drop-down menu and choose At End of Sheet or As Displayed on Sheet.

Selecting Cells in a Worksheet

To format, copy, move, or delete numbers or words in a worksheet, you have to select the numbers and words. Here are ways to select cells and the data inside them:

✦ **A block of cells:** Drag diagonally across the worksheet from one corner of the block of cells to the opposite corner. You can also click in one corner and Shift+Click the opposite corner.

✦ **Adjacent cells in a row or column:** Drag across the cells.

✦ **Cells in various places:** While holding down the Ctrl key, click different cells, drag across different cells, or click row numbers and column letters.

✦ **A row or rows:** Click the row number to select an entire row. Click and drag down the row numbers to select several rows.

✦ **A column or columns:** Click the column letter to select an entire column. Click and drag across letters to select several columns.

✦ **Entire worksheet:** Click the Select All button, the square to the left of the heading letters and above the row numbers, press Ctrl+A, or press Ctrl+Shift+Spacebar.

Press Ctrl+Spacebar to select the column that the active cell is in; press Shift+Spacebar to select the row where the active cell is.

You can enter the same data item in several different cells by selecting cells and then entering the data in one cell and pressing Ctrl+Enter. This technique comes in very handy, for example, when you want to enter a place-holder **0** in several different cells.

Deleting, Copying, and Moving Data

To empty cells of their contents, select the cells and then either press the Delete key or right-click and choose Clear Contents.

To copy or move data in a worksheet, use those old standbys, the Cut, Copy, and Paste commands. When you paste the data, click where you want the first cell of the block of cells you're copying or moving to go. Be careful not to overwrite cells with data in them when you copy or move data.

After you paste data, you see the Paste Options button. Click this button and choose an option from the menu to format the data in different ways.

As for the drag-and-drop method of copying and moving text, you can use it as well. Move the pointer to the edge of the cell block, click when you see the arrow, and start dragging.

Finding the Missing Data

In a large workbook, finding data can be difficult. You scroll and scroll, look under the couch pillows, and look under the chaise lounge, but you still can't find it. In times like these, you have to rely on the <u>E</u>dit⇔<u>F</u>ind command to find the data you're looking for. Follow these steps:

1. **Choose <u>E</u>dit⇔<u>F</u>ind or press Ctrl+F.**

2. **You see the Fin<u>d</u> tab of the Find and Replace dialog box, as shown in Figure 2-3.**

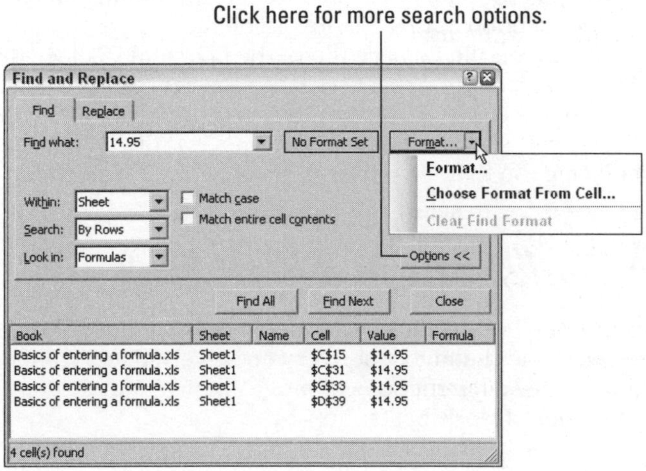

Click here for more search options.

Figure 2-3:
Finding missing data.

3. **Enter the characters you're searching for in the Fi<u>n</u>d What text box.**

4. **If you know how the data you're looking for is formatted, you can click the For<u>m</u>at button and, in the Find Format dialog box, select options to describe the format you want.**

Sometimes an easier way to describe formats is to click the arrow beside the For_mat button, select Choose Format from Cell on the drop-down menu, and select a cell with the formats you're looking for (refer to Figure 2-3).

5. **Click the F_ind What button to find the next instance of the thing you want, or the F_ind All button to generate list of all instances of the thing (refer to Figure 2-3).**

If you clicked the F_ind All button to generate a list, click an item on the list to scroll there in your worksheet or workbook.

These days, computers are awfully fast, and it isn't as though you have to help the search along by describing it, but you can do that by clicking the Op_tions button and choosing among the extra search options. You can use wildcards in searches. Chapter 3 in Book VI explains how wildcard characters work.

Finding and Replacing Data

Finding and replacing data is the mirror image of finding data (explained in the previous section of this chapter). The difference is, you enter the replacement data on the Re_place tab of the Find and Replace dialog box. Choose Edit⇨Replace (or press Ctrl+H) to see the Replace tab. Just be sure that you can replace data with confidence before clicking the Replace A_ll button. Better yet, click the R_eplace button a few times to make sure that you're replacing the right data in your workbook or worksheet.

Handling the Worksheets in a Workbook

As a glance at the bottom of the worksheet tells you, each workbook comes with three worksheets named, not very creatively, Sheet1, Sheet2, and Sheet3. Follow these instructions to move among, add, delete, rename, and change the order of worksheets:

`/ Sheet2 /`

✦ **Moving among worksheets:** To go from one worksheet to another, click a tab along the bottom of the screen. You can also press Ctrl+PgUp or Ctrl+PgDn to go from worksheet to worksheet.

✦ **Renaming a worksheet:** Right-click the worksheet tab, choose R_ename on the shortcut menu, type a new name, and press Enter. Spaces are allowed in names, and names can be 31 characters long. Brackets ([]) are allowed in names, but you can't use these symbols: / \ : ? * .

✦ **Selecting a worksheet:** Click the worksheet's tab. To select several worksheets, Ctrl+click their tabs or click the first tab and Shift+click the last tab in the set.

✦ **Rearranging worksheets:** Drag the worksheet tab to a new location. As you drag, a tiny black arrow and page icon appear to show you where the worksheet will land when you release the mouse button.

✦ **Deleting a worksheet:** Right-click the worksheet tab and choose <u>D</u>elete. To delete more than one worksheet, hold down the Ctrl key, click the tabs of the worksheets you want to delete, and then choose <u>E</u>dit⇨De<u>l</u>ete Sheet.

✦ **Inserting a new worksheet:** Choose <u>I</u>nsert⇨<u>W</u>orksheet or press Shift+F11.

✦ **Copying a worksheet:** Hold down the Ctrl key and drag the worksheet tab to a new location. You can also choose <u>E</u>dit⇨<u>M</u>ove or Copy Sheet and, in the Move or Copy dialog box, choose where to place the copy.

✦ **Color-coding a worksheet:** Right-click a worksheet tab and choose <u>T</u>ab Color. Then select a color in the Format tab color dialog box.

To change the size of columns or apply numeric formats to the same addresses in different worksheets, select all the worksheets and format one of them. The formats will apply to all the worksheets you selected. Being able to format several different worksheets simultaneously comes in handy, for example, when your workbook tracks monthly data and each worksheet pertains to one month. Of course, another way to handle worksheets with similar data is to create the first worksheet and copy it to the second, third, and fourth worksheets with the Copy and Paste commands.

Hiding a worksheet

Hide a worksheet when you don't want others to see or tamper with it. People with savvy and foresight sometimes set up workbooks so that one worksheet holds raw data and the other worksheets hold formulas that calculate the data. Keeping the raw numbers on the same worksheet discourages people from messing with the raw numbers, and if those numbers are hidden, the temptation to mess around is even smaller.

To hide a worksheet, select it and choose F<u>o</u>rmat⇨<u>S</u>heet⇨<u>H</u>ide. To unhide a worksheet, choose F<u>o</u>rmat⇨<u>S</u>heet⇨<u>U</u>nhide and, in the Unhide dialog box, select a worksheet and click OK.

Chapter 3: Formulas and Functions for Crunching Numbers

In This Chapter

✓ Constructing a formula

✓ Using cell ranges in formulas

✓ Naming cell ranges

✓ Referring to cells in other worksheets

✓ Copying formulas to other columns and rows

✓ Tracing a formula's cell references

✓ Using functions in formulas

Formulas are where it's at as far as Excel is concerned. After you know how to construct formulas — and constructing them is pretty easy — you can put Excel to work. You can make the numbers speak to you. You turn a bunch of unruly numbers into meaningful figures and statistics.

This chapter explains what a formula is, how to enter a formula, and how to enter a formula quickly. You also discover how to copy formulas from cell to cell and how to trace formulas to see how numbers in your worksheet generate formula results. Finally, this chapter explains how to make use of the hundred or so functions that Excel offers.

How Formulas Work

A *formula,* you may recall from the sleepy hours you spent in the back of math class, is a way to calculate numbers. For example, 2+3=5 is a formula. When you enter a formula in a cell, Excel computes the formula and displays its results in the cell. Click in cell A3 and enter **=2+3**, for example, and Excel displays the number 5 in cell A3.

Referring to cells in formulas

As well as numbers, Excel formulas can refer to the contents of different cells. When a formula refers to a cell, the number in the cell is used to compute the formula. In Figure 3-1, for example, cell A1 contains the number 2; cell A2 contains the number 3; and cell A3 contains the formula =A1+A2. As shown in cell A3, the result of the formula is 5. If I change the number in cell A1 from 2 to 3, the result of the formula in cell A3 (=A1+A2) becomes 6, not 5. When a formula refers to a cell and the number in a cell changes, the result of the formula changes as well.

Formula in Formula bar

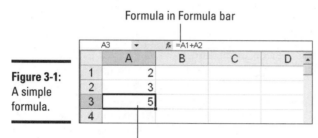

Figure 3-1:
A simple
formula.

Results of the formula

To see the value of using cell references in formulas, consider the worksheet shown in Figure 3-2. The purpose of this worksheet is to track the budget of a school's Parent-Teacher Association. Column C lists income from different sources; column D shows what the PTA members thought income from these sources would be; and column E shows how actual income compares to projected income from the different sources. As the figures in the Actual Income column (column C) are updated, figures in the Over/Under Budget column (column E) and the Total Income row (row 8) change instantaneously. These figures change instantaneously because the formulas refer to the numbers in cells, not to unchanging numbers (known as *constants*).

Figure 3-2:
Using
formulas
in a
worksheet.

	A	B	C	D	E
1					
2	Income		Actual Income	Projected Income	Over/Under Budget
3		Book Fair	4,876.40	5,500.00	-623.60
4		Dances	1,476.95	1,800.00	-323.05
5		Fundraising	13,175.00	5,000.00	8,175.00
6		Merchandise Sales	5,888.50	7,000.00	-1,111.50
7		PTA Membership	3,918.00	3,000.00	918.00
8	Total Income		$ 29,334.85	$ 22,300.00	$ 7,034.85

Figure 3-3 shows the formulas used to calculate the data in the worksheet in Figure 3-2. In column E, formulas deduct the numbers in column D from the numbers in column C to show where the PTA over- or under-budgeted for the different sources of income. In row 8, you can see how the SUM function is used to total cells in rows 3 through 7. The end of this chapter explains how to use functions in formulas.

Figure 3-3: The formulas used to generate the numbers in Figure 3-2.

	A	B	C	D	E
1					
2	Income		Actual Income	Projected Income	Over/Under Budget
3		Book Fair	4876.4	5500	=C3-D3
4		Dances	1476.95	1800	=C4-D4
5		Fundraising	13175	5000	=C5-D5
6		Merchandise Sales	5888.5	7000	=C6-D6
7		PTA Membership	3918	3000	=C7-D7
8	Total Income		=SUM(C2:C7)	=SUM(D2:D7)	=SUM(E2:E7)

Excel is remarkably good about updating cell references in formulas when you move cells. To see how good Excel is, consider what happens to cell addresses in formulas when you delete a row in a worksheet. If a formula refers to cell C1 but you delete row B, row C becomes row B, and the value in cell C1 changes addresses from C1 to B1. You would think that references in formulas to cell C1 would be out of date, but you would be wrong. Excel automatically adjusts all formulas that refer to cell C1. Those formulas now refer to cell B1 instead.

To display formulas in worksheet cells instead of the results of formulas as was done in Figure 3-3, press Ctrl+` (the grave accent, the key above the Tab key on your keyboard). Press Ctrl+` to see formula results again.

Referring to formula results in formulas

Besides referring to cells with numbers in them in a cell, you can refer to formula results in a cell. Consider the worksheet shown in Figure 3-4. The purpose of this worksheet is to track scoring by the players on a basketball team. The Totals column shows the total points each player has scored in the three games. The Average column, using the formula results in the Totals column, determines how much each player has scored on average. The Average column does that by dividing the results in column E by 3, the number of games played.

Averages returned from the formula results in column E.

	A	B	C	D	E	F
1		Game 1	Game 2	Game 3	Totals	Average
2	Jones	4	3	7	14	4.7
3	Sacharsky	2	1	0	3	1.0
4	Mellon	11	13	8	32	10.7
5	Gomez	8	11	6	25	8.3
6	Riley	2	0	0	2	0.7
7	Pealer	3	8	4	15	5.0
8	Subrata	13	18	18	49	16.3
9		43	54	43	140	46.7

Figure 3-4: Using formula results as other formulas.

	A	B	C	D	E	F
1		Game 1	Game 2	Game 3	Totals	Average
2	Jones	4	3	7	=B2+C2+D2	=E2/3
3	Sacharsky	2	1	0	=B3+C3+D3	=E3/3
4	Mellon	11	13	8	=B4+C4+D4	=E4/3
5	Gomez	8	11	6	=B5+C5+D5	=E5/3
6	Riley	2	0	0	=B6+C6+D6	=E6/3
7	Pealer	3	8	4	=B7+C7+D7	=E7/3
8	Subrata	13	18	18	=B8+C8+D8	=E8/3
9		=SUM(B2:B8)	=SUM(C2:C8)	=SUM(D2:D8)	=B9+C9+D9	=E9/3

Operators in formulas

Addition, subtraction, and division aren't the only operators you can use in formulas. Table 3-1 explains the arithmetic operators you can use and the key you press to enter each operator. In the table, operators are listed in the order of precedence.

Table 3-1	Arithmetic Operators for Use in Formulas	
Operator	*Symbol*	*Example Formula*
Percent	%	=50%, 50 percent, or 0.5
Exponentiation	^	=50^2, or 50 to the second power, or 2500
Division	/	=E2/3, the number in cell E2 divided by 3
Multiplication	*	=E2*4, the number in cell E2 multiplied by 4
Addition	+	=F1+F2+F3, the sum of the numbers in those cells
Subtraction	–	=G5–8, the number in cell G5 minus 8

Another way to compute a formula is to make use of a function. As "Working with Functions" explains later in this chapter, a function is a built-in formula that comes with Excel. SUM, for example, adds the numbers in cells. AVG finds the average of different numbers.

The order of precedence

When a formula includes more than one operator, the order in which the operators appear in the formula matters a lot. Consider this formula:

$=2+3*4$

Does this formula result in 14 (2+[3*4]) or 20 ([2+3]*4)? The answer is 14, because Excel performs multiplication before addition in formulas. In other words, multiplication takes precedence over addition. The order in which calculations are made in a formula that includes different operators is called the *order of precedence*. Be sure to remember the order of precedence when you construct complex formulas with more than one operator:

1. Percent (%)

2. Exponentiation (^)

3. Multiplication (*) and division (/); leftmost operations are calculated first

4. Addition (+) and subtraction (-); leftmost operations are calculated first

5. Concatenation (&)

6. Comparison (+, <, <=, >, >=, <>)

To get around the order of precedence problem, enclose parts of formulas in parentheses. Operations in parentheses are calculated before all other parts of a formula. For example, the formula =2+3*4 equals 20 when it is written this way: =(2+3)*4.

The Basics of Entering a Formula

No matter what kind of formula you enter, no matter how complex the formula is, follow these basic steps to enter it:

1. **Click the cell where you want to enter the formula.**

2. **Click in the Formula bar.**

3. **Enter an equal sign (=).**

You must be sure to enter the equal sign before you enter a formula. Without it, Excel thinks you're entering text, not a formula.

4. **Enter the formula.**

For example, enter =B1*.06. Make sure that you enter all cell addresses correctly. By the way, you can enter lowercase letters in cell references. Excel changes them to uppercase when you finish entering the formula. The next section in this chapter explains how to enter cell addresses quickly in formulas.

5. **Press Enter or click the Enter button (the green check mark).**

The result of the formula appears in the cell.

Warning: Does not compute!

Sometimes you enter a formula but it doesn't compute and you get an error message, a cryptic three or four letters preceded by a pound sign (#). Here are common error messages and what you can do about them:

- ✔ **#DIV/01:** You tried to divide a number by 0 or an empty cell.

- ✔ **#NAME:** You used a cell range name in the formula, but the name hasn't been defined. Sometimes this error occurs because you typed the name incorrectly. (Later in this chapter, "Naming cell ranges so that you can use them in formulas" explains how to name cell ranges.)

- ✔ **#N/A:** The formula refers to an empty cell, so no data is available for computing the formula. Sometimes people enter NA in a cell as a placeholder to signal the fact that data has not been entered yet. Revise the formula or enter a number or formula in the empty cells.

- ✔ **#NULL:** The formula refers to a cell range that Excel can't understand. Make sure that the range is entered correctly.

- ✔ **#NUM:** An argument you used in your formula is invalid.

- ✔ **#REF:** The cell or range of cells that the formula refers to are not there.

- ✔ **#VALUE:** The formula includes a function that's used incorrectly, takes an invalid argument, or is misspelled. Make sure that the function uses the right argument and is spelled correctly.

Speed Techniques for Entering Formulas

Entering formulas and making sure that all cell references are correct is a tedious activity, but, fortunately for you, Excel offers a few techniques to make entering formulas easier. Read on to find out how ranges make entering cell references easier and how you can enter cell references in formulas by pointing and clicking. You'll also find instructions here for copying formulas.

Clicking cells to enter cell references

The hardest part about entering a formula is entering the cell references correctly. You have to squint to see which row and column the cell you want to refer to is in. You have to carefully type the right column letter and row number. However, instead of typing a cell reference, you can click the cell you want to refer to in a formula. As soon as you click the cell, Excel enters its address on the Formula bar. What's more, shimmering marquee lights appear around the cell to show you which one you're referring to in the formula.

In the worksheet in Figure 3-5, I clicked cell F3 instead of entering its address on the Formula bar. The reference F3 appears on the Formula bar and the marquee lights appear around cell F3.

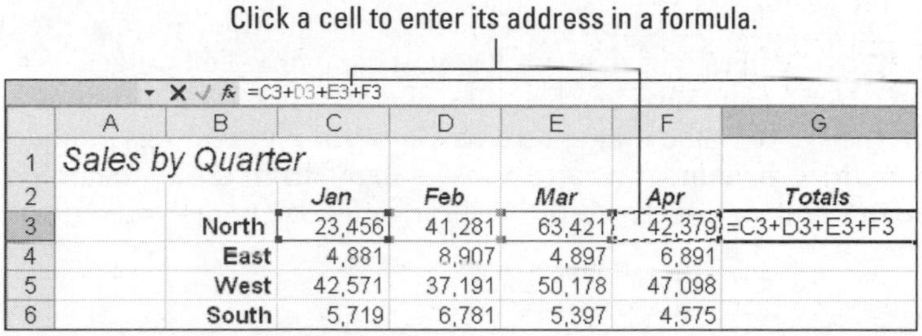

Click a cell to enter its address in a formula.

Figure 3-5:
Clicking to
enter a cell
address.

	A	B	C	D	E	F	G
						fx =C3+D3+E3+F3	
1	Sales by Quarter						
2			Jan	Feb	Mar	Apr	Totals
3		North	23,456	41,281	63,421	42,379	=C3+D3+E3+F3
4		East	4,881	8,907	4,897	6,891	
5		West	42,571	37,191	50,178	47,098	
6		South	5,719	6,781	5,397	4,575	

Entering a cell range

A *cell range* is a line or block of cells in a worksheet. Cell ranges come in especially handy where functions are concerned (see "Working with Functions," later in this chapter). To create a cell range, select the cells. In Figure 3-6, I selected cells C3, D3, E3, and F3 to form cell range C3:F3. The formula in the Figure 3-6 uses the SUM function to total the numeric values in cell range C3:F3. Notice the marquee lights around the range C3:F3.

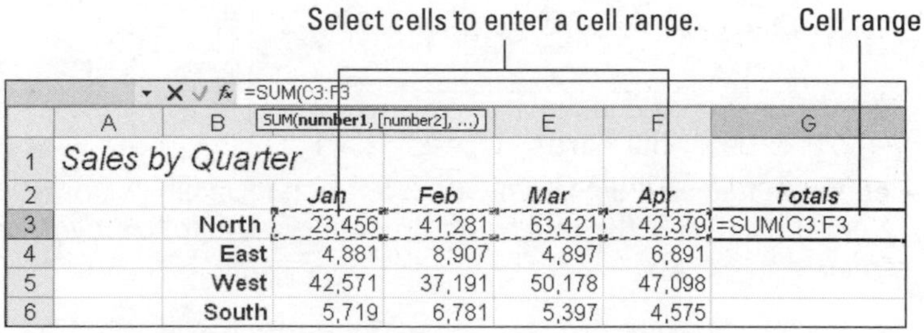

Select cells to enter a cell range.   Cell range

Figure 3-6:
Using a cell
range in a
formula.

	A	B	C	D	E	F	G
			fx =SUM(C3:F3				
			SUM(**number1**, [number2], ...)		E	F	G
1	Sales by Quarter						
2			Jan	Feb	Mar	Apr	Totals
3		North	23,456	41,281	63,421	42,379	=SUM(C3:F3
4		East	4,881	8,907	4,897	6,891	
5		West	42,571	37,191	50,178	47,098	
6		South	5,719	6,781	5,397	4,575	

To identify a cell range, Excel lists the outermost cells in the range and places a colon (:) between cell addresses. You can enter cell ranges on your own without selecting cells. To do so, list the first cell in the range, enter a colon, and list the last cell. A cell range comprising cells A1, A2, A3, and A4 has this address A1:A4. A cell range comprising a block of cells from A1 to D4 has this address: A1:D4.

**Book IV
Chapter 3**

**Formulas and
Functions**

Naming cell ranges so that you can use them in formulas

Whether you type them yourself or drag across cells, entering cell references is a chore. Entering =C1+C2+C3+C4, for example, can cause a finger cramp. Entering =C1:C4 is no piece of cake, either. To take the tedium out of entering cell ranges in formulas, you can name cell ranges. When you want to enter a cell range in a formula, all you have to do is double-click a name in the Paste Name dialog box, as shown in Figure 3-7. Naming cell ranges has an added benefit. You can choose a name from the Name Box drop-down menu and go directly to the cell range whose name you choose, as shown in Figure 3-7.

Choose a name to move there.   Double-click to enter the named range in a formula.

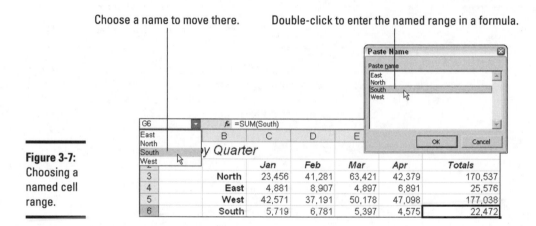

Figure 3-7: Choosing a named cell range.

Cell range names must begin with a letter, backslash (\), or underscore (_). Select the cells for the range and do either of the following to name a cell range:

✦ Click in the Name Box (you'll find it to the left of the Formula bar), enter a name for the range, and press the Enter key.

✦ Choose Insert➪Name➪Define and, in the Define Name dialog box, enter a name and click OK.

To insert a range name in a formula, press F3 or choose Insert➪Name➪ Paste to open the Paste Name dialog box (refer to Figure 3-7) and then double-click the range name.

Naming cell ranges has one disadvantage, and it's a big one. Excel doesn't adjust the cell references when you copy a formula with a range name from one cell to another. A range name always refers to the same set of cells. Later in this chapter, "Copying Formulas from Cell to Cell" explains how to copy formulas.

Referring to cells in different worksheets

Excel gives you the opportunity to use data from different worksheets in a formula. If one worksheet lists sales figures from January and the next lists sales figures from February, you can construct a "grand total" formula on either worksheet to tabulate sales in the two-month period. A reference to a cell on a different worksheet is called a *3-D reference*.

Construct the formula as you normally would, but when you want to refer to a cell or cell range in a different worksheet, click a worksheet tab to move to the other worksheet and select the cell or range of cells there. Without returning to the original worksheet, complete your formula in the Formula bar and press Enter. Excel returns you to the original worksheet, where you can see the results of your formula.

The only thing odd about constructing formulas across worksheets are the cell references. As a glance at the Formula bar tells you, cell addresses in cross-worksheet formulas list the sheet name and an exclamation point (!) as well as the cell address itself. For example, this formula in Worksheet 1 adds the number in cell A4 to the numbers in cells D5 and E5 in Worksheet 2:

```
=A4+Sheet2!D5+Sheet2!E5
```

This formula in Worksheet 2 multiplies the number in cell E18 with the number in cell C15 in Worksheet 1:

```
=E18*Sheet1!C15
```

This formula in Worksheet 2 finds the average of the numbers in the cell range C7:F7 in Worksheet 1:

```
=AVERAGE(Sheet1!C7:F7)
```

Copying Formulas from Cell to Cell

Often in worksheets, the same formula but with different cell references is used across a row or down a column. For example, take the worksheet shown

**Book IV
Chapter 3**

**Formulas and
Functions**

in Figure 3-8. Column F of the worksheet totals the rainfall figures in rows 5 through 9. To enter formulas for totaling the rainfall figures in column F, you could laboriously enter formulas in cells F5, F6, F7, F8, and F9. But a faster way is to enter the formula once in cell F5 and then copy the formula in F5 down the column to cells F6, F7, F8, and F9.

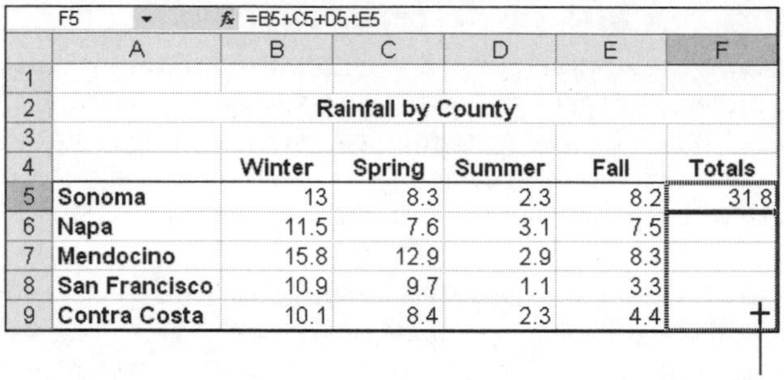

F5	▾	fx =B5+C5+D5+E5				
	A	B	C	D	E	F
1						
2		Rainfall by County				
3						
4		Winter	Spring	Summer	Fall	Totals
5	Sonoma	13	8.3	2.3	8.2	31.8
6	Napa	11.5	7.6	3.1	7.5	
7	Mendocino	15.8	12.9	2.9	8.3	
8	San Francisco	10.9	9.7	1.1	3.3	
9	Contra Costa	10.1	8.4	2.3	4.4	+

Figure 3-8:
Copying a
formula.

Drag the AutoFill handle.

When you copy a formula to a new cell, Excel adjusts the cell references in the formula so that the formula works in the cells to which it has been copied. Astounding! Opportunities to copy formulas abound on most worksheets. And copying formulas is the fastest and safest way to enter formulas in a worksheet.

Follow these steps to copy a formula:

1. **Select the cell with the formula you want to copy.**

2. **Drag the AutoFill handle across the cells to which you'll copy the formula.**

This is the same AutoFill handle you drag to enter serial data (see the section in Chapter 1 of this mini-book about entering lists and serial data with the AutoFill command). The AutoFill handle is the small black square in the lower-right corner of the cell. When you move the mouse pointer over it, it changes to a black cross. Figure 3-8 shows a formula being copied.

3. **Release the mouse button.**

If I were you, I would click in the cells to which you copied the formula and glance at the Formula bar to make sure that the formula was copied correctly. I'd bet you it was.

You can also copy formulas with the Copy and Paste commands. Just make sure that cell references refer correctly to the surrounding cells.

Tracing Cell References

In a complex worksheet in which formulas are piled on top of one another and the results of some formulas are computed into other formulas, it helps to be able to trace cell references. By tracing cell references, you can see how the data in a cell figures into a formula in another cell or, if the cell contains a formula, which cells the formula gathers data from to make its computation.

Figure 3-9 shows how cell tracers describe the relationships between cells. A *cell tracer* is a blue arrow that shows the relationships between cells used in formulas. You can trace two types of relationships:

	A	B	C	D	E	F
1						
2		Game 1	Game 2	Game 3	Totals	Average
3	Jones	4	3	7	14	4.7
4	Sacharsky	2	1	0	3	1.0
5	Mellon	11	13	8	32	10.7
6	Gomez	8	11	6	25	8.3
7	Riley	2	0	0	2	0.7
8	Pealer	3	8	4	15	5.0
9	Subrata	13	18	18	49	16.3
10		43	54	43		
11						
12		Total Points		140		
13						
14		Average Per Game		46.7		
15						

Figure 3-9: Tracing the relationships between cells.

✦ **Tracing precedents:** Select a cell with a formula in it and trace the formula's *precedents* to find out which cells are computed to produce the results of the formula. Trace precedents when you want to find out where a formula gets its computation data. Cell tracer arrows point from the referenced cells to the cell with the formula results in it.

✦ **Tracing dependents:** Select a cell and trace its *dependents* to find out which cells contain formulas that use data from the cell you selected. Cell tracer arrows point from the cell you selected to cells with formula results in them. Trace dependents when you want to find out how the data in a cell contributes to formulas elsewhere in the worksheet. The cell you select can contain a constant value or a formula in its own right (and contribute its results to another formula).

To trace a cell's precedents or dependents, select it and do one of the following:

✦ Choose Tools➪Formula Auditing➪Trace Precedents.

✦ Choose Tools➪Formula Auditing➪Trace Dependents.

Choose Tools➪Formula Auditing➪Remove All Arrows to wipe the arrows off the worksheet.

Working with Functions

A *function* is a canned formula that comes with Excel. Excel offers hundreds of functions, some of which are very obscure and fit only for use by rocket scientists or securities analysts. Other functions are very practical. For example, you can use the SUM function to quickly total the numbers in a range of cells ("Entering a cell range," earlier in this chapter, describes cell ranges). Instead of entering =C2+C3+C4+C5 on the Formula bar, you can enter =SUM(C2:C5), which tells Excel to total the numbers in cell C2, C3, C4, and C5. To obtain the product of the number in cell G4 and .06, you can use the PRODUCT function and enter =PRODUCT(G4,.06) on the Formula bar. Table 3-2 lists the most common functions.

Table 3-2	Common Functions and Their Use
Function	*Returns*
AVERAGE(*number1,number2,...*)	The average of the numbers in the cells listed in the arguments.
COUNT(*value1,value2,...*)	The number of cells that contain the numbers listed in the arguments.
MAX(*number1,number2,...*)	The largest value in the cells listed in the arguments.
MIN(*number1,number2,...*)	The smallest value in the cells listed in the arguments.
PRODUCT(*number1,number2,...*)	The product of multiplying the cells listed in the arguments.
STDEV(*number1,number2,...*)	An estimate of standard deviation based on the sample cells listed in the argument.
STDEVP(*number1,number2,...*)	An estimate of standard deviation based on the entire sample cells listed in the arguments.
SUM(*number1,number2,...*)	The total of the numbers in the arguments.
VAR(*number1,number2,...*)	An estimate of the variance based on the sample cells listed in the arguments.
VARP(*number1,number2,...*)	A variance calculation based on all cells listed in the arguments.

A function takes one or more *arguments* — the cell references or numbers, enclosed in parentheses, that the function acts upon. For example, AVERAGE(B1:B4) returns the average of the numbers in the cell range B1 through B4; PRODUCT(6.5,C4) returns the product of multiplying the number 6.5 by the number in cell C4. When a function requires more than one argument, enter a comma between the arguments.

To get an idea of the numerous functions that Excel offers, click the Insert Function button or choose Insert➪Function. You see the Insert Function dialog box, shown in Figure 3-10. Choose a function category in the dialog box, select a function name, and read the description. You can click the Help on This Function link to open the Help program and get a thorough description of the function and how it's used.

Choose a category.   Choose a function.

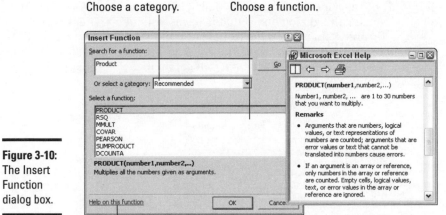

Figure 3-10:
The Insert Function dialog box.

Click to learn more.

Manually entering a function in a formula

If you know a function well, you can enter it yourself in the Formula bar along with the rest of the formula. Be sure to enclose the argument or arguments in parentheses. Don't enter a space between the function's name and the first parenthesis. And please, please, please be sure to start your formula by entering an equal sign (=). Without it, Excel thinks you're entering text.

You can enter function names in lowercase. Excel converts function names to uppercase after you click the Enter button or press Enter to complete the formula. Entering function names in lowercase is recommended because doing so gives you a chance to find out whether you entered a function name correctly. If Excel doesn't convert your function name to uppercase, you made a typing error.

To quickly total the numbers in cells, click the cell where you want the total to appear and then click the AutoSum button on the Standard toolbar. Marquee lights appear around the cells that Excel wants to add up. If these are the cells you want to add up, press Enter immediately. Otherwise, select the cells you want to add up and then press Enter. You can also enter the AVERAGE, COUNT, MAX, or MIN function and their arguments this way. Click the arrow next to the AutoSum button and choose AVERAGE, COUNT, and so on from the drop-down menu.

Getting Excel's help to enter a function

Besides entering a function the conventional way by typing it, you can do it by way of the Function Arguments dialog box, shown in Figure 3-11. The beauty of using this dialog box is that it warns you if you enter arguments incorrectly and it spares you the trouble of typing the function name without making an error. What's more, the Function Arguments dialog box shows you the results of the formula so that you get an idea whether you're entering the formula correctly.

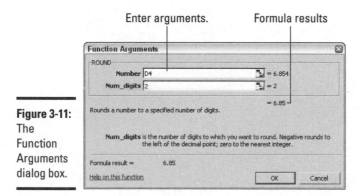

Figure 3-11: The Function Arguments dialog box.

Click the cell where you want to enter a formula, enter an equals sign (=) in the Formula bar, and do one of the following to bring up the Function Arguments dialog box:

✦ Open the Functions drop-down menu (it appears on the left side of the Formula bar after you enter the equals sign) and choose a function.

♦ Click the Insert Function button or choose <u>I</u>nsert⇨<u>F</u>unction and, in the Insert Function dialog box (refer to Figure 3-10), find and double-click the name of the function you need for your formula.

Enter arguments in the spaces provided by the Function Arguments dialog box. To enter cell references or ranges, you can click or select cells in the worksheet. If necessary, click the Go to Worksheet button (you'll find it to the right of an argument text box) to shrink the Function Arguments dialog box and get a better look at your worksheet. Click OK when you have finished fooling with the function.

Chapter 4: Making a Worksheet Easier to Read and Understand

In This Chapter

- Aligning numbers and text
- Changing the size of columns and rows
- Splashing color on a worksheet
- Drawing borders between cells and titles
- Applying styles to the data in cells
- Making worksheets fit well on the page
- Printing your worksheet

This short but pithy chapter explains how to dress a worksheet in its Sunday best in case you want to print it and present it to others. It explains how to align numbers and text, as well as insert rows and columns and change the size of rows and columns. You find out how to decorate a worksheet with colors and borders, as well as create and apply styles to make formatting tasks go more quickly. Finally, this chapter describes everything you need to know to print a worksheet, including how to make it fit on one page and repeat row labels and column names.

Laying Out a Worksheet

Especially if you intend to print your worksheet, you may as well dress it in its Sunday best. And you can do a number of things to make worksheets easier to read and understand. You can change character fonts. You can draw borders around or shade important cells. You can also format the numbers so that readers know, for example, whether they're staring at dollar figures or percentages. This part of Chapter 4 is dedicated to the proposition that a worksheet doesn't have to look drab and solemn.

Aligning numbers and text in columns and rows

To start with, numbers in worksheets are right-aligned in cells and text is left-aligned. Numbers and text sit squarely on the bottom of cells. You can, however, change the way that data is aligned. For example, you can make data float at the top of cells rather than rest at the bottom, and you can center or justify data in cells. Figure 4-1 illustrates different ways to format text and numbers.

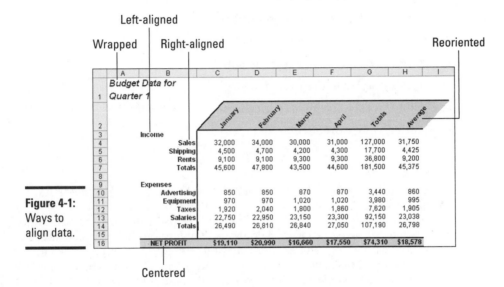

Figure 4-1: Ways to align data.

Select the cells whose alignment needs changing and follow these instructions to realign data in the cells:

✦ **Changing the horizontal (side-to-side) alignment:** Click an Align or Center button on the Formatting toolbar. You can also choose Format⇨Cells and, on the Alignment tab of the Format Cells dialog box, choose an option on the Horizontal drop-down list. Figure 4-2 shows the Format Cells dialog box.

✦ **Changing the vertical (top-to-bottom) alignment:** Choose Format⇨Cells and, on the Alignment tab of the Format Cells dialog box (refer to Figure 4-2), choose an option on the Vertical drop-down list. The Distribution option makes all the letters or numbers fit in a cell, even if it means wrapping text to two or more lines.

✦ **Reorienting the cells:** Choose Format⇨Cells and, on the Alignment Tab of the Format Cells dialog box (refer to Figure 4-2), drag the diamond in the Orientation box or enter a number in the <u>D</u>egrees text box.

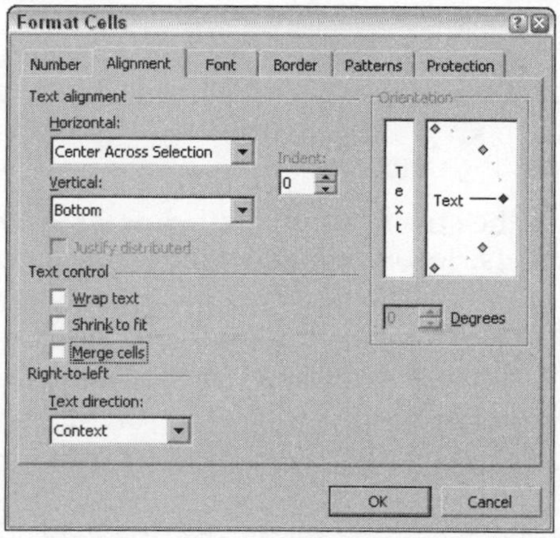

Figure 4-2:
The Format
Cells dialog
box.

Changing the orientation of text in cells is an elegant solution to the problem of keeping a worksheet from getting too wide. Numbers are usually a few characters wide, but heading labels can be much wider than that. By changing the orientation of a heading label, you make columns narrower and keep worksheets from growing too fat to fit on the page.

Merging and centering text across several cells

In the illustration shown here, "Sales Totals by Regional Office" is centered across four cells. Normally, text is left-aligned, but if you want to center it across several cells, drag across the cells to select them and then click the Merge and Center button. Merging also permits you to create large cells that span several columns.

The only way to "unmerge" cells is to select the merged cells, choose Format⇨Cells, and uncheck the <u>M</u>erge Cells check box on the Alignment tab of the Format Cells dialog box.

	C	D	E	F
	Sales Totals by Regional Office			
	North	West	East	South

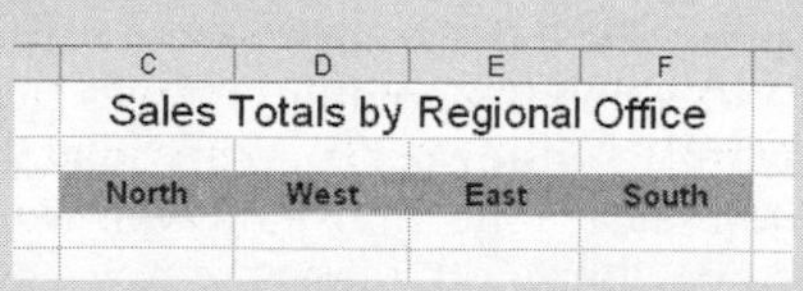

Inserting and deleting rows and columns

At some point, everybody has to insert new columns and rows and delete ones that are no longer needed. Make sure before you delete a row or column that you don't delete data that you really need. Do the following to insert and delete rows and columns:

✦ **Deleting rows or columns:** Drag across the row numbers or column letters of the rows or columns you want to delete; then right-click and choose <u>D</u>elete or press the Delete key.

✦ **Inserting rows:** Right-click the row number below where you want the new row to be and choose Insert. For example, to insert a new row above row 11, right-click row 11's number and choose Insert. You can also click in the row below where you want the new row to appear and choose Insert⇨Rows.

✦ **Inserting columns:** Right-click the column letter to the right of where you want the new column to be and choose <u>I</u>nsert. You can also click in the worksheet and choose <u>I</u>nsert⇨<u>C</u>olumns. A fast way to insert several columns is to insert one and keep pressing F4 (the Repeat command) until you've inserted all of them.

After you insert rows or columns, the Insert Options button appears. Click it and choose an option from the drop-down menu if you want your new row or column to have the same or different formats as the row or column you selected to start the Insert operation.

To insert more than one row or column at a time, select more than one row number or column letter before giving the Insert command.

Changing the width of columns and height of rows

By default, columns are 8.43 characters wide. To make columns wider, you have to widen them yourself. Rows are 12.75 points high, but Excel makes them higher when you enter letters or numbers that are taller than 12.75 points (72 points equals one inch).

Here are ways to change the height of rows:

✦ **One at a time:** Move the mouse pointer onto the boundary between row numbers and, when the pointer changes to a cross, drag the boundary between rows up or down. A pop-up box tells you how tall the row will be when you release the mouse button. You can also double-click the bottom of a cell border to make the row as tall as its tallest entry.

✦ **Several at a time:** Select the rows and choose Format➪Row➪Height. In the Row Height dialog box, enter a measurement and click OK.

Here are ways to make columns wider or narrower:

✦ **One at a time:** Move the mouse pointer onto the boundary between column letters and, when the pointer changes to a cross, drag the border between the columns. A pop-up box tells you what size the column is.

✦ **Several at a time:** Select the columns, choose Format➪Column➪Width and, in the Column Width dialog box, enter the number of characters you want to fit in the column. You can also select the columns and drag a column border. Doing so changes the size of all the columns you selected.

Rather than dicker with the width of columns, you can tell Excel to make columns as wide as their widest entries. This way, you can be certain that the data in each cell appears on-screen. To make columns as wide as their widest entries, select the columns and choose Format➪Column➪AutoFit Selection. You can also double-click the right border of the columns after you select them.

To change the 8.43-character standard width for columns in a worksheet, choose Format➪Column➪Standard Width and enter a new measurement in the Standard Width dialog box.

Decorating a Worksheet with Borders and Colors

The job of gridlines is simply to help you line up numbers and letters in cells. Gridlines aren't printed when you print a worksheet, and because gridlines are not printed, drawing borders on worksheets is absolutely necessary if you intend to print your worksheet. Use borders to steer the reader's eye to the most important parts of a worksheet — the totals, column labels, and heading labels. You can also decorate worksheets with colors. This part of the chapter explains how to put borders and colors on worksheets.

Decorating a worksheet requires clicking buttons on the Drawing toolbar. Click the Drawing button on the Standard toolbar to display the Drawing toolbar.

Choosing an "autoformat"

Rather than go to the trouble of decorating a worksheet with borders and colors, start by seeing whether one of Excel's "autoformats" does the trick.

An *autoformat* (where do they get these ridiculous names?) is a prefabricated spreadsheet design. Excel offers no less than 19 different autoformats. Trying them on for size takes about a second.

To try on an autoformat, select the data in your worksheet and choose Format⇨AutoFormat. You see the AutoFormat dialog box, shown in Figure 4-3. Scroll through the autoformats and find one that tickles your fancy. Clicking the Options button in the dialog box provides you with a few extra options for tinkering with the worksheet design.

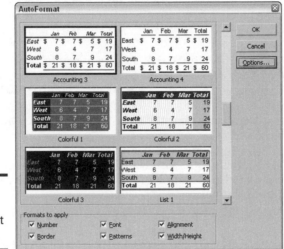

Figure 4-3:
The
AutoFormat
dialog box.

Decorating worksheets with colors

Select the cells that need color and try one of these techniques to splash color on your worksheet:

✦ Click the down arrow beside the Fill Color button and choose a color from the drop-down menu. Choose No Fill to remove a color.

✦ Choose Format⇨Cells and, on the Patterns tab of the Format Cells dialog box, select a color.

Slapping borders on worksheet cells

To draw borders on a worksheet, start by selecting the cells around which you want to place borders. Then click the down arrow beside the Borders button (you'll find it on the Formatting toolbar) and choose a border.

Usually, you have to wrestle with the Borders buttons until you come up with borders you like. By the way, don't be afraid to click the Undo button and start all over, or select a new set of cells and press F4 to apply the same kind of border a second time.

As shown in Figure 4-4, the Border tab in the Format Cells dialog box offers different lines for borders and colors for borders as well. Choose Format⇔Cells and select the Border tab if you want to try your hand at applying borders by way of the dialog box.

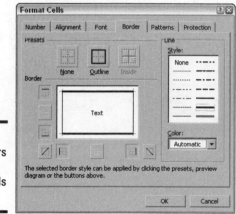

Figure 4-4:
The Borders tab of the Format Cells dialog box.

Saving formats in a template

If you go to the trouble to lay out a very fine workbook, you may as well save it as a template. That way, you can call upon your new-fangled design next time you want to create a new Excel workbook. Follow these steps to save a file as a template and be able to call upon its formats later on:

1. **Choose File⇔Save As to open the Save As dialog box.**

2. **Enter a descriptive name for your template in the File Name text box.**

3. **In the Save As Type drop-down menu, choose Template.**

4. **Click the Save button.**

5. **Back in your worksheet, delete the extraneous data that you don't need when you create a file from your template, and click the Save button to save the template again.**

To call upon the template you created, choose File⇔New (or press Ctrl+N) and, on the New Workbook task pane, select the On My Computer link (find it under "Other Templates.") Then, on the General tab of the Templates dialog box, select your template and click OK.

Styles for Quickly Formatting a Worksheet

A *style* is a collection of formats — boldface text, a background color, a border around cells — that can be applied all at one time to cells without having to visit a bunch of different dialog boxes or give a bunch of different commands. Styles save time. If you find yourself choosing the same formatting commands time and time again, consider creating a style. That way, you can apply all the formats simultaneously and go to lunch earlier.

Excel already comes with several built-in styles. To see what they are, choose Format⇨Style. You see the Style dialog box, shown in Figure 4-5. Open the Style Name drop-down menu to see the names of built-in styles. By putting a style of your own on this menu, you can apply the style quickly by choosing its name in the Style dialog box..

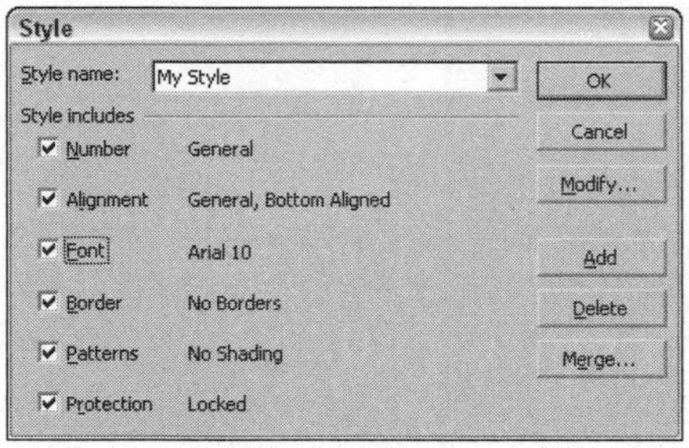

Figure 4-5:
Creating a
new style.

The easiest way to create a new style is to do it by example. Follow these steps:

1. **Apply the formatting commands you want for your style to a single cell.**

Click the Align Left button to left-align cell data. Or open the Fill Color drop-down menu and choose a color. Knock yourself out. Choose all the formatting commands you want for your new style.

2. **Choose Format⇨Style to open the Style dialog box (refer to Figure 4-5).**

3. **Enter a descriptive name for your style in the Style Name box and click OK.**

To apply a style, select cells, choose Format⇨Style, and choose a style on the Style Name drop-down menu in the Style dialog box.

Printing a Worksheet

Printing a worksheet isn't simply a matter of giving the Print command. A worksheet is a vast piece of computerized sprawl. Most worksheets don't fit neatly on a single page. If you simply click the Print button to print your worksheet, you wind up with page breaks in unexpected places, both on the right side of the page and the bottom. Read on to discover how to print a worksheet so that the people you hand it to can read and understand it easily.

Making a worksheet fit on the page

Unless you tell it otherwise, Excel prints everything from cell A1 to the last cell with data in it in the southeast corner of the worksheet. Usually, it isn't necessary to print all those cells because some of them are blank. And printing an entire worksheet often means breaking the page up in all kinds of awkward places. To keep that from happening, here are some techniques for making a worksheet fit tidily on one or two pages.

 As you experiment with the techniques described here, click the Print Preview button (or Shift+click the Print button) from time to time to see what your worksheet will look like when it's printed.

Printing part of a worksheet

To print part of a worksheet, select the data you want to print and choose File⇨Print Area⇨Set Print Area. This command tells Excel to print only the cells you selected. On the worksheet, a dotted line appears around cells in the print area. To remove the dotted lines from your worksheet, choose File⇨Print Area⇨Clear Print Area.

Adjusting the page breaks

Reading a worksheet is extremely difficult when it's broken awkwardly across pages. To decide for yourself where page breaks occur, choose View⇨Page Break Preview. As shown in Figure 4-6, you switch to Page Break view. In this view, dashed lines show you where Excel wants to break the pages.

Here's everything a body needs to know about page breaks:

✦ **Changing break positions:** In Page Break view, drag a dashed line to adjust the position of a page break. After you drag a dashed line, it ceases being a default page break and becomes a manual page break.

Manual page breaks are marked by solid lines, not dashed lines. You can drag them, too. Excel shrinks the numbers and letters on your worksheet if you try to squeeze too much data on a worksheet by dragging a page break.

✦ **Introducing a page break:** Select the cell directly below where you want the horizontal break to occur, and directly to the right of where you want the vertical break to be, and choose Insert⇨Page Break. Drag a page break to adjust its position.

✦ **Removing page breaks:** Select a cell directly below or directly to the right of the page break and choose Insert⇨Remove Page Break. To remove all the page breaks, click the Select All button (or press Ctrl+A) and choose Insert⇨Reset All Page Breaks.

Drag to change page breaks.

Default page break

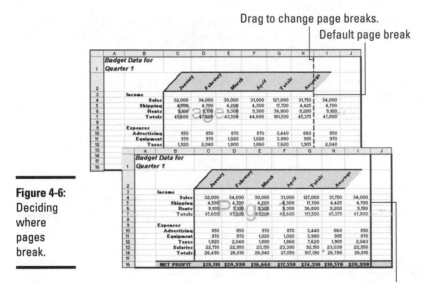

Figure 4-6: Deciding where pages break.

Manual page break

Choose View⇨Normal to return to Normal view after you're done fooling with page breaks. In Normal view, manual page breaks are marked by a dotted line. (If you don't care to see these dotted lines on your worksheet, choose Tools⇨Options, select the View tab in the Options dialog box, and unselect the Page Breaks check box.)

As the next section explains, you can use the Fit To option to scale data and make it small enough to fit on a page. However, the Fit To option and manual page breaks don't get along. Excel cancels manual page breaks if you select the Fit To option.

Scaling data to make it smaller

To scale the number and letters in the worksheet and make them a bit smaller, choose File➪Page Setup. You see the Page Setup dialog box, shown in Figure 4-7. On the Page tab, select the Fit To option button. Excel shrinks the data as much as necessary to make it fit on one page. The Fit To option is excellent for shrinking a worksheet that's just a little too big. Click the Print Preview button in the Page Setup dialog box to look at the Preview screen and see whether shrinking your worksheet this way is a help.

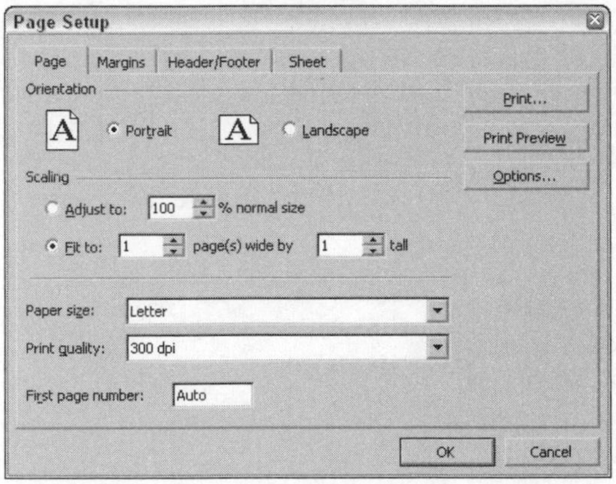

Figure 4-7:
The Page Setup dialog box.

Printing a landscape worksheet

If your worksheet is too wide to fit on one page, try turning the page on its head and printing in landscape mode. Choose File➪Page Setup and, on the Page tab of the page Setup dialog box (refer to Figure 4-7), select the Landscape option button.

Adjusting the margins

Another way to stuff all the data onto one page is to narrow the margins. Use either of these techniques to adjust the size of the margins:

✦ Choose File➪Page Setup and, on the Margins tab of the page Setup dialog box, change the size of margins.

**Book IV
Chapter 4**

**Making a
Worksheet Easier
to Read**

✦ Click the Print Preview button (or choose File➪Print Preview) to switch to the Print Preview window. From there, you can drag the margin lines to adjust the size of margins (margin lines are the outermost lines). If you don't see the margin lines, click the Margins button.

Making a worksheet more presentable

Before you print a worksheet, visit the Page Setup dialog box and see what you can do to make your worksheet easier for others to read and understand. To open the Page Setup dialog box, choose File➪Page Setup or click the Setup button in the Print Preview window. Here are your options:

✦ **Including page numbers on worksheets:** On the Page tab of the Page Setup dialog box (refer to Figure 4-7), enter **1** in the First Page Number text box. Then, on the Header/Footer tab, choose a Header or Footer option that includes a page number (for example, Page 1 of ?).

✦ **Putting headers and footers on pages:** On the Header/Footer tab of the Page Setup dialog box, choose options from the Header and Footer drop-down menus. You'll find options for listing the file name, page numbers, the date, and your name. By clicking the Custom Header or Custom Footer button, you can open the Header or Footer dialog box and construct a header or footer there. Figure 4-8 shows the Header dialog box.

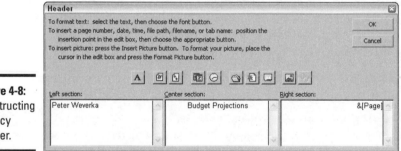

Figure 4-8: Constructing a fancy header.

✦ **Centering worksheet data on the page:** On the Margins tab, choose Horizontally or Vertically to center the worksheet relative to the top or bottom or sides of the page. You can select both check boxes. The preview screen shows what your choices mean in real terms.

✦ **Printing gridlines, column letters, and row numbers:** By default, the gridlines, column letters, and row numbers you know and love in a worksheet aren't printed, but you can print them by selecting the Gridlines and Row and Column Headings check boxes in the Sheet tab of the Page Setup dialog box.

Solving the Letter, A4 dilemma

The Page tab of the Page Setup dialog box (refer to Figure 4-7) offers an option for printing on size A4 paper (210 by 297mm), the paper standard favored in Europe. To choose the option, open the Paper Size drop-down menu and choose A4. However, you probably don't need to bother, because Excel automatically adjusts worksheets laid out for 8 1/2 by 11-inch paper to the A4 standard when printing on that size paper. The program also adjusts A4 layouts for the 8 1/2 by 11-inch standard when printing on that size paper.

If you prefer Excel not to make these adjustments because you want to make them on your own, choose Tools➪Options and, on the International tab of the Options dialog box, unselect the Allow A4/Letter Paper Resizing check box.

Repeating row labels and column names on each page

If your worksheet is a big one that stretches beyond one page, you owe it to the people who will view your worksheet to repeat row labels and column names from page to page. Without the row labels and column names, no one can tell what the data in the worksheet means. Follow these steps to repeat row labels and column headings from page to page:

1. **Choose File➪Page Setup.**

   You see the Page Setup dialog box.

2. **Select the Sheet tab.**

3. **Select the Row and Column Headings check box.**

4. **To repeat rows, click the Return to Worksheet button next to the Rows to Repeat at Top text box; to repeat columns, click the Return to Worksheet button next to the Columns to Repeat at Left text box.**

   The dialog box shrinks so that you can get a better look at your worksheet.

5. **Select the row or column with the labels or names you need.**

   You can select more than one row or column, as long as they're next to each other.

6. **Click the Return to Dialog Box button to enlarge the dialog box and see it again.**

   The text box now lists a cell range address.

7. **Repeat Steps 4 through 6 to select column names or row labels.**

8. **Click OK to close the Page Setup dialog box.**

   If I were you, I would click the Print Preview button to make sure that row labels and column names are indeed repeating from page to page.

To remove row labels and column names, return to the Sheet tab of the Page Setup dialog box and delete the cell references in the Rows to Repeat at Top text box and the Columns to Repeat at Left text box. You can also press Ctrl+F3 and delete Print_Titles in the Define Name dialog box.

Chapter 5: Seeing Data in Charts

In This Chapter

⮑ **Creating charts with the Chart Wizard**

⮑ **Changing chart types and chart elements**

⮑ **Customizing a chart's appearance**

⮑ **Annotating a chart**

⮑ **Customizing tick marks, tick-mark labels, and 3-D displays**

⮑ **Entering a chart in the Chart Wizard Gallery**

One of the fastest ways to impress impressionable people is to create a chart from worksheet data. Excel makes it very, very easy to create charts. All you have to do to create a chart is select data and choose a few menu commands. And if you're fickle and don't like the chart you created, you can simply choose another type of chart. And if you're in the mood to do something out of the ordinary with a chart, you can do that, too.

This chapter explains how to create a chart and customize it in various ways to make the chart your very own.

Building Charts from Your Data

Herewith is an explanation of creating a chart. Believe me, creating a chart is easier than you think. All you have to do is paint by numbers. You will also find an explanation here for positioning a chart on the page.

Creating a chart with the Chart Wizard

Figure 5-1 shows an "Elvis Sightings" worksheet and a column chart that I created from data in the worksheet. You can create charts like these with the Chart Wizard dialog box. As you fill in the dialog boxes, you watch your chart take shape. You can always go back to the Chart Wizard dialog boxes and edit your chart, as the rest of this chapter explains in excruciating detail.

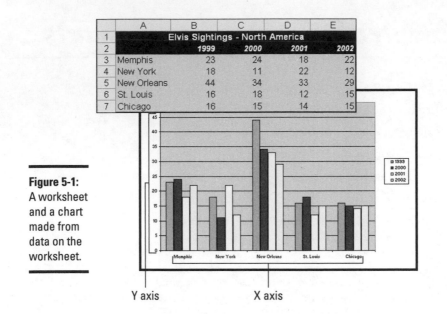

	A	B	C	D	E
1	Elvis Sightings - North America				
2		1999	2000	2001	2002
3	Memphis	23	24	18	22
4	New York	18	11	22	12
5	New Orleans	44	34	33	29
6	St. Louis	16	18	12	15
7	Chicago	16	15	14	15

Figure 5-1:
A worksheet and a chart made from data on the worksheet.

Y axis   X axis

Follow these steps to create a chart:

1. Select the data that you want to chart.

Don't select a totals column or row for your chart. The purpose of a chart is to compare and contrast data. Including a totals column or row creates an unrealistic comparison, because the totals data is inevitably much, much larger than the other data and you end up with an extra-large pie slice or bar, for example, in your chart.

2. Click the Chart Wizard button or choose Insert➪Chart.

You see the first of four Chart Wizard dialog boxes, as shown in Figure 5-2.

3. Clicking the Next button as you go along, construct your chart.

And don't worry about getting it right the first time. Charts usually need a bit of tinkering before they can be made into masterpieces.

You encounter four dialog boxes in your journey to a perfect chart: Chart Type, Chart Source Data, Chart Options, and Chart Location. Keep reading.

Chart Type

Choose a chart type. You can click the Press and Hold to View Sample button to see what the data you selected looks like in the chart type you chose. Be sure to scroll to the bottom of the list to look at all the chart types. The Custom Types tab offers some interesting choices.

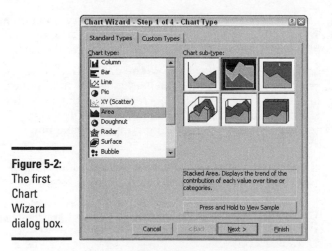

Figure 5-2:
The first
Chart
Wizard
dialog box.

Chart Source Data

From here, you can select source data from your chart, but you already did that in Step 1 if you followed my directions. Choose a Series In option to change the data series on which the chart is plotted. Keep your eye on the sample chart — it shows what your choices mean in real terms.

If you choose the wrong cell range for a data source or you want to choose a different cell range, follow these steps:

1. **Select the Series tab in the Chart Wizard dialog box.**

2. **In the Series box, select the data series that needs replotting.**

 3. **Select the Go to Worksheet button next to the Values text box.**

   The dialog box shrinks so that you can see your worksheet.

4. **Drag to select a different data series in your worksheet.**

5. **Press Esc to return to the Chart Wizard dialog box.**

Chart Options

This is where you decide what your chart looks like. There are six tabs in this dialog box:

✦ **Titles:** Enter a title for your chart in the Chart Title text box. If need be, enter descriptive labels for the data being plotted in the Category (X) and Axis, Value (Y) Axis text boxes (pie and doughnut charts don't have axes). However, axes descriptions aren't absolutely necessary. Sometimes including them crowds the chart and makes it smaller. Again, keep your eye on the sample chart to see what your choices mean in real terms.

✦ **Axes:** This is where you tell Excel how to scale the chart. In most cases, Excel recognizes whether it's dealing with category labels or time values, but if the program gets it wrong, select the correct option button. Later in this chapter, "Handling tick marks and tick-mark labels" describes how to change the points of a scale — the minimum and maximum values plotted on a chart.

✦ **Gridlines:** Click check boxes to decide how many vertical and horizontal gridlines you want.

✦ **Legend:** Select an option button to decide where on the chart to place the legend, if the chart needs a legend. The *legend* is the explanatory list of the symbols on the chart.

✦ **Data Labels:** If you so desire, select a check box to attach a data label to one of the data markers in the chart. Keep your eye on the Preview chart. It shows plainly what your choices are. If you choose a data label, choose one, not two or three. Two or three data labels per chart element can congest a chart and make it hard to understand, but if you have to choose two or three, open the Separator drop-down menu and choose a punctuation mark for separating the labels.

✦ **Data Table:** Select the Show <u>D</u>ata Table option if you want a replica of your Excel worksheet to appear on the page with the chart.

If you make a decision on the Chart Options tab that you regret later on, you can return to the Options tab by choosing <u>C</u>hart⇨Chart Opt<u>i</u>ons.

Chart Location

Choose where to place the new chart, on the worksheet where the data is or on another worksheet in the workbook.

Later in this chapter, I explain how to alter different parts of a chart, but if you want to start all over again, you can always do so by revisiting the Chart Wizard dialog boxes. Just select your chart and click the Chart Wizard button.

Adjusting a chart's position on the page

If you opted to place the chart on the same worksheet as the data from which you created the chart, your chart probably needs to be moved down the page. Click the perimeter of the chart to select it and then drag to move the chart elsewhere. While you're at it, select the chart and use one of these techniques to change the chart's size:

Creating an overlay chart

An *overlay chart* is a secondary chart that appears over another chart, the idea being to contrast two sets of data. Create an overlay chart by selecting one data series in a chart you already created and instructing Excel to use the data in the series for the overlay chart. To create an overlay chart, the original chart must plot more than one data series.

Follow these steps to create an overlay chart:

1. **In a chart you created, click to select the data that will be contrasted with the other data.**

For this chart, for example, I selected data that tracks Elvis sightings in 2002.

2. **Right-click the data series and choose Chart Type.**

You see the Chart Type dialog box.

3. **Choose a chart type for the overlay chart and click OK.**

Be sure to click a chart type different from the one in the mother chart.

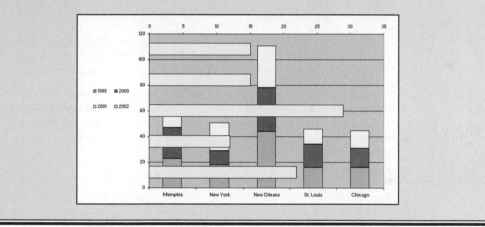

♦ Drag a corner handle to make it larger or smaller but keep its proportions.

♦ Drag a corner handle while holding down the Ctrl key to keep the center of the chart in the same position as you change its size.

By default, Excel creates a two-dimensional column chart. If you prefer a different kind of chart to be the default chart, create the kind of chart you like, select it, choose Chart⇨Chart Type, and click the Set As Default Chart button in the Chart Type dialog box.

Editing a Chart

Most charts need to be retooled, kneaded, massaged, and prodded a few times before they are just-so. These pages explain the specifics of editing a chart.

The Chart toolbar appears on-screen after you create a chart (click your chart if you don't see the toolbar, or right-click any toolbar and choose Chart). As I explain in the following pages, the Chart toolbar comes in handy for fiddling with a chart's appearance.

Choosing a different chart type

So you chose the wrong chart type? It happens in the best of families. To undo the damage, click to select your chart and do one of the following:

✦ Click the arrow beside the Chart Type button and choose a new type from the drop-down menu.

✦ Click the Chart Wizard button or choose Insert➪Chart to open the Chart Wizard dialog box (refer to Figure 5-2). On the Standard Types or Custom Types tab, choose a new chart type and click the Finish button.

To select a chart, click its outermost border. If you click inside the chart, you are liable to select a part of the chart — the legend, a data series — rather than the chart itself. You know when you have selected a chart because the black selection handles appear on the chart's corners and sides.

Adding and removing chart elements

Suppose that you construct a chart with the Chart Wizard but discover to your dismay that you forgot to include a title or legend? Suppose that you include a title or legend but regret doing so? Don't despair. With Excel, you always get a second chance. Click to select your chart and follow these steps to add or remove a title, legend, or other element:

1. **Click the Chart Wizard button.**

   You see the Chart Wizard dialog box. Does it look familiar? This is the same dialog box you used to create the chart in the first place.

2. **Revisit the different tabs in the Chart Wizard dialog box, and be careful this time to include or exclude chart elements.**

3. **Click the Finish button.**

   Earlier in this chapter, "Creating a chart with the Chart Wizard" explains the Chart Wizard.

You can click the Legend button on the Chart toolbar to add or remove the chart's legend, the box with explanations as to what everything on the chart is.

If you're in a hurry to remove an element from a chart, simply select it and press the Delete key. If you know which part of a chart you want to alter, select it and choose Chart⇨Chart Options. This command opens the third of the four Chart Wizard dialog boxes, the one that pertains to the chart's appearance.

The basics of changing a chart's appearance

A chart is composed of different so-called objects — the legend, the plot area, the different data series, and others. To see what I mean, try clicking part of the chart. Black selection handles appear around the object, or part of the chart, that you clicked. As shown in Figure 5-3, you can open the Chart Objects drop-down menu on the Chart toolbar to see a list of all the objects in your chart.

To change the size, shape, fonts, or colors of any part of a chart, follow these basic steps:

1. **Select the part of the chart you want to change by clicking it or by choosing its name on the Chart Objects drop-down menu.**

You find this menu on the Charts toolbar.

2. **Open the Format dialog box (refer to Figure 5-3) to start giving Format commands.**

Excel offers no fewer than five ways to open the Format dialog box:

- Click the Format button on the Chart toolbar.

- Double-click the part of the chart you selected.

- Right-click the part of the chart you selected and choose Format on the shortcut menu.

- Press Ctrl+1.

- Choose Format⇨Selected *object name*.

3. **Change formats in the Format dialog box.**

Again, which options you get in the dialog box depends on which part of your chart you selected in Step 1. You can find options in the Format dialog box to change the font, color, border, background, and alignment of text.

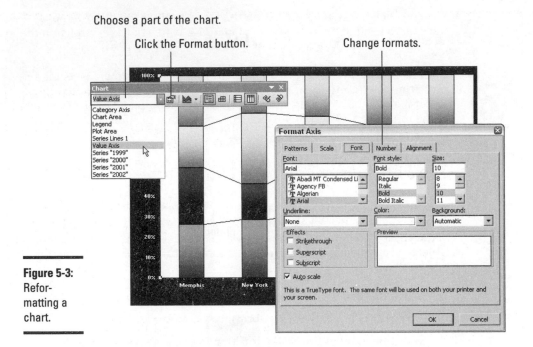

Choose a part of the chart.

Click the Format button.

Change formats.

Figure 5-3:
Reformatting a chart.

Choose Edit➪Undo (or press Ctrl+Z) and start all over if your changes to the chart didn't work out. Usually, you have to wrestle with Format dialog boxes for five minutes or so before the chart starts smelling like a rose.

Seeing as how all parts of a chart are objects, you can select and drag them to new locations. When you see the black selection handles, start dragging. A dotted line shows where the object will land when you release the mouse button.

You can click the By Row or By Column button on the Chart toolbar at any time to experiment with changing the data axes of the chart.

To make one slice in a pie chart stand out from the rest, click to select it, and then drag. Be sure to select a single slice and not the whole pie.

Putting Pizzazz in Your Charts

The rest of this chapter deals with how to make your charts stand out in a crowd. Be sure to read the previous section of this chapter, "Editing a Chart," before you delve into the extracurricular activity I describe in the following pages. You need to understand the basics before you can undertake the baroque and rococo.

Decorating a chart with a picture

A picture looks mighty nice on the plot area of a chart, especially a column chart. If you have a picture on your computer that would serve well to decorate a chart, you are hereby encouraged to start decorating. Follow these steps to place a picture on the plot area of a chart:

1. **Either select the plot area or choose Plot Area on the Chart Objects drop-down menu.**

2. **Click the Format Plot Area button or double-click the plot area.**

   You see the Format Plot Area dialog box.

3. **Click the Fill Effects button to open the Fill Effects dialog box.**

4. **Select the Picture tab.**

5. **Click the Select Picture button to open the Select Picture dialog box.**

6. **Locate the picture you need, select it, and click the Insert button.**

   Try to select a light-colored picture that will serve as a background.

7. **Click OK in the Fill Effects dialog box and click OK again in the Format Plot Area dialog box.**

Handling text and titles

Right-click text or a title and choose Format on the shortcut menu to open the Format dialog box and select a new font or font size for letters. Beyond that, Excel offers a couple of neat acrobatic stunts you can do with text and titles:

✦ **Aligning text:** To align text, click an Align button on the Formatting tool-bar. You can also go to the Alignment tab of the Formatting toolbar and choose from several vertical and horizontal alignment options.

✦ **Angling the text:** In Excel, "angling" means to turn text at a different angle, not to fish for text, as shown in Figure 5-4. To turn text at a 45-degree angle, click the Angle Clockwise or Angle Counterclockwise button on the Chart toolbar. You can also open the Format dialog box and, on the Alignment tab, enter a number in the <u>D</u>egrees text box or drag in the Orientation box to turn text to any angle.

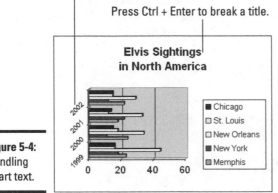

Figure 5-4: Handling chart text.

✦ **Creating a two-line title:** Long titles sometimes need to go on two lines. To break a title and move part of it to a new line, click where you want the break to occur and press Ctrl+Enter.

Handling tick marks and tick-mark labels

Like the lines on a ruler, *tick marks* are the lines on a chart that indicate what the data values are on the axis. *Tick-mark labels* are the number labels that accompany tick marks. These pages explain how to change tick-mark labels and alter the scale by which tick marks plot data.

Changing the numeric format of tick mark labels

Follow these steps to change the numeric format of tick-mark labels:

1. **Choose Value Axis on the Chart Objects drop-down menu.**

You find this menu on the Chart toolbar.

Annotating a chart

To highlight part of a chart — an especially large pie slice, a tall column, a bar showing miniscule sales figures — annotate it with a text box and place the text box beside the pie slice, column, or bar. Excel makes it very easy to annotate charts:

1. **Click anywhere on the chart.**

2. **Start typing the annotation text.**

   Your words appear on the Formula bar. You can edit the text while it's in the Formula bar.

3. **Press Enter.**

   The text box appears on your chart.

4. **Move the pointer over the text box and, when you see a four-pointed arrow, click and drag the text box where you want it to be.**

5. **Right-click the text box and choose Format Text Box.**

6. **In the Format Text Box dialog box, choose a font and font size for the letters, and a background color and border for the text box.**

   Book IX describes text boxes in detail.

7. **Click the Line or Arrow Style button on the Drawing toolbar and draw a line from the text box to the pie slice, column, or bar.**

   Book IX also describes line drawing.

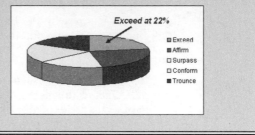

2. **Click the Format Axis button or press Ctrl+1.**

3. **Select the Number tab of the Format Axis dialog box.**

4. **Choose a new number format and click OK.**

Changing the tick-mark value-axis scale

As a general rule, Excel does a good job of scaling the values in a chart. Sometimes, however, the value-axis scale doesn't allow the chart to demonstrate clear differences in values. Sometimes the values being plotted are so similar, it's hard to tell which bar is taller than the next.

Take note of the highest and lowest value on your chart and follow these steps to choose a more representative range of values for the tick-mark scale:

1. **Choose Value Axis on the Chart Objects drop-down menu.**

   Look for this menu on the Chart toolbar.

2. **Click the Format Axis button or choose Format➪Selected Axis.**

3. **Select the Scale tab of the Format Axis dialog box.**

4. **In the Minimum text box, enter a number that represents where you want the scale to begin.**

5. **In the Maximum text box, enter a number that represents where you want the scale to end.**

   This number should be slightly above the largest value being plotted.

6. **Click OK.**

When you enter a value of your own on the Scale tab, Excel clears the check mark in the Auto box. To get a default value back, select an Auto check box. By selecting all the Auto check boxes, you can re-create a default chart.

Changing the look and frequency of gridlines

If you're not happy with the look or frequency of gridlines on your chart, don't just sit there, do something:

✦ **Changing the frequency of gridlines:** Select the chart and choose Chart➪Chart Options. On the Gridlines tab of the Chart Options dialog box, select or unselect check boxes to change the frequency of gridlines in your chart. Keep your eye on the preview chart in the dialog box. It shows exactly what you're getting.

✦ **Changing the look of gridlines:** Choose Value Axis Major Gridlines or Value Axis Minor Gridlines (depending on which you want to change) on the Chart Objects drop-down menu. This menu is available on the Chart toolbar. Next, click the Format button or press Ctrl+1. On the Patterns tab of the Format Gridlines dialog box, choose a style, color, and weight for the gridlines and click OK.

Changing the display of 3-D charts

In some kinds of three-dimensional charts, one bar or column gets in the way of another. When this happens, it's hard to compare bars or columns, because all of them can't be seen clearly. To remedy this problem, follow these steps to change the order in which data series are plotted:

1. **Click any bar or column.**

2. **Click the Format Data Series button or choose Format➪Selected Data Series.**

   You see the Format Data Series dialog box.

3. **Select the Series Order tab.**

4. **Select a data series and click the Move Up or Move Down button until the preview chart looks just right.**

5. **Click OK.**

On the subject of three-dimensional charts, one way to solve the problem of not being able to see all the bars or columns is to change the chart's viewing angle. To change it, select Corners on the Chart Objects drop-down menu on the Chart toolbar. Then drag a chart corner ever so slightly, as shown in Figure 5-4. You can also choose Chart⇨3-D View and tinker with the esoteric options in the 3-D View dialog box, also shown in Figure 5-5.

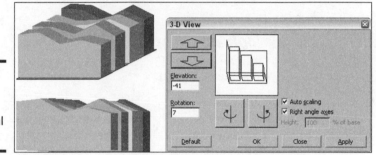

Figure 5-5:
Altering the three-dimensional view.

Putting your new-fangled chart in the Chart Wizard gallery

After you go to the significant trouble of changing the various aspects of a chart — the colors, fonts, gridlines, and so on — you may as well enter your chart in the Chart Wizard Gallery. That way, you can call upon it when you want to make your next chart. Select the chart and follow these steps to immortalize it in the gallery:

1. **Choose Chart⇨Chart Type.**

   You see the Chart Type dialog box.

2. **Select the Custom Types tab.**

3. **Under Select From, select the User-Defined option button.**

4. **Click the Add button, enter a name and description for your chart in the Add Custom Chart Type dialog box, and click OK.**

5. **Click OK again in the Chart Type dialog box.**

   To destroy a chart you created, return to the Custom Types tab of the Chart Type dialog box, select the User-Defined option button, select your chart, and click the Delete button.

When you want to put your chart to work, click the Chart Wizard button as usual, go to the Custom Types tab in the Chart Wizard dialog box, select the User-Defined option button, and select your chart.

Chapter 6: Analyzing Data

In This Chapter

✔ Sorting information in a worksheet list

✔ Filtering a list to find the information you need

✔ Using the Goal Seek command to produce formula results

✔ Performing what-if analyses with data tables

*T*his chapter offers a handful of tricks for analyzing the data that you so carefully and lovingly entered in a worksheet. Delve into this chapter to find out how to manage, sort, and filter worksheet lists. You also discover how the Goal Seek command can help you target values in different kinds of analysis, and how you can map out different scenarios with data by using one- and two-input data tables.

Managing Information in Lists

Although Excel is a spreadsheet program, many people use it to keep and maintain lists — address lists, product lists, employee lists, and inventory lists, among other types of list. These pages deal with all the different things you can do with a worksheet list. They explain the difference between a conventional worksheet and a list, constructing a list, sorting a list, and filtering a list.

Constructing a list

To sort and filter data in a worksheet, your worksheet must be constructed like a list. Make sure that your worksheet has these characteristics:

✦ **Column labels:** Enter column labels along the top row, as shown in Figure 6-1. Excel needs these labels to identify and be able to filter the data in the rows below. Each label must have a different name. The row along the top of the worksheet where the column labels are is called the *header row*.

	Product ID	Product Name	Production Cost	Packaging	Ship Cost	Sale per Unit	Profit	Warehouse	Supervisor
2	11100	Widget	1.19	0.14	0.45	4.11	2.33	Trenton	Munoz
3	11101	Gasket	2.24	0.29	0.89	4.14	0.72	Pickford	Salazaar
4	11102	Tappet	4.13	1.11	0.18	7.12	1.70	Trenton	Munoz
5	11103	Widget	8.19	3.40	0.45	14.80	2.76	LaRue	Smith
6	11104	Pludget	6.41	0.29	0.32	7.89	0.87	Massy	Yee
7	11105	Placker	7.39	0.98	1.11	12.14	2.66	Pickford	Salazaar
8	11106	Stacker	11.00	1.14	0.89	14.89	1.86	LaRue	Smith
9	11107	Knacker	14.31	3.14	0.45	20.98	3.08	Massy	Yee
10	11108	Tipplet	2.11	0.14	0.32	5.81	3.24	Trenton	Munoz
11	11109	Culet	4.16	0.17	0.32	6.01	1.36	Trenton	Munoz
12	11110	Ropper	13.44	2.89	0.79	21.43	4.31	LaRue	Smith
13	11111	Knocker	23.08	2.10	0.89	32.89	6.82	Trenton	Munoz
14	11112	Topper	1.14	0.09	0.11	4.02	2.68	Pickford	Salazaar
15	11113	Rammer	2.15	0.16	0.32	5.10	2.47	Massy	Yee
16	11114	Cricker	3.34	0.27	0.33	6.12	2.18	LaRue	Smity
17	11115	Knicker	8.78	1.01	0.89	10.79	0.11	Trenton	Munoz
18	11116	Stamler	2.14	0.53	0.20	6.78	3.91	LaRue	Smith
19	11117	Doublet	9.46	1.01	0.99	14.33	2.87	Pickford	Salazaar
20	11118	Crumpet	2.99	0.24	0.18	7.00	3.59	Trenton	Munoz

Figure 6-1:
A worksheet
as list.

✦ **No empty rows or columns:** Sorry, but you can't put an empty row or column in the middle of the worksheet list.

✦ **No blank columns on left:** Don't allow any empty columns to appear to the left of the list.

✦ **A single worksheet:** The list must occupy a single worksheet. You can't keep more than one list on the same worksheet.

If you know anything about databases, the rules for constructing a worksheet list no doubt sound familiar. These are the same rules that apply to constructing a database table. You might consider managing your list as a database if it's a long and complex one. Book VI explains how to use Access, the database program in Office.

Sorting a list

Sorting means to rearrange the rows in a list on the basis of data in one column. Sort a list on the Last Name column, for example, to arrange the list in alphabetical order by last name. Sort a list on the ZIP Code field to arrange the rows in numerical order by Zip Code. Sort a list on the Birthday field to arrange it chronologically from earliest born to latest born. Here are all the ways to sort a list:

✦ **Sorting on a single column:** Click in any cell in the column and click the Sort Ascending or Sort Descending button.

+ **Sort on more than one column:** Choose <u>D</u>ata⇨<u>S</u>ort. You see the Sort dialog box. Choose Sort By and Then By columns, and select option buttons to tell Excel to sort in ascending or descending order.

Be careful about sorting rows with formula results. Sorting discombobulates the rows. If a formula refers to a cell that *isn't* in the same row and you give a sort command, you get a #VALUE! error because the formula won't compute using the correct cell address.

Filtering a list

Filtering means to scour a worksheet list for certain kinds of data. To filter, you tell Excel what kind of data you're looking for, and the program assembles rows with that data to the exclusion of rows that don't have the data. You end up with a shorter list with only the rows that match your criteria. Filtering is similar to the Find command, except that you get more than one row in the results of the filtering operation.

To filter a list, you select options from column header drop-down lists to tell Excel what you're looking for. Follow these steps:

1. **Choose <u>D</u>ata⇨<u>F</u>ilter⇨Auto<u>F</u>ilter.**

As shown in Figure 6-2, you see a drop-down list on each column header in your list.

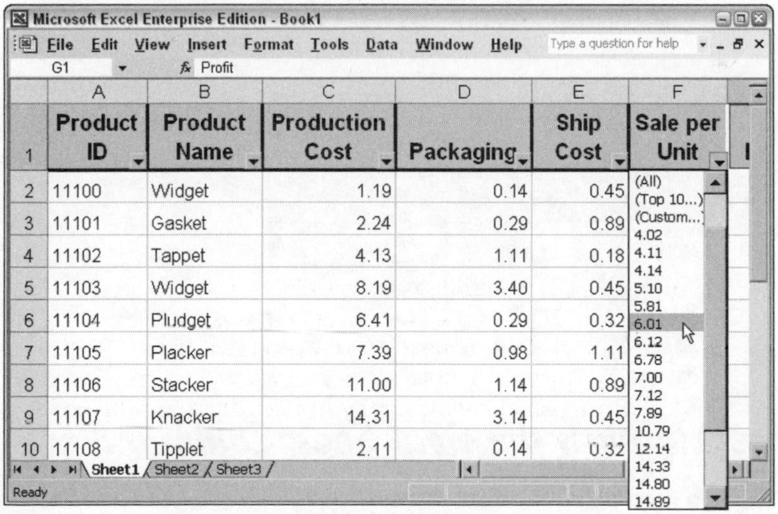

Figure 6-2:
Selecting
criteria from
the drop-
down
menus.

	A	B	C	D	E	F	
1	Product ID	Product Name	Production Cost	Packaging	Ship Cost	Sale per Unit	
2	11100	Widget	1.19	0.14	0.45	(All)	
3	11101	Gasket	2.24	0.29	0.89	(Top 10...) (Custom...) 4.02	
4	11102	Tappet	4.13	1.11	0.18	4.11	
5	11103	Widget	8.19	3.40	0.45	4.14 5.10	
6	11104	Pludget	6.41	0.29	0.32	5.81 6.01	
7	11105	Placker	7.39	0.98	1.11	6.12 6.78	
8	11106	Stacker	11.00	1.14	0.89	7.00 7.12	
9	11107	Knacker	14.31	3.14	0.45	7.89 10.79	
10	11108	Tipplet	2.11	0.14	0.32	12.14 14.33 14.80 14.89	

Microsoft Excel Enterprise Edition - Book1

<u>F</u>ile <u>E</u>dit <u>V</u>iew <u>I</u>nsert F<u>o</u>rmat <u>T</u>ools <u>D</u>ata <u>W</u>indow <u>H</u>elp — Type a question for help

G1 — ƒ<u>x</u> Profit

Sheet1 / Sheet2 / Sheet3 /

Ready

**Book IV
Chapter 6**

Analyzing Data

2. **Open a drop-down list and choose what you're looking for.**

   You can choose from more than one drop-down list to narrow your search to a few rows. When you're done, you see only rows that match the criteria you established when you chose options from the drop-down lists. The status bar tells you how many rows — or records, to use database terminology — were found.

To see all the data in the list again, choose Data⇨Filter⇨Show All or open a drop-down list you selected from previously and choose All.

Here are a few variations on the AutoFilter command:

✦ **Filtering for top or bottom items:** On the column header drop-down menu, choose Top Ten. You see the Top 10 AutoFilter dialog box. Choose whether you want to see the top or bottom items, how many items to bring up in the search, and whether you want to search for items by percentage. Then click OK.

✦ **Finding blank or nonblank cells:** Scroll to the bottom of the column header drop-down list and choose Blanks or NonBlanks.

✦ **Using operators to define search criteria:** Open a drop-down list and choose Custom. You see the Custom AutoFilter dialog box, shown in Figure 6-3. Choose an operator from the drop-down menu and a target criteria from the menu beside the operator menu. You can search by more than one criterion. Select the And option button if a row must meet both criteria to be selected, or the Or option button if a row can meet either criterion to be selected.

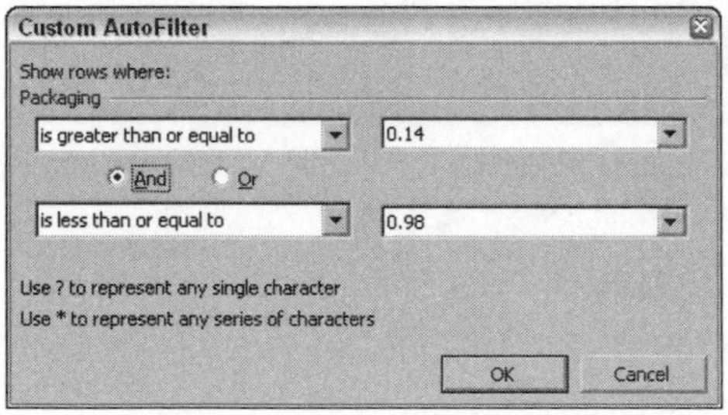

Figure 6-3:
The Custom
AutoFilter
dialog box.

Custom AutoFilter	⊗
Show rows where:	
Packaging	
is greater than or equal to ▼	0.14 ▼
⊙ And ○ Or	
is less than or equal to ▼	0.98 ▼
Use ? to represent any single character	
Use * to represent any series of characters	
OK	Cancel

Forecasting with the Goal Seek Command

In a conventional formula, you provide the raw data and Excel produces the results. With the Goal Seek command, you declare what you want the results to be, and Excel tells you the raw data you need to produce those results. The Goal Seek command is especially useful in financial analyses when you want the outcome to be a certain way and you need to know which raw numbers will produce the outcome that you want.

Figure 6-4 shows a worksheet designed to find out the monthly payment on a mortgage. Using the PMT function, the worksheet determines that the monthly payment on a $250,000 loan with an interest rate of 6.5 percent and to be paid over a 30-year period is $1,580.17. Suppose, however, that the person who calculated this monthly payment determined that he or she could pay more than $1,580.17 per month? Suppose the person could pay $1,750 or $2,000 per month. Instead of an outcome of $1,580.17, the person wants to know how much he or she could borrow if monthly payments — the outcome of the formula — were increased to $1,750 or $2,000.

Changing to the results you want

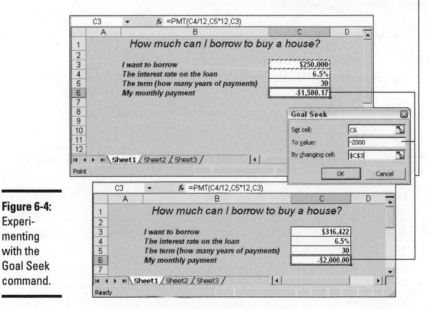

Figure 6-4: Experimenting with the Goal Seek command.

To make determinations such as these, you can use the Goal Seek command. This command lets you experiment with the arguments in a formula to achieve the results you want. In the case of the worksheet in Figure 6-4, you can use the Goal Seek command to change the argument in cell C3, the total amount you can borrow, given the outcome you want in cell C6, $1,750 or $2,000, the monthly payment on the total amount.

**Book IV
Chapter 6**

Analyzing Data

Entering the data in a form

After you have entered the header row (the column labels at the top of the list), you can enter the data in the list by means of a form. Forms are more convenient for entering data than worksheet cells are. To enter the data on a form, choose Data⇨Form. You see a form like the one in this figure. Click the New button to clear the form and start entering data. Columns in which data is derived from calculations are blank on the form. When you're done entering the information about a person, place, or thing, click the New button again.

Sheet1		
Product ID:	11119	New Record
Product Name:	Sprucer	New
Unit Production Cost:	2.27	Delete
Packaging:	.29	Restore
Ship Cost:	.89	
Sale per Unit:	5.99	Find Prev
Profit:		Find Next
Warehouse:	Pickford	Criteria
Supervisor:	Salazaar	Close

Follow these steps to use the Goal Seek command to change the inputs in a formula to achieve the results you want:

1. **Select the cell with the formula whose arguments you want to experiment with.**

2. **Choose Tools⇨Goal Seek.**

   You see the Goal Seek dialog box, shown in Figure 6-4.

3. **In the To Value text box, enter the target results you want from the formula.**

   In the example in Figure 6-4, you enter **1750** or **2000**, the monthly payment you can afford for the 30-year mortgage.

4. **In the By Changing Cell text box, enter the address of the cell whose value is unknown.**

   To enter a cell address, select a cell on your worksheet. In Figure 6-4, you select the address of the cell that shows the total amount you want to borrow.

5. **Click OK.**

   The Goal Seek Status dialog box appears. It lists the target value you entered in Step 3.

6. **Click OK.**

On your worksheet, the cell with the argument you wanted to alter now shows the target you're seeking. In the case of the worksheet in Figure 6-4, you can borrow $316,422, not $250,000, by raising your monthly mortgage payments from $1,580.17 to $2,000.

Performing What-If Analyses with Data Tables

For something a little more sophisticated than the Goal Seek command (described in the previous section), try performing what-if analyses with data tables. With this technique, you change the data in input cells and observe what effect changing the data has on the results of a formula. The difference between the Goal Seek command and a data table is that you can experiment with many different input cells simultaneously, and in so doing experiment with many different scenarios.

Using a one-input table for analysis

In a *one-input table,* you find out what the different results of a formula would be if you changed one *input cell* in the formula. In Figure 6-5, that input cell is the interest rate on a loan. The purpose of this data table is to find out how monthly payments on a $250,000, 30-year mortgage are different, given different interest rates. The interest rate in cell B4 is the input cell.

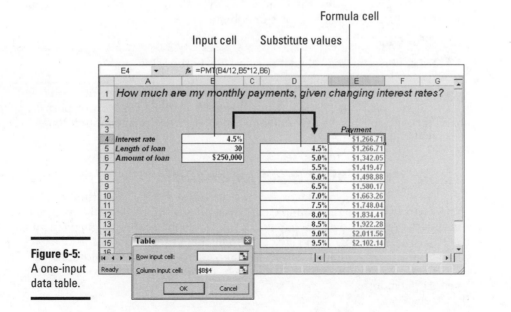

Figure 6-5:
A one-input
data table.

Book IV
Chapter 6

Analyzing Data

Follow these steps to create a one-input table:

1. **On your worksheet, enter values that you want to substitute for the value in the input cell.**

   To make the input table work, you have to enter the substitute values in the right location:

   - **In a column:** Enter the values in the column starting one cell below and one cell to the left of the cell where the formula is located (refer to Figure 6-4).

   - **In a row:** Enter the values in the row starting one cell above and one cell to the right of the cell where the formula is.

2. **Select the block of cells with the formula and substitute values.**

   In the case of a column, select the formula cell, the cell to its left, as well as all the substitute values directly below. In the case of a row, select the formula cell, the cell above it, as well as the substitute values in the cells directly to the right.

3. **Choose Data⇨Table.**

   You see the Table dialog box.

4. **In the Row Input Cell or Column Input Cell text box, enter the address of the cell where the input value is located.**

   Which box you enter the input cell address in depends on whether you put substitute values in rows or columns.

5. **Click OK.**

   Excel performs the calculations and fills in the table.

To generate the one-input table, Excel constructs an array formula with the TABLE function. If you change the cell references in the first row or plug in different values in the first column, Excel updates the one-input table automatically.

Using a two-input table for analysis

In a two-input table, you can experiment with two input cells rather than one. Getting back to the example of the loan payment in Figure 6-5, you can calculate not only how loan payments change as interest rates change, but how payments change if the life of the loan changes. Figure 6-6 shows a two-input table for examining monthly loan payments given different interest rates and two different terms for the loan, 15 years (180 months) and 30 years (360 months).

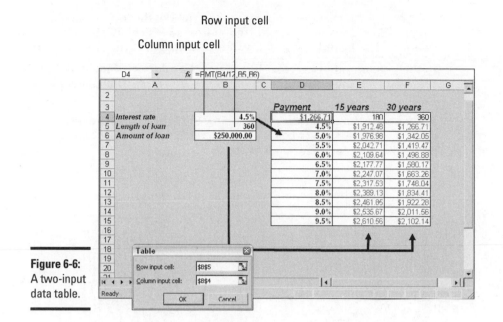

Figure 6-6:
A two-input
data table.

Follow these steps to create a two-input data table:

1. **Enter one set of substitute values below the formula in the same
column as the formula.**

In Figure 6-6, different interest rates are entered.

2. **Enter the second set of substitute values in the row to the right of the
formula.**

In Figure 6-6, 180 and 360 are entered. These numbers represent the
number of months of the life of the loan.

3. **Select the formula and all substitute values.**

Do this correctly and you'll select three columns, including the formula,
the substitute values below it, and the two columns to the right of the
formula.

4. **Choose Data⇨Table.**

The Table dialog box appears (refer to Figure 6-6).

5. **In the Row Input Cell text box, enter the address of the cell referred
to in the original formula where substitute values to the right of the
formula will be plugged in.**

**Book IV
Chapter 6**

Analyzing Data

In Figure 6-6, for example, the rows to the right of the formula are for length of loan substitute values. Therefore, I select cell B5, the cell referred to in the original formula where the length of the loan is listed.

6. **In the Column Input Cell text box, enter the address of the cell referred to in the original formula where substitute values below the formula are.**

In Figure 6-6, the substitute values below the formula cell are interest rates. Therefore, I select cell B4, the cell referred to in the original formula where the interest rate is entered.

7. **Click OK.**

Excel performs the calculations and fills in the table.

Book V

FrontPage

The 5th Wave   By Rich Tennant

"IT'S ANOTHER DEEP SPACE PROBE FROM EARTH,
SEEKING CONTACT FROM EXTRATERRESTRIALS.
I WISH THEY'D JUST INCLUDE AN E-MAIL ADDRESS."

Contents at a Glance

Chapter 1: Introducing FrontPage

In This Chapter

✔ Getting acquainted with FrontPage

✔ Understanding the FrontPage Server Extensions

✔ Tips for designing Web page and Web sites

✔ Creating Web sites and Web pages

✔ Switching views

✔ Managing a Tasks List

This chapter takes the proverbial bull by the horns and shows you how to create a Web site and people your Web site with Web pages. Along the way, you get a brief lesson in how to design Web pages and Web sites, discover how to switch views, and find out how to manage a Task List.

What Is FrontPage, Anyway?

FrontPage is a computer program for creating Web sites and the Web pages of which a Web site is composed. As Figure 1-1 shows, the FrontPage screen looks a little like Microsoft Word. Many of the same buttons and commands for formatting text and pages are found on the main menu and toolbars. The commands for inserting text and graphics are the same as well.

FrontPage offers windows for entering text and laying out Web pages, windows for viewing HTML codes, windows for examining hyperlinks, and other windows. The program makes it possible to create full-fledged Web sites without having to be an expert in coding or programming.

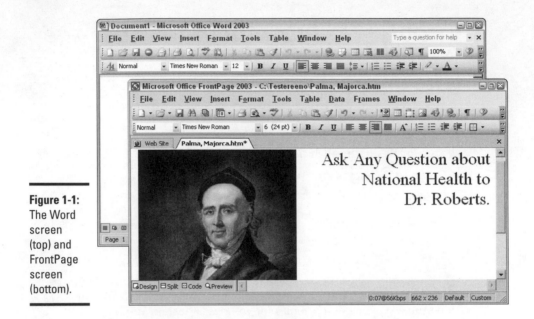

Figure 1-1:
The Word
screen
(top) and
FrontPage
screen
(bottom).

What You Should Know Before You Begin

With the idea that you should look before you leap, these pages explain a
few things worth knowing before you start constructing a Web site. Read on
to find out what HTML is, how easy creating a Web site can be, how to keep
organized, what the FrontPage Server Extensions are, and how to choose a
Web-service provider.

This is easier than you think

Creating a Web site is not as hard as people make it out to be. True, if you
want to make a fancy Web site with all kinds of interactive gizmos, you need
to know FrontPage well. You need to know how to write scripts and code in
hypertext markup language. But if your aim is to create a simple Web site
with a handful of Web pages, a few graphics, and buttons for getting from
place to place, you can do it very easily with FrontPage.

All in all, FrontPage works like a word processing program. You lay out the
page, write the words, and stick the images on the page, and what you see is
pretty much what others will see when they view your Web pages over the
Internet. If you know your way around Microsoft Word, you will soon make
yourself at home in FrontPage.

You don't have to deal with HTML codes

Unless you want to, you don't have to concern yourself with the dreaded HTML codes to create a Web page. HTML, or *hypertext markup language,* is the code that browsers read in order to display Web pages on computer screens. In FrontPage, HTML coding is done in the background. All you have to do is enter the text, graphics, and other items on your Web pages. FrontPage enters the codes for you.

However, FrontPage *does* permit you to do HTML-coding on your own. To see HTML codes in action and perhaps enter a code or two, click the Split or Code button in Page view (choose View⇒Page to switch to Page view). Figure 1-2 shows the HTML codes that produce the Web page shown in Figure 1-1. Scary, aren't they? Fortunately, these codes are entered for you as you format text, insert graphics, and do other layout chores. You don't have to enter HTML codes unless you want to.

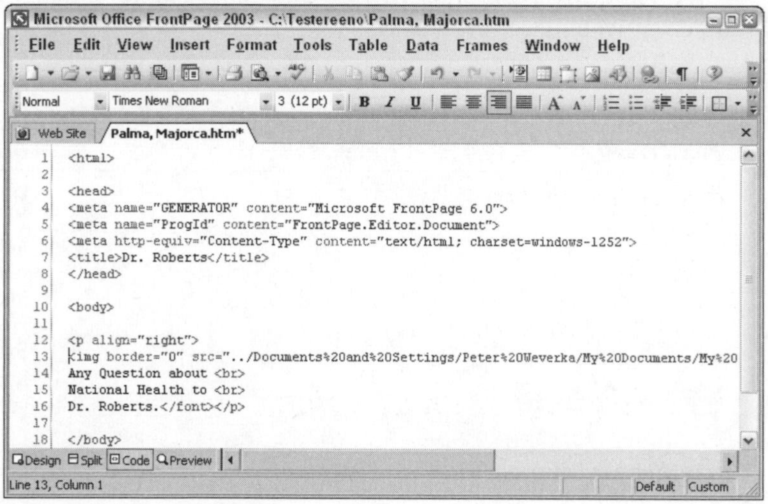

Figure 1-2:
The HTML codes that produced the Web page in Figure 1-1.

Staying organized

The difference between a Web page and Word document or Publisher publication is that Web pages are actually composed of several different files. The Web page you see on-screen with four photographs of a camping trip is actually composed of five files: one for the page itself and four for the photographs. HTML codes tell the browser where to fit the photographs on the page when it is displayed. When you send your Web page or pages to a Web server provider so that your pages can be displayed on the Internet, you send all the files that are needed to display the Web pages.

Because a Web page is composed of different files, misplacing a file or two can render a Web page unintelligible. If you accidentally move or delete a graphic that is part of a Web page, you end up with an empty hole where the graphic is supposed to be. To prevent that from happening, organizing files into folders is more important than ever.

Choosing where to publish a Web site

For others to see your Web site, it must be uploaded to a *Web server*, a powerful computer that holds Web-site files. In Web-site lingo, *publish* means to upload your Web site to a Web server (Chapter 4 of this mini-book explains how) so that others can view the pages that make up the site. Obviously, creating a bunch of nifty Web pages doesn't do much good unless you publish them. Table 1-1 summarizes the advantages and disadvantages of the different Web server providers.

Table 1-1	Different Kinds of Web-Server Providers	
Provider	*Advantages*	*Disadvantages*
Free Web sites (ad-supported)	Free	Limited disk space (usually 3 to10 megabytes); annoying ads; may not support FrontPage Server Extensions; may not be able to use your own domain name
Free Web site (ISP provided)	Free, no ads	Limited disk space; may not support FrontPage Server Extensions; may not be able to use your own domain name
Professional Web hosting	FrontPage Server Extensions; can use your own domain name; extra e-mail accounts, lots of disk space	Monthly fee

Your needs and budget will determine which is the best Web server for you. As part of the monthly subscription fee, most Internet service providers (ISPs) — the companies that connect computers to the Internet — offer their subscribers space on a Web server for hosting a Web site. If yours is one such ISP, by all means take advantage of the free server space that is provided for you. However, if your ISP doesn't give you space on a Web server, your options for publishing your Web site are

✦ Use a free Web-hosting service, such as www.tripod.com or www.geocities.com, and make visitors to your Web site suffer the annoying pop-up advertisements.

✦ Pay for a professional Web-server provider. Go this route if you're serious about creating a Web site or your Web site pertains to a business or other important organization.

A Word about FrontPage Server Extensions

Microsoft makes a set of programs called the FrontPage Server Extensions. These programs run on Web servers, the computers where Web sites are hosted so that they can be viewed on the Internet. The Server Extensions are designed to make certain FrontPage features work. For example, FrontPage Server Extensions make it possible to create Web forms and hit counters.

However, the FrontPage Server Extensions are not installed on every Web server. For various reasons, some technicians who run Web servers choose not to install FrontPage Server Extensions. And this is an important issue for you, someone building a Web site with FrontPage, because you can't do certain things in FrontPage unless the Server Extensions are installed on the Web server where you publish your Web site.

The first thing to do before you start creating a Web site is to find out from your Web server provider whether FrontPage Server Extensions are installed on the Web server where your Web site will go. Call your provider to find out. You don't need the FrontPage Server Extensions to create and publish basic Web sites — FrontPage works just fine with Web servers that use *file transfer protocol,* or FTP, the basic protocol for uploading files to a Web server. But if you want to create Web forms to gather information from visitors, for example, make sure that your Web server provider has installed the FrontPage Server Extensions. You also need FrontPage Server Extensions if you want to include a hit counter on a Web page or view Web site usage data from within FrontPage. Table 1-2 lists FrontPage features that require FrontPage Server Extensions as well as SharePoint Services, the software needed to collaborate with others over an intranet.

Table 1-2	FrontPage Features that Require the Server Extensions or SharePoint Services
FrontPage Feature	*Required Service*
Discussion board	SharePoint Services
Document check in and check out	FrontPage 2000 Server Extensions or later; or (Web) DAV support
File uploading for visitors	FrontPage 2002 Server Extensions
Forms (User input forms, search forms, discussion forums)	FrontPage 98 Server Extensions or later
Hit counter	FrontPage 98 Server Extensions or later
List and document library views	SharePoint Services
Nested sub webs (Web sites stored within Web sites)	FrontPage 2000 Server Extensions or later
SharePoint team Web site wizard	SharePoint Services
Surveys	SharePoint Services
Top Ten List Web component	FrontPage 2002 Server Extensions
Web site usage analysis reports	FrontPage 2002 Server Extensions

You can find a list of Web server providers that support FrontPage Server Extensions at this address: http://www.microsoft.com/frontpage/wppsearch/.

Designing Web Pages and Web sites

Before you create your Web site, take a moment to consider what it will look like. These pages are devoted to that very topic. They explain how to make professional-looking Web pages that others will admire. By heeding this advice, you can create Web pages that are useful, pleasant to look at, and easy to read.

Consider the audience

The cardinal rule for developing Web sites is to always remember who your audience is. Obviously, a Web site whose purpose is to publicize an amusement park needs to be livelier than a Web site whose purpose is to compare mortality rates in different orphanages. Likewise, a Web site that posts pictures of a newborn baby should be brighter and more colorful than one that promotes a small business.

A corollary to the "Who's my audience?" question, and one that's good to ask yourself as well, is "Why exactly am I developing this Web site?" You're doing the hard work of creating a Web site for a good reason. Ask yourself what that reason is and then you can think of compelling ways to present the topic so that others become as passionate about it as you are.

Remember to be consistent

If you opened a magazine at a newsstand and discovered that the text on each page had a different font, each page was laid out differently, and each page was a different size, you wouldn't buy the magazine. The same goes for Web sites. A Web site that isn't consistent from Web page to Web page gives a bad impression. Visitors will conclude that little thought was put into the site, and they won't stick around.

To be consistent, lay out all your Web pages in a similar manner. Make sure that headings are the same size. Use similar dividers on each page. Pages don't have to have the same background, but backgrounds should be similar. For example, you can use the same pattern but a different hue. Or you can use different shades of the same color. The point is to give visitors the impression that a lot of thought was put into your Web site and that you care very much about its presentation.

The home page as introduction

The *home page* is the first page, or introductory page, of a Web site. Usually the home page offers hyperlinks that you can click to go to other pages on the Web site. Because most visitors go to the home page first, be sure that the home page makes a fine introduction to your Web site. The home page should include lots of hyperlinks to the other pages on the site. It should be enticing. It should be alluring. It should make people want to stay and explore your Web site in its entirety.

However, to make the home page serve as an introduction, you have to do a little planning. You might sketch a diagram showing how the introductory stuff you will write on the home page will be linked to the other pages on the Web site.

Divide your Web site into distinct topics, one to a page

An unwritten rule of Web site developers is to never create such a long Web page that you have to scroll far to reach the bottom. Topics on Web pages should be presented in small, bite-sized chunks. Rather than dwell upon a topic at length, divide the topic across several pages.

What's more, a Web site isn't like a book or article. No one reads Web sites from start to finish. A Web site is like a garden of forking paths in that visitors can click hyperlinks and take different routes through a Web site. (Visitors don't hesitate to try different routes because they know they can always click the Back button or a navigation button to return to where they came from.)

When you build your Web pages, be sure to include hyperlinks and buttons like the ones shown in Figure 1-3. Hyperlinks and buttons give visitors the chance to go to different pages in the Web site or other Web sites altogether. Instead of presenting long pages that visitors have to scroll to read, let visitors choose what to read next. Navigation buttons and hyperlinks are explained in Chapter 2.

Figure 1-3: Navigation buttons and hyperlinks let visitors choose where to go next.

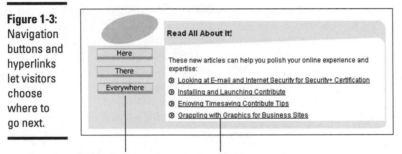

Navigational buttons   Hyperlinks

Write the text and assemble the graphics beforehand

Before you start constructing your Web site, write the text. Rewriting and editing text after it has been placed on a Web page isn't easy. Open your word processor, start typing, say exactly what you want to say on your Web pages, correct all misspellings and grammatical errors, and save the file. Later, you can copy and paste the text from the word-processed file to the Web page.

If you intend to use graphics or pictures on your Web site, set them aside in a folder where you can find them easily. While you're at it, take a good look at them. Which graphics you use will influence the design decisions you make as you construct your Web page. Make sure that you intimately know the graphics you intend to use so that you can use them wisely and well. Chapter 3 explores the issue of choosing art for a Web site.

Keep it clean

Maybe it's just me, but I prefer clean, easy-to-read Web pages to pages that are crowded with gizmos and fancy graphics. In the early days of the World Wide Web, Web site designers tended to load their Web sites with fancy stuff, but today's designers take their cue from the people who design magazines and newspapers. They keep it simple. The idea is to communicate, not to show off or demonstrate your technical skill. Make it easy for visitors to stick around and find out what you have to say. You can do that by making liberal use of empty space, balancing the elements on Web pages, and not overloading Web pages with too much stuff.

Creating and Opening a Web Site

Creating a Web site entails creating a *Web,* the FrontPage word for a Web site. To begin with, a Web is actually a shell for holding Web pages. When you create a new Web, FrontPage creates a Web-page file called index.htm and two subfolders for you — _private and images.

✦ **index.htm:** The home page, the one that most visitors come to first. Do not change the name of this Web page file. By convention, a Web site's home page is always called index.htm. You will create your home page in the index.htm file.

✦ **_private:** A folder for storing files that you need for your Web site but you don't want visitors to see. Visitors cannot view the contents of this folder.

✦ **images:** A folder for storing the pictures and photographs you will place on the Web pages in your Web site.

You can change the name of the subfolders and create subfolders of your own for storing text files or graphics (I explain how shortly). But allow me to repeat myself: Do not change the name or location of the index.htm file, and use this file as your home page. If somewhere down the road you want to make a different Web page the home page for your Web site, right-click it in Folders view and choose Set As Home Page. FrontPage will rename the file index.htm and give your old home page file the name index-old.htm.

Creating a so-called Web

Before you create a Web, create a new folder on your computer for storing it (Book IX, Chapter 2 explains how to create folders). Then follow these steps to create a Web in the folder you created:

1. **Open the Web Site Templates dialog box, shown in Figure 1-4.**

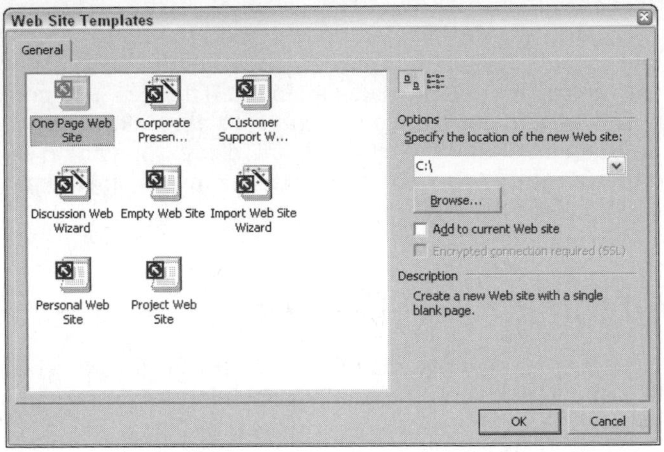

Figure 1-4:
Creating
a new
Web site.

How you do that is up to you. Try one of these techniques:

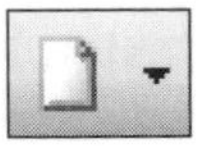

- Click the down arrow beside the Create a Normal Page button and choose <u>W</u>eb Site on the drop-down menu.

- Choose File⇨New and, on the New task pane, click the One Page Web Site hyperlink.

2. **In the Web Site Templates dialog box, click the <u>B</u>rowse button and, in the New Web Site Location dialog box, find and select the folder you created; then click the <u>O</u>pen button.**

In the Web Site Templates dialog box, the folder you selected appears in the <u>S</u>pecify the Location of the New Web Site text box.

3. **Make sure that One Page Web Site is selected in the Web Site Templates dialog box; then click OK.**

You see the new Web site in Folders view (views are explained later in this chapter). Notice the index.htm file and the two subfolders.

Click the Save button, press Ctrl+S, or choose <u>F</u>ile⇨<u>S</u>ave to save a Web site and all its pages. To close a Web site, choose <u>F</u>ile⇨Clos<u>e</u> Site or click the Close button in the upper-right corner of the window.

Folders that store Web sites are marked with the Web Site icon, the standard manila folder with a blue globe on it. If you open Windows Explorer or My Computer and look at the folder you created for your new Web site, you will see the blue globe.

Creating Webs from a template or wizard

You may have noticed several templates and wizards in the Web Site Templates dialog box (refer to Figure 1-4). Yes, you can create a Web site from a template or wizard, but I don't recommend it. You end up with a full-fledged Web site that needs all kinds of tweaking. Boilerplate text needs replacing. Headings have to be rewritten. Worst of all, you end up tailoring your text and graphics to work with a design, when ideally it should work the other way — the ideas you want to communicate should determine what kind of design you create.

Still, if templates and wizards are your cup of tea, simply double-click the template or wizard that interests you in the Web Site Templates dialog box and take it from there.

Opening a Web site so you can work on it

Here are the ways to open a Web site:

✦ Choose File➪Recent Sites and select the Web site's name on the sub-menu.

✦ Click the down arrow beside the Open button and choose Open Site on the drop-down menu. You see the Open Site dialog box. Find and select the folder that holds the site you want to open (it is marked with a Web Site icon) and click the Open button.

The last Web site you worked on appears on-screen when you start FrontPage, but if you prefer to see a blank Web page instead, choose Tools➪Options and, on the General tab of the Options dialog box, unselect the Open Last Web Site Automatically When FrontPage Starts check box.

Handling the subfolders in a Web

Although FrontPage creates images subfolders and private subfolders for you, most people require more subfolders than that. Here are instructions for creating, deleting, and changing the names of subfolders:

✦ **Creating a new subfolder:** Choose View➪Folders to switch to Folders view and display the folders in the Web site. Then click the New Folder button or right-click and choose New➪Folder, and enter a folder name beside the folder icon that appears.

✦ **Deleting a subfolder:** In Folders view, right-click the folder and choose Delete. Then click the Yes button in the confirmation dialog box. Items stored in the folder are deleted as well.

✦ **Moving from subfolder to subfolder:** Double-click a folder to display its contents. To close a folder and move up the folder hierarchy, click the Up One Level button. You will find this button on the right side of the Folders window.

✦ **Changing the name of a subfolder:** In Folders view, right-click the folder, choose Rename, and enter a new name.

Importing files and folders to a Web

To import files and folders into the Web site you're working on, start in Folders view by selecting the folder where you want to store the files or folders and then choose File➪Import. You see the Import dialog box. Take it from there, compadre:

✦ **Importing a file:** Click the Add File button and, in the Add File to Import List dialog box, select the file you want to import and click the Open button. You can Ctrl+click to select more than one file.

✦ **Importing a folder and its contents:** Click the Add Folder button and, in the File Open dialog box, locate and select the folder and click the Open button. The files in the folder appear in the Import dialog box.

In the Import dialog box, you can remove files from the batch you're going to import by selecting them and clicking the Remove button. Click the OK button to import the files or folders.

Deleting and renaming Web sites

Before you delete a Web site, make sure that you can really do without it. A deleted Web site is gone for good and can't be recovered. Here are instructions for deleting and renaming Web sites:

✦ **Deleting:** Choose View➪Folders or click the Toggle Pane button to display the folders in your Web site. Then right-click the topmost folder and choose Delete. You see the Confirm Delete dialog box. Choosing the second option button, Delete This Web Site Entirely, is tantamount to deleting a folder and all its contents in Windows Explorer. Choosing the first option button, Remove FrontPage Information from This Web Site Only, retains all files but removes hyperlinks and all else that pertains to Web sites and Web pages.

✦ **Renaming:** Choose Tools➪Site Settings and, on the General tab of the Site Settings dialog box, enter a new name in the Web Name text box and click OK.

All about Web Pages

Now you're getting somewhere. After you create a Web site — or "Web," as the tight-lipped engineers at Microsoft call it — you can create the Web pages. Herewith are instructions for (take a deep breath) creating, naming, titling, saving, opening, closing, deleting, moving, and renaming Web pages.

Creating and naming Web pages

A *Web page* is simply a hypertext markup (.htm) file that can be viewed through a Web browser. A Web site can include one page or many pages. Creating a Web page is a two-step business. First you create the page and then you save, name, and title it. Better read on.

Choosing a title for a Web page

Choose a descriptive title for your Web pages. Lycos, Yahoo, and other search engines keep careful track of the words on Web pages, and the word or words in the title bar are given extra weight. If you enter "Welcome to Madagascar" in the title, for example, a Web surfer who enters the keyword "Madagascar" in order to conduct a search of the Web is more likely to find your page than he or she is if you make "Welcome to Greenland" the title. Including the word "Madagascar" in the title red-flags the page for people searching about information pertaining to Madagascar.

To change the title of a Web page, right-click it in Folders view and choose Properties, or right-click it in Page view and choose Page Properties. Then, on the General tab of the Properties or Page Properties dialog box, enter a new title in the Title text box.

To create one Web page from another — in other words, to create a new Web page from a prototype — choose View➪Folders to switch to Folders view, right-click the page you want to copy, and choose New From Existing Web Page.

Creating a Web page

In Folders view (choose View➪Folders to get there), select the folder or sub-folder where you want to keep the new Web page and then use one of these techniques to create it:

✦ **A blank Web page:** Click the New Page button. Figure 1-5 shows where the New Page button is located.

New page button

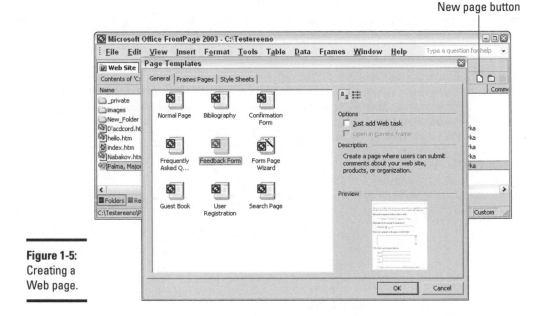

Figure 1-5:
Creating a
Web page.

✦ **A predesigned Web page from a template:** Click the down arrow beside the Create a Normal Page button and choose Page on the drop-down menu, or choose File➪New and click the More Page Templates hyperlink in the New task pane. You see the Page Templates dialog box, shown in Figure 1-5. Select a template and click OK.

Saving, naming, and titling a Web page

The next step is to save, name, and title your new Web page:

1. **Click the Save button or right-click the tab of the Web page you just created and choose Save.**

You see the Save As dialog box.

2. **In the File Name text box, enter a descriptive name for the Web page file you created.**

Names can't include these characters: / \ * : ? # > < |.

3. **Click the Change Title button, enter a name in the Set Page Title dialog box, and click OK.**

A visitor who comes to your Web page will see the title you entered on the title bar at the top of his or her browser.

4. **Click the Save button.**

Instead of new_page_1.htm or some such, the page tab now bears the filename you entered.

To rename a Web page file, right-click its name in Folders view, choose Rename, and enter a new name.

Handling and managing Web pages

Following are instructions for doing this, that, and the other thing with Web pages. To handle and manage Web pages, start by choosing View➪Folders to switch to Folders view:

✦ **Opening a Web page:** Double-click the page's name or right-click it and choose Open. You can also choose File➪Recent Files➪and the name of a Web page on the submenu. The submenu lists the last eight files you worked on.

✦ **Closing a Web page:** Right-click the page tab and choose Close or choose File➪Close while the page is displayed.

✦ **Deleting a Web page:** Select the page in Folders view and press the Delete key, choose Edit➪Delete, or right-click and choose Delete.

✦ **Moving a Web page to another folder:** Drag the file to another folder.

✦ **Renaming a Web page:** Right-click the file and choose Rename. Then enter a new name.

To open a Web page in its own window far from the distractions of the other pages in the Web site, right-click it and choose Open in New Window.

Exploring the Different Views

The seven views and when to employ them are explained throughout this book. Rather than bore you with a detailed description of each view, here are the seven views in a nutshell:

View	*What it does*
Page	For laying out Web pages, entering text, and entering graphics. You can also enter HTML codes in this view and see what a Web page looks like in a browser window.
Folders	For handling and managing folders and Web page files.
Remote Web Site	For managing Web sites that aren't kept on your computer.
Reports	For generating different reports about the health and well-being of your Web site. Chapter 4 of this mini-book explains the different reports.
Navigation	For seeing how Web pages fit together in the hierarchy of folders and files. You can drag pages to new folders in this view.
Hyperlinks	For seeing how hyperlinks connect the Web pages in your site to one another, as shown in Figure 1-6.
Tasks	For viewing the lists of tasks that need completing. The next section in this chapter explains tasks.

To change views, choose an option on the View menu. In all views except Page view, you can also change views by clicking a View button — Folders, Remote Web Site, Reports, Navigation, Hyperlinks, or Tasks — along the bottom of the window, as shown in Figure 1-6.

In Page view, click one of these buttons along the bottom of the window to undertake your work in different ways:

✦ **Design:** For laying out Web pages, entering the text, and entering graphics.

✦ **Split:** For seeing layouts and HTML code. The HTML codes appear in the top of the window and the Web page appears in the bottom. Select an item in either half of the window, and the other half scrolls to the item you selected.

✦ **Code:** For viewing the HTML codes on which a Web page is based.

✦ **Preview:** For seeing roughly what the Web page will look like on a Web browser.

You can see the Folder List on the left side of the window at any time by pressing Alt+F1, choosing View➪Folder List, or clicking the Toggle Pane button.

Choose a view option.

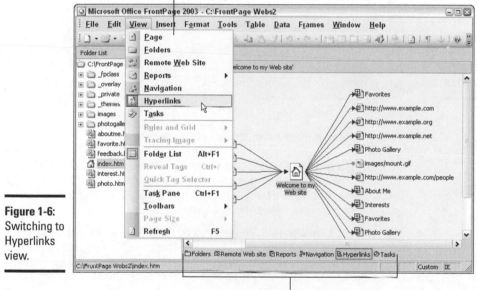

Figure 1-6:
Switching to
Hyperlinks
view.

Click a view button

Tracking and Prioritizing Tasks

Especially if more than one person is working on a Web site, the Tasks List can be a convenient way of determining what needs to be done, dividing tasks, prioritizing tasks, and tracking your progress. Figure 1-7 shows the Tasks List along with the New Task dialog box, where you describe a task that needs doing. Choose View➪Tasks or click the Tasks button to see the list. If a task is associated with a Web page, you can right-click the task, choose Start Task, and go immediately to the Web page that pertains to the task.

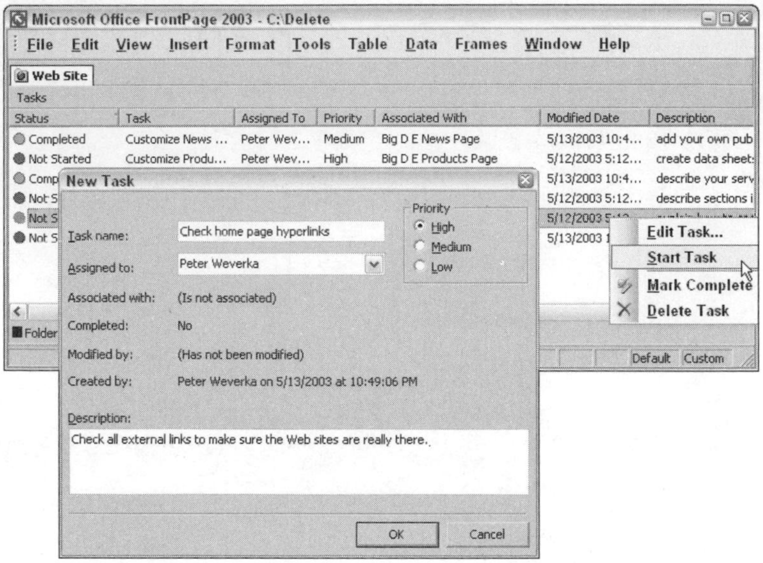

Figure 1-7:
A Tasks List.

Here is everything a mere mortal needs to know about tasks:

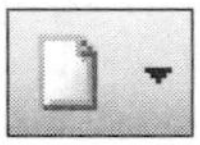

✦ **Assigning a new task:** Click the down arrow beside the Create a New Normal Page button and choose Task, or choose Edit➪Tasks➪Add Task. You see the New Task dialog box (refer to Figure 1-7). Name the task, assign it to a person, describe it, prioritize it, and click OK.

✦ **Associating a task with a Web page:** To associate a task with a Web page and be able to open the Web page from the Tasks List, select a Web page in Folders view before assigning the task. To go to a Web page from the Tasks List, right-click a task and choose Start Task.

✦ **Marking a task as complete:** Right-click the task in the Tasks window and choose Mark Complete.

✦ **Deleting tasks:** Right-click the task in the Tasks window and choose Delete Task.

Chapter 2: Laying Out a Web Page

In This Chapter

✓ **Using tables, shared borders, layers, and Dynamic Web templates to lay out pages**

✓ **Testing your Web site in different browsers**

✓ **Choosing a theme for a Web page**

✓ **Giving a background color or image to a Web page**

✓ **Inserting hyperlinks in Web pages**

✓ **Creating a mail-to hyperlink so that others can get in touch with you**

1 n this chapter, your Web site starts to take shape. You discover how to lay out Web pages so that headings, text, graphics, and other elements appear on a Web page precisely where you want them. You find out how to peer into your Web site through different Web browsers. You get to play interior decorator. In these pages, you find out how to splash color on a Web page or give it a theme. This chapter also explains how to hyperlink the pages of your Web site with one another and with pages on the Internet at large.

Techniques for Laying Out Web Pages

Laying out a Web page means to set up the page so that you can put items — headlines, text, and graphics — in the right places. The easiest way to lay out a Web page is to treat the page as though it were a page in a word-processing document and, as they say in New York City and parts of New Jersey, *fuhged-daboudit.* Under this scheme, visitors to your Web site scroll down the page and read it in much the same way they read a page in a book.

If your Web page calls for a simple layout like that, more power to you, but if you want something more sophisticated, you have to look into layout tables, shared borders, layers, and Dynamic Web templates. With these techniques, you can place items in different parts of a Web page and rest assured that they will stay there. For example, you can place navigation buttons on the side, a copyright notice along the bottom, and graphics with captions. The following pages examine and compare the different ways to lay out Web pages. I suggest reading these pages carefully to choose the layout technique that works best for you.

Using layout tables for block layouts

One way to arrange items on a Web page is to create a *layout table* like the one in Figure 2-1 and place text, graphics, and whatnot in the table cells. Layout tables make putting text and items in the right place easier. People who visit your Web site need not know that you created a table for layout purposes. They can't see the table because the table borders — they appear as dotted lines in the figure and the FrontPage window — are invisible. What's more, the layout table changes shape to accommodate different browsers and screen resolutions, but as it changes shape, the items in the table cells remain in the same positions relative to one another. (By the way, don't confuse a layout table with a standard table like the kind for presenting data. You can create those as well in FrontPage with the Insert Table button and commands on the T<u>a</u>ble menu.)

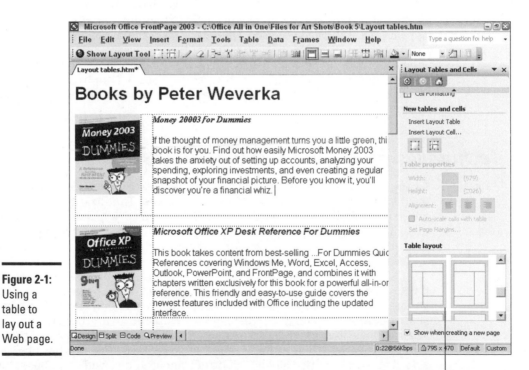

Figure 2-1:
Using a
table to
lay out a
Web page.

Choose a table layout.

Creating a layout table

Follow these steps to create a layout table for arranging items on a Web page:

1. **Choose Table➪Layout Tables and Cells.**

   The Layout Tables and Cells task pane opens.

2. **Choose a predefined table layout from the bottom of the task pane or click the Insert Layout Table hyperlink and create your own table.**

   You can save a lot of time by choosing a predefined table layout, but if that doesn't work for you, drawing the layout table can be done, but it requires work, as the next section in this chapter explains.

After you create a table in the Layout and Tables Cells task pane, the so-called Layout Tools appear on-screen. These blue and green lines are meant to help you lay out the table, but they are very, very unwieldy. To turn them off and construct your table using commands on the Tables toolbar, click the Show Layout Tool button on the Tables toolbar.

Drawing and rearranging layout tables

Unlike the standard tables you use for presenting data, layout tables are "dynamic." They are designed to change shape and size to accommodate different browsers and screen resolutions, which is great, of course, but it makes changing the size of and inserting columns and rows difficult. Layout tables are slippery and hard to wrestle with. Here are techniques for handling layout tables:

✦ **Inserting a column or row:** Click in the column to the left of where the new column will be or the row below where the new row will be and then click the Insert Rows or Insert Columns button.

✦ **Merging and splitting rows and columns:** To join cells in the table or split a cell into more than one cell, click the Merge Cells or Split Cells button. If you split cells, you see the Split Cells dialog box, where you enter the number of columns or rows you want to split the cell into.

✦ **Aligning text items in table cells:** To align items horizontally, click an Align or a Center button on the Formatting toolbar. To align items vertically, click the Align Top, Center Vertically, or Align bottom button on the Table toolbar.

✦ **Changing the size of columns and rows:** Drag borders between columns and rows to change column and row size.

✦ **Making space between borders and text:** If text is too close to a border, it can crash into another item on the page and be hard to read. To put extra space between text and table borders, choose Table⇨Table Properties⇨Table and, in the Table Properties dialog box, enter a pixel measurement in the Cell Spacing text box to put extra space between table cells and in the Cell Padding text box to put space between items and the interior border of cells.

Using shared borders for consistent layouts

Another way to handle a table layout is to use *shared borders*. With this technique, space on the border of some Web pages in your Web site or all the pages in your Web site hold the same elements — a navigation bar, a company name, or a company logo, for example. Shared borders save you layout work. Instead of laboriously putting the same navigation bar on several Web pages, you can create shared borders for the Web pages and place the navigation bar in the shared border. The navigation bar will appear on all the pages. Microsoft uses the word "shared" to describe this layout technique because different Web pages share the same items. Shared borders are a bit like headers and footers in word-processed documents in that the same items appear along the borders — the top, left, right, or bottom — of several pages.

Setting up shared borders

Choose Tools⇨Page Options and, on the Authoring tab, select the Shared Borders check box (unless it's already selected) to activate shared borders. Then, if you want a handful, not all, of the pages in your Web site to have shared borders, switch to Folders view and select the Web pages. Follow these steps to place a shared border on more than one page in a Web site:

1. **Choose Format⇨Shared Borders.**

FrontPage displays the Shared Borders dialog box. If you're giving borders to a handful of pages, select the Selected Page(s) option button.

2. **Select a check box or check boxes that describe where you want the border to appear on the Web pages.**

3. **Click OK.**

FrontPage creates a new folder called borders for holding the .htm files on which the elements on the shared border are kept. To remove shared borders from Web pages, select the pages with shared borders in Folders view, choose Format⇨Shared Borders, and unselect check boxes in the Shared Borders dialog box.

Putting stuff in a shared border

After you've created a shared border, it's time to stuff it like a Thanksgiving turkey:

✦ **Inserting a column or row:** Open any Web page for which you've created a shared border and enter the element — a navigation bar, a company name — that you want. Insert text and images as though the shared borders were table cells. The shared borders expand to make room for the content you place in them (this is the only way to resize shared borders).

✦ **Choosing a background color or picture:** Choose Format➪Shared Borders and click the Border Properties button in the Shared Borders dialog box. Then use the Border Properties dialog box to select a background color or picture.

Unless your Web server supports FrontPage 2002 (or newer) server extensions, changes you make to the background of a shared border are lost when you publish your Web site. To work around this problem, insert a one-cell table with no borders (so that it's invisible) into a shared border and then change the background properties of the table. Or use dynamic Web templates instead of shared borders.

Using layers to place elements on-screen

With layers, you can place screen elements such as graphics, headings, and text anywhere you choose on a Web page. Each element appears in a layer box, and you can move the boxes at will. You can even overlap different screen elements, as shown in Figure 2-2. Layers permit you to create very elegant and sophisticated Web pages. However, not all browsers are capable of handling layers, and browsers that can handle layers sometimes get it wrong and display the pages incorrectly. Layers aren't very good about handling different screen resolutions, either. Depending on screen resolution, a visitor to your Web page may have to scroll here and there to view the page or gaze at a lot of empty screen space.

In deciding whether to use layers or tables, consider the all-important target audience. Is the audience likely to have up-to-date browsers that are capable of handling layers? If not, use another technique for laying out Web pages. On the other hand, if you want a sophisticated layout, you don't care to muck around with tables, or you don't mind designing the Web page for a single screen resolution, go with layers.

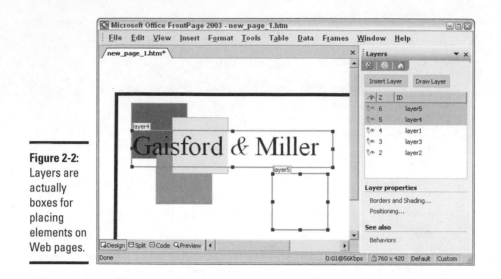

Figure 2-2:
Layers are
actually
boxes for
placing
elements on
Web pages.

Follow these instructions to work with layers:

✦ **Creating a layer:** Choose Insert⇨Layer. A blue layer box appears. Drag a corner or side handle to adjust the size of a layer box. Start typing in the box to insert text. To insert an object such as a clip art image or picture, insert it using the standard commands.

✦ **Adjusting the position of layers:** Click the layer and move the pointer over its perimeter. When you see the four-headed arrow, click and start dragging.

✦ **Displaying the Layers task pane:** Right-click a layer's ID number — layer1, layer2, and so on — and choose Layer Properties.

✦ **Making layers overlap:** Double-click a Z number in the Layers task pane. Numbers in the Z column determine the order in which layers appear. Layers with high numbers overlap those with lower numbers. After you double-click, you can enter a number in the Z column. The higher the number, the higher it appears in the stack.

✦ **Borders and shading for layer boxes:** Click the Borders and Shading link in the Layers task pane to open the Borders and Shading dialog box and make selections there.

You can group layers together so that they can be treated as a single unit. To group two layers, go to the Layers task pane and drag a layer onto the ID of another layer. When you move or change the visibility of a "parent" layer, all "child" layers are affected as well.

Using Dynamic Web templates

Most Web sites include elements that appear on all or most of the Web pages. A navigation bar with hyperlinks to different pages is an example of one such element. Obviously, creating the same element on each page is a hassle. To get around the problem, you can use frames, shared borders (explained earlier in this chapter), or Dynamic Web templates.

Dynamic Web templates have one advantage over shared borders: You can alter part of the page if you want. By designating part of a Web template an *editable region,* you make it possible to change elements in the region without disturbing the layout of the page you're working on or any other page in the Web site. However, if you want to change the layout of all the pages, you can do so very quickly by changing the template on which the pages are based. By the way, Dynamic Web templates are compatible with Macromedia Dreamweaver 4's templates.

Creating a dynamic Web template

Follow these steps to create a dynamic Web template:

1. **On a new or existing Web page, insert the content that you want to appear on all the pages or several pages in your Web site.**

    For example, insert a navigation bar, company logo, or copyright information.

2. **Create table cells or layers for the "editable region."**

    In other words, create space for material that will differ from page to page. Most of the time, this will be a single, empty table cell or layer.

3. **Choose Format⇨Dynamic Web Template⇨Manage Editable Regions and click Yes to save the page as a Dynamic Web Template.**

    You see the Save As dialog box.

4. **Enter a descriptive name for the template in the File Name text box and click the Save button.**

    You see the Editable Regions dialog box, shown in Figure 2-3. Commit to memory the name you choose: You will select it when you attach the template to a Web page.

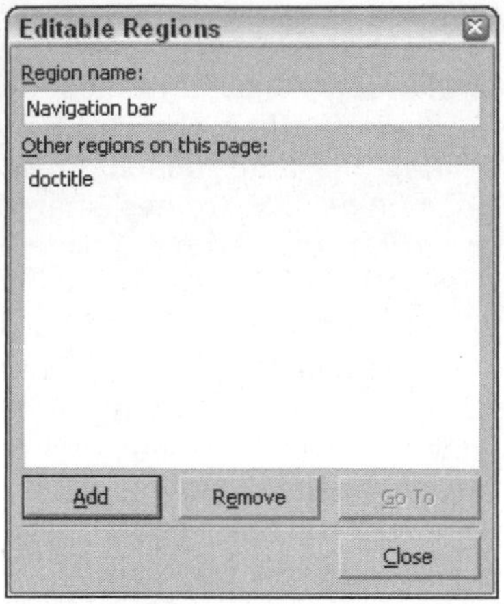

Figure 2-3:
Naming an editable region in a Dynamic Web template.

5. **Enter a name for the region, click the Add button, and click Close.**

   Putting placeholder text or images inside the editable regions is a good way to show others who work on your Web site what kind of content or layout you want in the editable regions.

A few words about frames

In effect, a *frame* is a mini-Web page that, together with other frames, forms a Web page. Frames permit you to display several Web pages in the same browser window. In most cases, one frame, a navigation bar, appears along the side of the window, and the rest of the Web site appears in another, larger frame. Frames were extremely popular a few years back. You could hardly visit a Web site without encountering a frame or two.

However, frames make Web sites too complex — for the visitor and the designer. The designer must worry about what page goes in what frame. As for visitors, they never know quite which Web page they are looking at, which makes bookmarking Web pages difficult.

Frames take longer to download. They can look vastly different from one Web browser to the next.

For these reasons, this book does not cover frames, which I consider an out-of-date technology. If you want to experiment with frames, however, choose File⇨New, click More Page Templates link in the New Task pane, select the Frames Pages tab, and then choose a frame design that you like. FrontPage creates the necessary frame structure. Your job is to create frames or specify which page should be loaded in each frame. After you've created your frames, test the pages carefully to make sure that hyperlinks open in the correct frame (this is the tricky part).

Attaching a dynamic Web Template to a Web page

After you've created a Dynamic Web template, you can attach it to a new or existing page. The content on the template will appear on the page and move aside content in the editable region. Follow these steps to attach a dynamic Web template to a new or existing page:

1. **On a new page or existing one, choose Format⇨Dynamic Web Template⇨Attach Dynamic Web Template.**

   You see the Attach Dynamic Web Template dialog box.

   To attach a dynamic Web Template to more than one file, select the files in the Folders view before undertaking Step 1.

2. **Select the template you want to attach and click the Open button.**

3. **If you're attaching the template to an existing page, specify where to place existing content.**

   FrontPage is pretty good about placing existing content in the correct editable region, so you can probably just click OK in the Choose Editable Regions for Content dialog box. Alternatively, select a region from the old page, click the Modify button, select in which region (from the template) existing content should be placed, and then click OK.

4. **Add content to the editable regions.**

   Insert text, images, tables, and layers into the editable regions. As you do so, they expand to make room for the content you place in them (this is the only way to resize editable regions without modifying the attached dynamic Web template).

To detach a Dynamic Web Template from a Web page, choose Format⇨ Dynamic Web Template⇨Detach from Dynamic Web Template. Although FrontPage detaches the dynamic Web Template, it leaves all content from the template on the Web page. You can delete this content or leave it.

Making Sure Your Web Site is Compatible with Different Web Browsers

To read your Web site, visitors must see it properly in their Web browsers. A *Web browser* is a software program for viewing Web pages and surfing the Internet. Being a Microsoft product, FrontPage creates Web pages that are optimized for viewing in Internet Explorer 6.0, the browser that comes with Windows. However, Internet Explorer is not the only browser out there.

Although roughly 90 percent of computer users travel the Internet with Internet Explorer, a handful use Netscape Navigator, Mozilla, Opera, and Safari (an Apple creation). Most Web pages look fine in browsers apart from Internet Explorer, but complex pages that include tables, layers, or themes require a little tweaking in order to display properly.

These pages explain the three things that you can do to make sure that your Web pages appear properly in different browsers:

✦ Configure FrontPage to optimize its pages for different browsers.

✦ Use FrontPage's new Browser Compatibility tool to check pages for potential problems.

✦ Manually test your pages in a variety of browsers.

Ninety percent of people traveling the Internet travel with Internet Explorer, the Web browser made by Microsoft that comes with Windows. As long as your Web site isn't too complicated, simply create your site for Internet Explorer and leave it at that. You will serve 90 percent of the people 100 percent of the time. Not bad, if I say so myself.

Viewing a Web page at different resolutions

Besides viewing Web pages in different Web browsers, people also view Web pages at different screen resolutions. As Book IX, Chapter 3 explains, things are bigger and easier to see at low screen resolutions such as 640 x 480, but more items appear on-screen at high resolutions such as 800 x 640. People whose eyesight isn't the best prefer low screen resolutions, whereas high screen resolutions are favored by people who like to put many programs on-screen and by people who have high-tech monitors that display at 1024 x 768 pixels or larger.

As you construct your Web site, take a moment from time to time to see what your Web pages look like at different resolutions. People whose monitors display at low resolutions may have to scroll from side to side to see your Web pages if those pages are too wide. And your Web

pages may look too small to people whose monitors display at high resolutions.

FrontPage offers two ways to quickly find out what pages look like at different resolutions:

✓ Choose View➪Page Size and an option on the submenu.

✓ Click the Page Size button on the Status bar and choose an option on the pop-up menu.

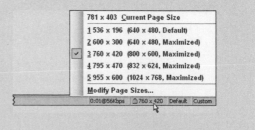

Optimizing pages for a particular browser

FrontPage gives you the opportunity to tailor Web pages for one or two Web browsers. Follow these steps to select the Web browsers that your target audience is most likely to use:

1. **Choose <u>T</u>ools⇨<u>P</u>age Options.**

   You see the Page Options dialog box.

2. **Select the Authoring tab.**

3. **On the <u>B</u>rowsers drop-down menu, choose the Web browser with which you want to make your Web pages compatible.**

4. **On the B<u>r</u>owser Versions drop-down menu, choose the browser version that you want to target.**

   Depending on which browser you chose, FrontPage may disable certain Web technologies so that you don't include an element that the browser you chose can't handle. You can tell which elements are disabled by looking at the check boxes directly below the <u>B</u>rowsers and B<u>r</u>owser Versions drop-down menus.

Changing FrontPage's compatibility settings disables FrontPage features that are incompatible with the Web browsers you specify, and changes the way that FrontPage creates the HTML code for layers and tables. However, it doesn't remove existing elements, even if they are incompatible with the browser.

You can use the Check Browser Behavior to redirect visitors using an incompatible browser to a special version of your page designed to work with that browser. This page could simply tell users that they need a newer version of Internet Explorer, Netscape Navigator, or a compatible browser in order to properly view the Web site. Browser behaviors are discussed in Chapter 5 of this mini-book.

Checking for browser compatibility problems

Follow these steps to use the Browser Compatibility tool to check Web pages for Web browser compatibility problems:

1. **If you want to run the test on a handful of pages rather than all the pages in your Web site, open the pages or switch to Folders view and select the pages.**

   Or, to run the test on a single page, simply open it.

2. **Choose Tools⇨Browser Compatibility.**

   You see the Browser Compatibility dialog box.

3. **Choose which pages to run the test on.**

   Choose All Pages, Open Page(s), Selected Pages, or Current Page.

4. **Click the Check button.**

   FrontPage checks the pages and displays a list of pages with compatibility errors, if any can be found. A summary of the error and the line on which it is found (in the HTML code) appear in the Browser Compatibility dialog box.

   To create a Web page with a compatibility report, click the Generate HTML Report button.

You can create Web pages that are compatible with Internet Explorer and Netscape Navigator versions 4.0 and later without sacrificing nifty features such as Themes and Layers. If permitting all visitors to view your Web site is critical, use the 3.0 browsers and later settings, and place a link on your home page to a text-only version of your Web site as well.

Manually testing pages in different browsers

Despite FrontPage's nifty tools for optimizing and testing pages for compatibility problems, the only reliable way to make sure pages look right in different browsers is to actually open the pages in different browsers. Here's what's what:

✦ **Download and install the browsers you want to test:** At minimum, test your Web pages in Microsoft Internet Explorer versions 5 or 6, and Netscape Navigator 7 (or Mozilla 1.*x*). Table 2-1 describes which versions to test and where to download Web browsers. Yes, you can download these browsers at no cost! To run Safari, however, you need a Macintosh computer.

Table 2-1	**Different Web Browsers**	
Web Browser	*Versions to Test*	*Download Site*
Microsoft Internet Explorer	6.*x* or 5.*x*	`http://www.microsoft.com`
Netscape Navigator	7.*x*, 4.7*x*, or 4.8	`http://www.netscape.com`
Mozilla	Newest released version	`http://www.mozilla.com`
Opera	7.*x*	`http://www.opera.com`
Apple Safari	1.*x*	`http://www.apple.com/macosx`

✦ **Preview your pages in each browser at different screen resolutions:** Open the pages in FrontPage, click the down arrow next to the Preview in Microsoft Internet Explorer button, and choose the browser and screen resolution.

✦ **Test your pages after you've published your site:** Sometimes pages look different when they're published on the Internet, especially if you're using features that require FrontPage Server Extensions. Chapter 5 of this mini-book explains how to publish a Web site.

✦ **Test your pages on alternate platforms:** For bonus points, open your site on computers running Mac OS X and Linux, and look for fonts and colors that don't look right. If you don't have access to these types of computers, ask around for someone who has one. Also consider testing your site on TV-based browsing devices (such as WebTV) and hand-held computers.

When testing a Web page, look for tables and layers that aren't placed correctly, as well as interactive objects such as hover buttons, link bars, and forms that don't work right. While you're at it, make sure that visitors aren't required to scroll horizontally very far at the 640 x 480 or 800 x 600 screen resolutions (many developers believe that scrolling at 640 x 480 is acceptable). Tables and layers shouldn't look strange at 1024 x 768, either. Earlier in this chapter, the "Viewing a Web page at different resolutions" sidebar explains how you can quickly see Web pages at different resolutions in Page view.

You don't have to test your whole Web site every time you create a new page, but quickly testing pages in Netscape Navigator and Internet Explorer is recommended. Just to be on the safe side, test the entire Web site every once in a while and when a new browser or browser version is released.

Applying Themes and Background Colors to Web Pages

FrontPage offers two ways to change the look of a Web page. You can choose a color or picture or you can visit the Theme task pane and select a full-blown design for the various elements — the headings, bulleted items, and hyperlinks, for example. Read on to see how to turn a simple Web page into a high-fashion boutique.

To apply a theme or background color to a handful of Web pages, select them first in Folders view.

Applying a color or shade to page backgrounds

Color backgrounds are a great way to "code" the various pages in a Web site. Visitors know they have come to a new page and are embarking on a new topic when they see a different background color. Just make sure the colors are similar to one another so that the contrast between one page and the next isn't too harsh.

To spruce up a Web page by giving it a color background or a picture background, start by choosing Format⇨Background. You see the Formatting tab of the Page Properties dialog box, as shown in Figure 2-4. Here are some ways to change the look of a Web page or Web pages:

✦ **Color background:** Select a color on the Background drop-down list. If none of the colors tickles your fancy, select More Colors at the bottom of the menu and choose a color in the More Colors dialog box.

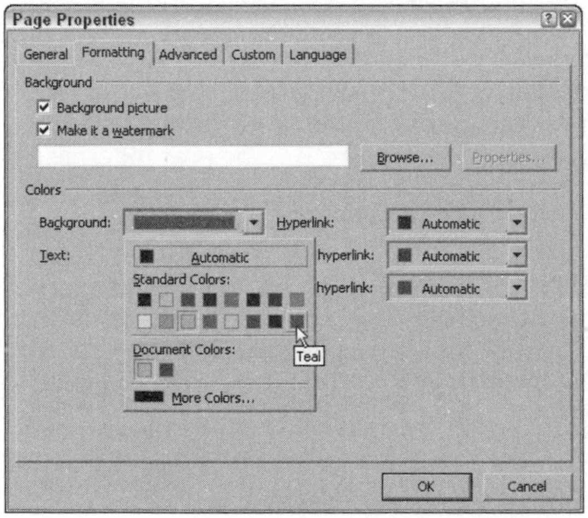

Figure 2-4: Choosing a background image or color for a Web page.

✦ **Picture background or logo:** With the Background Picture check box selected, click the Browse button. In the Select Background Picture dialog box, select the picture you want for a background. You can use .BMP, .GIF, .JPG, or any other Windows-compatible graphic file as a background. .GIF files are best. They require the least disk space, so viewers don't have to wait long for them to appear. Pictures are "tiled" — they repeat themselves in the background. To make the picture appear faintly in the background, select the Make It a Watermark check box.

Web-safe colors

When choosing colors for a Web page or theme, be careful which colors you choose. Not all colors appear properly on every platform (PCs, Macs , and Linux), and color blind people can't see some colors at all. Fortunately, FrontPage makes use of so-called *Web-safe* *colors* for all its Themes. Web-safe colors appear as well on main color wheels from which you choose colors. Web-safe colors are supposed to look the same on all platforms, except to color blind people, of course.

If you regret choosing a background for your Web page and you want to start all over, choose Format⇨Background and choose Automatic on the Background drop-down menu.

To borrow a background from a Web page you like, right-click it and choose Save Background As on the shortcut menu. If the background is copyrighted, however, you are obliged to obtain permission before you use the background image for your own purposes. (P.S. You won't know whether it's copyrighted unless you ask.)

Applying a theme to different pages

A background theme is a "ready-to-wear" design. When you choose a background theme, all elements of the Web page are overhauled — the headings, bulleted items, and the background as well. If you created your Web site with the help of a template or the Web Page Wizard, you already know about themes, because templates come with a theme.

Follow these steps to choose a theme for your Web page:

1. **Choose Format⇨Theme.**

The Theme task pane appears, as shown in Figure 2-5. Scroll through the themes and look for ones that catch your eye.

2. **Until you find one you like, click a few theme names to see what they do to your Web pages.**

When you select a theme, the Web page adopts it.

When you have found your theme, you can tweak it to your liking by checking or unchecking the three check boxes at the bottom of the Theme task pane:

✦ **Vivid Colors:** Offers muted or vibrant variations of graphic elements in the theme.

✦ **Active Graphics:** Turns off and on the .GIF animations or animated cartoons in the theme, if the theme includes animations.

✦ **Background Image:** Removes or restores the page background.

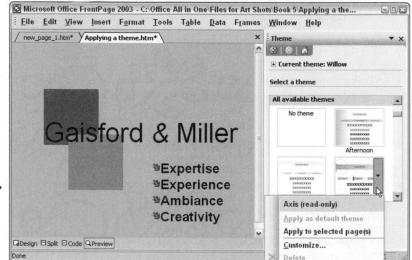

Figure 2-5:
Choosing a theme for a Web page.

 Theme files remain as part of your Web site when you abandon one theme for another. To remove these files and save on disk space, choose View⇨Reports⇨Site Summary. Then, in the Site Summary window, click the Unused Themes link.

Style sheets for customizing themes

 When you apply a theme to a Web site or page, FrontPage creates a separate file called a *style sheet* for storing the theme information. The style sheet file, which uses the industry standard Cascading Style Sheet (CSS) specification, is linked to all pages to which you apply the theme. Unless you want to create your own style sheets, though, you don't need to know this.

To create a style sheet, choose File⇨New, click More Page Templates in the New task pane, select the Style Sheets tab in the Page Templates dialog box, and then choose the style sheet template you want to use.

Including Hyperlinks in Web Pages

A *hyperlink* is an electronic shortcut from one place on the Internet to another. Hyperlinks can go from one Web page to

✦ The top of another Web page in the same Web site

✦ A spot apart from the top of another Web page in the same Web site

✦ A different spot on the same Web page

✦ A Web page in another Web site altogether

Clicking a hyperlink is the fastest way to go elsewhere. By convention, text hyperlinks are blue when first seen and purple after they have been clicked, but you can change the convention for your Web site if you want. You can also create hyperlinks from buttons, graphics, clip art images, shapes, layers, and other so-called objects. You can tell when you have encountered a hyperlink because when you move the pointer over it, a pop-up box tells where the link goes.

The next pages of this chapter explain how to create a hyperlink to the top of a different Web page, to the middle of a different Web page on your site, or to a Web page on the Internet. Finally, this section explains how to edit hyperlinks.

The rules of hyperlinking

Observe these rules about hyperlinking before you attempt to create a hyperlink:

✦ For a hyperlink to go to a page on another Web site, you must know the URL of the Web page. Each page on the Internet has an address, also known as a *URL*, or *uniform resource locator.* You can tell the address of a Web page by looking in the Address bar in the Web browser (right-click the main menu in Internet Explorer and choose Address Bar if you don't see the Address bar). For example, the URL of the Dummies Press is `http://www.dummies.com/WileyCDA`.

✦ For a hyperlink to go from one place to another on the same Web page or to a location apart from the top of another Web page in your site, the target of the link must be marked with a bookmark. Later in this chapter, "Entering a bookmark on a Web page" explains how to put a bookmark on a Web page.

Inserting a hyperlink

To insert a hyperlink, start by selecting the word, phrase, button, graphic, or other object that will form the hyperlink. Visitors to your Web site will activate the hyperlink when they click the thing you select. Then click the Insert Hyperlink button, press Ctrl+K, or choose Insert⇨Hyperlink. You see the Insert Hyperlink dialog box, shown in Figure 2-6.

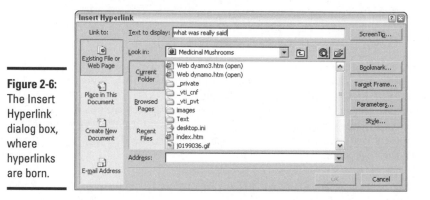

Figure 2-6:
The Insert Hyperlink dialog box, where hyperlinks are born.

Changing the look of hyperlinks on a Web page

By convention, text hyperlinks are blue, links that have been visited are purple, and links that have been selected are red. Some people do not hold with convention and want to change this color scheme. Sometimes changing it is necessary to accommodate page backgrounds. On a blue page, for example, blue text hyperlinks don't show up well.

To change the hyperlink color scheme on a Web page, choose File⇨Properties in Design view and select the Formatting tab in the Page Properties dialog box. Then choose new colors on the Hyperlink drop-down menus.

Enter the target of your hyperlink — the place where you want visitors to go when they click the link:

✦ **The top of a different page on your Web site:** Select the name of the Web page file. To find the file, click the Current Folder button, if necessary, and click folders to open them. If worse comes to worst and you can't find the file anywhere, click the Browse for File button to locate the Web page file in the Link to File dialog box.

✦ **A different place on the same page where the link is:** Click the Bookmark button. You see the Select Place in Document dialog box. Select the bookmark target of your hyperlink and click OK.

✦ **A place on another Web page apart from the top:** Select the name of the Web page file and then click the Bookmark button. Bookmark targets in the Web page you selected appear in the Select Place in Document dialog box. Select a bookmark and click OK.

✦ **A Web page in a different Web site:** Enter the address of the Web page in the Address text box. To enter it, use one of these techniques:

   • Type it in the box.

   • Click the Browse the Web button and, in your Web browser, go to the Web page you want to link to. Its URL will appear in the Address box.

   • Open the Address drop-down list and choose it from the list of URLs you entered recently in your browser's Address bar.

   • Click the Browsed Pages button and select from the list of pages you visited in the last 90 days.

The next step is to click the ScreenTip button and enter a phrase or a short sentence in the Set Hyperlink ScreenTip dialog box that describes the who, the what, or the where of your hyperlink. When a visitor moves the pointer over the hyperlink you're creating, he or she will see the text you enter. This brief description will help the viewer decide whether the link is worth clicking. Without the ScreenTip, visitors see a cryptic pathname instead of a tidy description.

Test your hyperlink by clicking the Preview button, moving the mouse pointer over the link, and clicking. If all goes well, the page you linked to appears in FrontPage. You can also Ctrl+click a link in the Design window to test a hyperlink, but you can't read ScreenTips, the short descriptions of where a link takes you, in the Design window.

Editing and removing hyperlinks

For you and you only, here are techniques for editing and removing hyperlinks:

✦ **Editing a hyperlink:** Right-click the link in Design view and choose Hyperlink Properties. You see the Edit Hyperlink dialog box, which looks and works exactly the same as the Insert Hyperlink dialog box (see Figure 2-6). Change the link destination, change the ScreenTip, or do what you will and click OK.

✦ **Removing a hyperlink:** Right-click the link in Design view and choose Hyperlink Properties. In the Edit Hyperlink dialog box, click the Remove Link button. Removing a hyperlink does not delete the words or graphic that formed the link. Removing a link merely takes away the words' or graphic's hyperlink status.

Entering a bookmark on a Web page

To hyperlink to any part of a page except the top, it is necessary to place a bookmark on the page as a target for the hyperlink. When a visitor clicks the link, the Web page opens and scrolls to the bookmark's position. In long Web pages, targeting a hyperlink to a bookmark is essential. Without the bookmark, visitors have to search long and hard for the item they are looking for. Follow these steps to enter a bookmark:

1. **Click in the Web page where you want the bookmark target to be.**

2. **Choose Insert⇨Bookmark or press Ctrl+G.**

The Insert Bookmark dialog box appears.

3. **Enter a name for the bookmark and click OK.**

In Design view, the bookmark icon appears where bookmarks have been entered. Right-click this icon and choose Bookmark Properties to open the Bookmark dialog box and remove a bookmark.

Making It Easy for Visitors to E-Mail You

Usually, you will find the means to send an e-mail message to the person who maintains a Web site somewhere on the home page. Sometimes you see an e-mail address, but more often you see an e-mail icon. When a visitor clicks an address or e-mail icon, his or her default e-mail program opens. And if the person set up the address or icon correctly, the e-mail message is already addressed and given a subject line.

A hyperlink that opens an e-mail program is called a *mail-to hyperlink,* or sometimes an *e-mail link*. Follow these steps to put a mail-to hyperlink on your home page so that others can get in touch with you:

1. **Select the words, graphic, or other object that will constitute the link.**

2. **Click the Insert Hyperlink button or choose Insert⇨Hyperlink.**

The Insert Hyperlink dialog box appears (refer to Figure 2-6).

3. **Under Link to, click the E-Mail Address icon.**

As shown in Figure 2-7, text boxes appear for entering an e-mail address and subject message.

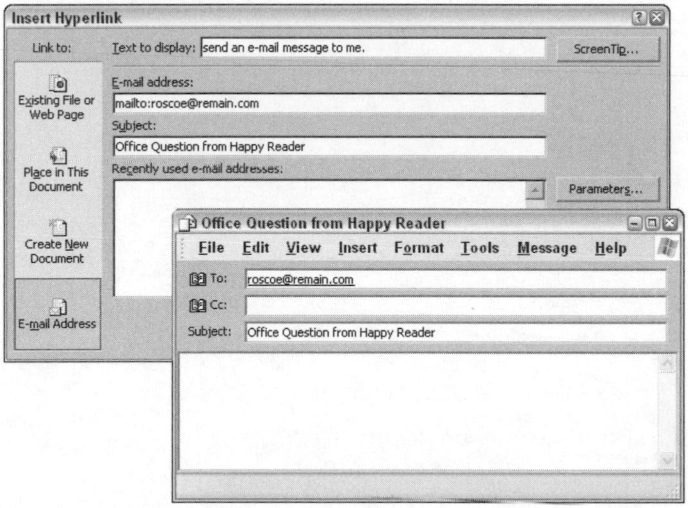

Figure 2-7:
A mail-to
hyperlink
opens the
default
e-mail
program.

4. **Enter your e-mail address and a subject for the messages that others will send you in the text boxes.**

FrontPage inserts the word *mailto:* before your e-mail address as you enter it.

5. **Click OK.**

Test the link by clicking it. Your default e-mail program — probably Outlook — will open. The e-mail message is already addressed and given a subject.

Chapter 3: Presenting the Content

"Content" is the droll term that Web site developers use to describe the text and images that are presented on a Web site. The person responsible for writing the text and choosing and creating the images is sometimes called the "content provider." Don't let anyone tell you otherwise: Content is everything. People don't return to a Web site to see new Web technologies or marvel at page designs. They return because something on the Web site interests or intrigues them. If Web site developers spent more time putting interesting material on their Web sites and less time worrying about their Web sites' appearance, the Internet would be a much better place to visit.

This chapter is devoted to entering the contents on a Web site. It explains how to lay out and enter text, choose images for a Web site, and insert the images. You also find out how to wrap text around images, handle thumbnail images, and create a navigation bar, a series of buttons that visitors can click to get from place to place quickly in your Web site. Finally, this chapter shows how to make a clickable image map.

Formatting and Positioning Text

When it comes to entering, editing, and positioning text, FrontPage works very much like its cousin, Microsoft Word. If you know your way around Word, you've got it made. You already know nearly everything there is to know about formatting and positioning text. Don't blame me if the following pages elicit spooky feelings of déjà-vu.

Formatting and aligning text

Here are techniques for handling text on Web pages:

+ **Choosing fonts and fonts sizes:** Select the text and choose a font and font size from the Font and Font Size menus on the Formatting toolbar. You can also click the Increase Font Size and Decrease Font Size buttons to change the size of text. (See the sidebar "A word about fonts" before choosing a font for text.)

Instead of fonts being measured in points, font sizes in FrontPage are measured using a 1 to 7 scale. This way, no matter whether visitors change the size of text in their browsers, text and headings on your Web pages remain the same size relative to each other.

+ **Choosing a font color for text:** Click the down arrow next to the Font Color button to choose a color on the drop-down list. To change the default text color used throughout a Web page, choose File➪Properties, select the Formatting tab in the Page Properties dialog box, and choose a color on the Text drop-down list.

+ **Choosing text effects:** Click the Bold, Italic, or Underline button to boldface, italicize, or underline text. You can also choose Format➪Font and select from several text effects — strikethrough, superscript, and others — in the Font dialog box.

+ **Aligning text:** Click the Align Left, Center, Align Right, or Justify button to align text relative to the margins of the Web page, the table cell, the layer, or whichever object the text is in.

+ **Indenting text:** Click the Decrease Indent or Increase Indent button to move paragraphs further from or closer to the margin.

+ **Making bulleted and numbered lists:** Click the Numbering or Bullets button. To change the look of bullets or choose a different numbering scheme, select the list, choose Format➪Bullets and Numbering, and make choices in the List Properties dialog box.

+ **Constructing a table:** Tables work the same way in Word as in FrontPage (Book I, Chapter 5 explains tables in detail). The difference between FrontPage and Word tables, however, is that tables in a Web page can change shape to accommodate the browser window in which they are shown. To tell FrontPage to let tables stand or permit them to change shape, right-click your table and choose Table Properties. In the Table Properties dialog box, select the In Pixels option button if you want the table to always remain the same size; select the In Percent option button to permit the table to change shape.

To break a line before it reaches the right margin, click where you want the break to be and press Shift+Enter.

A word about fonts

Although using fancy fonts such as Brush Script or Elephant on Web pages is tempting, stick to common fonts that most people have on their computers. To display fonts on a Web page, Web browsers must rely on font files that are installed on visitors' computers. Because the same fonts aren't installed on every computer, you run a risk if you use Brush Script, Elephant, or another fancy font. If a file for the font in question isn't installed on a visitor's computer, the Web browser substitutes another font. The lovely and enticing font you wanted for your Web page may not appear because it's an obscure font — and something you wouldn't want at all may show up in its place.

If you're a fan of fancy fonts, you have two choices for getting around the problem of having to use common fonts:

✓ **Hand-code a list of alternate fonts so that visitors who are missing the fancy font get a close relative.** Going this route requires knowing how to code in HTML. Builder.com offers advice for coding fonts in HTML. The site's address is `http://builder.cnet.com`.

✓ **Use a FrontPage theme.** Bundled into every theme are HTML codes directing visitors' computers how to substitute for a font that isn't installed. With a theme, the HTML codes for substituting fonts are written for you. Chapter 2 of this mini-book explains themes.

Formatting with paragraph styles

One way to change the look of text is to assign text a paragraph style. A *style* is a collection of formats that have been bundled under one name. Instead of assigning a font, font size, and font color, you can simply choose a style and be done with it. Styles help make headings and text consistent from Web page to Web page. You can change the look of text in one place on a Web site and rest assured that the text looks like text elsewhere that was assigned the same style.

To apply a style, click the text and choose a style from the Style drop-down menu on the Formatting toolbar, as shown in Figure 3-1. Styles apply to entire paragraphs.

I don't recommend altering a style, because people can adjust text settings in their Web browsers. As the sidebar "A word about fonts" explains, substitute fonts in the form of HTML codes are a part of every style, but if you alter a style, you void those substitute fonts, because no substitutes are built into the new style you created. As a result, a visitor to your Web site who does not have the proper font files on his or her computer for displaying the font you want may not see your font or a reliable substitute. What's more, if you adjust the font size when you alter the style, text that has been assigned the style won't be able to resize if a visitor adjusts the text size in his or her browser. A visitor won't be able to do this because fonts are assigned a 1-to-7 value on a relative scale, not a distinct point-size measurement.

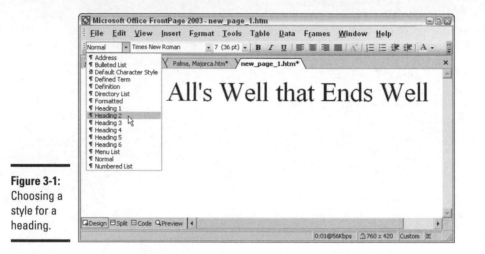

Figure 3-1:
Choosing a
style for a
heading.

Working with Images

A picture is worth a thousand words, or so they say, and a picture or two on a Web page is very attractive indeed. In fact, people expect to see pictures on Web pages. Following is advice for choosing Web page art, arranging pictures and images on Web pages, changing image formats, changing an image's size, and wrapping text around an image.

Advice for choosing Web page art

Here is some advice for choosing and using images:

✦ **Consider how long the image takes to download:** The Estimated Time To Download indicator on the status bar tells you how long it takes for a Web page to download. FrontPage considers a page "slow" if it takes 30 seconds to download over a 56K modem, but I believe 30 seconds is slower than slow. Pages should download faster than that. Try to keep download times under 16 seconds at 56K (30 seconds over a 28.8 Kbps modem).

✦ **Choose images that fit easily on the page:** Visitors have to scroll from side to side to see images that are too large to fit on the screen. If an image is larger than 320 x 240 pixels, create a thumbnail of it (see "Creating Thumbnail Images," later in this chapter). Photo albums are an exception to the rule; the largest images in a photo album should be no larger than 760 x 420 (for display at 800 x 600 resolution), or 955 x 600 (for display at 1024 x 768 resolution).

✦ **Take image formats into consideration:** Use the JPEG image format for pictures; use the GIF format for small graphics. The newer *portable network graphic*, or PNG, image format isn't widely compatible as of this writing. I recommend waiting a year or two to use PNG graphics.

✦ **Use animated GIFs sparingly:** Animated GIFs, the little graphics that dance on the page like bobble-head dolls, should be used sparingly if they are used at all. The little things can be very annoying.

Placing art on a Web page

Here's some good news for people who have read Book VIII, Chapter 3 of this book: Inserting a clip art image or picture file requires the same steps whether you're using Word, Excel, PowerPoint, Publisher, or FrontPage. The details of inserting pictures and clip art images are explained in the aforementioned chapter, but to spare you the strain of turning to Book VIII, Chapter 3, here are shorthand instructions for placing art on a Web page:

✦ **Inserting a graphic:** Click the Insert Picture from File button on the Drawing toolbar or choose Insert➪Picture➪From File. In the Picture dialog box, find and double-click the name of the graphic file whose image you want.

✦ **Inserting a clip art image:** Click the Insert Clip Art button on the Drawing toolbar or choose Insert➪Picture➪Clip Art. The Clip Art task pane opens. Book VIII, Chapter 4 describes the Clip Art task pane in detail.

Resampling to reduce download times

Reducing the size of an image shrinks the image on the page but doesn't shrink the file size of the image. Shrink a few large images, place them on a Web page, and pretty soon you have a bunch of small pictures that take forever to download.

To keep download times from growing too long, resample images after you resize them.

Resampling not only reduces the file size of an image but also usually improves the appearance of the image as well, because resized images tend to look ragged and resizing prevents that. To resample an image, right-click it and choose Resample.

Changing an image's size

Images are usually too large to fit on the Web page, and that's good because images retain their clarity better when they're shrunk than when they're enlarged. Whether you want to shrink or enlarge an image, do it the standard Office way — by dragging a selection handle on the image's border. Drag a corner to retain the image's proportions or drag a side to scrunch or stretch the image. You can also right-click the image, choose Picture Properties, and, in the Picture Properties dialog box, enter measurements in the Width and Height text boxes.

Don't specify the size of an image by percentage. Doing so causes the image to be pixilated, strangely proportioned, and the wrong size to boot.

Positioning an image beside the text

FrontPage offers two techniques for positioning images on Web pages:

✦ **Putting the image in a layer:** As Chapter 2 of this mini-book explains, a layer is a box that you can drag on-screen to any location on a Web page. To place an image in a layer, select it and click the Position Absolutely button on the Pictures toolbar. Now you can drag the image at will. Not all Web browsers can handle layers, so go this route only if you're certain that the people who will view your Web pages have advanced browsers.

✦ **Dragging the image:** Drag the image where you want it to go.

Wrapping text around an image

Unless you tell FrontPage to wrap text around an image, only one line of text appears next to an image before FrontPage wraps the text to a new line underneath the image. Follow these steps to choose precisely where text appears with respect to an image:

1. **Double-click the image (or right-click it and choose Picture Properties).**

You see the Picture Properties dialog box, shown in Figure 3-2.

2. **Choose a wrapping style — None, Left, or Right.**

Wrapping styles determine where text goes when it runs into an image.

3. **Choose an option on the Alignment drop-down menu.**

Table 3-1 explains the Alignment options. These options determine where text falls horizontally with respect to the image.

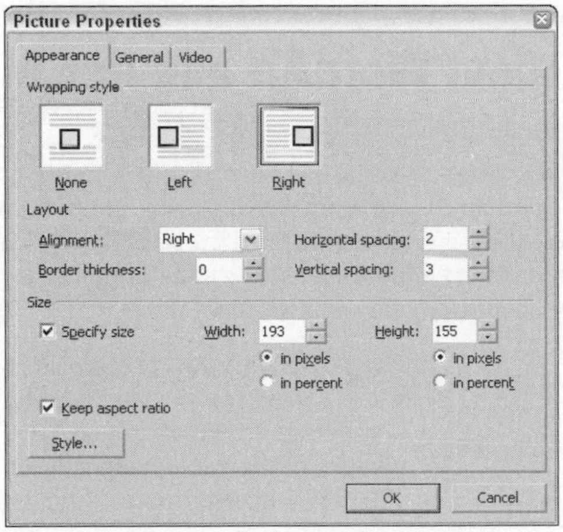

Figure 3-2:
Wrapping
text around
an image.

4. **On the Horizontal Spacing and Vertical Spacing text boxes, enter in pixels how close you want text to come to the image.**

Be sure to leave space between text and the image. Without the space, your Web page may suffer from claustrophobia.

5. **Click OK.**

Table 3-1	Alignment Options for Wrapping Text around Images
Option	*What It Does*
Left	Places the graphic on the left side of the browser window and wraps text around the right side of the graphic
Right	Places the graphic on the right side of the browser window and wraps text around the left side of the graphic
Top	Aligns the top of the graphic with the top of the tallest element on the same line
Texttop	Aligns the top of the graphic with the top of the tallest character on the same line
Middle	Aligns the middle of the graphic with the middle of the surrounding text
Absmiddle	Aligns the middle of the graphic with the middle of the largest item on the current line
Baseline and Bottom	Aligns the bottom of the graphic with the bottom of the surrounding text
Absbottom	Aligns the bottom of the graphic with the bottom of the nearest line of text
Center	Centers the graphic horizontally in the browser window

A few words about WordArt and line art

Like most of the Office programs, FrontPage provides some nifty tools for creating stylized text called WordArt and simple line drawings. You can find these tools on the Drawing toolbar (Book VIII, Chapter 3 explains them). To present WordArt and line drawings, FrontPage converts them into vector markup language, or VML. VML files are actually simple text files that tell Web browsers how to draw an image using VML. Because VML files are so simple, they download quickly and display quite well even when enlarged.

That's the good news. The bad news is that only one Web browser, Internet Explorer, knows how to display VML files (although rumor has it that Mozilla might support VML files at some point).

Visitors who view your Web site through Mozilla, Netscape Navigator, or another browser apart from Internet Explorer see GIF images rather than VML files. These GIF images aren't quite as pretty and they take longer to download. Still, they do the trick.

If you think that most of the visitors to your Web site are likely to use Internet Explorer, go ahead and include line art and WordArt images. Ninety percent of the public uses Internet Explorer. If you have apprehensions about using WordArt and line art made with the Drawing toolbar, make images such as logos and graphics the way the pros do — with an image-editing program.

Changing image formats

Two image formats are widely supported by Web browsers: JPEG (.jpg), which is used for pictures, and GIF (.gif), which is used for line art and graphics that are partially transparent. FrontPage also supports the higher-quality portable network graphics (PNG) file format, but PNG files are quite large and, moreover, not all Web browsers can handle them (in other words, don't use PNG files).

Convert images to the JPEG or GIF format before you place them on a Web page, or else convert them with FrontPage. In fact, FrontPage converts files that aren't JPEG, GIF, or PNG to JPEG or GIF automatically. Follow these steps to change graphic file formats on your own:

1. **Right-click the image and choose Change Picture File Type.**

You see the Picture File Type dialog box, shown in Figure 3-3.

2. **Choose an image format.**

Choose GIF for small, line-art images; otherwise choose JPEG. Don't use PNG format unless your images need to be of exceptionally high quality and the audience for your Web site is likely to use the latest model browsers.

3. **Click OK.**

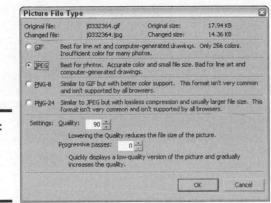

Figure 3-3:
Changing
the file
format of
an image.

Creating Thumbnail Images

When you're tempted to place an image larger than about 500 x 300 pixels on a Web page, consider using thumbnail images instead. A *thumbnail image* is a small image that a visitor can click to see the image in its entirety. To create "thumbnails," as they're sometimes called, create small versions of each image and hyperlink each image to its full-size version or else use the Auto Thumbnail feature.

The AutoThumbnail feature creates a second file from the original. The file is called by the name of the original followed by the letters *_small.* The *_small file,* a thumbnail, appears on your Web page, and when a visitor double-clicks it, the original, full-size image appears in its own Web page.

 To create a thumbnail image with the Auto Thumbnail feature, select the image and click the Auto Thumbnail button on the Pictures toolbar or right-click and choose A<u>u</u>to Thumbnail. The image shrinks to the size of a thumbnail. You can adjust the thumbnail by dragging one of its corner handles and moving it as you would any image.

 To adjust the default size of thumbnails created with the Auto Thumbnail feature, choose <u>T</u>ools ⇨<u>P</u>age Options, select the AutoThumbnail tab in the Page Options dialog box, and fiddle with the options there.

Inserting a Ruled Line

A ruled line is a horizontal line that separates one part of a Web page from another, as shown in Figure 3-4. Use ruled lines, also known as a *dividers,* to let readers know that you're changing subjects in the middle of a Web page. FrontPage offers two ways to draw a ruled line:

✦ **A plain horizontal line:** Choose Insert➪Horizontal Line. To change the color or size of the line, double-click it or right-click it and choose Horizontal Line Properties. Then, in the Horizontal Line Properties dialog box, choose a new width, height, alignment, or color for the line.

✦ **A line from a clip-art image:** Click the Insert Clip Art button on the Drawing toolbar or choose Insert➪Picture➪Clip Art. In the Clip Art task pane, enter the word **dividers** in the Search For text box and click the Go button. Then scroll in the task pane and select a divider that interests you. Change a divider's shape and position as you would any clip-art image.

Figure 3-4: Examples of ruled lines, also known as dividers.

Artful transitions for Web pages

A *page transition* is a cinematic effect that appears as one page leaves the screen and the other takes its place. Examples of page transitions include "wipe right" and "blend." FrontPage makes it easy to apply transitions to Web pages. To test-drive a page transition, choose Format➪Page Transition to open the Page Transitions dialog box. Then choose among these options:

✔ **Event:** Choose when the transition is to begin. Most people choose Page Enter to make the transition appear as the Web page lands on-screen.

✔ **Duration (Seconds):** Enter how long the transition occurs.

✔ **Transition Effect:** Choose a transition (choose No Effect to go without a page transition).

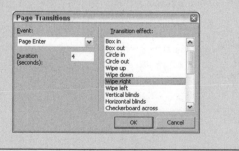

Creating a Navigation Bar

A *navigation bar,* also known as a *link bar,* is a set of buttons or tabs that visitors can click to go quickly from page to page in a Web site. In reality, each button or tab is a hyperlink to a different Web page in the Web site. Figure 3-5 shows an example of two navigation bars, one composed of tabs and one composed of buttons. Typically, the first button or tab is called "Home" and takes you to the home page. Visitors can't get lost in a Web site with a navigation bar because they can always click a navigation bar button or tab to go where they want.

Navigation bar with buttons.

Navigation bar with tabs.

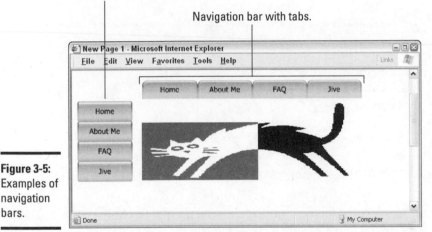

Figure 3-5:
Examples of
navigation
bars.

To create a navigation bar, you create the buttons — FrontPage calls them *interactive buttons* — one at a time and link them to different pages in your Web site. The easiest way to lay out a navigation bar is to start by creating a table for holding the buttons. To create a button, click in a table cell and choose Insert➪Interactive Button. You see the Interactive Buttons dialog box, shown in Figure 3-6. Fashion your button in the dialog box's three tabs. As you go along, the Preview box shows precisely what your button will look like.

✦ **Button tab:** Choose a button or tab style in the Buttons list, enter the text in the Text box, and, in the Link box, enter the filename of the Web page that will open when visitors click the button. You can click the Browse button and select the filename in the Edit Hyperlink dialog box (Chapter 2 of this mini-book explains how to create hyperlinks, including hyperlinks between Web pages on the same site, in this dialog box).

✦ **Text:** Choose a font and font size for the button or tab text. In the Font Color drop-down lists, choose what the button or tab will look like when it's idle, when the mouse pointer hovers over it, and when it's clicked. Click or move the pointer over the sample button or tab to see what your choices do. The alignment menus are for aligning text inside the button or tab.

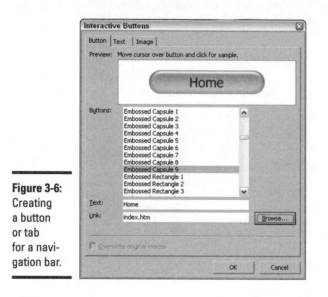

Figure 3-6: Creating a button or tab for a navigation bar.

✦ **Image:** Change the size of the button on this tab. You can also deactivate the hover or pressed mechanism.

To tinker with the button settings, double-click the button or tab or right-click it and choose Button Properties. Doing so opens the Interactive Buttons dialog box.

If you laid out your navigation bar inside a table, you probably need to adjust the amount of space between buttons and remove the table borders. To do so, right-click the table and choose Table Properties. In the Table Properties dialog box, enter **0** in the Size text box (under Borders) to remove the table borders. To adjust the amount of space between the buttons or tabs in the navigation bar, play with the Cell Padding and Cell Spacing measurements.

Creating an Image Map

An *image map* is a graphic that you can click in different places to go to different Web pages. Often, image maps literally are maps. In Figure 3-7, for example, a visitor can click a number on the city map to go to a Web page with information about landmarks in a city. To create an image map, you insert the graphic that serves as the map, draw *hotspots* on it, and link the hotspots to different Web pages.

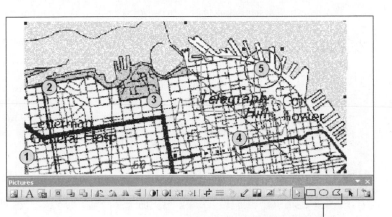

Figure 3-7: Drawing a hotspot on an image map.

Click a hotspot button and start drawing.

Make sure that the graphic you use for the image map is large enough to accommodate the hotspots. While you're at it, plan for hotspots that are large and easy to find. Scouring an image map for hotspots is an unpleasant experience. One way to help visitors recognize hotspots is to number them and simply create the hotspot on the number, as shown in Figure 3-7.

Creating a hotspot and hyperlink

Follow these steps to create a hotspot and a hyperlink to go with it:

1. **Insert the graphic.**

   "Working with Images" near the start of this chapter explains how to insert a graphic on a Web page.

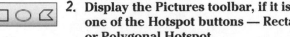
2. **Display the Pictures toolbar, if it isn't already displayed, and click one of the Hotspot buttons — Rectangular Hotspot, Circular Hotspot, or Polygonal Hotspot.**

   The pointer changes into a pencil.

3. **Draw the hotspot on the graphic by dragging the pencil.**

   To draw a perfect rectangle or circle, hold down the Shift key as you drag.

   If you want to draw an irregularly shaped hotspot, click the Polygonal Hotspot button. Rather than drag to create the hotspot, draw one line at a time. As you finish drawing each line, release the mouse button, click, and draw the next line. To enclose the polygon, return to the point where you started drawing and double-click.

   When you finish drawing the hotspot, the Insert Hyperlink dialog box appears.

4. **Enter the hyperlink.**

   Chapter 2 of this mini-book explains how to insert a hyperlink and how the Insert Hyperlink dialog box works. Be sure to click the ScreenTip button and enter a description of what happens when you click the hotspot. This way, visitors to your Web site will understand that they can click the image and travel elsewhere.

Adjusting the hotspots

To adjust or delete a hotspot, start in Design view and click the image map to display its hotspots; then click the hotspot that needs changing. Boxes appear on the image to show you where the hotspots are. Here's how to move, resize, or delete a hotspot on an image map:

✦ **Moving a hotspot:** Click inside the hotspot and drag it to a new location.

✦ **Resizing a hotspot:** Click and drag a hotspot handle. If you're dealing with a polygonal hotspot, dragging a handle changes the hotspot's shape as well as its size.

✦ **Deleting a hotspot:** Press the Delete key.

If you have trouble finding a hotspot in an image, click the Highlight Hotspots button on the Drawing toolbar. The image will blank out and you'll clearly see where the hotspots are.

Chapter 4: Publishing and Maintaining a Web Site

In This Chapter

✔ Generating a Site Summary report

✔ Recalculating and verifying the accuracy of hyperlinks

✔ Introducing FrontPage to your Web server

✔ Publishing and republishing a Web site

✔ Ideas for promoting a Web site

✔ Tracking visitors to your Web site

A t last, the moment of truth has arrived. The work on your Web site is done. You have put together a little masterpiece. Now is the time to publish it on the Internet. This chapter explains how to do that and how to do the little chores that must be done before you publish. You will also find suggestions here for promoting a Web site and tracking the number of visitors.

Getting Ready to Publish a Web Site

Before publishing a Web site to the Internet, check it over to make sure that everything is in its place and there is a place for everything. Checking for broken and invalid hyperlinks is vital, because nothing irks a Web site visitor more than clicking a hyperlink that goes nowhere. The following pages explain different ways to make sure that a Web site is ship-shape. Read on to discover how to run Site Summary reports, verify and fix hyperlinks, and check for uncompleted tasks.

Running a Site Summary report

Run a *Site Summary report* to get an overview of your Web site and find out whether any problem will keep it from working properly. A Site Summary report is actually several reports, each dealing with a different aspect of your Web site. To run a Site Summary report, choose View➪Reports➪Site Summary. You see the Site Summary window, shown in Figure 4-1. Pay special attention to the following items:

Click a link to see a report.　　　　　　　　　　Click to verify hyperlinks.

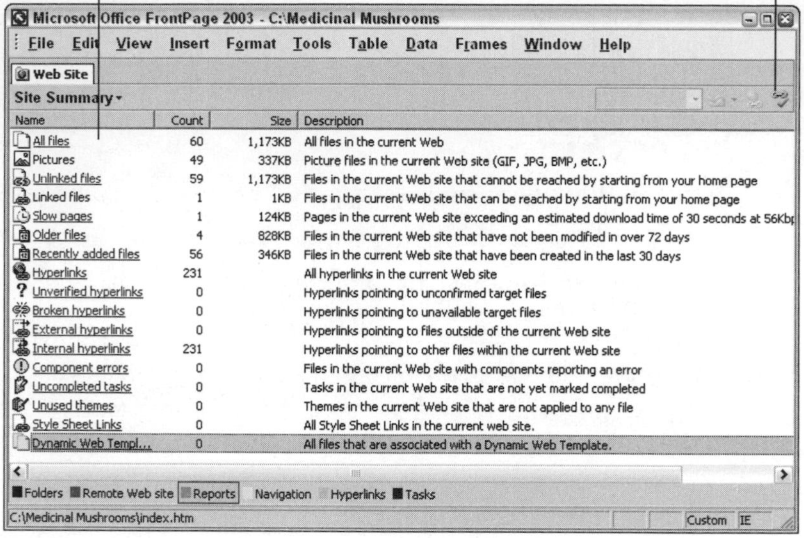

Figure 4-1:
A Site
Summary
report.

Report	What It Tells You
All Files	How many files are in your Web site and how much disk space they occupy. The number in the Size column cannot exceed the amount of disk space your ISP provides for your Web site.
Slow Pages	The number of Web pages that take longer than 30 seconds to download over a 56 Kbps modem. Click the Slow Pages report hyperlink to open slow pages and resize or delete some images.
Unverified Hyperlinks	The number of hyperlinks that haven't been tested.
Broken Hyperlinks	The number of hyperlinks to pages or files that no longer exist or have been moved.
Component Errors	The number of problems with any components (such as forms) that you've placed in your Web site.
Uncompleted Tasks	The number of uncompleted tasks in your Web site.

Recalculating the hyperlinks

Before you publish your Web site, recalculate all the hyperlinks. In FrontPage parlance, *recalculating* means to update all the hyperlinks that FrontPage creates automatically. (FrontPage creates hyperlinks automatically when you create navigation bars, create a photo album, or create thumbnail images.)

To recalculate the hyperlinks, choose Tools⇨Recalculate Hyperlinks and then click Yes.

Verifying and fixing hyperlinks

Especially if more than one person is working on a Web site, hyperlinks can get broken as files are moved. And if someone enters a URL for a hyperlink incorrectly, you get a dud hyperlink. Read on to discover how to generate a list of broken hyperlinks and, starting from the list, repair the broken links one at a time.

Generating a list of broken hyperlinks

Follow these steps to check all hyperlinks in your Web site and generate a list of the hyperlinks that are broken:

1. **Choose View⇨Reports⇨Site Summary.**

   The Site Summary window appears (refer to Figure 4-1).

2. **Click the Verifies Hyperlinks in Current Web button.**

   This hard-to-find button is located on the right side of the Site Summary title bar (refer to Figure 4-1). After you click it, you see the Verify Hyperlinks dialog box.

3. **Select the Verify All Hyperlinks option button and click the Start button.**

   FrontPage methodically goes through your Web site, testing each and every hyperlink. Finally, if FrontPage finds links that don't work, you see a Hyperlinks report similar to the one in Figure 4-2.

Repairing a broken hyperlink

After you have generated a list of broken hyperlinks, select a hyperlink in the list and double-click it or click the Edit Hyperlink button to repair the link. You see the Edit Hyperlink dialog box shown in Figure 4-2. Starting here, you can fix the broken link in different ways:

✦ **Fix the link by going to its Web page:** Click the Edit Page button to open the Web page on your site where the hyperlink is found and fix it there.

✦ **Fix the link by entering a new target address:** Click the Browse button to open the Edit Hyperlink dialog box and fix the hyperlink there. Chapter 2 of this mini-book explains how hyperlinking works.

✦ **Repair some instances of the hyperlink:** If a broken link to the same target is found in more than one place in your Web site, each page where the broken link appears is listed at the bottom of the Edit Hyperlink dialog box. If you want to repair some, not all, instances of the broken hyperlink, select the Change in Selected Pages option button and select the pages where you want to correct the link.

Check for uncompleted tasks

As Chapter 1 of this mini-book explains, the Tasks list is a handy way to keep track of what needs to be done on your Web site. Before you publish your Web site, check to see whether any essential tasks still need completing. Choose View➪Tasks to examine the Tasks list.

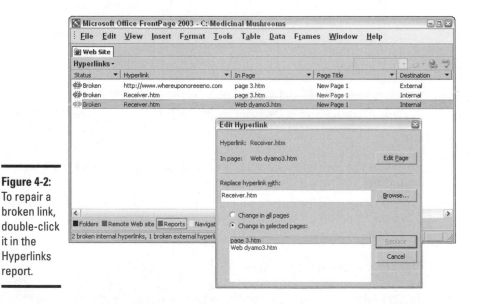

Figure 4-2: To repair a broken link, double-click it in the Hyperlinks report.

Setting Up FrontPage to Work with Your Web Server

Before you can upload a Web site, you need to open the Remote Web Site Properties dialog box and tell FrontPage what kind of Web server will hold your Web pages and where the Web server is located. Figure 4-3 shows the Remote Web Site Properties dialog box. Before you open this dialog box, get the address of the Web server where you will upload your Web site from your Internet service provider. And remember: Your ISP is obliged to help you upload Web pages, so don't hesitate to ask questions of your ISP or seek its assistance if anything goes wrong.

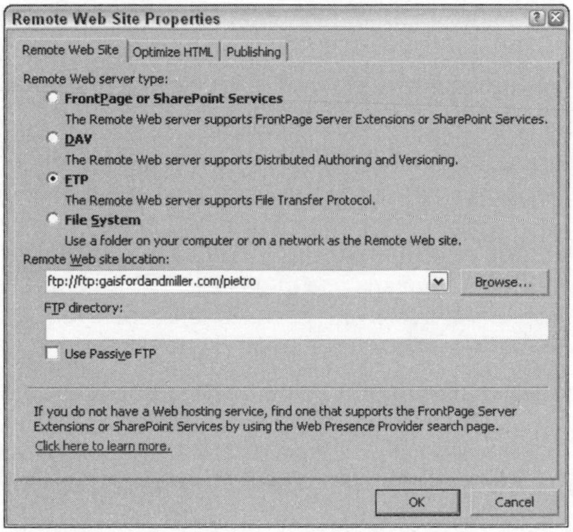

Figure 4-3: Telling FrontPage where to publish a Web site.

The Remote Web Site Properties dialog box appears automatically the first time you click the Publish Site button to try to publish a Web site. However, you can always return to the dialog box by following these steps:

1. **Choose View⇨Folders.**

2. **Click the Remote Web Site button.**

   You can find this button along the bottom of the Folders window next to Folders, Reports, Navigation, and the other buttons.

3. **Click the Remote Web Site Properties button.**

   You can find this button in the middle of the FrontPage window. The Remote Web Site Properties dialog box appears.

Choose a Remote Web Server Type option to describe the Web server where you will publish your Web pages:

✦ **FrontPage or SharePoint Services:** If the FrontPage server extensions are installed on your ISP's Web server or you're using SharePoint Services (a topic not covered in this book), select this option button and enter the address that your ISP provided in the Remote Web Site Location text box. Select the Encrypted Connection Required (SSL) check box if you're required to enter a password to publish your Web site.

✦ **DAV:** Distributed authoring and versioning (DAV or WebDAV) is an industry standard that makes it easy to track who is editing what Web page by way of a checkout and versioning scheme. If a Web server supports HTTP uploading, it most likely supports DAV. Enter a password and select the Encrypted Connection Required (SSL) check box if you're required to enter a password to publish the Web site.

✦ **FTP:** File Transfer Protocol (FTP) provides basic uploading capabilities and works fine for simple Web sites that don't use forms or other dynamic content. Enter the address of the Web server in the Remote Web Site Location text box. If your ISP requires you to enter an FTP directory, or if the ISP makes use of passive FTP to handle firewalls, enter the directory address and click the Use Passive FTP check box (your ISP will explain what these are and whether you need them).

✦ **File System:** Select this option if you want to publish your Web site to another folder on your computer or on a network. Do this, for example, if you're creating a series of Web pages for a CD. Click the Browse button and, in the New Publish Location dialog box, select a folder on your computer or on a network.

After you click OK, the Publish Web site window appears. This is the same window you see when you click the Publish Web button and tell FrontPage to publish your Web site. Keep reading.

Publishing a Web Site

 After you have done the preliminary work, you can upload your Web site to a remote Web server. Start by clicking the Publish Web button, choosing File⇨Publish Site, or pressing Alt+P. You see the Publish Site window, shown in Figure 4-4. The left side of the window lists the folders and files on your computer that make up your Web site. The right side shows the folders and files on the Web server that have already been published there (if you have not yet published your Web site, no folders or files appear on the right side of the window).

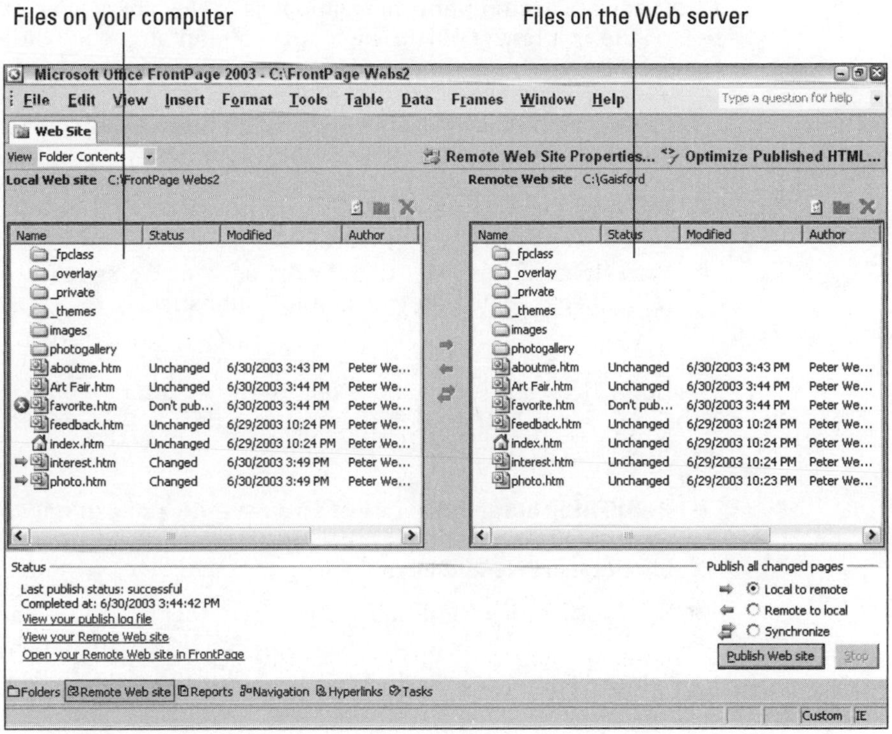

Files on your computer   Files on the Web server

Figure 4-4:
The Publish Site window shows which folders and files have been uploaded to the Web server.

Follow these steps to publish a Web site for the first time:

1. **Make sure that the Local to Remote option button is selected.**

   You can find this button under "Publish All Changed Pages" in the lower-right corner of the Publish Site window.

2. **Click the Publish Web Site button.**

   What happens next depends on your connection to the Internet and whether you must enter a password to publish your Web pages. However, the names of all files that are published successfully on the Web server appear on the right side of the window.

   Click the View Your Remote Web Site link (it's in the lower-left corner of the window) to view your Web site in a Web browser.

Republishing a Web site

The Publish Site window (refer to Figure 4-4) is designed to help you understand which files have been published already, which files have changed and therefore need republishing, and which files are new and need publishing for the first time. Look in the Status column on the left side of the Publish Site window to find out where each file stands:

✦ **Unchanged:** These files are identical to files already published on the Web server and don't need republishing.

✦ **Changed:** These files have been updated since the last time you published the Web site.

✦ **Unmatched:** These files didn't exist on your Web site the last time you published the site. They need to be published.

By default, only new files and files that have changed since the last time you published your Web site are sent to the Web server when you click the Publish Web Site button. However, you can decide for yourself which files are published by using these techniques:

✦ **Publishing a handful of files:** To save time, publish only the files you want to publish by Ctrl+clicking their names, right-clicking, and choosing Publish Selected Files.

✦ **Preventing files from being published:** Right-click a filename and choose Don't Publish. An X icon appears beside the names of files that aren't meant to be published. To see only not-to-be-published files in the window, open the View menu and choose Files Not to Publish.

Synchronizing files on your computer and the Web server

In computer lingo, *synchronizing* means to compare two files with the same name to see which one was saved more recently and then replace the older file with the newer one. If you copy files back and forth between your computer and the Web server, the files will need synchronizing now and then. To synchronize files, click the Synchronize option button in the Publish Site window (refer to Figure 4-4) and then click the Publish Web Site button.

Promoting Your Web Site

Obviously, you want your Web site to be more popular than Britney Spears, but to do that, your site needs promoting. These pages look at various ways to publicize a Web site. You'll discover how to ingratiate yourself with search engines, publicize your site online, and publicize your site the old-fashioned way — by pounding the proverbial pavement.

Helping search engines find your Web site

Search engines — Yahoo, Lycos, Google, and the rest of them — are always scouring the Internet and recording information about Web pages. The search engines work a little differently in that some record information about every word on a Web page and some look only at titles and headings. The search engines store this information in giant databases. When you conduct a search of the Internet, you're really searching a database that the search engine you're using maintains. Obviously, you should do all you can to help search engines find and index your Web site — and that is the subject of the next several pages.

TIP

Searchengines.com offers a superb explanation of search engines, how they work, and what they are. The Web site is located at this address: `www.searchengines.com`.

The different types of search engines

Here's a quick rundown of the different kinds of search engines:

✦ **Crawler-based:** This type of search engine sends out a *crawler* (also known as a *spider*), an automated computer program that analyzes Web sites and captures pertinent information about Web sites for the search engine's database.

✦ **Directories:** This type of search engine works much like a card catalog at a library. Rather than rely on computer programs, people compile information about Web sites and store it in the search engine's database.

✦ **Hybrid:** This type of search engine combines the crawler-based and directory approach. A search is usually performed first in the directory, and if the results aren't satisfactory, the searcher is presented with information gathered by a crawler.

✦ **Meta-search:** This type of search engine rides piggyback on other search engines. It searches other search engines and returns summaries of the results it has found.

Providing meta information

Crawler-based search engines, when they record information about a Web page, record the meta information. The *meta information* — found in the HTML code — includes the Web page's title, its description, and the keywords that you provide. A *keyword* is a word that a person types in a search engine to look for information about a certain topic. Enter the keyword

Madagascar in the Lycos.com search engine, for example, and you get Web pages about Madagascar. By entering keywords that describe your Web pages in the meta information, you help others find your Web pages.

FrontPage offers a special command for entering meta information without having to muck around in the HTML code. Follow these steps to enter meta information that helps people find your Web pages:

1. **Choose Format⇨Background.**

You see the Page Properties dialog box.

2. **Select the General tab.**

Figure 4-5 shows where to enter meta information in the General tab of the Page Properties dialog box.

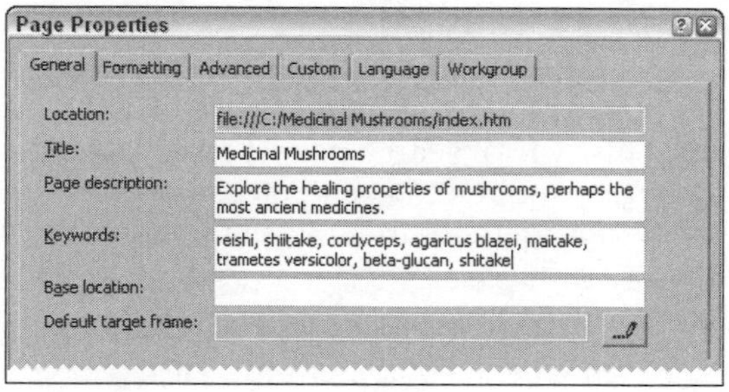

Figure 4-5:
Entering
the meta
information.

Page Properties	
General	Formatting	Advanced	Custom	Language	Workgroup
Location:	file:///C:/Medicinal Mushrooms/index.htm
Title:	Medicinal Mushrooms
Page description:	Explore the healing properties of mushrooms, perhaps the most ancient medicines.
Keywords:	reishi, shiitake, cordyceps, agaricus blazei, maitake, trametes versicolor, beta-glucan, shitake
Base location:	
Default target frame:	

3. **In the Title text box, enter a title for the Web page if you haven't already entered one.**

As I explain in Chapter 1 of this mini-book, the page title appears in the title bar of the Web browser. The title is the most important piece of meta information.

4. **In the Page Description text box, enter a description of the Web page.**

Some search engines display the description you enter, word for word, in the results of an Internet search, so enter the description carefully. Keep the description under 25 words.

You can't check for spelling errors in the Page Properties dialog box, and the Page Description text box isn't a comfortable place to type a description. Try typing the description in Word and pasting it into the text box. To do so, right-click the text box and choose Paste.

5. **In the Keywords text box, enter some keywords.**

Put yourself in the place of someone searching the Internet and enter all keywords that people searching for a Web site like yours might enter when conducting a search. When someone enters a keyword that matches a keyword you enter, your site will appear in the search results.

People often make spelling errors when they enter keywords. To help your site get found, enter misspelled words as well as correctly spelled words in the Keywords text box.

Submitting your Web site to search engines

Most search engines invite you to submit your Web site for inclusion in their catalog. Crawler-based search engines usually request the URL; directory-based engines usually request more information. Table 4-1 lists some search engines to which you can submit your site. You must pay a fee to submit your Web site to search engines whose names are marked with an asterisk in the table.

Table 4-1	Search Engines	
Name	*Type of Search Engine*	*Address*
Altavista	Hybrid using Open Directory	http://www.altavista.com
AOL Search	Hybrid using Open Directory and Google	http://search.aol.com
Google	Hybrid using Open Directory	http://www.google.com
Lycos	Hybrid using Open Directory	http://www.lycos.com
MSN Search*	Hybrid using Looksmart	http://www.msnsearch.com
Open Directory	Directory	http://www.dmoz.org
Teoma*	Crawler	http://www.teoma.com
Yahoo!	Hybrid using Google	http://www.yahoo.com

You must pay a fee to submit to these search engines.

Other ways to publicize a Web site

Here are some other ways to publicize a Web site:

✦ **Include your site in link exchanges and Web rings:** Link exchanges and Web rings are methods of exchanging hyperlinks with other Web sites, as long as you can find an exchange or Web ring that pertains to the topic your Web site covers. A good place to start looking for Web rings is http://www.webring.com.

✦ **Post your Web site on newsgroups:** Place a notice about your Web page on newsgroups where members might be interested in a Web site like yours. If you answer questions or post helpful and informative information to the newsgroup, the participants will appreciate it and probably come visit your site.

✦ **Link your site to other sites and hope they reciprocate:** Include a "Links" Web page on your site where hyperlinks to sites similar to yours are listed. Then send an e-mail message to the developer at each Web site to which your Web site is linked and hope that he or she reciprocates.

✦ **List your Web site address at the bottom of e-mail messages:** Casually, at the bottom of the e-mail messages you send, enter a link to your Web site. Doing so encourages more people to visit your site.

The Hit Parade: Keeping Track of Visitors

Obviously, you want to find out how many people are visiting your Web site. To obtain this information, you can take advantage of FrontPage Usage Reports, examine site statistics from your Web provider, or use a hit counter. Better keep reading.

FrontPage usage reports

Find out whether your Web provider has installed FrontPage Server Extensions and whether FrontPage usage analysis has been enabled. If the answer is "yes" to both queries, you can use the various FrontPage Usage reports to track how many visitors are coming to your site.

To run these reports, choose Reports⇨Usage and a report on the submenu. There are thirteen reports in all.

Site statistics provided by your Web host

Few Web providers support FrontPage's built-in usage analysis tools, but most can offer usage statistics for you. How you access these statistics varies from company to company, but the same information is there — hit counts, Web browser statistics, search engine terms, and more.

Placing a hit counter on a page

A *hit counter* keeps track of and displays the number of people who have visited a Web page. As long as your Web provider has installed the FrontPage Server Extensions, you can include a hit counter on a Web page by following these steps:

1. **Click the Web Component button or choose Insert⇨Web Component.**

   You see the Insert Web Component dialog box.

2. **Under Component Type, select Hit Counter.**

   Several hit counter styles appear on the right side of the dialog box.

3. **Select a style and click the Finish button.**

   The Hit Counter Properties dialog box, shown in Figure 4-6, appears.

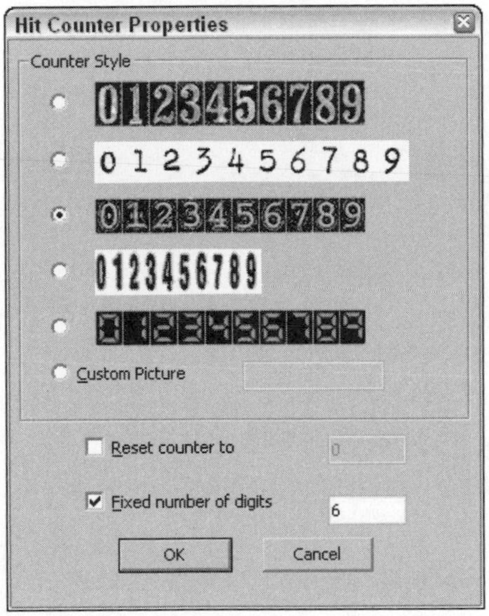

Figure 4-6:
Deciding
what the hit
counter
looks like.

4. **Choose a style, enter the number of digits you want, and click OK.**

To reset a hit counter, double-click it in Design view. You see the Hit Counter Properties dialog box. Select the Reset Counter To check box and enter **0** in the accompanying text box.

Chapter 5: Forms and Behaviors

This short chapter offers a little extra something to make your Web pages stand out in the crowd. It explains how to include a user-input form on a Web page and, in so doing, solicit information from the people who visit your Web pages. This chapter also explains how behaviors can make your Web pages more dynamic and exciting.

Creating User-Input Forms

As shown in Figure 5-1, a *user-input form* is a means of soliciting information from visitors to a Web page. After a visitor enters information in the form and clicks a button, the information is sent to the Web page developer. For conducting surveys and getting address and other types of useful information, user input forms can be invaluable.

As long as the Web-host provider where your Web site is published has installed the FrontPage Server Extensions or Sharepoint Services, you can include user-input forms on your Web pages. Creating the forms is easy, although linking the forms to the Web server so that you can accept input from visitors and store the results can be a chore.

Creating the form

To create a form, you can choose Insert⇨Form and select an option on the submenu, or you can make use of the Form Page Wizard. I strongly suggest using the Form Page Wizard. This gizmo queries as to what kind of form you want and what kind of information you want to solicit, and it does all the layout work for you. Creating a form with the Insert⇨Form command, on the other hand, is a sticky business. Here are instructions for creating a form:

✦ **With the Insert⇨Form command:** Choose Insert⇨Form and a submenu option that describes how you want to solicit information. For example, choose Checkbox to create a check box or Textbox to create a text box that visitors to your Web site can type into. FrontPage inserts the item you selected. To enter the text or values in the item, double-click it and fill in the Properties dialog box.

✦ **With the Form Page Wizard:** Choose File⇨New and, in the New task pane, click More Page Templates. You see the Page Templates dialog box. Double-click Form Page Wizard and, in the Form Page Wizard dialog boxes, answer questions and keep clicking Next as you go along.

To alter any part of a form, double-click the text box, option button, check box, or whatever. You see a Properties dialog box for changing values, the size of the form field, and other things. To change the name of a button, double-click it in Design view and, in the Push Button Properties dialog box, enter a new name in the Value/Label text box.

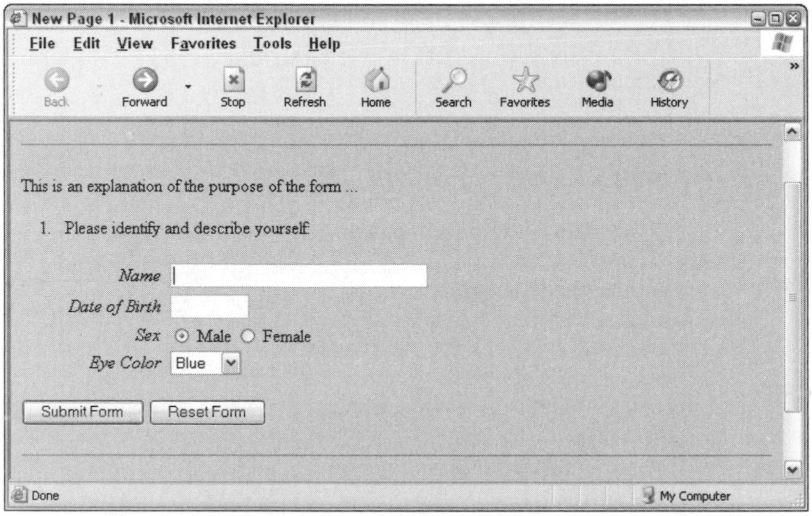

Figure 5-1:
A typical user-input form.

Specifying where form data is stored

When a visitor to your Web site fills in a form and clicks the Submit or Submit Form button, the information is stored in a file called formrslt.htm (form result) in the _private folder. However, you can decide for yourself where and how the information is stored and, for that matter, you can tell FrontPage to send the information to you in an e-mail message.

Follow these steps to decide where information entered on a user-input form is stored:

1. **Right-click the form and choose Form Properties.**

You see the Form Properties dialog box, shown in Figure 5-2.

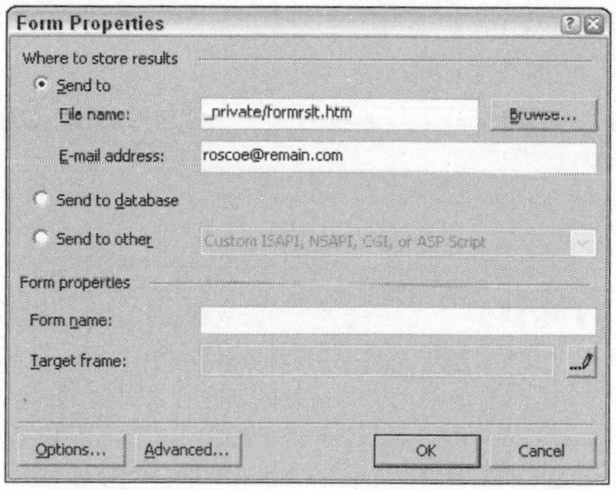

Form Properties

Where to store results
- Send to
  - File name: _private/formrslt.htm   Browse...
  - E-mail address: roscoe@remain.com
- Send to database
- Send to other   Custom ISAPI, NSAPI, CGI, or ASP Script

Form properties

Form name:

Target frame:

Options...   Advanced...   OK   Cancel

Figure 5-2:
Choosing
where form
data is
stored.

2. **Enter the name of the file where you want to store form data in the File Name box.**

   You can change the filename that FrontPage uses for form results if you want. Just be sure to leave the _private/ part.

3. **Optionally, enter an e-mail address where form data is to be sent in the E-Mail Address text box.**

   While you're at it, you can click the Options button and, on the E-Mail Results tab of the Saving Results dialog box, choose a format and enter a subject line for the e-mail that will be sent to you.

4. **Click OK.**

To retrieve form data stored on a Web server, use the Publish Web Site window to copy form data from the remote server back to your local Web site, and then open the file there.

Behaviors for More Dynamic Web Pages

If you've spent any time on the Internet, you've no doubt had the experience of seeing the screen come to life or a sound play when you move the pointer over a part of a Web page. Almost certainly you've seen pop-up boxes, usually advertisements, appear as you surf the Internet. To make these kinds of things happen, programmers write scripts in the Java programming language. These scripts cause something to happen on the computer screen — a new browser window to open, a new Web page to appear, a sound file to play — when a visitor, for example, moves the mouse pointer over a graphic or presses a certain key.

Writing complex Java script is beyond the ability of most people who use FrontPage, but that doesn't mean that you can't make dynamic things happen on your Web pages. To make them happen, FrontPage offers behaviors and events. This section describes them.

Behaviors aren't compatible with Internet Explorer and Netscape Navigator versions 3.*x* and earlier. However, few people still use these outdated browser versions.

Behaviors and events

A *behavior* is a prewritten, canned piece of Java code that makes something happen on-screen. Table 5-1 describes the different behaviors. Without writing a lick of Java script, you can make the actions in Table 5-1 happen on your Web pages (I tell you how in the next section).

Table 5-1	Behaviors Available for Use in FrontPage
Behavior	*What It Does*
Call Javascript	Executes the Javascript code that you type.
Change Property	Changes the properties of the selected object (for example, you can change the font or hide a layer).
Change Property Restore	Restores the properties of an object back to the way it was before the Change Property Behavior was used.
Check Browser	Checks the visitor's Web browser type and version, and loads a different page.
Check Plug-in	Checks what type of media plug-in the visitor's Web browser uses (Flash, QuickTime, and so on) and loads a different page.
Control Flash	Controls a Flash animation on the Web page.
Go To URL	Opens a new Web page in the visitor's Web browser.
Jump Menu	Creates a drop-down menu with a number of options, each of which loads a different Web page. This is handy for a Table of Contents.
Jump Menu Go	Loads the URL associated with the specified Jump Menu entry.
Open Browser Window	Opens a new Web browser window with the desired dimensions, name, and URL.
Play Sound	Plays a sound file.
Popup Message	Displays a pop-up message box.
Preload Images	Preloads images (great for photo albums).
Set Text	Places the specified text in the frame, layer, status bar, or text field.
Swap Image	Replaces one image with another image.
Swap Image Restore	Restores the original image after a Swap Image behavior.

A behavior happens on-screen when the computer detects a certain kind of *event* occurring. Examples of events include a page appearing on-screen or a visitor moving the mouse pointer over a graphic. Table 5-2 lists the different events that can trigger a behavior. The section that follows describes how to get visitors to your Web pages to see a certain behavior when one of these events occurs.

Table 5-2	Some Events That Can Trigger Behaviors
Event	*Action That Triggers the Event*
onbeforeunload	The visitor closes the browser window, leaves the page, or presses the Refresh button. This event occurs before the new page is loaded.
onblur	The visitor presses Tab on the keyboard to move to another object in the page, or switches to another application.
onchange	The visitor changes the text in a text box, or chooses a different option in a form, and then moves to another form field.
onclick	The visitor clicks the object.
ondlbclick	The visitor double-clicks the object.
onerror	A script error occurs, or an error occurs while downloading an object or image.
onfocus	The visitor clicks or moves the cursor to the object by pressing the Tab key.
onhelp	The visitor presses F1.
onkeydown	The visitor presses any key.
onkeypress	The visitor presses a key in the numeric keypad.
onkeyup	The visitor releases a key.
onload	The page loads in a Web browser.
onmousedown	The visitor presses a mouse button while the pointer is over an object.
onmousemove	The visitor moves the mouse over an object.
onmouseout	The visitor moves the mouse away from an object.
onmouseover	The visitor moves the mouse over an object.
onmouseup	The visitor releases a mouse button while the pointer is over an object.
onresize	The visitor resizes the object or Web browser window.
onscroll	The visitor scrolls down, using the scroll bar or the keyboard.
onunload	The visitor closes the browser window, leaves the page, or clicks the Refresh button. This event occurs after the new page is loaded.

Making a behavior occur on a Web page

Follow these steps to make a behavior occur when a certain event transpires on a Web page:

1. **Choose Format➪Behaviors.**

You see the Behaviors task pane, as shown in Figure 5-3.

2. **Select the text, image, or object to which you will assign a behavior.**

3. **Click the Insert button in the Behaviors task pane and, on the drop-down menu, choose the behavior that you want to insert.**

Table 5-1 explains these behaviors.

4. **In the dialog box that appears, describe how you want the behavior to unfold.**

Which dialog box you see depends on which behavior you chose. If you want to play a sound, for example, you will be asked to locate and select a sound file. If you want to display a pop-up message, you will be asked to enter the message.

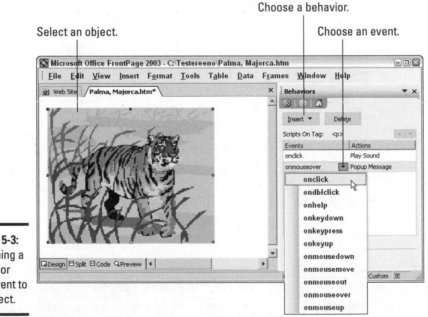

Figure 5-3:
Assigning a
behavior
and event to
an object.

5. **On the Events drop-down menu, choose the event that will trigger the behavior.**

   Table 5-2 describes several of the different events. To begin with, onclick or onmouseover is usually the event, and the behavior is triggered when the user clicks or moves the mouse over the text, image, or object you chose in Step 2. However, you can open the Event drop-down menu and choose a different event to trigger the behavior, as shown in Figure 5-3.

   You can assign as many behaviors as you want to an object or a page. In the Behaviors task plane, behaviors are listed in the order in which they will occur. Just don't get carried away and enter too many behaviors. To change the order in which behaviors occur, right-click in the Actions column in the Behaviors task pane and choose Move Row Up or Move Row Down.

To remove a behavior, right-click the Actions column in the Behaviors task pane and choose Delete.

Book VI

Access

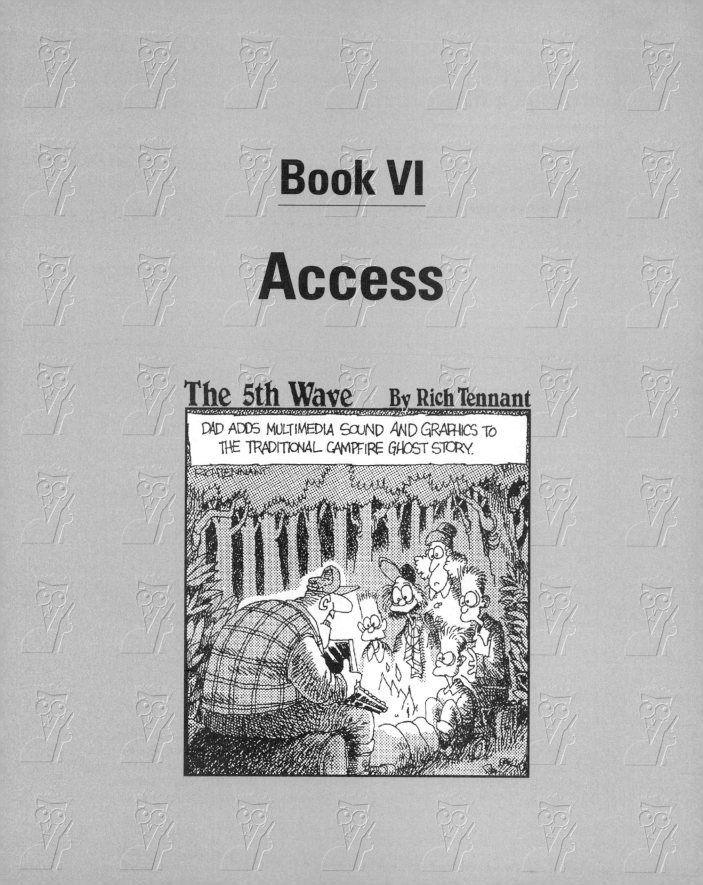

The 5th Wave   By Rich Tennant

DAD ADDS MULTIMEDIA SOUND AND GRAPHICS TO THE TRADITIONAL CAMPFIRE GHOST STORY.

Contents at a Glance

Chapter 1: Introducing Access

In This Chapter

✔ **Understanding how databases work**

✔ **Looking at tables, queries, and other database objects**

✔ **Creating a database**

✔ **Opening and closing tables**

✔ **Designing the tables, queries, and the other parts of a database**

The word "database" is prone to making most people feel kind of queasy. Can you blame them? Database terminology — *record, field, filter* — is the worst of the worst. It even puts other computer terminology to shame. Databases intimidate most people. Even brave souls with a considerable amount of experience in Word and Excel shy away from Access, the Office database program. However, Access can be invaluable for storing and organizing customer lists, inventories, addresses, payment histories, donor lists, and volunteer lists. What's more, Access is easy to use, after you get the hang of it. No kidding!

This chapter starts you down the road to the Land of Oz. In truth, it introduces databases and the concepts behind databases. It shows how to create a database and database tables for storing information. The second half of this chapter explains how to design databases. Sorry, but you have to know about database design before you can start fooling with databases. You can't jump right in as you can with the other Office programs.

Access offers a practice database that you can experiment with as you learn your way around databases. To open this database, choose Help⇨Sample Databases⇨Northwind Sample Database. The Main Switchboard of the Northwind database opens. Click the Display Database Window button to see the Database window.

What Is a Database, Anyway?

Whether you know it or not, you are no stranger to databases. The address book on your computer is a database. The telephone directory in the desk drawer is, too. A recipe book is also a database in that recipes are categorized under different headings. If you've ever arranged a CD collection in a certain way — in alphabetical order or by musical genre — you've created a database of CDs, one that makes finding a particular CD easier. Any place where information is stored in a systematic way can be considered a database. The only difference between a computerized database and a conventional database such as a telephone directory is that storing, finding, and manipulating data is much easier in a computerized database.

Imagine how long it would take to find all of the New York addresses in an address list with ten-thousand entries. In Access, you can query a ten-thousand-entry database and find all New York addresses in a matter of seconds. For that matter, you can query to find all the addresses in a certain ZIP Code. You can put the list in alphabetical order by last name or in numerical order by ZIP Code. Doing these chores without a computer requires many hours of dreary, monotonous labor.

Tables, Queries, Forms, and Other Objects

One of the problems with learning a database program — and the primary reason that people are intimidated by databases — is that you can't jump right in. You have to know how data is stored in a database and how it is extracted, to use programmer terminology. You have to know about objects, Access's bland word for database tables, queries, and all else that makes a database a database. To help you get going, these pages offer a crash course in databases. They explain the different *objects* — database tables, queries, forms, and reports — that make up a database. Fasten your seatbelt. If you complete the crash course without crashing, you will be ready to create your first database.

Database tables for storing information

Information in databases is stored in *database tables* like the one in Figure 1-1. In a database table, you include one field for each category of information you want to keep on hand. *Fields* are the equivalent of columns in a table. Your first duty when you create a database table is to name the fields and tell Access what kind of information you propose to store in each field. The database table in Figure 1-1 is for storing names and addresses. It has six fields: Last Name, First Name, Street, City, State, and ZIP Code.

Access Database terminology

Stumbling over database terminology is easy. To keep yourself from stumbling, fold back the corner of this page and return here when one of these database terms puzzles you:

Cell: In a database table, a place for entering one piece of data. Cells appear in a database table where a field and record intersect.

Database: A systematic way of organizing information so that it can be retrieved and manipulated easily.

Database table: A collection of data records arranged into well-defined categories, or fields. Most databases have more than one table.

Dynaset: The results of a search for data in a database (the term is short for "dynamic set"). A dynaset is not to be confused with a dinosaur.

Field: One category of information in a database table. Fields are the equivalent of columns in a conventional table.

Filtering: Finding the records in a database table that have the same or nearly the same field value. Filtering is a more convenient but not as sophisticated means of querying a database.

Foreign field: In a relationship between two database tables, the field that is on the "many" side of a one-to-many relationship. The primary key field is on the "one" side.

Form: Similar to a dialog box, a place with text boxes and drop-down menus for entering records in a database table.

Module: A Visual Basic procedure whose job is to perform a certain task in Access.

Object: The catch-all term for the tables, queries, forms, and reports that you create and open starting in the Database window.

Page: In Access, a means of presenting data on a company intranet so that others can view and edit it. Also known as a *data access page.*

Primary key field: The field in a database table where unique, one-of-a-kind data is stored. To query more than one database table at a time, the tables must have primary key fields.

Query: A question asked of a database that yields information. Queries can be made of a single database table, several tables, and even other queries.

Record: In a database table, all the data that is recorded about one person or thing. A record is the equivalent of a row in a conventional table.

Relational database: A database program in which data is kept in more than one database table, relationships are established between tables, and queries can be conducted and reports made by assembling data from different tables. Access is a relational database. A database that permits only one table is called a *flat-file database.*

Report: Information gathered from a database and laid out in such a way that it's easy to read and understand. Reports are meant to be printed and distributed.

Sort: To rearrange records in a database table so that the records appear in alphabetical, numerical, or date order in one field.

**Book VI
Chapter 1**

Introducing Access

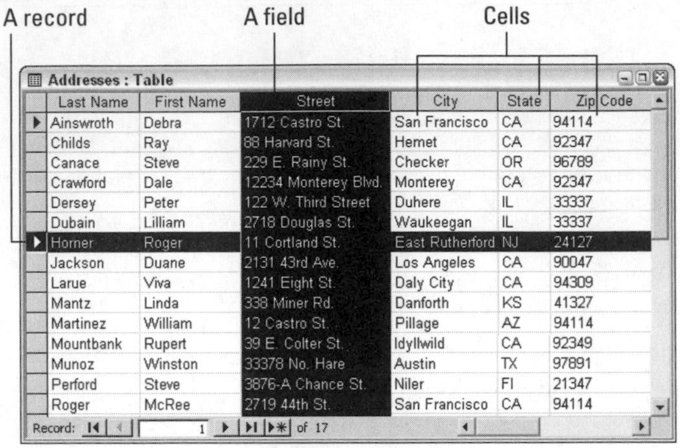

A record   A field   Cells

Last Name	First Name	Street	City	State	Zip Code
Ainswroth	Debra	1712 Castro St.	San Francisco	CA	94114
Childs	Ray	88 Harvard St.	Hemet	CA	92347
Canace	Steve	229 E. Rainy St.	Checker	OR	96789
Crawford	Dale	12234 Monterey Blvd.	Monterey	CA	92347
Dersey	Peter	122 W. Third Street	Duhere	IL	33337
Dubain	Lilliam	2718 Douglas St.	Waukeegan	IL	33337
Horner	Roger	11 Cortland St.	East Rutherford	NJ	24127
Jackson	Duane	2131 43rd Ave.	Los Angeles	CA	90047
Larue	Viva	1241 Eight St.	Daly City	CA	94309
Mantz	Linda	338 Miner Rd.	Danforth	KS	41327
Martinez	William	12 Castro St.	Pillage	AZ	94114
Mountbank	Rupert	39 E. Colter St.	Idyllwild	CA	92349
Munoz	Winston	33378 No. Hare	Austin	TX	97891
Perford	Steve	3876-A Chance St.	Niler	Fl	21347
Roger	McRee	2719 44th St.	San Francisco	CA	94114

Record: 1 of 17

Figure 1-1:
A database
table.

A database can comprise one database table or many different tables that are linked together. If you're dealing with a lot of information, storing data in more than one table is to your advantage. Later in this chapter, "Separating information into different database tables" explains why storing data across several database tables is advantageous.

Forms for entering data

After you create the fields in the database table, you can start entering the records. A *record* describes all the data concerning one person or thing. In Figure 1-1, 17 records have been entered in the database table. Each record comprises a person's last name, a person's first name, a street address, a city, a state, and a ZIP Code. Records are the meat of the database. Information is stored in records.

Although you can enter records straight into a database table, the easiest way to enter a record is to do so on a *form*. Similar to a dialog box, a form has convenient text boxes and drop-down lists for entering information. Figure 1-2 shows the form for entering a record in the database table shown in Figure 1-1. Notice that the form has one place for entering data in each field in the database table: First Name, Last Name, and so on. On a form, you can see clearly what kind of information needs entering in each field.

Queries for getting the data out

Figure 1-3 shows a simple query for finding out which people in the database table shown in Figure 1-1 live in California. A *query* is a question you ask of a database. The question here is, "Who lives in California?" Notice the criterion "CA" in the State field on the Query grid.

Fields

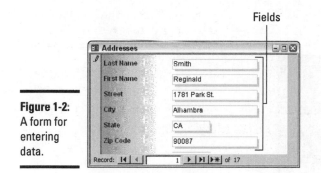

Figure 1-2:
A form for
entering
data.

In an address database, you can find all the people in a particular ZIP Code or state. If information about contributions is stored in the database, you can find out who contributed more than $500 last year. Queries can get very complex. For example, you could find all the people in a particular city who contributed between $50 and $500 and who volunteered more than eight hours in the past year. You can construct the query so that it produces these people's names and their telephone numbers, or you can construct it so that all the information you have concerning each of these people appears in the query results.

Table being queried

Query criteria

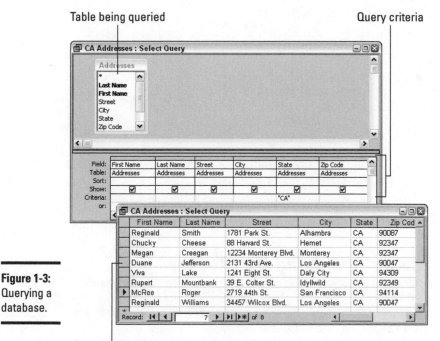

Figure 1-3:
Querying a
database.

Results of the query

When you get junk mail, it likely came to your mailbox as the result of a query. Companies routinely buy and sell customer databases. They query these databases to gather the names of people who they believe will be well-disposed to the products they sell. Next time you get a junk mail solicitation, study the letter and ask yourself, "How did I get in this database, and which database query produced my name?" Probably the junk-mailer was targeting extraordinarily beautiful, intelligent people.

After you create a query, you can save it and run it again. You can use it as the basis of constructing new queries. The information in database tables usually changes over time. Customers change addresses. New products come online and others are discontinued. But no matter how much the data changes, you can find out exactly what you want to know from a database by running a well-crafted query.

Reports for presenting and examining data

Figure 1-4 shows a *report*. Reports can be made from database tables or from the results of queries. Reports are usually read by managers and others who don't get their hands dirty in databases. They're meant to be printed and distributed so that the information can be scrutinized and analyzed. Access offers many attractive reports. Don't worry — the program does most of the layout work for you, and exporting reports to a Word file is easy.

CA Addresses

First Name	Last Name		Street
Reginald	Smith		1781 Park St.
City	State	Zip Code	
Alhambra	CA	90087	

First Name	Last Name		Street
Chucky	Cheese		88 Harvard St.
City	State	Zip Code	
Hemet	CA	92347	

First Name	Last Name		Street
Megan	Creegan		12234 Monterey Blvd.
City	State	Zip Code	
Monterey	CA	92347	

Figure 1-4: A report gathers data for scrutiny and analysis.

Pages, macros, and modules

Pages, macros, and modules are not covered in this book, but they are also database objects. A *page* is a means of presenting data on a company intranet so that co-workers can view and manipulate the data. A macro is a series of commands. You can store macros for running queries and doing other Access tasks (Book VIII, Chapter 2 explains macros). A *module* is a collection of Visual Basic procedures and declarations for performing tasks in Access.

Creating a Database File

Creating a database is a lot of work, at least in the beginning. You have to design the database (a subject explained shortly). You have to enter the raw information into the table. You have to construct queries that allow yourself and others to read meaning into the data (explained in Chapter 4). By contrast, creating a database file for storing the information is the easy part.

Access offers two ways to create a new database file. You can do it from scratch or get the help of a template. With a template, some of the work is done for you. The template comes with prefabricated queries and reports. However, templates are for people who already know their way around Access databases. To make use of a template, you have to know how to modify a pre-existing database.

Before you create a database file, start by deciding where on your computer to store it. Unlike other Office programs, Access requires you to save and name a new file as soon as you create it.

Creating a blank database file

Follow these instructions to create a blank database file:

1. **Click the New button or choose File⇨New.**

The New File task pane opens.

2. **Click the Blank Database link.**

3. **In the File New Database dialog box, find the folder where you want to keep the database file, enter a name in the File Name text box and click the Create button.**

The Database window appears. Later in this chapter, "Finding Your Way around the Database Window" explains what this window is all about. I suggest you go there without delay or deferral.

Getting the help of a template

As I explained earlier, templates are wonderful if you have the wherewithal to modify them. Access offers prefabricated databases for tracking assets, keeping an inventory, scheduling resources, and doing other things.

Unfortunately, the only way to find out whether one of the templates is worthwhile is to go to the trouble to create a database from a template, open up the databases file, and look around.

Follow these steps to create a database file from a template:

1. **Click the New button or choose File⇨New.**

The New File task pane opens.

2. **Click the On My Computer link.**

The Templates dialog box appears.

3. **Select the Databases tab.**

The tab lists templates. There are databases here for tracking assets, expenses, orders, and other data.

4. **Select a template and click OK.**

5. **Answer questions in the series of Database Wizard dialog boxes.**

Which questions need answering depends on which database template you chose.

6. **In the File New Database dialog box, select a folder for storing the database file, enter a name in the File Name text box, and click the Create button.**

You see the Database window. Later in this chapter, "Finding Your Way around the Database window" explains what it's all about.

Finding Your Way around the Database Window

The first thing you see when you open a database file is a Database window like the one in Figure 1-5. This is the starting point for doing all your work in Access. From here, you can select an object — that horrible word again! — and begin working. You also create new objects in the Database window.

Here are shorthand instructions for doing this, that, and the other thing in the Database window:

✦ **Choosing an object type:** Under Objects, select what type of object you want to work with. In Figure 1-5, for example, the Tables object type is selected and the Database window lists tables created for this database.

✦ **Creating a new object:** Select an object type and click the New button to create a certain kind of object. You can also click one of the Create icons at the top of the window.

✦ **Opening an object:** To open a database table, a query, form, or report, either double-click it or select it and click the Open button.

✦ **Opening an object in Design view:** The task of formulating database tables, forms, and queries is done in Design view. If an object needs reformulating, select it and click the Design button to open it in Design view.

Select an object type.

Open the object.

Design the object.

Change views.

Figure 1-5:
The
Database
window.

```
Little League : Database (Access 2000 file format)

Open  Design  New  ×

Objects          Create table in Design view
  Tables         Create table by using wizard
  Queries        Create table by entering data
  Forms          Coaches
  Reports        Divisions
  Pages          Players
  Macros         Products
  Modules        Teams
Groups
  Favorites
```

✦ **Changing views:** Click one of the four buttons on the right side of the toolbar — Large Icons, Small Icons, List, and Details — to view the object icons in different ways. You can also choose View➪Arrange Icons and make a choice on the submenu to rearrange the icons in the window.

✦ **Manipulating the Database window:** Click the Minimize button on the Database window when you want to shrink it and get it out of the way. You can treat this window like any other. Change its size, for example, or maximize it when you're having trouble finding an object icon.

Similar to the files that are stored on your computer, tables, queries, reports, and other objects appear in their own windows on-screen after you open them, and Access places a new button on the taskbar each time you open a new table, query, or whatnot. To go from window to window, click the buttons on the taskbar. Click the Close button in a window to close a table, query, or report.

Access file formats

Surprisingly, the default file format for database files you create with Access 2003 is Access 2000. In other words, database files you create with your version of Access are nonetheless saved in the older, Access 2000 file format. Files are saved in the older format so that people who have earlier versions of Access can open and work on the files you create with your program, the latest, greatest Access.

If you work on your own or work with people who have the latest version of Access, you needn't worry about your Access files being compatible with older versions of the program. Use one of the following methods to save your files in the latest version of Access:

✦ **Converting a file to a different Access version:** Choose Tools➪Database Utilities➪Convert Database and, on the submenu, choose which version of Access to save the file in. The Convert Database Into dialog box appears. Choose a folder and name for the database file and click the Save button.

✦ **Saving all files by default in a different version:** Choose Tools➪Options, select the Advanced tab in the Options dialog box, and choose a different version in the Default File Format drop-down list.

No matter how cluttered the Access window gets with database tables, queries, and forms, you can quickly return to the Database window with these techniques:

✦ Click the Database Window button on the Database toolbar.

✦ Press F11.

✦ Click the Database Window button on the taskbar.

Designing a Database

Being a database designer is not nearly as glamorous as being a fashion designer, but it has its rewards. If you design your database carefully and correctly, it will be very useful to you and others. You'll be able to enter information accurately. When the time comes to draw information from the database, you'll get precisely the information you need. These pages explain everything you need to consider when designing a database. Pay close attention to "Separating information into different database tables." The hardest part about designing a database is deciding how to distribute information across database tables and how many database tables to have.

Deciding what information you need

The first question to ask yourself is what kind of information you want to get out of the database. Customers' names and addresses? Sales information? Information for inventory tracking? Interview your co-workers to find out what information would be helpful to them. Give this matter some serious thought. Your goal is to set up the database so that every tidbit of information that your organization needs can be recorded there.

A good way to find out what kind of information matters to an organization is to examine the paper forms that the organization uses to solicit or record information. These forms show precisely what the organization deems worthy of tracking in a database. Figure 1-6, for example, shows the paper form that players fill out to sign up for the little league whose database tables appear in Figure 1-7. Compare Figure 1-6 and 1-7 and you can see that the Players, Teams, and Divisions database tables all have fields for entering information from this form.

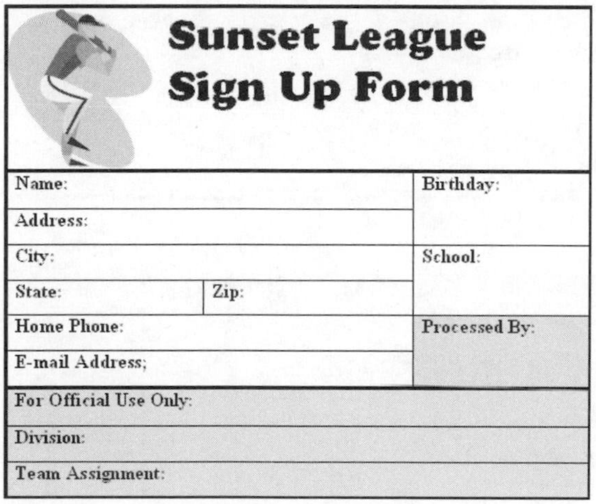

Figure 1-6:
Paper forms also have fields.

Sunset League Sign Up Form

Name:		Birthday:
Address:		
City:		School:
State:	Zip:	
Home Phone:		Processed By:
E-mail Address:		
For Official Use Only:		
Division:		
Team Assignment:		

Separating information into different database tables

After you know the information you want to record in the database, think about how to separate the information into database tables. Many are tempted to put all the information into a single database table, but Access is a *relational database*, which means that you can query more than one table at a time and, in so doing, assemble information from different tables.

Keeping object shortcuts in groups

In a database with many tables, queries, and reports, finding the one you want to work on can be a chore. To help you find objects, Access gives you the opportunity to create shortcuts to objects and keep these shortcuts in groups. After you create a group, its name appears under *Groups* at the bottom of the Objects menu in the Database window. By clicking a group name, you can make the shortcut icons you assigned to the group appear in the Database window. Then, to open an object, all you have to do is double-click its shortcut.

Follow these instructions to handle groups:

✦ **Creating a new group:** Right-click an object that belongs in a group and choose Add to Group⇨New Group on the shortcut menu. You see the New Group dialog box. Enter a name for the group and click OK.

✦ **Putting a shortcut in a group:** Right-click the object that needs a shortcut, choose Add to Group, and choose the group's name on the submenu.

✦ **Opening a group:** If necessary, click the word *Groups* on the task pane of the Database window and then select a group name to display its shortcuts.

✦ **Removing a shortcut from a group:** Select the object, press the Delete button, and click Yes when Access asks whether you really want to do it. Before you click Yes, make sure that you're deleting a shortcut, not the original object. If you look closely, you'll see small arrows on the shortcut icons.

Figure 1-7:
Plans for
database
tables and
field names.

Players	Coaches	Teams	Divisions
Player Number	Coach Number	Team Name	Division Number
First Name	Team Name	Division Number	Division Name
Last Name	First Name	Sponsor	
Street Address	Last Name	Team Colors	
City	Street Address	Practice Field	
State	City	Practice Day	
Zip Code	State	Practice Time	
Telephone No	Zip Code		
E-Mail Address	Telephone No		
Team Name	E-Mail Address		
Fee Paid?			
Birthday			
Sex			
School Attended			

To see how it works, consider the simple database shown in Figure 1-7. The purpose of this little database and its four tables is to store information about the players, coaches, and teams in a little league. The Team Name field appears in three tables. It serves as the link between the tables and permits more than one to be queried. By querying individual tables or combinations of tables in this database, I can assemble team rosters, make a list of coaches and their contact information, list teams by division, put together a mailing list of all players, find out which players have paid their fee, and list players by age group, among other things. The database comprises four tables:

Players	Includes fields for tracking players' names, addresses, and birthdays, which teams they are on, and whether they paid their fees.
Coaches	Includes fields for tracking coaches' names, addresses, and the names of the teams they coach.
Teams	Includes fields for tracking team names and which division each team is in.
Divisions	Includes fields for tracking division numbers and names.

Deciding how many database tables you need and how to separate data across the different tables is the hardest part of designing a database. To make the task a little easier, do it the old-fashioned way with a pencil and eraser. Here are the basic rules for separating data into different tables:

✦ **Restrict a table to one subject only:** Each database table should hold information about one subject only — customers, employees, products, and so on. This way, you can maintain data in one table independently from data in another table. Consider what would happen in the little league database (refer to Figure 1-7) if Coaches and Teams data were kept in a single table, and one team's coach was replaced by someone new. You would have to delete the old coach's record, including information about the team, enter information about the new coach, and re-enter the information about the team that you just deleted. But by keeping team information separate from coach information, you can update coach information but still maintain the team information.

✦ **Avoid duplicate information:** Try not to keep duplicate information in the same database table or duplicate information across different tables. By keeping the information in one place, you have to enter it only once, and if you have to update it, you can do so in one database table, not several.

Deciding how many tables to include in a database and how the tables relate to one another is probably the hardest task you will undertake in Access. Entire books have been written about database design, and this book cannot do the subject justice. You can, however, store all your data in a single table if the data you want to store is not very complex. The time you lose entering all the data in a single table will be made up by the time you save by not having to design a complex database with more than one table.

Choosing fields for database tables

As I explained earlier, fields are categories of information. Each database table needs at least one field. If the table itself is a subject, you could say that its fields are facts about the subject. An Address database table needs fields for recording street addresses, cities, states, and postal codes. A Products database table needs fields for product ID numbers, product names, and unit prices. Just the facts, ma'am. Within the confines of the subject, the database table needs one field for each piece of information that is useful to your organization.

While you're planning which fields to include in your database tables, follow these guidelines:

✦ **Break up the information into small elements.** For example, instead of a Name field, create a First Name field and a Last Name field. This way, you can sort database tables by last name more easily.

✦ **Give descriptive names to fields so that you know what they are later on.**

✦ **Think ahead and include a field for each piece of information your organization will need.** Adding a field to a database table late in the game is a chore. You have to return to each record, look up the information to enter, and enter it.

✦ **Don't include information that can be derived from a calculation.** As I explain in Chapter 4 of this mini-book, calculations can be performed as part of a query. For example, you can total the numbers in two fields in the same record or perform mathematical calculations on values in fields.

Deciding on a primary key field for each database table

Each database table must have a *primary key field.* This field, also known as the *primary key,* is the field in the database table where unique, one-of-a-kind data is stored. Data entered in this field — an employee ID number, a part number, a bid number — must be different in each record. If you try to enter the same data in the primary key field of two different records, a dialog box warns you not to do that. Primary key fields prevent you from entering duplicate records. They also make queries more efficient. In a query, you tell Access what to look for in database tables, Access searches through the tables, and the program assembles information that meets the criteria. Primary key fields help Access recognize records and not collect the same information more than once in a query.

Social security numbers make great primary key fields, because no two people have the same social security number. Invoice numbers and serial numbers also make excellent primary key fields. Returning to the sample little league database (refer to Figure 1-7), which fields in the little league database tables are primary key fields? In the Teams table, Team Name can be the primary key field because no two teams have the same name. Division Number can also be a primary key field because divisions in the league are numbered and no two divisions have the same number.

The Players and Coaches database tables, however, present a problem when it comes to choosing a primary key field. Two players might have the same last name, which rules out Last Name as the primary key field. A brother and sister might have the same telephone number, which rules out the Telephone No. field. Because no field holds values that are certain to be different from record to record, I introduced fields called Player Number and Coach Number. For the purpose of this database, players and coaches will be assigned numbers (Chapter 2 explains how Access can assign sequential numbers for you in a database table).

Mapping the relationships between tables

If your database includes more than one table, you have to map how the tables relate to one another. Usually, relationships are formed between the primary key field in one table and the corresponding field in another, called the *foreign key*. Figure 1-8 shows the relationships between the tables in the little league database. Because these tables are linked by common fields, I can gather information from more than one table in a query or report. Chapter 2 takes up the subject of linking tables in more detail. For now, as you design your database, consider how to connect the various tables with common fields.

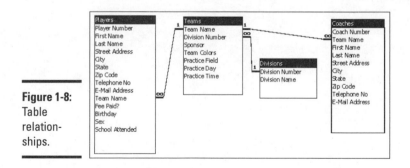

Figure 1-8:
Table
relation-
ships.

To get an idea how database tables can be linked, open the Northwind sample database that comes with Access and look in the Relationships window. To open the Northwind database, choose <u>H</u>elp⇨<u>S</u>ample Databases⇨ Northwind Sample Database; then close the Switchboard (by clicking its Close button). Click the Relationships button (you can find it on the right side of the Database window) to open the Relationship window. The Relationships window shows you how the various tables are related to one another.

Chapter 2: Building Your Database Tables

In This Chapter

✓ **Creating database tables**

✓ **Creating fields for a database table**

✓ **Choosing a primary key field**

✓ **Using field properties to make data entries more accurate**

✓ **Indexing fields in a table**

✓ **Forming relationships between tables**

Database tables are the building blocks of a database. They hold the raw data. Relationships between the tables permit you to query and generate reports from several different tables. How well your database tables are put together and how accurately data was entered in the tables determine whether your database is a thing of beauty or a wilted flower.

This chapter explains how to create database tables and fields for the tables. It explains what primary key fields are and how primary key fields and indexed fields make it easier for Access to sort, search, and query a database. This chapter describes how to forge relationships between tables. Fasten your seatbelts. In this chapter, you can find numerous tips and tricks for making sure that data is entered accurately in your database tables.

Creating a Database Table

Raw data is stored in database tables (or in a single table if you decide to keep all the data in one place). The first and most important part of setting up a database is creating the tables and entering the data. After you have entered the data, you can harass your database for information about the things and people your database keeps track of. If you haven't done so already, read the sections in Chapter 1 that pertain to storing information and designing a database before you create a database table. Chapter 1 explains what database tables are and how to fashion a splendid one.

The business of creating a database table starts on the Tables tab of the Database window, as shown in Figure 2-1.

Select tables.

Click New or select an icon.

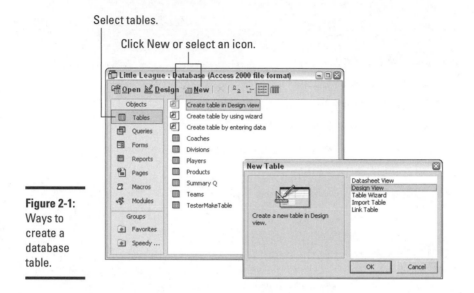

Figure 2-1:
Ways to
create a
database
table.

Select Tables on the Objects tab to view tables. As I explain in detail in the upcoming pages, Access offers three ways to create a database table:

+ **Create the database table from scratch:** Enter and format the fields one at a time on your own.

+ **Get the help of a wizard:** Get prefabricated fields and assemble them in a table. This is the way to go if you know Access well and you can modify database tables and table fields.

+ **Import the database table from another database:** This technique can be an enormous time saver if you can recycle data that have already been entered in a database table in another Access database.

Creating a database table from scratch

Creating a table from scratch entails creating the table and then entering the fields one by one. Follow these steps to create a database table from scratch:

1. **On the Objects tab of the Database window, select Tables (refer to Figure 2-1).**

2. **Double-click the Create Table in Design View icon.**

   New

   Or, if you are so inclined, click the <u>N</u>ew button, select Design View in the New Table dialog box (refer to Figure 2-1), and click OK.

   The Design window appears. From here, you enter fields for your database table. I hate to be like a City Hall bureaucrat who gives everybody the runaround, but I can't help myself. Turn to "Entering and Altering Table Fields" later in this chapter to find out how to enter fields in a database table.

3. **Click the Save button.**

   The Save As dialog box appears.

4. **Enter a descriptive name for your table and click OK.**

   Return to the Database window and you'll see the name of the table you created. If you don't believe me, click Tables on the Objects tab to see the names of tables in your database.

Creating a database table with a wizard

If you know your way around Access and know how to modify database tables, you can do worse than create a database table with a wizard. Access offers 45 different tables (20 in the Personal category and 25 in the Business category). You can pick and choose which fields you want from these tables. Usually, you can find fields that do the trick.

To create a table with a wizard, select Tables on the Objects tab of the Database window, and double-click the Create Table by Using Wizard icon (refer to Figure 2-1). The first Table Wizard dialog box appears, as shown in Figure 2-2.

In this dialog box, you describe the table you want, clicking the <u>N</u>ext button as you go along:

✦ **Business or Personal:** Select the Bu<u>s</u>iness or <u>P</u>ersonal option button to describe what kind of table you want to create.

✦ **Choosing a table type:** Under Sample <u>T</u>ables, choose the table that best describes the table you need.

✦ **Selecting fields for the table:** A list of fields appears in the <u>S</u>ample Fields box. Go down the list, selecting the fields you need and clicking the > button to list the fields in the Fields in <u>M</u>y Table list. You can rename a field by selecting it, clicking the <u>R</u>ename Field button, and entering a new name in the Rename Field dialog box.

Select a table.   Choose fields.   Arrange fields.

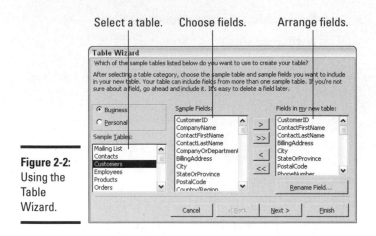

Figure 2-2:
Using the
Table
Wizard.

♦ **Naming your table:** Enter a descriptive name for the table.

♦ **Choosing the primary key field:** Click <u>Y</u>es to let Access choose the primary key field, or No to choose one on your own from the drop-down list. You can always change the primary key field later on. See the section about deciding on a primary key field for each database table in Chapter 1, and see "Designating the primary key field," later in this chapter.

♦ **Relationships:** Save the task of relating the new table to others in your database for later. This task is too important to take care of in a Wizard dialog box. See "Establishing Relationships between Database Tables," later in this chapter.

Importing a table from another database

Few things are more tedious than entering records in a database table. If the records you need have already been entered elsewhere, more power to you. Follow these steps to get a database table from another Access database:

1. **Select Tables on the Objects tab of the Database window (refer to Figure 2-1).**

2. **Click the <u>N</u>ew button to open the New Table dialog box (refer to Figure 2-1).**

3. **Select Import Table and click OK.**

The Import dialog box opens.

4. **Find the Access database with the table you need, select it, and click the Import button.**

   You see the Import Objects dialog box, shown in Figure 2-3.

5. **On the Tables tab, select the database table you want and click OK.**

   You can import more than one database table by Ctrl+clicking table names in the dialog box or clicking the Select All button.

Figure 2-3:
Getting data
from
another
database.

```
Import Objects                                    ⊠
Tables | Queries | Forms | Reports | Pages | Macros | Modules |

Account Types                          [    OK     ]
Accounts
Switchboard Items                      [  Cancel   ]
Transactions
                                       [ Select All ]

                                       [ Deselect All ]

                                       [ Options >> ]
```

If the table you want to import includes lookup fields, import the tables or queries that the lookup fields refer to as well as the table itself. Without those tables or queries, the lookup fields won't be able to obtain any values. Later in this chapter, "Creating a lookup data-entry list" explains what lookup fields are.

You can import a table structure — its field names and formats — without importing the data in the table. To do so, select the Options button in the Import Objects dialog box and, under Import Tables, select the Definition Only option button.

Opening and Viewing Tables

As with all the so-called objects in a database, you open tables by starting in the Database window. Select Tables on the Objects tab to view the database tables you created in the Database window. How you open a table depends on whether you want to open it in Datasheet view or Design view. Figure 2-4 illustrates the difference between these views. Datasheet view is for entering and examining data in a table; Design view is for creating fields and describing their parameters.

Select a table and follow these instructions to open it:

Design

◆ **Opening in Design view:** Click the <u>D</u>esign button or right-click and choose <u>D</u>esign view.

Open

◆ **Opening in Datasheet view:** Click the <u>O</u>pen button, double-click the table, or right-click and choose <u>O</u>pen.

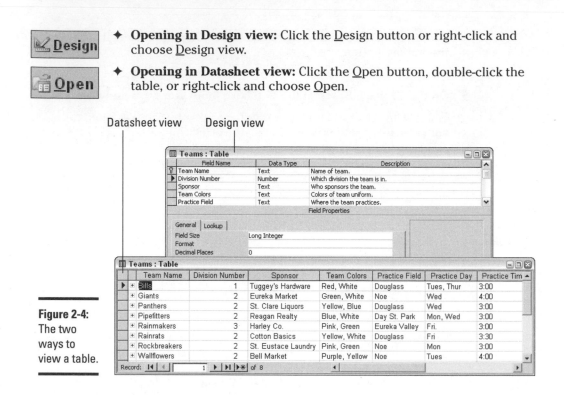

Datasheet view   Design view

Figure 2-4:
The two
ways to
view a table.

◆ **Switching views:** Click the View button. This button changes appearance, depending on whether you're in Design or Datasheet view. The View button is the leftmost button on the Table toolbar. You can also change views by choosing <u>V</u>iew➪<u>D</u>esign View or <u>V</u>iew➪<u>D</u>atasheet View.

Entering and Altering Table Fields

After you create a database table, the next task is to enter the fields or, if Access created the table for you, alter the fields to your liking. As Chapter 1 of this mini-book explains, fields represent categories of information in a database table. They are the equivalent of columns in a conventional table. Fields determine what kind of information is stored in a database table.

These pages explain how to create a field, choose the right data type, display data in fields, and designate the primary key field in a table. While I'm on the subject of fields, W.C. Fields said, "Horse sense is the thing a horse has which keeps it from betting on people."

The Field Builder

To get Access's help in creating a field, select an empty row and click the Build button. You see the Field Builder dialog box. Do the sample tables and sample fields in this dialog box look familiar? These are the same fields you get the opportunity to enter when you create a database table with the Table Wizard. Select a sample table, select one of its fields, and click OK to enter the field in your database table.

> **Field Builder**
>
> Select a sample table, then select the sample field you want.
>
> Sample Tables:
> - Addresses
> - Guests
> - Categories
> - Household Inventory
> - Recipes
> - Plants
> - Exercise Log
>
> ○ Business
> ● Personal
>
> Sample Fields:
> - DietLogID
> - PersonID
> - DietType
> - DateAcquired
> - WhichMeal
> - GramsCarbohydrates
> - GramsProtein
> - GramsFat
> - TotalCalories
> - MilligramsSodium
>
> OK
> Cancel

Creating a field

Follow these steps to create a new field in a database table:

1. **Open the table and switch to Design view if you aren't already there.**

You can click the View button to change views.

2. **If necessary, insert a new row for the field.**

To do so, click in the field that is to go after the new field; then click the Insert Rows button or choose Insert⇨Rows. A blank row appears.

3. **Enter a name in the Field Name column.**

Names can't include periods or be longer than 64 letters, but you would be foolish to enter a long name anyway because it wouldn't fit very well along the top of the table.

Some database programs don't permit spaces in field names. If you intend to export Access data to other database programs, don't include spaces in field names. Instead, run the words together or separate words with an underscore character, like this: underscore_character.

4. **Press the Tab key or click in the Data Type column, and choose a data type from the drop-down menu, as shown in Figure 2-5.**

Data types classify what kind of information is kept in the field. The next section in this chapter explains data types.

5. **Enter a description in the Description column if you desire.**

These descriptions can be very helpful when you need to reacquaint yourself with a field and find out what it's meant to do.

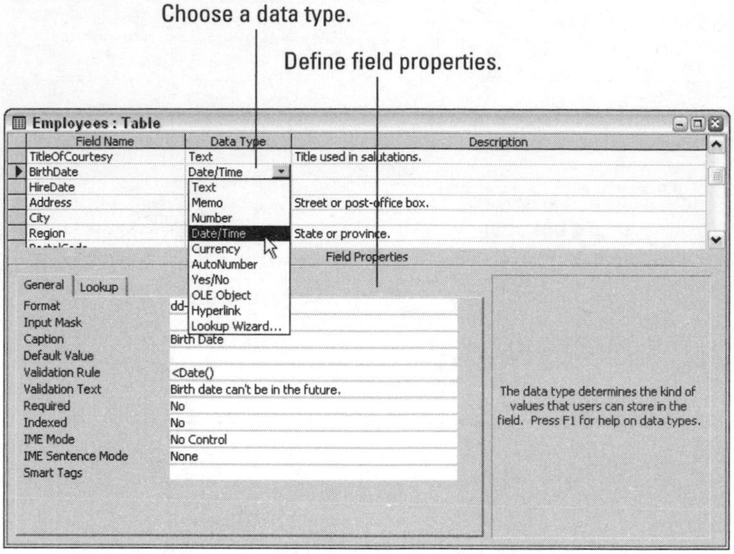

Choose a data type.

Define field properties.

Figure 2-5:
Choosing a
data type.

TIP

In case the name you chose for your field isn't descriptive enough, you can give the field a second name. The name appears in Datasheet view, on forms, and on reports. To enter a second, descriptive field name, enter the name in the Caption field on the General tab of the Design View window.

Later in this chapter, "Field Properties for Making Sure Data Entries Are Accurate" demonstrates how to define field properties in the Design View window to make it easier for data-entry clerks to enter the data.

All about data types

To choose a data type for a field, open the Data Type drop-down menu in the Design View window and choose a data type (refer to Figure 2-5). Data types are the first line of defense in making sure that data is entered correctly in a table. Try to enter text in a field assigned the Currency or Number data type and Access tells you that your entry is invalid. You get the chance to fix your mistake as soon as you make it.

Table 2-1 explains the ten options on the Data Type menu. Choose data types carefully, because how you classify the data that is entered in a field determines how you can query the field for information. Querying for a number range is impossible, for example, if the field you're querying was not classified as a Number or Currency field on the Data Type menu.

Table 2-1	Data Types for Fields
Data Type	*What It's For*
Text	For storing text (city names, for example), combinations of text and numbers (street addresses), and numbers that won't be calculated or used in expressions (telephone numbers and social security numbers). By default, a Text field is 50 characters long, but Text fields can be 255 characters if you need that many. If you need that many characters, however, you probably need the Memo data type, not the Text data type.
Memo	For storing long descriptions. Fields assigned this data type can hold 65,535 characters, not that anyone needs that many.
Number	For storing numbers to be used in calculations or sorting. (If you're dealing with monetary figures, choose the Currency data type.)
Date/Time	For storing dates and times and being able to sort data chronologically or use dates and times in calculations.
Currency	For storing monetary figures for use in calculations and sorting.
AutoNumber	For entering numbers in sequence that will be different from record to record. Use the AutoNumber data type for the primary key field if no other field stores unique, one-of-a-kind data. (See "Designating the primary key field," later in this chapter.)
Yes/No	For storing True/False, Yes/No, On/Off type data. Choose this data type to enter a box in the field. When the box is selected, the data in the field is True, Yes, or On, for example.
OLE Object	For embedding an OLE link in your Access table to another object — an Excel worksheet or Word document.
Hyperlink	For storing hyperlinks to other locations on the Internet or on the company intranet.
Lookup Wizard	For creating a drop-down menu with choices that a data-entry clerk can choose from when entering data. See "Creating a lookup data-entry list," later in this chapter.

Book VI Chapter 2

Building Your Database Tables

Designating the primary key field

As explained in the previous chapter of this mini-book, no database table is complete without a primary key field (see the section about deciding on a primary key field for each database table in Chapter 1). The primary key field identifies which field in the table is unique and contains data that differs from record to record. Duplicate values and null values can't be entered in the primary key field (a null value indicates a missing or unknown value). So important is choosing a primary key field that Access doesn't let you close a table unless you choose one.

Deciding how the data in fields is displayed

To decide how numbers, times, dates, currency values, and Yes/No data are displayed in fields, open the Format drop-down menu on the Field Properties part of the Design window and choose an option. These display options are useful indeed. Choose a number format with a dollar sign and comma ($3,456.79), for example, and you don't have to enter the dollar signs or commas when you enter data in the field. These marks are entered for you. You just enter the numbers.

✦ @ (at symbol): A character or space is required. For example, @@@@-@@ inserts a hyphen between the first set of numbers and the second. You don't have to enter the hyphen — only the text or numbers.

✦ & (ampersand): A character or space is optional. For example, @@@@@-&&&& in a ZIP Code field tells Access that either entry is correct, a five-character ZIP Code or a five-character plus the four extra characters ZIP Code.

✦ > (right bracket): Convert all characters in the field to uppercase. Merely by entering this symbol in the Format text box, you can convert all entries in the field to uppercase without the data-entry clerk having to hold down the Shift or Caps Lock key.

✦ < (left bracket): Convert all characters in the field to lowercase. Enter this symbol to make all characters lowercase in the field.

If no field in your table holds one-of-a-kind data that will be different from record to record, get around the problem with one of these techniques:

✦ **The AutoNumber data type:** Create a new field, give it a name, choose AutoNumber from the Data Type menu (refer to Figure 2-5), and make your new field the primary key field. This way, as you enter data, Access enters a unique number to identify each record in the field. (To generate random numbers instead of sequential numbers in an AutoNumber field, go the Field Properties tab of the Design View window and choose Random instead of Increment on the New Values drop-down menu.)

✦ **A multiple-field primary key:** Combine two or more fields and designate them as the primary key. For example, if you're absolutely certain that no two people whose names will be entered in your database table have the same name, you can make the First Name and Last Name fields the primary key. The problem with multiple-field primary keys, however, is that it takes Access longer to process them, and you run the risk of entering duplicate records.

Follow these steps to designate a field in a database table as the primary key field:

1. **In Design view, select the field or fields you want to be the primary key.**

To select a field, click its row selector, the small box to its left; Ctrl-click row selectors to select more than one field.

2. **Click the Primary Key button or choose Edit⇨Primary Key.**

A small key symbol appears on the row selector to let you know which field is the primary key field.

To remove a primary key, click its row selector and then click the Primary Key button all over again.

Moving, renaming, and deleting fields

Suppose that you need to move, rename, or delete a field. To do so, switch to Design View and follow these instructions:

✦ **Moving a field:** Select the field's row selector (the box to its left) and drag the selector up or down to a new location.

✦ **Renaming a field:** Click in the Field Name box where the name is, delete the name that's there, and enter a new name.

✦ **Deleting a field:** Right-click the field and choose Delete Rows on the shortcut menu.

Field Properties for Making Sure That Data Entries Are Accurate

Unfortunately, entering the data in a database table is one of the most tedious activities known to humankind. And because the activity is so dull, people are prone to make mistakes when they enter data in a database table. One way to cut down on mistakes is to take advantage of the Field Property settings on the General tab in the Design View window. Figure 2-6 shows the General tab.

These properties determine what can and can't be entered in the different fields of a database table. Some of the settings are invaluable. The Field Size property, for example, determines how many characters can be entered in a field. In a State field where two-letter state abbreviations are to be entered, make the Field Size property 2 to be certain that no one enters more than two characters. If the majority of people you're tracking in an address database live in New York, enter NY in the Default Value property. That way, you spare data-entry clerks from having to enter NY the majority of the time. They won't have to enter it because NY will already be there.

Enter the properties.

What the property is.

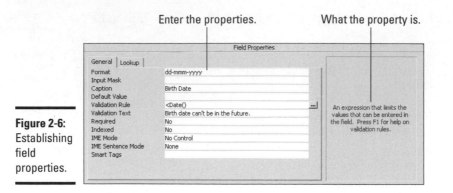

Figure 2-6:
Establishing
field
properties.

The Lookup tab in the Field Properties part of the Design View window is for creating a data-entry drop-down list. It, too, is invaluable. If you happen to know that only four items can be entered in a field, create a drop-down list with the four items. That way, data-entry clerks can choose from a list of four valid items instead of having to enter the data themselves and perhaps enter it incorrectly.

A look at the Field Properties settings

Especially if yours is a large database, you're encouraged to study the field properties carefully and make liberal use of them. The Field Properties settings safeguard data from being entered incorrectly. Following is a description of the different properties (listed here in the order in which they appear in the Design View window) and instructions for using them wisely. Which properties you can assign to a field depends on which data type the field was assigned.

Field Size

In the Field Size box, enter the maximum number of characters that can be entered in the field. Suppose that the field you're dealing with is called "ZIP Code" and you want to enter five-number ZIP Codes. By entering **5** in the Field Size text box, only five characters can be entered in the field. A sleepy data-entry clerk couldn't enter a six-character ZIP Code by accident.

Format

Earlier in this chapter, "Deciding how the data in fields is displayed" explains the Format property. Open the drop-down menu and select the format in which text, numbers, and dates and times are displayed.

TIP

Here's a neat trick: You can make text in a field appear in color by entering [*color name*] in the Format text. Enclose the word Black, Blue, Cyan, Green, Magenta, Red, Yellow, or White in square brackets ([]).

Decimal Places

For a field that holds numbers, open the Decimal Places drop-down list and choose how many numbers can appear to the right of the decimal point. This property affects how numbers and currency values are displayed, not their real value. Numbers are rounded to the nearest decimal point. The Auto option displays the number of decimal places that the format you chose on the Format drop-down menu permits.

Input Mask

For Text and Date field types, this feature provides a template with punctuation marks to make entering the data easier. Telephone numbers, social security numbers, and other numbers that typically are entered along with dashes and parentheses are ideal candidates for an input mask (another ridiculous database term!). On the datasheet, blank spaces appear where the numbers go, and the punctuation marks stand at the ready to receive numbers, as shown in Figure 2-7.

Phone Numbers : Table

Last Name	First Name	Phone Number	Social Security Number
Williams	Reginald	(415) 555-6431	111-22-3344
Wong	Mariam	(000) 000-0000	___-__-____

Record: 17 of 17

Figure 2-7: Input masks.

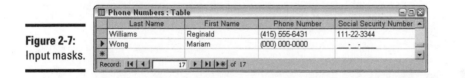

In the Input Mask text box, enter a 0 where numbers go, and enter the punctuation marks where they go. For example, enter **(000) 000-0000** or **000/000-0000** to enter an input mask for a telephone number like the one shown in Figure 2-7. You can also create input masks by clicking the three dots beside the Input Mask text box. Doing so opens the Input Mask Wizard dialog box, where you can fashion a very sophisticated input mask.

Caption

If the field you're working on has a cryptic or hard-to-understand name, enter a more descriptive name in the Caption text box. The name will appear in Datasheet view, on forms, and on reports in place of the field name. People entering data will understand what to enter after reading the descriptive caption.

Default Value

When you know that the majority of records will require a certain value, number, or abbreviation, enter it in the Default Value text box. That way, you save yourself the trouble of entering the value, number, or abbreviation most of the time, because the default value will already appear in each record as you enter it. You can always override the default value by entering something different.

Validation Rule

As long as you know your way around operators and Boolean expressions, you can establish a rule for entering data in a field. For example, you can enter an expression that requires dates to be entered in a certain time frame. Or you can require currency figures to be above or below a certain value. To establish a validation rule, enter an expression in the Validation Rule text box. To use dates in an expression, the dates must be enclosed by number signs (#). Here are some examples of validation rules:

>1000	The value entered must be over 1000.
<1000	The value entered must be under 1000.
>=10	The value entered must be greater than or equal to ten.
<>0	The value entered cannot be zero.
>=#1/1/1990#	The date entered must be January 1, 1990 or later.
>=#1/1/1990# And <#1/1/1990#	The date entered must be in the year 1990.

 To get help forming expressions, click the Build button to open the Expression Builder, shown in Figure 2-8, and build an expression there. Try clicking the Help button in the Expression Builder dialog box. Doing so opens the Access Help program, where you can get advice about building expressions.

Validation Text

If someone enters data that violates a validation rule that you entered in the Validation Rule text box, Access displays a standard error message. The message reads, "One or more values are prohibited by the validation rule set for [this field]. Enter a value that the expression for this field can accept." If this message is too cold and impersonal for you, you can create a message of your own for the error message dialog box. Enter it in the Validation Text text box.

Required

By default, no entry has to be made in a field, but if you choose Yes instead of No in the Required box and you fail to make an entry in the field, a message box tells you to be sure to make an entry. Choose Yes in the Required box if you want to be certain that entries are made in a field.

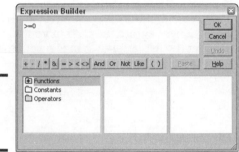

Figure 2-8:
Creating a
validation
rule.

Allow Zero Length

This property allows you to enter zero-length strings in a field. A *zero-length string* — two quotation marks with no text between them ("") — indicates that there is no value for a field. To see how zero-length strings work, suppose that your database table calls for entering e-mail addresses. If you didn't know whether one person had an e-mail address, you would leave the E-Mail Address field blank, but if you knew that the person didn't have an e-mail address, you could indicate as much by entering a zero-length string. Choose Yes on the drop-down menu to permit zero-length strings to be entered in the field.

Indexed

Indicates that the field has been indexed. As "Indexing for Faster Sorts, Searches, and Queries" explains later in this chapter, indexes make sorting a field and searching through a field go faster. The word *Yes* appears in this text box if the field has been indexed.

Unicode Expression

Choose Yes from the Unicode Expression drop-down menu if you want to compress data that is now stored in Unicode format. Storing data this way saves on disk space.

Smart Tags

If you intend to enter smart tags in the field, indicate which kind you will enter by clicking the three dots next to the Smart Tags box and choosing an option in the Smart Tags dialog box. Book VIII, Chapter 1 explains smart tags.

Creating a lookup data-entry list

Perhaps the best way to make sure that data is entered correctly is to create a data-entry drop-down list. Whoever enters the data in your database table has only to choose an item from the list, as shown in Figure 2-9. This saves time and prevents invalid data from being entered. Access offers two ways to create the drop-down list:

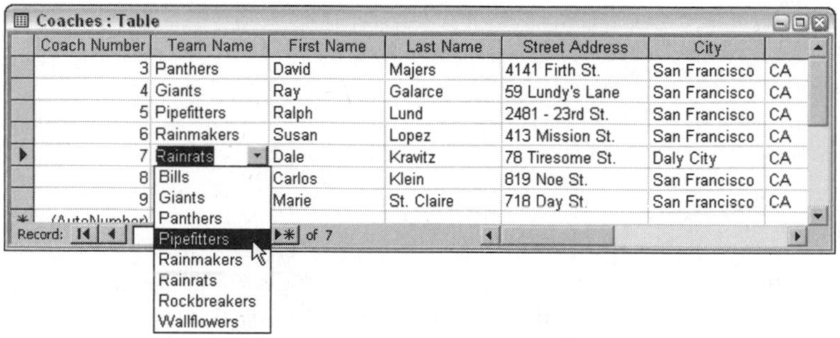

Figure 2-9:
A so-called
lookup list.

+ **Create the list by entering the items yourself:** Go this route when you're dealing with a finite list of items that never change.

+ **Get the items from another database table:** Go this route to get items from a column in another database table. This way, you can choose from an ever-expanding list of items. As the number of items in the other database table changes, so do the number of items in the drop-down list, because the items come from the other database table. This is a great way to get items from a primary key field in another table.

Creating a drop-down list on your own

Follow these steps to create a drop-down, or lookup, list with entries you type:

1. **In Design view, click the field that needs a drop-down list.**

2. **Open the Data Type drop-down menu and choose Lookup Wizard, the last option on the menu.**

   You see the Lookup Wizard dialog box.

3. **Select the second option, I Will Type in the Values that I Want, and click the Next button.**

4. **Under Col1 in the next dialog box, enter each item you want for the drop-down list; then click the Next button.**

   You can create a multicolumn list by entering a number in the Number of Columns text box and then entering items for the list.

5. **Enter a name for the field, if necessary, and click the Finish button.**

   Switch to Datasheet view and open the drop-down list in the field to make sure that it displays properly.

To see what's on a drop-down list, start in Design view, select the field for which you created the list, and select the Lookup tab. As shown in Figure 2-10, you can edit the list by editing or removing items in the Rows Source text box. Be sure that a semi-colon (;) appears between each item. To remove a lookup list, choose Text Box on the Display Control drop-down menu.

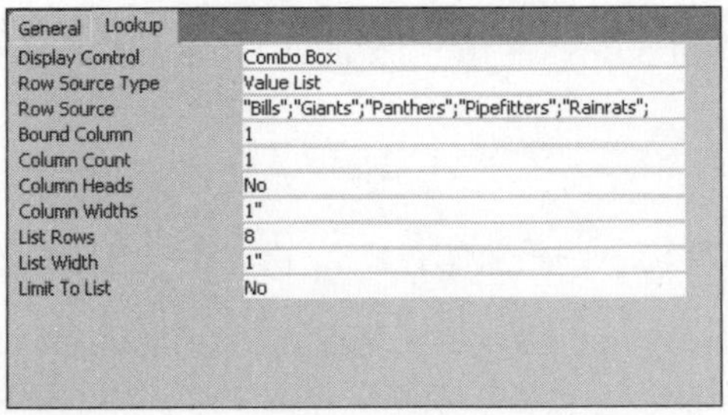

Book VI Chapter 2

Building Your Database Tables

General	Lookup	
Display Control	Combo Box
Row Source Type	Value List
Row Source	"Bills";"Giants";"Panthers";"Pipefitters";"Rainrats";
Bound Column	1
Column Count	1
Column Heads	No
Column Widths	1"
List Rows	8
List Width	1"
Limit To List	No

Figure 2-10:
Editing a
lookup list.

Getting list items from a database table

Before you can get list items from another database table, you have to define a relationship between the tables. The next section of this chapter explains how to do that. Follow these steps to get items on a drop-down list from another database table:

1. **In Design view, click the field that needs a list, open the Data Type drop-down menu, and choose Lookup Wizard.**

   The Lookup Wizard dialog box appears.

2. **Select the first option, I Want the Lookup Column to Look Up the Values in a Table or Query; and click Next.**

    You see a list of tables in your database.

3. **Select the table with the data you need and click the Next button.**

    The dialog box shows you a list of fields in the table.

4. **Select the field where the data for your list is stored.**

5. **Click the > button.**

    The name of the list appears on the right side of the dialog box, under Selected Fields.

6. **Click the Next button.**

    Normally, lists are displayed in ascending order, but you can click the Descending button to reverse the order of the list.

7. **Click the Finish button.**

    If you're so inclined, you can change the width of the list before clicking Finish, but you can always do that on the datasheet, as the section about changing the appearance of the datasheet explains in Chapter 3.

 Suppose that you obtained the items from the wrong field or wrong database table? To fix that problem, select the field for which you created the list and, in Design view, select the Lookup tab (refer to Figure 2-10). Choose Text Box instead of Combo Box on the Display Control drop-down menu and start all over.

Indexing for Faster Sorts, Searches, and Queries

Indexing means to instruct Access to keep information about the data in a field or combination of fields. Because Access keeps this information on hand, it doesn't have to actually search through every record in a database table to sort data, search for data, or run a query. In a large database table, indexes make sorting, searching, and querying go considerably faster because Access looks through its own data rather than the data in tables. The performance difference between querying a database table that has and has not been indexed is astonishing. That's the good news. The bad news is that indexes inflate the size of Access files.

By default, the field you choose as the primary key field is indexed. Choosing other fields for indexing is recommended if you often conduct queries and searches. When you choose a field to index, choose one with data that varies from record to record and is likely to be the subject of searches, sorts, and queries. That way, the index will mean something. However, a field with data that is mostly the same from record to record is a waste of a good index, not to mention disk space. By the way, Access automatically indexes fields whose names include the words *ID, Code, Num,* and *Key*, the idea being that these fields store essential information worthy of indexing.

Indexing a field

To index a field, switch to Design view, select the field you want to index, and, on the General tab of the Field Properties part of the Design window, open the Indexed drop-down menu and choose one of these options:

✦ **Yes (Duplicates OK):** Indexes the field and allows duplicate values to be entered in the field.

✦ **Yes (No Duplicates):** Indexes the field and disallows duplicate values. If you choose this option, the field works something like a primary key field in that Access does not permit you to enter the same value in two different records. Not many fields can be indexed this way.

**Book VI
Chapter 2**

**Building Your
Database Tables**

Indexing based on more than one field

Generate an index on more than one field at the same time if doing so will make sorting, querying, and searching the database table go faster. A multi-field index is especially valuable in sorting operations where records in one field are often the same but records in a companion field are different. In a long address database table, for example, many names in Last Name field are inevitably the same, so indexing the Last Name field isn't worthwhile, but indexing the First Name and Last Name fields helps Access distinguish the records from one another.

Follow these steps to generate a multifield index:

1. **Starting in Design view, click the Indexes button or choose View⇨Indexes.**

You see the Indexes dialog box, shown in Figure 2-11. The dialog box already lists the primary key field, because it's indexed by default.

2. **On a blank line in the dialog box, enter a name for the index you will generate with more than one field.**

3. **In the Field Name column, open the drop-down list and choose the first field you want for the multifield index.**

Access sorts the records first on this field and then on the second field you choose.

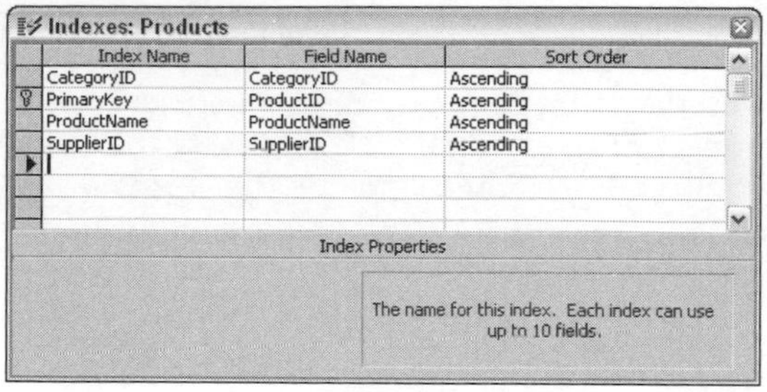

Figure 2-11:
A multi-field
index.

4. **In the next row of the Field Name column, choose the second field you want for the index.**

   You can use as many as ten different fields in a multifield index. In Figure 2-11, four fields are in the index.

5. **Choose Descending in the Sort Order column if you want some of the fields to be sorted in descending order.**

6. **Click the Close button.**

   Click the Indexes button in Design view if you need to return to the Indexes dialog box and change how fields are indexed.

Establishing Relationships between Database Tables

As the section about mapping the relationships between tables in Chapter 1 explains, you have to establish relationships between tables if you want to query or generate reports with data from more than one database table. Relationships define the field that two separate tables have in common. To understand why relationships between tables are necessary, consider the query shown in Figure 2-12. The purpose of this query is to list all companies that ordered items in 1997, list the companies by name, and list the city and country where each company is located. Figure 2-13 shows the results of the query.

Consider what Access does to run this query:

✦ Access deals with two database tables, Customers and Orders.

✦ In the Orders table, Access looks in the OrderDate field to isolate all records that describe orders made in the year 1997. The expression for finding these records is shown on the Criteria line in Figure 2-12: Between #1/1/1997# And #12/31/1997#.

Tables being queried   Table relationship

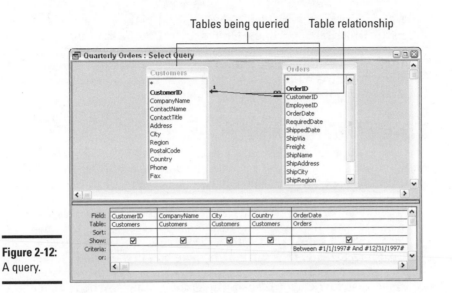

Book VI
Chapter 2

Building Your
Database Tables

Figure 2-12:
A query.

✦ Because there is a relationship between the CustomerID field in the Customers table and the CustomerID field in the Orders table — because the two fields hold the same type of information — Access can match the 1997 records it has found in the Orders table with corresponding records in the Customers table. Where the CustomerID of a 1997 record in the Orders table and a CustomerID in the Customers table match, Access assembles a new record and places it in the query results. As Figure 2-13 demonstrates, the query records list Customer IDs, company names, cities, and countries.

Figure 2-13:
Results of
the query
from Figure
2-12.

	Customer ID	Company Name	City	Country	Order Date
▶	ALFKI	Alfreds Futterkiste	Berlin	Germany	25-Aug-1997
	ALFKI	Alfreds Futterkiste	Berlin	Germany	03-Oct-1997
	ALFKI	Alfreds Futterkiste	Berlin	Germany	13-Oct-1997
	ANATR	Ana Trujillo Emparedados y helados	México D.F.	Mexico	08-Aug-1997
	ANATR	Ana Trujillo Emparedados y helados	México D.F.	Mexico	28-Nov-1997
	ANTON	Antonio Moreno Taquería	México D.F.	Mexico	15-Apr-1997
	ANTON	Antonio Moreno Taquería	México D.F.	Mexico	13-May-1997
	ANTON	Antonio Moreno Taquería	México D.F.	Mexico	19-Jun-1997
	ANTON	Antonio Moreno Taquería	México D.F.	Mexico	22-Sep-1997
	ANTON	Antonio Moreno Taquería	México D.F.	Mexico	25-Sep-1997
	AROUT	Around the Horn	London	UK	21-Feb-1997
	AROUT	Around the Horn	London	UK	04-Jun-1997
	AROUT	Around the Horn	London	UK	16-Oct-1997
	AROUT	Around the Horn	London	UK	14-Nov-1997
	AROUT	Around the Horn	London	UK	17-Nov-1997
	AROUT	Around the Horn	London	UK	08-Dec-1997
	AROUT	Around the Horn	London	UK	24-Dec-1997

Record: 14 ◀ 1 ▶ ▶I ▶* of 404

✦ Data for determining which records appear in the query results is found in the OrderDate field in the Orders table. But the information compiled in the query results — customer IDs, company names, cities, and countries — comes from fields in the Customers table. Thanks to the relationship between the CustomerID fields in these tables, Access can draw upon information from both tables.

Types of relationships

The vast majority of relationships between tables are *one-to-many relationships* between the primary key field in one database table and a field in another. Table relationships fall in these categories:

✦ **One-to-many relationship:** Each record in one table is linked to many records in another table. The relationship in Figure 2-12 is a one-to-many relationship. Each CustomerID number appears only once in the CustomerID field of the Customers table but, in the Orders table, the same CustomerID number can appear in many records, because the same customer can order many different products. When you link tables, Access creates a one-to-many relationship when one of the fields being linked is either a primary key field or an indexed field assigned the No (No Duplicates) setting (see "Indexing for Faster Sorts, Searches, and Queries," earlier in this chapter).

✦ **One-to-one relationship:** Two fields are linked. This relationship is rare and is sometimes used for security purposes.

✦ **Many-to-many relationship:** This complex relationship actually describes crisscrossing relationships in which the linking field is not the primary key field in either table. To create a many-to-many relationship, an intermediary table called a junction table is needed. This relationship is rare.

Usually, fields in separate tables that hold the same data also have the same name, but that isn't necessary. For example, a field called ZIP Code in one table might be called Postal Code in another. What matters is that fields that are linked hold the same kind of data.

Finding your way around the Relationships window

To display the tables in a database and link tables to one another or see how they are related to each other, click the Relationships button or choose Tools⇨Relationships. You see the Relationships window, as shown in Figure 2-14. Notice the field names in each table. The primary key field is shown in boldface. Lines in the window show how relationships have been established between tables.

Placing tables in the Relationships window

The first time you open the Relationships window, you see the Show Table dialog box. The purpose of this dialog box is to find out which tables to put in the Relationships window. Ctrl+click to select tables and then click the Add button.

 If you create a new database table and need to place it in the Relationships window, click the Relationships button to display the Relationships window; then click the Show Table button or choose Relationships➪Show Table. The Show Table dialog box appears. Select your new table and click the Add button.

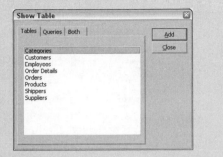

Book VI Chapter 2

Building Your Database Tables

Figure 2-14: The Relationships window.

Right-click a line to edit or delete a relationship.

Apart from linking tables in the Relationships window (a subject explained shortly), here's all you need to know about the window:

✦ **Handling the tables:** Each table appears in its own window. Drag tables from place to place, drag a border to change a window's size, and scroll to see field names.

✦ **Removing a table from the window:** Right-click the table and choose <u>H</u>ide Table on the shortcut menu.

✦ **Removing all tables from the window:** Click the Clear Layout button and select <u>Y</u>es in the confirmation box.

✦ **Placing tables back on the window:** To put selected tables back in the window, click the Show Table button and, in the Show Table dialog box, select the tables and click the <u>A</u>dd button. To put all the tables back in the window, click the Show All Relationships button.

✦ **Studying a table's relationships:** Click the Clear Layout button to remove all tables from the window; then place the table back in the window, select it, and click the Show Direct Relationships button.

Forging relationships between tables

Make sure that both tables are on display in the Relationships window, and follow these steps to forge a relationship between them:

1. **Click to select the field in one table; then hold down the mouse button and drag the mouse pointer to the field in the other table where you want to forge the link, and release the mouse button.**

   You see the Edit Relationships dialog box shown in Figure 2-15. This dragging between table fields is probably the most awkward thing you will undertake in Office! If you do it right, a bar appears where the mouse pointer is as you move it over the second table, and the names of the two fields appear in the Edit Relationships dialog box.

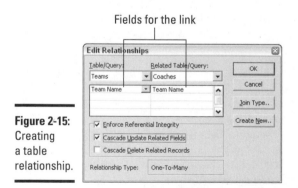

Figure 2-15: Creating a table relationship.

   Notice the relationship type at the bottom of the dialog box. If you accidentally created a link to the wrong field, choose the correct field from the drop-down menu in the dialog box.

2. **Select the Enforce Referential Integrity check box.**

If you don't select this box, the relationship between the tables is inde-terminate, instead of being a one-to-many relationship. *Referential integrity* (another hideous database term!) has to do with whether values in the two different fields corroborate each other.

3. **Choose Cascade options, if you want.**

One of these options is excellent and the other is dangerous:

- **Cascade Update Related Fields:** If you change a value on the "one" side of the relationship, a matching value on the "many" side is changed as well to preserve referential integrity. In Figure 2-15, for example, if I change a team's name in one table, the name is changed as well in the other table. This is a great way to make sure that infor-mation is up to date.

- **Cascade Delete Related Records:** If you delete a record in the "one" table, all records in the "many" table to which the deleted record is linked are also deleted. In Figure 2-15, for example, if I delete a team name in the "one" table, all records in the "many" table that include that team name in a field are deleted! Access warns you before making the deletion, but still! This option is dangerous and I don't recom-mend selecting it.

4. **Click the Create button to forge the relationship.**

In the Relationships window (refer to Figure 2-14), a line is drawn between the table fields. The number 1 appears on the "one" side of the relationship and the infinity symbol (∞) appears on the "many" side.

If you mistakenly establish a relationship between the wrong fields, right-click the line between the fields, choose Delete on the shortcut menu (refer to Figure 2-14), and select Yes in the confirmation box. Choose Edit Relationship to open the Edit Relationship dialog box and rethink the link (hey, that rhymes!).

After you create a one-to-many relationship between tables, you can't enter a value in the "many" table unless it's already in the "one" table. For exam-ple, suppose that the "one" table includes a primary key field called Employee Number and this field is linked to a field in the "many" table that's also called Employee Number. If you enter an Employee Number in the "many" table that isn't in the "one" table, Access warns you that it can't be done without violating referential integrity. The best way to solve this problem is to create a lookup data-entry list in the "many" table with values from the primary key field in the "one" table. See "Creating a lookup data-entry list," earlier in this chapter.

TIP

To generate and print an Access report that shows how tables in your database are linked, open the Relationships window and choose File⇨Print Relationships. Then save the report and print it. Access reports are explained in Chapter 5 of this mini-book.

Subdatasheets

In Datasheet view, Access gives you the opportunity to view the "many" records that are linked to a field when a relationship has been established between tables. The records appear on a *subdatasheet*. In the database shown in this illustration, the Divisions and Teams tables are linked on the Division Number field, the primary key of the Divisions table and the "one" side of the relationship. In the Divisions table, I can click the plus sign in a record to see the "many" records that are linked to Division Number, the primary key field. For this illustration, I clicked the plus sign (+) to see the teams in Division 2. The information on the subdatasheet comes from the Teams table. Click the minus sign (–) to hide a subdatasheet.

Divisions : Table						
Division Number	**Division Name**					
1 ▼	Bronco					
2	Pony					
	Team Name	**Sponsor**	**Team Colors**	**Practice Field**	**Practice Day**	**Practice Time**
+	Giants	Eureka Market	Green, White	Noe	Wed	4:00
+	Wallflowers	Bell Market	Purple, Yellow	Noe	Tues	4:00
+	Panthers	St. Clare Liquors	Yellow, Blue	Douglass	Wed	3:00
+	Pipefitters	Reagan Realty	Blue, White	Day St. Park	Mon, Wed.	3:00
+	Rainrats	Cotton Basics	Yellow, White	Douglass	Fri	3:30
+	Rockbreakers	St. Eustace Laundry	Pink, Green	Noe	Mon	3:00
*						
+	3	Colt				
+	4	Junior				

Record: 14 ◄ 1 ► ►I ►* of 5

Chapter 3: Entering the Data

A t last — you can start entering the data. You've set up your database tables, named the fields, and established relationships between the tables. Now you're ready to go. This short chapter explains how to enter the data in a database table. It shows you how to enter data on a datasheet or enter data by way of a form. This chapter also describes how to find missing records in case one goes astray.

There's no getting around it. Entering data truly is a tedious activity. But if you set up the fields well, and if you take advantage of input masks and other field properties, it isn't so bad. It's better than stepping on a shovel blade, anyway.

The Two Ways to Enter Data

When it comes to entering data in a database table, you can take your pick between Datasheet view and a form. Figure 3-1 compares and contrasts the two. Here are the advantages of entering data in Datasheet view:

✦ Many records appear at one time.

✦ You can copy and paste data.

✦ You can sort by column (right-click a column heading and choose Sort Ascending or Sort Descending).

✦ You can scroll up or down to locate records.

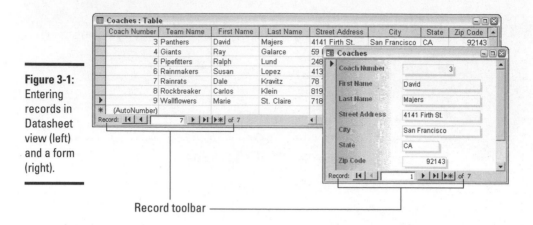

Record toolbar ──────────────

Here are the advantages of entering the data in a form:

✦ You can don't have to scroll left or right to see all the fields.

✦ Getting from field to field is easier.

✦ Fields are clearly labeled so that you always know what to enter.

Entering the Data in Datasheet View

Entering data in Datasheet view is like entering data in a conventional table. As with a table, a datasheet has columns and rows. Records are entered in rows, and each column represents a field. Fans of Datasheet view like being able to look at a dozen records simultaneously. They like being able to open subdatasheets (the end of the previous chapter explains what those are). For fans of Datasheet view, these pages explain how to enter data in a datasheet and change a datasheet's appearance.

 Database tables open in Datasheet view when you double-click their names in the Database window. But if you happen to be gazing at a table in Design view, click the View button or choose <u>V</u>iew⇨Data<u>s</u>heet View to switch to Datasheet view.

Entering data

In Datasheet view, the bottom of the Datasheet View window tells you how many records have been entered in the datasheet and which record the cursor is in. To enter a new record, create an empty row and start entering the data. To create a new row, do one of the following:

+ Click the New Record button (this button is found on the Table Datasheet toolbar and the Record toolbar at the bottom of the window).

+ Choose Insert⇨New Record or Edit⇨Go To⇨New Record.

+ Press Ctrl+the plus key.

A pencil icon appears on the row selector to let you know which record you're dealing with. To get from field to field, click in a field, press the Tab key, or press Enter. Table 3-1 lists keyboard shortcuts for getting around a datasheet.

Table 3-1	Datasheet Shortcuts
Press. . .	*To Move. . .*
↑	To the previous record. You can also press the Previous button on the Record toolbar.
↓	To the next record. You can also press the Next button.
Tab or Enter	To the next field in the record.
Shift+Tab	To the previous field in the record.
Ctrl+Home	To the first field in the first record. You can also press the First button.
Ctrl+End	To the last field in the last record. You can also press the Last button.
PgUp	Up one screen.
PgDn	Down one screen.

To delete a record, click its row selector and then click the Delete Record button or press the Delete key. Access asks whether you really want to delete the record. Click Yes in the confirmation box.

Two tricks for entering data quicker

In a database table with many fields, it's sometimes hard to tell what data to enter. When the cursor is in the sixth or seventh field, for example, you can lose sight of the first field, the one on the left side of the datasheet that usually identifies the person or item whose record you're entering. To "freeze" a field so that it appears on-screen no matter how far you travel toward the right side of the datasheet, click the name of the field at the top of the datasheet and choose Format⇨Freeze Columns. To "unfreeze" the field, choose Format⇨Unfreeze All Columns. You can freeze more than one field by dragging across field names at the top of the data sheet before choosing Format⇨Freeze Columns.

Entering data in the Zoom box

To make putting a long entry in a field a little easier, Access offers the Zoom box. Instead of having to stay within the narrow confines of a datasheet field, you can press Shift+F2 to open the Zoom box and enter the data there. After you click OK, the data is entered in the field. The Zoom box is especially convenient for entering data in a Memo field. As Chapter 2 explains, Memo fields can hold a whopping 65,535 characters. Move the cursor into a field and press Shift+F2 to open the Zoom box and read all the text in the field.

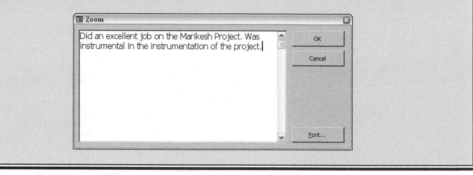

Another way to handle the problem of not being able to identify where data is supposed to be entered is to hide columns in the datasheet. To perform this trick, select the columns you want to hide by dragging the pointer across their names; then choose Format⇨Hide Columns. To see the columns again, choose Format⇨Unhide Columns, select column names in the Unhide Columns dialog box, and click the Close button.

The fastest way to hide a column is to drag the border between it and the next column to the left until the column disappears.

Changing the appearance of the datasheet

To make the datasheet a little less cluttered and unwieldy, try experimenting with its appearance. Access offers a few handy shortcuts for doing just that:

✦ **Rearranging columns:** To move a column to a different location, click its name at the top of the datasheet and drag it to the left or right.

✦ **Resizing columns:** Move the mouse pointer between column names at the top of the datasheet and, when you see the double-headed arrow, click and start dragging. To make a column just large enough to fit its widest entry, move the mouse pointer between column names and double-click when you see the double-headed arrow.

+ **Changing fonts:** Fonts are Arial 10-point, but you can choose options on the Font and Font Size menus to perhaps make entering data a little less mind-numbing.

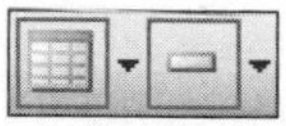

+ **Changing the look of gridlines:** Open the drop-down menus on the Gridlines and Special Effects buttons and choose options to change the number and thickness of gridlines.

To experiment all at one time with the many options for changing a datasheet's appearance, choose Format➪Datasheet and play with options in the Datasheet Formatting dialog box, shown in Figure 3-2. If you want a customized look for all the datasheets you work on, choose Tools➪Options, select the Datasheet tab in the Options dialog box, and go to town.

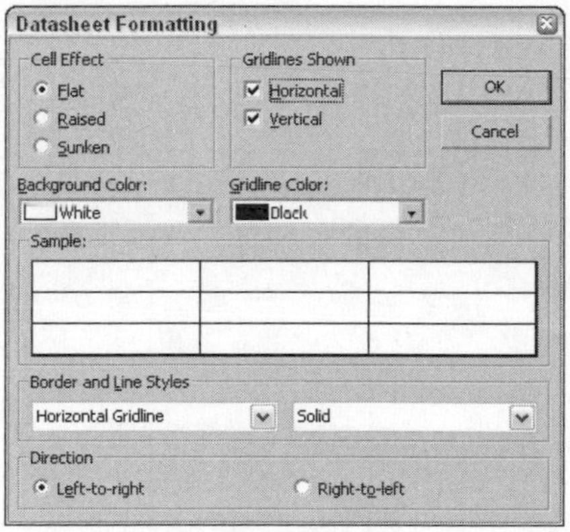

Figure 3-2:
The
Datasheet
Formatting
dialog box.

Datasheet Formatting		
Cell Effect	**Gridlines Shown**	
○ Flat	☑ Horizontal	OK
○ Raised	☑ Vertical	Cancel
○ Sunken		
Background Color:	**Gridline Color:**	
White	Black	
Sample:		
Border and Line Styles		
Horizontal Gridline	Solid	
Direction		
⊙ Left-to-right	○ Right-to-left	

Entering the Data in a Form

Forms like the one shown in Figure 3-3 are very convenient for entering data. The labels tell you exactly what to enter. Personally, I prefer entering data in a form to entering data on a datasheet. On a form, you take it one step — make that one record — at a time. Not having to look at a dozen records makes the task of entering data a little easier. These pages explain how to create a form for entering information in a database table. You also get tried-and-true advice for moving around with the Record toolbar.

Creating a form

Fortunately, the Form wizard makes it very simple to create a form for entering information in a database table. All you have to do is give a command, choose the table, and make a couple of design decisions. To create a form, start in the Database window and select Forms in the Objects pane. Then double-click the Create Form by Using Wizard icon. You see the first of several Form Wizard dialog boxes. Answer these questions and keep clicking the Next button until the time comes to click Finish:

+ **Tables/Queries:** From the drop-down menu, choose the name of the database table you need to enter data in.

+ **Selected Fields:** Click the >> button to enter all the field names in the Select Fields box.

+ **Layout:** Select the Columnar option button. The other layouts aren't much good for entering data in a table. If you choose Tabular or Datasheet, you may as well enter data straight into the datasheet rather than rely on a form.

+ **Style:** Choose a look for the form.

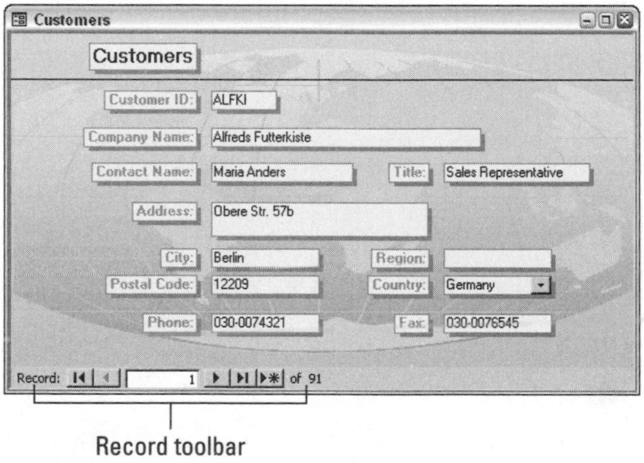

Figure 3-3:
A form.

Record toolbar

Click the Save button to save and name your form (I suggest naming it after the database table you created it for). When you want to enter data by way of the form you created, select the Forms object in the Database window and, in the list of forms, double-click the form.

If you're in a hurry to create a form, choose Insert⇨Form and, in the New Form dialog box, select AutoForm:Columnar. Then choose a table in the Choose the Table or Query drop-down menu and click OK.

Entering the data

To enter data in a form, click the New Record button on the Record toolbar and start typing. Press the Tab key, press the Enter key, or click to move from field to field. You can move backwards through the fields by pressing Shift+Tab. If you enter half a record and want to start all over, click the Esc key to empty all the fields.

The Record toolbar (refer to Figure 3-3) at the bottom of the form window tells you how many records are in the database table and which record you're looking at. Click buttons on the Record toolbar to do the following:

Book VI
Chapter 3

✦ Go to the first record in the database table. You can also press Ctrl+Home.

✦ Go to the previous record.

✦ Go to the next record.

✦ Go to the last record. You can also press Ctrl+End.

Finding a Missing Record

Sometimes data goes astray. You scroll through a datasheet but simply can't find the item or record you need so bad. For times like those, Access offers the Find command. Use the command to scour a database for errant information.

Open the database table with the data that needs finding. If you know in which field the data is located, click in the field. You can save a little time that way. Then choose Edit⇨Find, click the Find button, or press Ctrl+F. You see the Find and Replace dialog box, shown in Figure 3-4. Fill in the dialog box as follows:

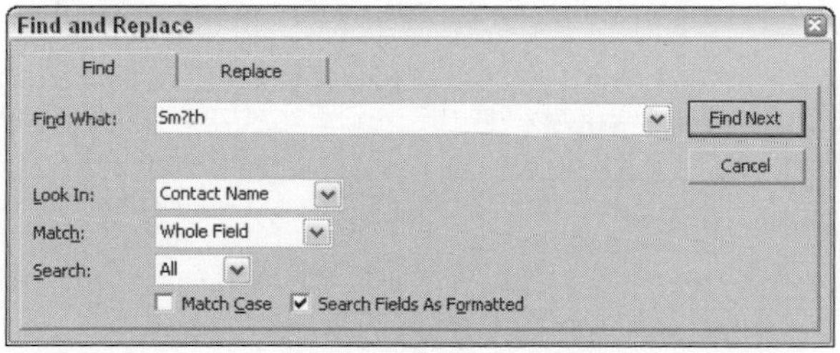

Figure 3-4:
Finding
data.

Find and Replace

| Find | Replace |

Find What: Sm?th   Find Next

Cancel

Look In: Contact Name
Match: Whole Field
Search: All
☐ Match Case ☑ Search Fields As Formatted

✦ **Find What:** Enter the item you're looking for. If you're looking for a null value, enter **null** in this text box. Enter "" (two double-quotation marks) to find zero-length strings. Table 3-2 describes the wildcard characters you can use in searches.

✦ **Look In:** If you clicked in a field before choosing Edit➪Find, the field's name appears in this box. To search the entire database table, select its name from the drop-down list.

✦ **Match:** Choose the option that describes what you know about the item. Choosing the Any Part of Field option can make for a long search. For example, a search for the letters *chin* finds, among others, China, Ching, and itching — any word with the consecutive letters *chin*.

✦ **Search:** Choose an option that describes where to start searching.

✦ **Match Case:** If you know the combination of upper- and lowercase letters you're after and you entered the combination in the Find What text box, select this check box.

✦ **Search Fields As Formatted:** If you're searching for a field that has been formatted a certain way, select this check box and make sure that the text or numbers you entered in the Find What text box are formatted correctly. For example, if you're searching for a record with the date July 31, 1958, and you chose the *mm/dd/yyyy* format, enter the date as 07/31/1958.

Click the Find Next button to conduct the search. The item might be found in more than one location. Keep clicking Find Next until you find the item or you die of thirst on the hot sands of the digital desert.

Table 3-2	Wildcard Characters for Searches	
Character	*Description*	*Example*
?	A single character	**b?t** finds bat, bet, bit, and but.
#	A single numeric digit	**9411#** finds 94111, 94112, 94113, and so on.
*	Any group of consecutive characters	**t*o** finds to, two, and tattoo.
[*xyz*]	Any character in the brackets	**t[aio]pper** finds tapper, tipper, and topper, but not tupper.
[!*xy*]	Any character *not* in the brackets	**p[!io]t** finds pat and pet, but not pit and pot.
x–z	Any character in a range of characters	**[1–4]000** finds 1000, 2000, 3000, and 4000, but not 5000. The range must be in ascending order.

Finding and Replacing Data

Finding and replacing data is remarkably similar to finding data. The difference is, you enter data in the Replace With text box as well as the familiar Find What and other option boxes. Figure 3-5 shows the Replace tab of the Find and Replace dialog box. Does it look familiar? If it doesn't, read the previous section in this chapter.

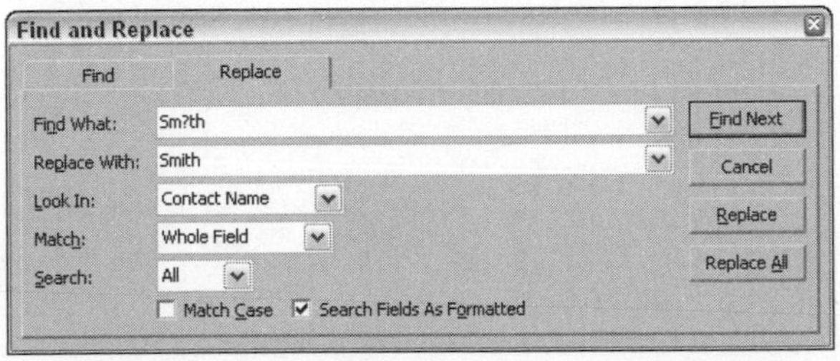

Figure 3-5:
Replacing data.

[Find and Replace dialog box showing the Replace tab with Find What: Sm?th, Replace With: Smith, Look In: Contact Name, Match: Whole Field, Search: All, with Match Case unchecked and Search Fields As Formatted checked. Buttons: Find Next, Cancel, Replace, Replace All]

Choose Edit➪Replace (or press Ctrl+H) to open the Replace tab of the Find and Replace dialog box. After you enter the replacement data in the Replace With text box, make sure that Whole Field is selected in the Match drop-down menu. Conducting a find-and-replace operation with Any Part of Field or Start of Field selected in the Match drop-down menu can have unintended consequences. For example, a search for *Brook* will also find *Brooklyn, Middlebrook,* and other words that include the letters *brook.* Blindly replacing the *brook* text string with *stream* produces, for example, *Streamlyn* and *Middlestream.*

Unless you're as confident as a gambler with four aces, don't click the Replace All button to replace all instances of the text or numbers in the database table or field you're searching in. Instead, click the Replace button to find and replace text or numbers one instance at a time.

You can't replace zero-length strings in null values in a find-and-replace operation. You can, however, find zero-length strings in null values one at a time and replace them on your own.

You can also find and replace data with an update query. See the section about update queries in Chapter 4 of this mini-book.

Chapter 4: Sorting, Querying, and Filtering for Data

In This Chapter

✔ **Sorting, or rearranging, records in a database table**

✔ **Filtering records in a table to see only the records you need**

✔ **Querying to collect and examine information stored in a database**

✔ **Looking at the different kinds of queries**

*N*ow that you've laid the groundwork, you can put your database through its paces and make it do what databases are meant to do — provide information of one kind or another. This chapter explains how to pester a database for names, addresses, dates, statistical averages, and what not. It shows how to sort records and filter a database table to see records of a certain kind. You also find out how to query a database to get it to yield its dirty little secrets and invaluable information.

Sorting Records in a Database Table

Sorting means to rearrange records in a database table (or subdatasheet) so that the records appear in alphabetical, numerical, or date order in one field. By sorting the records in a database, you can locate records faster. What's more, being able to sort data means that you don't have to bother about the order in which you enter records, because you can always sort them later to put them in a particular order.

Records can be sorted in ascending or descending order:

✦ **Ascending order:** Arranges records in alphabetical order from A to Z, numbers from smallest to largest, and dates from earliest in time to latest.

✦ **Descending order:** Arranges text from Z to A, numbers from largest to smallest, and dates chronologically from latest to earliest.

The database tables shown in Figure 4-1 present the same information. In the table on the left, records have been sorted in ascending order in the Last Name field. In the table on the right, records have been sorted in descending order in the Birthdate field.

Addresses : Table

Last Name	First Name	Street	City	State	Zip Code	Birthdate
Cheese	Chucky	88 Harvard St.	Hemet	CA	92347	11/10/1962
Clark						
Creegan						
Danforth						
Dubain						
Hornsby						
Jefferson						
Lake						
Manfred						
Martinez						
Mountbank						
Munoz						
Perford						
Roger						
Smith						

Addresses : Table

Last Name	First Name	Street	City	State	Zip Code	Birthdate
Williams	Reginald	34457 Wilcox Blvd.	Los Angeles	CA	90047	3/24/1949
Danforth	Peter	122 W. Third Street	Duhere	IL	33337	6/3/1950
Creegan	Megan	12234 Monterey Blvd.	Monterey	CA	92347	2/2/1951
Perford	Steve	3876-A Chance St.	Niler	Fl	21347	7/12/1953
Hornsby	Roger	11 Cortland St.	East Rutherford	NJ	24127	8/3/1953
Manfred	Linda	338 Miner Rd.	Danforth	KS	41327	9/10/1953
Lake	Viva	1241 Eight St.	Daly City	CA	94309	7/31/1958
Wong	Mariam	178 E. Lansing	Checkers	NY	02134	8/8/1962
Cheese	Chucky	88 Harvard St.	Hemet	CA	92347	11/10/1962
Mountbank	Rupert	39 E. Colter St.	Idyllwild	CA	92349	4/27/1963
Clark	Wilma	229 E. Rainy St.	Checker	OR	96789	12/12/1963
Roger	McRee	2719 44th St.	San Francisco	CA	94114	7/7/1971
Smith	Reginald	1781 Park St.	Alhambra	CA	90087	11/11/1971
Dubain	Lilliam	2718 Douglas St.	Waukeegan	IL	33337	1/23/1972
Munoz	Winston	33378 No. Hare	Austin	TX	97891	4/27/1973

Record: 8 of 17

Figure 4-1: Sorting a database table.

Follow these steps to sort the records in a database table:

1. **In Datasheet view, click anywhere in the field by which you want to sort the records.**

2. **Click the Sort Ascending button or Sort Descending button.**

   You can also right-click a field name at the top of a column and choose Sort <u>A</u>scending or Sort <u>D</u>escending on the shortcut menu.

As long as the fields are adjacent to one other, you can sort on more than one field. Access sorts the leftmost field, then the one to its right, then the one to that one's right. For example, in a database table whose first three fields are Last Name, First Name, and Middle Initial, records are sorted first by last name, then by first name, then by middle initial. To sort on more than one field, move the fields so that they are next to each other, select the fields, and click a Sort button.

Filtering to Find Information

Filtering means to isolate all the records in a database table that have the same field values or nearly the same field values. Instead of all the records in the table appearing on the datasheet, only records that meet the search criteria appear, as shown in Figure 4-2. The basic idea behind filtering is to choose a field value in the database table and use it as the standard for finding or excluding records. For example, you can find all the people who live in California, all the people under age 30, or all the people who live in California who are under the age of 30. For that matter, you can filter by exclusion and see the records of all the people in a database table who do *not* live in California and who are *not* under the age of 30. Filtering is useful when you need to find records with specific information in a single database table.

Figure 4-2:
Results of
a filtering
operation.

	Last Name	First Name	Street	City	State	Zip Code	Birthdate
▶	Williams	Reginald	34457 Wilcox Blvd.	Los Angeles	CA	90047	3/24/1949
	Creegan	Megan	12234 Monterey Blvd.	Monterey	CA	92347	2/2/1951
	Lake	Viva	1241 Eight St.	Daly City	CA	94309	7/31/1958
	Cheese	Chucky	88 Harvard St.	Hemet	CA	92347	11/10/1962
	Mountbank	Rupert	39 E. Colter St.	Idyllwild	CA	92349	4/27/1963
	Roger	McRee	2719 44th St.	San Francisco	CA	94114	7/7/1971
	Smith	Reginald	1781 Park St.	Alhambra	CA	90087	11/11/1971
	Jefferson	Duane	2131 43rd Ave.	Los Angeles	CA	90047	11/1/1974

Addresses : Table

Record: 1 of 8 (Filtered)

Number of filtered records

Different ways to filter a database table

Here are shorthand descriptions of the five ways to filter a database table. These techniques are described in detail in the coming pages.

✦ **Filter by Selection:** Select all or part of a field in the database table and click the Filter by Selection button. Access isolates all records with the data you selected. This method works best when you can't quite decide what you're looking for. It's the only filtering method that permits you to look for data found at the start of a field or in part of a field.

✦ **Filter by Form:** With the database table displayed, click the Filter by Form button. You see a form with one drop-down menu for each field in your table. From the drop-down menus, make choices to describe the records you're looking for; then click the Apply Filter button. This method is superior to filtering by selection in that you can choose more than one field to filter with, and you can search for different kinds of information in the same field. For example, you can isolate the records of people named Smith who also live in California, or the people who live in California or New York.

✦ **Filter Excluding Selection:** Select all or part of a field and choose Records➪Filter➪Filter by Excluding Selection. You see all the records in the database *except* those with the value or text you selected. This method is great for isolating a handful of records when the majority of records in the database table have the same value or text.

✦ **Filter For Input:** Starting in a datasheet or on a form, right-click the field you want to search, choose Filter For on the drop-down menu, enter a value or term in the text box on the menu, and press Enter. With this technique, you can use comparison operators such as greater than (>) and less than (<) to troll for records. And you can filter a database without having to click a Filter button.

✦ **Advanced Filter/Sort:** Choose Records➪Filter➪Advanced Filter/Sort and, in the Filter window, drag the name of the field you're filtering onto the grid. Then enter a search criterion, choose a Sort option, and click the Apply Filter button. This filtering technique has more in common with queries than filters. Truth be told, the Advanced Filter/Sort command is merely a way to query a single table.

You can tell when you're looking at a subset of filtered records rather than a database table because the word *filtered* and the number of filtered records appears beside the Record toolbar (refer to Figure 4-2). What's more, the letters FLTR appear on the Status bar.

When you have finished filtering a database table and you want to see all the records in the table again, choose Records➪Remove Filter/Sort or click the Remove Filter button. This button looks exactly like the Apply Filter button. It changes names but not its appearance. You can reapply the filter you most recently used by clicking the Apply Filter button.

Some kinds of filtering operations can be saved and run again, but to save them, you must save them as queries. With the results of the filtering operation in the Datasheet window, choose File➪Save As Query; then enter a name in the Save As Query dialog box. Later in this chapter, "Querying: The Basics" explains how to run queries.

Filtering by selection

Filtering by selection is the fastest way to filter a database table. It's also the best way when you're not sure what you're looking for, because you can search for partial words and phrases. Follow these steps to filter by selection:

1. **Display the database table that needs filtering in Datasheet view.**

2. **Tell Access how to filter the records.**

To find all records with the same value or text in a particular field, simply click in a field with the value or text. If you aren't quite sure what to look for, select part of a field. For example, to find all names that start with the letters *St*, select **st** in one of the name fields.

3. **Click the Filter By Selection button or choose Records➪Filter➪Filter By Selection.**

Filtering by form

Filtering by form permits you to search more than one field in a database table, as well as search the same field more than once. For example, you can tell Access to look in the Last Name field for people named Martinez, as well as look in the City field for Martinezes who live in Los Angeles *or* San Francisco. Searching twice in the same field is called an *OR search*. To be included in the filtering results, a record has only to satisfy one *or* the other criterion. Follow these steps to filter by form:

1. **In Datasheet view, click the Filter By Form button or choose Records➪Filter➪Filter By Form.**

   Only field names appear on the datasheet, as shown in Figure 4-3.

Choose or enter a criterion.

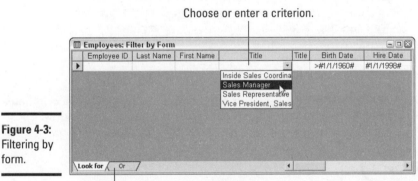

Figure 4-3:
Filtering by form.

Click to search more then once in the same field.

2. **Click in a field, open its drop-down menu, and choose the value or text you want to search for.**

   To search in more than one field, open another drop-down menu and choose a value or text entry from it. In number and currency fields, you can enter comparison operators to search for values. Table 4-1 explains the comparison operators.

Table 4-1	Comparison Operators for Filtering and Querying	
Operator	*Name*	*Example*
<	Less than	**<10**; any number smaller than 10
<=	Less than or equal to	**<=10**; 10 as well as any number smaller than 10
>	Greater than	**>10**; any number larger than 10
>=	Greater than or equal to	**>=10**; 10 as well as any number larger than 10
=	Equal to	**=10**; 10, not any other number
<>	Not equal to	**<>10**; all numbers except 10 (instead of <>, you can enter the word *not*)
Between...And...	Between	**Between 10 And 15**; A number between 10 and 15

3. **To search twice in the same field with different criteria, click the OR tab and then choose a value or text from the drop-down menu in a field you're already searching in.**

   As soon as you click the OR tab, the search choices you made previously disappear from the screen. Don't worry — Access remembers them. You can click the OR tab again if you want to enter yet more criteria for searching in a field you're already searching in.

4. **Click the Apply Filter button.**

   The results of the filtering operation appear in the datasheet.

If you click the Filter by Form button to try to filter by form a second time, the criteria you entered previously appear in the datasheet window. Click the Clear Grid button to empty the datasheet and start all over.

Filtering by exclusion

Filter by exclusion to isolate the records in a database table that don't belong to the majority. For example, in an Address database table in which most of the records show people living in the same ZIP Code, you can filter the ZIP Code field to exclude those records and have left the handful of records belonging to people who *don't* live in the majority ZIP Code.

Filtering by exclusion is very much like filtering by selection, except that you select all or part of a field whose data you want to temporarily eliminate from the table, not target in the table. In the datasheet, select the data to exclude and choose Records➪Filter➪Filter Excluding Selection.

Filtering for Input

As shown in Figure 4-4, filtering by input is a means of filtering a database table starting in Datasheet view or on a form. Right-click the field with data you want to isolate and, on the shortcut menu, enter a value or text in the Filter For text box. You can use comparison operators with numeric and currency fields (see Table 4-1, earlier in this chapter). To filter the database table, press the Enter key after you enter the value or text. Immediately right-click and enter another value or text string in the Filter For text box if you want to filter the results of the filtering operation.

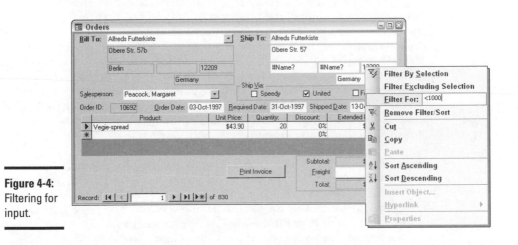

Figure 4-4:
Filtering for input.

The difference between a filter and a query

The biggest difference between filtering and querying is that you can save a query and call upon it more than once. Queries are kept at the ready in the Database window. A filter, on the other hand, is as good as the first time you use it, although you can save and run it as a query. Filters apply to a single database table, whereas you can query to assemble information from more than one table. In the results of a query, you can include as many fields as you want, but the results of a filtering operation show all the fields in the database table, whether you want them or not.

When it comes to examining data, a query is more sophisticated than a filter. Although you can use standard comparison operators to find records by filtering, querying gives you the opportunity to use complex expressions as well as comparison operators. You can filter, for example, to find people whose income is greater than or less than a certain amount. However, because you can write expressions in queries, you can query to find people whose income falls within a certain range.

Running an Advanced Filter/Sort

This command — choose Records⇨Filter⇨Advanced Filter Sort to activate — works exactly like a query, except that it works on only one database table. If you're tempted to use this command, resist the temptation. Run a query instead.

Querying: The Basics

Querying means to ask a question of a database and get an answer in the form of records that meet the query criteria. Query when you want to ask a detailed question of a database. "Who lives in Los Angeles and donated more than $500 last year?" is an example of a query. So is, "Which orders were purchased by people who live in California and therefore have to pay sales tax, and how much sales tax was charged with these orders?" A query can search for information in more than one database table. For that matter, you can query other queries for information. A query can be as sophisticated or as simple as you need it to be. In the results of the query you can show all the fields in a database table or only a few necessary fields.

Access offers several different ways to query a database (the techniques are described later in this chapter in "Six Kinds of Queries"). Still, no matter which kind of query you're dealing with, the basics of setting up and running a query are the same. You start in the Database window by selecting Queries on the Objects pane to make the window display queries. From there, you can open a query you already created by double-clicking its name, or create a new query. The following pages introduce you to queries, how to create them, and how to construct them.

Creating a new query

To create a new query, start from the Queries tab in the Database window and click the New button. You see the New Query dialog box. Do one of the following:

✦ **Create the query in Design view:** Select Design View and click OK. You see the Query Design window, shown in Figure 4-5, as well as the Show Table dialog box for telling Access which database tables to query. Construct your query in the Design window (the following pages explain how to do it).

✦ **Create the query with a wizard:** Choose a Query Wizard option (there are four possible Query Wizards) and answer the questions that the Query Wizard dialog boxes ask. You're asked which table or tables to query, which fields to include in the query, and which fields to include in the query results (the following pages explain these issues).

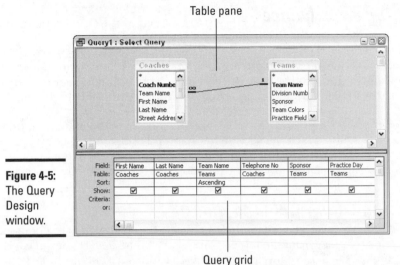

Table pane

Query grid

Figure 4-5:
The Query
Design
window.

Finding your way around the Query Design window

The Query Design window (refer to Figure 4-5) is where you construct a query or retool a query you already constructed. You see this window straightaway when you click the Design button to construct a new query. Select a query in the Database window and click the Design button to open the Query Design window and fiddle with the query design to make it better.

The Query Design window is divided into halves:

✦ **Table pane:** Lists the database tables you are querying, as well as the fields in each table. You can drag the tables to new locations or drag a table border to change its size and view more fields.

✦ **Design grid:** Lists which fields to query from the tables, how to sort the query results, which fields to show in the query results, and criteria for locating records in fields.

To run a query starting in the Query Design window, click the Run button or choose Query⇔Run.

Choosing which database tables to query

To choose which database tables (and queries as well) to get information from, click the Show Table button or choose Query⇔Show Table. You see the Show Table dialog box. The Tables tab lists all the database tables you created for your database. Ctrl+click to select the tables you want to query and then click the Add button. To query a query, go to the Queries tab and select it.

The tables and queries you chose appear in the Table pane of the Query Design window (refer to Figure 4-5). To remove a table from a query, right-click it in the Table pane and choose Remove Table on the shortcut menu.

In order to query more than one table, you must have established relationships between tables (see the section in Chapter 2 of this mini-book about establishing relationships between database tables). So-called join lines in the Query Design window show how the tables are related to one another.

Choosing which fields to query

Now that you've selected which tables to query, the next step is to choose which fields to query from the tables you selected. The field names in each table appear in the Table pane. The object is to list fields from the Table pane in the first row of the Design grid, as shown in Figure 4-6. As the figure shows, the fields whose names you enter in the Design grid are the fields that produce query results.

Field:	First Name	Last Name	Team Name	Telephone No	Sponsor	Practice Day
Table:	Coaches	Coaches	Teams	Coaches	Teams	Teams
Sort:			Ascending			
Show:	☑	☑	☑	☑	☑	☑
Criteria:						
or:						

Query1 : Select Query

	First Name	Last Name	Team Name	Telephone No	Sponsor	Practice Day
▶	Ray	Galarce	Giants	(415) 555-8971	Eureka Market	Wed
	David	Majers	Panthers	(415) 555-1244	St. Clare Liquors	Wed
	Ralph	Lund	Pipefitters	(415) 555-8191	Reagan Realty	Mon, Wed
	Susan	Lopez	Rainmakers	(415) 555-3612	Harley Co.	Fri.
	Dale	Kravitz	Rainrats	(650) 555-3281	Cotton Basics	Fri
	Carlos	Klein	Rockbreakers	(415) 555-3879	St. Eustace Laundry	Mon
	Marie	St. Claire	Wallflowers	(415) 555-3891	Bell Market	Tues
*						

Record: ◀◀ ◀ 1 ▶ ▶▶ ▶✳ of 7

Figure 4-6: How query fields translate into query results.

Access offers these techniques for listing field names in the first row of the Design grid:

✦ **Dragging a field name:** Drag a field name into a column on the Design grid. The field name appears on the grid, as does the name of the table you dragged it from.

✦ **Double-clicking a field name:** Double-click a field name to place it in the next available column in the Design grid.

✦ **Choosing a table and field name:** Click in the Table row and choose the name of a table from the drop-down list. Then, in the Field box directly above, choose a field name from the drop-down list.

✦ **Selecting all the fields in a table:** In the unlikely event that you want all the fields from a table to appear in the query results, either double-click the asterisk (*) at the top of the list of field names or drag the asterisk into the Design grid. Access places the name of the table followed by an asterisk in the Field text box. The asterisk signifies that all the fields from the table are included in the query.

To remove a field name from the Design grid, select it and press the Delete key or click the field name and choose Edit➪Delete Columns. To remove all field names from the Design grid, choose Edit➪Clear Grid.

Sorting the query results

At the start of this chapter, "Sorting Records in a Database Table" explains what sorting is. Open the Sort drop-down list in a field and choose Ascending or Descending to sort the results of a query on a particular field. To sort the results on more than one field, make sure that the first field to be sorted appears to the left of the other fields.

You can move fields in the query grid by clicking above the field name and dragging the field to the left or right.

Choosing which fields appear in query results

Although you've included a field in the Query grid, it isn't always necessary to display information from the field in the query results. Consider the Query grid shown in Figure 4-7. The object of this query is to find out which children in the Players database table are eligible to play this year. To be eligible, a player must have been born in the year 1989. The Criteria line of the Birthday field, therefore, shows the expression Between #1/1/1989# And #12/31/1989#. However, when the query results are generated, it isn't really necessary to list the players' birthdays, because the object of the query is to find out whether they are eligible to play, not when they were born.

When a field's Show check box is selected, results from the field appear in Query results. If a field is necessary for producing records in a query but not necessary in the query results, uncheck its Show check box. Access moves unchecked fields to the right side of the Query grid (and you usually have to scroll to see them).

Moving field columns on the Query grid

The order in which field names appear in the Query grid is also the order in which they appear in the query results (refer to Figure 4-6). Follow these steps to move field columns to the right order in the Query grid:

1. **Click a column's selector button to select a column.**

This button is the narrow gray box directly above the field name. The pointer turns into a downward-pointing arrow when you move it over the selector button.

2. **Now that the column is selected, click the selector button again and drag the column to the left or right.**

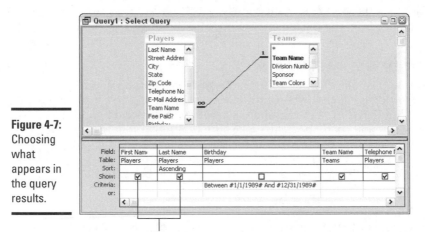

Figure 4-7: Choosing what appears in the query results.

Check or uncheck to show data in query results.

Entering criteria for a query

What separates a run-of-the-mill query from a supercharged query is a *criterion,* an expression or value you enter on the Criteria line under a field. Enter criteria on the Criteria line of the Query grid. By entering criteria, you can pinpoint records in the database with great accuracy. In Figure 4-8, the Query grid instructs Access to search for people born before January 1, 1950, whose income is over $85,000 per year. Notice the OR values in this query. By entering values in the OR text boxes, you can tell Access to search in the same field for more than one value. The query in Figure 4-8 instructs Access to look in the State field for people who live in three states: Connecticut, New York, and New Jersey.

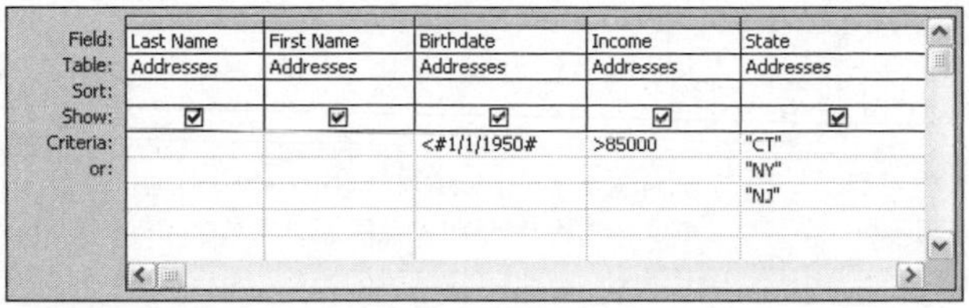

Field:	Last Name	First Name	Birthdate	Income	State
Table:	Addresses	Addresses	Addresses	Addresses	Addresses
Sort:					
Show:	☑	☑	☑	☑	☑
Criteria:			<#1/1/1950#	>85000	"CT"
or:					"NY"
					"NJ"

Figure 4-8:
Including criteria in a query.

As Figure 4-8 shows, Access places double quotation marks ("") around text criteria and number signs (#) around date criteria. When you enter text or date criteria, don't enter the double quotation marks or number signs yourself. Access enters them for you.

When you need help writing an expression for a query, try clicking the Build button and constructing your query in the Expression Builder dialog box.

Entering numeric criteria

Enter numeric criteria in Number and Currency fields when you want to isolate records with specific values. Earlier in this chapter, Table 4-1 describes comparison operators you can use for querying and filtering. These operators are invaluable when it comes to mining a database for information. Use the greater than (>) and less than (<) operators to find values higher or lower than a target value. Use the Between operator to find values between two numbers. For example, *Between 62 And 55* in a currency field isolates records with all items that sell for between $62.00 and $55.00.

Do not include commas in numbers when you enter them. For example, enter **3200**, not **3,200**. Enter a comma and you get a "The expression you entered contains invalid syntax. . ." error message.

Entering text criteria

To enter a text criterion, type it in the Criteria text box. For example, to find students who attended Wake Forest, enter **Wake Forest** in the Criteria text box of the University field. Access places double quotation marks ("") around the text you entered as soon as you move the cursor out of the Criteria text box.

Wildcards and the Not operator can come in very handy when entering text criteria:

✦ **Wildcards:** Wildcards make it possible to query for data whose spelling you aren't quite sure of (in the previous chapter, Table 3-2 explains what the wildcard characters are and how to use them). For example, entering

Sm?th in the Criteria box of the Last Name field finds all Smiths and Smyths. Entering **E*** in the Company field finds all company names that begin with the letter *E*.

✦ **Not operator:** Use the Not operator to exclude records from query results. For example, to exclude records with Belgium in the Shipped To field, enter **Not Belgium** in the Criteria text box. This is a great way to strip unneeded records from a query.

Entering date criteria

All the operators that work for numeric data (see Table 4-1 earlier in this chapter) also work for data entered in a Date field. For example, enter **>7/31/58** in a Birth Date field to find all people born after (greater than) July 31, 1958. Enter **Between 1/1/20 And 12/31/29** to retrieve data about people born in the Roaring Twenties.

Access places number signs (#) around date criteria after you enter it. You can enter dates in these formats:

✦ 11/2/03

✦ 2-Nov-03

✦ November 2, 2003

For the purpose of entering two-digit years in dates, the digits 30 through 99 belong to the 20th Century (1930–1999), but the digits 00 through 29 belong to the 21st Century (2000–2029). For example, *>4/1/24* refers to April 1, 2024, not April 1, 1924. To enter a date in 1929 or earlier, enter four digits instead of two to describe the year: >4/1/1929. To enter a date in 2030 or later, enter four digits instead of two: >4/1/2030.

The Date() function can come in very handy when you want to retrieve data relative to today's date, whatever it happens to be. For example, to retrieve purchase orders made between January 1, 2004 and today's date, enter this expression: **Between 1/1/04 And Date()**.

At last — running and saving a query

After you have laboriously constructed your query, take it for a test drive. To run a query:

✦ **Starting from the Query Design window:** Click the Run button or choose Query➪Run.

+ **Starting from the Database window:** Double-click the query's name, or select its name and click the <u>O</u>pen button.

If the query doesn't work the way you want it to, click the Design button to return to the Query Design window, and start tinkering.

To save a query and inscribe its name forever in the Database window, click the Save button and enter a descriptive name in the Save As dialog box. The name you enter will appear on the Queries tab of the Database window.

Six Kinds of Queries

For your pleasure and entertainment, these pages describe six useful types of queries. Access offers a handful of other queries, but let's not go there. Those queries are pretty complicated. If you become adept at querying, however, you're invited to look into the Help system for advice about running the query types that aren't explained here.

Select query

A *select query* is the standard kind of query, the one explained in the previous dozen pages of this book. A select query gathers information from one or more database tables and displays the information in a datasheet. A select query is the Ur query, the primal query, the starting point for all other queries.

Top-value query

A *top-value query* is an easy way to find out, in a numeric or currency field, the highest or lowest values. On the Query grid, enter the name of the numeric or currency field you want to learn more about; then choose Ascending or Descending on the Sort menu to rank values from highest to lowest or lowest to highest. Finally, in the Top Values box on the Query Design toolbar, enter a value or choose a value from the drop-down menu:

+ **Highest or lowest by percentage:** Enter or choose a percentage to find, for example, the highest or lowest 25 percent of the values. To enter a percentage, type a percent sign (%) after your entry and press the Enter key.

+ **Highest or lowest by ranking number:** Enter or choose a number to find, for example, the top-ten or lowest-ten values. Press the Enter key after you enter a number.

Summary query

Similar to a top-value query, a summary query is a way of getting cumulative information about all the data in a field. In a field that stores data about sales in Kentucky, for example, you can find the average amount of each sale, the total amount of all the sales, the total number of all the sales, and other data.

Σ

To run a summary query, click the Totals button on the Query Design toolbar or choose View⇨Totals. A new row called Group By appears on the Query grid. Open the Total drop-down menu in the field whose contents you want to summarize and choose a function. Table 4-2 describes the functions.

Table 4-2	Summary Query Functions
Function	*Returns*
Sum	The total of all values in the field
Avg	The average of all values
Min	The lowest value
Max	The highest value
Count	The number of values
StDev	The standard deviation of the values
Var	The variance of the values
First	The first value
Last	The last value

Calculation query

A *calculation query* is one in which calculations are performed as part of the query. For example, you can calculate the sales tax on items sold, or total the numbers in two fields in the same record. The beauty of a calculation query is that the data is recomputed each time you run the query. If the data used to make a calculation changes, so does the result of the calculation. If you were to include the calculation in a database table, you would have to recalculate the data yourself each time one of the values changed. With a calculation query, Access does the math for you.

To construct a calculation query, create a new field in the Query grid for storing the results of the calculation; then enter a name for the field and a formula for the calculation itself. Follow these steps to create a calculation query:

1. **Create a query as you normally would, and be sure to include the fields you want to use for calculation purposes in the Query grid.**

2. **In the Field box of a blank field, enter a name for the calculation field and follow it with a colon.**

In Figure 4-9, I entered **Sales Tax:**. The purpose of the new Sales Tax field is to calculate the 6 percent sales tax on the items in the Sales Totals field.

Field in calculations

New field's name

Field:	Product	Sales Totals	Sales Tax: [Sales Totals]*0.3
Table:	Products	Products	
Total:	Group By	Group By	Group By
Sort:		Ascending	
Show:	☑	☑	☑
Criteria:			
or:			

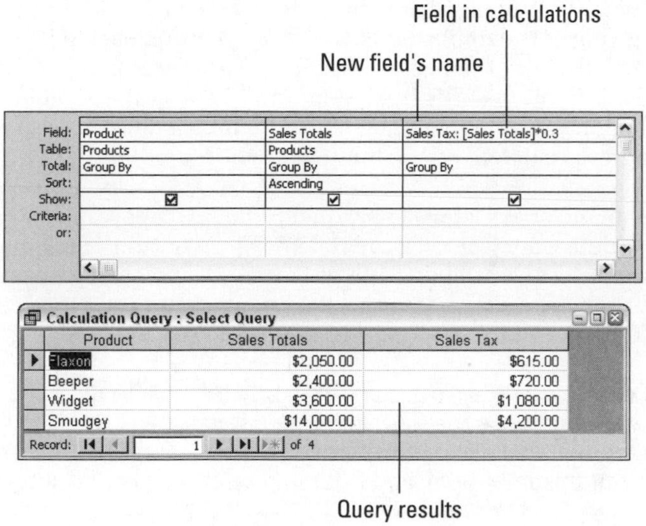

Figure 4-9:
A
calculation
query.

Calculation Query : Select Query

Product	Sales Totals	Sales Tax
Flaxon	$2,050.00	$615.00
Beeper	$2,400.00	$720.00
Widget	$3,600.00	$1,080.00
Smudgey	$14,000.00	$4,200.00

Record: ◄ ◄ 1 ► ►► ►* of 4

Query results

3. **After the colon, in square brackets ([]), enter the name of a field whose data you will use for the calculation.**

In Figure 4-9, data from the Sales Totals field is used in the calculation, so its name appears in square brackets: [Sales Totals]. Be sure to spell field names correctly so that Access can recognize them.

4. **Complete the calculation.**

How you do this depends on what kind of calculation you're making. In Figure 4-9, I entered ***.03** to calculate the sales tax. The equation multiplies the values in the Sales Totals field by 3 percent. You can add the data from two different fields by putting their names in brackets and joining them with a plus sign, like so: [Sales Totals]+[Sales Tax].

Sometimes the results of the query are not formatted correctly on the datasheet. To assign a new format to a field you created for the purposes of making a calculation query, right-click the field on the Query grid and choose Properties. You see the Field Properties dialog box. On the General tab, open the Format drop-down menu and choose the correct format for your new, hand-crafted field.

Delete query

Be careful about running delete queries. A *delete query* deletes records and doesn't give you the opportunity to get the records back if you change your mind about deleting them. If used skillfully, however, a delete query is a great way to purge records from more than one database table at the same time. Back up your database file before running a delete query. Edith Piaf didn't regret her delete query, but you might regret yours.

To run a delete query, start a new query and, in Query Design view, choose Query⇨Delete Query or click the Delete Query button (click the arrow beside the Select Query button to get to the Delete Query button). Then make as though you're running a select query, but target the records you want to delete. Finally, click the Run button to run the query.

You can delete records from more than one table as long as the tables are related and you chose the Cascade Delete Related Records option in the Edit Relationships dialog box when you linked the tables (see the section in Chapter 2 of this mini-book about forging relationships between tables).

Update query

An *update query* is a way to reach into a database and update records in several different tables all at one time. Update queries can be invaluable, but, as with Delete queries, they can have untoward consequences. Back up your database before you run an Update query; then follow these steps to run it:

1. **Starting in Design view, choose Query⇨Update Query or click the Update Query button.**

   A new line, Update To, appears on the Query grid.

2. **Set up the query as you normally would; then click the View button to see which records the query collects.**

   The records appear in Datasheet view. Take this step to make sure that you're updating the records correctly.

3. **Click the View button again to return to Design view.**

4. **In the field with the data that needs updating, enter text or a value in the Update To line.**

   What you enter in the Update To line replaces what's in the field of the records you collected.

5. **Click the Run button.**

To update records in more than one table, you must have chosen the Cascade Update Related Fields option in the Edit Relationships dialog box when you linked the tables (see the section in Chapter 2 about forging relationships between tables).

**Book VI
Chapter 4**

Sorting, Querying, and Filtering for Data

Chapter 5: Presenting Data in a Report

In This Chapter

- ✔ Creating a new report
- ✔ Opening a report
- ✔ Changing the look of a report

The prettiest way to present data in a database table or query is to present it in a report. Even people who are allergic to databases can put up with database material in a report. Reports are easy to read and understand. They succinctly present the data so that you and others can interpret it. This brief chapter explains how to create reports, open them, and edit them.

Creating a Report

Access comes with all kinds of complicated tools for fashioning your own report — for laying out the pages in different ways and making data fields show up in different parts of the page. If ever a task called for relying on a wizard, creating a report is it. You can save yourself a lot of trouble, and fashion sophisticated-looking reports as well, by dispensing with the fancy report-making tools and letting the wizard do the job.

What's more, the easiest and best way to make a report is to base your report on a query. As part of fashioning a report with a wizard, you can tell Access which database tables and which fields to get the data from — in other words, you can query your database from inside the Report Wizard. However, doing that requires turning somersaults and cartwheels. It's far easier to run a query to produce the results you want in your report, save your query, and then fashion a report from the query results. The previous chapter explains how to run a query.

To create a report with the Report Wizard, start in the Database window by clicking the Reports tab. Then double-click the Create Report by Using Wizard icon. You see the first of several Report Wizard dialog boxes. Negotiate the dialog boxes as follows, clicking the Next button as you go along:

✦ **Tables/Queries:** Open this drop-down menu and choose the query where the information in the report will come from. A list of fields in the query appears in the Available Fields box.

✦ **Available Fields:** Select the fields whose data you want in the report by selecting the fields one at a time and clicking the > button. Doing so moves field names to the Selected Fields box.

✦ **How Do You Want to View Your Data?:** Choose a field to define the grouping level. A grouping level is like a report subheading. For example, if you make Last Name the grouping level, information in the report is presented under people's last names.

✦ **Do You Want to Add Any Grouping Levels?:** To include sub-subheadings in your report, select a field name and click the > to make it a sub-subheading.

✦ **What Sort Order Do You Want?:** Your fields are already sorted, because you're fashioning your report from a query. Aren't you smart? Just click Next.

✦ **How Would You Like to Lay Out Your Report?:** Experiment with the options, and watch the Preview box, to choose a layout for your report.

✦ **What Style Would You Like?:** As shown in Figure 5-1, this dialog box asks you to choose a design for your report. Click all six options and choose the one that makes you happiest. (Later in this chapter, "Tweaking a Report" explains how to change designs.)

✦ **What Title Do You Want for Your Report?:** Enter a descriptive title. The name you choose will appear on the Form tab of the Database window. You double-click the name when you want to see the report.

✦ **Preview the Report:** Select this option button and click Finish. The report appears in the Preview window. How do you like it?

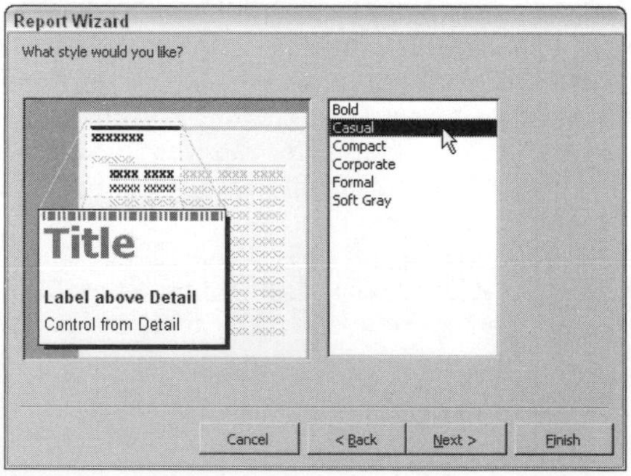

Figure 5-1:
Choosing a design for the report.

Opening and Viewing Reports

If you've spent any time whatsoever in Access, you know the drill for opening a so-called object. Follow these steps to open a report:

1. **On the Objects tab in the Database window, click Reports.**

You see the names of reports you created.

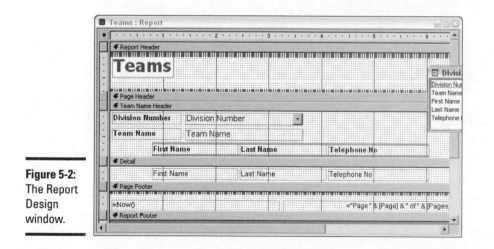

2. **Either double-click a report name or select a name and click the Preview button.**

The report appears in the Preview window. Experiment with the Zoom settings to examine your report. Click the Close button when the examination is over.

Tweaking a Report

As mentioned at the start of this chapter, Access offers a bunch of complex tools for changing the layout and appearance of a report. If you're courageous and have lots of time on your hands, you're invited to take these tools in hand and go to it. On the Reports tab of the Database window, select a report and click the Design button. You see your report in the Report Design window, shown in Figure 5-2. Have you ever seen anything scarier?

Figure 5-2:
The Report
Design
window.

I tell you how to create a report with the Report Wizard in order to avoid your having to visit this imposing window. However, you can change a report's appearance in the Report Design window without going to very much trouble if you follow these instructions:

✦ **Choosing a new design:** If the design you chose in the Report Wizard isn't cutting it, click the AutoFormat button or choose Format➪AutoFormat. You see the AutoFormat dialog box and its design choices. Select a new design and click OK.

✦ **Removing the footer:** Access places today's date and page numbers in the footer of reports. To remove these items, choose View➪Page Header/Footer and click Yes in the confirmation dialog box.

✦ **Including page numbers:** To include page numbers on the report, choose Insert➪Page Numbers. You see the Page Numbers dialog box, shown in Figure 5-3. Choose Page N to display a page number only, or Page N or M to display a page number as well as the total number of pages in the report (as in "page 2 of 4"). Choose Alignment and Position options to describe where on the page to put the page number. To remove a page number, scour the Report Design window to find an ="Page" code, and delete it.

✦ **Changing the margins:** Choose File➪Page Setup and, on the Margins tab of the Page Setup dialog box, enter new margin settings. (You can click the Setup button in the Preview window to open the Page Setup dialog box.) Figure 5-4 shows the Page Setup dialog box.

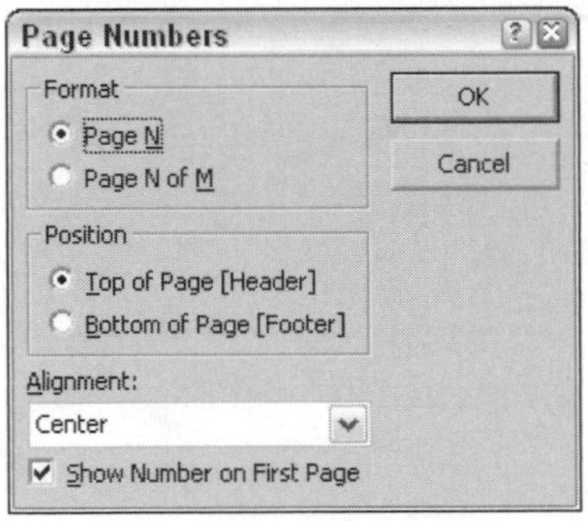

Figure 5-3:
Putting on
the page
numbers.

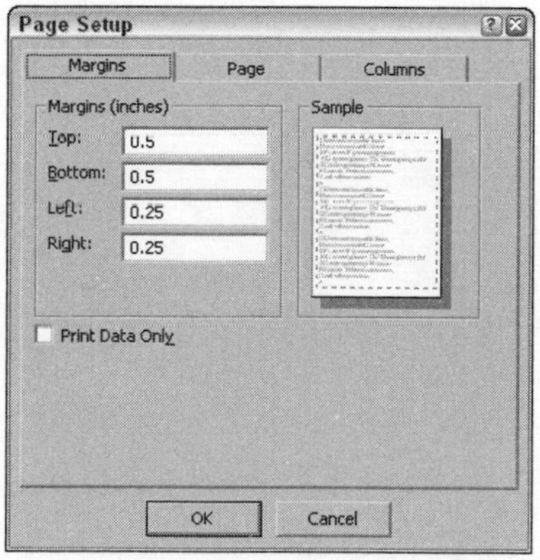

Figure 5-4:
Setting the margins.

An easier way to tweak a report — in Word

If you aren't comfortable in the Report Design window (who is?), try transferring your report to Microsoft Word and editing it there. Choose Tools➪Office Links➪Publish It with Microsoft Word. In a moment, your Access report appears in Word in the form of a table. You can find the new Word file in the same folder as the Access database you're working in. The file is an RTF (rich text format file). To save it as a Word file, choose File➪Save As and, in the Save As dialog box, name your file and choose Word Document on the Save As Type drop-down menu. Book I, Chapter 5 describes how to edit tables in Word.

Book VII

Publisher

The 5th Wave   By Rich Tennant

"Sometimes I feel behind the times. I asked my 11-year old to build a web site for my business, and he said he would, only after he finishes the one he's building for his ant farm."

Contents at a Glance

Chapter 1: Introducing Publisher

In This Chapter

- Understanding frames
- Creating a new publication
- Entering your personal information
- Changing view of the Publisher window
- Putting grid guides on pages
- Drawing a ruler guide

Welcome to Publisher. Not so long ago, creating professional publications like the kind you can create with Publisher required sophisticated printing equipment and a background in graphic design. However, even a novice can now create professional-looking publications with Publisher. As long as you rely on a publication design — a template that comes with Publisher — most of the layout work is done for you. All you have to do is enter the text and the other particulars.

"A Print Shop in a Can"

Publisher has been called "a print shop in a can" because the program is great for creating prefabricated brochures — business cards, calendars, newsletters, resumes, posters, and the like. To make these publications without going to a great deal of trouble, however, you have to stick to the publication designs. Similar to a template, a *publication design* is a ready-made brochure, calendar, and so on. Chances are you can find a suitable publication design for whatever kind of publication you want to create. Figure 1-1 shows some examples of the publication designs for creating flyers. The designs include placeholders for graphics and text. To create a publication, you choose a publication design, enter graphics and text in the publication design where the placeholders are, and tweak the publication to your liking.

Choose a kind of publication.   Click your choice.

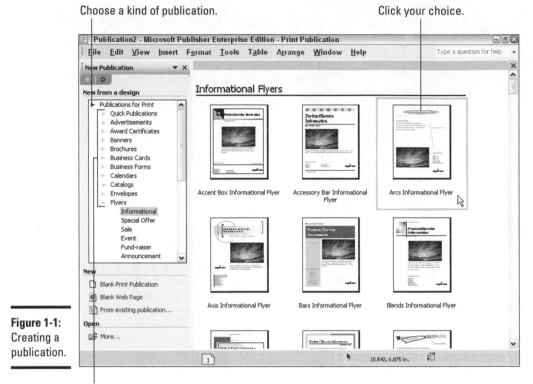

Figure 1-1:
Creating a
publication.

Choose publication type.

Striking out on your own and designing publications like those in Figure 1-1 can be done, but you need a thorough knowledge of Publisher and a full head of hair. You need the hair because much of it will have been pulled out in frustration by the time you finish your design. I venture to say that the people who invented Publisher expect everyone to work from ready-made publication designs. Designing publications from scratch is simply too difficult. Don't be discouraged, however, because you can almost always find a publication design for whatever you want to communicate.

Introducing Frames

The publications that you make with Publisher are composed of frames. A *frame* is a placeholder for text, a graphic, or a table. Complex publications have dozens of frames; simple publications have only a few. Frames keep text and graphics from overlapping. They make sure that everything stays on the page where it should be. As you create a publication, you enter your own text or graphics in frames.

The publication in Figure 1-2 is made up of several frames that have been latched together to form a poster. On the right side of the figure, you can see the frame boundaries; the left side of the figure shows what the poster looks like after it is printed. Frames make laying out publications easier. When you want to move text, a picture, a table, or an image, you simply drag its frame to a new location. After you select a frame, the commands you give apply to the text or graphic in the frame. Frames do not appear in the finished product — they are meant strictly to help with the laying out of text and graphics.

Selected frame

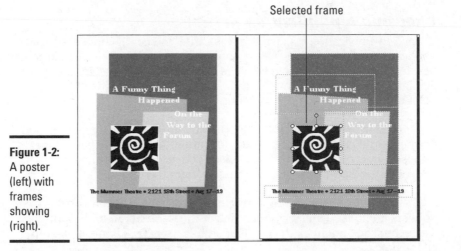

Figure 1-2:
A poster
(left) with
frames
showing
(right).

Creating a Publication

To create a new publication, choose File⇨New (or press Ctrl+N) to display the New Publication task pane (if necessary) and then choose the kind of publication you want, choose a color scheme, and choose design options. The details of making these all-important choices are explained in the pages that follow.

Make your design choices carefully. In theory, you can change publication designs, color schemes, and design options when you are well along in a project, but in practice, changing these designs can have unforeseen consequences. If you change the color of a headline, for example, and then choose a new color scheme, the headline might be swallowed or rendered invisible by a background color in the new scheme. If you enter a bunch of text, change the size of a few frames, and then choose a new publication design, you will likely turn your publication into corned-beef hash and have to start over.

You can create a new publication by starting from one you've already designed. In the New Publication task pane, click the From Existing Publication link. Then, in the Create New from Existing Publication dialog box, select the prototype publication and click the Create New button.

Choosing a publication design

In the New Publication task pane (press Ctrl+N to see it), choose the kind of publication you want, along with a publication type. Where a triangle appears beside a name, you can click the name and choose from specific kinds of publications. Click to select a publication design on the right side of the dialog box Publisher window (refer to Figure 1-1).

Not happy with the publication design you chose? To change it, choose Format➪Publication Designs. The Publication Designs task pane appears. Choose a new design there. The choices you see are the same ones that appear in the New Publication task pane (refer to Figure 1-1).

If you prefer *not* to see the New Publication task plane when you start Publisher, choose Tools➪Options, select the General tab in the Options dialog box, and uncheck the Use New Publication Task Pane at Startup check box.

Choosing a color scheme

After choosing a publication design, the next step is to choose a color scheme. Figure 1-3 shows the Color Schemes task pane where you select a scheme for publications. Choose Format➪Color Schemes to display the Color Schemes task pane, and then select a scheme. If your document has more than one page, be sure to click page number buttons and examine the colors on all the pages before making a final choice.

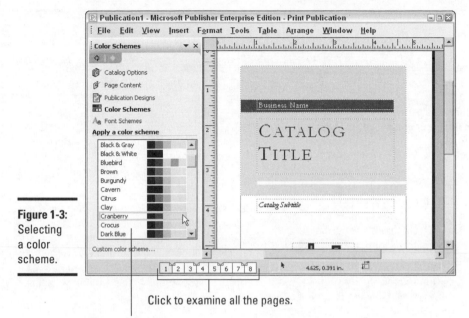

**Book VII
Chapter 1**

**Introducing
Publisher**

Figure 1-3:
Selecting
a color
scheme.

Click to examine all the pages.

Choose a scheme.

Choosing a font scheme

You will be glad to know that most of the text-formatting techniques that are available in Word are also available in Publisher on the Standard toolbar and Format menu. To boldface text, select it and click the Bold button. To change font sizes, choose an option from the Font Size drop-down menu. To center or right-align a heading in a frame, click the Center or Align Right button.

To avoid going to the trouble of formatting text, you can choose a *font scheme,* an assortment of fonts for the body text, headings, and other text in a publication. Font schemes spare you the trouble of having to format the text on your own. The schemes were designed by people who know what they're doing. They look good.

Shrink your document to 50 percent or so to get a good look at all the text; then choose Format➪Font Schemes and select a scheme from the Font Schemes task pane. Experiment with different schemes until you find one that tickles your fancy.

Personal Information

Brochures, newsletters, letterheads, envelopes, and a handful of other publication types include what Publisher calls "personal information." Publisher plugs personal information — a company name, company motto, address, and phone number — into the publication without your having to enter it by hand. The information comes from the Personal Information dialog box. As long as the information in this dialog box is up-to-date, you needn't be concerned whether the information appears in the right places in a publication or whether it's accurate. And you don't have to enter the information directly into the publication you're working on.

To enter personal information, choose Edit⇨Personal Information, fill in the Personal Information dialog box, and click the Update button.

The information you enter will be plugged into all publications you create in the future, as well as the publication you're working on. Notice the Select a Personal Information Set drop-down menu in the dialog box. By default, information from the Primary Business set is entered, but you can choose an option from this menu to enter information about a secondary business or about yourself.

Publisher offers an unwieldy command for quickly entering personal information: Choose Insert⇨Personal Information and the appropriate piece of personal information on the submenu. Then adjust the frame that the information appears in (Chapter 2 of this mini-book explains how).

Choosing design options

The last important step in creating a publication is to choose design options. These options vary depending on the kind of publication you are working on. When you're working on a brochure, for example, choose Format⇨Brochure Options to decide how many panels the brochure needs and whether to include an order form or sign-up form. Choose Format⇨ Banner Options when you are working on a banner and you want to make the banner a certain height or width.

Getting Around in Publisher

The Publisher window can get kind of cluttered. In fact, the place has been known to cause claustrophobia. These pages are meant to help you conquer your fear of the Publisher window. They explain how to get from page to page and, more important, change view of the publication you are working on.

Going from page to page

Use these techniques to get from page to page in a publication:

 ✦ **Click a page navigation button:** In a publication with more than one page, click a page navigation button to go to a different page. The buttons are located on the status bar along the bottom of the window. (If you don't see them, choose View⇨Status Bar.)

 ✦ **The Go to Page dialog box:** Choose Edit⇨Go to Page (or press Ctrl+G) and enter a page number in the Go to Page dialog box.

To help you identify pages, you can name them. When you move the pointer over a page navigation button whose page has been given a name, the name appears in a pop-up bubble. To name a page, right-click its navigation button on the status bar and choose Rename on the shortcut menu. In the Rename Page dialog box, enter a descriptive name.

Zooming in and zooming out

Because seeing the little details as well as the big picture matters so much in a publication, Publisher offers special Zoom In and Zoom Out buttons as well as the Zoom menu. Click a Zoom button to quickly peer at or lean away from a document. You can also choose View⇨Zoom and choose one of the intriguing options on the submenu. For example, select a frame and choose View⇨Zoom⇨Selected Objects when you want to focus on a single frame.

The View menu offers a command called View⇨Two-Page Spread for seeing facing pages in newsletters, brochures, and other publications with more than one page. Choose this command early and often. It permits you to see what readers of your publication will see when they open it to the second page and view facing pages like the ones in Figure 1-4.

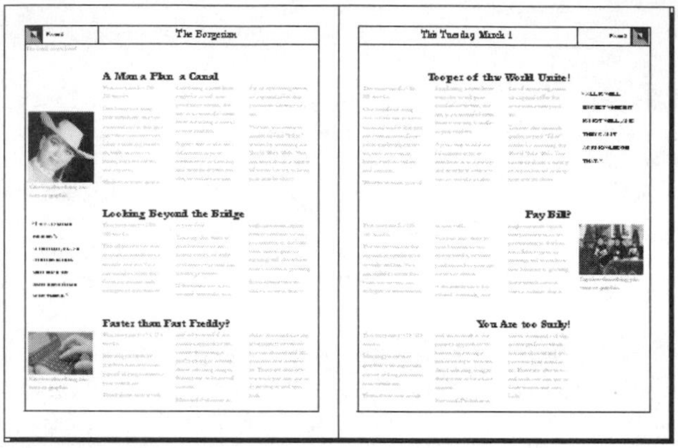

Figure 1-4:
A two-page spread.

Understanding and Using the Layout Guides

Making frames, graphics, and lines of text line up squarely on the page is essential if your publication is to look smart and snappy. Readers tend to go cock-eyed when they see side-by-side columns with the text in one column slightly askew of the text in the column beside it. A graphic or text frame that spills into the margin is a breach of etiquette punishable by death. A row of graphics has to be just that — a row, not a crooked line.

As shown in Figure 1-5, Publisher offers a bunch of different tools for making objects and frames line up squarely. To wit, Publisher offers these tools:

✦ **Margin guides:** Blue lines that show where the margins begin and end.

✦ **Grid guides:** Blue lines that appear in grid form across the page. Frames and objects can be made to "snap to" the grid. Because the objects "snap," you're spared the trouble of aligning them, because they line up on grid guides.

✦ **Ruler guides:** Green horizontal or vertical lines that you can place on the page for assistance in aligning frames and objects. Frames and objects can be made to "snap to" ruler guides, too.

✦ **Baseline guides:** Baselines are green horizontal lines that appear on the page to help with aligning frames and objects.

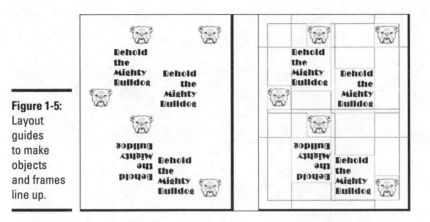

Figure 1-5:
Layout
guides
to make
objects
and frames
line up.

Choose <u>V</u>iew⇨<u>B</u>oundaries and Guides (or press Ctrl+Shift+O) to hide or display margin guides, grid guides, and ruler guides. To hide or display baseline guides, choose <u>V</u>iew⇨Bas<u>e</u>line Guides (or press Ctrl+F7).

These commands make frames and objects "snap to" ruler guides or grid guides: <u>A</u>rrange⇨<u>S</u>nap⇨To Ruler <u>M</u>arks and <u>A</u>rrange⇨<u>S</u>nap⇨To <u>G</u>uides (press Ctrl+W). Book VIII explains all the details of placing objects such as graphics and text frames on pages.

Laying out the margin and grid guides

Unless you create a new section (choose <u>I</u>nsert⇨Se<u>c</u>tion), margin settings and grid guides apply to every page in a publication. Follow these steps to draw blue margin and grid guides:

1. **Choose <u>A</u>rrange⇨<u>L</u>ayout Guides.**

You see the Layout Guides dialog box.

2. **On the Margin Guides tab, enter measurements to determine how wide to make the margins; on the Grid Guides tab, enter numbers to determine how many rows and columns form the grid.**

The Preview box shows you precisely what your grid will look like and where the margins are. Think carefully about entering a number less than .2 in the <u>S</u>pacing boxes. If you enter 0, for example, object and frames will touch each other when they "snap to" the grid.

3. **Click OK.**

To remove grid guides, return to the Grid Guides tab of the Layout Guides dialog box and enter **1** in the <u>C</u>olumns text box and **1** in the <u>R</u>ows text box.

Handling the Rulers

Rulers, when they aren't coming in very handy, get in the way. To hide or display rulers, choose View⇨Rulers. For precision work, you can drag a ruler into the middle of the screen. Simply move the pointer onto the ruler, click, and drag.

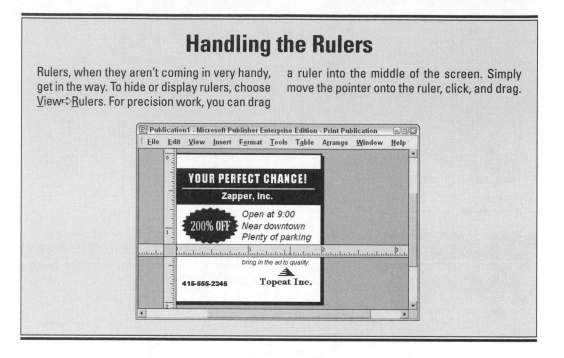

Setting down ruler guides

Use a ruler guide to line up frames or objects in a row. Ruler guides can go anywhere on the page. You can draw ruler guides where you need them and remove the guides very easily when they get in the way. Whereas grid guides appear on every page in a publication, ruler guides appear on one page. You can, however, place the same ruler guide on every page by choosing View⇨Master Page and drawing the ruler guide on the master page.

Publisher offers three ways to draw ruler guides:

✦ **Shift+dragging from a ruler:** Move the pointer over the vertical or horizontal ruler, hold down the Shift key, and drag a guide onto the page. (Choose View⇨Rulers if you don't see the vertical and horizontal rulers.)

✦ **Ruler Guides commands:** Choose Arrange⇨Ruler Guides and, on the submenu, choose Add Horizontal Ruler Guide or Add Vertical Ruler Guide. A guide appears across the page. Drag it to a new location, if necessary.

✦ **Ruler Guides dialog box:** Choose Arrange➪Ruler Guides➪Format Ruler Guides. In the Ruler Guides dialog box, enter horizontal or vertical measurements for the guides and click OK.

Now you know all there is to know about ruler guides, except this stuff:

✦ **Moving a ruler guide:** Click and drag the guide to a new location.

✦ **Removing ruler guides:** Drag the guide off the page. To remove all guides, choose Arrange➪Ruler Guides➪Clear All Ruler Guides.

Chapter 2: Refining a Publication

In This Chapter

- ✓ Entering and editing text
- ✓ Making text fit in frames
- ✓ "Flowing" text from frame to frame
- ✓ Wrapping text around frames and graphics
- ✓ Putting graphics in a publication
- ✓ Manipulating frames

his chapter picks up where the previous chapter left off. In Chapter 1, you discovered how to create a publication, find your way around the screen, and use the different guides. In this chapter, you find out how to make a publication your own. This chapter offers speed techniques for entering and editing text. It explains how to handle frames, make text "flow" from frame to frame, and put graphics and other kinds of art in a publication. Bon voyage!

Entering Text on the Pages

The placeholder text that appears in publication designs has to go, of course. One of your first tasks is to replace the generic text with your own words. In the case of a newsletter story, you have a lot of writing to do. If you are putting together a sign, you have but a handful of words to write. *Story* is Publisher's word for an article that reaches across several text frames.

To select all the text in a frame or story, click in the frame and press Ctrl+A (or choose Edit⇨Select All). Here's another trick that comes in handy when you are entering text: Click in the text and press F9 to zoom in and display text at its actual size.

Publisher offers these techniques for handling large blocks of text:

✦ **Writing the text in Microsoft Word:** Choose Edit⇨Edit Story in Microsoft Word. Microsoft Word opens, and you see the placeholder text in its entirety. Delete the text and enter your own text. You can call on all of the Word commands to edit the text. You can also copy text from elsewhere into the Word document. When you're finished writing, choose File⇨Close & Return to *Your Publication*.

Notice that the placeholder text tells you roughly how many words will fit into the story. As you compose the story in Word, choose Tools⇨Word Count from time to time to see how many words are in the story, and try to keep to the number of words you are allotted.

✦ **Inserting a text file:** Delete the placeholder text and choose Insert⇨Text File. In the Insert Text dialog box, select a file and click OK.

The problem with the techniques just described is that files you worked on in Microsoft Word or imported land in Publisher with their formats intact. If the text is bold and 26 points high, it is bold and 26 points high in your publication in spite of the publication design you chose. To fix the problem, choose Format⇨Font Schemes and select a font scheme in the task pane.

Making Text Fit Text Frames

One of the biggest challenges in a publication is making text fit in text frames. What happens if the headline at the top of the story is too long to fit in the frame? Suppose that a story in a newsletter is too long to fit in the text frames that the publication design you are working in has allotted for the article? These pages explain how to make text fit elegantly in frames.

Handling "overflow" text

The Text in Overflow icon appears at the bottom of a text frame when text doesn't fit in the frame and needs to go elsewhere, as shown in Figure 2-1. When you see this icon, it means that you must make decisions about how to fit the heading or story in your publication.

If you're dealing with a story that reaches across more than one frame, these are your options for handling overflow text:

✦ **"Flow" text from frame to frame on your own:** Direct the text from one frame to another. See "Making text jump from frame to frame," the next section in this chapter.

✦ **Use the "autoflow" mechanism:** Let Publisher suggest where to "flow" the text. After you insert a long story, you see the Autoflow dialog box. By clicking the <u>Y</u>es button in this dialog box, you can tell Word to "flow" the story into different frames in the publication. I don't recommend this technique. Publisher merely picks the next available text frame without regard to whether more than one story appears on the same page. Click <u>N</u>o in the Autoflow dialog box to flow the text on your own.

Connect text boxes toolbar

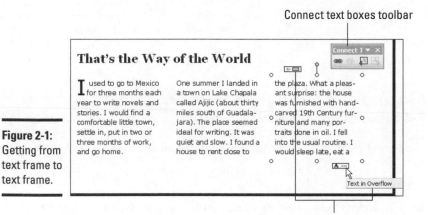

Figure 2-1: Getting from text frame to text frame.

That's the Way of the World

I used to go to Mexico for three months each year to write novels and stories. I would find a comfortable little town, settle in, put in two or three months of work, and go home.

One summer I landed in a town on Lake Chapala called Ajijic (about thirty miles south of Guadalajara). The place seemed ideal for writing. It was quiet and slow. I found a house to rent close to

the plaza. What a pleasant surprise: the house was furnished with hand-carved 19th Century furniture and many portraits done in oil. I fell into the usual routine. I would sleep late, eat a

Text in Overflow

Previous and next text box icons

Book VII Chapter 2

Refining a Publication

If you're dealing with a heading or paragraph that you want to fit in a single frame, try one of these techniques for making the heading or paragraph fit into the text frame:

✦ **Shrink the text automatically:** Choose F<u>o</u>rmat⇨AutoFit Text⇨<u>S</u>hrink Text On Overflow. This command shrinks the point size of text so that all text fits in the frame. Sometimes, however, shrinking the text this way makes the heading or paragraph hard to read.

✦ **Edit the text:** Snip out a word or sentence here and there to make the text fit. Have you ever wondered why magazine articles always fill the page and never end in the middle? That's because skillful editors and typesetters remove and add words here and there to make the story fit the page.

✦ **Make the text frame larger:** See "Changing the size and position of frames," later in this chapter.

✦ **Make the text frame margins smaller:** Like a page, text frames have internal margins to keep text from getting too close to the frame border. To shrink these margins and make more room for text, right-click the text frame and choose Format Text Box. Then, on the Text Box tab of the Format Text Box dialog box, enter smaller measurements for the margins.

One way to handle large blocks of text that don't fit text frames well is to try out a Tracking command. Select the text (press Ctrl+A) and choose Format⇨ Character Spacing. In the Character Spacing dialog box, choosing a Tracking option — Normal, Very Tight, Loose, and so on — to shrink or enlarge the text. The same tracking options are also available on the Measurement toolbar.

Making text jump from frame to frame

Follow these steps to direct text from frame to frame in a publication:

1. **Select the text frame with overflowing text.**

You can tell when text is overflowing because the Text in Overflow icon appears at the bottom of the text frame.

2. **Click the Create Text Box Link button on the Connect Text Boxes toolbar.**

If you don't see this toolbar, right-click any toolbar and choose Connect Text Boxes. The pointer turns into an overflowing pitcher — or is that a beer stein? — after you click the button.

3. **Move the pointer over the box that you want the text to flow into.**

4. **Click in the target text box to make the text flow there.**

As I mention earlier, text frames linked this way are known as a story in Publisher-speak. Here are techniques for handling text frames that are linked in a story:

✦ **Going from text frame to text frame so that you can edit text:** When text travels from frame to frame, the Go to Previous Text Box and Go to Next Text Box icons appear above and below the frames (refer to Figure 2-1). Click an icon to go to the previous or next frame in the chain. You may also click the Previous Text Box or Next Text Box button on the Connect Text Boxes toolbar.

✦ **Selecting the text in all the text frames:** Press Ctrl+A or choose Edit⇨ Select All.

✦ **Breaking the link between frame:** Select the frame that you want to be the last one in the chain and click the Break Forward Link button on the Connect Text Boxes toolbar.

Continuation slugs

A *continuation slug* is a notice that tells the reader where to turn to continue reading an article or where an article is continued from. Publisher offers a nifty command for entering continuation slugs at the bottom or top of text frames:

1. **Right-click the text frame that needs a slug and choose Format Text Box.**

2. **On the Text Box tab of the Format Text Box dialog box, select the Include "Continued on Page" or Include "Continued from Page" check box and click OK.**

Be sure to enter page numbers on slugs. If you decide down the road that you don't care for the formatting of continuation slugs, select a slug, reformat it, click in the Style menu on the Formatting toolbar, press the Enter key, and select the Change the Style Using the Selection as an Example check box. Doing so changes the Continued-On Text style.

In a crowded publication, it's easy to overlook a text frame with "overflowing" text. To find these text frames, choose Tools⇨Design Checker. Then, in the Design Checker task pane, look for "Story with Text in Overflow Area."

Filling out a text frame

The opposite of an "overflow" problem is a text frame with too much blank space. Here are some techniques for handling vacant text frames:

✦ **Use an AutoFit Text option to fill the frame:** Choose Format⇨AutoFit Text⇨Best Fit. This command enlarges the text so that it fills the frame. Sometimes, however, the command makes text too big.

✦ **Edit the text:** Add a word or sentence here or there. In the case of headings, write a subheading as well.

✦ **Insert a graphic or Design Gallery object:** Placing a small graphic or Design Gallery object makes the page more lively and fills the dead space. See "Inserting a new frame," later in this chapter.

Book VII Chapter 2

Refining a Publication

Making Text Wrap Around a Frame or Graphic

Wrap text around a frame, clip art image, picture, or WordArt image and you get a very elegant layout. Figure 2-2 shows text that has been wrapped around a clip art image. Looks nice, doesn't it? Wrapping text may be the easiest way to impress innocent bystanders with your layout prowess. As Figure 2-2 shows, text wrapped to a picture follows the contours of the picture, whereas text wrapped to a frame runs flush with the frame.

Figure 2-2:
Text
wrapped to
a picture
(left) and
frame
(right).

Techniques for wrapping text apply throughout the Office programs and are explained in Book VIII, Chapter 3. Here are shorthand instructions for wrapping text:

1. **Select the item that text is to wrap around.**

In Figure 2-2, you would select the clip art image.

2. **Display the Picture toolbar, click the Text Wrapping button on the toolbar and choose a wrapping option on the drop-down menu.**

For Figure 2-2, I chose Tight for the picture on the left, and Square for the picture on the right. As the figure shows, you can drag the Text Wrapping drop-down menu away from the toolbar. Doing so makes it easier to click buttons and experiment with wrapping options. If you want to be a great wrapper, be sure to visit Book VIII, Chapter 3.

Replacing the Placeholder Graphics

As you must have noticed by now, publication designs are littered with generic clip art images and graphics. Besides writing your own words where the generic words are, replace the generic graphics with graphics of your own. Well, do it if you please. You are welcome to pass off the generic pictures as your own. I won't tell anybody.

Follow these steps to put a graphic where a placeholder graphic is now:

1. **Right-click the picture and choose Change Picture.**

2. **On the submenu, choose what kind of picture you want to import.**

What happens next depends on what kind of picture you're dealing with. Book VIII, Chapter 3 describes how to handle graphics in all the Office programs. You'll be delighted to discover that graphics are handled the same way, no matter which program you're toiling in.

The next section in this chapter explains how to put a graphic on the page without the benefit of a placeholder graphic.

Inserting Frames on the Pages

Publications are made of frames — text frames, table frames, WordArt frames, picture frames, and Design Gallery frames. Nothing appears on the pages of a publication unless it appears within the confines of a frame. These pages explain everything you need to know about frames. You can find out how to insert a new frame, adjust the size of a frame, align frames, and place borders around frames. You can also see how to make frames and the words or images inside them overlap.

Inserting a new frame

To insert a new frame, click one of the five frame tool buttons — Text Box, Insert Table, Insert WordArt, Picture Frame, or Design Gallery Object — on the Objects toolbar, click in your publication, and drag. As you drag, you form a rectangle. Release the mouse button when the frame is the right size. (The next section in this chapter explains how to adjust the size and position of a frame.) Do the following to create a text, table, WordArt, picture, or clip art frame:

✦ **Text frame for paragraphs, headings, and stories:** Click in the frame and start typing. Earlier in this chapter, "Entering Text on the Pages" offers speed techniques for entering text.

✦ **Table frame for tables:** You see the Create Table dialog box, shown in Figure 2-3. Choose the number of rows and columns you want and, in the Table Format list, a layout for your table. Book I, Chapter 5 explains techniques for handling tables.

✦ **WordArt frame for WordArt images:** The WordArt Gallery dialog box opens when you create a WordArt frame. Select an image and click OK. Book VIII, Chapter 3 explains WordArt.

✦ **Picture frame for clip art:** Click the Picture Frame button and choose Insert Clip Art on the drop-down menu. In the Clip Art task pane, find and select a clip art image. Book VIII, Chapter 3 explains clip art.

✦ **Picture frame for art from a file:** Click the Picture Frame button and choose Picture from File on the drop-down menu. The cursor changes to a cross-hair. After you drag to form the picture frame, the Insert Picture dialog box appears so that you can choose a picture.

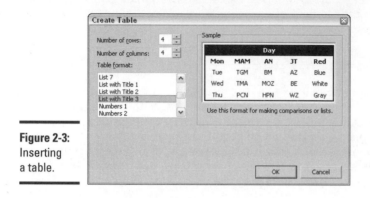

Figure 2-3:
Inserting
a table.

To delete a frame, all you have to do is select it and press the Delete key. You can tell when a frame is selected because round selection handles appear on the corners and sides.

Changing the size and position of frames

After you click a frame and can see the selection handles, you're ready to change the size of the frame or adjust its position on the page. Use these standard techniques for resizing and moving frames:

✦ **Changing the size of a frame:** Move the pointer over a round selection handle and start dragging. If you're dealing with anything but a text frame, be careful about dragging a selection handle on the side of the frame. Dragging a side handle changes the frame's size as well as its proportions. Images can blur or become distorted when you change their proportions.

✦ **Changing the position of a frame:** Move the pointer onto the frame, and click and drag when you see the four-headed arrow. To move more than one frame simultaneously, Ctrl+click the frames you want to move. As explained in Chapter 1, frames snap to the grid as you move them, but you can hold down the Alt key as you drag to adjust frames with precision.

Making Frames Overlap

When frames overlap, you have to tell Publisher which frame goes in front of the other. And you are hereby invited to overlap frames, because overlapping frames are artful and look good on the page. Figure 2-4 shows a portion of a newsletter. If you look closely, you can see where frames overlap in the figure. Overlapping frames like these make for a sophisticated layout.

Figure 2-4:
Examples of overlapping frames.

Order toolbar

**Book VII
Chapter 2**

Refining a
Publication

Making frames like the ones in Figure 2-4 overlap requires doing a delicate balancing act with these commands:

✦ **Text wrapping:** Wrapping must be turned off for frames to overlap. Select the frames, click the Text Wrapping button on the Picture toolbar, and choose <u>N</u>one on the drop-down menu.

✦ **Fill Color:** For frames and objects on the bottom of the stack to show through, the frames and objects below cannot have a fill color that would obscure other objects. To remove the fill color, select the object, open the Fill Color drop-down menu on the Formatting toolbar, and choose No Fill.

✦ **Object and frame order:** To tell Publisher which object goes where in the stack, select each object, open the Order drop-down menu on the Standard toolbar, and choose an option (the Order button is to the right of the Redo button). As Figure 2-4 shows, you can drag this menu onto the screen and thereby have the Order toolbar at your command. Click buttons on the toolbar until objects are in the right order in the stack.

Inserting, Removing, and Moving Pages

Suppose that you have too many pages or you need to add a page or two. Follow these instructions to insert, remove, or move a page:

✦ **Inserting a new page:** Click a page navigation button to move to the page where you want to insert pages; then choose Insert➪Page or press Ctrl+Shift+N. In the Insert Page dialog box, enter the number of pages you want to insert and click an option button to put the new pages before or after the page you're on. Then, under Options, choose an option to tell Publisher what to put on the new page or pages and click OK.

✦ **Removing a page:** Go to the page you want to remove and choose Edit➪Delete Page.

✦ **Moving a page:** Go to the page you want to move and choose Edit➪Move Page. Give instructions for moving the page in the Move Page dialog box.

Chapter 3: Putting on the Finishing Touches

In This Chapter

- ✔ Using horizontal rules and drop caps
- ✔ Decorating frames with borders and color backgrounds
- ✔ Putting a background on a page
- ✔ Putting objects and frames on the master page
- ✔ Inserting a Design Gallery object
- ✔ Preparing publications so that they can be printed commercially

This final chapter in Book VII is devoted to the Project to Beautify Publications, a joint effort of the Dummies Press and the author to try to make publications less bland and more original. The author has noticed, on the bulletin boards and lampposts in his neighborhood, that the rummage sale and lost pet notices look a little rough around the edges. The neighbors are using sophisticated software to produce their notices, but they're not using it well. They are relying solely on templates, which makes the publications look alike. These pages explain a few simple tricks for making publications more sophisticated.

This chapter explores drop caps and horizontal rules, page backgrounds and borders, borders and backgrounds for frames, and how to place a logo in the same place on each page in a publication. The chapter shows you Publisher's excellent Design Checker and Graphics Checker. Finally, this chapter offers advice for printing publications at a commercial print shop.

Decorating the Text

Herewith are a couple of tricks to amaze your friends and intimidate your enemies. These pages explain how horizontal rules and drop caps can make a publication a little livelier. Don't worry — horizontal rules have nothing to do with which side of the bed to sleep on, and drop caps don't explode when you unroll them on the sidewalk and strike them with a hammer.

Drawing a horizontal rule

A *horizontal rule* is a horizontal line that divides one part of a page from another and directs the reader's eye on the page. There are four horizontal rules in Figure 3-1. By varying the width of the lines — the width is known as the *weight* — and placing lines in strategic places, you can make a publication look more elegant and graceful. How you draw a horizontal rule depends on whether you want to draw it above or below a frame, or above or below a text paragraph. The horizontal rules in Figure 3-1 appear above and below frames. Rules appear between paragraphs to mark an abrupt transition between paragraphs. In a mystery story, for example, the horizontal rule appears right after the murderer gets away.

MODERN LIBRARIAN

Volume 3, Issue 2   Building happy, healthy libraries

What's on the Horizon

INSIDE THIS ISSUE:

To the Max   2

The Angels   2

Martians Ahoy   3

Letters   5

Obit Oboy   5

Sorry I can't be there to deliver this in person and answer your questions, but after you have read this memo you will understand why it is utterly impossible for me to leave the Gates Mansion. The news isn't good, John. It's not good on several fronts. In fact, the Gates heirs have not been completely honest with us. We were charged with finding out whether Bill Gates is still alive inside his vast mansion. The answer: he through the east wing, the former servants' quarters. As you know, Gates built the place at the turn of the century as "the first electronic smart house." The inhabitants wore computer-badges so that the house would know exactly where they were at all times. The house would open doors for its inhabitants as they came to doorways, would play

Figure 3-1: Examples of horizontal rules.

Usually where horizontal rules come in pairs, the bottommost rule is thicker than its twin. The thicker bottom line encourages the reader's eye to move down the page and find an article to read.

Horizontal rule on a frame

Follow these steps to draw a horizontal rule on a frame:

1. **Select the frame, right-click it, and choose Format.**

   The format command changes names, depending on what type of frame or object you are working with. You see the Format dialog box.

2. **Select the Color and Lines tab.**

3. **In the Preview box, click the top of the box if you want to draw a rule above the frame, or the bottom of the box if you want to draw a rule below.**

   By clicking part of the Preview box, you tell Publisher where you want to draw the rule.

4. **On the Color menu, choose a line color for the horizontal rule.**

5. **On the Style menu, choose the kind of line you want.**

   If you want a dashed line, select it from the Dashed drop-down menu. You can adjust the thickness of the line in the Weight text box, if necessary.

6. **To draw a second rule on the frame, click again in the Preview box and repeat steps 4 and 5.**

7. **Click OK.**

To remove a horizontal rule on a frame, select the frame, open the Format dialog box, and choose No Line on the Color drop-down menu.

Horizontal rule on a paragraph

Follow these instructions to draw a horizontal rule above or below a paragraph:

1. **Click in the paragraph and choose Format⇨Horizontal Rules.**

   You see the Horizontal Rules dialog box.

2. **Select the Rule Before Paragraph or Rule After Paragraph check box, or both check boxes if you want to draw two horizontal rules.**

3. **Choose options to describe the thickness, color, and style of the line you want.**

   Lines extend from margin to margin or column to column, but you can shorten the lines by entering measurements in the From Left Margin and From Right Margin text boxes.

   To put more distance between the rule and paragraph text, enter a measurement in the Before Paragraph or After Paragraph text box.

4. **Click OK.**

   To remove horizontal rules from a paragraph, click the paragraph, choose Format⇨Horizontal Rules, and remove the check marks from the Rule Before Paragraph and Rule After Paragraph check boxes.

Dropping in a drop cap

As shown in Figure 3-2, a *drop cap* is a large capital letter that "drops" into the text. Drop caps are usually found in the first paragraph of an article or chapter. Pound for pound, considering how little effort is required, a drop cap yields the most reward for the least amount of work.

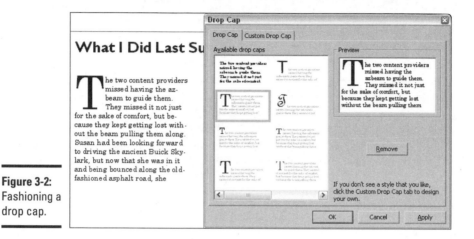

Figure 3-2:
Fashioning a drop cap.

Follow these steps to place a drop cap in a publication:

1. **Click the paragraph that is to get the drop cap and choose Format⇨Drop Cap.**

   You see the Drop Cap dialog box, shown in Figure 3-2.

2. **Select one of the drop caps and click OK.**

   If the drop caps on the Drop Cap tab don't do the trick, visit the Custom Drop Cap tab, where you can choose how far to drop the capital letter or select a font for the letter.

Techniques for Decorating Pages

No one likes a dull publication. Following are some simple techniques to make pages a little bit livelier. Read on to find out how to put borders and color backgrounds on frames. You will also find instructions for painting an entire page with a background color or gray shade.

Putting borders and color backgrounds on frames

As shown in Figure 3-3, putting borders and background colors on text frames makes the frames stand out. Everybody knows what a border is. A background color is a color or gray shade that fills a frame. Borders and background colors are ideal for calling readers' attention to important notices and items in publications. To really get readers' attention, for example, try using black for the background and white for the font color.

Figure 3-3:
Examples
of filled-in
frames.

Select a frame and follow these instructions to give it background color or a border:

✦ **Background color:** Click the Fill Color button and select a color on the drop-down menu. Choose No Fill to remove the background color or to create no background color so that frames below the frame you are dealing with can show through.

✦ **Color for the border:** Click the Line Color button and choose a color from the drop-down menu. You must have chosen a line for the border in order to choose a color.

✦ **Line or dashed-line border:** Click the Line Style button or Dash Style button to open the drop-down menu and choose a line. Or choose More Lines to open the Format dialog box and choose from many different lines or to put a border on only one, two, or three sides of the frame (earlier in this chapter, "Drawing a horizontal rule" explains how to draw a border on different sides of a frame).

Instead of clicking buttons on the Formatting toolbar, you can handle borders and backgrounds in the Format dialog box. Right-click a frame and choose Format on the drop-down menu to open this dialog box. The Colors and Lines tab offers all kinds of commands for borders and backgrounds.

Backgrounds for pages

Yet another nifty trick is to put a color or gray-shade background on the page. Be sure to choose a light color or gray shade that doesn't get in the way of your publication or render it impossible to read. Shrink the publication to 50 percent so that you can see what backgrounds really look like; then follow these steps to give your publication pages a background:

1. **Choose Format➪Background.**

The Background task pane opens, as shown in Figure 3-4.

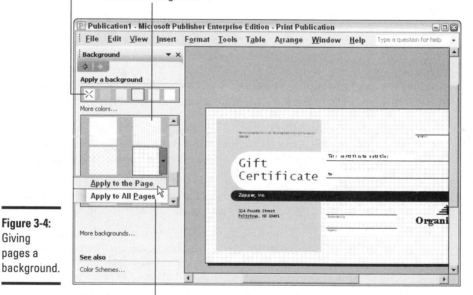

Choose a tint

Select a background

Figure 3-4:
Giving
pages a
background.

Apply to one or all the pages

2. **Experiment with the Tint buttons and Color choices until you find a suitable background.**

   To remove the background color, return to the Background task pane opens and select No Fill, the first Color choice.

The Master Page for Handling Page Backgrounds

In a publication with many pages, the same object sometimes goes on every page. A company logo on the corner of each page looks mighty elegant. Page numbers and copyright information are also found on all the pages of some publications. The good news is that you don't have to place the objects on each page individually. Instead, you can place the objects on the *master page*. Objects on the master page show up on the background of every page.

 To open the master page, choose <u>V</u>iew⇨<u>M</u>aster Page (or press Ctrl+M). Place objects and frames on the master page as if you were putting them on run-of-the-mill pages. You can tell when you're looking at a master page because the page navigation buttons show letters instead of numbers.

In a publication with facing pages, creating two master pages, one for the left-facing pages and another for the right-facing pages, is convenient. To create a second master page, select choose A<u>r</u>range⇨<u>L</u>ayout Guides and, in the Layout Guides dialog box, choose T<u>w</u>o-Page Master. The original master becomes the master page for right-facing pages, the new master page becomes the one for left-facing pages, and Publisher copies everything on the original master page (right) to the second master page (left).

 When background objects on the master page get in the way, choose <u>V</u>iew⇨<u>I</u>gnore Master Page to prevent them from appearing on-screen.

Taking Advantage of the Design Gallery

The Design Gallery is a collection of objects — logos, pull quotes, accent boxes, and thingamajigs — that you can throw into your publications. Figure 3-5 shows some examples of Design Gallery objects. They are great for filling blank spaces in a publication. After you've placed the object, you can change its size or shift its position by using the same techniques you use with other objects.

Figure 3-5:
Examples
of Design
Gallery
objects.

 To insert a Design Gallery object, click the Design Gallery Object button on the Objects toolbar or choose Insert⇨Design Gallery Object. You see the Microsoft Publisher Design Gallery dialog box. Select an object that tickles your fancy — there are about 250 objects in 22 categories — and click the Insert Object button.

Running the Design Checker

When at last your publication is ready for printing, be sure to run the Design Checker. This helpful tool can alert you to frames that fall on nonprinting parts of the page, stories that "overflow" without finding a text frame to go to, invisible objects, and a host of other problems.

Choose Tools⇨Design Checker to run the Design Checker. As shown in Figure 3-6, the Design Checker task pane opens and lists items that need your attention. Open an item's drop-down menu and choose Go to This Item to go to it in your publication. Sometimes the drop-down menus offer quick fixes as well.

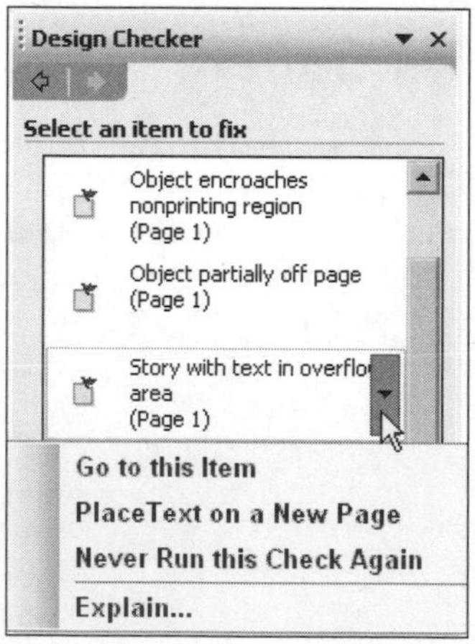

Figure 3-6:
Running
the Design
Checker.

Design Checker ▼ ✕

Select an item to fix

  Object encroaches
  nonprinting region
  (Page 1)

  Object partially off page
  (Page 1)

  Story with text in overflow
  area
  (Page 1)

Go to this Item

PlaceText on a New Page

Never Run this Check Again

Explain...

To see which design flaws the Design Checker looks for, click the Design Checker Options hyperlink in the Design Checker task pane. Then, in the Design Checker Options dialog box, select the Checks tab and read the list.

Commercially Printing a Publication

You know the routine for printing a publication on your computer: Click the Print button; or, choose File⇨Print, negotiate the Print dialog box, and click OK.

Sending a publication to a commercial printer is a different story. Commercial printers either print with process colors (also known as CMYK) or spot colors. To put it simply, process colors are made by mixing cyan, magenta, and yellow to make colors, whereas spot colors are premixed before printing begins. Before you hand over your publication to a commercial printer, find out which color system the printer prefers. It costs more to print with process colors than spot colors because process-color printing requires each color to be created on a different color plate. Process colors, however, produce color photographs much better than spot colors do.

Follow these steps to convert the colors in your publication to the color system that the commercial printer prefers:

1. **Choose Tools⇨Commercial Printing Tools⇨Color Printing.**

You see the Color Printing dialog box.

2. **Under Define All Colors As, choose Spot Colors or Process Colors (CMYK).**

3. **Click OK.**

Publisher also offers the Pack and Go command for copying large files onto floppy disks and embedding fonts in the file. Whereas normally Publisher calls upon instructions from the computer to display fonts, embedded fonts make those instructions part of the file itself. As such, the fonts display the same on all computers — including the computer your printer uses. Embedding fonts, however, makes files grow bigger.

To use the Pack and Go command, choose File⇨Pack and Go⇨Take to a Commercial Printing Service. The Pack and Go dialog box appears. Keep clicking Next and following the directions in the dialog box until your publication is "packed and gone."

Book VIII

One Step Beyond Office

The 5th Wave   By Rich Tennant

"Oh, that's Jack's area for his paper crafts. He's made some wonderful US Treasury Bonds, Certificates of Deposit, $20's, $50's, $100's, that sort of thing."

Contents at a Glance

Chapter 1: Customizing an Office Program

In This Chapter

✔ Creating a new toolbar

✔ Creating toolbar buttons for different commands

✔ Deleting and renaming toolbars

✔ Adding and removing commands from menus

✔ Creating your own menus

✔ Changing the keyboard shortcuts in Word

✔ Deciding what to do about Smart Tags

*Y*ou are hereby invited to make like a software developer and rearrange the toolbars, toolbar buttons, menus, and keyboard shortcuts in the Office programs you like best. You're also invited to invent your own toolbars, toolbar buttons, menus, and keyboard shortcuts. Many people are wary of retooling an Office program this way, but changing the toolbars and menus can save a lot of time. Instead of having to fish around for your favorite commands, you can locate them right away on a toolbar or menu. What's more, you can't do any damage to Word, Excel, PowerPoint, or any other Office program, because if you make a hash of your menus, toolbars, or keyboard shortcuts, you can get the originals back in about two seconds flat.

This chapter explains how to create your own toolbars and toolbar buttons. It shows how to rearrange the buttons on a toolbar, remove buttons, and add buttons. You also discover how to customize the menu system by rearranging menu commands, creating your own menus, and creating your own shortcut menus. Finally, this chapter shows how to change keyboard shortcuts in Word and how to handle Smart Tags, the data snippets that sometimes get mysteriously underlined in Office documents.

What Can 1 Customize?

If you like to use a particular font or command, run a certain macro, or apply a certain style to text, consider putting that font, command, macro, or style on a toolbar or menu. For that matter, assign it a shortcut key combination. You can save a lot of time by customizing the interface of an Office program this way. Customizing makes it easier to give commands. Instead of burrowing into a menu, opening a dialog box, and finding the command, you can simply click a toolbar button, press a shortcut key combination, or open a menu of your own invention and choose a command there. Customizing gives you the opportunity to assemble your favorite commands on a toolbar or menu.

To find out how many commands, styles, and so on can be placed on toolbars and menus, choose Tools⇨Customize in your favorite Office program and, in the Customize dialog box, select the Commands tab (you can also right-click a toolbar and choose Customize to open this dialog box). Figure 1-1 shows the Commands tab of the Customize dialog box. Every command is listed by category here. Select a category and scroll through the Commands list to see the different commands. At the bottom of the Categories list are macros, fonts, AutoText entries, and other esoteric stuff. Each of these commands, macros, fonts, and so on can be put on a menu, made into a toolbar button, or assigned a keyboard shortcut (in Word). Kind of makes you feel like a kid in a candy store, doesn't it?

Select a category.   Review the commands.

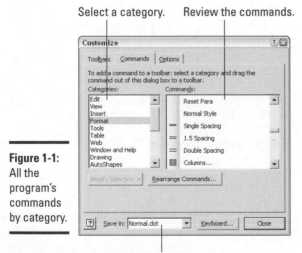

Figure 1-1:
All the program's commands by category.

In Word, choose a template.

Choosing a template in Word for your customizations

Microsoft Word is a little peculiar when it comes to customizing toolbars, menus, and keyboard shortcuts. As part of customizing Word, you have the opportunity to assign the customizations you make to the template you're working in. As Book 1, Chapter 4 points out, each Word document is founded on a template, a collection of styles and formats. If you assign your new toolbars, menus, or keyboard shortcuts to a template, your menus, toolbars, and keyboard shortcuts are made available to all documents founded on the template you're using.

Customizations are made in the Customize dialog box. When you're done Customizing, visit the Commands tab in the dialog box and choose a template from the Save In drop-down list (refer to Figure 1-1) if you want your customizations to be available to all documents founded on the template you're using in your document.

Creating Your Own Toolbars and Toolbar Buttons

For all I know, you never do some of the tasks that the buttons on some of the toolbars were put there to help you do. If you're not using a button, you may as well take it off the toolbar and replace it with a button that you do use. Adding buttons to and removing buttons from toolbars is easy. Creating your own toolbar is a piece of cake, too. Read on to find out the fast way as well as the slow-but-thorough way to remove or add toolbar buttons. You also find out how to create your own toolbars, restore a toolbar to its original condition, and create a hyperlink button for a toolbar.

To see larger buttons on toolbars, right-click a toolbar and choose Customize. Then, on the Options tab of the Customize dialog box, select the Large Icons check box.

Adding buttons to and removing buttons from toolbars

Sometimes, adding and removing buttons from toolbars is merely a matter of clicking the Toolbar Options button and taking it from there. Other times, you have to open the ominous and all-powerful Customize dialog box. Better read on. Office provides three ways to handle toolbars.

Handling toolbars the easy way

Before you add or remove toolbar buttons with the Customize dialog box, see whether you can do it the easy way with the Toolbar Options button. Display the toolbar you want to fool with, click its Toolbar Options button, choose <u>A</u>dd or Remove Buttons on the drop-down menu, and choose the name of the toolbar you're working with. As shown in Figure 1-2, you see a drop-down list with the names of buttons currently on the toolbar and a short list of buttons you can add to the toolbar. Select or unselect buttons on the drop-down list to decide which buttons belong on the toolbar. Select <u>R</u>eset Toolbar if you go overboard and remove too many buttons.

The Toolbar Options button doesn't appear on a toolbar unless the toolbar is docked to a side of the screen. To dock a toolbar, double-click its name.

Select or unselect buttons.   Toolbar options button.

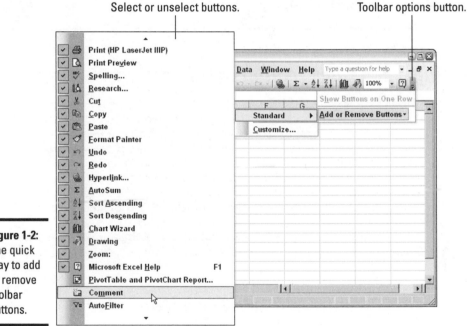

Figure 1-2:
The quick
way to add
or remove
toolbar
buttons.

Handling toolbars in the Rearrange Commands dialog box

The Toolbar Options button technique of handling toolbar buttons is fine and dandy, but what if you want to place a toolbar button on a toolbar and the button isn't on the drop-down list? To do a more thorough job of customizing toolbars, follow these steps:

1. **Choose Tools⇨Customize or right-click a toolbar and choose Customize.**

The Customize dialog box appears (refer to Figure 1-1).

2. **Select the Commands tab.**

3. **Click the Rearrange Commands button.**

You see the Rearrange Commands dialog box, shown in Figure 1-3.

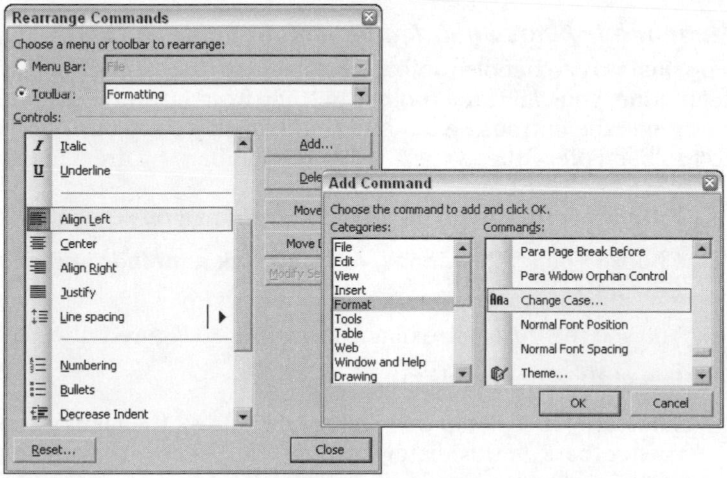

Figure 1-3: Customizing toolbars in the Rearrange Commands dialog box.

4. **Select the Toolbar option button and, from the Toolbar drop-down list, select the name of the toolbar you want to customize.**

The names of commands on the toolbar appear in the dialog box.

5. **Customize your toolbar.**

The Rearrange Commands dialog box offers commands for doing just that:

- **Adding a new button:** Click the Add button and, in the Add Command dialog box (refer to Figure 1-3), find and select the command you want to add. Then click OK.

- **Removing a button:** Select the button and click Delete.

- **Rearranging buttons:** One at a time, select buttons and click the Move Up or Move Down button to change the order of buttons on the toolbar.

If all goes wrong and you need to start over, click the Reset button in the Rearrange Commands dialog box.

Handling toolbars by dragging and dropping buttons

The final way to handle toolbar buttons is to drag and drop them. With this technique, you can trade toolbar buttons from faraway toolbars, drag to rearrange the buttons on a toolbar, and quickly copy buttons from toolbar to toolbar. Follow these steps to handle toolbars by dragging and dropping:

1. **Put the toolbar that you want to customize on-screen.**

2. **Choose Tools⇨Customize, or right-click a toolbar and choose Customize.**

You see the Customize dialog box (refer to Figure 1-1).

3. **Select the Commands tab.**

The Categories list in this dialog box lists all the menus and several of the toolbars. In this dialog box, you can find every command in the program in which you're working by clicking an item in the Categories box and then scrolling in the Commands box. Depending on which program you're working in, at the bottom of the list may be styles, macros, AutoText entries, and fonts.

4. **Remove, move, or add a button to the toolbar.**

The Customize dialog box is a sort of backstage pass that lets you do all kinds of things you can't normally do. As long as the Customize dialog box is on-screen and open, you can magically do these things to toolbar buttons:

- ✦ **Removing buttons:** Drag the button off the toolbar. As you drag, a gray rectangle appears above the pointer and an *X* appears below it. Release the mouse button and the toolbar button disappears.

- ✦ **Moving buttons along a toolbar:** Drag the button to a new location.

- ✦ **Copying buttons:** Hold down the Ctrl key and drag the button from one toolbar to another.

- ✦ **Adding buttons:** Find the button in the Customize dialog box by clicking categories and scrolling in the Commands box. When you have found the button, carefully drag it out of the Customize dialog box and place it on the toolbar where you want it to appear. A gray rectangle appears above the cursor. A plus sign appears below it when you move the button onto the toolbar.

To quickly remove buttons from toolbars or slide them into new locations, hold down the Alt key as you click and drag the button you want to remove or move.

Resetting a toolbar

If you make a boo-boo and wish that you hadn't fooled with the buttons on a toolbar, take one of these actions:

- ✦ Click the Toolbar Options button of the toolbar that needs restoring, choose <u>A</u>dd or Remove Buttons, choose the name of the toolbar that needs restoring, and choose <u>R</u>eset Toolbar at the bottom of the drop-down list.

- ✦ Choose <u>T</u>ools⇨<u>C</u>ustomize or right-click a toolbar and choose Customize to get to the Customize dialog box. From there, select the Tool<u>b</u>ars tab, select the toolbar whose buttons you fooled with, and click the <u>R</u>eset button.

Creating your own toolbar

You can also create a new toolbar and put your favorite buttons on it. If you want, you can even create toolbar buttons for styles, fonts, AutoText entries, and macros. Follow these steps:

1. **Choose <u>T</u>ools⇨<u>C</u>ustomize, or right-click a toolbar and choose <u>C</u>ustomize to open the Customize dialog box.**

**Book VIII
Chapter 1**

Customizing an
Office Program

2. **Select the Toolbars tab.**

Figure 1-4 shows the Toolbars tab of the Customize dialog box.

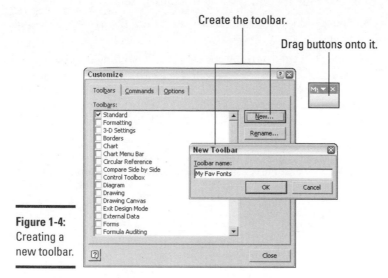

Figure 1-4:
Creating a
new toolbar.

3. **Click the New button.**

The New Toolbar dialog box appears, as shown in Figure 1-4.

4. **Enter a name for your toolbar in the Toolbar Name box.**

The name you type here will appear on the View⇨Toolbars submenu.

5. **Click OK.**

A puny toolbar with the name you entered appears on the screen, as shown in Figure 1-4. Locating this toolbar can be difficult; have a good look-see and you will find it. At this point, the thing is hardly bigger than a toolbar button. Drag it to a convenient location.

6. **Place buttons on your toolbar.**

Earlier in this chapter, "Adding buttons to and removing buttons from toolbars" describes the different ways to place buttons on toolbars.

Creating a hyperlink toolbar button

Here's a neat little trick: You can put a hyperlink button on a toolbar and in so doing be able to click the button and go straight to another file or a Web site. A hyperlink is an electronic shortcut between two documents or two Web sites. Follow these steps to put a hyperlink button on a toolbar:

1. Choose Tools➪Customize to open the Customize dialog box; then place a button on the toolbar. For the time being, it doesn't matter which button you put on because it will soon change functionality. Name the button after the file or Web site to which the link will go.

2. Right-click your new button and choose Assign Hyperlink➪Open. You see the Assign Hyperlink: Open dialog box.

3. Enter the address of the Web page or document you want to link to, or choose it in the dialog box.

To remove the hyperlink from a button, right-click it while the Customize dialog box is open and choose Edit Hyperlink➪Remove Link. Then right-click and choose Assign Hyperlink➪Open to establish a new link for the button.

 If you've added styles or fonts to your toolbar, you may want to shorten their names to make them fit better. To do so, right-click the button whose name you want to shorten and enter a new name in the Name text box on the drop-down list. Also on the shortcut menu are commands for changing the appearance of buttons.

Deleting and renaming toolbars you created

Only toolbars you invented yourself can be deleted or renamed. Follow these instructions to delete or rename them:

✦ **Deleting a toolbar:** Choose Tools➪Customize or right-click a toolbar and choose Customize to get to the Customize dialog box. Then select the Toolbars tab, select the toolbar you want to extinguish (self-made toolbars are at the bottom of the list), and click the Delete button.

✦ **Renaming a toolbar:** Select the toolbar you want to rename on the Toolbars tab of the Customize dialog box, click the Rename button, and enter a new name in the Rename Toolbar dialog box.

Book VIII
Chapter 1

Customizing an
Office Program

Choosing images for toolbar buttons

When you borrow or take buttons from other toolbars, images appear on the buttons. Images also appear when you put certain commands on toolbars. But not all commands have images associated with them. Follow these steps to choose an image for a toolbar button:

1. **Choose Tools➪Customize to open the Customize dialog box.**

2. **Display the toolbar whose button or command needs a change of face.**

3. **Right-click the button or command, choose Change Button Image, and select an image on the submenu.**

   You can always right-click a button and choose Reset Button Image to see the original image — the one that appeared on the toolbar button or menu command before you started tinkering.

To put an image of your choosing on a button, find a bitmap image that suits you, select it, and copy it to the Clipboard. Then right-click the toolbar button that needs an image and choose Paste Button Image.

Customizing the Menu Commands

Customize your own menus to place the commands you need most often on a single menu, remove unneeded commands from menus, or gather commands for a specific task in one place. Commands aren't the only items you can put on a menu. You are invited to put macros, fonts, AutoText entries, styles, and hyperlinks on a menu to get at them more quickly. You can even customize shortcut menus, the menus you see when you right-click a part of the screen. Better keep reading.

Microsoft Word offers a quick but scary way to remove a command from a menu. Press Ctrl+Alt+hyphen and, when the cursor changes into an ominous black bar, simply select the menu command that you want to remove. Press Esc, by the way, if you decide after you press Ctrl+Alt+hyphen that you don't want to remove menu commands this way.

Removing commands from and adding commands to menus

Office provides two techniques for customizing menus and menu commands. You can start from the Rearrange Commands dialog box or use the drag-and-drop method. Keep reading.

Handling menu commands in the Rearrange Commands dialog box

The Toolbar Options button technique of handling toolbar buttons is fine and dandy, but what if you want to place a toolbar button on a toolbar and the button isn't on the drop-down list? To do a more thorough job of customizing toolbars, follow these steps:

1. **Choose Tools⇨Customize or right-click a toolbar and choose Customize.**

    You see the Customize dialog box.

2. **Select the Commands tab.**

3. **Click the Rearrange Commands button.**

    You see the Rearrange Commands dialog box (refer to Figure 1-3).

4. **Make sure that the Menu Bar option button is selected and, from the Menu Bar drop-down list, choose the name of the menu or submenu you want to customize.**

    The names of commands on the menu appear in the dialog box.

5. **Customize the menu to the extent that you prefer.**

    You will find commands in the Rearrange Commands dialog box for doing these tasks:

    *   **Adding a new command:** Click the Add button and find and select a command in the Add Command dialog box.

    *   **Removing a menu command:** Select the command and click Delete.

    *   **Rearranging commands:** Select commands and click the Move Up or Move Down button to change the order in which they appear on the menu.

You can always click the Reset button in the Rearrange Commands dialog box if all goes awry and you need to start over.

Handling menu commands by dragging and dropping

As I explain earlier in this chapter, the Customize dialog box is like a back-stage pass to Office programs. As long as this dialog box is open, you can drag and drop menu commands and toolbar buttons at will. Follow these steps to remove commands from or add commands to menus by dragging and dropping:

1. **Choose Tools⇨Customize to open the Customize dialog box.**

2. **Select the Commands tab.**

What you do next depends on whether you want to remove a command from a menu, add a command to a menu, or change its position on a menu. Changing menu commands requires moving the pointer out of the Customize dialog box and clicking menus on the menu bar.

 ✦ **Removing menu items:** To remove a menu command, move the pointer over the menu that holds the command you want to remove and click. That's right — click the menu name as if you were pulling it down to choose one of its commands. When the menu appears, select the menu command you want to remove and drag it off the menu. You see a gray rectangle above the pointer and an *X* below it. Release the mouse button after you have dragged the menu command away from the menu.

 ✦ **Adding menu items:** To add a menu command to a menu, find the command in the Commands list on the Commands tab of the Customize dialog box and drag it from the Commands list to the menu itself. As you do this, you see a gray rectangle above the pointer and a plus sign below it. Move the pointer over the menu to which you want to add the command. The menu appears. Gently drag the pointer down the menu to the spot where you want the command to be listed. A black line appears on the menu to show where your command will go. When the command is in the right spot, release the mouse button.

✦ **Changing the position of menu items:** To change the position of a command on a menu, move the pointer out of the Customize dialog box and gently click on the menu whose command you want to move. Then drag the pointer up or down the list of commands. A black line shows where the command will move when you release the mouse button. When the black line is in the right spot, let up on the mouse button.

Seeing full menus, not abridged versions

Whether you know it or not, Office keeps track of how often you use menu commands in each program. When you open a menu, commands you used recently appear. The idea is not to overwhelm you with too many menu choices. To make all the commands on the menu appear, click the double chevrons at the bottom of the menu.

Some people find the abridged menus annoying and wish they could see full menus when they click to open them. If you're one of those people, take heed of the two ways to display full menus in an Office program:

✔ Double-click menu names instead of clicking them. Double-clicking a menu name on the menu bar opens the full menu, not the abridged version.

✔ Choose Tools➪Customize and, on the Options tab of the Customize dialog box, select the Always Show Full Menus check box.

Customizing the shortcut menus

Shortcut menus are menus that appear when you right-click part of the screen. In Word, PowerPoint, and Access, you can customize these menus, starting from the Toolbars tab in the Customize dialog box. On the Toolbars list, select Shortcut Menus. The Shortcut Menus toolbar appears on-screen. Open a drop-down list of shortcut menus and select the shortcut menu you want to customize. After the shortcut menu is displayed on-screen, you can change or rearrange its menu commands using the standard techniques described in this chapter.

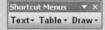

Resetting the menus

If you wish that you hadn't messed with the menus and you want to repent, choose Tools➪Customize, select the Commands tab, move the pointer out of the dialog box, right-click the name of the menu whose commands you fooled with, and choose Reset on the shortcut menu.

Creating your own menu

Follow these steps to create your own menu and place it on a menu bar or a toolbar:

1. **If your plan is to place the menu on a toolbar, display the toolbar.**

2. **Choose Tools➪Customize to open the Customize dialog box.**

3. **Scroll to the bottom of the Categories list on the Commands tab and select New Menu.**

   The name New Menu appears in the Commands list.

4. **Click New Menu in the Commands list and drag it off the Customize dialog box and onto the menu bar or toolbar where you want your new menu to be.**

   A black line shows where the menu will land when you release the mouse button. The name "New Menu" appears on the menu bar or toolbar. Not much of a menu name, is it?

5. **Right-click the words "New Menu" and, in the Name text box on the shortcut menu that appears, enter a descriptive name for your menu and press Enter.**

6. **Add commands to your new menu.**

Earlier in this chapter, "Removing commands from and adding commands to menus" explains how to do it.

To delete a menu you created, choose Tools⇨Customize to open the Customize dialog box and then right-click the menu and choose Delete, or simply drag the new menu off the toolbar.

Changing the Keyboard Shortcuts in Word

In Microsoft Word, you can change the keyboard shortcuts. A *keyboard shortcut* is a combination of keys that you press to give a command. For example, pressing Ctrl+P opens the Print dialog box. Pressing Ctrl+S gives the Save command. If you don't like a keyboard shortcut in Word, you can change it and invent a keyboard shortcut of your own. You can also assign keyboard shortcuts to symbols, macros, fonts, AutoText entries, and styles.

Follow these steps to choose keyboard shortcuts of your own in Microsoft Word:

1. **Choose Tools⇨Customize.**

You see the Customize dialog box.

2. **Click the Keyboard button.**

You see the Customize Keyboard dialog box, shown in Figure 1-5.

3. **In the Categories list, choose the menu with the command to which you want to assign the keyboard shortcut.**

At the bottom of the list are the Macro, Font, AutoText, Style, and Common Symbols categories.

4. **Choose the command name, macro, font, AutoText entry, style, or symbol name in the Commands list.**

5. **In the Press New Shortcut Key box, type the keyboard shortcut.**

Press the actual keys. For example, if the shortcut is Ctrl+~, press the Ctrl key and the ~ key — don't type out C-t-r-l-+~.

If you try to assign a shortcut that is already assigned, the words "Currently assigned to" and a command name appear below the Press New Shortcut Key box. You can override the preassigned keyboard assignment by entering a keyboard assignment of your own.

6. **Click the Assign button.**

7. **When you're done, close the Customize Keyboard dialog box.**

To delete a keyboard shortcut, display it in the Current Keys box, select it, and click the Remove button.

You can always get the old keyboard shortcuts back by clicking the Reset All button in the Customize Keyboard dialog box.

Select a command.

Enter the shortcut.

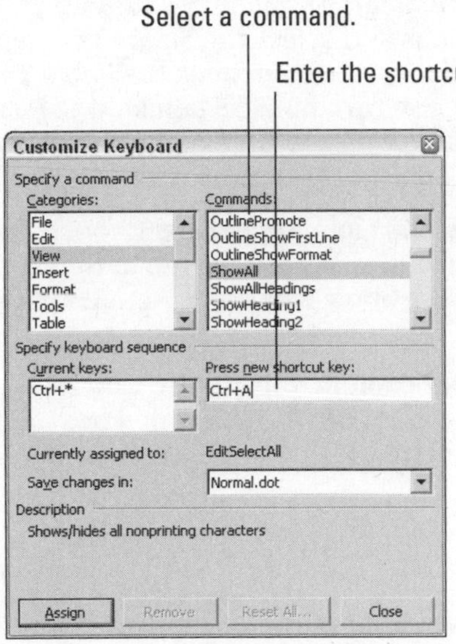

Figure 1-5:
Assigning
keyboard
shortcuts to
commands.

Smart Tags, Smart Alecks

A *Smart Tag* is a snippet of data that Office programs recognize as a date, an address, a company ticker name, a place, a telephone number, or a person to whom you recently sent e-mail. If Word recognizes one of these entities, it places a purple dotted line underneath the data. Move the pointer over the purple dotted line and you see the Smart Tag icon. Click this icon and you see a shortcut menu with tasks, as shown in Figure 1-6.

**Book VIII
Chapter 1**

**Customizing an
Office Program**

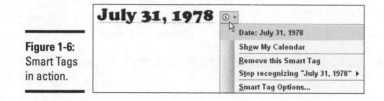

Not everyone likes Smart Tags, however. Here's how to handle them:

✦ **Turning off Smart Tags:** If Smart Tags aren't your cup of tea, choose Tools⇨AutoCorrect Options and select the Smart Tags tab in the AutoCorrect dialog box. From there, uncheck the Label Text with Smart Tags check box. You can also turn off a certain kind of Smart Tag in the Smart Tags tab. Smart Tags remain with text you entered already, but this option prevents the Smart Tags of the future from bothering you.

✦ **Keeping the Smart Tag icons from appearing:** Choose Tools⇨ AutoCorrect Options, select the Smart Tags tab in the AutoCorrect dialog box, and uncheck the Show Smart Tag Actions Buttons check box.

✦ **Putting Smart Tags in a document you pass to others:** Choose Tools⇨ Options, select the Save tab in the Options dialog box, and uncheck the Embed Smart Tags check box.

Chapter 2: Automating Tasks with Macros and VBA

In This Chapter

✔ Understanding Visual Basic for Applications (VBA)

✔ Recording and running macros

✔ Finding your way around the Visual Basic Editor

✔ Editing and fashioning macros in the Visual Basic Editor

✔ Including message boxes and input boxes with macros

✔ Moving, renaming, and deleting macros

*E*xcept for this chapter, this book deals with creating and editing Office files — Word documents, Excel workbooks, PowerPoint presentations, Access databases, and so on. This chapter explains how to streamline and automate your work with macros and a programming language called VBA (*Visual Basic for Applications*). Entire books have been written about macros and VBA, and a short chapter like this can't really do the subject justice. However, macros and VBA are simply too good to overlook. This chapter just scratches the surface of macros and VBA, but it scratches deep enough to give you the basics and whet your appetite for further investigation.

This chapter explains various aspects of VBA, including the language's procedures, functions, modules, and methods. You discover how to record a macro and run macros. This chapter has you create two sample macros, one in Word and one in Excel, and examine them closely to see how code is written in Visual Basic Editor, the program in which VBA code is written and edited. This chapter looks at adding message boxes and input boxes to macros and, finally, how to copy, move, rename, and delete macros and modules in the Visual Basic Editor.

What Is a Macro?

A *macro* is a set of command instructions recorded under a name. When the macro is activated, the application you're working in carries out the instructions in the macro. Macros help automate repetitive and complex tasks. Instead of your entering commands yourself, the macro does it for you — and it enters the commands faster and more efficiently. Instead of reaching into several dialog boxes to get the task done, you can run a macro and let the macro do the work.

As I explain later in this chapter, you can record a macro by choosing Tools⇨Macro⇨Record New Macro. After you choose this command, the application you're running records the commands you give and saves them as a macro. When you later run the macro, those same commands are carried out. Most people don't know it, but recording a macro actually involves recording command sequences in Visual Basic for Applications. Behind the scenes, the application you're working in writes VBA codes when you record a macro. When you run the macro, you're really executing VBA codes — the same codes that were written when you recorded your macro.

What Is VBA?

Visual Basic for Applications (VBA) is a programming language built into all the major Office applications: Word, Excel, PowerPoint, Access, Outlook, and FrontPage. You can create VBA code by using the VBA Macro Recorder to record a macro or by typing the code into the Visual Basic Editor. For that matter, you can combine the two approaches. You can start by recording actions with the Macro Record and then edit the resulting code in the Visual Basic Editor. VBA code is a sort of mini-computer program, one that operates inside another computer program.

Programming — or writing code — with VBA presents a way to automate complex and long-winded tasks. If you know your way around VBA, you can construct command sequences for working interactively in Office applications — for opening dialog boxes, giving commands, and moving data, for example. You can even perform actions automatically that *can't* be performed when working interactively. For example, you can construct VBA code to enter data in an Excel workbook apart from the active workbook you're working in. You can hide an application such that the person sitting at his or her computer can interact with the application without actually seeing it. All the person sees is VBA dialog boxes.

VBA and VB

VBA is an offshoot of *Visual Basic* (VB), the computer language in which Office and other Microsoft programs are written. VBA is different in each Office application because each Office application contains different objects (objects are explained shortly). Because VBA is different in each application, VBA is more a family of dialects than a computer language, but when you understand how the language works in one application — you know the grammar of VBA, so to speak — you can quickly transfer your knowledge to and be able to work with VBA in another application. What's more, getting acquainted with VBA is an excellent introduction to learning Visual Basic, in case you want to tackle that programming language.

Unlike VB, which is used to create standalone applications, VBA always runs inside another application. All the major Office applications can run VBA code, as can Microsoft applications such as Visio and Project. Some applications produced by software companies apart from Microsoft can also run VBA. For example, you can use VBA to automate tasks in WordPerfect and AutoCAD. If you've worked with VB, you'll find working with VBA very easy. In VBA and VB, you use the same application, the Visual Basic Editor, to create and test programming code. The Visual Basic Editor is explained later in this chapter.

Understanding VBA Components

Using VBA, you create the code that tells the computer application — Excel or Word, for example — what you want it to do. Before you can create this code, you need to know the different components of Visual Basic for Applications. Read on to acquaint yourself with basic VBA components. And don't worry about understanding this abstract stuff right away. Later in this chapter you can get your hands dirty creating and editing macros, and then most of this stuff will start making real sense.

Procedures, subprocedures, and functions

VBA code consists of procedures. A *procedure* is a chunk of code that can stand on its own. Procedures come in two types:

✦ **Subprocedures:** A *subprocedure* (also called a *subroutine*) is a standalone chunk of code whose purpose is to execute an action of some kind. Subprocedures start with the VBA keyword `Sub` and end with the keywords `End Sub`.

✦ **Functions:** A *function* is also a standalone chunk of code, but it returns a value. Functions start with the keyword `Function` and end with the keywords `End Function`. VBA functions are like Excel functions in that they take arguments and produce values. If you're familiar with Excel functions, you have a head start using VBA functions.

A macro is an example of a subprocedure (*macro* is just a friendlier and less clumsy word than subprocedure). Some people argue that *macro* refers only to code recorded with the Macro Recorder, but that isn't true. You can write macros as well as record them. For the sake of simplicity, I use the word *macro* rather than *subprocedure* throughout this chapter.

The Object model: Objects, methods, and properties

Consider what happens when you work interactively with an application. In Excel, for example, you bring up the Open dialog box, choose a file to open, click a tab to select a worksheet in the file, press arrow keys to move to a cell, type a formula in the cell, and then press Enter to enter the formula.

Telling VBA to perform this same sequence of actions requires using the object model for the Excel application. The *object model* defines how VBA interacts with an application. In the context of VBA, each application is made up of a number of *objects* — identifiable entities to which VBA code can refer. The object model describes how the objects are arranged in relation to each other. Getting back to the example of the Excel worksheet, to create a macro for the command sequence described earlier, you tell VBA to open the appropriate Workbook object, select the appropriate Worksheet object, select the appropriate Cell object, and enter a formula in the cell.

Much the same as in the Windows file system, the object model for a typical application is arranged in the form of an inverted tree:

✦ **Application object:** At the root is an Application object. It represents the entire application. The Application object is used for setting general properties and for accessing other objects contained in the Application object. These objects in turn contain other objects.

✦ **Collection objects:** Objects of the same type are arranged into *collection* objects or, more simply, *collections*. For example, Excel's Workbook objects (which represent workbooks) are arranged in a Workbooks collection that represents all open workbooks. To access a workbook, you go through the Workbooks collection.

✦ **Object properties:** A *property* is an object characteristic that you can return, set, or in some cases do both. For example, the Workbook object in Excel has a Path property whose purpose is to list the path to the folder on a computer where a workbook is stored. The Path property is read-only — you can check it from VBA, but you can't set it.

✦ **Object methods:** A *method* is an action you can take with an object. For example, the Workbook object includes a SaveAs method whose purpose is to save a workbook under a different filename or save a workbook for the first time. In VBA, the SaveAs method is the equivalent of the File➪Save As command.

To avoid having to go through the Application object for every command, most object models include top-level objects that you can access directly. In Excel, for example, you can directly access the ActiveWorkbook object (it represents the active workbook) and the Workbooks collection.

In most Office applications, the best way to understand how the Object model works is to consult the Help program, as shown in Figure 2-1. This figure shows the Object model for Excel. To see a diagram like this, open an Office application, press Alt+F11 to open the Visual Basic Editor, press F1 to start the Help program, and type **object model** in the Help program's Search text box. Diagrams such as the one in Figure 2-1 show precisely how objects are related to each other. You can click an object in the diagram to learn more about it.

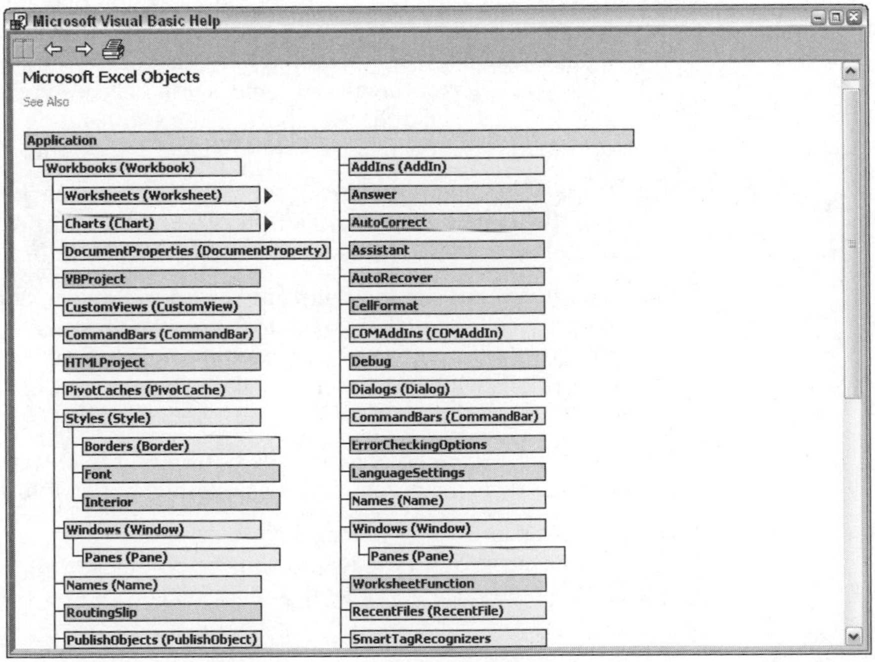

Figure 2-1:
An Object model diagram.

**Book VIII
Chapter 2**

Automating Tasks

I'm sure that this object-properties-method business seems very abstract at the moment, but don't worry about it. By recording the sample macros in this chapter, you'll quickly reach the objects, properties, and methods you need. By editing the macros, you'll soon understand how properties and methods differ and what you can do with them.

Recording a Macro

As I explain at the start of this chapter, recording a macro in an Office application is a matter of turning on the Macro Recorder and giving commands. The Macro Recorder is modeled after a tape recorder. You turn on the recorder, choose commands, and turn the thing off. Herewith are the ground rules for recording macros and instructions for recording macros.

Ground rules for recording macros

Before you record a macro, observe these ground rules:

✦ Plan ahead. If the actions you intend to record in the macro are complex, write them down beforehand so that you can execute the commands without making any mistakes.

✦ Set up the application the way it will be when you play back the macro. Before creating a macro that manipulates information in a worksheet, for example, open a worksheet that is typical of the kind of worksheet on which you will run the macro. Unless you prepare yourself this way, you may have to pause the Macro Recorder (you can do that in Word) as you record or edit the macro in the Visual Basic Editor later on.

✦ Close open files that might get in the way. For example, before creating a macro that copies information from one PowerPoint presentation to another, close any open presentations that might confuse the issue.

✦ If you intend to choose the Edit⇨Find or Edit⇨Replace command in Word, open the Find dialog box before you start recording the macro and click the More button. This way, you can get to all the find-and-replace options when you open the dialog box as part of recording the macro.

✦ In Excel, click the Relative Reference button on the Macro Recorder if you want to record cell references as relative, not absolute, references.

✦ Toggle commands that you can switch on and off have no place in macros, because when the macro starts running, the Macro Recorder can't tell whether the command is on or off.

Recording a macro

Having read and followed the ground rules, follow these steps to record a macro in Word, Excel, or PowerPoint:

1. **Choose Tools⇨Macro⇨Record New Macro.**

The Record Macro dialog box opens, as shown in Figure 2-2.

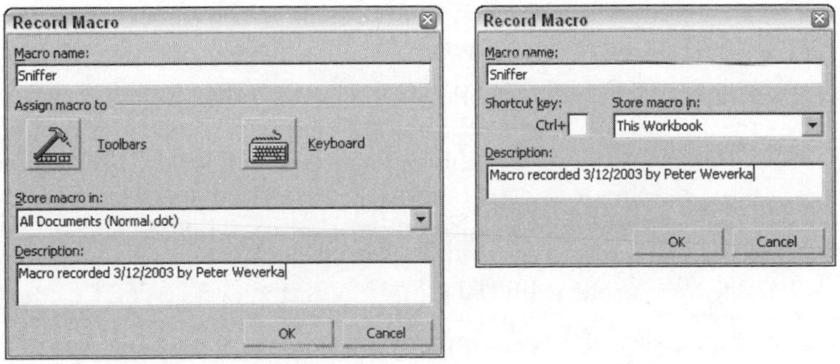

Figure 2-2:
The Macro
Recorder in
Word (left)
and Excel
(right).

If you can't find the <u>M</u>acro command on the <u>T</u>ools menu, chances are an administrator removed it to prevent you from using or recording macros. Depending on which version of Windows you have, administrators can remove all macro and VBA functionality from Office by not installing the VBA component, or they can install the component but prevent individuals from accessing macros and VBA. If you administer your computer, run the Office setup program again, choose a custom installation, and select the Visual Basic for Applications check box to install the VBA components.

2. **In the <u>M</u>acro Name text box, enter a name for your macro.**

Macro names can be 80 characters long, must begin with a letter, and can include numbers and underscores. Blank spaces, symbols, and punctuation are not allowed.

3. **If you desire, assign a toolbar button or keyboard shortcut to the macro.**

In Word, you can click the <u>T</u>oolbars or the <u>K</u>eyboard button and assign a toolbar button or keyboard shortcut for activating the macro. Click either of these buttons and you go to a Customize dialog box. The previous chapter in this mini-book describes the Customize dialog boxes.

In Excel, you can assign a Ctrl key combination or Ctrl+Shift key combination to a macro. However, the key combination won't work if you subsequently move the macro to a different module.

4. **In the Store Macro In drop-down list, decide where to store the macro you're about to record.**

   In Word, you can store macros in the document you're working on, the template the document is attached to, or the Normal template (the global template that's always loaded). Store a macro with a template if you would like to be able to run the macro from other documents to which this one is attached.

   In Excel, you can store macros in the workbook you're working on (choose the This Workbook menu item), a new workbook, or the Personal.Macro Workbook. The Personal.Macro Workbook is designed expressly for storing macros. It is created automatically the first time you choose Personal Macro Workbook. The workbook, called Personal.xls, is stored in the C:\Documents and Settings*Your Name*\Application Data\Microsoft\Excel\XLSTART folder.

   In PowerPoint, you can store macros in the active presentation, another open presentation, or a template.

5. **In the Description text box, type a concise description of what the macro does.**

6. **Click the OK button.**

   The Record Macro dialog box closes. In its place, you see the Macro Recorder toolbar. Notice the Stop Recording button. Click that button when you finish recording your macro.

   In Word, the Macro Recorder toolbar includes a Pause Recording button. You can click it to suspend recording. Click it again to resume recording.

   In Excel, the Macro Recorder toolbar includes a Relative References button. Click it to switch between recording absolute cell references and relative cell references.

7. **Perform the actions you want to record in the macro.**

   Avoid using the mouse as you record a macro (although you can use it to open menus and select menu commands). The Macro Recorder interprets some mouse actions ambiguously. Select data by using key presses (in Excel, you can select cells with the mouse, because the Macro Recorder is able to recognize cell addresses). Similarly, you can use the mouse to select objects on a PowerPoint slide.

When you visit a dialog box as part of recording your macro, take into account all the dialog box settings. For example, if you visit the Font dialog box and choose 12 points on the Font Size list, the Macro Recorder duly records the 12-point font size, but it also records the Times Roman font in the macro if Times Roman happens to be the font that is chosen in the Font dialog box. The moral: Take account of all the settings in a dialog box when you visit it while recording a macro.

In dialog boxes with tabs, you cannot click tabs to switch from tab to tab and choose commands. Instead, click OK to close the dialog box, then reopen it, click a different tab, choose a command on the tab, and close the dialog box again.

8. **Click the Stop Recording button.**

The Macro Recorder records every action you take, but it doesn't record actions in real time. Take your time when recording a macro. Concentrate on taking the actions in the right order so that you don't need to adjust the code afterwards.

Running a Macro

If you assigned a macro to a toolbar button or keyboard shortcut, you can run it by clicking the button or pressing the shortcut keys. You can always run a macro by following these steps:

1. **Choose Tools⇨Macros⇨Macros or press Alt+F8.**

The Macros dialog box appears, as shown in Figure 2-3.

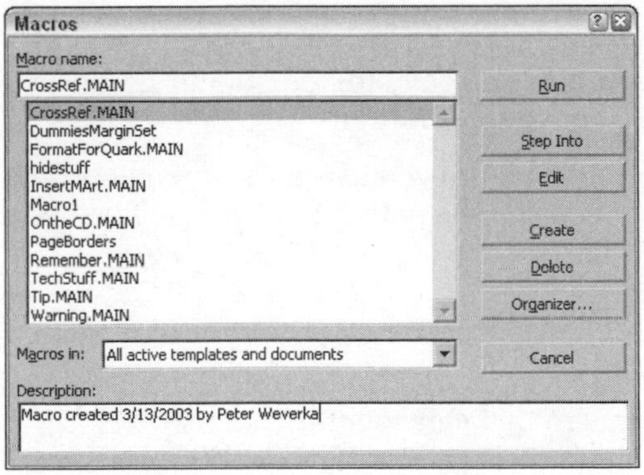

Figure 2-3:
The Macros
dialog box.

Book VIII
Chapter 2

Automating Tasks

2. **If the macro you want isn't shown in the dialog box, open the Macros In drop-down list and choose an option.**

3. **Select the macro you want to run.**

4. **Click the Run button.**

If your macro is a long one and you need to stop it from running, press Ctrl+Break (on most keyboards, the Break key is located along with the Pause key on the right side of the keyboard to the right of key F12).

Building Sample Macros for This Chapter

The rest of this chapter explains how to examine and edit macros in the Visual Basic Editor. To help you get acquainted with the Visual Basic Editor, create two macros, one in Word and one in Excel. Later in this chapter, you use these sample macros as you explore the various features of the Visual Basic Editor. You also combine the Word and Excel macros to build a third macro for use in both applications.

Creating a sample macro in Word

In Microsoft Word, create a new document and follow these steps:

1. **Enter** Sales Report: September 2003, **press the Enter key to go to the next line, and enter** Total Sales: $108,000.

2. **Select the text 108,000 (without the dollar sign), choose Insert⇨ Bookmark to open the Bookmark dialog box, enter** Sales_Total **in the Bookmark Name text box, and click the Add button to create the bookmark around the number.**

   The Bookmark dialog box closes.

3. **Click the Save button and save the document under the name Sales Report.doc in a convenient folder.**

   Remember the folder where you saved the document; you need it later. In this chapter, I'm using the path Z:\Users\Public\Reports\, but you need to substitute the correct path in your macros.

4. **Close your new document.**

Now that you've created and saved the sample document, you're ready to record the sample macro by following these steps:

1. **Choose Tools⇨Macro⇨Record New Macro to open the Record Macro dialog box.**

2. **Enter** Sales_Report_basis **in the <u>M</u>acro Name text box.**

3. **In the <u>S</u>tore Macro In drop-down list, make sure that the All Documents (Normal.dot) item is selected.**

4. **In the <u>D</u>escription text box, write a description along these lines:**
   Opens the Sales Report document, selects data, and then closes the document. Macro recorded 8/28/2003 by Jane Phillips.

5. **Click the OK button.**

   The Record Macro dialog box closes and the Macro Recorder appears.

6. **Choose <u>F</u>ile⇨<u>O</u>pen and, in the Open dialog box, navigate to where you saved the Sales Report.doc document, select the document, and click the <u>O</u>pen button.**

   Word opens the document.

7. **Press Ctrl+Home to move the insertion point to the start of the document (in case it's not already located there).**

8. **Press Ctrl+→ three times to move the insertion point to just before the words "September 2003."**

9. **Press Ctrl+Shift+→ once to select the word "September" (including the trailing space) and then press Shift+← once to deselect the trailing space.**

10. **Choose <u>I</u>nsert⇨<u>B</u>ookmark to open the Bookmark dialog box, select the Sales_Total bookmark, and click the <u>G</u>o To button.**

    Word selects the Sales_Total bookmark.

11. **Click the <u>C</u>lose button to shut down the Bookmark dialog box.**

12. **Choose <u>F</u>ile⇨Close to close the Sales Report.doc document.**

13. **Click the Stop Recording button.**

    The Macro Recorder stops recording the macro.

Creating a sample macro in Excel

Create the Excel workbook by taking the following steps:

1. **Click the New button to create a new workbook.**

2. **Name the first worksheet** North.

   To rename a worksheet, right-click its worksheet tab, choose <u>R</u>ename, and type the new name.

3. **Enter** January **in cell A2 and then drag the AutoFill handle to cell A13 to enter the rest of the months in column A.**

4. **Format column B with the Currency format and no decimal places.**

   To do that, choose Format➪Cells and, on the Number tab of the Format Cells dialog box, choose Currency in the Category list and enter **0** in the Decimal Places text box.

5. **Press Ctrl+Home to move the pointer to cell A1.**

6. **Click the Save button and save the document under the name Sales Report.xls in a convenient folder.**

   Remember the folder where you saved the document. In this chapter, I'm using the path Z:\Users\Public\Reports\, but you need to substitute the correct path in your macros.

7. **Close your new workbook.**

Now that you've created the sample worksheet, record the Excel macro by following these steps:

1. **Create a new workbook, name it Macro.xls, and save it in the same folder as the Sales Report.xls workbook.**

2. **Choose Tools➪Macro➪Record New Macro to open the Record Macro dialog box.**

3. **Enter** Temporary_Excel_Macro **in the Macro Name text box.**

4. **In the Store Macro In drop-down list, make sure that This Workbook is selected.**

   Leave the description in the Description text box. You'll delete this macro before long.

5. **Click the OK button.**

   The Record Macro dialog box closes and you see the Macro Recorder.

6. **Choose File➪Open and, in the Open dialog box, navigate to where you saved the Sales Results.xls workbook, select the workbook file, and click the Open button.**

   Excel opens the workbook.

7. **If the Relative References button in the Macro Recorder doesn't appear pushed in, click the button to start recording relative references rather than absolute references.**

When you move the pointer over the button, the pop-up box should say "Relative Reference."

8. **Choose Edit⇨Find and, in the Find and Replace dialog box, enter** September **in the Find What text box, and click the Find Next button.**

9. **Click the Close button to close the Find and Replace dialog box.**

10. **Press ← once to select the cell to the right of the cell with "September" in it.**

11. **Choose File⇨Save to save the workbook.**

12. **Choose File⇨Close to close the workbook.**

13. **Click the Stop Recording button to stop recording the macro.**

Making sure that the sample macros work

Before going any further, verify that the macros work as they should. Run the macros by following these steps from inside Word or Excel:

1. **Choose Tools⇨Macro⇨Macros or press Alt+F8 to open the Macro dialog box.**

2. **If necessary, open the Macros In drop-down list to specify where the macro is located.**

3. **Select the macro you want to test.**

   Scroll with the mouse or else type the first few letters of the macro's name to select it automatically.

4. **Click the Run button.**

   Which works faster, you or the macro? No offense, but I bet the macro runs faster than you do.

All about the Visual Basic Editor

The Visual Basic Editor, or VBE as it's known to the people who know and love it, is a program for creating and editing macros. These pages explain how to open a macro in the Visual Basic Editor, handle the Editor's Code window, find your way around the Editor, and construct a macro in the Editor. You also find out how to read macro codes and what all that mumbo-jumbo is.

**Book VIII
Chapter 2**

Automating Tasks

Opening a macro in the Visual Basic Editor

Open a macro in the Visual Basic Editor by following these steps:

1. **Choose Tools⇨Macro⇨Macros or press Alt+F8.**

You see the Macros dialog box.

2. **Select the macro you want to open.**

If your Macros dialog box lists many macros, typing the start of the macro's name in the Macro Name text box takes you to a macro faster than does scrolling to find it.

3. **Click the Edit button.**

The Visual Basic Editor opens, as shown in Figure 2-4. In the Code window, it displays the text of the macro.

Project Explorer window

Object drop-down list   Procedure (macro) drop-down list

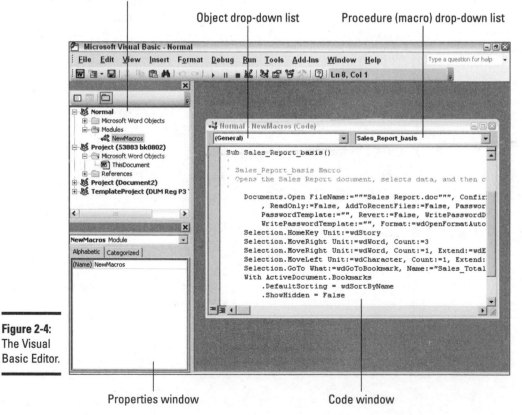

Figure 2-4:
The Visual
Basic Editor.

Properties window   Code window

When you close the application you were running when you opened the Visual Basic Editor, the Basic Editor closes as well.

Opening a macro by way of the Macros dialog box is the most convenient way to open the Visual Basic Editor, because the macro appears in the VBE window. However, you can also launch the Visual Basic Editor by choosing Tools⇨Macro⇨Visual Basic Editor or pressing Alt+F11. In the VBE window, you see the same Code windows that were open last time you saved your document, although the Code windows may be stacked in an unfamiliar order.

Displaying a macro in a Code window

To display the macro you want to work with in a Code window, do one of the following:

+ In the Project Explorer window (refer to Figure 2-4), scroll to a Modules folder, open it, and either double-click a macro name or select a name and click the View Code button.

+ Choose Tools⇨Macros. In the Macros dialog box, select the macro and click the Edit button. Use this technique when you can't remember which module houses the macro you want.

+ Open the Procedure drop-down list (refer to Figure 2-4) and select the macro's name.

Getting acquainted with the Visual Basic Editor

By default, the Visual Basic Editor displays three windows: the Project Explorer window, the Properties window, and the Code window (refer to Figure 2-4). The Project Explorer window and Properties window are on the left side of the screen; the Code window occupies the rest of the available space.

Again by default, the Project Explorer and the Properties window are *docked,* or snapped into position the way toolbars are in an Office application. To undock a window and be able to drag it elsewhere, double-click its title bar. You can resize undocked windows by dragging their borders. I suggest reducing the size of the Project Explorer to see more properties in the Properties window. To redock a window, double-click its title bar again.

You can prevent the VBE from docking the Project Explorer and Properties windows, and most other windows as well, by choosing Tools⇨Options and, on the Docking tab of the Options dialog box, clearing the appropriate check boxes.

The Project Explorer window

In the Project Explorer window is a list of the projects currently available to you. In VBA terminology, a *project* is an entity that contains VBA code. The word *Project* was inherited from Visual Basic, in which code is saved in a project file. Each project is the VBA part of a document, template, presentation, or workbook. In VBA, the word "project" is used more loosely to mean a storage container that is saved as part of another file.

VBA host applications — Word, Excel, PowerPoint, and so on — create different kinds of files, and they store VBA code in different ways. Table 2-1 explains how each Office application stores VBA projects. Depending on the host application you're working in, a single project or a dozen projects may be available to you.

Table 2-1	How Office Applications Store VBA Projects
Application	*How VBA Projects Are Stored*
Access	Each Access file can contain only one VBA project.
Excel	Each workbook or template can contain one VBA project.
FrontPage	FrontPage uses only the Microsoft_FrontPage project. This project stays open all the time you're running FrontPage.
Outlook	Outlook can have one project or multiple projects. Each project stays open all the time you're running Outlook.
PowerPoint	Each presentation or template can contain one VBA project.
Word	Each document and template can contain one VBA project. The Normal template (the global template that's always loaded) and any other global templates can each contain one VBA project as well.

As Figure 2-5 shows, items in the Project Explorer window are arranged in a collapsible tree in the finest Windows tradition. Each project appears as a separate item at the root level, and you can expand each project to display its contents in the same way you can open folders in Windows Explorer or My Computer. In the Project Explorer window, shown in Figure 2-5, two Word projects can be seen, one for the Normal document template and one for a document called Sales Report.

Each project can contain three VBA-standard object types: the Forms collection, the Modules collection, and the Class Modules collection, as well as other items peculiar to the host application. For example, each Word project (document or template) contains an item called Microsoft Word Objects;

each Excel project (workbook or template) contains an item called Microsoft Excel Objects.

Projects

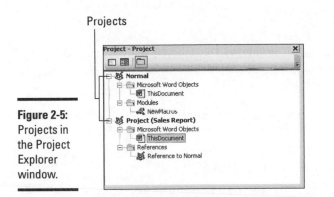

Figure 2-5:
Projects in
the Project
Explorer
window.

Here are brief explanations of the Modules collection, the Forms collection, and the Class Modules collection:

✦ **Modules collection:** Contains all the regular modules stored in the project. These modules contain macros that you record or write, and functions that you write. (You can't record a function with the Macro Recorder.) Each module can contain multiple macros and functions.

✦ **Forms collection:** Contains all the userforms stored in the project. A *userform* is essentially a blank dialog box on which you can position controls (text boxes, list boxes, command buttons, and so on) to create custom dialog boxes. You attach code to the userform and its controls to specify what they do. This chapter doesn't cover creating userforms.

✦ **Class modules collection:** Contains all the class modules stored in the project. Briefly, a *class* is a custom object that you create to store or process information. Class objects are an advanced topic and are not covered in this book.

The Properties window

The Properties window provides quick access to the properties of the object you're currently working with. When you're working in a code module, the only property you can set is the name of the module. By contrast, userforms and their controls each have numerous properties for specifying their appearance and behavior. For example, you specify the size of a userform by setting its Height property and its Width property.

The Code Window

The Code window is where you create and edit code. You'll start working in the Code window shortly.

Other windows in the Visual Basic Editor

Beyond the Project Explorer window, the Properties window, and the Code window (which are displayed by default), the VBE presents other windows that you need to use from time to time:

✦ **Object Browser:** For finding your way through an application's object model to the objects, methods, and properties you need.

✦ **Immediate window:** For executing a single line of code. Use this window to tweak or test code.

✦ **Locals window:** For displaying the value of expressions and variables. Following these values helps determine when errors creep into code.

✦ **Watch window:** For keeping tabs on expressions. For example, you can tell VBA to alert you when the value of an expression changes.

✦ **Call Stack window:** For seeing when one procedure calls another so that you can see trace code being executed by a procedure.

Examining the Word sample macro in the Code window

Reading the mumbo-jumbo codes in the Code window takes some getting used to, but there is method in this madness. Figure 2-6 shows code for the Word macro that you created earlier in this chapter (see "Creating a sample macro in Word"). Using that macro as an example, note the following in the Code window. (For Figure 2-6, I numbered the lines to make referring to lines easier; line numbers don't actually appear in the Code window.)

Figure 2-6: Codes for the Word sample macro.

```
 1. Sub Sales_Report_basis()
 2. '
 3. ' Sales_Report_basis Macro
 4. ' Opens the Sales Report document, selects data, and then closes
       the document. Macro recorded 8/28/2003 by Jane Phillips.
 5. '
 6.     Documents.Open FileName:="""Sales Report.doc""", _
           ConfirmConversions:=False, ReadOnly:=False, AddToRecentFiles:=False, _
           PasswordDocument:="", PasswordTemplate:="", Revert:=False, _
           WritePasswordDocument:="", WritePasswordTemplate:="", Format:= _
           wdOpenFormatAuto
 7.     Selection.MoveRight Unit:=wdWord, Count:=3
 8.     Selection.MoveRight Unit:=wdWord, Count:=1, Extend:=wdExtend
 9.     Selection.MoveLeft Unit:=wdCharacter, Count:=1, Extend:=wdExtend
10.     Selection.GoTo What:=wdGoToBookmark, Name:="Sales_Total"
11.     With ActiveDocument.Bookmarks
12.         .DefaultSorting = wdSortByName
13.         .ShowHidden = False
14.     End With
15.     ActiveDocument.Close
16. End Sub
```

The Visual Basic Editor applies different colors to different items. Most text is black, but keywords are dark blue by default, comments are green, and errors are red. (You can change this color scheme by choosing Tools⇨Options and, on the Editor Format tab of the Options dialog box, choosing new colors.)

Each macro begins with a *Sub line* (line 1) that contains the Sub keyword followed by the name you gave the macro (Sales_Report_basis in the sample macro), and parentheses. Each macro ends with an End Sub line (line 16) that consists of the End Sub keywords.

After the Sub line are four lines (lines 2–5) that begin with a single quotation mark ('). These are *comment lines*. Comment lines explain the macro and are strictly for the benefit of human beings. The VBA runtime system ignores them. You can write a comment about any line by starting the line with a single quotation mark and entering the line yourself. Another way to enter a comment is to display the Edit toolbar, click the Comment Block button, and type the comment. To "uncomment" a line, delete the single quotation mark manually; to uncomment a block, select it, display the Edit toolbar, and click the Uncomment Block button.

Line 6 opens the document by using a Documents.Open command. The key argument here is FileName, which specifies the filename of the document to be opened. Notice that the filename appears in three pairs of double-quotation marks ("). The outer set of double quotation marks indicates a text string. The inner two sets are a VBA convention for showing that the string itself starts and ends with double quotation marks. (The string includes these quotes because the filename contains spaces.) The document becomes the active document, which is represented in VBA by the ActiveDocument object.

The Visual Basic Editor has automatically broken line 6 into five lines and marked the end of each line with a blank space following by an underscore (_). You can break any line this way to make it fit in the Code window or make it easier to read. To break a long string, split it into two parts and join them with the & character, like so:

```
strMyString =  "First part of string " _ & "and second part
    of string"
```

Line 7 uses the MoveRight method to move the selection right by three "words." The Selection in VBA represents either the current selection (for example, a selected paragraph) or the current position of the insertion point (with nothing selected).

Line 8 also uses the `MoveRight` method, but with the `Extend:=wdExtend` argument to specify that the selection is extended rather than moved.

Line 9 uses the `MoveLeft` method with the `Extend:=wdExtend` argument to reduce the selection by one character (and thereby eliminate the space after the word "September").

Line 10 uses the `GoTo` method to move the selection to the `Sales_Total` bookmark.

Lines 11 –14 specify that the bookmarks are sorted by name and that hidden bookmarks are not displayed. These lines are superfluous, but notice the `With... End With` statement. Line 11 specifies that the lines up to the `End With` statement refer to the Bookmarks collection inside the `ActiveDocument` object. Lines 12 and 13 can then refer to items within the Bookmarks collection more briefly — for example, `.DefaultSorting` instead of `ActiveDocument.Bookmarks.DefaultSorting`.

Line 15 uses the `Close` method to close the active document.

Examining the Excel sample macro in the Code window

Figure 2-7 shows code for the Excel macro that you created earlier in this chapter (see "Creating a sample macro in Excel"). Using this macro as an example, note the following in the Code window. (Once again, I numbered the lines to make referring to lines easier.)

Figure 2-7: Codes for the Excel sample macro.

```
1. Sub Temporary_Excel_Macro()
2. '
3. ' Temporary_Excel_Macro Macro
4. ' Macro recorded 8/28/2003 by Jane Phillips
5. '
6. '
7.     Workbooks.Open Filename:= _
        " Z:\Users\Public\Spreads\Sales Results.xls"
8.     Cells.Find(What:="September", After:=ActiveCell, LookIn:=xlFormulas, _
       LookAt:=xlPart, SearchOrder:=xlByRows, SearchDirection:=xlNext, _
       MatchCase:=False, SearchFormat:=False).Activate
9.     ActiveCell.Offset(0, 1).Range("A1").Select
10.    ActiveWorkbook.Save
11.    ActiveWorkbook.Close
12. End Sub
```

Line 7 opens the workbook by using a `Workbooks.Open` command. As does the `Documents.Open` command in the Word macro, the `Filename` argument contains the name of the file to be opened. The workbook becomes the active workbook, represented in VBA by the `ActiveWorkbook` object.

Line 8 executes a Find command for the cell containing "September."

Line 9 uses the `Offset` method of the ActiveCell object (which represents the active cell) to select the cell to the right of the active cell.

Line 10 uses the `Save` method to save the active workbook, and line 11 uses the `Close` method to close the active workbook.

Fashioning a new macro in the Visual Basic Editor

To create a macro inside the Visual Basic Editor, you start by creating a new module to hold the macro. Then you manually enter code in the module or else copy the code from other macros. Better read on.

Creating a new module

Before you can create a new macro in the Visual Basic Editor, you need to create a new module to store the macro. Follow these steps to create a new macro:

1. **Decide which project to put the module in.**

   If you're working with Microsoft Word, for example, you can create the module in the Normal project (the Normal template) or a project attached to a document.

2. **Select the project in the Project Explorer window where you want to put the module.**

3. **Choose Insert⇨Module.**

   The Visual Basic Editor adds a new module to the Modules list, assigns it an automatic name (such as Module1), and displays an empty Code window for the module.

4. **In the Properties window, delete the automatic name in the (Name) box, enter a name of your own, and press Enter.**

   The Properties window, you remember, is located directly below the Project Explorer window. Module names can't include blank spaces or begin with a number.

   See that empty Code window to your right? That's where you enter the code for the new macro.

**Book VIII
Chapter 2**

Automating Tasks

Entering code in the Code window

The Visual Basic Editor offers these ways to enter macro code in a Code window:

✦ **Copy it:** Open a macro, copy code with the Edit➪Copy command, and then paste the code in the Code window. To select text in a Code window, drag over it.

✦ **Enter the code yourself:** Of course, you can always type the code on your own, provided that you know what you're doing and you have nimble fingers.

You can type VBA code in lowercase if you like. The Visual Basic Editor applies the correct case — uppercase or lowercase — to most terms when you move the insertion point to another line. However, some terms remain in lowercase.

As you enter the code, keep in mind the following rules and regulations:

✦ **Sub lines:** Macros begin with the key word Sub followed by the macro name, and end with the keywords End Sub.

✦ **Comments:** Comment lines begin with a single quotation mark ('). The Visual Basic Editor turns them green after you enter them. (If the line goes red and you get a "Compile Error: Expected End of Statement" message, you forgot to enter the single quotation mark.)

You don't have to indent code in the Visual Basic Editor, but indenting helps make code easier to read. Indent code by pressing the Tab key or clicking the Indent button on the Edit toolbar. "Outdent" code by pressing the Backspace key or clicking the Outdent button on the Edit toolbar.

Saving a macro you created

To save the macro you created, make sure that the Normal template (or one of its components) is selected in the Project Explorer; then click the Save button or press Ctrl+S.

Adding Message Boxes to a Macro

In the context of macros, a *message box* is a small dialog box that appears before the macro runs and offers the users a handful of options in the form of command buttons. Typically, the message box presents a choice of buttons such as OK, Yes, No, Ignore, Retry, and, of course, Cancel. The user must dismiss the message box or else make a choice in the message box before he or she can run the macro.

Message boxes give you an opportunity to let users decide how the macros run. A typical message box includes a preliminary statement that explains what the macro does and asks the user to decide whether to run the macro. Some message boxes ask the user to choose among different courses of action for the macro to take. Message boxes also notify the user when a macro has finished running and sometimes summarize the actions taken by the macro.

Message boxes in VBA

VBA provides considerable flexibility in its message boxes. The best way to display a message box in a macro is to use the `MsgBox` function. The basic syntax for this statement is

```
Result = MsgBox(Prompt[, Buttons] [, Title])
```

+ `Result` is the result that the message box returns. It tells you which command button the user clicked in the message box, and hence which course of action the macro should take.

+ `Prompt` is the text that appears in the message box. It can be 1,023 characters long.

+ `Buttons` is an optional argument that you can use to specify which command buttons the message box includes and whether it includes an icon. If you omit the `Buttons` argument, VBA displays a message box with only an OK button and no icon. Table 2-2 lists the main options for the `Buttons` argument.

+ `Title` is an optional argument that places the text in the message box's title bar. For example, you might put the macro's name in the title bar. If you omit `Title`, VBA puts the application's name in the title bar, which isn't particularly helpful to the person running the macro.

Table 2-2	Options for the Buttons Argument in Message Boxes	
Value	*Constant*	*Effect*
Controlling which buttons the message box includes		
0	vbOKOnly	OK button only
1	vbOKCancel	OK button, Cancel button
2	vbAbortRetryIgnore	Abort button, Retry button, Ignore button
3	vbYesNoCancel	Yes button, No button, Cancel button
4	vbYesNo	Yes button, No button
5	vbRetryCancel	Retry button, Cancel Button

(continued)

Table 2-2 *(continued)*

Value	Constant	Effect
Controlling which button is the default		
—	[No entry]	First button is the default
0	vbDefaultButton1	First button is the default
256	vbDefaultButton2	Second button is the default
512	vbDefaultButton3	Third button is the default
768	vbDefaultButton4	Fourth button is the default
Controlling which icon is displayed in the message box		
16	vbCritical	Displays a Stop icon
32	vbQuestion	Displays a question-mark icon
48	vbExclamation	Displays an exclamation-point icon
64	vbInformation	Displays an Information icon

As you can see from Table 2-2, the `Buttons` argument can consist of one, two, or three parts: the first part specifies which buttons are displayed; the second part which button is the default (if none is specified, the first button is the default); and the third specifies which icon (if any) accompanies the buttons. Icons give the user an idea of the nature of the message box. You can use the values or the constants to specify the details of the message box. Constants are best because they're easier to read and understand when you review code in the Code window. Use the Auto List Members drop-down list to enter the constants quickly without typing their full names.

Using a message box to control whether the macro runs

To make sure that no user runs your macro by accident, add a message box to the start of the macro after the variable declarations. Here's an example of how to do so:

```
lngResult = MsgBox("Enter your description of the message box
    here", _
    vbOKCancel + vbQuestion + vbDefaultButton2, "Transfer
    Info Macro")
If lngResult = vbCancel Then End
```

The first line displays a message box that contains a Yes button and a No button, with the No button the default, and a question mark icon. Figure 2-8 shows what the message box looks like.

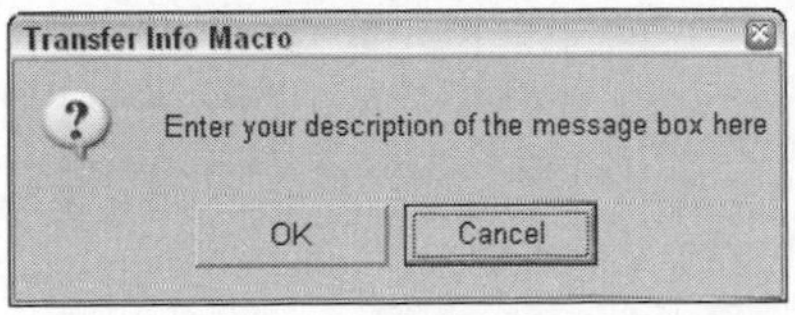

Figure 2-8:
Sample
message
box.

Checking which choice the user made in a message box

The MsgBox function returns a value or constant that represents the button the user clicked in the message box. Table 2-3 explains these values and constants. As before, using the constants is usually easier and clearer than using the values, even though doing so involves a little more typing.

Table 2-3	Values and Constants for the Buttons in a Message Box	
Value	*Constant*	*User chose this button*
1	vbOK	OK
2	vbCancel	Cancel
3	vbAbort	Abort
4	vbRetry	Retry
5	vbIgnore	Ignore
6	vbYes	Yes
7	vbNo	No

You can find out which button the user chose in the message box in two ways:

+ Assign the result of the message box to a variable that uses the variable lngResult. If lngResult is vbCancel, the End command ends the macro; otherwise, the macro continues.

✦ Build the message box into an If statement that checks which button was chosen (see the next section in this chapter).

To implement more choices than a single message box can offer, you can string multiple message boxes and input boxes together in sequence. But usually you'll do better to bite the bullet and learn to work with userforms so that you can create a single dialog box that offers all the choices you need. Few users tolerate struggling through a confusing sequence of message boxes and input boxes to make a few simple choices, but you may countenance this minor inconvenience in your own macros if you're reluctant to get up-to-speed with userforms or you simply need to produce quick-and-dirty macros in a short amount of time. For complex sequences of choices, you can even create your own wizards and let users move backward through the sequence of options so that they can amend the choices they've already made.

Presenting decisions in your code

In the previous section, you saw how to make a quick decision in your code by using an If...Then condition to evaluate the result of a message box. If...Then statements are very flexible and are the easiest way to present decisions in macro code.

If...Then is the simplest form of If condition. To give yourself more flexibility, you'll want to use either an If...Then...Else condition or an If...Then... ElseIf...Else condition.

If...Then...Else conditions let you specify what happens if a condition isn't met. Here's an example using simple message boxes:

```
Dim lngButton As Long
lngButton = MsgBox("Do you like chocolate?", vbYesNo +
    vbQuestion, "Chocolate")
If lngButton = vbYes Then
    MsgBox "Okay, we'll share.", vbOK + vbExclamation,
    "Chocolate"
Else    'the user must have clicked the No button
    MsgBox "Your loss, my gain.", vbOKOnly + vbExclamation,
    "Chocolate"
End If
```

If... Then... ElseIf... Else conditions let you specify one or more extra conditions by using one or more ElseIf statements. Here's an example using message boxes:

```
Dim lngClicked As Long
lngClicked = MsgBox("Click a button!", vbYesNoCancel, "Demo")
If lngClicked = vbYes Then
    MsgBox "You clicked the Yes button.", vbOKOnly, "Demo"
ElseIf lngClicked = vbNo Then
    MsgBox "You clicked the No button.", vbOKOnly, "Demo"
Else    'the user must have clicked the Cancel button
    MsgBox "You clicked the Cancel button.", vbOKOnly, "Demo"
End If
```

Using input boxes to get information from the user

You can get a single item of input from the person using the macro by using an input box. Depending on how you look at it, an input box is a message box with an extra text field or an ultra-simplified dialog box.

To display an input box in a macro, you use an InputBox statement. The basic syntax for this statement is as follows:

```
String = InputBox(Prompt[, Title], [Default])
```

+ String is the result the input box returns (more on this in a moment).

+ Prompt is a required argument that you use to specify the text that appears in the input box.

+ Title is an optional argument that specifies the text that appears in the input box's title bar.

+ Default is an optional argument that enters default text in the text box so that if the default text is right, the user can accept it by clicking the OK button.

Four other optional arguments are sometimes needed for special effects: XPos and YPos for specifying where the input box appears on-screen, and HelpFile and Context for adding a Help button linked to a topic in a Help file.

**Book VIII
Chapter 2**

Automating Tasks

For example, the following code creates a string variable named strUserName, displays the input box shown in Figure 2-9, and assigns the result of the input box to strUserName:

```
Dim strUserName As String
strUserName = InputBox("Please enter your name:",
    "Personalization Macro")
```

Figure 2-9:
A sample
input box.

When using an input box in your macros, make sure to take into consideration what happens if the user dismisses the input box without entering text. The user can dismiss the input box by clicking the Cancel button or by leaving the text box empty and clicking the OK button. Either action makes the input box return an empty string, which you represent in VBA by a pair of double quotation marks with no space between them:

```
CheckUserName:
strUserName = InputBox("Please enter your name:",
    "Personalization Macro")
If strUserName = "" Then GoTo CheckUserName
```

Here, CheckUserName is a *label* — a named location in the code — to which the If statement returns execution if the condition is met. In this case, the effect is to keep displaying the input box until the user enters text in the text box and clicks the OK button rather than the Cancel button.

Organizing Macros in the Visual Basic Editor

The Visual Basic Editor and the host applications provide various methods of organizing your macros. These are the easiest ways to copy, move, rename, and delete macros and modules:

✦ **Deleting a module:** Right-click the module in the Visual Basic Editor and choose <u>R</u>emove. To make sure that you don't lose any code accidentally, the VBE offers you the chance to export the module before removing it.

✦ **Copying a macro:** Display the macro in the Code window, select it, and give a Copy command. Display the module into which you want to paste the macro, position the insertion point, and then give a Paste command.

✦ **Moving a macro:** Make like you're copying a macro, but give the Cut command instead of the Copy command.

✦ **Renaming a macro:** Display the macro in the Code window and then type the new name in the Sub line. Alternatively, choose Tools⇨Macro⇨ Macros or press Alt+F8. In the Macros dialog box, select the macro and click the Delete button.

✦ **Deleting a macro:** Display the macro in the Code window, select it, and then press the Delete key.

✦ **Copying an entire module:** Drag the module from the source project to the destination project.

When you move, rename, or delete a macro, any associated menu item, toolbar button, or call from another procedure stops working.

Chapter 3: Embellishing Your Files with Art and Graphics

In This Chapter

- ✔ **Putting graphics and clip art images in files**
- ✔ **Creating and drawing lines, shapes, autoshapes, and WordArt images**
- ✔ **Changing an image's color and border**
- ✔ **Selecting, moving, and resizing objects**
- ✔ **Aligning and distributing objects on a page, slide, or worksheet**
- ✔ **Wrapping text around images in a Word document**

All the Office programs except Access and Outlook provide drawing tools that you can use to doodle, draw lines, draw shapes, and create autoshapes, not to mention import graphics and clip art images. This chapter is meant to bring out the artist in you. You may be pleasantly surprised to find out how easy dropping a clip art image or shape into a file really is.

This chapter explains how to put clip art images and graphics in files, draw lines and shapes, and create what Office calls "autoshapes" and WordArt images. You also find out how to tweak these lines and shapes in various ways. For example, this chapter explains how to fill a shape with a different color, crop it, and give it a third dimension. The last half of this chapter explains how to manipulate lines, shapes, and clip art images. You discover how to move, resize, rotate, align, distribute, and hogtie the images.

Inserting Clip Art and Graphics in Files

One of the easiest ways to spruce up an Office file — even an Excel worksheet — is to include a clip art image or graphic. Putting clip art images and graphics images in files is ridiculously easy. If you keep clip art, graphics, and photographs on your computer, you have a golden opportunity to embellish your files with something beyond the usual.

Table 3-1 lists the graphic file formats that are compatible with Office programs. The upcoming sidebar, "Bitmaps vs. vector graphics," describes the differences between the bitmap and vector graphics, the two types of graphics. You can bring a graphic into an Office file as long as it's in one of the formats listed in the table. (In some cases, however, you must have installed a graphics filter to import a graphic. Usually, you can install the graphics filters you need by re-installing Windows.)

Table 3-1	Graphic File Formats You Can Use in Office Files	
Format	*File Extension*	*Bitmap/Vector*
Bitmap File in RLE Compression Scheme	RLE	Bitmap
Computer Graphics Metafile	CGM	Vector
CorelDRAW	CDR	Vector
Device Independent Bitmap	DIB	Bitmap
Encapsulated PostScript	EPS	Vector
Enhanced Metafile	EMF	Vector
FashPix	FPX	Bitmap
Graphics Interchange Format	GIF	Bitmap
Interchange Format	JPG	Bitmap
Kodak Photo CD	PCD	Bitmap
Macintosh PICT	PCT	Vector
Microsoft Windows Bitmap	BMP	Bitmap
PC Paintbrush	PCX	Bitmap
Portable Network Graphics	PNG	Bitmap
Tagged Image File Format	TIF, TIFF	Bitmap
Windows Metafile	WMF	Vector
WordPerfect Graphics	WPG	Vector

Click where you want the image to go and use one of these techniques to insert it in your file:

✦ **Get the image from the Clip Art task pane:** Choose Insert⇨Picture⇨ Clip Art or click the Insert Clip Art button on the Drawing toolbar to open the Clip Art task pane and get the image there. Chapter 4 of this mini-book describes the Clip Art task pane in detail.

✦ **Use a file on your computer:** Click the Insert Picture from File button on the Drawing toolbar or choose Insert⇨Picture⇨From File and, in the Insert Picture dialog box, find and double-click the name of the graphic file whose image you want to insert.

Bitmap vs. vector graphics

All graphic images, including the ones listed in Table 3-1, fall in either the bitmap or vector category. A *bitmap graphic* is composed of thousands upon thousands of tiny dots called *pixels* that, taken together, form an image (the term "pixel" comes from "picture image"). A *vector graphic* is drawn with the aid of computer instructions that describe the shape and dimension of each line, curve, circle, and so on.

As far as Office is concerned, the difference between the two formats is that vector graphics do not distort when you enlarge or shrink them, whereas bitmap graphics lose resolution when their size is changed. Furthermore, vector images don't require nearly as much disk space as bitmap graphics. Drop a few bitmap graphics in a file and soon you're dealing with a file that is 500KB or 750KB in size.

Later in this chapter, "Handling Objects in Files" explains how to move an image or change its size. When you import a graphic into a Word document, it arrives as an inline graphic and can't be moved on the page. You can change that, however, by displaying the Picture toolbar, clicking the Text Wrapping button on the toolbar, and choosing an option besides In Line With Text on the pop-up menu.

Creating and Tweaking Shapes and Lines

Next in our tour of the Office Art Gallery are pointers for creating lines, arrows, shapes, autoshapes, curves, and WordArt images. And because you're so fussy and want things to be just so, you can also find out how to tinker with the appearance of the objects you can create with Office. Here, you discover how to change the color of lines, fill shapes with different colors, change the brightness and contrast of clip art images, crop an image, and give images a three-dimensional look.

Starting from the Drawing toolbar

To create a shape, line, or arrow, start by clicking a button on the Drawing toolbar, shown in Figure 3-1. To display this toolbar, choose View➪ Toolbars➪Drawing or right-click a toolbar and choose Drawing. Some Office programs also offer a button for displaying the Drawing toolbar — the Drawing button.

Figure 3-1:
The Drawing toolbar and two so-called objects (a clip art image and text box).

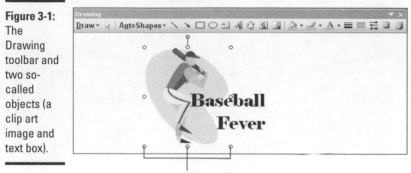

Selection handles

After you click the appropriate button, start dragging. As you drag, you can see the thing you're drawing take shape on-screen. Release the mouse button when your drawing is the right size. When drawing a rectangle or oval, you can hold down the Shift key as you drag to make a perfect circle or square.

When you click to select them, all lines and shapes — all objects — display drawing handles, as shown in Figure 3-1. Shapes have eight handles, one at each corner and one on each side. Lines have two drawing handles, one on each end. By dragging a drawing handle, you can change the size of a shape or line, as "Handling Objects in Files" explains, later in this chapter.

Creating AutoShapes

Besides the standard shapes that you can draw with the Rectangle and the Oval tool on the Drawing toolbar, you can draw *autoshapes* — unusual shapes such as polygons and stars. To draw an autoshape, click the AutoShapes button on the Drawing toolbar, choose an option on the pop-up menu, and select the shape you want to draw on the submenu. Figure 3-2 shows examples of different autoshapes you can draw. Hold down the Shift key as you draw an autoshape if you want it to retain its symmetry.

A yellow diamond, and sometimes two or three, appear on some autoshapes. By dragging the diamond, you can change the symmetry of the autoshape. Figure 3-2, for example, shows the same autoshape — the Quad Arrow Callout on the Block Arrows submenu — twisted into four different shapes. Notice where the diamonds are. By dragging a diamond even a very short distance, you can do a lot to change the symmetry of an autoshape.

Drawing lines and arrows

Your average user of Office has to draw an arrow now and then to point out, in a PowerPoint presentation or Word document, how well everything is going in some endeavor or another. Read on to find out how to draw a line, change its angle, and attach an arrow to the end of a line. You also discover how to draw curves, draw freeform, and draw a closed shape.

Drag a diamond to change an autoshape's appearance.

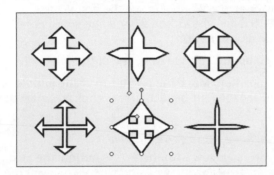

Figure 3-2:
A few so-called autoshapes, none shaped like an auto.

A word about Word's drawing canvas

When you start drawing a line or shape in Microsoft Word, the *drawing canvas* appears. The drawing canvas is meant to help you place objects such as lines and shapes on the page. Objects inside the drawing canvas are treated the same, meaning that you can move all the objects or change their size simultaneously with a single command. Here are techniques for handling the drawing canvas:

✔ **Drawing without the canvas:** To dispense with the drawing canvas, draw your line or shape outside the canvas or, if you've already drawn it, drag it outside the canvas. Then delete the drawing canvas if you care to do that.

✔ **Shrinking the drawing canvas:** When more than one object is in the drawing canvas, you can click the Fit button on the Drawing Canvas toolbar to make the canvas as large

as it needs to be to take in all objects. If necessary, right-click the drawing canvas and choose Show Drawing Canvas Toolbar on the shortcut menu to see the toolbar.

✔ **Changing the size of objects on the canvas:** To shrink or enlarge all the objects on the canvas simultaneously, click the Scale Drawing button on the Drawing Canvas toolbar and drag a selection handle on the canvas.

✔ **Dispensing with the drawing canvas:** The drawing canvas appears when you create a line, shape, or autoshape, but if you prefer that it not appear, choose Tools➪Options, select the General tab in the Options dialog box, and uncheck the Automatically Create Drawing Canvas when Inserting AutoShapes check box.

Drawing and editing a line or arrow

Drawing a line or arrow is much like creating a shape or autoshape: Select the Line or Arrow button on the Drawing toolbar, click in your document, and start dragging. The tricky part is getting line or arrow just right:

+ **Changing the angle:** Move the pointer over the selection handle at one end of the line or arrow. When you see the double-arrow, click and start dragging. A dotted line shows you what angle your line will have when you release the mouse button.

+ **Changing the length:** Click and drag one of the selection handles.

+ **Changing the position:** Move the pointer over the middle of the line and, when you see the four-headed arrow, click and start dragging.

Choosing an arrowhead style for an arrow

After you have drawn an arrow with the Arrow button, the next step is to choose what style arrowhead you want and where you want the arrowheads to go. Click to select the arrow and do one of the following:

+ Click the Arrow Style button on the Drawing toolbar and choose an arrow style from the pop-up menu.

+ Click the Arrow Style button and choose More Arrows on the Arrow Style pop-up menu. The Format AutoShape dialog box appears. Under Arrows, choose a Begin Style and End Style option for the arrows on either side of the line. Choose a Begin Size and End Size option as well.

Drawing curves and arcs

To draw a curve or arc, click the AutoShapes button on the Drawing toolbar, choose Lines on the pop-up menu, and choose Curve on the submenu. Then start dragging and click when you want to draw a curve. Each time you click, an *edit point* is made on the line, as shown in Figure 3-3. Double-click to complete the drawing.

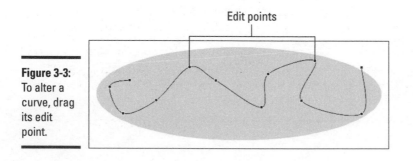

Figure 3-3: To alter a curve, drag its edit point.

Edit points

To change the angle of a curve, click to select it, click the D__r__aw button on the Drawing toolbar, and choose __E__dit Points on the pop-up menu. Edit points appear on the line, as shown in Figure 3-3. Drag an edit point to change the angle of a curve.

Suppose that you want to close off a drawing you have made to turn it into a shape, not a line. To close off a line and connect its beginning and end, right-click one end of the line and choose Close __P__ath.

WordArt for bending, spindling, and mutilating text

A *WordArt image* consists of a word that has been stretched, crumpled, or squeezed into an odd shape. Actually, it can have more than one word. Figure 3-4 shows the WordArt Gallery, where WordArt images are made, and an example of a WordArt image. After you insert a WordArt image, you can fool with the buttons on the WordArt toolbar and torture the word or phrase even further. Read on.

Figure 3-4:
A WordArt image.

Creating a WordArt Image

You can get a head start creating a WordArt image by typing and selecting the text you want in the image. Anyhow, follow these steps to insert a WordArt image in a document:

1. **Click in the page where you want the WordArt image to go and choose __I__nsert➪__P__icture➪__W__ordArt or click the Insert WordArt button on the Drawing toolbar.**

You see the WordArt Gallery dialog box, shown in Figure 3-4.

2. **Select a WordArt style and click OK.**

Don't worry about selecting the right style — you can choose a different one later on. You see the Edit WordArt Text dialog box.

3. **Enter the text for the image (if you didn't select it to begin with), choose a font and font size, and apply boldface or italics to the letters if you want.**

As I explain shortly, returning to the Edit WordArt Text dialog box later is easy, so don't agonize over choosing the right font and font size. You can amend your choices later.

4. **Click OK.**

The following sections in this chapter explain how to change the appearance and words in a WordArt image. See "Handling Objects in Files," later in this chapter, to move a WordArt image on the page or otherwise fiddle with it. As far as Office is concerned, the same commands apply to WordArt images, text boxes, and clip art when it comes to manipulating objects.

Editing a WordArt image

Usually, you have to wrestle with a WordArt image before it comes out right. By clicking buttons on the WordArt toolbar, you can win the wrestling match. (The WordArt toolbar is displayed when you click a WordArt image, but if for some reason you don't see it, choose <u>V</u>iew⇨<u>T</u>oolbars⇨WordArt.) Here are some pointers to help you wrestle with a WordArt image:

✦ **Changing the text, font, and font size:** Click the Edit Text button on the WordArt toolbar or double-click the image. You see the Edit WordArt Text dialog box that you used in the first place to create your image. Type new words, choose a new font or font size, and click OK.

 ✦ **Changing the Style of an image:** You don't like the WordArt style you chose when you created the image? You can choose a new one by clicking the WordArt Gallery button on the WordArt toolbar. In the WordArt Gallery dialog box (refer to Figure 3-4), select a new style and click OK.

 ✦ **Changing the color of the letters:** Click the Format WordArt button and choose new colors on the Colors and Lines tab of the Format WordArt dialog box. Experiment with the Fill Color list and the Line Color list, not to mention the Transparency slider, until your WordArt image is just so. Increase or decrease the weight of lines to make the letters in the image thicker or spindlier.

✦ **Stretching and skewing images:** To change the shape of an image, click and drag the diamond to stretch or scrunch the image, drag a selection handle, or click the WordArt Shape button on the WordArt toolbar and choose a new shape from the menu.

Click the WordArt Vertical Text button on the WordArt toolbar to flip an image so that letters appear one below the other instead of the usual way across the page.

Lines, line widths, and line colors for shapes

After you have drawn a line, arrow, shape, or autoshape, you can use tools on the Drawing toolbar to choose a line type, line width, and line color for the drawing, as shown in Figure 3-5. Here are techniques for selecting lines and colors:

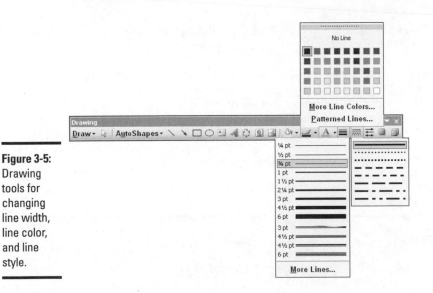

Figure 3-5:
Drawing
tools for
changing
line width,
line color,
and line
style.

✦ **Choosing a line type:** Click the Dash Style button and choose an option from the drop-down list, as shown in Figure 3-5.

✦ **Choosing a line width:** Click the Line Style button and choose an option. By choosing <u>M</u>ore Lines, the last option on the menu, you can open the Format dialog box and choose from many different kinds of lines on the <u>S</u>tyle drop-down list.

✦ **Choosing a line color:** Open the drop-down list on the Line Color button and select a color.

The other way to handle lines, line widths, and line colors for lines and shapes is to do so by choosing Line options on the Colors and Lines tab of the Format dialog box. To open this dialog box, double-click the line or shape you're dealing with.

Filling a shape with color

Filling a shape with color is easy: Select the shape, open the drop-down list on the Fill Color button on the Drawing toolbar, and choose a color. If no color suits you, you can choose More Fill Colors or Fill Effects on the pop-up menu:

✦ **More Fill Colors:** Opens the Color dialog box, where you can choose from 256 colors.

✦ **Fill Effects:** Opens the Fill Effects dialog box, where you can choose a fill effect, a gradient, texture, or pattern for the shape.

The Colors dialog box — the one you see when you choose More Fill Colors on the Fill Colors pop-up menu — offers a way to make transparent color. Transparent colors are especially useful in text boxes, because the text shows through and can be read easily. In the Colors dialog box, choose a color and then use the Transparency slider to choose how transparent a color you want. At 100%, the color is completely transparent and, in fact, not there; at 1%, the color is hardly transparent at all and you can't read anything underneath it.

Designating a design for all the objects you will work with

A command on the Draw menu called Set AutoShape Defaults makes putting borders and fills on shapes and autoshapes a little easier. To use this command, select an object with a border and fill what you want for the majority of the shapes and autoshapes you will work with in the file you're working on. Then choose the Set AutoShape Defaults command on the Draw menu (this menu is located on the Drawing toolbar). When you create a new shape or autoshape, it is given the same border and fill as the object that you chose as your official default object.

Experimenting with brightness and contrast

A clip art image or graphic can be a collaboration, not the work of a single artist. By selecting an image, displaying the Picture toolbar, and playing with the Image Control, More Contrast, Less Contrast, More Brightness, and Less Brightness buttons, you can collaborate with the original artist and create something new. Display the Picture toolbar and start experimenting with these options:

✦ **Changing the chromatics:** Click the Color button and choose <u>G</u>rayscale to see the image in shades of gray, <u>B</u>lack & White to see the *film noir* version, or <u>W</u>ashout to see a bleached-out image.

✦ **Changing the contrast:** Click the More Contrast or Less Contrast button as many times as necessary to either heighten or mute line and color distinctions. Use the aforementioned buttons in combination with the More Brightness and Less Brightness buttons to make the image clearer and easier to behold.

✦ **Changing the brightness:** Click the More Brightness or Less Brightness button as necessary to lighten or darken the image. These buttons are especially useful when you are experimenting with black-and-white images.

To get the original picture back if you experiment too enthusiastically, click the Reset Picture button on the Picture toolbar or click the Color button and choose Automatic on the drop-down list.

You can also experiment with contrast and brightness on the Picture tab of the Format dialog box. Right-click the image and choose Format to open this dialog box, where you find a <u>B</u>rightness and Co<u>n</u>trast slider for entering percentage settings. For the images in Figure 3-6, I chose (from left to right): 33% brightness, 66% contrast; 50% brightness, 50% contrast; and 66 % brightness, 33% contrast.

Figure 3-6: Experiments in brightness and contrast.

Putting a shadow or third dimension on an object

Yet another way to play interior decorator with your files is to give text boxes, shapes, autoshapes, WordArt images, or clip art images a shadow or third-dimension, or both, as shown in Figure 3-7. To call attention to an object this way, select it, click the Shadow Style or 3-D Style button on the Drawing toolbar, and choose an option on the pop-up menu.

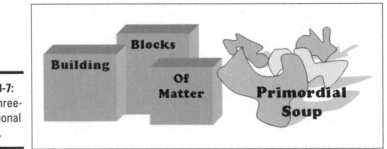

Figure 3-7:
Some three-dimensional objects.

If you want to get down and dirty with Shadow or 3-D effects, click the Shadow Style or 3-D Style button and select Shadow Settings or 3-D Settings on the pop-up menu. You see the Shadow Settings or 3-D Settings toolbar. These toolbars offer numerous commands for tweaking shadows and 3-D effects. Experiment at will. In the time it would take me to explain what these buttons do, you will have found one you like.

To remove a shadow from an object, click the Shadow Style button and choose the No Shadow option. To remove the third-dimension from an object, click the 3-D Style button and choose No 3-D.

Cutting off part of a graphic

You can *crop* — that is, cut off parts of — a graphic, but not very elegantly. To do that, select a graphic and click the Crop button on the Picture toolbar. The pointer changes into an odd shape with two intersecting corners on it. Move the pointer to a selection handle and start dragging. The dotted line tells you what part of a graphic you're cutting off. Sorry, you can crop off only the sides of a graphic. You can't cut a circle out of the middle, for example, proving once again that the computer will never replace that ancient and noble device, the scissors.

Suppose that you regret cropping your graphic. Besides clicking the Undo button, you can restore it to its original condition by selecting it and clicking the Reset Picture button on the Picture toolbar.

By the way, when you crop a graphic, you don't really cut off a part of it, not as far as your computer is concerned. All you do is tell Office not to display part of a graphic. The graphic is still whole. You can, however, compress a graphic after you crop it and in so doing truly shave off a part of the graphic and thereby decrease the size of the file you're working with. Deleting the cropped areas of a file can greatly decrease the size of a file when you're working with bitmap images, which take up a lot of disk space.

To truly delete part of a graphic, select it and click the Compress Pictures button on the Picture toolbar. In the Compress Pictures dialog box, make sure that the Delete Cropped Areas of Pictures check box is selected, uncheck the Compress Pictures check box, and choose the No Change option button under Change Resolution.

Handling Objects in Files

After you place a clip art image, graphic, text box, line, shape, autoshape, drawing canvas, or WordArt image in a document, it ceases being what it was before and becomes an *object*. That's good news, however, because the techniques for manipulating objects are the same whether you're dealing with a clip art image, graphic, text box, line, shape, autoshape, drawing canvas, or WordArt image. To move, reshape, draw borders around, fill in, align, distribute, or overlap an object, use the techniques described on the following pages.

Selecting objects

Before you can do anything to an object, you have to select it. To do so, click the object. You can tell when an object has been selected because *selection handles* appear on the sides and corners (for lines, only two selection handles appear, one on either side of the line). Follow these instructions to select more than one object at the same time:

✦ Hold down the Ctrl key and click the objects one at a time.

✦ Click the Select Objects button on the Drawing toolbar and drag slantwise across the objects to draw a box around them with the Select Objects pointer. All objects in the box are selected.

Moving an object

Moving an object on a page is easy enough. All you have to do is select the graphic, text box, shape, or whatever, wait till you see the four-headed arrow, click, hold down the mouse button, and drag the pointer where you want the object to be on the page or the drawing canvas. Dotted lines show where you're moving the object. When the object is in the right position, release the mouse button.

Grouping objects to make working with them easier

The Group command assembles different objects into a single object to make moving, copying, and reshaping objects easier. The Group command is a great way to enlarge or shrink different objects to the same degree. After objects have been grouped and made one object, drag a selection handle to enlarge or shrink all of them simultaneously. To use the Group command, select the objects that you want to "group" by Ctrl+clicking them or by drawing a box around them with the Select Objects pointer on the Drawing toolbar. Then do either of the following:

✔ Click the Draw button on the Drawing toolbar and choose Group on the pop-up menu.

✔ Right-click one of the objects you selected and choose Grouping⇨Group.

After objects are grouped, they form a single object with the eight selection handles. To add an object to a group, select the object and the grouped objects by Ctrl+-clicking; then choose the Group command again.

What are the Ungroup and Regroup commands on the Draw menu and shortcut menu for? To "ungroup" an object and break it into its components parts, perhaps to fiddle with one of the objects in the group, select the object and choose the Ungroup command. To reassemble the objects in a group, click an object that was formerly in the group and then choose the Regroup command. By the way, clip art images are composed of many different parts that have been grouped, as shown here:

If you have trouble easing an object into the right position, try one of these techniques:

✦ Hold down the Alt key as you drag. Doing so overrules the Grid settings in some Office programs and lets you move the object by smaller increments.

✦ Select the object, click the Draw button on the Drawing toolbar, choose Nudge, and then choose Up, Down, Left, or Right. Keep pressing F4 (the Repeat command) until the object looks just so.

If you can't move an object in a Microsoft Word document, it's because Word thinks that it is an inline image and shouldn't be moved. On the Picture toolbar or Drawing Canvas toolbar, click the Text Wrapping button and then click any button on the pop-up menu except In Line With Text. See also "Wrapping text around objects in Microsoft Word," later in this part, if you need to know how text wrapping works.

Resizing an object

How you change an object's size depends on whether you want to keep its proportions:

- ✦ **Changing size but not proportions:** To change the size of an object but keep its proportions, click the object and move the cursor to one of the selection handles on the *corners*. The cursor changes into a double-headed arrow. Click and start dragging. Dotted lines show how you're changing the size of the frame. When it's the size you want, release the mouse button.

- ✦ **Changing size and proportions:** To change both the size of an object *and* its proportions, move the cursor to a selection handle on the *side*. When the cursor changes into a double-headed arrow, click and start dragging. Dotted lines show how the object is being changed. When it is the size and shape you want, release the mouse button.

Figure 3-8 shows the same graphic at three different sizes. The original graphic is on the left. For the middle graphic, I pulled a corner selection handle to enlarge it but keep its proportions. For the one on the right, I pulled a selection handle on the side to enlarge it and change its proportions.

Figure 3-8:
Resizing a
graphic
image.

 If you want to get very specific about how big an object is, go to the Size tab of the Format dialog box. To do that, double-click the object to display the Format dialog box and select the Size tab. Then enter measurements in the Height and Width boxes. Go this route if you want to make objects the exact same size.

Rotating and flipping objects

To turn an object on its ear, as shown in Figure 3-9, start by selecting it. Then do either of the following:

✦ Move the pointer over the rotation handle, the green circle near the object. When the pointer turns into a curving arrow, click and start dragging.

✦ Click the Rotate Left 90° button on the Picture toolbar to turn the object 90 degrees.

Rotation handle

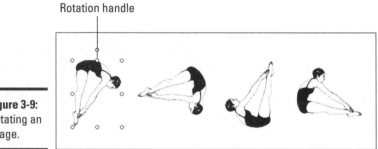

Figure 3-9: Rotating an image.

Aligning and distributing objects

The Align and Distribute commands come in handy when you want objects to line up with one another or be the same distance from one another. In Figure 3-10, for example, I used the Align and Distribute commands to make sure that the portraits are all lined up and an equal distance from one another. Use the Align and Distribute commands to give objects on a page, Web page, slide, or worksheet an orderly appearance.

Figure 3-10: The Align and Distribute commands at work.

Follow these instructions to align or distribute objects:

✦ **Align objects:** Ctrl+click to select the objects and then click the D<u>r</u>aw button on the Drawing toolbar, choose <u>A</u>lign or Distribute, and select an Align option.

✦ **Distribute objects:** Arrange the objects so that the outermost objects — the ones that go on the top and bottom or left side and right side — are where you want them to be. Then Ctrl+click to select all the objects, click the D<u>r</u>aw button on the Drawing toolbar, choose <u>A</u>lign or Distribute, and select a Distribute option. Office distributes the objects equally between the top and bottom object (if you chose Distribute <u>V</u>ertically) or the left-most and rightmost object (if you chose Distribute <u>H</u>orizontally).

Handling objects that overlap

Chances are, objects such as the ones in Figure 3-11 overlap when more than one appears on the same page, slide, or worksheet. And when objects are placed beside text, do you want the text to appear in front of the objects, or do you want the objects to cover up the text?

Figure 3-11: You can get interesting effects by overlapping objects.

The Office programs offer special Order commands for determining how objects overlap with one another and with text. Follow these steps to determine whether an object should overlap text or overlap other objects:

1. **Click the object to select it.**

2. **Click the D<u>r</u>aw button on the Drawing toolbar, choose O<u>r</u>der, and choose a Send or Bring command on the Order submenu.**

   You can also right-click an object, choose O<u>r</u>der, and choose a submenu command that way.

The commands on the O<u>r</u>der submenu can be confusing, but keep trying until the objects look just so. While you're at it, try displaying the Order toolbar and clicking the convenient buttons found there. To display this toolbar, move the pointer over the top of the Order submenu, click, and drag when you see the four-headed arrow.

Book VIII
Chapter 3

Embellishing Your
Files with Art

Making text appear in front of a graphic or clip art image

Follow these steps to make words and letters appear over a clip art image or graphic:

1. **Create a text box and enter the words in the text box.**

2. **Drag the text box on top of the image.**

3. **With the text box still selected, open the Fill Color pop-up menu on the Drawing toolbar and choose No Fill.**

4. **Open the Line Color pop-up menu on the Drawing toolbar and choose No Line.**

5. **If the image appears in front of the words, right-click the image, click Order on the** shortcut menu, and choose Send Behind Text on the submenu.

6. **If the image still appears in front of the words, right-click it again, click Order on the menu, and choose a Send command in the submenu to place the image behind the words.**

A dark image can obscure the words, even if it's placed behind them. To fix that problem, display the Picture toolbar and experiment with the Image Control, Contrast, and Brightness buttons to make the image less opaque (see "Experimenting with brightness and contrast," earlier in this chapter).

Wrapping text around objects in Microsoft Word

Word gives you lots of interesting opportunities to wrap text around text boxes, graphics, drawing canvases, and other objects in a document. By playing with the different ways to wrap text, you can create very sophisticated layouts. When you wrap text, you pick a wrapping style and the side of the object around which to wrap the text. Figure 3-12 figure demonstrates several of the wrapping styles and directions that text can be wrapped.

 The fastest way to wrap text is to select the object around which text is to be wrapped, click the Text Wrapping button, and choose an option from the drop-down list. You find the Text Wrapping button on the Picture and Drawing Canvas toolbars.

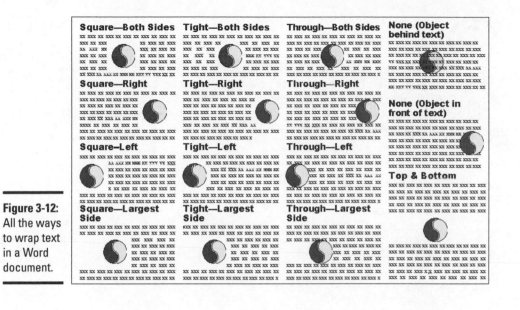

Figure 3-12:
All the ways
to wrap text
in a Word
document.

Follow these steps to wrap text around an object:

1. **Select the object by clicking it.**

2. **Right-click and choose Format, or else choose F̲ormat on the menu bar and then choose the last option on the F̲ormat menu (the option is named after the kind of object you're dealing with).**

3. **Select the Layout tab in the Format dialog box.**

4. **Select a box under Wrapping Style to tell Word how you want the text to behave when it reaches the graphic or text box.**

   The I̲n Line with Text option keeps text from wrapping around objects.

5. **Under Horizontal Alignment, tell Word where you want the object to be in relation to the text.**

   For example, choose the L̲eft option button to make the object stand to the left side of text as it flows down the page.

   If you want text to wrap to the largest side or to both sides without the object being centered, click the O̲ther option button and then click the A̲dvanced button. In the Advanced Layout dialog box, select the Text Wrapping tab, choose the Both S̲ides or the L̲argest Only option button, and click OK. The Text Wrapping tab also offers choices for telling Word how close text can come to the object as it wraps around it.

6. **Click OK.**

**Book VIII
Chapter 3**

Embellishing Your
Files with Art

Wrapped text looks best when it is justified and hyphenated. That way, text can get closer to the object that is being wrapped.

Click the Text Wrapping button on the Picture toolbar and choose <u>E</u>dit Wrap Points to choose precisely how close or far text is from the object. After you choose the command, *wrap points* — small black squares — appear around the object. Click and drag the wrap points to push text away from or bring text closer to the object in question.

Chapter 4: Managing the Microsoft Clip Organizer

In This Chapter

✔ Starting the Microsoft Clip Organizer program

✔ Cataloging the media files on your computer

✔ Finding and inserting a media clip in the file you are working on

✔ Organizing your media files so you can find them easily

As computers get faster and better, media files — graphics, video clips, and sound files — will play a bigger role in computing. Dropping a clip art image in a Word document or PowerPoint presentation won't be a big deal. Attaching a video clip to an e-mail message will be commonplace. Word-processed files will include sound icons that you can click to hear voice comments, whisperings, and grunts.

Microsoft, well aware that the future is closing in on us, created the Clip Organizer to help you manage the media on your computer. Using the Clip Organizer, you can place graphics, video clips, and sound in files in Word documents, Excel worksheets, PowerPoint presentations, Publisher publications, and FrontPage Web pages (but not Access databases or Outlook anythings). More important, the Clip Organizer is the place to organize media files on your computer so that you can find them and make good use of them. This chapter explains how to manage the Microsoft Clip Organizer.

Opening the Microsoft Clip Organizer

Do either of the following to open the Microsoft Clip Organizer:

✦ **Open the Clip Organizer:** Click the Start button and choose All Programs⇨Microsoft Office⇨Microsoft Office Tools⇨Microsoft Clip Organizer. As shown in Figure 4-1, the Clip Organizer window opens with the My Collections folder open and the Favorites folder selected (if this is the first time you've opened the Clip Organizer, see the sidebar "Automatically cataloging the media files on your computer," later in this chapter). As you will find out shortly, you can keep your favorite media files and images in the Favorites folder and be able to find them there quickly when you want to insert them in files.

Click a button to change views.

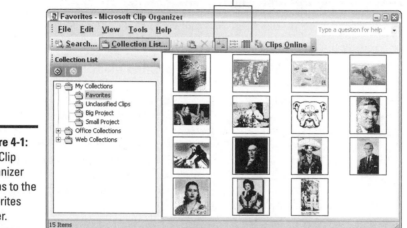

Figure 4-1: The Clip Organizer opens to the Favorites folder.

✦ **Open the Clip Organizer within the program you are running:** Choose Insert⇨Picture⇨Clip Art or click the Insert Clip Art button on the Drawing toolbar. The Clip Art task pane opens. This task pane gives you an entrée into the Clip Organizer.

Although media files appear to be organized into folders in the Clip Organizer, those folders don't really exist on your computer. The folders really represent categories. Inside each category are shortcuts similar to the shortcuts on the Windows desktop that tell your computer where the files are located on your computer. When you place a file in the Clip Organizer window, what you are really doing is placing a shortcut to a file located somewhere on your computer or network.

Media files are classified into three folders in the Collection List. In the Clip Art task pane, you can see these folders by opening the Search In drop-down menu.

Automatically cataloging the media files on your computer

The first time you open the Clip Organizer, you see the Add Clips to Organizer dialog box, which asks whether you want to catalog the clip art, sound, and video files on your computer. Don't do it! If you click OK, you will crowd the Clip Organizer with all kinds of extraneous files. You'll end up with sound files and graphics from every trivial program that is installed on your computer.

For now, click the Later button to postpone cataloging your media files. When you're ready to start cataloging, use one of these techniques for doing it:

✔ **Pick and choose which files to catalog:** Choose File➪Add Clips to Organizer➪On

My Own and select files in the Add Clips to Organizer dialog box. See "Putting your own media files in the Clip Organizer," later in this chapter, for details.

✔ **Catalog media files in folders:** Choose File➪Add Clips to Organizer➪Automatically to open the Add Clips to Organizer dialog box; then click the Options button. You see the Auto Import Settings dialog box. It lists every folder on your computer that holds media files. Go down the list, unselecting folders with meaningless media files and selecting folders with media files you may find useful. Then click the Catalog button to catalog the media files you really need.

Add Clips to Organizer

Add Media Clips

Clip Organizer can catalog picture, sound, and motion files found on your hard disk(s) or in folders you specify.

Click OK to catalog all media files. Click Cancel to quit this task. Click Options to specify folders.

[OK]   [Cancel]   [Options...]

✦ **My Collections:** Your favorite media files (in the Favorites folder), collections you organized yourself, the names of folders on your computer where the Clip Organizer found media files if you cataloged the media files on your computer (the next section in this chapter describes cataloging), and files you downloaded from Microsoft.

✦ **Office Collections:** Media files you installed along with Office.

✦ **Web Collections:** Media files from third-parties who provide clips online.

Locating Media Files in the Clip Organizer

Before you can insert a media file from the Clip Organizer, you have to find it. Find it by conducting a keyword search or by digging into a Clip Organizer folder. Better read on.

Before you conduct a search, connect your computer to the Internet. By doing so, you can access the numerous media files that Microsoft maintains at its Web site.

The Thumbnails, List, and Details buttons in the Clip Organizer come in very handy when you are rummaging around for a media file. Click the Thumbnails button to see thumbnail images of graphic files (refer to Figure 4-1), the List button to get a simple list of file names, or the Details button to see file types and file sizes.

Searching by keyword for a media file

Click the Search button in the Clip Organizer (or choose View⇨Search) to open the Search task pane. If you are working out of the Clip Art task pane, you're ready to go. Negotiate these text boxes or drop-down menus to describe the file or files you are looking for:

✦ **Search For:** Enter a keyword that describes what you're looking for.

✦ **Search In:** Select the folder that you want to search in (select the Everywhere folder to search in all the Clip Organizer folders).

✦ **Results Should Be:** Choose which type of media you're seeking — clip art, photographs, movies, or sounds. By clicking the plus sign (+) next to a media type, you can look for files of a certain kind. To look for JPEG photographs, for example, click the plus sign next to Photographs and select the check box beside JPEG File Interchange Format.

Click the Go button to begin the search. If the Clip Organizer can find what you're looking for, files appear in the window.

Getting a file from a Clip Organizer folder

If you know where the media file you need is catalogued in the Clip Organizer, click the Collection List button (or choose View⇨Collection List) and open the folder where the file is found. The file appears on the right side of the window.

Getting media files from Microsoft

Microsoft has ambitious plans for permitting users of Office to get their clip art, sound files, and video clips from the Microsoft Web site. To see what kind of media Microsoft offers online, click the Clip Art on Office Online hyperlink (or the Clips Online button). After your machine connects to the Internet, you come to a Web page where you can download collections of clip art and other media files to your computer.

When you find a file you like, open its drop-down list and choose Add to Selection Basket. To download the files to your computer, click the Download Items link. Items you download from the Microsoft Web site land in the My Documents\My Pictures\Microsoft Clip Organizer folder on your computer. In the Clip Organizer, you will find the files in the My Collections\Downloaded Clips folder.

Inserting a Media File

After you've found the file you want, the next step is to insert it into a Word document, Excel worksheet, PowerPoint slide, Publisher publication, or FrontPage Web page:

✦ **Clip Organizer:** Open the file's drop-down list and choose <u>C</u>opy. Then click in your file where you want the clip art image, graphic, sound file, or video clip to go and choose <u>E</u>dit⇨<u>P</u>aste (or press Ctrl+V).

✦ **Clip Art task pane:** Open the file's drop-down list and choose <u>I</u>nsert.

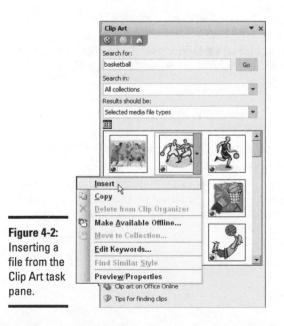

Figure 4-2:
Inserting a file from the Clip Art task pane.

Organizing Files in the Clip Organizer

The Clip Organizer can be a mighty convenient place for storing the media files you use in your work. And as good as it is, it can be made even better. These pages explain how to put media files in the Favorites folder where you can get them quickly, create a folder of your own for storing media files, and catalog the media files on your computer.

Copying or moving files to the Favorites or other folder

Suppose you come upon a media file in the Clip Organizer that looks intriguing. You tell yourself, "Maybe I'll use that one someday." In moments like that, be sure to copy or move the file to the Favorites folder or another folder of your choosing. That way, you can find it easily when you need it.

Follow these steps to copy or move a media file to the Favorites folder or another folder in the Clip Organizer:

1. **Find and select the files you want to copy or move.**

   To select more than one file, switch to List or Details view (click the List or Details button, or choose an option on the View menu); Then Ctrl+click the files to select them.

2. **Give the Copy to Collection or Move to Collection command.**

   How you give this command depends on how many files you selected:

   - **One file in Thumbnails view:** Open the file's drop-down list and choose Copy to Collection or Move to Collection.

   - **More than one file in List or Details view:** Right-click any file you selected and choose Copy to Collection or Move to Selection.

   You see the Copy to Collection or Move to Collection dialog box, as shown in Figure 4-3.

3. **Select a folder in the dialog box.**

   If necessary, click the plus sign (+) beside a folder to display its subfolders.

4. **Click OK.**

To remove a file from a folder, select it and click the Delete from Clip Organizer button or press the Delete key.

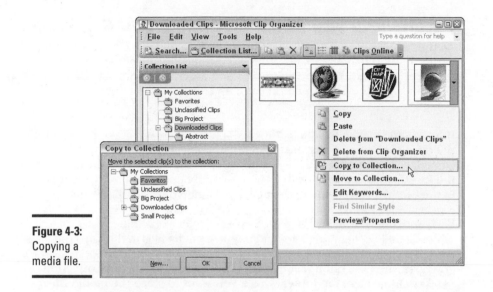

Figure 4-3:
Copying a
media file.

Creating your own folder for the Clip Organizer

If you work with a lot of media files, organize them into folders. Put photographs in a Photographs folder. Put music files in a Music folder. That way, you can find media files simply by going to the folder where you placed them. Follow these steps to create a new folder in the Clip Organizer:

1. **Choose File⇨New Collection.**

   The New Collection dialog box appears.

2. **Select the folder in which to place your new folder.**

   Selecting "My Collections" is the best choice, probably, but place your new folder wherever you want.

3. **Enter a name for the folder in the Name box.**

4. **Click OK.**

If you need to rename a folder, select it in the Collection List, choose Edit⇨ Rename, and type a new name. To remove it, choose Edit⇨Delete from Clip Organizer.

Book VIII
Chapter 4

Managing the
Clip Organizer

Putting your own media files in the Clip Organizer

As the "Automatically cataloging the media files on your computer" sidebar earlier in this chapter explains, the Clip Organizer can scour your computer for clip art, sound files, and video files and enter their names in the Clip Organizer. But the Clip Organizer can't inventory all the media files on your computer.

How would you like to catalog the media files you keep on your computer — the ones that the Clip Organizer couldn't inventory, that is — in the Clip Organizer? Remember: The files in the Clip Organizer are merely pointers to the locations of real files on your computer. By putting your own media files in the Clip Organizer, you make it easier to find your own media files.

You can store your own files in the Favorites folder or a folder you created yourself. Follow these steps to put your own media files in the Clip Organizer:

1. **Click the Collection List button, if necessary, to see the Collection List, and select the folder where you want to store the media files.**

2. **Choose File➪Add Clips to Organizer➪On My Own.**

   The Add Clips to Organizer dialog box appears.

3. **Select the file or files whose names you want to store in the Clip Organizer.**

   If you change your mind about which folder to put the files in, you can click the Add To button and, in the Import to Collection dialog box, choose a different folder.

4. **Click the Add button.**

To remove a media file from the Clip Organizer, select it and click the Delete from Clip Organizer button or press the Delete key.

Chapter 5: Note Taking with OneNote

In This Chapter

✔ Getting acquainted with OneNote

✔ Storing notes in sections, pages, and subpages

✔ Writing and drawing notes

✔ Organizing and finding stray notes

✔ Using OneNote in conjunction with other Office programs

Microsoft OneNote is designed for taking notes at meetings and conferences and taking notes while you're talking on the telephone. Rather than scribble notes indiscriminately in a Word document, you can enter them in OneNote, organize them into sections and pages so that they can be retrieved easily, and copy them very easily into Excel, PowerPoint, Word, or another Office program. OneNote comes with all sorts of amenities for finding and filing notes. I could be wrong, but I think the program was designed chiefly for people who are fond of brainstorming at their computers.

This chapter explains what OneNote is, how you can use it to write notes, and how to organize and find notes. Finally, this chapter explains a couple of tricks for recycling notes into other Office programs.

Running OneNote

Do one of the following to run OneNote:

✦ Click the Start button and choose All Programs➪Microsoft Office➪ Microsoft Office OneNote.

 ✦ Double-click the OneNote icon in the notification area of the taskbar (it's located in the lower-right corner of the screen next to the clock). If you don't see the icon in the system tray and you want to see it there, choose Tools➪Options, select Other in the Options dialog box, and select the Place OneNote icon in the Notification Area of the Taskbar check box.

OneNote opens to the section and page or subpage that was open the last time you closed the program. What is a section, page, and subpage? Better keep reading.

Introducing OneNote

Figure 5-1 shows the OneNote window with three sections open. In OneNote lingo, all notes are kept in the Notebook, the Notebook is divided into *sections,* and each section is divided into *pages* and *subpages.* Besides confusing you, the idea behind storing notes in sections, pages, and subpages is to help you organize and locate notes. Create a section for each new task you will undertake — for each new staff meeting, conference, or client. Within the sections, store your notes in pages and subpages (if using subpages proves really necessary).

Page title   Section tabs   Page header   Page and subpage

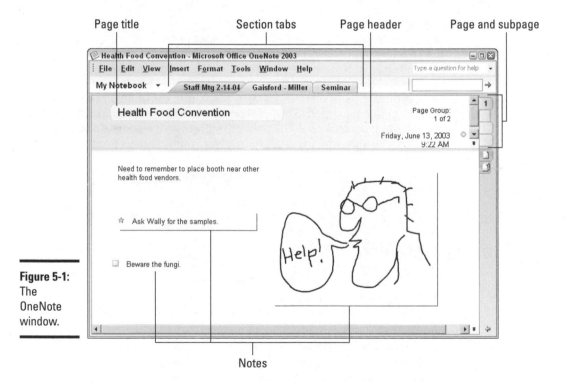

Figure 5-1: The OneNote window.

Notes

Here are ways to get from section to section or page to page in the OneNote window:

✦ **Go to a different section:** Click a section tab along the top of the window (refer to Figure 5-1), or click the My Notebook button and choose a section name on the drop-down list.

✦ **Go to a different page:** Click a page or subpage tab on the right side of the window (refer to Figure 5-1). Page tabs are large and have round corners; subpage tabs are square. You can also click the Back and Forward buttons on the Standard toolbar to revisit pages.

Move the pointer over a page tab and you see a pop-up message with the page's title, its number, and its creation date. To make page titles rather than page numbers appear on page tabs, choose View➪Titles in Page Tabs or click the Show Page Titles button in the lower-right corner of the window.

Creating Sections and Pages for Storing Notes

Before you jot down your first note, create a section and page or subpage for storing it:

✦ **Creating a new section:** Click the New Section button or choose Insert➪New Section. Then type a name for the section on its section tab. To rename a section, right-click its tab, choose Rename, and start typing.

You can color-code sections to distinguish one section from the next. To change a section's color, right-click its tab, choose Section Color, and choose a color on the submenu.

✦ **Creating a new page:** Each section comes with one page, but if you need more pages, press Ctrl+N or click the New Page button. A new page appears, as does a Title text box for entering a descriptive title for the new page (refer to Figure 5-1). Enter a page title to help identify the notes you will put on the page.

✦ **Creating a new subpage:** Display the page under which you will create a subpage and choose Insert➪New Subpage or press Ctrl+Shift+N. Subpages adopt the title of the pages to which they are subordinate. In OneNote terminology, a page and all its subordinate pages is called a *group*.

Most people don't need subpages. A subpage is subordinate to another page, and unless you're taking a copious number of notes, you don't need subpages.

Each time you create a new section, you also create a new OneNote Sections (.one) file. These files are stored in the C:\Documents and Settings*Your Name*\My Documents\My Notebook folder, in case you're looking for them and want to back them up.

Opening and Closing Sections

Do the following to open and close sections:

✦ **Opening a section:** Choose File⇨Open and select a section name in the File Open dialog box. You can also open the File menu and choose from the last five sections you opened at the bottom of the menu.

✦ **Closing a section:** Right-click a section tab and choose Close, or choose File⇨Close (or press Ctrl+W).

OneNote is unusual among Office programs in that it doesn't have a Save button or Save command. Every 30 seconds, OneNote saves all the notes for you. You needn't concern yourself with whether notes are being saved.

Writing Notes

Although the program is called OneNote, you can enter two kinds of notes — typed notes and drawings. Moreover, if you're using a Tablet PC to scribble your notes, OneNote can (at least in theory) recognize whether you're writing by hand or drawing. These pages explain how to write and draw notes.

Notes appear in what are called *containers,* as shown in Figure 5-2. Move the pointer over the top of a container and you see the four-headed arrow. At that point, you can click and drag a note elsewhere. Drag the little arrows in the upper-right corner of a container to change the container's width.

Typing a note

To type a note, simply click and start typing. Press the Enter key to begin a new paragraph in a note. You can draw upon the commands on the Formatting toolbar — do you recognize them from Microsoft Word? — to format the text or change its color.

Drag the bar to move a note.   Drag an arrow to change size.

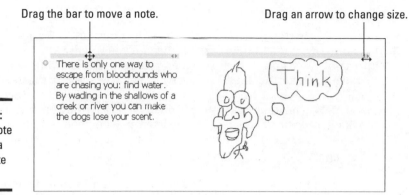

Figure 5-2:
A typed note
(left) and a
drawn note
(right).

To get more room on a page for notes, try removing the page header. To
remove or display page titles, choose View⇨Page Header.

Jotting down a side note

Suppose you're brainstorming and you come up
with an idea that cries out to be preserved in a
note. To quickly jot down your note, write a
"side note" in the small but convenient Side
Note window. This window works in cahoots
with OneNote to help you record ideas before
you forget them. When you enter a note in the
window, it's entered as well in the OneNote
window in a special section called Side Notes.
Next time you open OneNote, you can open the

Side Notes section and see the notes you
wrote. From there, you can read the note you so
hurriedly jotted down and perhaps copy or
move it to another section.

To open the Side Note window, click the
OneNote icon in the notification area or press
Windows key+N. Enter your note and click the
Close button in the Side Note window when
you're finished jotting down the note.

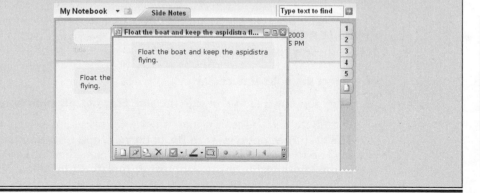

Drawing a note

Use the Pen button to draw a note. Click the down arrow beside the button to choose a color and thickness for the line you will draw. The pointer turns into a dot. Click and start drawing. As you draw, the drawing canvas enlarges to make room for the lines. Press the Esc key when you're finished drawing.

If you make a mistake in a drawing, click the Eraser button and then click the line you want to erase. Press the Esc key when you're finished erasing. You can also erase the last line you drew by choosing Edit➪Undo Inking (or pressing Ctrl+Z).

To get a better look at all the pens and highlighters you can choose among when drawing, display the Pens toolbar. To do so, choose View➪Toolbars➪Pens or right-click a toolbar and choose Pens.

Finding and Keeping Track of Notes

If you're an habitual note taker, you may find yourself drowning in notes. You won't be able to find the note you're looking for. The great idea you had may be lost forever. To keep notes from getting lost, these pages explain how to find stray notes and how to organize notes so that they don't get lost in the first place.

Flagging notes for follow up

The best way to keep notes from getting lost is to carefully place them in sections and pages. Short of that, you can flag notes to make it easier to follow up on them. OneNote offers five ways to flag notes. After you flag a note, you can search for it by opening the Note Flags Summary task pane, arranging notes according to how they were flagged, and pinpointing the note you want, as shown in Figure 5-3.

Flagging a note

Follow these steps to flag a note:

1. **Select the note, if necessary.**

2. **Click the down arrow beside theNote Flag button and choose a flag option.**

   The first three options — To Do, Important, and Question — place an icon on the note. The last two options — Remember for Later and Definition — highlight the note text, respectively, in yellow or green.

Arrange notes by flag.

Choose a flag.

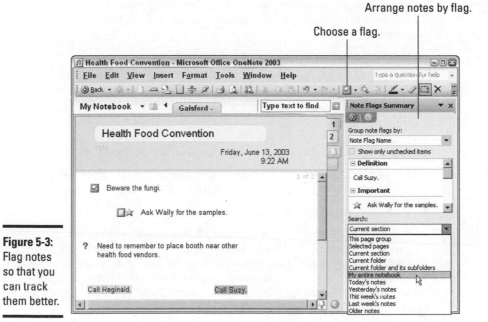

Figure 5-3:
Flag notes
so that you
can track
them better.

Arranging flagged notes in the task pane

Follow these steps to arrange notes in the Note Flags Summary task pane:

1. **Click the Note Flags Summary button or choose View⇨Note Flags Summary.**

You see the Note Flags Summary task pane (refer to Figure 5-3).

2. **Open the Group Notes By drop-down list and choose an option.**

These options determine the order in which flagged notes appear in the task pane. Note Flag Name, for example, arranges notes according to which icon they have been tagged with; Section arranges notes under section names; Note Text arranges the notes in alphabetical order.

3. **Open the Search drop-down list and choose an option.**

These options determine which notes appear in the task pane. Current Section, for example, assembles flagged notes only from the section that appears on-screen; My Entire Notebook puts flagged notes from all sections in the task pane.

**Book VIII
Chapter 5**

**Note Taking with
OneNote**

To remove flags from notes, select the notes and press Ctrl+0 or open the drop-down list on the Note Flag button and choose R̲emove Note Flags from Selection.

Finding a lost note

To find a lost note, you must be able to remember a word or two in the note. Open the sections you want to search in and follow these steps to chase down a lost note:

1. **Enter the word or phrase you're looking for in the Search box.**

This box is located in the upper-right side of the OneNote window. If you don't see it, press Ctrl+F or choose E̲dit⇨F̲ind.

 2. **Click the Find button.**

If the search text can be found, OneNote moves to the first instance of the search text. If the text is found in more than one note, click the Next Match (or Previous Match) button to go to the next or previous instance of the search text. You can also click the View List button to see a list of all notes with the search terms in the Page List task pane. Select a note in the task pane to view a note.

3. **Click the Close button beside the Search box when the search is complete.**

Some Housekeeping Chores

Unless you play loud soul music while you're doing it, housekeeping can be a tedious and irksome activity. Here are methods for handling a few housekeeping chores:

✦ **Selecting notes:** Click the bar along the top of a note to select it. Ctrl+click to select several notes. If you have trouble selecting notes, click the Selection Tool button and drag across the notes.

✦ **Moving notes to another page:** Use the tried-and-true cut-and-paste method. Select the note, right-click, choose Cu̲t, right-click on the page where you want to move the note, and choose P̲aste.

✦ **Moving a page to another section:** Before you can move or copy a page from one section to another, both sections must be open. To move or copy a page, right-click the page's tab and choose M̲ove Page To⇨A̲nother Section. You see the Move or Copy Pages dialog box. Select a section name and click the M̲ove or C̲opy button.

+ **Deleting notes:** Select the notes you want to delete and click the Delete button or press the Delete key.

+ **Deleting a section:** Right-click the section tab and choose <u>D</u>elete. Because each section is actually a file, you can recover a section you deleted accidentally by retrieving it from the Recycle Bin.

+ **Deleting a page or subpage:** Right-click the page tab and choose <u>D</u>elete. Pages you delete land in the Deleted Pages folder, where they remain until you close OneNote and the Deleted Paged folder is emptied. To recover a deleted page, click the My Notebook button and choose Deleted Pages on the drop-down list. Deleted pages reappear.

To keep deleted pages on hand after you close OneNote, choose <u>T</u>ools➪ <u>O</u>ptions and, in the Options dialog box, click Editing and then unselect the Empty Deleted Pages Folder on OneNote Exit check box.

OneNote and Other Office Programs

OneNote works hand in hand with its brothers and sisters in the Office suit. These pages describe how to copy notes into other programs, send notes by e-mail, turn a note into a Web page, and make a note into an Outlook task.

Copying a note into another Office program

To copy a note into another program, use the copy-and-paste command. Select the note, right-click it, and choose <u>C</u>opy. Then go to the other program, right-click, and choose <u>P</u>aste. Typed notes land in the other program in the form of text. Drawn notes taking the form of, you guessed it, drawings.

Sending notes by e-mail

As long as Outlook is installed on your computer, you can send the notes on a page by e-mail to someone else. The notes are sent both in the body of the e-mail message and as file attachments. Follow these steps to send notes:

1. **Open the page with the notes you want to send.**

Unfortunately, you can't send a single note unless it's the only one on the page.

2. **Click the E-Mail button on the Standard toolbar or press Ctrl+Shift+E.**

You see a dialog box for sending the note.

3. **In the Introduction text box, enter a message to accompany the notes.**

4. **Click the Send a Copy button.**

   The page of notes is sent by way of Outlook.

If you prefer to send notes in e-mail messages rather than attach them as files, choose <u>T</u>ools⇨<u>O</u>ptions, select E-Mail in the Options dialog box, and unselect the Attach a Copy of the Original Notes as a OneNote E-Mail file check box.

Turning a note into an Outlook task

As Book II, Chapter 5 explains, an Outlook task is a reminder to do something. To place a note in the Outlook Tasks window and make a note into a task, start by clicking the Create Outlook Task button or pressing Ctrl+Shift+K. The Task dialog box appears. Enter a description of the task and click the <u>S</u>ave and Close button.

Publishing section notes on a network

You can place all the notes in a section in a network folder so that your co-workers can read the notes. When you publish notes this way, you can publish them in a Web page file or a OneNote section. Publish notes in a OneNote section if you're certain that the people who will need to view your notes have OneNote on their computers.

To publish section notes on a network, choose <u>F</u>ile⇨Pu<u>b</u>lish Pages. You see the Publish dialog box. Locate and select the network folder where you want to place the section notes. To publish them as a Web page, choose Single File Web Page on the Save As <u>T</u>ype drop-down list; choose OneNote Sections to publish the notes in such a way that people with OneNote can read them.

Book IX

Windows XP

The 5th Wave   By Rich Tennant

"ALL THIS STUFF? IT'S PART OF A SUITE OF INTEGRATED SOFTWARE PACKAGES DESIGNED TO HELP UNCLUTTER YOUR LIFE."

Contents at a Glance

Chapter 1: Windows Basics

In This Chapter

✓ Finding your way around the screen

✓ Opening and closing programs

✓ Installing and uninstalling software

✓ Loading and removing fonts

✓ Making your system run better with the system utilities

Windows XP is not a standard computer program. To get technical about it, Windows XP is an *operating system,* or OS for short. Operating systems such as Windows XP make it possible to print a file, connect to the Internet, and run several programs simultaneously without the computer getting a hernia. They make computer programs work harmoniously. According to Microsoft, the XP in Windows XP stands for "experience," but some think the letters stand for "exasperating."

Chapter 1 of this mini-book introduces Windows XP. It shows how to find your way around the screen, install and uninstall software, and use the many Windows XP utility programs that were designed to make computer systems run better.

A Short Geography Lesson

Glance at Figure 1-1 to find out what the different parts of the Windows screen are called. Before you can make Windows do your bidding, you need to know where this, that, and the other thing are located.

Icons and shortcut icons   Desktop

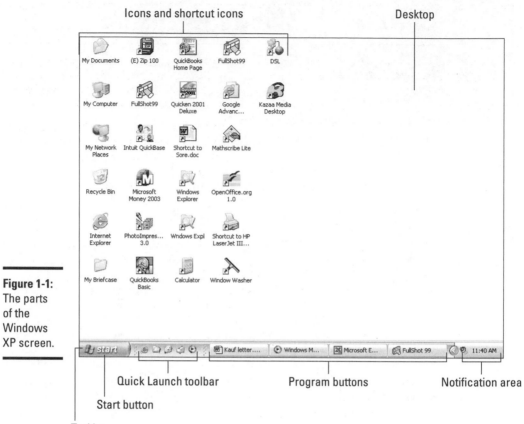

Figure 1-1:
The parts
of the
Windows
XP screen.

Quick Launch toolbar   Program buttons   Notification area

Start button

Taskbar

✦ **Desktop:** The catchall name for the place where icons and windows are found. When you open a program, its window appears on the desktop. No matter how many windows cover the desktop, you can make it appear right away by clicking the Show Desktop button on the Quick Launch toolbar.

✦ **Shortcut icons:** Double-click (or click) a shortcut icon to open a program, open a file, or connect to a Web site. Notice the little arrow in the lower-left corner of some shortcut icons. The arrow appears on icons that you create and icons that are created for you when you install a computer program.

Cleaning bric-a-brac from the Notification area

To call attention to themselves, programs you install on your computer sometimes drop an icon in the Notification area. As a result, the Notification area can get crowded with all kinds of bric-a-brac. You can, however, sweep the Notification area clean by following these steps:

1. **Right-click the clock and choose Properties on the shortcut menu.**

2. **In the Taskbar and Start Menu Properties dialog box, click the Customize button.**

3. **In the Customize Notification dialog box, open the Behavior drop-down menu next to each icon name and choose Hide When Inactive, Always Hide, or Always Show.**

   Don't hide the Volume icon if you play sounds on your computer. You need it for raising and lowering the volume.

4. **Click OK and then click the Apply button.**

To see icons you've hidden, you can always click the Show Hidden Icons button, the arrow on the left side of the Notification area.

✦ **Start button:** Click the Start button (or press Ctrl+Esc) to open the Start menu.

✦ **Taskbar:** The taskbar is the stripe along the side of the desktop. The Start button, Quick Launch toolbar, and Notification area are found on the taskbar. You can drag the taskbar to a side of the desktop, burden it with program buttons, and change its size and shape, as Chapter 3 of this mini-book explains.

Kauf letter....

✦ **Program buttons:** One program button appears on the taskbar for each program you opened. Click a button to get from one program to another or, if you opened more than one file in a program, click the button and choose a filename from the pop-up menu. You can also switch programs by pressing Alt+Tab and choosing an icon from the dialog box that appears.

✦ **Quick Launch toolbar:** Make a shortcut icon for the programs you know and love and place the icon on the Quick Launch toolbar. This way, you can open your favorite programs without opening the Windows menu or clicking an icon on the desktop. Chapter 3 of this mini-book explains how to customize the Quick Launch toolbar.

✦ **Notification area:** Here you will find the clock as well as icons put there by programs you loaded on your computer. The notification area is also called the *system tray*.

Starting, Closing, and Switching between Programs

All the gizmos that come with Windows XP are nice, but starting programs and getting down to work is what really matters. Read on to find out how to start computer programs, close them, and switch among the programs that are open.

Starting a computer program

Windows XP offers no fewer than six ways to start a computer program:

✦ **Open the Start menu:** Click a program name on the Start menu. The menu lists the last six programs you worked with. (You can remove a name from the list by right-clicking it and choosing Remove from This List.)

✦ **Open the All Programs menu:** Click the Start button, select the All Programs menu, locate the program you want to open, and click its name.

✦ **Double-click a shortcut icon:** Double-click an icon on the desktop (Chapter 3 of this mini-book explains how to create these icons).

✦ **Double-click a filename:** In My Computer or Windows Explorer, locate the file you want to open and double-click its name. With this technique, you open the file and a program at the same time.

✦ **Open the Recent Documents Menu:** Click the Start button, choose My Recent <u>D</u>ocuments, and select from the last several files you opened. This way, you open a file and a program at the same time.

✦ **Right-click a filename and choose a program:** In My Computer or Windows Explorer, right-click a filename, choose Open <u>W</u>ith on the shortcut menu, and choose a program name on the submenu. Go this route when a file can be opened in more than one program.

TIP

To place a program name permanently on the Start menu, find its name on the All Programs menu, right-click its name, and choose P<u>i</u>n to Start Menu on the shortcut menu.

TIP

The Start menu lists the last six programs you worked with, but you can list fewer or more than six program names. Right-click the Taskbar and choose Properties. In the Taskbar and Start Menu Properties dialog box, select the Start Menu tab, click the <u>C</u>ustomize button (the first one), and, on the General tab of the Customize Start Menu dialog box, enter a number in the <u>N</u>umber of Programs on Start Menu box.

Choosing which program opens certain types of files

Sometimes when you double-click a filename in My Computer or Windows Explorer, the file opens in the wrong program. That happens because Windows XP has preconceived ideas about which programs are supposed to open which files. DOC files, for example, are supposed to open in Microsoft Word. JPEG files are supposed to open in the Windows Picture and Fax Viewer. Most files, however, can be opened in more than one program. To open a file in the program you want it to open in, right-click its name and choose the program from the Open Wit<u>h</u> shortcut menu.

Suppose that the program's name doesn't appear on the list or you want the file to open automatically in a different program when you double-click its name. Follow these steps to "associate" a file or file type with a program:

1. **Right-click the filename and choose Open With➪Choose Program (see Figure 1-2).**

You see the Open With dialog box, shown in Figure 1-2. It lists programs that are capable of opening the file you right-clicked, as well as all the programs that are installed on your computer.

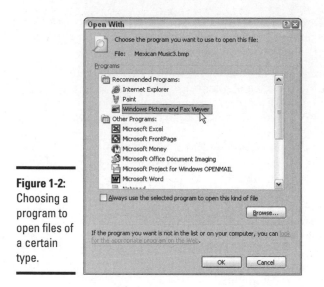

Figure 1-2:
Choosing a
program to
open files of
a certain
type.

2. **Select the program you want to open the file with.**

3. **If you want files of this type to open automatically in the program you selected, select Always Use the Selected Program to Open This Kind of File check box.**

Switching among programs

To switch among programs, click a program button on the Taskbar. Windows XP places a new button on the Taskbar whenever you open a new program. If more than one file is open in a program, click a program button and choose a filename on the pop-up menu. In Figure 1-3, two Word files are open.

Figure 1-3:
Switching
among
programs.

Starting a favorite program when you start your computer

Is there a computer program you run each time you sit down at your computer? If there is, you can kill two birds with one stone and make the program start automatically whenever you turn on your computer. Windows XP makes it very easy to carry out this magic trick.

To find out which programs are already slated to start running whenever you turn on your computer, click the Start button, choose All Programs, and move the pointer over Startup on the on the menu. The Startup submenu displays a list of programs that are "auto-started," to use Windows terminology. Your task now is to add a favorite program to the Startup menu:

1. **Click the Start button and, on a menu, move the pointer over the name of the program you want to start automatically.**

2. **Hold down the Ctrl key and drag the menu name over the Startup submenu.**

   Whether you know it or not, with this action you're copying a shortcut from one menu to another.

3. **When the Startup submenu appears, carefully move the shortcut onto the menu, and release the mouse button and the Ctrl key.**

To keep a program from starting automatically, remove its name from the Startup submenu. To do so, open the Startup submenu, right-click the name, and choose Delete.

Laptop users and others who are fond of keyboard techniques can also switch among files by pressing Alt+Tab and holding down the Alt key. A dialog box appears with icons that represent each file that is open (see Figure 1-3). Still holding down the Alt key, press Tab until you have selected the file you want; then release the Alt key.

To make more room for program buttons on a crowded Taskbar, try enlarging the Taskbar. If necessary, right-click the Taskbar (be careful not to click a program button) and unselect the Lock the Taskbar option to unlock the Taskbar. Then move the pointer over the top of the Taskbar, click when you see the double arrow, and drag the top of the taskbar higher on the screen.

Closing a program
Save and close files you're working on, and then close the program with one of these techniques:

✦ Click the Close button (the *X*) in the upper-right corner of the program window.

✦ Choose File⇨Exit (or File⇨Close).

✦ Press Alt+F4.

You can right-click a program button and choose Close or Close Group on the pop-up menu to close a program without displaying its window on-screen. Choose Close Group when more than one file is open in a program and you want to close all the files.

Suppose that a program hangs and you can't close it. In that case, press Ctrl+Alt+Del or right-click the Taskbar and choose Task Manager. You see the Windows Task Manager dialog box with a list of programs that are open, as shown in Figure 1-4. Programs that are hanging show the words "Not Responding" beside their names. Select the program that needs closing and click the End Task button.

Figure 1-4:
Closing a
frozen
program.

Installing Software Programs

Software manufacturers have made it very easy to install their software programs. In many instances, you can download programs straight from the Internet without having to fumble with CDs, or worse, floppy disks.

To install a program from a CD, put the CD in the CD-ROM drive on your computer and see what happens. If all goes well, the program starts installing itself in a half-minute. Sometimes, however, the CD is incapable of "auto-starting" and you have to start the installation on your own. To do so, open Windows Explorer or My Computer, select the CD-ROM drive, look for a file on the CD called setup or install, and double-click it. If you still can't install the program, you need to look for a file on the CD called ReadMe and read it for more instruction.

Numerous programs can be downloaded from the Internet. When you download a program, you see a dialog box similar to the one in Figure 1-5. In this dialog box, click the Save button and choose a folder on your computer to store the program. When you have retrieved it from the Internet, go to the folder and double-click the file to start the installation process.

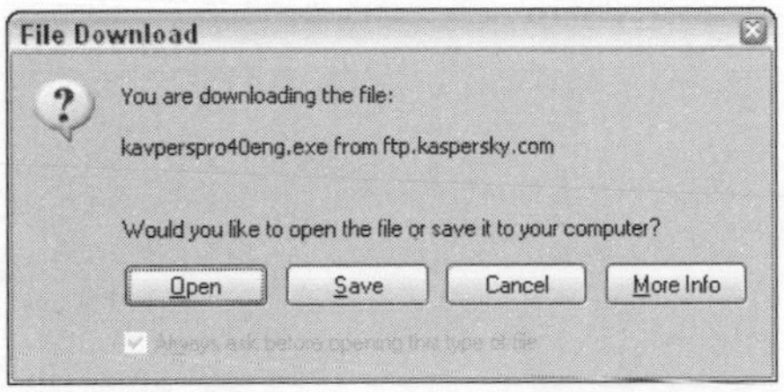

Figure 1-5:
Download-
ing a
program
from the
Internet.

I have a folder on my computer called "Downloaded" for storing programs from the Internet. If I need to re-install a program I downloaded, I know where to find it. I'm not suggesting that you also create a "Downloaded" folder, but you could do worse than follow my stellar example.

Here are some Web sites where you can sample and download computer programs:

✦ CNET (www.download.com)

✦ Network of Minds (www.networkofminds.com)

✦ Tucows (www.tucows.com)

Uninstalling Software Programs

When you no longer need a program, remove it from your computer. You save disk space that way. Windows XP tracks which programs have been installed and can remove them cleanly. Remember, however, that uninstalling a program usually erases its folders from your computer. If you keep files of your own making in those folders, they may disintegrate along with the program. If need be, move the files you want to keep to a safe place before you uninstall software.

Follow these steps to uninstall a software program:

1. **Click the Start button and choose Control Panel.**

2. **Select the Add or Remove Programs icon.**

   The Add or Remove Programs dialog box, shown in Figure 1-6, appears. This dialog box lists the names of all programs that are installed on your computer.

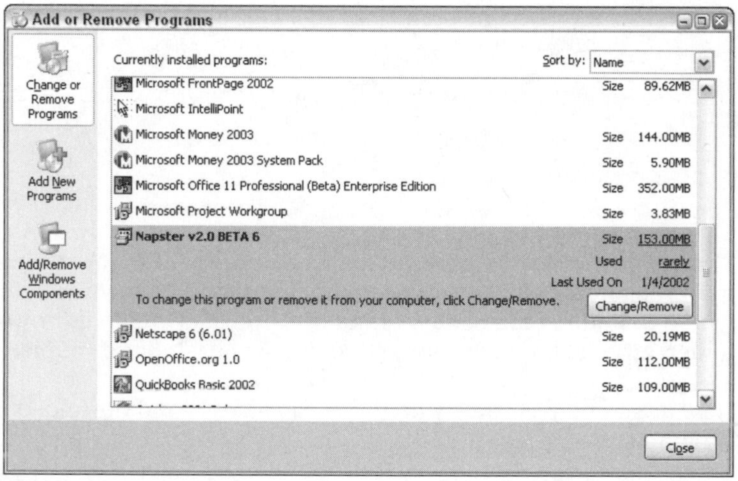
Add or Remove Programs
Change or Remove Programs
Add New Programs
Add/Remove Windows Components
Currently installed programs:
Sort by:
Name
Microsoft FrontPage 2002
Size 89.62MB
Microsoft IntelliPoint
Microsoft Money 2003
Size 144.00MB
Microsoft Money 2003 System Pack
Size 5.90MB
Microsoft Office 11 Professional (Beta) Enterprise Edition
Size 352.00MB
Microsoft Project Workgroup
Size 3.83MB
Napster v2.0 BETA 6
Size 153.00MB
Used rarely
Last Used On 1/4/2002
To change this program or remove it from your computer, click Change/Remove.
Change/Remove
Netscape 6 (6.01)
Size 20.19MB
OpenOffice.org 1.0
Size 112.00MB
QuickBooks Basic 2002
Size 109.00MB
Close

Figure 1-6: Uninstalling a software program.

3. **Scroll through the list and select the program you want to uninstall.**

   The dialog box tells you how often you use the program and when you last used it.

4. **Click the Change/Remove button.**

5. **Choose Automatic if you're given the opportunity to choose a method of uninstalling the software.**

6. **Follow the on-screen instructions for removing the software.**

   Sometimes you have to restart your computer to make the uninstallation official.

Meet the Character Map

The Office programs that are explained in this book all offer the Insert⇨Symbol command for entering unusual symbols — Greek letters, double daggers, smiling faces, and the like. However, if you need to enter an unusual symbol and you can't resort to the Insert⇨Symbol command in an Office program, you can always insert it by way of the Windows Character Map:

1. **Click the Start button and choose All Programs⇨Accessories⇨System Tools⇨ Character Map.**

2. **In the Character Map window, find the symbol you need and click the Select button.**

3. **Click the Copy button to copy the symbol to the Clipboard.**

4. **Close the window, return to your file, and click the Paste button or press Ctrl+V to enter the symbol in your file.**

The following third-party programs for uninstalling software do a more thorough job than Windows XP of hunting down and removing programs. If you're in dire need of more disk space, investigate these programs:

✦ EasyUninstall (www.alladinsys.com/easyuninstall)

✦ Norton CleanSweep (www.symantec.com/sabu/sysworks/basic)

✦ QuickClean (www.mcafee.com/myapps/qc3)

Installing and Removing Fonts on Your Computer

A *font* is a collection of letters, numbers, and symbols in a particular typeface, including all italicized and boldfaced variations of the letters, numbers, and symbols. When you installed Windows XP on your computer, you installed numerous fonts as well. In Word, PowerPoint, FrontPage, and the other Office programs, you can choose these fonts for text and headings. But suppose you want to load a new font on your computer? Or you want to remove fonts to keep the Font menus from being overcrowded?

As shown in Figure 1-7, font files are kept in the C:\Windows\Fonts folder on your computer. Windows Explorer and My Computer offer the File⇨Install New Font command for loading font files into this folder, but here's the easiest way to handle fonts:

✦ **Installing new fonts:** Place the font file in the C:\Windows\Fonts folder.

✦ **Removing a font:** Move its font file out of the C:\Windows\Fonts folder.

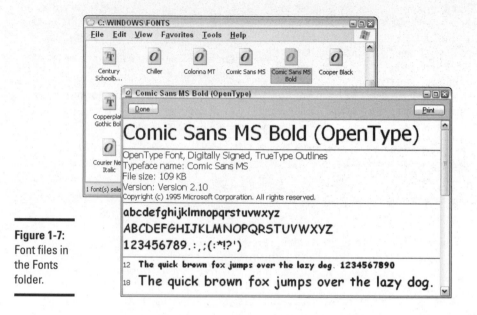

Figure 1-7:
Font files in
the Fonts
folder.

The Fonts folder provides these amenities for handling fonts:

✦ **Examining fonts:** Double-click a font file to examine a font more closely. As shown in Figure 1-7, a window opens and you see precisely what the font looks like. Do you know why "the quick brown fox jumped over the lazy dog"? Because that sentence includes every letter in the alphabet.

✦ **Finding similar fonts:** To list fonts that look similar to a certain font, click the Similarity button and choose the font's name on the List Fonts by Similarity To drop-down list. The list of fonts is arranged so that very similar fonts come first, fairly similar fonts come next, and dissimilar fonts come last in the list. Use this command to familiarize yourself with fonts or decide which fonts to remove when you have many that look nearly the same.

✦ **Shortening the font list:** To shrink the list of fonts and make font hunting a little easier, choose View⇨Hide Variations. Doing so removes boldface and italicized versions of fonts from the list.

Maintaining Your System and Making It Run Better

Windows XP offers about a half-dozen utility programs whose purpose is to maintain your computer system and make your computer run better. Most of these utility programs are found on the All Programs⇨Accessories⇨System Tools menu. Table 1-1 briefly describes these utility programs. The remainder of this chapter is devoted to the utility programs that are of interest to the average user (not network administrators, technicians, or self-styled computer guru geeks).

Table 1-1	Windows XP Utility Programs	
System Tool	*What It Does*	*How Often to Use It*
Disk Cleanup	Removes temporary files and files downloaded from the Internet from the hard disk	Every week
Disk Defragmenter	Stores files more efficiently on the hard disk so that they can be accessed faster	When the computer is sluggish
Error Checking	Checks a disk for bad sectors and logical errors	After a computer crash, frequent program failures, or a "bad sector" or "unable to read" error
Power Schemes	Switches the monitor and computer into standby or hibernation mode to save power	Make these settings once
System Information	Presents information about your computer, its components, and its resources	When you talk to a technician
System Restore	Restores your system to a previous incarnation	After a system crash
Windows Task Manager	Shows you what kind of a workout your computer's central processing unit is getting (Processes and Performance tabs)	When you talk to a technician

Disk Cleanup

Certain kinds of files behave like barnacles on the hull of a ship, cluttering the hard disk and making it slow down. Temporary files are the biggest culprits. When a computer crashes, Windows XP turns unsaved files into temporary files. When you surf the Internet, temporary files also come to stay on the hard disk. You can clean these files from the disk with Disk Cleanup:

1. **Click the Start button and choose All Programs⇨Accessories⇨System Tools⇨Disk Cleanup.**

The Disk Cleanup For dialog box appears, as shown in Figure 1-8.

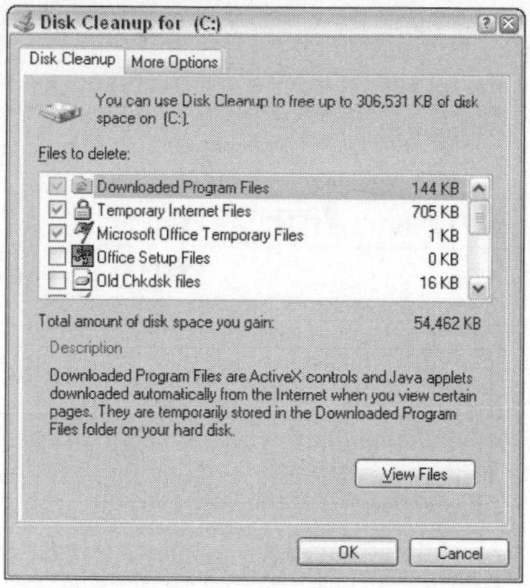

Figure 1-8:
Cleaning
unnecessary
files from
the hard
disk.

2. **Select the kinds of files you want to remove and click OK.**

Click a file type and read the description if you're not sure what a file type is.

Disk Defragmenter

When you save a file, your computer places data on the hard disk wherever it can find room for it. Over time, the data in the file is spread hither and yon, or *fragmented,* on the hard disk. To assemble a file and display it on-screen, the computer has to work harder and harder, and eventually it slows down.

You can *defragment* a sluggish hard disk to make it work faster. Defragmenting, however, can take an hour, depending on how fast your computer is. One more thing: Before you start the Disk Defragmenter, remove files and computer programs you don't need anymore. That way, you make defragmenting go faster.

Close all open programs and follow these steps to run the Disk Defragmenter:

1. **Click the Start button and choose All Programs⇨Accessories⇨System Tools⇨Disk Defragmenter.**

The Disk Defragmenter window opens, as shown in Figure 1-9.

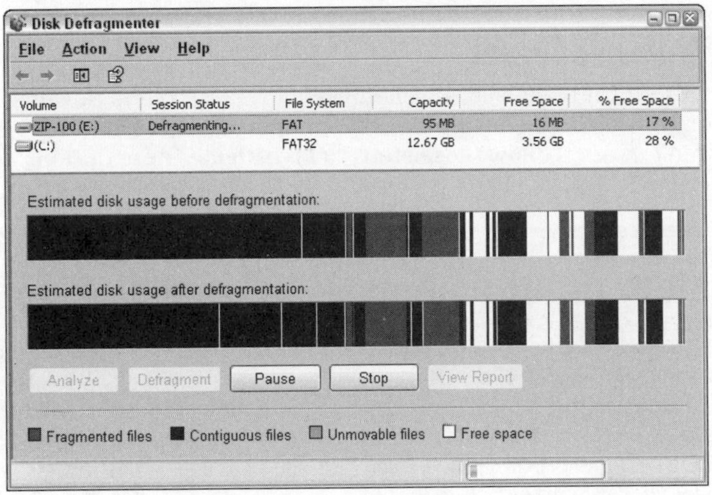

Volume	Session Status	File System	Capacity	Free Space	% Free Space
ZIP-100 (E:)	Defragmenting...	FAT	95 MB	16 MB	17 %
(C:)		FAT32	12.67 GB	3.56 GB	28 %

Figure 1-9:
Defrag-
menting a
hard disk.

2. **Choose which disk to defragment.**

3. **Click the Analyze button to see a graph that shows how many defragmented files are on the disk.**

4. **Click the Defragment button.**

Error Checking

Hard disks are susceptible to logical errors and bad sectors. Data on a hard disk is stored in *sectors*. When a sector is damaged, the data stored in it is irretrievable. A *logical error* describes data on a hard disk that is not associated with a file and merely wastes storage space. Follow these steps to get Windows XP to repair logical errors and map bad sectors so that data can't be stored on them:

1. **In My Computer or Windows Explorer, right-click the icon of the drive you want to check (probably Local Disk [C:]), and choose Properties.**

You see the Local Disk Properties dialog box.

2. **Select the Tools tab.**

3. **Click the Check Now button to open the Check Local Disk dialog box.**

4. **Choose to fix logical errors (the first option), repair bad sectors (the second option), or do both; then click the Start button.**

Power schemes

In the spirit of conserving energy, Windows XP offers power scheme options for slowing down or turning off your computer and monitor when they aren't in use. Follow these steps to investigate these options:

System requirements: RAM and disk space

As you shop for software, be sure to look at "system requirements," the list of conditions a computer must meet in order to run a software program. Usually, system requirements are listed on the box the software comes in. Software you purchase should be able to run on Windows XP. Usually, the system requirements state how much RAM (random access memory) a computer needs and how much disk space is required to run the software. You can find this information by following these instructions:

✔ **RAM (random access memory):** Click the Start button, choose Control Panel, select

Performance and Maintenance, and click the System icon. You see the System Properties dialog box. On the General tab, look for the amount of RAM on your computer and its speed in megahertz (MHz).

✔ **Disk space:** Open My Computer or Windows Explorer, right-click the Local Disk (C: drive) icon, and choose Properties. The General tab of Local Disk Properties dialog box tells you how much used and free space is on your computer.

1. **Click the Start button and choose Control Panel.**

2. **Select Performance and Maintenance.**

3. **Click the Power Options icon.**

   You see the Power Options Properties dialog box.

4. **On the Power Schemes drop-down menu, choose the option that best describes your computer and how you use it.**

5. **If you want, choose Settings For options as well.**

   All four options aren't available on every computer.

   • **Turn Off Monitor:** Turns off the monitor after a certain amount of time to conserve power.

   • **Turn Off Hard Disks:** Turns off the hard disk on the computer after a certain amount of time.

   • **System Standby:** Puts the computer in Standby mode after a certain amount of time. In this mode, the computer uses minimal power.

   • **System Hibernates:** Works like Standby mode, except the computer keeps a record of what is in random access memory. If a power failure occurs, on-screen work can be recovered.

System Restore

It so happens in your computing adventures that sometimes you install a new software program or make a change to the system only to discover that the computer now runs sluggishly. For times like that, you can run the System Restore utility. It tracks changes to your computer system by marking each change with a *restore point*, a record of your computer system as it stood at a certain point in time. When you want to restore your system to a previous incarnation, you choose a restore point and turn back the clock to when your computer ran better. You can create restore points on your own, and Windows creates them for you under these conditions:

✦ You run your computer for ten hours.

✦ You install a new program.

✦ You change a system setting in the Control Panel.

✦ You delete a program file (an .exe or .dll file, for example).

Word-processed files, spreadsheets, e-mail messages, and other files with commonly known file extensions are not deleted or altered when you roll back your computer system. Only system settings and system files are affected. If you don't like your system after you roll it back, you can have your system as it stood before you decided to restore it (see "Reversing a restoration"). You can, in other words, eat your cake and have it, too.

Restoring your system

Follow these steps to restore your system to a previous incarnation:

1. **Close all open programs.**

2. **Click the Start button and choose All _P_rograms⇨Accessories⇨System Tools⇨System Restore.**

   The Welcome to System Restore window appears.

3. **Make sure that the first option button, _R_estore My Computer to an Earlier Time, is selected; then click the _N_ext button.**

4. **Choose a restore point on the calendar, click the _N_ext button, and follow the on-screen instructions.**

   Calendar dates shown in boldface are restore points.

System Restore restores your system to a previous incarnation. Sooner or later, depending on how much restoring needs to be done, your computer shuts down and restarts, and you see the Restoration Complete window.

As mentioned earlier, you can create a restore point on your own. To do so, choose Create a Restore Point in the Welcome to System Restore window and click Next. You're asked to enter a descriptive name for the restore point. You can select this restore point later on.

If System Restore isn't tracking changes to your system, click the Start button, choose _C_ontrol Panel, select Performance and Maintenance, and click the System Icon. You see the System Properties dialog box. On the System Restore tab, make sure that the _T_urn Off System Restore check box is unselected. While you're on this tab, you can drag the slider to adjust the amount of disk space that is devoted to System Restore.

Reversing a restoration

If you restore your computer to a previous incarnation but you aren't happy with the results, you can reverse the restoration. Click the Start button and choose All _P_rograms⇨Accessories⇨System Tools⇨System Restore. In the Welcome to Restore window, select the _U_ndo My Last Restoration option button and take it from there. System Restore creates a "Restore Operation" restore point whenever you restore your system. When you reverse a restoration, you're returned to the "Restore Operation" restore point — the state your computer was in before you restored it.

Chapter 2: Working with Files and Folders

In This Chapter

- ✓ **Strategizing how to store your work on-disk**
- ✓ **Finding your way around Windows Explorer and My Computer**
- ✓ **Selecting, moving, copying, and deleting files and folders**
- ✓ **Recovering a file you accidentally deleted**
- ✓ **Searching for lost files**
- ✓ **Compressing and uncompressing files**
- ✓ **Wrestling with read-only files**

his chapter makes the most of what can be a very dreary subject — how to handle files and folders. All data are stored in files. Files are stored in folders. Folders are stored in other folders. If you're not careful, you can get lost in the labyrinth.

To keep you from getting lost, this chapter describes how to use Windows Explorer and My Computer to organize data on your computer. You discover how to select, copy, delete, move, bend, spindle, and mutilate files. You also find out how to track down stray files and resuscitate files you deleted by accident. Finally, this chapter explains how to compress files and in so doing be able to send them more swiftly over the Internet and store them more efficiently on your computer.

Devising a Strategy for Storing Your Work

Before you create any folders and begin moving files here and there, take a moment to devise a strategy for storing your work. As you know, Windows XP maintains a structure, or hierarchy, of folders. At the top are the *root directories* — the A drive, C drive, and other big-league folders. As you dig deeper into the hierarchy, you encounter other folders and subfolders. Figure 2-1 shows a sample folder hierarchy.

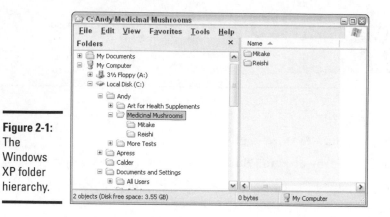

Figure 2-1:
The
Windows
XP folder
hierarchy.

Your first task when you start a new project is to create folders for the different kinds of work you do and arrange the folders on-disk in such a way that you can find them easily. This way, when you need to open, delete, copy, move, or back up a file, you'll know where to find it.

By the way, some people mistakenly believe that the Office files created with Word, Excel, or another Office program have to be stored on-disk either in the same folder as the program itself or in a nearby folder. That is not so. You can store the Office files you create yourself anywhere you want. And you should store them in a convenient place where you can find them easily.

Taking advantage of the My Documents folder

Nearly everywhere you go on a computer, you run into the My Documents folder. Microsoft planned it that way. The idea is for you to keep the files you're currently working on in the My Documents folder and move the files elsewhere when you're done with them. The My Documents folder and its subfolders — My Music, My Pictures, and so on — is the easiest folder to open in Windows XP. Here are four ways for opening the folder so that you can get at the files inside:

✔ Double-click the My Documents icon on the desktop. My Computer opens to show the contents of the My Documents folder. Double-click the file that you want to open.

✔ Click the Start button and choose My Documents on the Start menu.

✔ In the program you're working in, choose File➪Open. In the Open dialog box, click the My Documents button. You see the files and folders in the My Documents folder.

✔ In the Explorer bar of My Computer or Windows Explorer, click My Documents. You can find this link under "Other Places."

Introducing My Computer and Windows Explorer

Windows XP is littered with folders and files. They are everywhere. Files are kept in folders. Folders are kept inside other folders. Getting lost in the vast computer labyrinth of folders and subfolders is easy, but Windows XP has come to the rescue with two programs that take the sting out of exploring a computer: My Computer and Windows Explorer. These pages explain how to use these venerable programs to burrow into your computer and see what's there.

Meet My Computer and Windows Explorer

My Computer and Windows Explorer are computer programs in their own right. Their purpose is to help you locate folders and files, create new folders, copy and move files and folders, and delete files and folders. These programs work identically. The difference between the two is simply this: When you open a new folder in My Computer, it opens in a new window, but when you open a new folder in Windows Explorer, the contents of the window appear in the window you are looking in. Figure 2-2 shows the My Computer window.

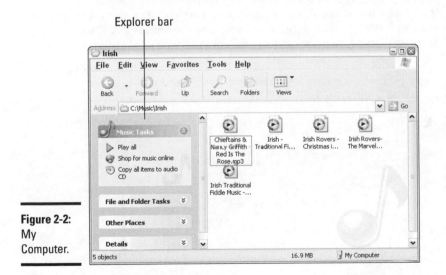

Explorer bar

Figure 2-2:
My
Computer.

To open Windows Explorer:

✦ Click the Start button and choose My Documents. Windows Explorer opens to the contents of the My Documents folder.

✦ Click the Start button and choose All Programs⇨Accessories⇨Windows Explorer. (If ever a program were a candidate for a shortcut icon, it's Windows Explorer. Chapter 3 explains how to create shortcut icons.)

To open My Computer:

✦ Double-click the My Computer icon on the desktop.(If you don't see this icon, click the Start button, right-click My Computer, and choose Show on Desktop on the shortcut menu.)

✦ Click the Start button and choose My Computer.

✦ If you're in Windows Explorer, click My Computer under "Other Places" in the Explorer bar.

On the left side of the My Computer and Windows Explorer window is the Explorer bar (refer to Figure 2-2). This gizmo — new in Windows XP — is a convenient means of doing tasks, opening new folders, and getting information about your computer system.

Nice as it is, the Explorer bar isn't for everybody. To make it go away, click the Folders button. As shown in Figure 2-3, you see the major folders on your computer where the Explorer bar used to be. You can copy and move files and folders by dragging them from one side of the My Computer or Explorer Window to another, as I explain later in this chapter.

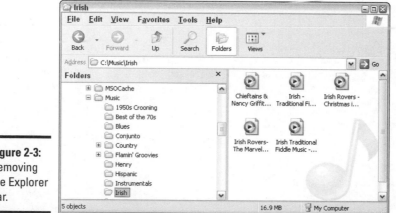

Figure 2-3: Removing the Explorer bar.

To permanently remove the Explorer bar, choose Tools⇨Folder Options, select the Use Windows Classic Folder option button on the General tab of the Folder Options dialog box, and click OK.

Going from folder to folder

Before you can move or copy a folder or file, you have to find the folder in which it resides. That means rooting around in Windows Explorer or My Computer until you find the darn thing. By far the easiest way to do that is to click the Folders button, display folders on the left side of the window, and click around until you find the file or folder you're looking for:

✦ Click a folder or drive icon on the left side of the window to display its contents on the right side. The contents are shown in alphabetical order, with the folders first and files second.

✦ Click the plus sign (+) next to a drive or folder you want to investigate. The folders inside that drive or folder appear below it. Click a minus sign (–) to keep the folders inside a drive or folder from being displayed.

You can also take advantage of the following toolbar buttons to get from folder to folder (right-click the menu bar and choose Standard Buttons if you don't see these buttons):

✦ **Back:** Takes you to the folder you saw previously (you can also press Alt+←). Click the down arrow beside the button to see a list of the folders you visited; click a folder's name to visit it again.

✦ **Forward:** Returns you to a folder you saw earlier (you can also press Alt+→). Click the down arrow to see a list of folders you retreated from and to return to a folder.

✦ **Up:** Climbs higher in the folder hierarchy (you can also press the Backspace key).

Here's a quick way to learn about a folder: Right-click it in Windows Explorer or My Computer and choose Properties on the shortcut menu. Among other juicy tidbits, the Properties dialog box tells you how large the folder is and when it was created.

Different ways of viewing folders and files

No matter where you go in Windows XP — My Computer, Windows Explorer, the Open dialog box, the Recycle Bin — you have the opportunity to change views and get a better idea of what is in the folder you are poking around in. Folders and files can be shown in the form of icons, thumbnail images, or in lists. And if you decide on a list, you can arrange it by name, file type, size, and so on. Figure 2-4 shows different ways of viewing folders and files.

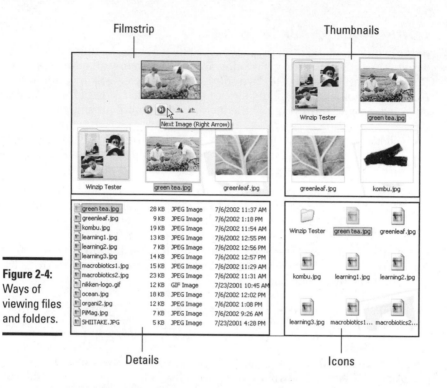

Figure 2-4:
Ways of
viewing files
and folders.

Selecting the default view

When you open a folder in Windows Explorer or My Computer, which view do you want to see it in? Personally, I like Details view, but that's because I work almost exclusively with text files and I want to know when they were created, how big they are, and when I last accessed them. If I worked entirely with graphics files, I would want folders to open by default in Filmstrip or Thumbnails view.

What's your favorite view? Windows Explorer and My Computer remember which view you chose last time you opened a folder and they give you that view next time you open it. Still, you can make your favorite view the default

view and rest assured that new folders you create open in the view you like so well. Follow these steps to designate your favorite view and make it the default:

1. **In Windows Explorer or My Computer, switch to the view you like most.**

2. **Choose Tools⇨Folder Options.**

3. **On the View tab of the Folder Options dialog box, click the Apply to All Folders button.**

4. **Click Yes when the dialog box asks whether you really want to change the default view.**

To change views:

1. Open the <u>V</u>iew menu or click the Views button to see the Views drop-
down menu.

2. Choose an option: Filmstri<u>p</u> (available only with graphics files),
<u>T</u>humbnails, Ti<u>l</u>es, Ico<u>n</u>s, <u>L</u>ist, or <u>D</u>etails.

All these views have their advantages. You can't beat Filmstrip or
Thumbnails view when peeking at graphics files. Icons and List view are
good for copying and moving files. Switch to Details view when you need to
look at file types, see when a file was created, or find out how big a file is.

In Details view, click a button at the top of a column — Name, Size, Type,
and so on — to arrange the files in different ways. If need be, drag the
border between the buttons to widen the columns. The columns you see in
Details view aren't the only ones you can see in a folder window. Choose
<u>V</u>iew➪<u>C</u>hoose Details to open the Choose Details dialog box and select
other means of examining files.

Usually, Windows Explorer and My Computer present an accurate picture
of what's in a folder, but if you move a few files around, update a file or two,
or move a folder, the picture might not be an accurate one. To see what's
really in a folder, choose <u>V</u>iew➪<u>R</u>efresh. Choose this command when you
suspect that all is not what it seems in a Windows Explorer or My Computer
window.

Choosing How to List Files and Folders

Here's a little bit of esoterica that can be very helpful as you go about your
computer chores: Windows XP gives you the opportunity to display filenames and paths in different ways.

✦ **File extensions:** A *file extension* is a three-letter designation that tells
you what kind of file you're dealing with. Hawaii.jpg, for example, is a
JPEG file, a kind of graphics file. In My Computer, Windows Explorer, and
dialog boxes where filenames are displayed, three-letter file extensions
don't normally appear on filenames, but you can change that. Being able
to see file extensions can be helpful when you're working with different
types of files because the extension identifies each kind of file you're
dealing with.

✦ **Paths:** A *path* is a list of the successive folders in which a file is located.
For example, C:\My Stuff\My Book\Chapter 1 is a path. For the naviga-
tionally challenged, Windows XP provides the opportunity to list paths
in the title bar at the top of the My Computer and Windows Explorer
window.

If, like me, you find being able to see file extensions and paths helpful, follow these steps to make them visible:

1. **Click the Start button and choose Control Panel.**

2. **Select the Appearance and Themes Category.**

3. **Select the Folder Options icon.**

The Folder Options dialog box appears.

4. **On the View tab, select Display the Full Path in the Title Bar to see paths in title bars, and unselect Hide Extensions for Known File Types to see file extensions.**

5. **Click OK.**

The only drawback to displaying file extensions is having to enter the extension as well as the filename when you save and name a file. Normally, for example, you can simply type **Hawaii** to name a file, but you have to enter the extension as well, **Hawaii.jpg**, if extensions are displayed in the Save As dialog box.

Creating a New Folder

Now that you know how to rummage in your computer with Windows Explorer and My Computer, you can create a folder. Create a folder whenever you start a new project. Create folders for storing the different kinds of files you work with. Create folders in such a way that you always know where files are stored on your computer.

Follow these steps to create a folder:

1. **In Windows Explorer or My Computer, locate and select the folder in which to put your new folder.**

In other words, find the folder in the hierarchy to which the new folder will be subordinate.

2. **Right-click the right side of the window and choose New⇨Folder on the shortcut menu, or choose File⇨New⇨Folder.**

You see a folder icon with the label "New Folder."

3. **Type a descriptive name in place of "New Folder" and press Enter or click elsewhere on-screen.**

Tired of the drab manila folder?

Folders are represented by the standard folder icon, a manila folder, but you can choose a different icon for a folder if doing so will help you recognize the folder or make the folder stand out from others. For that matter, you can use a digital picture as a folder icon.

To change the icon by which a folder is identified, right-click the folder in Windows Explorer or My Computer and choose Properties. In the

Properties dialog box, click the Customize tab. From there, you can choose a picture from a graphics file or click the Change Icon button and choose an icon from the Change Icon For dialog box.

To change the name of a folder, right-click its name, choose Rename on the shortcut menu, and enter a new name.

 You can also create a folder in the Save As dialog box, the dialog box that appears when you save a file for the first time. In the Save As dialog box, select the folder to which your new folder will be subordinate. Then click the Create a New Folder button, enter a folder name in the New Folder dialog box, and click OK. This on-the-fly method of creating folders isn't the best. My Computer and Windows Explorer are the best places to create new folders. In those programs, you can see clearly where your new folder will fit in the hierarchy of folders.

Copying and Moving Files and Folders

Now that you're well acquainted with Windows Explorer and My Computer, you can use those valuable programs to move and copy files and folders from place to place. These pages take up that very topic. First, however, you need to know how to select files and folders. You can't move or copy them until you select them. Better read on.

Selecting files and folders

Before you can copy, move, or delete files or folders, you have to select them. As Figure 2-5 shows, Windows Explorer and My Computer offer a bunch of different methods for selecting files and folders:

✦ **Selecting various items:** Hold down the Ctrl key and click the files or folders one at a time.

✦ **Selecting neighboring items:** Click the first file or folder and, holding down the Shift key, click the last.

✦ **Selecting a group of items:** Click a blank space in the window and drag to lasso the items and form a box around the group.

✦ **Selecting all the items:** Choose Edit⇨Select All or press Ctrl+A. Suppose you want to remove one or two items after you've selected them all. In that case, Ctrl+click the ones you want to remove.

✦ **Selecting all but one or two items:** Click the items you *don't* want and then choose Edit⇨Invert Selection. This is a great technique to use when you want to select all but one or two items in a folder with many items.

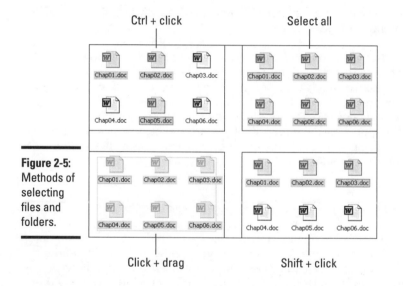

Figure 2-5:
Methods of selecting files and folders.

Some views are better than others when the time comes to select files. The Shift+click method, for example, works best in List and Details view. The Click+drag method works best in Tiles and Icons view. Earlier in this chapter, "Different ways of viewing folders and files" explains how to change views in My Computer and Windows Explorer.

The three ways to move and copy

Exactly three ways are available to move or copy files and folders: by dragging and dropping; cutting or copying and pasting; or starting from the

Explorer bar. Scholars debate about which method is best, but rather than recapitulate their spirited debates, you are invited to try all three methods and decide for yourself which one works best.

Book IX
Chapter 2

Working with Files and Folders

If you copy or move a folder or file and regret doing so, you can undo it with the Undo command. You can undo it, that is, if you haven't given any other commands since you moved or copied. The Undo command reverses your last action, whatever it happened to be. To undo a move or copy, press Ctrl+Z, choose Edit➪Undo, or right-click and choose the Undo command on the shortcut menu.

Dragging and dropping

Follow these steps to copy or move files and folders with the drag-and-drop method:

1. **In Windows Explorer or My Computer, select the files and folders you want to move or copy.**

In Figure 2-6, various files have been selected.

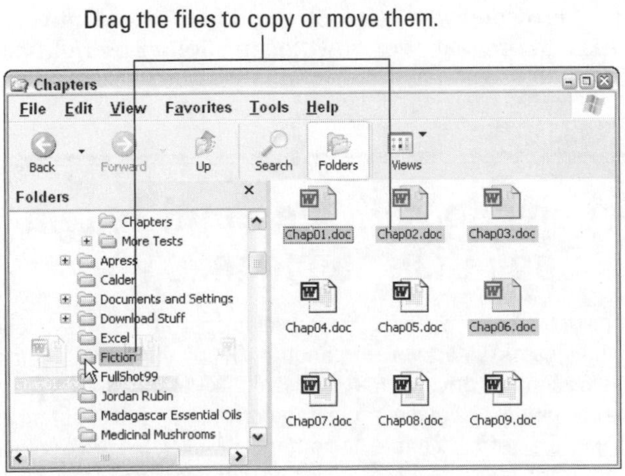

Drag the files to copy or move them.

Chapters		
File Edit View Favorites Tools Help		

Back · Forward · Up · Search · Folders · Views

Folders

- Chapters
- + More Tests
- + Apress
- Calder
- + Documents and Settings
- + Download Stuff
- Excel
- Fiction
- FullShot99
- Jordan Rubin
- Madagascar Essential Oils
- Medicinal Mushrooms

Chap01.doc Chap02.doc Chap03.doc

Chap04.doc Chap05.doc Chap06.doc

Chap07.doc Chap08.doc Chap09.doc

Figure 2-6: The drag-and-drop method.

2. **If necessary, click the Folders button to remove the Explorer bar and then display the folder on the left side of the window to which you want to copy or move the files and folders.**

Earlier in this chapter, "Going from folder to folder" explains how clicking a plus sign (+) next to a drive or folder displays its subfolders.

3. **Drag the files and folders to the folder you want to copy them to. If you're copying, hold down the Ctrl key as you drag.**

Ghostly images of the files or folders appear on-screen as you drag.

Here's some advice for backing up files or folders to a different drive: It isn't necessary to hold down the Ctrl key when copying files to another drive (3½ Floppy [A:], for example). You don't have to press Ctrl when copying to a different drive because a copy is made automatically when you move files from one drive to another. Suppose, however, that you *want to* move, not copy, files or folders to a different drive? In that case, hold down the Shift key as you drag. Holding down the Shift key tells Windows to move files and folders between drives without leaving the original copy behind.

4. **Release the mouse button.**

Some people prefer dragging and dropping with the secondary, or right, mouse button. With this technique, you hold down the right mouse button as you drag. When you release the mouse button, a small shortcut menu appears with options called Copy Here and Move Here. Choose one or the other and be done with it.

Folders can get crowded when new files and folders are moved or copied into them. You can prevent overcrowding in a folder by right-clicking an empty space and choosing Arrange Icons By⇨Auto Arrange.

Quick copying with the Send To and Copy Disk commands

Windows XP offers a neat command called Send To for quickly copying files or folders on the C: drive to the A: drive or another drive on your computer. To give the command, select the files or folders you want to move, right-click one of them, and choose a Send To command on the shortcut menu. For example, to copy a file to a floppy disk in the A drive, right-click and choose Send To⇨3½ Floppy (A).

You can also copy all the files on one floppy disk to another floppy disk if your computer has an A: and B: drive. Put the disk whose contents you want to copy in one drive, put an empty disk in the other, right-click the drive with to-be-copied files, and choose Copy Disk on the shortcut menu. The Copy Disk dialog box appears. Select the other drive's icon and click the Start button. This command copies all the content, including blank space, from one floppy disk to another.

The cut-and-paste and copy-and-paste commands

Another way to move or copy files or folders is to take advantage of the cut-and-paste and copy-and-paste commands:

1. **In Windows Explorer or My Computer, select the files and folders you want to move or copy.**

2. **Give the Cut or Copy command.**

Windows offers a bunch of ways to cut or copy items to the Windows clipboard:

- **Cut to move files or folders:** Choose Edit⇨Cut, right-click an item you selected and choose Cut, or press Ctrl+X.

- **Copy to copy files or folders:** Choose Edit⇨Copy, right-click an item you selected and choose Copy, or press Ctrl+C.

3. **Find and select the folder into which you want to copy the items.**

Earlier in this chapter, "Going from folder to folder" explains how to burrow into the folder hierarchy and locate a folder.

4. **Choose Edit⇨Paste, right-click and choose Paste, or press Ctrl+V.**

Phantom images of the files or folders appear on-screen as you drag.

Sometimes you need to keep a copy of a file in the same folder where the original is kept. Maybe you want to keep an earlier draft of a file in the same folder as the up-to-date draft. Or you want to keep one file as the starting point for creating other files.

To make a copy of a file to the same folder, right-click the file you want to copy and choose Copy on the shortcut menu. Windows XP drops a copy into the folder under the same name as the original but with the words *Copy of.* For example, a file called "January Report" is called "Copy of January Report." Now you can right-click the copy, choose Rename on the shortcut menu, and give the copy a more descriptive name.

Starting from the Explorer bar

Yet another way to copy or move folders or files is to let the Explorer bar do the work:

1. **In Windows Explorer or My Computer, select the files and folders you want to move or copy.**

2. **If necessary, display the Explorer bar by clicking the Folders button.**

3. **On the Explorer bar, select Move the Selected Items or Copy the Selected Items.**

You see the Move Items or Copy Items dialog box, as shown in Figure 2-7. Options for moving and copying are found under "File and Folder Tasks" on the Explorer bar. If you don't see these options, click the double arrows. You can give these commands without the help of the Explorer bar by choosing Edit⇨Move to Folder or Edit⇨Copy to Folder.

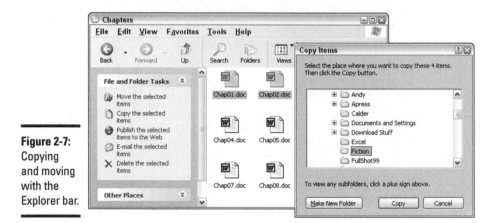

Figure 2-7: Copying and moving with the Explorer bar.

4. **Select the folder into which you want to copy the items.**

Click plus signs (+) until you burrow in and find the folder you're looking for.

5. **Click the Move or Copy button.**

Deleting Folders and Files

After you've gone to the trouble to select the folders and files you want to delete, deleting them is easy. Any of these ways will do:

✦ Press the Delete key.

✦ Choose File⇨Delete.

✦ Choose Delete on the Explorer bar (this command changes names, depending on what is to be deleted).

✦ Right-click an item you selected and choose Delete.

✦ Drag the items you selected over the Recycle Bin icon on the desktop.

A dialog box asks whether you're sure you want to delete the items and send them to the Recycle Bin. Take a good look at the names of the files you want to delete; click Yes if you really want to delete them. Files you delete are sent to the Recycle Bin (the subject of the next section in this chapter), but if you want to send them straight to oblivion, press Shift+Delete rather than Delete when you delete them.

Only files and folders you delete from your local hard dive (usually drive C:) are sent to the Recycle Bin when you delete them. In other words, only these files can be recovered. Files you delete from a floppy disk, a network drive, or a removable medium such as a Zip drive are not sent to the Recycle Bin. Take into consideration these provisos before deleting files and folders:

✦ When you delete a folder, you delete all the files that are stored inside it as well. Before deleting a folder, peer inside to make sure that the files are disposable.

✦ If you share your computer with others, be careful not to delete files or folders that are important to them.

✦ Never delete files in network folders that you share with others unless you have permission from your co-workers.

✦ Never delete a file that's necessary for running a program. Most of the files on your computer fall into this category. Leave 'em alone.

The Recycle Bin: Resuscitating Files and Folders You Deleted

Newspapers, bottles, and cans aren't the only items that can be recycled. You can also recycle files that have been deleted. Deleted files land in a folder called the Recycle Bin, where they remain until you either delete them or they are deleted automatically because they occupy too much disk space. You can, of course, restore a file from the Recycle Bin to its original location on your system.

To open the Recycle Bin, double-click the Recycle Bin icon on the desktop. The Recycle Bin folder appears in Windows Explorer. Be sure to try different views as you decide which files and folders to restore or delete permanently. As "Different ways of viewing folders and files" explains earlier in this chapter, some views are better than others when you're examining different types of files.

If you aren't a fan of the Recycle Bin, you can delete files and folders without sending them to the Recycle Bin first. Pressing Shift+Delete to delete files and folders destroys them permanently. You can also disable the Recycle Bin altogether. Right-click the Recycle Bin icon on the desktop, choose Properties on the shortcut menu, and, in the Recycle Bin Properties dialog box, select Do Not Move Files to the Recycle Bin.

Restoring files you deleted

Files that are restored are returned to the folders they were in when you deleted them. For example, if you delete a file from the My Documents folder, look for it there when you restore it. In Details view, you can see the original location of each item and the date it was deleted.

Here is how to restore files from the Recycle Bin:

+ **Restoring individual files:** Select the files you want to restore. Usually, the best way to do that is to Ctrl+click them. Then click the Restore the Selected Items button on the Explorer Bar, right-click and choose Restore on the shortcut menu, or choose File⇨Restore. (If you don't see the Restore the Selected Items button, click the Folders button to make the Explorer bar appear.)

+ **Restoring all the files:** Click the Restore All Items button on the Explorer Bar.

Permanently deleting files

From time to time, peer into the Recycle Bin and permanently delete files that are unwanted, unneeded, or unnecessary. Follow these instructions to permanently delete files:

+ **Delete selected files:** Select the files and press the Delete key, right-click and choose Delete, or choose File⇨Delete. Then click Yes in the confirmation box.

+ **Delete all files:** Click the Empty the Recycle Bin button in the Explorer bar, choose File⇨Empty Recycle Bin, or right-click the Recycle Bin icon on the desktop and choose Empty Recycle Bin on the shortcut menu. Then click Yes in the confirmation box.

Allocating disk space for deleted files

Windows XP devotes 10 percent of the disk space on your computer for storing deleted files in the Recycle Bin. When the 10-percent capacity is reached, the oldest files in the Recycle Bin are permanently deleted. If you work with multimedia programs whose files can be quite large, you might consider increasing the 10-percent capacity. And if you're running low on disk space, you might consider decreasing the Recycle Bin capacity to allow more room for undeleted files.

To change the Recycle Bin's capacity, right-click the Recycle Bin icon on the desktop and choose Properties. You see the Recycle Bin Properties dialog box shown in Figure 2-8. Drag the Maximum Size slider left or right and click OK.

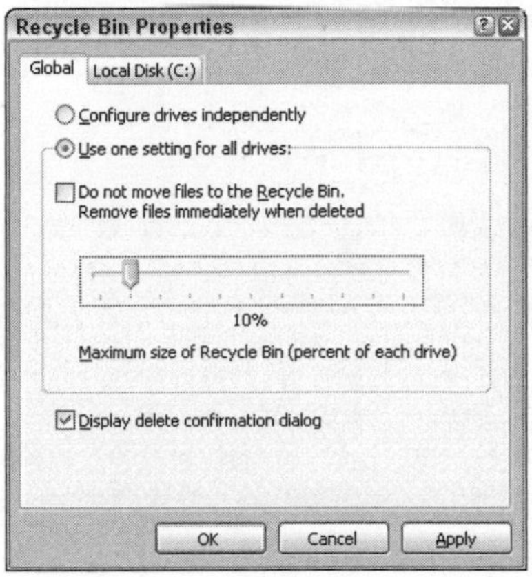

Figure 2-8:
Allocating
disk space
for the
Recycle Bin.

Searching for a Missing File

Files you need most tend to disappear, like socks in the laundry, without a trace. At least it seems that way when you're frantically searching for a file you know is there but can't find. To help you find errant files, Windows XP offers the Search command. Using this command, you describe the lost file as best you can, and Windows XP presents a list of files in Windows Explorer that fit your description, as shown in Figure 2-9.

Windows XP offers simple searches and advanced searches. Start with a simple search, and if it doesn't work out, go with an advanced search. To conduct a search, start by doing one of the following:

✦ Click the Start button and choose Search.

✦ In Windows Explorer, click the Search button, press Ctrl+E, or choose File➪Search. By right-clicking a folder and choosing Search, you can search exclusively in the folder your right-clicked as well as its subfolders.

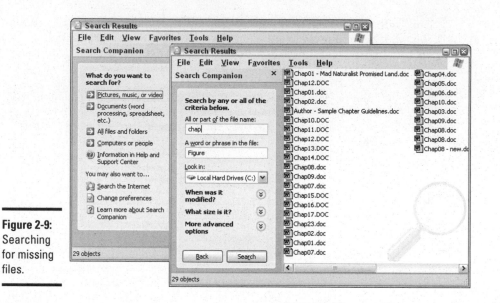

Figure 2-9:
Searching
for missing
files.

Office programs — Word, Excel, PowerPoint, and so on — offer search commands of their own. Choose File➪Search in an Office program to conduct a search there. I've found these Search commands better for searching on a network for Office files.

The Search command is a great way to assemble files from different folders in the same place. After the found files appear in the Windows Explorer window, you can move or copy them all simultaneously to a single folder. For that matter, you can delete them all. Use the Search command not only to search for errant files but also to collect and corral them.

Conducting a simple search

In a simple search, you describe what kind of file you're looking for, describe as best you can a few simple facts about the file, and click the Search button. The Search bar in Windows Explorer offers these basic means of searching for a file:

✦ **Pictures, Music, or Video:** Choose Pictures, Music, or Video and enter all or part of the filename.

✦ **Documents:** Describe when you last opened the document and enter all or part of its filename.

✦ **All Files and Folders:** Enter all or part of the file- or folder name and a word or phrase in the file or in a file in the folder.

The lower-left corner of Windows Explorer lists how many files were found. With any luck, the name of the file you're looking for appears in the window, but if it doesn't, click the Back button and start anew or take advantage of the advance search criteria that appear in the Search bar.

Conducting an advanced search

When you enter search criteria, you needn't make use of all the tools in the Search bar. To pinpoint a folder or file, accurately enter the information that you do know. Depending on which kind of search you are conducting, you can enter this information:

+ **All or Part of the Name:** Enter the entire name if you know it, but if you vaguely remember the name, enter the part of the name that you can remember. For example, entering **chap** finds *Chap*, *chap01*, *Chapter 9*, *chaplain*, and *Schapstuckle*.

You can use the * and ? wildcard characters in filename criteria. The ? finds any single character; the * finds zero or more characters. For example, entering **b?t** finds the filenames *bat, bet, bit*, and *but*; entering t*o finds the filenames *to, two*, and *tattoo*.

+ **A Word or Phrase in the File:** If you know a word in the file, enter it. Be sure to pick an obscure word. Telephone numbers and fax numbers, for example, are excellent choices. These numbers fall in the "one-of-a-kind" category and don't produce many search results.

+ **Look In:** Narrow the search to drives or folders on the drop-down menu. To search in a specific folder and its subfolders, right-click the folder in Windows Explorer and choose Search on the shortcut menu.

+ **When Was It Modified:** Choose the option that best describes when you created or last modified the file.

+ **What Size Is It:** Choose this option if you happen to know the size of the file you're looking for.

+ **Search System Folders:** Choose this in the unlikely event that you want to look in the folders where Windows XP stores its files.

+ **Search Hidden Files or Folders:** Includes files and folders that are normally hidden in the search.

+ **Search Subfolders:** Always search in subfolders. This option is a throwback to the days when computers were slow and searching in subfolders slowed down searches considerably.

✦ **Case Sensitive:** Takes into account capital letters in filenames. For example, entering **Chap** finds files named *Chapter 1* and *Chapel*, but not *chapstick* or *chapel*.

✦ **Search Tape Backup:** You can choose this option to search tape drives.

Compressing and Uncompressing Files

Compress files to make them smaller or to roll several files into a single file that's easier to manage. These days, hard disk space isn't as hard to come by, and most people don't compress files to save on disk space. Most people do it to send files more quickly over the Internet. Depending on what type of file you're dealing with, compressing files can shrink them by 50 to 90 percent. Sending several digital photographs over the Internet takes half to one-tenth the time that it takes to send digital photographs that haven't been compressed. The person to whom you send a compressed file doesn't have to wait as long to get it, nor do you have to wait as long to receive a compressed file. That's the good news. The bad news is that people to whom you send compressed files must have the software to uncompress them. Without the software, they can't open your compressed file. They can't *extract* it, to use file-compression terminology.

Compressed files are often called "Zip files" because they're usually compressed with WinZip, the most popular utility for compressing files. Everyone with a computer that runs Windows XP can compress and uncompress files. Windows XP offers the Compression utility for doing just that. What's more, the Compression utility can uncompress — or unzip — files that were compressed with WinZip. However, if WinZip or another third-party compression utility is installed on your computer, you can't use the Compression utility to compress files. You have to compress them using the third-party utility. If you try to use the Compression utility, Windows XP runs the third-party utility anyway.

After you compress files into a Zip file, Windows XP attaches a folder icon with a little zipper on it to the file. Zip files take some getting used to. A Zip file is a folder in the sense that it holds files and Windows XP treats it like a folder, but a Zip file is just that as well — it's a file. When you double-click a Zip file, its contents don't appear in My Computer or Windows Explorer. Because a Zip file is a hybrid between a folder and a file, I call it a folder-file. At any rate, look for folders with zippers on them when you try to locate Zip files.

Compressing files

Besides shrinking them, compressing files gives you the opportunity to roll them all together into one file. The twelve digital photographs you want to send to Aunt Enid can be sent in one file attachment rather than twelve. The fifty files you want to copy to a CD-R can be stored on the CD as one file rather than fifty.

Follow these steps to compress a file or files:

1. **Select the file or files you want to compress, as shown in Figure 2-10.**

Files of different types can be compressed into the same Zip file. Earlier in this chapter, "Selecting files and folders" explains how to select files.

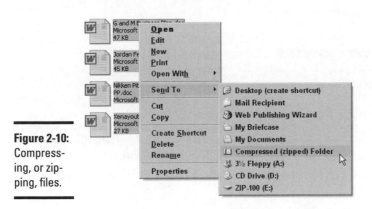

Figure 2-10:
Compress-
ing, or zip-
ping, files.

2. **Right-click and choose Send To➪Compressed (Zipped) Folder.**

What happens next depends on whether a third-party compression utility has been installed on your computer:

- **No third-party utility is installed:** You're done.

- **Third-party utility installed:** Click Yes or No — it doesn't matter — when the dialog box asks whether you want to associate compressed files with the Windows XP Compression utility, not the third-party utility.

As "Choosing which program opens certain types of files" explains in Chapter 1, Windows XP wants to associate each file type with one kind of program. Here, Windows XP is asking you to make its Compression utility the official compression program on your computer, but it doesn't matter what you decide, because you can't compress files with the Compression utility anyway if another compression utility is on your computer.

The third-party utility compresses the files, names the compressed file after the last file you selected, and places it in the same folder as the files you compressed. In other words, if the last file you selected is called Learning3, the folder-file is called Learning3 as well. To rename a compressed folder-file, right-click it and choose Rename.

Knowing that people like to send compressed files over the Internet, Windows XP offers a convenient command for sending compressed files right after you create them. Right-click the Zip folder-file and choose Send To➪Mail Recipient. Whichever e-mail program you use opens so that you can compose an e-mail message to go along with your compressed file. Book II explains how to send e-mail.

Uncompressing files

If someone sends you a Zip, or compressed, file, follow these steps to extract the files from the Zip file:

1. **Right-click the folder-file.**

Which command you choose on the shortcut menu depends on whether a third-party compression utility is installed on your computer:

- **No third-party utility is installed:** Choose Extract All on the short-cut menu.

- **Third-party utility installed:** Choose Open With➪Compressed (Zipped) Folders. Windows Explorer opens the Zip folder-file in a new window. Now you can see the names of the files that you're about to extract. Click Extract All Files in the Explorer bar.

The Extraction Wizard dialog box appears.

2. **Click the Next button.**

If you want, click the Browse button and choose a folder for the files you're about to extract in the Select a Destination dialog box. If you simply click Next, the extracted files will land in the folder-file where the Zip file is currently located.

3. **Click the Next button.**

The Extraction Complete dialog box appears.

4. **Click the Finish button.**

You see the extracted files in a new Windows Explorer window. From here, you can open a file or move files elsewhere. Click the Folders button to see where the folder with the extracted files is located on your computer.

Handling Read-Only Files

Occasionally you try to open a file and a message box tells you that it's "read-only." Read-only files can be read but cannot be changed in any way, shape, or form. Often these are files copied from the Internet or a CD-ROM.

Follow these steps to turn a read-only file into a read-write file that can be altered:

1. **Locate the file in Windows Explorer.**

2. **Right-click the File and choose Properties to open the Properties dialog box.**

3. **On the General tab, clear the Read-Only check box and click OK.**

Chapter 3: Making Windows XP Work Your Way

In This Chapter

✔ **Creating shortcut icons**

✔ **Changing the screen resolution**

✔ **Personalizing the desktop and screen**

✔ **Customizing the mouse**

✔ **Customizing the menu system**

✔ **Creating and switching among user accounts**

Seeing as how you have to stare at Windows XP as you work, you may as well stare at a pretty face as an ugly one. This chapter explains the numerous and sundry ways to change the look of the Windows desktop and Windows screens. It tells you how to customize the mouse and keyboard, and how to create user accounts so that the settings you make in Windows don't disturb the peace of mind of the people with whom you share your computer.

Creating Your Own Shortcut Icons

Shortcuts are one of the best things going in Windows XP. Why burrow into the All Programs menu to open a program when you can click a shortcut icon on the desktop? Create a shortcut icon to a Web page you visit regularly and all you have to do is click its icon to open your Web browser and go to the Web page. To quickly print a file, create a shortcut to a printer and then simply drop files to the shortcut icon on your desktop without having to open the files. Creating shortcuts, I'm happy to report, is easy.

Creating a shortcut icon

How you create a shortcut depends on what item you're dealing with:

✦ **Shortcut to a program:** Click the Start button, choose All Programs, and find the program name on the menu. When you have found it, right-click it and choose Create Shortcut. At the bottom of the menu, you see a shortcut item with the number 2 after its name. Drag the item with the 2 after its name onto the desktop. That's right — just drag it.

✦ **Shortcut to a file:** In My Computer or Windows Explorer, find the file, right-click it, and choose Send To⇨Desktop (Create Shortcut) on the shortcut menu. Windows creates a shortcut called "Shortcut to *Filename*" and places it on the desktop.

✦ **A Web page:** In Windows Explorer, go to the Web page that needs a shortcut. Then click and drag the Windows Explorer logo on the Address bar to the desktop. If you don't see the Address bar, right-click the menu bar and choose Address Bar. You can also create a Web page shortcut by opening the Favorites menu in Windows Explorer and dragging a favorite Web site on the menu to the desktop.

✦ **A printer:** Click the Start button and choose Control Panel. In the Control Panel window, choose Printers and Other Hardware. Choose View Installed Printers or Fax Printers. You land in the Printers and Faxes Folder. Your default printer shows a checkmark beside its name. Right-click the icon that represents the printer and choose Create Shortcut on the menu. Click Yes when Windows asks whether to create the shortcut on the desktop. To print a file, drag and drop it from the My Computer or Windows Explorer window to the printer shortcut icon.

Usually, shortcuts need renaming after they land on the desktop. To give a shortcut a descriptive name, right-click it, choose Rename, and enter the name.

Drag desktop icons where you prefer them to go. If they refuse to be dragged, right-click the desktop, choose Arrange Icons By, and unselect the Auto Arrange option.

Deleting a shortcut icon

To delete a shortcut icon, right-click it, choose Delete on the shortcut menu, and click Yes when Windows asks whether you really want to delete your shortcut icon. Don't worry about deleting the file, folder, or program that the shortcut goes to — you're merely deleting a shortcut when you delete a shortcut icon. You can delete several shortcut icons at one time by holding down the Ctrl key and clicking as you select them. As with files, shortcut icons go to the Recycle Bin after they are deleted.

A handful of shortcut icons on the desktop — My Computer, My Documents, My Network Places, and Recycle Bin — cannot be removed except by your jumping through a hoop while doing a back flip. To remove these icons:

1. **Right-click the desktop and choose Properties.**

2. **Select the Desktop tab in the Display Properties dialog box.**

3. Click the Customize <u>D</u>esktop button to open the Desktop Items dialog box.

4. As shown in Figure 3-1, unselect the desktop icons you no longer want and click the Apply button.

Practicing crowd control with a desktop folder

If you're not careful, the Windows desktop can get littered with shortcut icons. One way to handle this problem is to create a desktop folder and put shortcut icons inside it. When you want to take a shortcut, you open the desktop folder, see the icons all in a row, and click the one you want to activate.

To create a desktop folder, right-click in the desktop and choose New➪Folder. A folder icon appears. Type a name for your folder (how about "My Shortcuts"?) and press Enter. Double-click the desktop folder to open it; then drag shortcut icons into the new folder. When you need to double-click a shortcut icon, you'll know where to find it — in your Shortcuts folder on the desktop.

You can also let Windows XP do the work of creating a desktop folder for redundant shortcut icons. Windows puts the icons in a folder called Unused Desktop Shortcuts. Right-click the desktop and choose P<u>r</u>operties. In the Display Properties dialog box, select the Desktop tab and click the Customize <u>D</u>esktop button. Then, on the General tab of the Desktop Icons dialog box (refer to Figure 3-1), click the <u>C</u>lean Desktop Now button. A series of wizard dialog boxes appear so that you can choose which shortcuts get put in the Unused Desktop Shortcuts folder.

Desktop Cleanup Wizard		
Shortcuts
The shortcuts selected below will be moved to the Unused Desktop Shortcuts folder.		

To leave a shortcut on your desktop, clear its check box.

Shortcuts:

Shortcut to Clean Up	Date Last Used
☐ Internet Explorer	11/14/2002
☑ Calculator	Never
☑ Mathscribe Lite	Never
☑ OpenOffice.org 1.0	Never
☐ FullShot99	11/26/2002
☐ Window Washer	11/22/2002

< <u>B</u>ack   <u>N</u>ext >   Cancel

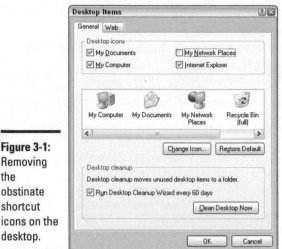

Figure 3-1:
Removing
the
obstinate
shortcut
icons on the
desktop.

Managing the Taskbar

Everybody knows that you can click program buttons on the Taskbar to switch from file to file, but few understand that you can tame the Taskbar and make it do your bidding with these nifty techniques:

✦ **Resizing:** To make the Taskbar fatter or thinner, move the mouse over the border of the Taskbar, and click and drag when you see the double-headed arrows. Resize the Taskbar to make more room for program buttons.

✦ **Moving:** Move the Taskbar to a side or the top of the screen by dragging it there. To accomplish this feat, click carefully between buttons, not on a program button.

✦ **"Auto-hiding":** The Auto-Hide option is a convenient way of grabbing more room for programs on-screen. When Auto-Hide is on, the Taskbar does not appear. To see it, move the mouse pointer to the very bottom of the desktop — the Taskbar comes out of hiding so that you can use it. To turn on the Auto-Hide option, right-click the Taskbar and choose Properties. You see the Taskbar and Start Menu Properties dialog box. Select the Auto-Hide the Taskbar check box.

Before you can start fooling with the Taskbar, you need to unlock it. A locked Taskbar stubbornly stays in one place no matter how hard you push or pull. To unlock the Taskbar, right-click it and unselect the Lock the Taskbar option.

Resetting the clock

On the right side of the Taskbar, the clock tells you the time. It also tells the date and day of the week if you point to it with the mouse pointer. If the clock needs resetting, simply double-click it. You see the Date and Time Properties dialog box. From there, you can reset the clock and change the date as well.

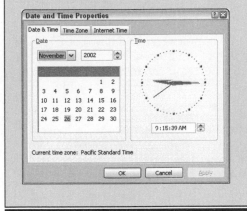

Use the Time Zone tab to tell Windows XP which time zone you're in. If your computer is connected to the Internet, you can synchronize your computer's time with Greenwich Mean Time on the Internet Time tab.

Follow these steps to change the format by which the date and time are displayed on the clock:

1. **Click the Start button and choose Control Panel.**

2. **Click the Date, Time, Language, and Regional Options icon.**

3. **Choose Change the Format of Numbers, Dates, and Times.**

   You see the Regional and Language Options dialog box.

4. **Choose a country from the drop-down list and click the Apply button.**

Tackling the Quick Launch Toolbar

The Quick Launch toolbar is the mini-toolbar on the Taskbar. Put shortcut icons for your favorite programs on the Quick Launch toolbar so that you can open the programs without having to visit the desktop or open the All Programs or Start menu. To place a shortcut icon on the Quick Launch toolbar:

1. **Create the shortcut icon and put it on the desktop ("Creating a short-cut icon" earlier in this chapter explains how).**

2. **Drag the shortcut icon onto the Quick Launch toolbar.**

   Could anything be easier?

Here are more techniques for tackling the Quick Launch toolbar:

✦ **Removing (or displaying) the Quick Launch toolbar:** Right-click the Taskbar and choose Toolbars➪Quick Launch to unselect (or select) the Quick Launch option.

✦ **Repositioning icons:** Drag the icon left or right.

✦ **Repositioning the toolbar:** Close all open programs (so that no program buttons are on the Taskbar) and drag the Quick Launch toolbar to one side or the other on the Taskbar.

✦ **Removing shortcut icons:** Drag the icon from the Quick Launch toolbar to the desktop.

✦ **Seeing large or small icons:** Right-click the Quick Launch toolbar and choose View⇨Large Icons or View⇨Small Icons.

Making the Screen Easier to See and Read

The eyes aren't meant to stare at a computer screen all day. The eyes are meant to gaze into the distance to detect the presence of protein-rich animals. You owe it to yourself to do the best you can to make gazing at the computer screen as easy on your protein-seeking eyes as possible.

Toward that goal, Windows XP offers numerous ways to change the appearance of the screen. They are explained in the pages that follow. Most screen-tinkering techniques start at the Display Properties dialog box. To get there, right-click the desktop and choose Properties. On the five tabs of the dialog box, you can change the look of Windows XP in these different ways:

✦ **Themes:** Select an overall design for Windows XP.

✦ **Desktop:** Choose a background color or design for the desktop.

✦ **Screen Saver:** Choose a screen saver, the picture that appears on-screen when your computer is idle.

✦ **Appearance:** Choose a color scheme and font for windows.

✦ **Settings:** Choose a screen resolution and change the color setting.

Choosing a screen size and screen resolution

In computer lingo, *screen resolution* describes how many pixels are used to display images and words on the computer screen. A *pixel* (the term stands for "picture element") is a tiny dot that, together with other dots, forms on-screen images. The more pixels, the larger the screen appears to be.

Figure 3-2 and Figure 3-3 compare two screens, one at the 800-by-600 pixel setting, and one at the 1024-by-768 pixel setting. As shown in Figure 3-3, the 1024-by-768 setting permits more stuff to be shown on-screen, but the 800-by-600 setting makes everything larger and easier to read, as Figure 3-2 demonstrates. Selecting screen resolutions is always a trade-off. What you gain by seeing things more clearly, you lose by not seeing as many things.

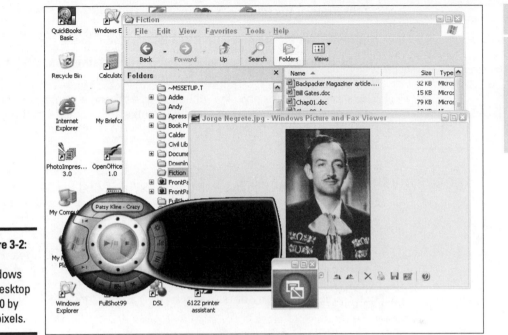

Figure 3-2:
The
Windows
XP desktop
at 800 by
600 pixels.

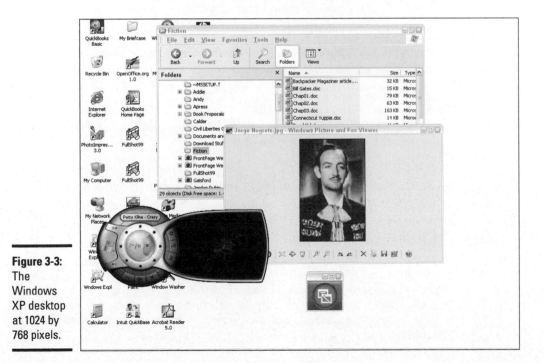

Figure 3-3:
The
Windows
XP desktop
at 1024 by
768 pixels.

Follow these steps to change screen resolutions:

1. **Right-click an empty place on the desktop and choose P̲roperties.**

2. **On the Settings tab of the Display Properties dialog box, drag the S̲creen Resolution slider to the setting you want.**

   The sample monitor gives an inkling of what these settings will look like on-screen. Which Screen Resolution settings are available in the Display Properties dialog box depends on what type of monitor is attached to your computer.

3. **Click OK.**

   The screen abruptly changes to the new setting, and the Monitor Settings dialog box asks what you think of this new arrangement.

4. **Click Y̲es to keep it or N̲o to beat a hasty retreat.**

To further experiment with screen resolutions, try clicking the Adv̲anced button on the Settings tab. Then, in the Default Monitor and Properties dialog box, choose an option from the D̲PI Setting drop-down list. This setting determines how many dots per inch (dpi) appear on-screen.

Choosing a color setting

The Color settings determine how many colors appear on-screen. How many choices you have for colors depends on your monitor and computer. The more colors that appear on-screen, the sharper the images. However, displaying too many colors can slow down a computer, especially if it's slow to begin with.

Follow these steps to choose a color scheme:

1. **Right-click an empty place on the desktop and choose P̲roperties to see the Display Properties dialog box.**

2. **Select the Settings tab.**

3. **Choose an option from the C̲olor Quality drop-down list and click the A̲pply button.**

Choosing a theme

As you're about to discover if you're brave enough to read the next half-dozen pages, Windows XP gives you numerous opportunities to change the look of the screen. You can change the appearance of the desktop, choose a screen saver, and, if you're truly brave, choose color schemes and font settings for every aspect of Windows — title bars, scroll bars, messages boxes, and more.

Rather than go to all the trouble of changing the appearance of different parts of the screen, why not choose a theme? In Windows terminology, a *theme* is a collection of screen settings that have been saved under a name. Chances are, you can find a theme that suits you. And if you know your way around the Display Properties dialog box, you can create a theme of your own and save it. This way, you can switch to a theme when the circumstances require it.

Follow these steps to choose a theme:

1. **Right-click the desktop and choose Properties to open the Display Properties dialog box.**

2. **Select the Themes tab.**

3. **Choose a Theme from the Theme drop-down list and click the Apply button.**

To create a theme of your own, start by choosing a name, and then, piece by piece, construct the theme and be sure to save it from time to time so that the construction work you do doesn't get lost. Follow these steps to create a theme of your own:

1. **Right-click the desktop, choose Properties to open the Display Properties dialog box, and select the Themes tab.**

2. **From the Theme drop-down list, choose the theme that most resembles the one you want to create.**

   This way, you get a head start and don't have to do as much work to create your theme. You can start with the settings in the theme you chose and modify them, rather than start from scratch.

3. **Click the Save As button and, in the Save As dialog box, choose a folder in which to store your theme, give the theme a descriptive name, and click the Save button.**

4. **Visit the Desktop, Screen Saver, Appearance, and Settings tabs, and make selections there to construct the theme you want.**

   The next handful of pages describe how these tabs work.

5. **From time to time as you construct your theme, return to the Themes tab, click the Save As button, and, in the Save As dialog box, click the Save button.**

   By doing this, you save the work you've done so far on your theme. Just be sure *not* to enter a new name in the Save As dialog box.

6. **Click the Apply button when you're done constructing your theme.**

   You can choose your theme from the Theme drop-down list whenever you need it.

Tinkering with the desktop's appearance

Yet another way to play interior decorator with Windows XP is to go to the Appearance tab of the Display Properties dialog box. To get there, right-click the desktop, choose Properties on the shortcut menu, and select the Appearance tab. You can choose different window and button schemes, color schemes, and font sizes from this dialog box. Just be sure to keep your eye on the sample window — it shows what your choices amount to.

If you're especially brave or you have a lot of time on your hands, click the Advanced button and choose screen colors and fonts for different parts of Windows XP — title bars, scroll bars, ToolTips, and more — in the Advanced Appearance dialog box. Go here only if you're confident and immortal.

Sharing themes with friends and co-workers

Settings you choose for a theme are stored in what's called a Windows Theme file. There is one Windows Theme file on your computer for every theme on the Themes tab of the Display Properties dialog box. When you choose a theme, you're really choosing a new Windows Theme file for your computer to work with.

If you create a theme and want to pass it along to a friend or co-worker, you can do so by passing along the Windows Theme file that holds the theme and instructing your friend or co-worker how to install the theme on their computer.

To find out where a Windows Theme file is located on your computer, open the Themes Tab of the Display Properties dialog box, select the theme you want to share with others, and click the Save As button. The Save As dialog box opens to the folder where the Windows Theme file is stored. You can also find Windows Theme files on your computer with the Search command: Click the Start button, choose Search, choose All Files and Folders, choose More Advanced Options, and choose Windows Theme

File on the Type of File drop-down list. After you locate the Windows Theme file, copy and send it to your friends or co-workers.

Friends and co-workers can load your Windows theme on their computers by following these steps:

1. **Place the Windows Theme file in a folder and remember where the folder is located.**

2. **Right-click the desktop, choose Properties to open the Display Properties dialog box, and select the Themes tab.**

3. **On the Theme drop-down list, choose Browse.**

    You see the Open Theme dialog box.

4. **Go to the folder where you placed the Windows Theme file, select the file, and click the Open button.**

    The name of the theme appears in the Display Properties dialog box.

5. **Click the Apply button.**

Dressing up the desktop background

Another way to make the Windows XP screen prettier is to change the look of the desktop background. As Figure 3-4 shows, you can choose from numerous colors and designs for the desktop background; you can also place a digital picture of your own on the desktop. Follow these instructions:

Figure 3-4:
Examples of
desktops.

✦ **Windows XP desktop background:** To choose a Windows XP desktop background, right-click the desktop and choose P̲roperties. Then, on the Desktop tab of the Display Properties dialog box, choose a design from the Bac̲kground list. In some cases, you can tweak the design by choosing options from the P̲osition and C̲olor menus.

✦ **Desktop picture:** Open the picture in the Windows Picture and Fax Viewer (find the picture in Windows Explorer or My Computer, right-click its filename, and choose Open Wit̲h⇨Windows Picture and Fax Viewer). Then right-click the picture and choose Set As Desktop B̲ackground. The picture you choose is added to the Background list on the Desktop tab of the Display Properties dialog box.

If you regret postering your desktop with a design or image, you can always return to the Display Properties dialog box and choose a different background image.

Here's a little trick: If you see an image on a Web page that you want as the background on your Windows XP desktop, right-click the image and choose Set As Background on the shortcut menu.

Choosing a screen saver

A *screen saver* is a picture that appears on-screen when your computer has been idle for a certain period of time, as shown in Figure 3-5. Once upon a time, computer screens suffered from burn-in if they were idle too long. The monitor's phosphorous lining would be damaged. Although burn-in is a thing of the past, people still like their screen savers. They express your personality. And they pop on-screen to let you know when you've been daydreaming too long and need to get back to work.

Figure 3-5:
Examples of
screen
savers.

Follow these steps to choose a screen saver and tell Windows XP how many minutes to let pass before putting it on-screen:

1. **Right-click an empty place on the desktop and choose Properties to see the Display Properties dialog box.**

2. **On the Screen Saver tab, choose a screen saver from the drop-down list and glance at the sample monitor to see what it is.**

3. **Click the Preview button if the sample screen saver doesn't appear. With some screen savers, you can click the Settings button and tweak the screen saver in the Settings dialog box.**

4. **In the Wait text box, enter how many minutes should elapse before the screen saver kicks in.**

   Enter **1** if you're lazy — the screen saver will burst on-screen after every minute you waste by dreaming.

5. **Click OK.**

Using a picture of your own as a screen saver

Instead of Microsoft's ready-made screen savers, how would you like to use one of your own? You can make your boss's face appear on-screen, or your mom's, or your special someone's. In fact, you can see a "slide show" with several pictures appearing in succession.

First, create a new folder and place the digital image or images you want to use as a screen saver in the folder. Then take note of where the folder is located on your computer and follow these steps to set up your own personal screen saver:

1. **Right-click the desktop and choose Properties.**

2. **On the Screen Saver tab of the Display Properties dialog box, open the Screen Saver drop-down menu and choose My Pictures Slideshow.**

3. **Click the Settings button to open the My Pictures Screen Saver Options dialog box.**

4. **Click the Browse button and, in the Browse for Folder dialog box, select the folder where the screen saver image or images are located; then click OK.**

5. **If you so desire, select other options in the My Pictures Screen Saver Options dialog box (they are self-explanatory).**

6. **Click OK and then click Apply.**

Preventing Eyestrain

After you reach the tender age of forty, the eyes start to go. Reading the small print becomes nearly impossible. While surfing the Internet, you can tell which Web sites were designed by brash, upstart twentysomethings — those Web sites have elaborate flash-screen animations and tiny words and letters that twenty-year-olds can read but you can barely see. What's with kids these days, anyway?

Here are some tips for preventing eyestrain as you sit at your computer:

✦ **Keep your monitor in the proper light:** Glare causes eyestrain. If yours is a conventional monitor, keep it out of direct light to reduce glare, and use an adjustable light to illuminate whatever it is you're working with besides your computer and monitor. If yours is an LCD (liquid crystal display) monitor, put the monitor in direct light. LCD displays — laptops have LCD monitors — do not produce glare.

✦ **Adjust the knobs on the monitor:** You know those knobs and buttons on your monitor? They can be helpful. Play with them until the screen looks just-so.

✦ **Choose a small screen resolution:** As "Choosing a screen size and screen resolution" explains earlier in this chapter, small screen resolutions make items look bigger on-screen.

✦ **Put large icons on the desktop:** Right-click the desktop and choose Properties. In the Display Properties dialog box, select the Appearance tab, click the Effects button, and choose Use Large Icons in the Effects dialog box.

✦ **Make icons on the Start menu larger:** Right-click the Taskbar and choose Properties. In the Taskbar and Start Menu Properties dialog box, select the Start Menu tab, click the Customize button (the first one), and, on the General tab of the Customize Start Menu dialog box, select Large Icons.

✦ **Take advantage of the Zoom command:** Every Office program has a Zoom command for making everything on-screen look larger. Use the Zoom command often.

✦ **Enlarge the mouse pointer:** Larger mouse pointers are easier to see on-screen, especially if you're using a laptop computer. Click the Start button and choose Control Panel. In the Control Panel window, select Switch to Classic View. Then click the Mouse icon to see the Mouse Properties dialog box. On the Pointers tab, Windows Standard (Extra Large) or Windows Standard (Large) from the Scheme drop-down menu.

✦ **Use pointer trails:** While you're in the Mouse Properties dialog box, go to the Pointer Options tab and check the Show Pointer Trails check box if you use a laptop. Pointer trails help you find the mouse on-screen.

If seeing and reading the computer screen is a serious problem for you, try out the Windows XP Accessibility options. These options are for people with physical impairments, including very poor eyesight. To experiment with the Accessibility options, click the Start button and choose Control Panel. Then choose Accessibility Options.

Making the Mouse Work Better

Windows XP offers a bunch of different options for fine-tuning the mouse. Examining these options and choosing the ones that will work for you is worthwhile. Strangely, however, you cannot get to these options in the Control Panel without switching to Classic view (I show you how shortly). What's with that?

Options for fine-tuning the mouse are found in the Mouse Properties dialog box shown in Figure 3-6. Follow this roundabout route to the dialog box:

1. **Click the Start button.**

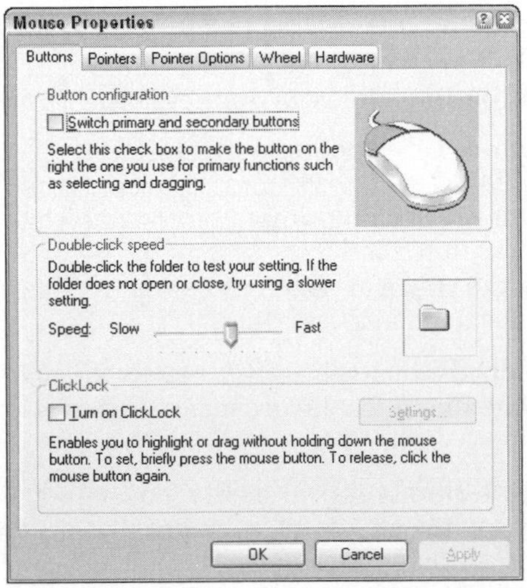

Mouse Properties

Buttons | Pointers | Pointer Options | Wheel | Hardware

Button configuration

☐ Switch primary and secondary buttons

Select this check box to make the button on the right the one you use for primary functions such as selecting and dragging.

Double-click speed

Double-click the folder to test your setting. If the folder does not open or close, try using a slower setting.

Speed: Slow ———————□——— Fast

ClickLock

☐ Turn on ClickLock   Settings...

Enables you to highlight or drag without holding down the mouse button. To set, briefly press the mouse button. To release, click the mouse button again.

OK   Cancel   Apply

Figure 3-6:
Fine-tuning
the mouse.

2. **Choose Control Panel to open the Control Panel in Windows Explorer.**

3. **Select Switch to Classic View.**

If you don't see this option, you're either in Classic view already or you need to click the Folders button. You find the Switch to Classic View option in the upper-left corner of the window.

4. **Double-click the Mouse icon to display the Mouse Properties dialog box (refer to Figure 3-6).**

The Buttons tab in the Mouse Properties dialog box offers these options:

✦ **Button Configuration:** For lefties, this option is for swapping the functions of the left and right mouse buttons.

✦ **Double-Click Speed:** For changing the time it takes to execute a double-click. Drag the slider and test your settings by double-clicking the sample folder.

✦ **ClickLock:** For dragging items without having to hold down the mouse button. With ClickLock on, you click an item and the pointer locks onto it so that you don't have to hold the button down. Click the Settings button and, in the Settings for ClickLock dialog box, choose the amount of time you will need to hold down the mouse button for Windows to recognize that you want to drag an item.

The Pointers tab provides options for changing the pointers' size and shape:

✦ **Scheme:** Choose a scheme to change all the pointers simultaneously. The dialog box shows what the new pointers are.

✦ **Customize:** If you want to change one pointer in the scheme, select it, click the Browse button, and choose a pointer in the Browse dialog box.

✦ **Enable Pointer Shadow:** Gives pointers a 3-D look.

The Pointer Options tab is for deciding what pointers look like on-screen:

✦ **Motion:** Determines the speed at which the pointer glides across the screen. Drag the slider to choose a setting.

✦ **Snap To:** When you open a dialog box, this places the pointer on the default option, the one that the software maker believes is most likely to be chosen.

 ✦ **Visibility:** Makes pointer trails appear as the mouse moves on-screen. A *pointer trail* is a series of ghostly pointer images that describe in which direction the pointer is traveling. Drag the slider to decide how many pointer ghosts to see. This option is very helpful on laptop computers.

✦ **Hide Pointer While Typing:** Makes the pointer disappear whenever you enter text on-screen.

✦ **Show Location of Pointer When I Press the Ctrl Key:** For people who often lose track of the pointer, this option lets you find it by pressing the Ctrl key. When you press the Ctrl key, circles appear around the pointer.

Whether to single-click or double-click

On the subject of clicking, Windows XP gives you the option of treating your computer screen like a Web site. On a Web site, you click a link to go to a new window. You click once, not twice. If you prefer single-clicking to double-clicking, you can dispense with double-clicking and single-click instead. Follow these steps:

1. **Click the Start button and choose Control Panel.**

2. **In the Control Panel window, select Appearances and Themes.**

3. **Choose Folder Options.**

   You see the Folder Options dialog box.

4. **On the General tab, choose Single-Click to Open an Item and click OK.**

The Wheel tab is for determining how far you scroll each time you rotate the wheel on your mouse, if your mouse has a wheel. Enter a setting in the text box or choose <u>O</u>ne Screen at a Time.

Customizing the Keyboard

Speedy typists and people with long, manicured fingernails can customize the keyboard and decide for themselves how sensitive or sticky to make the keys. You can also tell Windows XP how fast to make the cursor blink. The *cursor* is the vertical line that marks the place on-screen where text appears when you start typing.

Follow these steps to control the keyboard's responsiveness and the cursor blink rate:

1. Click the Start button and choose <u>C</u>ontrol Panel to open the Control Panel in Windows Explorer.

2. Select Switch to Classic View.

   Strangely, you can't get to the keyboard options without switching to Classic view. If you don't see the Switch to Classic View option in the upper-left corner of the window, you are in Classic view already or else you need to click the Folders button to see the Control Panel bar.

3. Double-click the Keyboard icon to display the Keyboard Properties dialog box, shown in Figure 3-7.

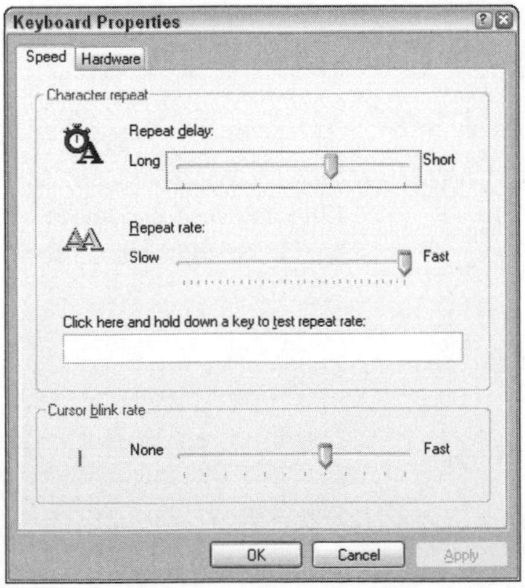

Figure 3-7:
Customizing
the
keyboard.

4. **Play with the Repeat <u>D</u>elay and <u>R</u>epeat Rate settings until you find a character repeat rate that's comfortable.**

   You can test your settings by typing in the text box.

5. **Under Cursor <u>B</u>link Rate, watch the sample cursor and drag the slider between None and Fast until you find a comfortable rate.**

   Eight out of ten doctors recommend a cursor blink rate that matches your heartbeat.

6. **Click OK to close the dialog box.**

Customizing the Menu System

The Windows XP menus can get terribly crowded. Finding the name of a program can sometimes be like finding the proverbial needle in the haystack. And sometimes the name of a program you want to open doesn't appear on any menu.

Fortunately, changing the menu system around is surprisingly easy because names on menus are really shortcuts. When you click a program name on a menu, you activate a shortcut to the executable file of the program that you want to open. Windows maintains these menu shortcuts in special folders in the C:\Documents and Settings\All Users\Start Menu folder and its subfolders. When you slide program names around in the menu system, all you really do is move shortcuts to new folders.

The My Recent Documents Menu

One of the easiest ways to open a file is to do it from the Start menu: Click the Start button, choose My Recent <u>D</u>ocuments, and select from the last several files you opened. If My Recent Documents doesn't appear on your Start menu, or for that matter if you don't want it to appear, follow these steps to tell Windows whether you want to open files from the My Recent Document submenu:

1. **Click the Start button to display the Start menu.**

2. **Right-click a blank space on the menu and choose Properties.**

You see the Taskbar and Start Menu Properties dialog box.

3. **Click the first Customize button, the one next to the Start Menu option.**

   The Customize Start Menu dialog box appears.

4. **Select the Advanced Tab.**

5. **Check or uncheck the List My Most Recently Opened Documents option and click OK.**

Adding a folder name to the Send To submenu

The Send To submenu is one of the nicest things going in Windows XP. By right-clicking a file or folder in Windows Explorer or My Computer, choosing Se̲nd To, and choosing a submenu command, you can send a file or folder any number of places very quickly — to a floppy disk, the My Documents folder, or a CD. Besides these conventional choices, you can place the name of a folder of your own on the Send To submenu. This way, instead of going to the trouble of moving files to the same folder over and over again, you can simply right-click, choose Se̲nd To, and select the name of your folder.

To place a folder of your own on the Send To submenu, create a shortcut to the folder. Then place the shortcut in the C:\Documents and Settings*Your Name*\SendTo folder.

Removing a program name from a menu

To remove a program name from a menu, simply open the menu, right-click the program name, and choose U̲nderline Delete. Removing a program name from a menu in no way removes the program from your computer. The program is removed in name only. Remove program names after you uninstall software.

Moving program names and submenus

To move a program name or submenu to a new location in the menu system, drag it. Click the icon beside its name and carefully drag it up or down the menu. When the black line is where you want the program name to be, release the mouse button. To move a program name onto a submenu, drag the name over the submenu, wait until the submenu opens, and drag the name onto the submenu.

Dragging can be problematic when you want to move a program or submenu a long distance on a crowded All Programs menu, but it can be done. Just drag slowly and patiently.

Creating a submenu for the All Programs menu

So, you want to create a new submenu on the All Programs and put all your favorite programs on it. To do that, follow these steps:

1. **Open Windows Explorer or My Computer to the C:\Documents and Settings\All Users\Start Menu\Programs folder.**

2. **Select the Programs folder.**

To do so, you might have to click the Folders button to display folders on the left side of the window.

3. **Choose File⇨New⇨Folder, enter a name for your new submenu, and press the Enter key.**

Now all you have to do is put program names on your new submenu (see the previous section "Moving program names and submenus").

Sharing Your Computer with Others

If you share your computer with others, you owe it to them and to yourself to create *user accounts.* With user accounts, family members and co-workers who share a computer can personalize the computer without risking the displeasure of others. Instead of the standard Welcome screen, you see a screen like the one in Figure 3-8 when you start your computer. From here, you choose the name of your user account, and Windows XP opens to a computer whose settings are yours and yours alone. As I explain shortly, you can switch from user account to user account without shutting down the computer.

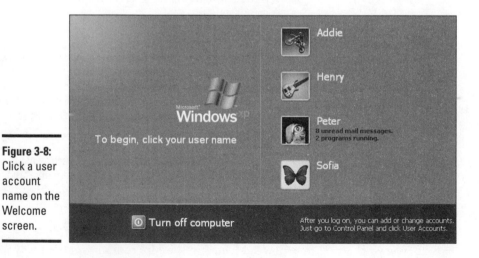

Figure 3-8: Click a user account name on the Welcome screen.

Creating a user account for each person who shares a computer has these advantages:

✦ Each person can change the screen settings — the screen saver, desktop appearance, and so on — to his or her liking.

+ Each user gets his or her My Documents folder for storing files. In the Save As dialog box, for example, you can click the My Documents button, save the file in the My Documents folder, and rest assured that your files and no one else's are stored there. (In case you need to move files, My Document folders for user accounts can be found at this location: C:\Documents and Settings*User Account Name*\\My Documents.)

+ Windows creates a Shared Documents folder so that people with different user accounts can keep their documents in the same folder if they want.

+ Each user gets a Favorites folder for storing Web site addresses and folder locations. You can assemble a library of Web sites that you like to visit and see your Web sites exclusively when, for example, you open the Favorites menu in the Internet Explorer browser.

+ Each user can choose his or her own View settings for examining files in folders in My Computer and Windows Explorer.

Three types of user accounts are available:

+ **Computer administrator account:** Can install and remove software and hardware, create new user accounts, delete user accounts, and change account names and passwords.

+ **Limited account:** Can change account passwords.

+ **Guest account:** Can use the computer but not change any settings.

Be sure to tell the others who use your computer that you intend to create user accounts. After you create one, users are greeted by a different Welcome screen (refer to Figure 3-8) and they follow different procedures for shutting down, as I explain shortly.

If you don't see a Welcome screen like the one in Figure 3-8 after you create user accounts, click the Start button, choose Control Panel, click the User Accounts icon, select Change the Way Users Log On and Off, and choose the Use the Welcome Screen option in the dialog box that appears.

Creating and changing a user account

Follow these steps to create a computer administrator or limited user account:

1. **Click the Start button and choose Control Panel.**

2. **Click the User Accounts icon in the Control Panel window.**

   The User Accounts dialog box opens.

3. **Choose Create a New Account.**

4. **Enter a name for the account and click the Next button.**

5. **Choose whether you want a Limited or Computer Administrator Account.**

6. **Click the Create Account button.**

 To create a Guest account, click the Guest account icon in the User Accounts dialog box and, in the following dialog box, click the Turn on the Guest Account button.

To change a user account, return to the User Accounts dialog box and select the name of the account that needs changing. You can change names, the picture beside the account name, and the account type. How to complete these tasks is self-explanatory.

Deleting a user account

Only users with computer administrator status can delete user accounts. When you delete an account, Windows XP gives you the opportunity to save the contents of the user's My Documents folder and his or her desktop settings.

To delete a user account, go to the User Accounts dialog box, select the account you want to delete, and select Delete the Account. Then click the Keep Files or Delete Files button. If you opt to keep the files, Windows XP places them on the desktop in a folder named after the person whose user account was deleted. You can copy or move the files elsewhere by double-clicking the folder on the desktop to open it in Windows Explorer. The files are found in this folder: C:\Documents and Settings*Computer Administrator Account Name*\Desktop*Deleted User Account Name*.

Logging off and switching users

Click the Start button and choose Turn Off Computer to cease working altogether. Otherwise, Windows XP offers two options for ceasing work:

 ✦ **Switching to another user account:** Go this route to switch to another account without closing programs and files. By switching, you make it possible to return at a later time to the files you're working on without having to reopen them. Click the Start button, choose Log Off, and click Switch User in the Log Off Windows dialog box. You soon see a screen with the names of user accounts on your computer. Click a name to

switch to an account. When this account logs off or switches back, you
see the files on-screen that were there when you switched user
accounts.

+ **Logging off:** When you log off, you close your user account altogether. It
doesn't wait for you in the background. After you log off, you get the
opportunity to switch to another account. Save and close all open files,
click the Start button, choose <u>L</u>og Off, and click the Log Off button.

If you don't see the Switch User button for switching between user
accounts, click the Start button, choose <u>C</u>ontrol Panel, click the User
Accounts icon, select Change the Way Users Log On and Off, and choose
User <u>F</u>ast User Switching.

Chapter 4: Let Me Entertain You

In This Chapter

✔ **Controlling the volume**

✔ **Playing CDs, audio files, and video files**

✔ **Burning a CD**

✔ **Listening the Internet radio**

✔ **Recording voices and sound**

For many years now, pundits have predicted that the television and the computer will merge into a supersonic entertainment monster. Whether this hybrid creature will really come to pass remains to be seen. For the time being, however, Windows XP permits you to treat your computer like an entertainment console. You can play music, play CDs, record sounds, burn CDs for your friends, and listen to faraway radio stations by way of the Internet. This chapter explains how Windows XP can entertain you, or at least keep you occupied on a rainy day.

Fine-Tuning the Volume

These days, nearly every computer comes with a sound card and speakers. That means you can play sounds and music, but the question is: How loudly do you want to play sound? And if more than one sound device is connected to your computer, which do you prefer to use? Follow these instructions to settle these all-important matters:

✦ **Master volume control:** Click the Volume Control icon — it looks like a speaker and is in the Notification area near the clock — to see the master volume control, as shown in Figure 4-1. From here, you can drag the slider to control the volume or select Mute to turn off the sound. All audio devices can be controlled from here.

✦ **Volume device controls:** Double-click the Volume Control icon on the Taskbar to display the Volume Control window shown in Figure 4-1. From here, you can drag sliders to adjust the volume of the different audio devices on your computer.

If a device isn't shown in the window, choose Options➪Properties, and, in the Properties dialog box, select the names of devices.

To control the bass and treble, choose Options⇨Advanced Controls and click the Advanced button. In the dialog box that appears, drag the Bass and Treble sliders.

✦ **Playback devices:** If more than one audio device is connected to your computer, tell Windows XP which ones to use. Click the Start button; choose Control Panel; select Sounds, Speech, and Audio Devices; and select Sounds and Audio Devices. On the Audio tab of the Audio Devices Properties dialog box, choose a Sound Playback, Sound Recording, and MIDI Music Playback option. Options appear on the drop-down menus if your computer can play sounds in different ways.

If the Volume Control icon doesn't appear on your Taskbar, click the Start button; choose Control Panel; select Sounds, Speech, and Audio Devices; and select Sounds and Audio Devices to open the Sounds and Audio Devices Properties dialog box. On the Volume tab, select Place Volume Icon in the Taskbar and click OK.

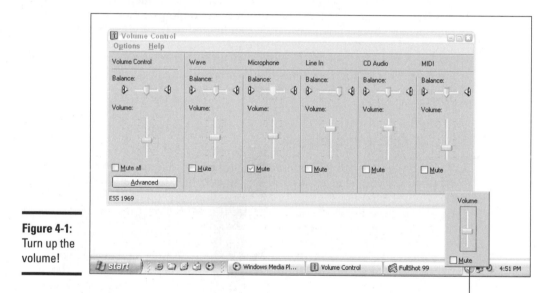

Figure 4-1: Turn up the volume!

Click or double-click the volume control

Windows Media Player: Playing Sound and Video

The Windows Media Player is an all-purpose gizmo for playing sound recordings and video. If you have a writeable CD player, you can even burn a CD with the Media Player. These pages explain how to find your way around the screen, play songs and videos from files on your computer, listen to the Internet radio, put together a media library of your favorite songs and videos, make a playlist, and burn a CD with audio files that are stored on your computer.

To open the Windows Media Player:

+ Double-click the Windows Media Player icon on the Quick Launch toolbar.

+ Click the Start button and choose All Programs⇨Accessories⇨Entertainment⇨Windows Media Player.

+ Open My Computer or Windows Explorer and double-click an audio or video file. Doing so opens the Windows Video Player and starts playing the file.

Introducing the Windows Media Player

Getting lost in the Windows Media Player is easy until you discover what's what, and to keep you from getting lost, Figure 4-2 shows what the most important parts of the Media Player are called:

Show/Hide taskbar

Task bar   Show/Auto Hide menu bar   Choose a CD, playlist, or file

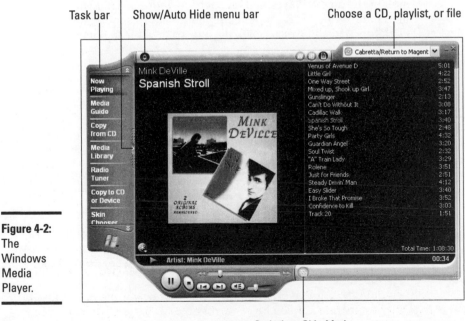

Switch to Skin Mode

Figure 4-2: The Windows Media Player.

✦ **Controls:** Controls for playing audio files and videos are found at the bottom of the window. These controls work like the ones on a tape player or video player.

✦ **Taskbar:** Click Taskbar buttons to open different windows in the Media Player and entertain yourself in various ways.

✦ **Playlists:** Open the Display Playlists, Audio, Video, or Radio Presets drop-down menu to see your playlists, play audio or video files, or turn on an Internet radio station. Later in this chapter, "Media Library: Creating playlists" explains what playlists are.

I could be wrong, but I believe that Microsoft expects you to play songs and videos on the Media Player while you do other things — such as your job, for example. To that end, the Media Player includes all kinds of buttons and gizmos to keep the Media Player from getting in the way of less entertaining computer programs:

✦ **Hiding the Taskbar:** Click the Show/Hide Taskbar button to display or remove the Taskbar.

✦ **Hiding the menu bar:** Click the Show/Auto Hide Menu Bar button to display or remove the menu bar.

✦ **Skin mode:** Click the Switch to Skin Mode button to see a compact version of the Media Player and an anchor window, as shown in Figure 4-3. Skin mode offers most of the commands that Full mode offers. Right-click the Media Player or click buttons to give these commands.

Figure 4-3:
The Media
Player in
Skin mode.

Do you want audio and video files to stop dead or repeat when they're finished playing? Choose Play➪Repeat (or press Ctrl+T) to select or unselect this command and decide what you want to happen when the song or video is finished playing.

Now Playing: CDs, music files, and videos

As long as speakers are attached to your computer and it's capable of playing sound and video, you can play commercial CDs, CDs that your friends burnt for you, music files such as MP3s, and video files. Go to the Now Playing tab to play CDs and music files. As shown in Figure 4-4, you can make the music sound even sweeter with these amenities:

✦ **Adjusting the sound:** Click the Show Equalizer button and, if necessary, the Select View button and choose Graphic Equalizer (refer to Figure 4-4). Controls for adjusting the sound appear in the window. You can also click the Select Preset button and choose settings for playing certain kinds of music — Rock, Jazz, Blues, and others.

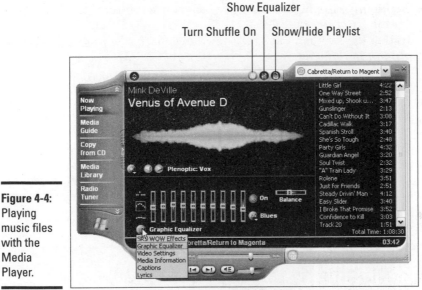

Figure 4-4:
Playing music files with the Media Player.

✦ **Ach! Visualizations!:** Visualizations, those psychedelic light shows in the Media Player, are nothing but a distraction, in my opinion. To turn them off, choose View⇨Now Playing Tools⇨Show Visualization. If visualizations are your idea of a good time, however, click the Select Visualization or Album Art button, or choose View⇨Visualizations and play with the options on the submenu to make your psychedelic experience a more enriching one. On some commercial CDs, you can choose Album Art on the submenu to see a picture of the CD cover (refer to Figure 4-2).

Playing CDs

To play a CD, insert it in your computer's CD-ROM drive. All things being equal, the Windows Media Player opens on-screen and plays the first song on the CD. If the CD doesn't start playing right away, click the Play button. If absolutely nothing happens, open My Computer or Windows Explorer, right click the CD-ROM icon, and click <u>P</u>lay.

Here's everything a sane person needs to know to play a CD on the Media Player:

✦ **Choosing which songs to play:** Double-click a song on the playlist. If you don't see a list of songs on the playlist, click the Show Playlist button (refer to Figure 4-4). You can also click the Previous or Next button to go from song to song on the list.

✦ **Randomly skipping from song to song:** Click the Turn Shuffle On button (refer to Figure 4-4).

Playing audio files

As mentioned earlier, you can double-click an audio file in Windows Explorer or My Computer to play it. Starting from the Media Player, you can also play audio files on your computer by making a choice from the Display Playlists, Audio, Video, or Radio Presets menu.

The names of playlists appear at the top of the menu. Choose a playlist to see a list of its songs on the right side of the window, and double-click a song to play it. Later in this chapter, "Media Library: Creating playlists" explains playlists. If you don't see a list of songs, click the Show Playlist in Now Showing button (refer to Figure 4-4).

Abiding by the copyright laws

The coming years will see an epic battle between the people who own the copyrights to music and video files and the people who download them from the Internet and copy them from CDs and DVDs. The matter of whether you can legally copy this material to your computer is still unresolved, but one thing is certain: Copying the material and then reselling it is a clear violation of the copyright laws. You can't copy this stuff and package it for resale. Remember as well that many people make a living by earning income or collecting royalties from the sale of music and video that is now being copied freely over the Internet. These people deserve your respect and consideration.

Now Playing: Playing a video file

Do one of the following to play a video in Windows Media Player:

✦ Open My Computer or Windows Explorer and double-click the video file.

✦ Choose a playlist with video files on the Display Playlists, Audio, Video, or Radio Presets menu, and select the video's name in the playlist, as shown in Figure 4-5. Later in this chapter, "Media Library: Creating playlists" explains what playlists are.

View Full Screen button

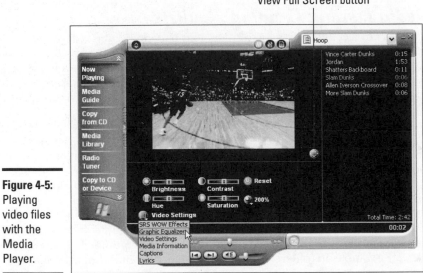

Figure 4-5: Playing video files with the Media Player.

To make watching videos on a computer screen more like watching movies in a drive-in theater, the Media Player offers these amenities:

✦ **Enlarging the movie:** Click the View Full Screen button (refer to Figure 4-5) to make the video fill the screen. You can also right-click this button to enlarge the screen by degrees.

✦ **Adjusting the brightness and contrast:** Click the Show Equalizer button and, if necessary, the Select View button and choose Video Settings. Controls for adjusting the picture appear (refer to Figure 4-5).

Copy from CD: Copying files from CDs

To copy audio files from a CD to your computer, insert the CD in the CD-ROM drive and click the Copy from CD tab in Windows Media Player. You see a list of the music tracks on the CD. Uncheck the tracks you *don't* want to copy, click the Copy Music button, and click OK in the dialog box that tells you the music is copyrighted, if the dialog box appears.

The files are copied to the C:\Documents and Settings\ *Your Name*\My Documents\My Music\ *Artist's Name* folder on your computer. They're converted from CD audio track (CDA) to Windows media audio (WMA) files.

Media Library: Creating playlists

Playlists are a convenient way to select and play audio and video files on your computer. All you have to do is choose a playlist on the Display Playlists, Audio, Video, or Radio Presets menu, and then select a filename in the playlist (see Figure 4-5). Playlists are also excellent for burning CDs. After you assemble files in a playlist, you can transfer them to a CD quite easily.

Playlists are convenient, all right, but assembling audio and video files for a playlist can be a chore. The song and video names on a playlist are actually shortcuts to audio and video files on your computer. To create a playlist, you tell Windows XP where on your computer these audio and video files are located — and that's where the trouble begins. After you create a playlist, you mustn't move its files, or else the Media Player won't be able to find or play them. To create playlists, therefore, your audio and video files must already be well organized in folders on your computer. I keep MP3 files, for example, in folders named after music genres — Country, Mexican, Jazz, and so on.

Creating a playlist

Creating a playlist is a two-step business. First you create and name the playlist; then you tell the Media Player which files on your computer belong in the playlist.

Follow these steps to create a playlist:

1. On the New Media tab, click the New Playlist button.

The New Playlist dialog box appears.

2. Enter a name for the playlist and click OK.

If you misnamed the playlist, right-click it, choose Rename, and enter a new name in the dialog box.

Follow these steps to enter filenames on a playlist:

1. **In Windows Explorer or My Computer, open the folder where you keep the audio or video files you want for the playlist.**

   Files are listed in the Media Player the same way they are listed in playlists. If you need to rename a file and give it a more descriptive name, now is the time to do it.

2. **Select the files you want for the playlist.**

   To select more than one file, either Ctrl+click different files or click the first in the bunch and then Shift+click the last.

3. **Right-click and choose Add to Playlist on the shortcut menu.**

   You see the Playlists dialog box. It lists each playlist you created.

4. **Select a playlist and click OK.**

   After you enter files on a playlist, the Media Player enters their names as well in these Media Library folders: Audio, Video, and their subfolders. Good luck finding anything in those crowded folders.

The Media Library tab offers a Search command for finding files and putting them in the library, but this command isn't worth very much if most of the files you're dealing with are MP3s or other audio or video files. With the Search command, you can search by these file properties: song title, album, artist, genre, or filename. Because most MP3 files have not been labeled precisely with these property settings, however, searches can find the wrong files, too many files, or no files at all.

Managing a playlist

After you create a playlist, you can start tinkering with it:

+ **Rearranging the titles:** To move a title up or down the list, select it and then start clicking the Moves the Media Up or the Moves the Media Down button. You can also drag titles up or down the list.

+ **Removing a title:** Select the title and then click the Delete Media From button and choose Delete from Playlist on the submenu. You can also right-click a title and choose Delete from Playlist.

+ **Deleting a playlist:** Select its name in the Media Library, click the Delete Media button, and choose Delete Playlist on the submenu. To find playlists, open the My Playlists folder in the Media Library.

Copy to CD or Device: Burning a CD

Don't ask me why copying audio files to a CD is called "burning." Maybe the term is used to make it seem more exciting than it really is. To burn a CD with the Media Player, create a playlist and copy it to a CD-R or CD-RW disc (the previous section in this chapter explains playlists). Don't worry about the order of songs. You'll get a chance to change the order around right before you burn the CD.

Take heed of these provisos before burning a CD:

✦ You need a CD-R or CD-RW disk burner to burn a CD. You can't burn a CD on a standard CD-ROM drive like the kind through which software is loaded on a computer.

✦ You can copy these types of audio files to the disc: MP3 (.mp3), Windows Media (.wma), and Wave Sound (.wav).

✦ Before actually copying the files to the disc, Media Player converts the files to the CDA (CD audio track) format.

✦ Files can be burned only once to a CD-R disc. After copying, files cannot be added or removed. A CD-RW disc, on the other hand, is similar to a floppy disk in that files can be copied there and erased later. On a CD-R disc, you have to get it right the first time, because erasing files and putting more files on the disc after the fact isn't permitted.

✦ The files must fit on the CD-R or CD-RW. To find out whether they will fit, take note on the packaging of how much space in megabytes is on the disk or how many minutes of music can be recorded.

To find out how many megabytes a playlist occupies and how many minutes of playing time it requires, go to the Media Library tab, select the playlist, and glance at the Total Time and MB figures in the lower-right corner of the window.

Burning a CD taxes the computer's central processing unit and memory cache. I recommend closing all programs except the Media Player when burning a CD. While you're at it, you might restart the computer to empty the memory cache. If your computer runs low on memory or has to strain, the burn may be interrupted. When that happens, the Media Player reports that more files "will not fit" on the CD, even if there is enough room for more files.

Place a CD-R or CD-RW in the disk burner drive on your computer and follow these steps to burn a CD:

1. **Select the Copy to CD or Device button in the taskbar of the Media Player.**

On the Copy to CD or Device tab, the Media Player window is divided in two. If you're copying to a CD-RW and files are already on the disc, their names appear on the right side of the window.

2. **On the Music to Copy drop-down menu, choose the name of the playlist whose songs you want to burn on a CD.**

The names of files on the playlist appear on the left side of the window, as shown in Figure 4-6. This is the order in which files will play on the CD-R or CD-RW. If you don't like the order, drag files up or down in the list, or right-click and choose Move Up or Move Down.

Figure 4-6:
Burning
a CD.

3. **Uncheck the names of files you *don't* want to burn into the CD.**

Files with a checkmark next to their names will be burned on the CD.

If the playlist is too long to fit on the CD, some files are marked "will not fit" in the Status column. Uncheck a few files, if necessary, to tailor the list and make the files fit on the CD.

4. **Click the Copy Music button.**

Twiddle your thumbs while the files are converted to CDA (CD audio track) format and then copied to the disc. When the job is done, the Status column next to each file you copied reads "Complete," not "Ready to Copy," "Copying to CD," or "Converted."

Smoothing over the pops, hisses, and bumps

Pops, hisses, bumps, and other sounds caused by scratches on a CD can get into the mix when you burn a CD or play it. Follow these steps to smooth over these faults when you play and burn CDs:

1. **Choose Tools➪Options in the Media Player.**

2. **Select the Devices tab in the Options dialog box.**

3. **Select the drive on which you burn CDs and click the Properties button.**

4. **Under Playback and Copy in the Audio CD Properties dialog box, select the Use Error Correction check boxes.**

On the CD, files are titled Track 1, Track 2, and so on. It's up to you to tap into your creative energy and decorate the CD case and label the CD. You can label the CD with a felt pen, but be sure to write on the top, not the bottom of the disc — that's where the data is.

Radio Tuner: Listening to the Internet radio

I'm a big fan of the Radio Tuner. With a good Internet connection, you can get radio stations from all over the world. You can explore musical genres you didn't know about. You can find out what's going on in Borneo and Bogotá. As long as your Internet connection is up to speed, the thing sounds like a real radio.

Select the Radio Tuner tab in the Windows Media Player to play a radio station over your computer. The stations on the Radio Tuner tab have made agreements with Microsoft to provide programming in digital form. When you select a radio station, your Web browser opens the station's Web page. Shortly after that, you hear the station in the Media Player, although in some cases the broadcast is made from the home page instead of the Media Player.

Here are the ins and outs of the Radio Tuner:

✦ **Playing a station:** Click a station's name to see its "details"; then click the Play button, as shown in Figure 4-7.

✦ **Compiling a list of favorite stations:** When you come across a station you like, click the Add to My Radio Stations button. The station's name is added to the My Stations list on the Radio Tuner tab.

Figure 4-7:
Playing the
digital radio.

✦ **Searching for stations:** The best way to find exciting radio stations is to click the Find More Stations button on the Radio Tuner tab (you'll find this button in the upper-right corner). You see the Search window, as shown in Figure 4-7. Enter search criteria to start exploring. To look for foreign-language stations, click the Use Advanced Search button.

Recording Sounds, Voices, and Music

Windows XP comes with an excellent gizmo for recording and editing sound: the Sound Recorder. Use it to record introductions to CDs, others snoring, or the mating cry of the yellow-bellied sapsucker. Sounds you record with Sound Recorder are saved as Wave Sound files (.wav), also known as waveform files. It goes without saying, but you must have a microphone and it must be connected properly to your computer before you can record anything. Play the sounds you've recorded either in the Sound Recorder or the Windows Media Player.

To open the Sound recorder, click the Start button and choose All Programs⇨ Accessories⇨Entertainment⇨Sound Recorder. Figure 4-8 shows the Sound Recorder in action. As you record or play sound, the wavy green line indicates roughly the volume at which you're recording or playing.

Here are general instructions for recording and editing sound files:

✦ **Recording:** Click the Record button. When you're finished recording, click the Stop button. Click the Play button to play the recording back. If the recording is a keeper, choose File⇨Save and save the sound file. Choose File⇨New to start a new recording.

✦ **Editing:** Play the recording or drag the slider to the point before which or after which you want to delete part of the file. Then choose Edit⇨ Delete Before Current Position or Edit⇨Delete After Current Position.

✦ **Inserting a file:** Move the slider where you want to insert the file and choose Edit⇨Insert File, locate the file in the Insert File dialog box, and click the Open button. You may insert only Wave Sound files this way.

✦ **Mixing, or overlaying, sound files:** Move the slider to the point where you want the second file to start being heard, choose Edit⇨Mix with File, locate and select the other file in the Mix With File dialog box, and click the Open button.

✦ **Changing the pitch:** To make voice recordings higher or lower in pitch, choose a speed option from the Effects menu.

✦ **Making it echo:** To make a voice recording sound as though it was made in a cave, choose Effects⇨Add Echo.

✦ **Playing it backward:** To reverse a recording and see whether it has a satanic message, choose Effects⇨Reverse.

✦ **Making it louder or softer:** To change the volume, choose a Volume option on the Effects menu.

Figure 4-8:
The Sound
Recorder

The Sound Recorder offers these options for deciding how clean and crisp the sounds should be:

✦ **CD Quality:** The highest quality sound, with the largest amount of space (172KB per second) required to store the sound on disk.

✦ **Radio Quality:** Medium-quality sound, with less disk space required (21KB per second).

✦ **Telephone Quality:** Low-quality sound, with the least amount of disk space required (10KB per second).

To choose a quality setting, choose File⇨Properties to open the Properties for Sound dialog box. Then, on the Choose From drop-down list, click the Convert Now button and, in the Sound Selection dialog box, choose a quality setting on the Name drop-down list.

Index

U

W

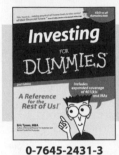 

FOR DUMMIES®

A world of resources to help you grow

TRAVEL

0-7645-5453-0

0-7645-5438-7

0-7645-5444-1

Also available:

America's National Parks For Dummies
(0-7645-6204-5)
Caribbean For Dummies
(0-7645-5445-X)
Cruise Vacations For Dummies 2003
(0-7645-5459-X)
Europe For Dummies
(0-7645-5456-5)
Ireland For Dummies
(0-7645-6199-5)

France For Dummies
(0-7645-6292-4)
Las Vegas For Dummies
(0-7645-5448-4)
London For Dummies
(0-7645-5416-6)
Mexico's Beach Resorts For Dummies
(0-7645-6262-2)
Paris For Dummies
(0-7645-5494-8)
RV Vacations For Dummies
(0-7645-5443-3)

EDUCATION & TEST PREPARATION

0-7645-5194-9

0-7645-5325-9

0-7645-5249-X

Also available:

The ACT For Dummies
(0-7645-5210-4)
Chemistry For Dummies
(0-7645-5430-1)
English Grammar For Dummies
(0-7645-5322-4)
French For Dummies
(0-7645-5193-0)
GMAT For Dummies
(0-7645-5251-1)
Inglés Para Dummies
(0-7645-5427-1)

Italian For Dummies
(0-7645-5196-5)
Research Papers For Dummies
(0-7645-5426-3)
SAT I For Dummies
(0-7645-5472-7)
U.S. History For Dummies
(0-7645-5249-X)
World History For Dummies
(0-7645-5242-2)

HEALTH, SELF-HELP & SPIRITUALITY

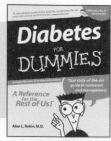

0-7645-5154-X

0-7645-5302-X

0-7645-5418-2

Also available:

The Bible For Dummies
(0-7645-5296-1)
Controlling Cholesterol For Dummies
(0-7645-5440-9)
Dating For Dummies
(0-7645-5072-1)
Dieting For Dummies
(0-7645-5126-4)
High Blood Pressure For Dummies
(0-7645-5424-7)
Judaism For Dummies
(0-7645-5299-6)

Menopause For Dummies
(0-7645-5458-1)
Nutrition For Dummies
(0-7645-5180-9)
Potty Training For Dummies
(0-7645-5417-4)
Pregnancy For Dummies
(0-7645-5074-8)
Rekindling Romance For Dummies
(0-7645-5303-8)
Religion For Dummies
(0-7645-5264-3)

Available wherever books are sold. Go to www.dummies.com or call 1-877-762-2974 to order direct